The
Severance
Genealogy

David C. Dewsnap

HERITAGE BOOKS
2007

IHERITAGE BOOKS

AN IMPRINT OF HERITAGE BOOKS, INC.

Books, CDs, and more—Worldwide

For our listing of thousands of titles see our website
at
www.HeritageBooks.com

Published 2007 by
HERITAGE BOOKS, INC.
Publishing Division
65 East Main Street
Westminster, Maryland 21157-5026

International Standard Book Number: 978-0-7884-0357-6

CONTENTS

ILLUSTRATIONS

iv

INTRODUCTION

This Severance compilation began as a search for my great great grandparents, Edwin Clark and Olive Naomi Roberts, who were born in New Hampshire and lived there until 1868 when they migrated to Wisconsin. My grandmother and mother provided proof of this New England family from photos, letters, and biographies which were carefully preserved and passed down within the family.

I was handed a direct opportunity to research this family as a series of events caused me to settle in Massachusetts in 1984. However, as I scoured the libraries, archives, genealogical societies, and numerous cemeteries, I was unable to locate any indication that they ever lived in the indicated area.

In 1986 I obtained a marriage record which indicated that Olive Naomi Roberts had married Elbridge G. Severance in Belmont, New Hampshire. This strange puzzle turned into a long detailed search which not only uncovered my own family history but also the entire genealogy of the John Severance and Abigail Kimball family starting around 1630 in Boston, Massachusetts.

A newly printed paper donated to the Kingston, New Hampshire public library, by Betty Johnsen, started me in the right direction. It also gave me early warning that much of the genealogy of the Severances had not been compiled in a printed format. John F. Severance, in 1893, had compiled the genealogy of John and Abigail Severance's son, John, but the other children were not followed. Several of the later biographies built upon errored research.

During the past 9 years with the help of countless Severance families and the use of every possible genealogical resource available, I have compiled the most complete genealogical history of the first 9 generations of the Severance's in America. Weekly trips through New England and travels throughout the United States allowed me to search each local area in fine detail and get a more accurate perspective into that family's place in the local history.

The various branches of the National Archives were used to obtained information in Revolutionary War Records and Federal Census Records. Each state's census records were researched from 1790 through 1920. Countless Libraries were searched for any available local Severance history.

This work is not perfect, but rather a beginning which the Severance family can build upon and improve. The author looks forward to any correspondence which will make this family history more accurate.

I am greatly indebted to everyone who has provided their family records and local history. The references give credit to this research where the family manuscripts were used to provide a better detail of that individual family line.

I am most indebted to Berenice G. Davis, who for the past 5 years has provided detailed research into all available census records, church records, bibliographies, vital records, and any other record that might provide a most accurate family history.

I dedicate this entire work to my parents who have given me support and encouragement and in particular to my mother and her Severance ancestors who provided the available family photos and records that helped make this project a reality.

THE BEGINNING

Nothing can exite an avid genealogist more than finding a past ancestors life or family preserved in the records. It is finding a piece of your very being and an indication of your past that goes to your very soul.

The early 1600's showed New England as a great magnet for many Europeans. Anyone who was willing to take the risk and accept the adventure could set sail and start an entirely new life.

However, for most of the New England settlers, they did not start a new life but tried to maintain as much of the old way of life without the burdens of taxes and religious persecution.

Boston was a port and city that provided the new arrivals with similarities of the old world and provided the abilities to get their lives in order before venturing out into the new frontier, which may have been just a few miles outside the Boston limits.

Reality soon caught up with the families that ventured out. The hardships were great since the frontier offered them no conveniences. The daily task of survival took all the energy those brave people could put out. Religion and family were the two stable forces that kept the people going forward. Therefore, the only early records concerning these settlers were the family Bibles and church records which usually indicated birth, baptism, marriage, and death. Some of the records also gave individuals achievements or standing within the community. These records also gave a location where the family lived and worked. If these records were lost, either to fire, flood, or deterioration, little was left for future generations to follow back their ancestry. When the records were rewritten from memory or recopied, many mistakes could occur and they often did.

Just the wrong spelling of the surname, which was written phonetically, could place a family into a whole different ancestry.

The Severance name, although compiled for several generations, has been the victim of frequent conjecture and unverified interpretations. Most of the information has turned out to be accurate. Unfortunately, the incorrect material has been proliferated through its use in more recent biographies and histories of the Severance family.

The spelling of the name, in part, has caused many researchers to confuse the various family lines within the family. The name has been found spelled as Leverance, Saverns, Saverance, Seabornes, Seaverans, Seaverns, Seberance, Serveran, **Severance**, Severence, Severens, Severn, Severnes, Severns, Severon, Sievernce, Siverence, Siverens, Sevrance, Sevrens, Sovereign, Soverin, Sufferance, and Sufference, among others. The name can be found spelled differently even within the same document.

The early records of Massachusetts will show four Severance families in the Massachusetts Bay Colony.

The first was John Seavorne, born circa 1619 and married to Mary___ in 1641. They had three daughters, Elizabeth, born 10-21-1642, Mary, born 9-15-1644, and Deborah, born 2-26-1645, all of Boston, MA. [MAVR] No other records could be found of this family.

The second family was Samuel Severans who married to Sarah Grant on 2-23-1665. [Charlestown, MAVR] Samuel died sometime after 1672 as indicated by a Deed transfer from Samuel Severns and Sarah Severns to Brimsdon, conveyed "all that small parcell of land lying and being at the south end of the town of Boston High Merryes Point, bounded south by Roger Rose, west by upland, and east by low water, 1-16-1672". Recorded 4-16-1672. [PRMA-Suffolk County] Samuel died relatively young and Sarah remarried to Thomas Sylvester after 5-9-1694. [Torrey p661][Bond p260,425,932]

This Samuel had at least one son, also named Samuel, who was born 11-19-1669. Samuel Severns Jr. was baptized, 11-28-1686. At this time, Samuel's mother, a widow, was also united with the church. [CRWMA] Samuel Jr. most likely married Rebecca Stratton. They were of Watertown, MA. This family spelled their last name as Seaverns.

John F.[6] Severance detailed this family of Samuel Jr. as part of the **John**[1] Severance and Abigail Kimball family. He reasoned that **Joseph**[2], a son of **John**[1] Severance and Abigail Kimball, married to Elizabeth _____, and had a son **Samuel**[3]. [JFS]

This could not be correct. **Joseph**[2] of **John**[1] Severance and Abigail Kimball removed to the Cape of Massachusetts and had a family at Harwich during this same time period. [Paine p107-108]

It has been suggested that this **Samuel**[2] (son of **John**[1] Severance and Abigail Kimball) married to the above Sarah Grant. However, **Samuel**[2] died relatively young. This was indicated when **Ebenezer**[2], a brother of **Samuel**[2], died young (1665) and left a Will. He mentioned all of his living brothers and sisters but **Samuel**[2] was not listed. [ECPR Vol 1 p2]

A third Severance family lived in Lynn, MA. This John Severance married Elizabeth Fuller on 4-10-1683. [MAVR-Lynn] She was born 5-30-1652, a daughter of John Fuller of Lynn, MA. Their children (born in the colonies) were John, born 3-22-1683; Edward, born 8-21-1685; William, born 2-20-1687; Joseph, born 9-19-1692 and died young; and Elizabeth, born 6-18-1690. [MAVR] Little information was left on this family indicating that they perhaps did not stay in this country or they died at sea. The name was spelled *Severus* in some documents. [Fuller p159] The only record found which might indicate the history of this family says, "in 1699 George Carr, Jr. was at this time building vessels at the Ferry, and took William Severance apprentice for four years", [Merrill II p94]

The fourth family, and the one that will be recorded with the descendants in this book, is the family of **John**[1] *Severans* and Abigail Kimball.

FIRST GENERATION...On April 10, 1634, when Richard Kimball was about 39 years old, his wife, Ursula Scott Kimball, her 60 year old mother, Martha Scott, Ursula's brother, Thomas, and his wife and children, embarked at Ipswich in the County of Suffolk, England in the ship *Elizabeth*, with William Andrews as the Master. Seven of the eight Kimball children, who had been born in Rattlesden, England, were with the family. Abigail Kimball, the eight child, followed three years later (1637) on

the same schooner, *Elizabeth*, with her husband
John[1] *Severns*. [White I p215-216]
     It is uncertain if **John**[1] also sailed on the
George. It has been stated that **John**[1] Severance was
a shipmaster and as master of the vessell *George*,
he brought a company of emigrants to New England in
1635. [Hotten p 124]
     John[1] Severance, our founding ancestor, was born
in Ipswich, England circa 1609/1615. He married
Abigail Kimball of Ipswich, in 1635. [JFS p1] When
they arrived in America in 1637, they probably
lived in Boston. Abigail's Uncle, Robert Scott, was
a merchant who owned a house and garden on
Washington Street, in the city. **John**[1] was admitted
a free man that same year. [Farmer p259] He and his
family later moved to Salisbury, where **John**[1]
settled as one of the original founders. [Hoyt
p314]
     John[1] moved to Salisbury in 1639 where he
received land in the first division. Salisbury, the
plantation at Merrimack, was begun in early 1638.
This was the first attempt at settlement north of
the Merrimack River. **John**[1] served the community
well as a member on the prudential committee, the
highway surveyor, and he was given the license to
keep the ordinary. He sold his old and new houses
to Thomas Bradbury in 1647 and became known as a
"planter, victualler and vinter". He subscribed to
the oath of fidelity in 1667. [Cutter p184]
     Abigail (Kimball) Severance died 6-19-1658 after
the birth of a child. **John**[1] remarried to Susanna
Ambrose on 10-17-1663. She was the widow of Henry
Ambrose. **John**[1] died 4-9-1682. His body was placed
in an unmarked grave in the Old Burying Ground at
East Salisbury, MA. Abigail (Kimball) Severance
died on 6-17-1658. Her death was only 1 month and
24 days after the birth of their last daughter who
lived 6 days. [ECPR micofilm]

Children of **John**[1] Severance and Abigail Kimball
     i   **Samuel**[2] b 9-19-1637 [MAVRS] d young. He
            was not mentioned in his brothers Will
            which was read in 1667. [ECPR Vol IIp82]
     ii   **Ebenezer**[2] b 3-7-1639 d 1667 unmarried.
            He left a Will and Testament indicating
            his brothers and sisters. The last Will
            and Testament of **Ebenezer**[2] Severance
            made the 22th of August '65, "I do give
            and bequeath unto my brothers **John**[2]
            Severans and **Joseph**[3] Severans all my

4

tooles to be divided equally between them, and to my brothers **Benjamin**[2] and **Ephraim**[2] Severans; each 40s, I give unto my sister **Mary**[2] Coffyns daughter, Mary, five pound, I give unto Abigail Ambross 20s, and the rest of my estate, I do give and bequeath unto my beloved sisters **Abigail**[2] Church and **Mary**[2] Coffin, And I do appoint my honered father **John**[1] Severans my sole executor to this my last will and testament". Proved in Salisbury Court, February 9, 1667. [ECPR Docket 25,068]

iii **Abigail**[2] b 1-7-1641 d same day

iv **Abigail**[2] b 5-25-1643 in Salisbury, MA m to John Church 11-29-1664. [MAVRS] Apparently **Abigail**[2] d relatively young because John Church m secondly as early as 1683 to Sarah ___. [MAVR-Hampton] John was b about 1641 and d 1696. John Church was the son of Jonathan Church

v **Mary**[2] b 6-8-1645 [MAVR] in Salisbury, MA m to James Coffin (son of Tristram Coffin and Dionis Stevens on 11-3-1663 Salisbury, MA. [NHVR] James Coffin was b in England on 8-12-1640 and d in Nantucket, MA on 7-28-1872. Mary d after 1680. They had 14 children. [Clapp p3]

To illustrate how these families would move, often over great distance; James Coffin was b in England, 8-12-1640. He m 12-3-1663, **Mary**[2], daughter of **John**[1] and Abigail Severance, of Salisbury, MA, and d at Nantucket 7-28-1720, aged 80 years. He (James Coffin) came to Nantucket with the first settlers, then removed to Dover, NH, where he lived in 1668, being a member of the church in 1671, and the same year, 5-31-1668, he was made freeman. Soon after this date, he returned to Nantucket and resided there until his death. [Clapp p3]

1 vi **John**[2] b 11-27-1647 m Mary__, 8-15-1672.

2 vii **Joseph**[2] b 2-15-1650 m Martha Warden

viii **Elizabeth**[2] b 4-8-1652 d 1656. The vital records of Salisbury, MA shows a birth date for **Elizabeth**[2] on 2-8-1652 and another birth date for **Elizabeth**[2] on 4-17-1658 both as daughters of **John**[1] and

Abigail. It also shows the death date
for **Elizabeth²**, daughter of **John¹** 4-17-
1658 and a death date of 4-23-1658.
However the records are read, it seems
obvious that two daughters were born
named **Elizabeth²** and both d young. It
has been stated that this **Elizabeth²** m
Samuel Eastman and their grand-daughter,
Abigail Eastman, b 7-10-1737, m Ebenezer
Webster and was the mother of Daniel
Webster. However, as noted above, this
could not be correct. Again, **Ebenezer²**
did not mention any **Elizabeth²** in his
Will and Testament and later research
indicates that Samuel Eastman married an
Elizabeth Scriven. "Per daughter of John
Scriven, of Dover" Elizabeth *Scrivens*
married Samuel Eastman. [Hoyt Vol I
p315]

ix **Benjamin²** b 1-13-1654 living in 1665 as
(listed in his brothers Will in 1665)
Benjamin² was listed on an imperfect
list of pound-keepers in Newtown (NY)
village. The records kept from that date
up to the Revolution, show **Benjamin²**
Severens , dated 2-4-1711. His widow
kept it after his death. In 1689.
Benjamin⁴ Severens retained his place as
constable, being at this time deputy
sheriff of Queen's County. The 1698
NY Census shows **Benjamin²** *Seavernes* as
head of a four member family. [O'Gorman]
The research, although incomplete, tend
to indicate that this **Benjamin²** was a
son of **John¹** and Abigail. **Benjamin²**
Severns probably m1 to Elizabeth Lynch,
who was b 2-24-1661/2 at Branford, CT.
[Jacobus Vol 1] Elizabeth's father was
Gabriel Lynch. **Benjamin²** *Severns* signed
the Will of Jonathan Strickland at Long
Island, NY [Jacobus Vol 1] Indications
are that the Severance family was from
Gill, Massachusetts. (The Connecticut
river was a route from New England to
New York) William Sallier and
Elizabeth³ Severance m 2-21-1710; **Joseph³**
Severance and Sarah Roberts m 3-4-1724;
and Jeremiah and **Rebecca³** Severance m
1731. [NYGBR] Elmhurst was formerly
Newton, Long Island, NY. from 1709 to

6

1881. On 1-21-1754, eight persons including William Sallier were found frozen in Jamaica Bay. Widow Severance d 10-6-1748 and Jeremiah North d 4-6-1750. [NYGBR] "consideration of 50 pounds John White convey and offers to Jeremiah North, mason, 8 acres, being the land formerly belonging to **James³** Severance. [O'Gorman]

It appears that **Benjamin²** married twice. The Will of **Benjamin²** written 4-22-1704 in which he left his entire estate to his son **John³** and his wife Mary and the wife was to be the sole executrix. It seems probable that **James³** was also a son who had a daughter **Rebecca⁴**. **Rebecca⁴** b circa 1714 in Newton, NY, was the Severance that married Jeremiah North, 1731. [IGI] The **Joseph³** Severance who married to Sarah Roberts of Queens, Newton Presbyterian Church, 3-4-1724, [IGI], was probably another brother of **James³**.

In the Will of Edward North, he gives to his son, Thomas, the house and land I now live on, as divided between him and his brother Jonathan in the presence of James Renne and Nathaniel Hazard, with a piece of salt meadow as already divided in presence of **Benjamin²** *Severns*, James Burroughs, and Benjamin Comforth. [O'Gorman] This tends to indicate that there was family interaction between the Norths and the Severance family. [MVM]

William Green formerly of Newton, Long Island but now from Hunterdon County, gives to his sons Joseph and William the house and Plantation that he bought from **John³** Severans. This is most likely the **John³** Severans, son of **Benjamin²**, of Newton, Long Island. [MVM]

3   x   **Ephraim²** b 4-8-1656 m Lydia Morrill 11-9-1682

     xi   **daughter** b 4-17-1658 d 4-23-1658 [Abigail (Kimball) Severance d on 6-17-1658]

SECOND GENERATION...(1) John², (John¹), was born 11-27-1647 in Salisbury, MA. The descent of **John²** Severans, son of **John¹** and Abigail Kimball, is followed through *The Severans Genealogy* [JFS] with minor revisions. The initial compilation was completed in 1893 by **John F.**[6] Severance.

About 1672, **John**[2] moved to Boston and settled there. At an early age he helped his father at his Inn and soon began to look after his fathers business matters. Four of his children were born in Boston. Then, in 1680, he removed to Suffield, CT where his last two children were born. The family was of Suffield in 2-14-1678. He stayed there only 9 years and then moved to Deerfield, MA. Next they went to Bedford, Westchester Co., NY about 1702. **John**[2] became a large land holder. He settled an account with Major Pynchon on August 13, 1717. After living at Bedford about 12 years, he moved back to Deerfield where he lived until his death with his son **Joseph**[3]. **John's**[2] wife, whom he married 8-15-1672 [MAVR], was named Mary but nothing else is known about her. She was born in 1650. [Cutter p184] He moved around like a moving planet. In 1710, **John**[2] Severance was age 63 and his wife Mary age 60. [TRBNY Vol I p149]

Children: [Sheldon p286]
4 i   **Ebenezer**[3] b 9-19-1673 [MAVR] m Mary.
   ii   **Abigail**[3] b 5-5-1675 d 1691 [MAVR]
        shows Abigail, daughter of **John**[2] and
        Mary, d 1--1691
5 iii **John**[3] b 9-22-1676. [MAVR] No further
        record of him in New England. It is
        thought that he was among the passengers
        of a ship which shipwrecked off Cape
        Fear, NC, were saved by Indians and
        later settled in SC. **Note** the
        information for **Mary**[3] (his sister) who m
        John Dibble. This could indicate how
        John[3] happened to be on a ship which
        sank off Cape Fear with passengers who
        later settled in Charleston, SC.
   iv   **Daniel**[3] b 6-3-1678, killed by Indians 9-
        15-1694 at Deerfield, MA. **"Daniel**[3]
        Severance, a lad, was killed in the
        meadow" when in 9-15-1694, Baron Saint
        Castrine and Indians attacked the fort
        at Deerfield, and were repulsed. The
        Indians, with the help of the French,
        implemented several massacres and
        maraudings on the English colonies in an
        effort to disrupt peace treaties made
        between the English and the eastern

Indians. It was **Daniel's³** timely warning that gave advanced warning to the fort. [Judd p253]

v   **Mary³** b 7-14-1681 Suffield, CT m John Dibble 11-26-1697 in Deerfield, MA [MAVR] The family lived in Bedford, NY. The interaction between the Severance's of MA and the other intermarried families of CT and Newton, Long Island, NY. would indicate the connection between **Benjamin²** Severance as the brother of **John²** and children of **John¹** and Abigail Kimball. Joseph Phillips m 1st to ____ Graves, a daughter of William Graves of Newton, L.I. and Stamford, CT. He m 2nd to Patience Higby, daughter of Capt. Edward and Jedediah Skidmore. (Capt Higby was engaged in the West India trade with his son-in-law, Joseph Phillips. [Furman p1]

John Dibble and **Mary³** Severance had at least three children, John, Abigail and Mary Dibble. William Graves m Sarah, the widow of John Dibble Sr., who d 1646, at Stamford, CT. William Grave was of Stamford, CT and later of Newtown, Long Island. He leaves all the rest of land and good to the little children of my daughter Hannah Graves, and to my grandchild, Abigail Dibble, now living in CT. [Furman p8]

An abstract of original bill of sale shows **John²** Severance of Deerfield, Hampshire Co., Province of Massachusetts Bay of late belonging to Bedford, Westchester, NY., "sold to Hezekiah Roberts of Bedford for y use of John Dibble's grandson" of above named **John²** Severance. [TRBNY p80-81]

A list of the names of persons within the District of the Town of Bedford, issued from the Clerk of the County in 1710 indicates **John²** Severance aged 63 years, Mary, his wife age 60, **Mary³** (Severance) Dibble, widow, age 29, her son John Dible age 7, and her daughter, Abigail Dible, age 5. [TRBNY p149]

John Dibble, miller, resided at Bedford by 1703. He died by 1710 and married **Mary³** who was born 1681,

daughter of **John²** and Mary Severance. He
purchased Crosses Vineyard in 2-4-1702.
John² Severance of Deerfield, Hampshire
Co. MA., 11-3-1715 cites the three
Dibble grandchildren, John born 1703;
Abigail born 1705; and Mary, living in
1715, [Davis p71]

6   vi   **Joseph³** was b 10-26-1682 [CTVR] m Anna
Kellogg.

(2) Joseph², (John¹), born 12-14-1649. [MAVR] He
died before 1725. He married Martha Warden before
1676 and they settled at Yarmouth and Harwich, MA
before 1700. [Torrey] Martha, born 1643, was the
daughter of Peter Warden Jr. of Yarmouth and
Harwich, MA. [MAVR] Peter Warden Jr. was born in
England circa 1608, and no doubt accompanied his
father to New England, becoming a resident of
Yarmouth, where he died 1-11-1680. His will,
recorded at Plymouth, names wife Mary, son Samuel,
and daughters Martha, wife of **Joseph²** Severance,
Mary, wife of Joseph Burgess, and Mercy, wife of
Kenelm Winslow. [Winslow p105]

   Joseph² bought land with Manoah Ellis and Elisha
Eldridge in 1693. By deed dated April 8, 1687, Mr.
Lumbert sold half interest in his farm to **Joseph²**
Severance of Yarmouth and the remaining one-half
interest was acquired by Manoah Ellis of Sandwich,
MA. [Smith II p115-116]

   Joseph² Severence was with the first expedition
under Capt. John Gorham's Company sent out of
Yarmouth against Mount Hope in the King Philips War
of 1675, He was from that part of Yarmouth which is
now East Dennis, MA. [Paine p107-108]

   Apparently **Joseph²** Severance died before 1725.
Martha died at her daughters, **Abigail³** Broadbrooks,
on 3-31-1725. [MAVR-Harwich]

Children:
No complete record appears for all of their
children.

   "**Abygall³** Sevarnes, the daughter of **Joseph³**
Sevarnes, borne in Yarmouth 9-11-1676, **Marsey³** born
3-1-1677/78, **Joseph³** Sevarnes born 3-20-1683"
[MAVR-Yarmouth]

      i   **Abigail³** b 9-11-1676 in Yarmouth m
Beriah Broadbrooks 11-17-1700. Beriah
Broadbrooks, the ancestor of the
Broadbrooks and Brooks family, was a
settler after 1700. He was twice

married. His first wife was **Abigail³** Severance, daughter of **Joseph²** and Martha Severance, to whom he was m 11-17-1700. They had at least nine children. [Paine]

ii   **Mary³** (Marsey) b 3-1-1678/9

iii   **Joseph³** b 3-20-1683 (settled in Chatham) He was living in 1753 age 69. A **Joseph³** Severance gave testimony in 1753 stating that he was 69 years old. [Smith II p209] **Joseph³** apparently had a son, **Joseph⁴**, probably b circa 1703-1720. He d in 1740 [PRMA Barnstable Co., dated 3-19-1740] It gave **Joseph³** Severance the power to dispose of the goods and chattel of **Joseph⁴** Severance Jr. late of Chatham who d intestate.

iv   **Martha³** b circa 1684, Barnstable Co. Harwich, MA. She m John Ellis 6-21-1706, they had at least four children, Benjamin, Joseph, John, and Thankful Ellis. [Smith II p162] **Martha³** (Severance) Ellis was appointed administratrix of his estate January 7, 1712-13, and on June 23, 1717, widow Ellis and her four children were baptized. John Ellis was born about 1680 at Harwich, Barnstable Co., MA. He d on 10-19-1712. John Ellis was b about 1680 d in Chatham 10-19-1712 m in Eastham 6-21-1706, **Martha³** Severance, daughter of **Joseph²** and Martha (Worden) Severance of Yarmouth and Harwich.

v   **Ebenezer³** m Rebecca Tomlin 2-14-1709/10 (MAVR) Rebecca was supposedly the daughter of John Tomlin and Sarah Barnes. The records do not directly show the name Rebecca but it is a family name and Sarah and Elizabeth were already used for other siblings.

vi   **Peter³** m Elizabeth Cole, September of 1724. [PRMA Barnstable Co] shows that **Joseph³** Severance Jr. was appointed as administrator and disolver of goods and chattel of **Peter³** Severance, late of Harwich in the County of Barnstable, who d intestate.

The Severances of New Bedford and Fairhaven, MA are probably descendants of the **Joseph²** family

11

although there is no direct proof of this assumption. The possibility exists that the Severances of Long Island resettled in this area. This genealogical line will be continued from **Joseph²** as unconnected.

The first residents of Pleasant Lake, a settlement at and near the west end of Long pond, and at Hinckley's pond, were Thomas Hinckly, Micah Philips, Reuben Philips, **James³** Severance, and James Cahoon. [Paine] Later additional residents of Monomoit were Isaac Atkins, Beriah Broadbrooks, John Ellis, **Joseph³** Severance Jr. and Samuel Nickerson Jr. [Smith II]

(3) Ephraim², (John¹), born 4-8-1656 in Salisbury, MA. He spent his early life in Salisbury. He married Lydia Morrill, the daughter of Abraham Morrill and Sarah Clements, 11-9-1682. [Williamson p21] [Hoyt p251] Lydia was born 3-8-1661. [MAVR-Salisbury] All of their children were born in Salisbury. Both **Ephraim²** and Lydia signed the Bradbury petition of 1692. [NHSP]

Ephraim² became one of the first settlers of the newly established town of Kingston, New Hampshire. His land was laid out by a chosen committee, August 17-1714. His name was listed of men sworn to Kingston, September 9, 1727. His wife, Lydia, was admitted to the First Church on September 25, 1726. She died 2-6-1727 and "died the aged Mr. Severans, October, Ye 24, 1734" [ECVR-microfilm of originals]

Ephraim² was among the constituent members, of the First Church of Kingston, New Hampshire where he is recorded as "Old Goodman Severance". [Tibbetts p131-133]

Children: [Hoyt p315]
  i   **Abigail³** b 8-29-1683. She m Joseph Abby 11-30-1706 of Exeter, NH. [Abbe p14-15] **Abigail³** m 2nd Phillip Greeley 12-11-1707.
  ii   **Mary³** b 7-2-1685 m Abraham Watson 3-14-1711/12 [MAVR]
  iii **Lydia³** b 1-15-1687, d young
7 iv   **Ephraim³** b 12-2-1689 m Mary Burnham 11-25-1714
  v   **Dinah³** b 9-3-1692 m John Dow 1-6-1713/14 [MAVR]
8 vi   **Ebenezer³** b 11-29-1694, bpt 1-3-1719/20 [FF p157] m Anna Fitts 1-8-1716/17 [NHVR]

vii   **Sarah³** b 2-7-1697/98 [MAVR] m John Marsh 12-11-1718

9   viii   **Jonathan³** b 4-21-1700 [MAVR] m Katherine Tucker 2-14-1725

ix   **Hannah³** b 12-13-1702, The [MAVR] shows a marriage of Hannah to John Davis on 9-22-1724

x   **Lydia³** b 9-9-1705 m William Fowler 10-8-1730

THIRD GENERATION (4) Ebenezer³, (John², John¹), born in Boston, MA on 9-19-1673. [MAVR] As his parents moved to Suffield, CT and then to Deerfield, MA so did **Ebenezer³**, where he settled and married Mary ____, on May 9, 1695. [MAVR] He served in Capt. Wright's Co., in 1709. In 1718, he settled in Northfield on a tract of land which he had purchased in 1703.

     Ebenezer³ was a farmer as well as a producer of turpentine. He held the positions of Selectman of the town during the years of 1719-21 and 1723. In March of 1723, the town voted him ten acres of land on Bennett Hill. On October 11, 1723, while harvesting his corn, he was killed by Indians. [Judd p332] Mary died on 6-20-1761. [MAVR-Deerfield] [JFS p2-3]

Children: [Sheldon p286]
born at Deerfield, Franklin Co. MA

i   **Abigail⁴** b 4-27-1696 [MAVR] d 12-18-1770 m John Allen 6-21-1716. John b 1-14-1683/4 d 11-30-1761. She d 12-18-1770 [MAVR Deerfield]

ii   **Ebenezer⁴** b 11-14-1697 d young [MAVR]

iii   **Sarah⁴** b 11-19-1699 [MAVR] m Ezekiel Bascom 12-21-1724 [D-MAVR]

10   iv   **Daniel⁴** b 1-4-1701/02 [MAVR] m Rebecca Jones 10-18-1733

v   **Mary⁴** b 10-7-1703 [MAVR]

vi   **Hannah/Harriet⁴** [MAVR] b 4-1-1706 m Benomi Wright 3-31-1724, Benomi was b 1702 [Spooner p95]]

vii   **John⁴** b 3-7-1708 [MAVR] It is not known if he married. He was reported to have enlisted in Col., Ephraim Williams Regiment at Northfield in 1759 with the Ticonderoga and Crown Point Expedition. No report was found of him after that.

11   viii   **Ebenezer⁴** b 7-24-1709 [MAVR] m Hannah ____ 9-23-1736

ix   **Elizabeth⁴** b 7-30-1712 {MAVR] m Josiah
             Davison 4-28-1737. They lived in
             Deerfield, MA

x   **Samuel⁴** b 12-27-1716 [MAVR] There was a
             Samuel⁴ Severance killed in Jamaica,
             VT., 6-1-1745 [VTVR] It is unclear if it
             was this **Samuel⁴**. [MBGD]

xi   **Martha⁴** b 10-20-1718 [MAVR] [MBGD]

(5) John³, (John², John¹), born on 9-22-1676 in
Boston, MA but his parents moved shortly after to
Suffield, CT. [Cutter p184] He married to Catherine
_____, who dyed on March 20, 1739 in Berkley County
South Carolina. [MgSC Vol 58 p38] **John³** died 4-20-
1740 [MgSC Vol 20, p 202] The name was found
spelled *Saverance*, *Severance*, and *Seaverance*.

    The fact that this **John³**, born in Massachusetts,
is the same as **John³**, living in South Carolina is
conjecture. The one missing piece in this puzzle is
the actual proof that **John³** was the son of **John²**
from New England. However the evidence seems fairly
clear. Judging from the fact that there was just
one **John** Severance in America at that time fitting
that description and given the similarity in regard
to time and placement, one has to come to the
conclusion that **John³**, is in fact the son of **John²**,
and the grandson of **John¹** and Abigail Kimball.

    John³ Saverance first lived in an area of the
Wappetaw Congregational Church. [MgSC Vol 58 p85]
This area later became Christ Church Parish of SC.

    John³ received a grant for 300 acres of Land in
Berkley Co on 3-2-1701. **John³** Saverance lived in
the area of the Wappetaw Congregational Church as
early as 1701. A note on the Wappetaw
Congregational church which was located near
Highway 17 about 14 miles from Mount Pleasant,
South Carolina. This church was planted here in
1698 by a colony of 52 who came from New England
and landed at Seawee Bay. The settlement had been
made by a group of adventurers from New England.
They were shipwrecked on the coast of North
Carolina and friendly Indians allowed some of them
to travel overland to see Governor Archdale in
Charlestown. He brought a vessel to bring them to
the north side of the Cooper River, where they
settled. [Salley p302]

    Mrs. McIver, in writing the history of Wappataw
church, tells of a letter written 6-26-1696 to
Governor Archdale of South Carolina from a group of

people in Ipswich, Massachusetts, in which they ask permission to relocate in South Carolina. She names **John³** and Catherine Saverance in Christ Church Parish, Wappataw at that time as well as other families such as Murrell, Huggins, Barkley, Barton, Watson, Whilden, Knowles, Legree, Woods, White, Fenwick, Tommer and Fairchild. Whilden and Legree are the only names with records showing that they came from Massachusetts. [MgSC Vol 58 p84-85]

John's³ reason for coming to South Carolina could have been adventure or "getting away" from the Indian threat, as his younger brother was killed by Indians in Deerfield, and his oldest brother was killed by the Indians while harvesting corn, although this was in the 1700's after **John³** would have gone to South Carolina. Perhaps a more logical reason was religion and the search for land and adventure.

John³, could have been among a group under Joseph Lord of Dorchester, MA. They gathered on "Ocktober y 22 (1695)" and set sail from Boston on December 14th. Among the names mentioned were Joshua Brooks, Nathaniel Billings, Simon Daken, Williams Adams, Increase Sumner, William Pratt, and George Foxe. This group of men were from Roxesbury, Milton, Charlestown, Concord, Reading, Sudbury, and Dorchester, all in MA. [The American Congregational Association, Bulletin, Vol 28 Winter 1977 No, 2 p6]

Children:

i   **Sarah⁴** b unknown d 8-17-1741 m John White. John White, son of William White, first lived in Christ Church Parish, Berkely Co., SC., and married **Sarah⁴** Saverance, daughter of **John³** and Catherine Saverance. **John³** Severance mentioned in his will of his daughter, **Sarah³** (Severance) White, and his son in law, John White. [PRCSC] The Whites had a total of 11 children as recorded in the Christ Church Parish Records

12   ii   **John⁴** b before 1718 d 4-4-1740 m Ann Barton 6-10-1735 [MgSC Vol 20 p66]

13   iii   **Joseph⁴** m Ann Watson 3-30-1732 [IGI] d 1-11-1750 [MgSC Vol 20 p66]

(6) Joseph³, (John², John¹), born in Suffield, CT on 10-26-1682. He lived almost his entire life either in Deerfield or Northfield, MA. He owned a house and a home lot and he was a tailor by trade. He

15

fought in the meadows in 1704 and served as a soldier in 1713. He was granted 200 acres of land east of Northfield on Mount Grace by the general court as compensation for being made a cripple when wounded by the Indians. **Joseph**[3] also served as Corporal in Captain Kellogg's Company in 1723. [JFS p3-4]

Joseph[3] Severance of Deerfield was wounded by the Indian enemy, as a soldier in the service of the Province. He was crippled. In 1735, the court granted him 200 acres of land east of Northfield, MA on Mt. Grace for his services. [Sheldon p286]

It was **Joseph**[3] who carried the news of the fall of Ft. Massachusetts in 1746 for which he received seven shillings, six pence from the Province treasury. Again he rode post to North Hampton in December of that year when the Snowshoe Scouts had seen Indian smoke in the north woods.

In the spring of 1747, he reported the peril of Shattuck's Fort in Hinsdale, NH and a little later he rode toward Ft. Massachusetts to bring in a soldier taken sick on the road. His father also gave him land in Deerfield.

Joseph[3] married Anna Kellogg 11-17-1712 [MAVR]. Anna was born 7-14-1689 in Hatfield, MA and died in Montague on 3-15-1780 [MAVR]. He owned both a house and home lot in Northfield, MA. He owned No. 36 in Deerfield in which he lived. **Joseph's**[3] father, **John**[2], lived with him in his older age after returning from Suffield, CT. [JFS] In his late life he divided his real estate among his children and he and his wife Anna Kellogg lived with their youngest son, **Moses**[3], in Montague, MA. Anna was the daughter of Martin Kellogg and Anna Hinsdale. **Joseph**[3] died April 10, 1766.

The vital records show "a tailor came from Wales 1706" husband of Anna Kellogg, d at Montague 1765". [MAVR] This has always bothered me. If he was born in CT, how could he have been from Wales?

Children: [Bates-Gen 10 p1] [MAVR-Deerfield]
14   i   **Joseph**[4] b 10-7-1713
     ii   **Anna**[4] b 11-25-1715 m Samuel Bardwell 10-21-1737 (a daughter of Samuel Bardwell and **Anna**[4] Severance, Tama or Zama Bardwell married to Elisa Nims 11-22-1776) [Suddaby p 541]
15   iii **Martin**[4] b 9-10-1718
16   iv   **John**[4] b 10-20-1720 [MAVR] m Esther Arms

	v	**Experience**[4] b 3-14-1723 m Phineas Nevers 7-23-1749, of Stafford, CT.

17	vi	**Jonathan**[4] b 6-12-1725
	vii	**Rebecca**[4] b 3-4-1728 m Samuel Smead 11-28-1734 in Deerfield, Franklin Co., MA. They had 9 children. He was the son of Samuel Smead and Mary Weld. He d 5-25-1809 and she d 1768. [MLCK]
18	viii	**Moses**[4] b 3-23-1730
	ix	**Abigail**[4] b 11-16-1732

It is in this spot where I am continuing the **Joseph**[2] line from the Cape Cod Severance's with names such as **James**[3], **Ebenezer**[3], **Joseph**[3], **Phillip**[3], **Thomas**[3], and **William**[3]. These Severance's are most probably of the Cape Cod or Long Island family. The available resources do not allow a concise record. The families will be continued in this context as unconnected until further research can verify the actual placement.

Hannah[3] Severance of Harwich married to Thomas Hinckly of Harwich, MA. Thomas Hinckley, son of Thomas, born 3-11-1708/09, married first, 3-31-1730, to Ruth Myrick of Harwich. He married second, 3-7-1765, to Lydia Nickerson of Chatham, and third on 7-31-1776 to **Hannah**[3] Severance of Harwich. Thomas died 1769, leaving a widow **Hannah**[3] and a minor son Elijah. His widow married perhaps in 1771 to John Burgess of Yarmouth. It appears that there were children of these families that continued the Severance name, however the records are very vague.

(7) Ephraim[3], (Ephraim[2], John[1]), born in Salisbury, Essex County, MA on 12-2-1689. [MAVR-Salisbury] He settled at a young age in Kingston, New Hampshire. He married to Mary Burnham 11-25-1714. [NHVR] She was believed to be the daughter of Lydia Pengry and Lt. Thomas Burnham Jr. of Ipswich, MA. [MDS]

Kingston, NH was still very much unsettled and **Ephraim**[3] had the adventure of being captured by the Indians and taken to Canada in May of 1724 during Three Years' War. [Coleman p338] Even after a treaty of peace in 1713, the Indians became restless and began renewing their attacks on the settlers. The young men were taken to Canada but soon released after a Peter Colcord escaped and a ransom was met. [Hazlett p493]

Ephraim[3] died at Kingston, NH, 5-31-1759 [NHVR] [Tibbetts]

Children: [Johnsen p12]
     i   **Mary**⁴ b 12-19-1719 m Elias Reno 4-5-1742
           [DARPI]
22   ii   **Benjamin**⁴ b around 1721 m Ruth Long 2-
           12-1744
     iii   **Elizabeth**⁴ bpt 7-23-1727 m Thomas
           Morrill 6-24-1740, Thomas b 9-19-1715,
           was the son of Ezekiel Morrill and
           Abigail Wadleigh of Salisbury, MA.
23   iv   **Joseph**⁴ bpt 7-23-1727 m Sarah Hills
     v   **John**⁴ bpt 7-23-1727
24   vi   **Ephraim**⁴ bpt 7-23-1727 m Elizabeth Sweat
           10-25-1749
25   vii   **Jacob**⁴ bpt 7-27-1729 m Sarah George 8-
           22-1735
     viii **Samuel**⁴ bpt 5-9-1731 d perhaps 1731
The parents of **Jacob**⁴ and **Samuel**⁴ are not listed in
the church records but the time and place would
tend to assure this as the correct placement.

(8) Ebenezer³, (Ephraim², John¹), born in Salisbury,
MA on 11-29-1694 and lived most of his life in
Kingston, NH and Ipswich, MA. He married Anna Fitts
on 1-8-1716/7. Anna was the daughter of Abraham
Fitts and Margaret Choate [NEHGR Vol 22 p71] Some
of the written accounts of this family indicate
that **Ebenezer³** married twice. Anna's maiden name
seems to be in question since it has been found as
Fitts or Choate. However, this appears to be an
error in reading the records.

Children: [MAVR-Ipswich]
     i   **Margaret**⁴ ("Margrit") bpt 7-30-1718
           [IGI] m William Coleman int 12-23-1739
     ii   **Sarah**⁴ bpt 12-21-1719 m Amos McIntire
           10-29-1741 [NHVR]
26   iii   **Abbe (Abraham⁴)** bpt 1721 m int Mary
           Stone 3-22-1745
27   iv   **Ephraim**⁴ bpt 11-17-1723 m Abigail Trask.
           Settled in Washington, NH
     v   **Hannah**⁴ bpt 10-24-1724 m Samuel Moody
           12-3-1755 [DAR Patriot Index]
     vi   **Matthew**⁴ bpt 12-22-1728 d 1737 age 9
           years [NHVR]
28   vii   **Ebenezer**⁴ bpt 8-29-1731 [MAVR] m
           Dorothy Eliot 4-6-1757 [MAVR]

(9) Jonathan³, (Ephraim², John¹), born 4-21-1700 in
Salisbury, MA. [Hoyt Vol 1 p315] **Jonathan³** married
to Katherine Tucker in Salisbury, MA 2-24-1726 (int

11-13-1725. [MAVR-Amesbury] The marriage also shows on the [MAVR-Salibury] and lists her name as Elizabeth Tucker. A later marriage to Katherine Tucker of 11-3-1725 in Amesbury would indicate that this was either the actual marriage date or perhaps it was just recorded later in Amesbury. This was indicative of several of the early records as they were recorded in several towns. The date they were recorded was given instead of the actual date. Katherine Tucker was the daughter of Ebenezer Nichols and Benoni Tucker.

It is possible that **Jonathan**[3] married a second time. The birth of **Judath**[4] Severance shows as the daughter of **Jonathan**[3] Severance and Mary Nickell's, born 8-2-1732 [MAVR-Amesbury]. This could be the only family at this time period.

Jonathan[3] died 5-14-1786, age 86. [NHVR] and is buried in the Plains Cemetery. [CRPCNH]

Children:
29	i	**Jonathan**[4] m Tryphena Nichols 9-5-1754. [NHVR]
30	ii	**Benjamin**[4] bpt 1-22-1731 m Jude Nichols 6-5-1755 [Harmond]
	iii	**Judith**[4] b 8-2-1732, daughter of Jonathan Severance and Mary Nickells. [MAVR]
	iv	**Hannah**[4] bpt 4-8-1733
	v	**Lidea**[4] d 9-6-1737
	vi	**Lydia**[4] b 1738 m Jonathan Sanborn 9-19-1758. **Lydia**[4] d 4-4-1827. [Sanborn p139]
	vii	**Elizabeth**[4] m Ebenezer Watson 7-25-1758
31	viii	**Samuel**[4] b 1741 m Hannah Winslow 8-1-1768
32	ix	**John**[4] b 12-2-1744 m Joanna Bartlett

FOURTH GENERATION (10) Daniel[4], (Ebenezer[3], John[2], John[1]), born in Northfield, MA, 1-24-1701. [MAVR] He married Rebecca Jones of Springfield, MA 10-18-1733. [MAVR] Rebecca was born 11-27-1705. [MAVR] They lived their lives in Northfield. **Daniel**[4] enlisted into the military at the age of 17 and vowed to kill every Indian in the hopes of avenging the death of his father who was killed at a corn harvest. [JFS p4] By 1747, **Daniel**[4] had attained the rank of Lieutenant, "his name appearing in a list posted in Colrain. 7-29-1748 at Deerfield. [Adams E p662] **Daniel**[4] died 12-15-1748. He was in the military service at the time. [MAVR]

Daniel[4] was a soldier under Capt. Kellogg from 1723-1730, he was a Lieut. under Capt. Ephraim

Williams in the brave defense of Fort Massachusetts on 8-2-1748. [Sheldon p286]

After the death of **Daniel⁴**, Rebecca remarried to Noah Alvord of Wilbraham, MA. The marriage was on 2-20-1752. Rebecca died 10-17-1793. [Alvord p51]

Rebecca (Jones) Severance Alvord was born 10-29-1712. She married to David Hall as his second wife on October 1774. She was the daughter of Ebenezer and Rebecca (Allis) Jones. [Jacobus 235]

Children: [Sheldon p286]
    i   **Sarah⁵** b 1-29-1734 [MAVR] m Nathaniel Hitchcock on 11-18-1755
33 ii   **Tabitha⁵** b 12-8-1736
   iii **Obed⁵** b 4-6-1739 d 1757, Hadley, MA. [MAVR] He was a soldier in the French War and was apparently killed in the war.

(11) Ebenezer⁴, (Ebenezer³, John², John¹), born 7-24-1709. He served with his brother **John⁴** in the military. He was a scout from the Connecticut River north of the line of forts at Charleston, NH and Fort Adams, MA. He was married in 9-23-1736 to Hannah ____. She died 12-16-1780 (MAVR) **Ebenezer⁴** died 3-24-1791. [MAVR]

Children: [JFS]
    i   **Mary⁵** b 12-1-1737 [MAVR] apparently d young
34 ii   **Ebenezer⁵** b 9-5-1739 [MAVR] m Azuba Smith 2-28-1764 removed to Middlebury, VT. Azuba was the daughter of Daniel Smith
   iii **Hannah⁵** b 1-19-1741 m David Risley 10-25-1764
35 iv **Abner⁵** b 11-5-1744 m Naomi Risley (Wrisley) settled in Northfield, MA
    v   **Mary⁵** b 9-9-1750 [MAVR] m Samuel Stoughton 7-12-1799 in Gill, MA

(12) John⁴, (John³, John², John¹), born at Christ Church Parish, Berkeley Co, SC. His birth date is not known, but it was before 1718. He married to Ann Barton, daughter of Thomas and Anne Barton on 6-10-1735. [MgSC Vol 20 p66] Anne was the daughter of Joseph Barton and Mary Barker and died before 1723. **John⁴** died on 4-4-1740 in Charleston, South Carolina. [MgSC Vol XX p 202]

Children: [MPN]
    i   **John⁵** b 3-31-1736 in SC but relatively little is known about him or his family. Records show a grant for 300 acres of land in 1775 in Craven County. [MWS] **John⁵** Saverance was in Christ Church Parish, with a wife and two daughters. [1790 SCFC] In the Will of Ann Humphrey's of Johns Island, SC, dated 1-28-1789, she mentions **Charlotte⁶** Saverance, grand daughter. **Charlotte⁶** Saverance, near eighty, shows with several slaves. [1830 SCFC] Another possible daughter is indicated as a marriage between John Bougler of Charleston and **Ann Elizabeth⁶** Saverance of Christ Church Parish by Rev. Mr. Frost shows in the [MgSC Vol 25]

36   ii   **Thomas⁵** b 2-8-1738/39 bpt 2-8-1738/9 [MgSC Vol XVIII p 174]

(13) Joseph⁴, (John³, John², John¹), born in SC. His birth date is not known. He married Ann Watson on 3-30-1732. He died on 1-11-1750 [MgSC Vol p 253] There is little evidence to show the families of **Joseph's⁴** children, however, **William¹⁰** Saverance believed that they settled in Alabama and Texas. However, little has been found to support that belief.

Children: [MWS]
    i   **Joseph⁵** b 7-12-1736
    ii   **William⁵** b 5-30-1739 IGI
   iii   **Sarah⁵** bpt 10-31-1747
   iv   **John⁵** bpt 5-13-1749

(14) Joseph⁴, (Joseph³, John², John¹), born 10-7-1713 in Greenfield, MA. [MAVR] He married Mary Clesson, daughter of Joseph Clesson 10-31-1731. Mary was born 5-9-1732 and died 7-25-1775, age 68. [MAVR] They settled in Deerfield, Franklin Co., MA. As a soldier in the French and Indian War, serving under Capt. Cheever, he was taken prisoner August 1757 at Fort William Henry at the head of Lake George, NY, and taken to Canada. He remained only a short time, escaped, and returned home. [JFS p6]
   He was a soldier in Father Rasle's War and in the service under Capt. Kellogg in 1730. [Sheldon p287]

Children: i-viii [Sheldon p287]
    i   **Joseph**[5] b 4-13-1733 d 5-29-1733
    ii   **Joseph**[5] b 6-15-1734 d 6-27-1734
37 iii   **Matthew**[5] b 6-15-1735 d 3-14-1816 m
            Experience Nash 1-24-1762
    iv   **Eunice**[5] b 1-5-1737 d 7-21-1802 m Moses
            Bascom 9-22-1760
    v   **Cloe**[5] b 4-7-1739 m Dan Corse November
            1759. [Suddaby p307] Dan was the son of
            James Corse and Thankful Munn
    vi   **Joanna**[5] b 9-13-1743 m David Allen
    vii   **Mary**[5] b 5-6-1745 d 5-8-1823 m Oliver
            Atherton 8-16-1756
    viii   **Ruel**[5] bpt 4-24-1747 d 9-17-1768
38 ix   **Jesse**[5] b 1751 [HOCoNY p195]

(15) Martin[4], (Joseph[3], John[2], John[1]), born 9-10-
1718. [MAVR] He married 9-10-1746 to Patience
Fairfield. [MAVR] She died 5-25-1809 age 81 [MAVR]
and he died on 4-8-1810. [MAVR] He is buried with
Patience in the Hill Cemetery, Old Deerfield, MA.
He was of Hinsdale, New Hampshire in 1749 [Sheldon
p287]
    When fighting between England and France was
renewed, **Martin**[4] became one of the famous Rogers's
Rangers who served around Lake George and Fort
Ticonderoga. Only the most experienced were
accepted by Captain Rogers. On June 25, 1758,
Martin[4] and three other rangers were captured by
the enemy at Sabbath Day Point and taken as
prisoners to Canada and then to France. [Burnham
p186]
    He left an amazing history as detailed by **John
F.**[6] Severance. **Martin's**[4] grandson, who was eighteen
years old when **Martin**[4] died, tells that; "he was
fearless, daring, shrewd, and wary. He was never
known to fall into an ambush or surprise in any
attack; never off his guard. He was never wounded
or captured but once." With his nephew, **Matthew**[6],
and a James Henry Smith, they were taken across the
lake to Canada. "In crossing the lake he was made
to row the boat, and during the passage the Indians
began to vex him which he resented, whereupon one
of the more daring ones slapped his face, knocking
his hat off. Raising his oar, he struck the Indian
over the head and knocked him overboard, leaving
him to his fate in the water. On their arrival in
Canada an effort was made to make the party run the
gauntlet during which his nephew and Smith nearly

lost their lives. **Martin**[4] stoutly refused and they excused him and he did not run."

Rev. Theophilus Packard, pastor of the 1st Congregational Church of Shelburn, Massachusetts for many years relates; "When a captive among the Indians, he was set to hoeing corn in the summer, and with apparent ignorance and honesty would hoe up the corn with the weeds to such an extent that he was released from that employment. He was held a captive for about two years and returned by the way of Quebec, France, and England, having served in both French Wars."

It is related of him by **John F.**[6] Severance, "that when in camp they were in great need of vegetables and that he and some of his comrades went on a foraging expedition with a box in the shape of a coffin, filled it with cabbages and bore it solemnly into camp, calling to all sentinels; "stand aside, dead man, small pox," and space was given at once for the corpse to pass." [JFS p6-8]

David Merrill, "says that his maternal great grandfather came to America during the early Colonial times and the story of his life is one of thrilling interest. He was a brave fearless man and twice served his country as a soldier. He enlisted in the French and Indian War and was twice captured by red men and sent to Canada. He also aided the Colonies in their struggle for independence and lived to a ripe old age and died in this ninety third year. Once while trying to cross a river, they felled a large tree and when the chief tried to cross, Mr. Severance rolled the log and caused the chief to fall into the water. The Chief would have killed Severance but the other Indians were greatly amused and saved him." [P&BRWI p976]

Martin[4] married Patience Fairfield, 9-10-1746. "Patience Severence, wife of **Martin**[4] Severance" was allowed cetain amounts (among others) in the Will of Thomas Allen. [Allen p17] She was the daughter of Samuel Fairfield and Patience Miller. She was born 6-14-1724 and died 5-25-1809, age 81. He moved his family to Shelburn Falls in 1760, taking all of his household goods on horseback in baskets.

Rev. Packard continues, "he was not a professor of religion but he was an habitual attendant upon public religious worship."

John F.[6] Severance relates, "He lived at the base of the west slope of the mountain near Salmon (now Shelburn) Falls. On one of his hunting excursions on the mountain he saw two bears run into a den among the rocks, and while endeavoring to find an opening through which he might get a shot at them, down went **Martin**[4], rocks and all among the bears, all of which left him without further ceremony than tearing his cloths in their efforts to get out." "He related later that it was the only time in this life he was ever scared." [JFS p8]

    Martin[4], in his old age, became quite a story teller and he passed on many tales of his experiences. He died April 8, 1810 and is buried at Shelburn Center.

    Notes from a letter to a Greenfield, MA newspaper in the 1800's or early 1900's written by Rev. **John F.**[6] Severance; "**Martin**[4] Severance was one of the first settlers at Salmon (now Shelburne Falls). At this time **John**[2] Severance Jr., **Martin's**[4] grandfather, was living at Bedford, Westchester Co., NY., having left Deerfield the last of 1702 or early in 1703. **Martin's**[4] father, **Joseph**[3], was 22 years of age at the time of the meadow fight.

    A few years after **Martin's**[4] father was made a cripple, his grandfather, **John**[2] came from Bedford to Deerfield and lived with him, about 1716. **Martin**[4] was born two years later, April 10, 1718; his brother **Joseph**[3] five years earlier. **John Jr.**[2] gave all of his Deerfield lands to **Joseph**[3], **Martin's**[4] father, with whom he lived and at whose home he died.

    Martin's[4] cousin, **Daniel**[4], son of **Ebenezer**[3], declared that "he would kill every Indian of whom he could get sight. This cousin **Daniel**[4] was 13 years older than **Joseph**[3], and 17 years older than **Martin**[4]. At the time **Ebenezer**[3] was killed, his son **Daniel**[4] was 22 years old, **Joseph**[3] 9, and **Martin**[4] was 5 years. Of the two brothers, **Martin**[4] was the most determined as well as the most vindictive. **Martin**[4] and his son **Samuel**[5] enlisted and served through the Revolutionary War."

    The **Martin**[4] Severance Chapter of the National Association of the Daughters of the American Revolution of Aneheim, CA was named in his honor.

Children:

    i   **Elisha**[5] bpt 5-18-1746 in Deerfield, Franklin Co., MA. "son of Martin Severance and Patience Fairfield," bpt 5-18-1746, "on account of his grandfather, **Joseph**[2] Severance of Shelburne, 1780 [MAVR-Church record].

The [MAVR-Shelburne] show the deaths of
Polly[6] d 4-13-1776 age 2 and **Nathaniel**[6]
8-20-178_ age 3, both of Shelburn, MA
and children of Elijah[5] and Bethia ____.
It is uncertain if they should be placed
here but there was no other section that
would fit them.

ii   **Catharine**[5] b 12-20-1747 d 4-8-1785 m
Elisha Hinsdale of Greenfield 11-13-1764

iii   **Experince**[5] b 10-8-1750 in Hinsdale, NH d
7-27-1828 m Eleazer Scott of Wendell 10-
1-1772 [Allen p39] says that they
married 10-6-1774. [DAR Patriot Index]

iv   **Abigail**[5] b 3-6-1753 at Fort Dummer m
David Hosley 10-13-1773

40   v   **Martin**[5] b 3-8-1755 in Hinsdale, NH, at
Fort Dummer d 12-29-1843 m Lucy Whitney
11-15-1781

vi   **Submit**[5] b 10-28-1758 in Deerfield, MA d
8-6-183_ m Asa Smith of Belchertown 9-
16-1782. [DARPI p624] **Submit**[5] was born
while her father was a captive and named
by her mother in recognition of the fact
of his captivity [JFS p9]

The following children were born at Shelburne, MA
[Sheldon p 287][MAVR-Shelburne and Deerfield]

41   vii   **Samuel**[5] b 1-12-1761 m Azuba Smith 9-7-
1786

viii   **Sophia**[5] b 2-12-1765 m Jacob Crosby

ix   **Sarah**[5] b 1-4-1767 d 10-27-1805 unm

x   **Mary**[5] b 8-1-1769 d 4-25-1785

42   xi   **Selah**[5] b 9-26-1771 d 10-8-1832 m Hannah
Putman 11-30-1797. Hannah was b 10-24-
1780 and d 5-30-1854 [Snow p12]

xii   **Patience**[5] b 5-13-1774 d 5-25-1809 unm
[MAVR]

(16) John[4], (Joseph[3], John[2], John[1]), born 12-15-1720.
[MAVR Deerfield] He married to Esther Arms,
daughter of Daniel Arms on 3-15-1742. [MAVR] She
was born 11-12-1723. "He moved from Deerfield to
Falltown about 1759, and with seven others
petitioned the General Court for incorporation with
the name of Bernardston. This was granted 3-6-1762
   He enlisted November 20, 1745, in Capt. John
Light's Co., Col. Thomas Moore's Regiment, in the
campaign against Louisburg. He was promoted to the
rank of Lieutenant; was a soldier in Capt. Salah
Barnard's Co., Col. Israel Williams Regiment, in

the French and Indian War in 1759; served under
Capt. Agrippa Wells, Col. Samuel William's
Regiment, in 1775." [JFS p9]
He bought and sold several pieces of land as is
indicated by the land transactions of Franklin Co.,
Massachusetts. His name is listed in 1800. [MAFC].
He died 12-25-1805 in Barnardston, MA. [MAVR-
Barnardston]

Children: [MAVR-Deerfield, Shelburne, Greenfield]
    i   **Esther**[5] b 4-26-1742
    ii   **Hanna**[5] bpt 2-5-1744 d 5-18-1838 m int
        Uriah Martindale 2-8-1817
43 iii **John**[5] bpt 1-19-1746 m int Zuriah Nichols
        5-22-1784
44 iv **David**[5] b 2-4-1747 d 11-25-1838 m Sarah
        Santer 1-15-1778 who died 6-14-1815 age
        55 m2 Lucy, probably the widow of Dr.
        Edward Billings of Guilford, daughter of
        Luke Hitchcock, she d 11-4-1844 age 77
        [MAVR]
    v   **Drucilla**[5] b 2-23-1750
    vi   **Achsah**[5] bpt 11-16-1752 [MAVR] m Thadeus
        Merrill
    vii **Eleaner**[5] b 9-3-1754 d 8-31-1777 m
        Adonijah Atherton 5-19-1777
    viii **Rachel**[5] b 1-9-1759
45 ix **Daniel**[5] b 12-18-1764/65 d 1-6-1728.

(17) Jonathan[4], (Joseph[3], John[2], John[1]), born 6-12-
1725 in Deerfield, MA. He married Thankful Stebbins
on 8-30-1749. [MAVR] "Thankful was the daughter of
John Stebbins and Mary___, born 4-1-1729 at
Deerfield, MA and died 12-8-1806 [MAVR] at
Greenfield." [Greenlee Vol I p206]
Jonathan[4] settled as a farmer in Greenfield, MA.
He owned land north of the village in Greenfield
Meadows. He held a Lieutenant's commission in the
French and Indian War. It was said that "after the
battle of Lexington he stood aloof from military
service." During the Revolutionary War he sent a
substitute for his eldest son who managed the
gristmill. The mill was the first erected in that
town.
Jonathan[4] "was a tall, well formed, broad
shouldered man; a keen black eye, erect, somewhat
stern in his bearing, yet of pleasant speech."
When, in 1800, his eldest son left with
Jonathan's[4] two grand-sons to make their home in
Truxton, NY., **Jonathan**[4] waived good-bye "wearing

his pig tail queue and dressed in his William Penn
cut of coat, long waistcoat and knee breeches, his
daily dress." [JFS p10-11] In 1800 he was living in
Hampshire Co. [MAFC]

Thankful died at the age of 77 on 12-8-1806
[MAVR] **Jonathan**[4] died 4-2- 1822, age 96 years at
Truxton, NY. [MAVR] He had been Town Collector and
chairman of patriot committees of Massachusetts.
[DARLR Vol 165 p122]

Children: [JFS p10]
46	i	**Jonathan**[5] b 3-31-1750 [MAVR-Greenfield] d 5-15-1845 m Elizabeth McClellan [Greenlee Vol I p206]
	ii	**Experience**[5] b 1-8-1752 m Reuben Wells 4-11-1772 [10-1-1772 Greenlee p206]
		Thirza[5] bpt 11-1-1753 died soon
	iii	**Thirza**[5] b 10-29-1754 d 12-25-1758
	iv	**Thankful**[5] b 1-17-1756 d 12-23-1829 m Ariel Hinsdale 1-13-1774 [DARLR Vol 165]
	v	**Dorotha**[5] b 10-8-1718 d 6-4-1816 unm
47	vi	**Joseph**[5] b 9-20-1760 d 11-24-1829 m Mercy Allen 9-28-1778
48	vii	**Solomon**[5] (Capt.) b 11-10-1762 (9-20-1762 Greenlee p206) d 11-12-1804 m Hannah Hoyt 11-21-1785
	viii	**Thirza**[5] b 11-15-1764 d 9-23-1827 m Elisha Wells Jr. 4-11-1782
49	ix	**Elihu**[5] b 9-1-1766 d 11-24-1841 m Patty (Martha) Hitchcock 11-26-1801
	x	**Abigail**[5] b 12-4-1768 m Amos Cornwall 10-14-1785
50	xi	**Rufus**[5] b 3-28-1770 d 9-10-1819 m Sarah Newton 1-7-1802 m2 Tirzah Root 1-1-1808
	xii	**Cynthia**[5] b 12-28-1772 d 9-17-1858 unm
	xiii	**Martha**[5] b 2-13-1774 d 12-19-1806 (12-13-1836 Greenlee p206) unm

(18) Moses[4], (Joseph[3], John[2], John[1]), the youngest
son of **Joseph**[3] and Ann Severance, born 3-23-1730 in
Deerfield, MA. (MAVR) He served in the service of
Capt. Burke's Co., of Rangers for about two years
and obtained the rank of Ensign. On 10-28-1762 he
married Joanna French at Deerfield, Massachusetts
[MAVR], daughter of Thomas French and Joanna Field.
Joanna was born 5-15-1740. They settled in Montague
around 1769. [1790 MAFC-Montague]

He was appointed a delegate from Montague to the
convention for the ratification of the Federal
Constitution. He voted "nay" and was then charged

27

as being a Tory. However, as many others also voted "nay" and they were by no means Tory's, it can be said that **Moses**[4] was neither a Tory or a supporter of any British interest in this country. As so many others at the convention, he did not agree with the wording "we the people" and not "we the states". They felt that the new plan was too costly and gave the power of taxation to the congress and not the people. It also did not assure the liberty of the press. One hundred and eighty seven of those voting "nay" did so to "ratify" the declaration. [JFS p11-12]

Moses[4] died on 8-1-1799. Joanna died 3-6-1812 at the age of 72 [MAVR-Montague]

Children: [JFS p12][MAVR-Montague-Deerfield]
51   i   **Moses**[5] b 10-10-1763 m Abigail Austin
     ii   **Joanna**[5] b 3-3-1765 m Aaron Taylor
     iii   **Elisha**[5] b 2-16-1767. Little is known, he
           d 3-7-1834, and was listed on a jury in
           1807 at Cazenovia, Madison Co, NY.
           [Tuttle p223] The [1800 NYFC] shows an
           Elisha[5] living in Chenango Co with a wife
           and 1 son under the age of one year old.
     iv   **Mercy (Mary)**[5] b 7-4-1769 m Arad Root
           (Arad Root, son of Elisha of Williston,
           Chittenden Co., VT) m **Mary**[5] Severance,
           she d 11-27-1800 ae 31 and he m2 to
           Lydia Shattuck) [Root p224]
     v   **Rebecca**[5] b 9-9-1770 d 1-6-1777
52   vi   **Elihu**[5] b 9-6-1773 d 3-5-1834 m Tryphena
           Gunn 9-10-1796
     vii   **Rebecca**[5] b 6-10-1778 m Rufus Green

(19) James[4], (unconnected, Joseph[2], John[1]), born circa 1730 m Jane Phillips of Lynn, Essex Co. MA, daughter of Thomas and Sarah Phillips, on 1-3-1761 at Harwich, Barstable Co., MA. [MAVR-Harwich] Jane was born 6-2-1737.

Children: conjecture
53   i   **James**[5] b circa 1760
54   ii   **Phillip**[5] b circa 1760
55   iii   **Joseph**[5] b circa 1760
56   iv   **Ebenezer**[5] b circa 1760

(19a) Joseph[4] (unconnected, Joseph[2], John[1]), b circa 1730, shows at New Bedford, MA. The records will show that **Joseph**[4] married to Mary Howland, 4-25-1776 and the intentions for marriage of **Joseph**[4] to

28

Amie Bennett, 3-18-1758, at Dartmouth, Bristol Co.,
MA
[MAVR]

Children:
57   i   **Joseph**[5] b 1760. The 1790 MA census for
                Greenfield, shows with 1 son and 1
                daughter.
58   ii   **Thomas**[5] b circa 1760
59   iii   **William**[5] b circa 1760
    There were most likely others of this line that
produced children. However the records are very
vague.
    Revolutionary War records show that **Joseph**[6],
Thomas[6], and **Nicholson**[6], privates, under Capt.
Thomas Crandon's Co., Col. John Hathaway's Regt,
entered service 8-2-1789, discharged 8-8-1780 on an
alarm at Rhode Island. Certified at Dartmouth, MA
under Capt. Henry Jenne's Co., Col. John Hathaway's
92nd (Bristol Co) Regt. [MASS]
    The records will show a **Nicholson** or **Nickerson**
of Colchester, in the District of Chittenden, VT,
who died intestate before 5-2-1820. A **Joseph,
Ebenezer**, and Hannah Severance gave up the right of
administration of his goods and chattel. [Vermont
Probate Records}

(22) Benjamin[4], (Ephraim[3], Ephraim[2], John[1]), of
Kingston, NH was bpt 9-11-1726 but probably was
born around 1721. He lived in Kingston until 1751
when he bought land in Chester, NH. [NHPSP Vol 46]
    Benjamin[4] married Ruth Long, on 2-12-1744/45.
[Tibbetts p42] She was born 4-15-1725 and died 6-
16-1816, [Chase p623] the daughter of William Long
and Deborah Tong. She was living in Chester with a
young son and 2 younger daughters in 1790. She was
living alone in 1800. [NHFC]
    Various land transactions from the New Hampshire
Provincial and State Papers show the family
connections and establish the residence as being in
Chester, NH. [MBJ]
    Benjamin[4] received land from John March on March
7, 1740/1, "land in Kingston which said March
bought of his grandfather Severance" [NHPSP Vol 53
p80-81] who was **Ephraim**[2] Severance Sr..
    Benjamin[4] and Ruth Severance gave land to
Ebenezer Long, October 1, 1754, "right in Kingston
of the late William Long, father of said Ruth."
[NHPSP Vol 45 p 82]

Ephraim[2], Severance Sr. gives land "for love and affection I bear" for his son **Ephraim[3]**, land in Kingston, New Hampshire (March 27, 1716). [NHPSP Vol 22 p235-236

Ephraim[2], Severance and John March purchase from Jedediah Philbrook land bounded by "Spectall Meadow" (April 4, 1731) [NHPSP Vol 53 p79-80]

John March sells to **Benjamin[4]**, Severance "land I bought of grandfather Severance late of Kingston", "half of the meadow at Spectall brook" that John March bought of Jedidiah Philbrook. **Ephraim[2]**, grandfather to **Benjamin[4]**. (March 7, 1741) [NHPSP Vol 53 p89-81]

Benjamin[4] Severance purchases land in the Township of Chester, New Hampshire formerly the estates of Mr. John Calf. (October 24, 1751) [NHPSP Vol 46 p33-34]

Children: [Johnsen p13]
    i   **Elizabeth[5]** bpt 9-8-1745 [Tibbetts p152]
            d 3-4-1771
60 ii   **Joseph[5]** b 7-21-1745 d 3-16-1813
            Salisbury, MA m Anna Currier
    iii   **Anna[5]** bpt 5-8-1748
    iv   **William[5]** b 1752 His life is rather
            elusive. He appears to have served in
            the military in several capacities.
            First he is found with Capt. Hutchin's
            Company, Col. Reed's Regt., This
            regiment was raised from men of Chester
            and surrounding towns,. He was listed
            living with **Peter[5]** Severance, age
            twenty-one of Chester, and **William[5]** was
            listed as age twenty three, husbandman,
            and living in Londonderry, NH. He was
            again in the continental line in 1777
            under Capt. Runnel's Co., Col. Nichol's
            Regiment with General Stark. [NHPSP Vol
            2] In 1791 he is on the tax list at
            Salisbury and it was reported that he
            later went to Sandwich, New Hampshire.
            It is not known if he ever married or
            had a family.
61 v   **Peter[5]** b 1754 d 5-30-1817 Chester, m
            Sarah Hall 11-28-1780. [DARRW #589678]

(23) Joseph[4], (Eprhaim[3], Ephraim[2], John[1]), bpt 9-11-1726. He was married circa 1749. He verified that he and his wife renewed their baptismal covenant with their son **Joseph[5]** on June 16, 1751 [Tibbetts]

Joseph⁴ Severance married Sarah Hills. Sarah was born on 10-7-1731, daughter of Nathaniel, born Dunstable, (afterwards Nottingham West, now Hudson, New Hampshire) married **Joseph⁴** Severance who died young (about 1757) and Sarah married second to John Hall. [DARPI p294] Sarah was the daughter of Nathaniel Hills and Ann Worn of Newbury, MA. Sarah Severance and John Hall moved to Tunbridge, VT about 1795. They had additional children (Hall surname) John, Thomas, Nathaniel, Sarah, and Moody. [Hills p275] [VTVR]

  Joseph⁵, Caleb⁵ and **Joshua⁵**, served and fought in the Revolutionary War. "**Anna⁵**, daughter of **Joseph⁴** was baptized, December 3, 1753". [Tibbetts]

Children:
62   i   **Joseph⁵** b Nottingham West 9-12-1750
             [IGI] bpt 6-16-1751 [Tibbetts] enlisted
             in the Continental Army in 1777 for 3
             years, m Mary Harper 11-22-1785.
     ii   **Anna⁵** b Nottingham West 11-14-1752 [IGI]
             bpt 12-3-1753 [Tibbetts] m William
             Abrams 4-19-1796 [IGI]
63   iii   **Caleb⁵** b Nottingham West 5-15-1753/55
             [PRME] He was in the Bennington
             campaign in 1777 for 2 months
64   iv   **Joshua⁵** b Nottingham West 12-22-1757
             [IGI] was in the army at Cambridge 8
             months, was in the battle of Bunker Hill
             and in the RI campaign in 1778 m
             Elizabeth Snow on 4-14(5-8)-1787, they
             lived in Brewer and Orrington, ME.

(24) Ephraim⁴, (Ephraim³, Ephraim², John¹), bpt 7-23-1727 at the First Church of Christ in Kingston, NH. At this period of history many families were on the move, claiming free land, raising large families, and fighting off hostile Indians. They had little time to record or leave record of their lives. As a result, very little is known about some of these early families. Church records and various town records give the only rough indications of their movement.

  Ephraim⁴ Severance was a native of NH. He married to Elizabeth Sweat at the Kingston First Church, 10-25-1749. [NHVR] Elizabeth was the daughter of John Sweet and Judith Young. She was born 12-24-1724 at Kingston, Rockingham Co., NH. [NHVR]

Widow Elizabeth Severance was granted Administration and Bond of her husband's estate and a license to sell as administratrix on 10-26-1757. She remarried to Ebenezer Watson [NHVR] at Kingston, NH, 7-25-1758. [Hosier p165] Elizabeth died in 1777 in Kingston of a fever.

Their children were born in Kingston, NH but the family was among the pioneers of Sandwich, New Hampshire, settling north-east of the town and north of Bear Camp Pond.

Ephraim[4] died 5-20-1757 and Elizabeth died 1777 [Tibbetts Vol. III p44]

Children: [NHVR]
65 i   **John**[5] bpt 9-9-1750 [Tibbetts Vol III p44](b 9-2-1750) m Susanna (Smith)
    ii   **Moses**[5] b 3-19-1752
66 iii   **Peter**[5] b 3-6-1754 m Abigail Pettengill 9-20-1779
    iv   **Judith**[5] b 3-25-1756 m Isreal Clifford [Draper Vol 75 p94]

(25) Jacob[4], (Ephraim[3], Ephraim[2] John[1]), bpt 7-27-1729 in Kingston, NH. (NHVR) Very little is known of his life. He married Sarah George on August 22, 1753. [Tibbetts Vol III p86] They had a daughter born at Kingston in 1755, and a son **Jacob**[5].

Children:
    i   **Mary**[5] b 8-12-1755
67 ii   **Jacob**[5] m Mary Tucker 3-12-1794

(26) Abbe[4](Abraham), (Ebenezer[3], Ephraim[2], John[1]), bpt 1721 married Mary Stone, (their intention of marriage was 3-22-1745). [MAVR] Mary was bpt 9-20-1724. [MAVR] **Abbey**[4] Severance and Mary Stone listed their intention of marriage in Ipswich, MA. [MAVR] **Abba**[4] Severance married 1745 to Mary Stone [Hammatt p349] In 1790 **Abby (Abbe)**[4] was at Temple, Hillsboro County with a wife and three daughters. [NHFC]

Abbe[6] Severance's name, of the Revolutionary War, NH line, was placed on the Vermont Roll under the law of March 18, 1818. [1820 U.S. War Department Pension List, National Archives]

(27) Ephraim[4], (Ebenezer[3], Ephraim[2], John[1]), bpt 11-17-1723 in Ipswich, MA [MAVR]. He married in Beverly, Essex Co., MA to Abigail Trask, daughter of John (Joshiah) Trask and Mary Woodbury, on 2-22-1747/48. [MAVR] He died in Topsham, Orange Co., VT

circa 1810 where he was living with his son
Daniel[5].

"On June 15, 1748, I **Ephraim[4]** Severance of
Groton, blacksmith for fifty pounds, paid by
Ebenezer of Groton, physician, paid by the said
Ebenezer Perry for and in behalf of his son Abijah
Perrs a minor, do sell unto him the said Abijah
Perry a certain piece of land in Groton, six acres,
with a mansionhouse thereon...signed by Abigail
Perry, Benjamin Hazen and wife, Betty Hazen, along
with **Ephraim[4]** and Abigail Severance. [Adams p16]

New Ipswich, Province of NH 1-8-1765 from
Ichabod How to Aaron Kidder Constable for Ipswich,
states that "whereas a family vix, **Ephraim[4]**
Severance and Abigail, his wife and **Abigail[5]**,
Daniel[5], **Abel[5]**, **Molly[5]**, and **Sarah[5]**, their children,
have for some time past resided in said Ipswich and
are likely to become inhabitants in said town
unless lawfully prevented". [TRNINH Vol 2 p831]

This is certainly the above family, however
where was **Ephraim Jr.[5]** (age 8), **Rufus[5]**, or
Ebenezer[5], sons of **Ephraim[4]** and Abigail, when the
family was sent out of New Ipswich?

They moved to Washington, NH (formerly called
Camden) at an early date. He was on the first board
of selectmen in 1777. [HWNH p596] His name was with
three daughters in 1790. [NHFC]

On 4-18-1777 **Ephraim[4]** sent a note to New
Ipswich, NH, apparently to verify his good
intentions, "This may certify to all whom it may
concern that I, **Ephraim[4]** Severance, of New Ipswich
am engaged and enlisted as a soldier in the
Continental Service for and during the term of
three years which service is to be reaconed and
acconned for unto Ebenezer Champney, Francis
Fletcher, John Cutter, and William Spear, the same
as tho either of the said person had served in
person." [TRNINH] It is believed that this **Ephraim[4]**
is the son of **Ephraim Sr.[3]**

Children:
68	i	**Daniel[5]** b 1752 d 3-10-1817 m Betsy Safford
69	ii	**Ebenezer[5]** b 1753 d 9-21-1819 m Lucy Nutter 4-9-1777
70	iii	**Abel[5]** b 1754 d 8-26-1842 Bradford, NH m Martha Bruce 8-26-1779
71	iv	**Rufus[5]** b 1755 d 1835 Washington, NH m Martha Flagg 4-20-1785
72	v	**Ephraim[5]** b 1759 d 3-4-1836 Knox, ME

vi   **Abigail**[5] d in Washington m Charles Brown 6-18-1795
vii   **Molly**[5] m Elijah Foster 1783
viii   **Sarah**[5] d in Washington

(28) Ebenezer[4], (Ebenezer[3], Ephraim[2], John[1]), born about 1721 in Kingston, NH. He was bpt 8-29-1731 [MAVR]. He married Dorothy Eliot on 4-6-1757 in Temple, Hillsboro Co., NH. [Tibbetts Vol I p89] Their three children were born in Kingston.

The following "warning out" was issued "from the Selectmen of Kingston" (signed by Josiah Bartlett and John Wadleigh) 5-27-1773 against **Ebenezer[4]** Severance and his wife Dorothy and the children **Naomi[5]**, **Dorothy[5]**, and **Ebenezer[5]**, from the town of Kingston, New Hampshire. The Severance's answered that they had come there from Hawke 12-24-1772. Again Dorothy Severance was "warned out of Raymond in 1795 (a widow) Dorothy (either the daughter or the above Dorothy)." **Ebenezer[6]** Severance was with his wife, a son and a daughter in 1790. [NHFC-Gilsum] He also is indicated in 1800. [NHFC]

Children: The family reportedly had five children but only four could be found in the research.
     i   **Naomi[5]** b 2-3-1758 m Samuel Haley 11-2-1777 [IGI] Kingston, NH
     ii   **Dorothy[5]** b 10-6-1760 [Tibbetts Vol I p89]
73   iii   **Asa[5]** b 11- -1761 (that he was a son of **Ebenezer[4]** is conjecture but is probably correct since he can't be placed with another family) **Asa[4]** was most likely born elsewhere. He also shows on the Census of Pensioners June 1, 1840 for Lancaster, Erie Co, New York, age 78. His Revolutionary War Pension Records #S15636 indicate that he was born in Alstead, Cheshire Co., NH, and transfered to Lancaster, Erie County, NY to be with his son.
74   iv   **Ebenezer[5]** b 9-8-1768 [Tibbetts Vol I p89] supposedly married first to Sarah Brown and 2nd to Sally Coolidge who was b 7-5-1779.

(29) Jonathan[4], (Jonathan[3], Ephraim[2], John[1]), was born in Kingston. He probably was a farmer. He married Tryphena Sarah Nichols on October 5, 1754. [NHVR] The Kingston First Church Records show that he died 4- -1776. All of there children were born in Kingston, NH. [NHVR]

Children: [Tibbetts Vol III p81-89][MBG]
    i   **Catten**[5] b 8-28-1755
75 ii   **Jonathan**[5] b 7-31-1757 in Kingston, NH m Mehitable Brown 7-4-1781
    iii **Mary**[5] b 7-26-1762
    iv **Lida**[5] b 7-13-1766 m Moses Sargent the 3rd, intentions of Marriage 11-26-1791. [Amesbury, MAVR]
    v   **Tryphena**[5] (Sarah) b 3-28-1769

(30) Benjamin[4], (Jonathan[3], Ephraim[2], John[1]), born in Salisbury, MA and bpt 1-22-1733 [MAVR-Salisbury] He was most likely a farmer in the new wilderness. He married Judith Nichols, June 5, 1755, at the 2nd Congregational Church, now Merrimac. [MAVR-Amesbury] She was born 8-2-1732 and the daughter of Jonathan Nichols and Mary Challis. All of their children were born in Kingston, NH. [NHVR]

Children: [MLSW]
    i   **Juda**[5] b 9-26-1756
    ii   **Sarah**[5] b 11-19-1758 d young
76 iii **Benjamin**[5] b 2-10-1760 bpt 2-15-1761 [Amesbury, NHVR] m Rebecca (Swett) Holcomb 12-16-1784
    iv **Lowes**[5] b 3-6-1764
77 v   **Nichols**[5] b 10-15-1766 m Louise Swett 9-21-1790 [IGI]
    vi **Sarah**[5] b 3-26-1769 m Nathaniel Kilborn 1788
    vii **Molly**[5] b 9-19-1771 m Isaac Fiske, son of Ebenezer Fiske. He was b 8-27-1769 [Pierce p127]

(31) Samuel[4], (Jonathan[3], Ephraim[2], John[1]), born 1741 in Kingston, NH and spent his entire life there. He was most likely a farmer. He served in the Revolutionary War. He married Hannah Winslow on August 1, 1768. [NEVR] Hannah was born 4-22-1743 at Kingston, NH, daughter of Samuel Winslow. All of their children were born in Kingston, NH. The [1790 and 1820 NH census] shows them living in Kingston.

    A letter submitted by E. George Adams of Newburyport, MA to The New England Historical and Genealogical Register in 1856, allows us to get an inside look into this family. It was written in 1775 by **Samuel**[4] Severance. He was a native of

Kingston, NH. He enlisted in the Revolutionary Army and served about three months. He was in the battle of Bunker Hill. The letter was addressed from Medford to his wife at Kingston. Her maiden name was Hannah Winslow. E. George Adams relates an incident to illustrate the social life and the privation of those times.

"When the postman came round to convey letters from the inhabitnats of Kingston, as well as any little necessaries from their friends, to the soldiers in the service, Mrs. Severance sent to her husband some green beans, with a piece of pork to cook with them, and some Indian meal to make him a pudding, while his little daughter, six years old, picked him a pint of berries to put in it; which he gratefully received, while the soldiers stood looking onwith tears in their eyes, wishing they had a wife or children to send them a like present. Mr. Severance was taken sick with the camp disease, and was forced to return home. This little daughter's name was Hannah, and married Henry Adams of Newbury. Henry Adams had a daughter Hannah who married Ebenezer Plumer of Newburyport, whose only child, Sarah Cobb Plumer, was E. George Adams' wife.

"madford July th 17, 1775"
"these lines comes to you, my loveing wife and dear children, hoping in the marcy of god that you are all well, and I hope in gods time I shall be restored home again; but if not, I beg of god that we may so live in this world that we may spend some day in each others preasents in a world of glory, for I put noe trust in the arm of flesh, by my trust is in god alone for life and mearcy, and I hope in the mearcy of god that he will cary you throu all your troble and dificiles that you have to pas throu in this life. my love to father and mother, to brother John and wife. I hope that you are all well, and the rest of my friends, to my wife; what money I send home to you, you may take care of it. if you have aney prospect of corn, I would have that old cow have a peas on her horns, so I have noe more at the preasent, so I remain your living housband till death peart."

(**Samuel**[4] Severance)

[NEHGR Vol XII p22]

Children: [NHVR-Kingston]

	i	**Hannah**[5] b 7-8-1769 d 3-23-1851 m Henry Adams as his third marriage 5-3-1799. Henry married first to Sarah Dole and secondly to Sarah Pulsifer of Ipswich, MA. [Adams A p49]
	ii	**Phebe**[5] b 3-31-1771
	iii	**Elizabeth**[5] b 8-5-1773 m Jonathan Shepard Int 1-2-1793 [Kingston, NH]
78	iv	**Samuel**[5] b 8-25-1775 m Judith Towle
	v	**Katherine**[5] b 5-9-1778 possibly married to James Banks of Newburyport, MA, Int. 3-19-1808.

(32) John[4], (Jonathan[3], Ephraim[2], John[1]), born 12-2-1744 in Kingston, NH. [NHVR] Very little is known about him or his family. He was probably a farmer and most likely supported the Revolutionary War as did his brother. He married Joanna Bartlett in 1765. [NHVR] Joanna was born 1742 and died in 1835 at Pembroke, NH. He died on 12-2-1827. Their known son was born in Kingston. [NHVR] In 1790 **John**[4] and his wife were living in Lyndborough. [NHFC]

Children:

79	i	**John**[4] b 7-23-1773 m Rachel Heath 11-4-1807. They had a son, **Nathan**[5], who married to Lydia Gould 9-19-1830.

FIFTH GENERATION (33) Tabitha[5], (Daniel[4], Ebenezer[3], John[2], John[1]), born on 12-18-1736. She married to Asa Miller on 12-12-1765 [MAVR West Springfield] (three years after **John**[6] was born). Apparently **Tabitha**[5] died relatively young as Asa Miller remarried to Eunice Sheroy (his second wife) in 1778. [DARLR Vol 75 p88]

Tabitha's[5] son, **John**[6] was bpt 7-18-1762 at Springfield, MA [MAVR]. The fathers name was not given.

Known children of **Tabitha**[5] Severance

80	i	**John/Abba**[6] bpt 7-18-1762 m Eunice Chase, both of Newbury, MA on 10-12-1781 [MAVR]

(34) Ebenezer[5], (Ebenezer[4], Ebenezer[3], John[2], John[1]), born 9-5-1739 in MA [MAVR] He settled in Northfield and married Azuba Smith, daughter of Daniel Smith on 2-28-1764.

All of their children were born there. He later removed to Middlebury, VT where some of his sons had settled at an earlier date. He was reportedly

an active member of the Congregational Church. [JFS
p12] In 1790 **Ebenezer⁵** had 8 children [MAFC] and in
1800 he is indicated at Middlebury, VT with one
son, 16-26 years old and 2 daughters, one below 10
years and one 16-26 years. [VTFC]

Ebenezer⁵ settled in Middlebury in 1790, west
end of home lots 16 and 17. He cleared and farmed
there until his death in 1812. There were land
transactions between his son **Samuel⁶**, Mr. Kirby,
Samuel's⁶ father in law, and **Ebenezer⁵**. [Swift p210]
Ebenezer⁵ died on 9-23-1812 [VTVR]

Children:
81   i   **Samuel⁶** b 2-2-1765 d 2-11-1851 m Mary
            Kirby 1-30-1791
      ii   **Eusebia⁶** b 2-8-1767 d 6-15-1790
      iii   **Arethusa⁶** b 2-8-1767 m Zephenia Buss
82   iv   **Daniel⁶** b 11-19-1768 d 1-22-1859 m Polly
            Starkweather 8-12-1807
      v   **Azubah⁶** b 11-1-1772
      vi   **Martha⁶** b 4-26-1775 d 2-24-1791
83   vii   **Enos⁶** b 11-24-1776 m Cloe Emerson and
            Mrs. Abigail Field, settled on the west
            end of home lots 14 and 15, built a
            house, and remained until his death in
            1842. [Swift p210]
84   viii   **Moses⁶** b 2-2-1779 d 8-13-1851 m Kezia
            Andrews 1-17-1799, came into town with
            his father but lived in another area for
            several years but returned to Middlebury
            with his family, to care for his father
            in his old age. [Swift]
      ix   **Hannah⁶** b 1-23-1781 d 10-3-1784
      x   **Adozia⁶** b 10-4-1783 m Rev. John Keep

(35) Abner⁵, (Ebenezer⁴, Ebenezer³, John², John¹),
born 11-5-1744 in Northfield, MA but settled in
Gill as a farmer. He was a member of the
Congregational Church and he filled most of the
offices that the town had to offer. He married
Naomi Wrisley on 12-25-1785. [JFS p13] **Abner⁵** lived
in Gill for most of his life. [1790-1820 MAFC-Gill]

Children: [MAVR-Gill]
      i   **Elijah⁶** b 3-2-1784 d young
85   ii   **Elijah (Elisha)⁶** b 2-6-1786 m Charlotte
            Starkweather. The Severans Genealogy
            listed this **Elijah⁶** as Eliza.

86 iii **Oren⁶** b 4-9-1788 d 12-20-1825 [MAVR] m
Chloe Munn 6-23-1809
iv **Philena⁶** b 3-1-1789 at Gill d 1-7-1872
at Gill, MA, age 84 yrs, single [MAVR]
v **Obed⁶** b 2-27-1791 d 2-28-1791 [MAVR]
87 vi **Obed⁶** b 6-22-1792 m Nancy Hale

(36) Thomas⁵, (John⁴, John³, John², John¹), born 2-8-
1738 in Charlestown, SC. [MgSC Vol 18 p174] He died
after 11-29-1798. In 1765 he married Susannah
Murrell [PRSC 1771-1774 p351] who was born 9-9-1732
and died after 11-29-1798 at Charlestown. [MPN]
The Will of **Thomas⁵** Saverance, written 11-1-1788
and proved 11-29-1798, [PRSC Will Book C 1793-1800
p525] list his wife Susannah, sons **Paul⁶**, **Robert⁶**,
and daughter **Sarah⁶**. Susannah was the daughter of
Robert Murrell and Susannah, she was born 9-9-1732.
[MgSC Vol 18 p174] The Will of Susannah Murrill's
father, Robert Murrill says that **Thomas⁵** Severance
(husband to Susannah) to live on the plantation and
to manage, oversee and carry on the planting
business on the said plantation. (proved 4-16-1773)
[PRSC Will Book 1771-1774 p351]

Children: [PRSC Will Book C 1793-1800 p525]
88 i **Robert⁶** b before 1780 d 1840
ii **Sarah⁶** (Sukey) b 7-15-1766
89 iii **Paul⁶** b 1770 d 5-11-1844 m Hannah
Huggins 2-27-1797

(37) Matthew⁵, (Joseph⁴, Joseph³, John², John¹), born
6-15-1735, at Fort Dummer, Brattleboro, VT. but
spent his early life in Greenfield, MA. He was the
first white child to be born in VT.
He served in the French War as a soldier under
Capt. Burbanks Company. He was taken as a prisoner
June 25, 1758 on Lake George while on a scouting
party and taken across the Lake into Canada.
According to Rev. **John⁶** Severance, he was compelled
to run the gauntlet between two files of Indians.
"He made a successful run nearly the whole length
of the line, when he was hit by a blow given by a
squaw, which felled him to the ground." "Quickly
recovering himself, he returned the blow with a
kick that prostrated her."
"He was with them but a short time before he
made his escape, and fled to the woods where he
secreted himself in a hollow log, backing into it
feet first and covering the opening with weeds and
brush; here he lay concealed for two days and three

nights." He was sought after by the Indians who even sat on the log, but they did not find him and he escaped." [JFS p13-14]

Matthew[5] married Experience Nash, daughter of Daniel Nash and Abigail Stebbins, of Greenfield, MA, on 3-10-1762. [MAVR] They settled in Greenfield and lived there until 1807, when they moved to Leyden, MA, where **Matthew**[5] died on 3-13-1816. **Matthew**[5] was the first generation to live in Leyden. He shows on the 1790-1810 MA census.

Children: [MAVR-Greenfield]]

	i	**Joseph**[6] b 4-27-1763. He was a Revolutionary Soldier in 1780. He m Lydia Nims on 11-28-1790. They settled in Shelburn, MA. **Joseph**[6] d 1-30-1852. [MAVR] He was a tailor by trade and kept a tavern at the center of town. He served as Town Clerk for 17 years. He was called **"Uncle Joe"**. He left no children.
90	ii	**Matthew**[6] b 7-11-1765
91	iii	**Zenas**[6] b 7-26-1767 m Eunice Wood
	iv	**Martha**[6] b 8-31-1769 d 5-29-1771 [Sheldon p 288]
92	v	**Consider**[6] b 12-25-1771 m Elizabeth Craige
93	vi	**Ruel**[6] b 12-29-1773 m Nancy Wilbur
	vii	**Experience**[6] b 3-6-1777 d 8-24-1828 m Richard Eason
	viii	**Erastus**[6] b in Leyden, MA 7-6-1779 d 9-22-1816. He m first to Mary Hall 3-3-1800 who d shorly after. He m2 to Elizabeth Lewis, 1-23-1810 [VTVR] who d on 9-16-1816. They had settled in Bennington, VT. **Erastus**[6] manufactured boots and shoes. He served as sheriff for two years. He d 9-22-1816, just six days after his wife died. They reportedly had children, **Erastus**[7] b 12-13-1817 and **Miranda**[7] b 6-27-1820. However these births would be after the death of their parents.
94	ix	**Asaph**[6] b 8-29-1781 m Amittai Eason
	x	**Ezra**[6] b 1-5-1784 [MAVR] d after 1830 in Leyden, MA. He m Jane Elliott 1-19-1807. The family lived in Greenfield and Leyden, MA. They had a daughter, **Almeda**[7] b 11-28-1807 m Enos Cooledge 10- -1838. [MAVR]

xi   **Sephas**[6] b 3-31-1786 d 1809
xii   **Abigail**[6] b 10-20-1791 m Rufus Foster

(38) Jesse[5], (Joseph[4], Joseph[3], John[2], John[1]), born
in Deerfield, MA in 6-2-1754. **Jesse**[5] married to
Lucy Mann on 12-1-1775 [MAVR]. He later lived in
Shelburne around 1780. **Jesse**[5] served as Sergeant,
under Capt. Benjamin Phillip's Co., Col. Elisha
Porter's (Hampshire Co.) Regt., engaged July 10,
1777, discharged 8-12-1777 in Northern Department.
[MASS]
He then settled in Conway where he served as
selectman and deputy sheriff. Before 1806 he moved
back to Deerfield and was a tavern keeper at Bloody
Brook. [HOCoNY p195] **Jesse**[5] died 12-21-1831 age 80
years. [MAVR] It is recorded that he first married
to Eunice. (see first child) Eunice (the mother)
must have died young. [Sheldon p290]

Children: [MAVR-Conway]
   i   **Eunice**[6] b 4-10-1776 d 5-17-1796 (Conway
           MAVR) "Eunice bpt 6-23-1776, by Parson
           Ashley, as "dau. to **Jesse**[5] Severance and
           Eunice his wife."
95   ii   **Jesse**[6] b 3-20-1778 m Sophia Abbott 8-23-
           1800
   iii   **Lucy**[6] b 1-28-1780 m Allen Mansfield. The
           [MAVR] shows the death of **Lucy**[6],
           daughter of **Jesse**[5] and Lucy, d on 10-18-
           1871 at Conway, MA, single, age 91 yrs 9
           months.
96   iv   **Elihu**[6] b 4-6-1782
97   v   **David**[6] b 2-22-1784 m Dolly Beals on 12-
           26-1807.
   vi   **Rufus**[6] b 2-12-1786
   vii   **Sarah**[6] b 2-15-1788
   viii **Ora**[6] b 2-3-1790 (Conway VR) m to Charles
           Lyon on 8-9-1821. [VTVR]
   ix   **Lois**[6] b 1-15-1792 m Capt. Nathan Frary
           2-19-1815
   x   **child**[6] b 1796 d 12-22-1815 age 19 yrs 16
           days
   xi   **Jennette E.**[6] m David Cooley Leonard 1-
           28-1825 [Sheldon p290]

(40) Martin[5], (Martin[4], Joseph[3], John[2], John[1]), born
3-8-1755 at Hinsdale, NH. He died on 12-29-1843.
[MAVR-Shelburne] He spent his life in Shelburne
Falls, MA. He purchased and lived on his fathers
farm. [1800-1840 MAFC-Shelburne]

It was said that he was a homebody, quite, and
devoted husband. He married to Lucy Whitney on
November 15, 1781 [MAVR], the daughter of Joseph
Whitney and Hannah Chandler. Lucy was born 3-20-
1762 at Shutesbury, MA and died 1-10-1844, buried
at Shelburne Falls. [MAVR-Shelburne] They lived
together for 62 years.

Martin[5] was a soldier and a scout for many
years. He also served during the Revolutionary War.
"Receipt given to the Selectmen of Shelburne, dated
Sept. 22-1777, signed by said Severance and others.
Capt. John Wells certifies that the men whose names
appear upon the above receipt went out of the town
with him, also Capt. John Well's Co., of Hampshire
Co., militia, enlisted 9-22-1777, discharged 10-23-
1777, service under Col. David Wells in the
Northern Department, roll dated Shelburne." [MASS]

In 1760, he came to Shelburne with Daniel Ryder
in search of farm land. They settled near the
springs on the hillside on the east of what is now
Maple Street. Each of these pioneers built log
cabins and the territory from up on the mountain to
the river comprised the Severance and Allis Farms.
The oldest residence in Shelburne Falls was built
by **Martin Jr.**[5] in 1784. **Martin**[5] bought the homestead
and farm of his father and lived there before he
died. [Bardwell p60]

Children: born in Shelburn Falls. [Whitney]

    i   **Joel**[6] b 9-24-1782 d 1-14-1785

    ii   **Achsa**[6] b 7-3-1784 d 1872 m Thadeus
               Merrill 8-6-1801. [MAVR] **Achsa**[6] d in
               1872 [Merrill III p440]

    iii   **Tirzah**[6] b 11-22-1786 d 9-18-1802 [MAVR]

    iv   **Rachel**[6] b 4-21-1789 m Moses Allen 11-26-
               1812, Moses was b 6-7-1781 and d 10-20-
               1822, the son of Sylvanus Moses Allen
               and Martha Stebbins. Moses was a
               saddler. [Suddaby p144]

    v   **Sophia**[6] b 5-11-1791 d 12-9-1815 m Samuel
               Anderson 12-3-1812

    vi   **Lucy**[6] b 7-13-1793 d 12-4-1822 m Allen
               Barnard 12-23-1815 [DAR Lineage Book Vol
               160]

    vii   **Laura**[6] b 10-5-1795 m David Fiske 10-31-
               1814, David was the son of Samuel Fiske
               and Rebecca Fiske, (Samuel's cousin)
               [Pierce p224] In it "Captain **Martin**[5]
               Severance, Laura's father, owned either

side of the Salmon Falls in Shelburne
Falls.

 viii **Patience**[6] b 3-11-1797
 ix **Rhoda**[6] b 2-1-1798 m Dexter Billings
   (Strongsville OH) 10-13-1825
 x **David**[6] b 3-4-1800 d 9-2-1802
98 xi **Asa**[6] b 10-9-1802 d 5-9-1851

(41) Samuel[5], (Martin[4], Joseph[3], John[2], John[1]), born
in Shelburn, MA on 1-12-1761 [MAVR] and spent his
first twenty years in that town. [1800 MAFC-
Hampshire Co] "He removed from Shelburne to
Bradford County, PA, settling at Springfield in
1815. At the age of 18 years he entered the
American Army as a cook for General Washington and
served in that capacity till 1781". [Heverly]

He served in the military until June 7, 1783
under Capt. Green's Co., and Col. Joseph Vose's
Regiment. His occupation was a farmer, 5' 6 in.,
complexion, light, hair, light. He was 19 yrs old
in 1781. He enlisted in the service at Shelburne in
March of 1781 into Capt. Green's Company and Col.
Varnum's Regiment and remained until 6-7-1783 when
he was discharged. [Bardwell p61] He was placed on
the pension roll, 1818, of Springfield, Bradford
County, PA, where he died. [DARLR Vol 63] He
married Azuba Smith, daughter of Moses Smith and
Sarah Catlin, on 9-7-1786. Azuba was born 4-18-
1763. They settled in the backwoods of Springfield,
PA.

The Census of Pensioners for the Western
District of Pennsylvania shows that Azuba Severence
age 77 received pension from Samuel Severence, her
husband in 1840. Rev. **John F.**[6] Severance, [JFS p15-
16], said that he "led a good christian life and
endured the hardships of a backwoods Man." **Samuel[5]**
died 8-28-1833.

Children: [MAVR-Shelburne]
 i **Sarah**[6] (Sally) b 5-28-1787 m David
   Phinney (Jefferson, NY)
 ii **Mary**[6] (Polly)b 3-4-1789 d 9-15-1852 m
   Oliver Gates
99 iii **Samuel**[6] b 3-22-1793 m Mary Parks 1-20-
   1850
100 iv **Elisha**[6] b 1-31-1795 m Martha Bangs 4-23-
   1823, m2 Phebe (Tracy) Morgan 5-7-1831
 v **Patience**[6] b 3-21-1797 m John Harkness 9-
   30-1815

vi   **Clarissa**[6] b 5-20-1799 m Almon L. Berry
        10-15-1827 [DARLR Vol 63]
vii   **Martin**[6] b 10-26-1801 d 8-27-1803

(42) Selah[5], (Martin[4], Joseph[3], John[2], John[1]), born
9-26-1771 in Shelburn, MA [MAVR] but later settled
in Heath, on a farm west of the centre, according
to **John F.**[6] Severance. Then about 1807 he moved to
Shelburn and lived in the large brick house which
was built by Enoch Dole [Bardwell p56] and then
eventually to a farm north of the center of that
town. [1800-1830 MAFC] He led a quite life and only
served as a Selectman two or three years. He was a
Whig and a member of the Congregational Church. He
married Hannah Putnam, daughter of Nathaniel Putnam
of Wilton, NH on 11-30-1797. [JFS p16]
    Hannah Putnam was born 10-24-1780 died 5-30-1854
at Shelburne, MA. **Selah**[5] died 10-8-1832. [MAVR]

Children:
101 i   **Fairfield**[6] b 5-26-1799 m Cynthia Davy
            Douglass
     ii   **Asaph**[6] b 1-1-1802 [MAVR] d 10-20-1802
     iii   **Emily**[6] b 1-20-1803 [MAVR] m William
            Ewing Bardwell 2-3-1831 [Snow p225]
     iv   **Asaph**[6] b 5-20-1805 [MAVR] d 7-18-1806
102 v   **Luther**[6] b 1-22-1807 [MAVR] bpt Heath, 3-
            13-1808 [Snow p12] m Polly Eddy
     vi   a daughter b 10-22-1809 d same day
     vii   **Calvin**[6] b 4-22-1811 d 9-29-1819
103 viii   **Lorenzo**[6] b 3-25-1813 m Amanda Stewart 3-
            27-1834. [MAVR-Shelburne]
     ix   **Hervey**[6] b 2-25-1815 at Shelburn, MA. He
            lived on his father's farm for some time
            after his fathers death. He later moved
            to South Deerfield, MA and then
            Lakewood, NJ where he used his knowledge
            as a farmer. He m Marian Packard on 5-
            28-1846. [MAVR-Shelburne] In 1870, he
            represented his district in the
            Massachusetts State Legislature. **Hervey**[6]
            d 5-16-1885. He left no family.
104 x   **John F.**[6] b 3-12-1817 resided in Chicago,
            IL. He was the author of The Severans
            Genealogy. He m Hannah Linsley.

JOHN F.[6] SEVERANCE

xi   **Carolina[6]** b 6-28-1819 d 4-17-1821
       [MAVR-Shelburne]
xii   **Hannah[6]** b 5-19-1821 at Shelburn, MA, she
       m Baxter Forbes, son of Nahum and Lucy
       Forbes, 5-17-1849 of Westboro, MA.
xiii   **Lucretia Scott[6]** b 9-6-1823 at
       Shelburne, MA and d at Raynham Center,
       MA on 12-23-1914 m Frederic Augustus
       Ball 3-22-1853. Frederic d at Raynham
       Center on 4-27-1906 [MAVR][DARGCLR]

(43) John[5], (John[4], Joseph[3], John[2], John[1]), bpt in
Bernardston, MA on 1-19-1745 [MAVR] and he lived
his entire life there on land purchased from his
father. [1790-1800 MAFC] A land transaction shows
"John[5] Severance Jr. sold to **David[5]** Severance (his
brother), lot number 5, 4th division containing
twenty five acres". **John[5]** married Zerhiah Nichols
in 1784 (the intentions were 5-22-1784 [MAVR] and
it is known that they had a least one daughter,
Sarah[6], who married Joseph Stebbins of Northfield,
MA. **Sarah[6]** died while she was relatively young.

    It appears that **John[5]** settled in Guilford, VT.
The records show that Lt. **John[5]** Severance collected
his son **David's[6]** Bounty in Guilford, VT. [HGVT
p139] It also shows that **John[5]** was the head of a
household of 5 people in 1790. [1790 VTFC Guilford]
In 1802, **John[5]** sold land to his son **Roger[6]** and

Roger[6] resold land to Joel Eddy in 1813. **Roger**[6] also sold land to Simon Aldrich in 1820. [HGVR p330-331]

He served as a private under Capt. Agrippa Well's Co., Col. Samuel William's Regt. of Minutemen, which marched 4-20-1775, in response to the alarm of 4-19-1775, he left the place of rendezvous 5-3-1775. [MASS]

John[5] signed a land transaction on 5-15-1793 with his wife in Bernardston, MA.

Children:

    i   **Sarah**[6] b circa 1785 m Joseph Stebbins of Northfield, MA [JFS]

    ii   **David**[6] [HGVT p139]

    iii   **Roger/Royer**[6] [HGVT p330-331] **Royer**[7] *Severens* b circa 1804 living in Guilford, VT on the [1820 VTFC] The IGI indicates that **Roger**[6] married to Hanna of Guilford, VT and they had children: **Seymour**[7] b 5-6-1810, **Eunice**[7] b 6-16-1811 and **Betsy**[7] b 8-9-1812.

(44) David[5], (John[4], Joseph[3], John[2], John[1]), born in Bernardston, MA on 1-10-1747. He died 11-25-1838. **David**[5] later settled on a farm called "Huckle Hill" as stated by Rev. **John F.**[6] Severance and shows on the [1790-1830 MAFC]

He served as a private under Capt. John Well's Co., Lieut. Col. Timothy Robinson's Detachment of Hampshire Co. militia, muster roll dated Garrison at Ticonderoga, 2-24-1777, enlistment to expire 3-23--1777, also same Company and Detachment, entered service 12-23-1776, discharged 4-1-1777, service 100 days at Ticonderoga. [MASS]

"He lead a quiet life, was everybody's uncle, and highly respected by all." He married first to Sally Sauter on 1-15-1778. Sally was born 5-10-1759 and died June 12, 1815 and **David**[5] then married Mrs. Lucy Billings in July of 1816 [the intentions were recorded 7-3-1816 MAVR]. Lucy died 11-14-1844 at Bernardston, MA. **David**[5] died on 11-25-1838. [JFS p17]

Children: [MAVR-Bernardston]

        i   **Guy**[6] b 3-12-1779 d 4-6-1782 [MAVR]

        ii   **Guy**[6] b 5-21-1784 d 6-23-1843 unm [MAVR]

 105 iii   **Seth**[6] b 1-6-1787 m Abigail Wells and Mary Wells

        iv   **Horace**[6] b 7-15-1790 d 11-8-1794

        v   **Oren**[6] b 5-10-1792 d 11-8-1811

	vi	**Lovina**[6] b 4-7-1794 d 9-15-1794
106	vii	**Horace**[6] b 6-23-1796 m Belinda Howard and Lucy Root
	viii	**Rachel**[6] b 9-2-1798 m Oliver____ of Long Island, NY.,
	ix	**Sarah**[6] b 2-12-1800 m Luther Clark
	x	**Sophronia**[6] b 4-11-1802 d 9-30-1805
	xi	**Lovina**[6] b 11-3-1804 d 6-25-1837 m Alden Eason 1-16-1827
	xii	**Sophronia**[6] b 12-23-1806 d 5-6-1844 m Polycarpus Cushman Alexander

(45) Daniel[5], (John[4], Joseph[3], John[2], John[1]), born 12-18-1764. He married Lydia Healy 1-3-1790. She was born 9-23-1767 and died 1-24-1846. They settled in Winchester, NH. It was said of him that "he was public spirited, energetic, and a philanthropist in every sense of the word." At the age of twenty-eight he sought aid from the General Court to raise money to build a road from Northfield, MA to Chesterfield, NH, passing through Hinsdale, NH. He served as a supervisor through-out the entire project. [JFS p18]

He served as private under Capt. Isaac Newton's Co., Col. S. Murray's Regt., enlisted 7-13-1780, discharged 10-10-1780. Regiment raised in Hampshire Co. to reinforce Continental Army for 3 months. Descriptive list dated Deerfield, 7-24-1780 of men detached from Hampshire Co., militia, agreeable to resolve of 6-22-1780 and returned by Maj. David Dickinson as mustered by him by order of Lieut. Col. David Wells, 4th or 15th Co., 5th Hampshire Co. Regt., 17 yrs, complexion light, engaged for the town of Bernardston. [MASS]

Daniel[5] and Lydia are buried in the Winchester, Evergreen Cemetery. [Goss p156] **Daniel**[5] died 1-6-1828 age 64 years and Lydia, wife of **Daniel**[5] died 1-24-1846 age 77 years. [NHVR]

Children: [JFS p18]
	i	**John Jenks**[6] b 10-15-1790 He m1 Martha Bently and m2 Sophia B. but left no family.
	ii	**Daniel Arms**[6] b 7-10-1793 d 9-27-1796
	iii	**Zama**[6] b 9-8-1795 d 9-28-1796
	iv	**Zama**[6] b 1-20-1798 d 3-22-1845
	v	**Lydia**[6] b 4-19-1800 d 1-5-1824
107	vi	**Daniel Arms**[6] b 10-29-1802 m Emily Willard

vii   **John Healy**[6] b 1-6-1805 d 1-4-1869. He m
Mrs. Elvira Anderson, daughter of
Timothy Anderson and Betsey Hastings, 1-
1-1842 at Winchester, NH. They left no
family. Elvira d 2-12-1898 at Barre, MA.
The [MAVR] states that **John**[6] m Elvira
Alexander 11-24-1844 at Hardwick, MA,
she was a widow
viii   **Cynthia**[6] b 12-13-1806 d 10-12-1823
ix   **Ezra**[6] b 11-23-1808 d 8-8-1823

(46) Jonathan[5], (Jonathan[4], Joseph[3], John[2], John[1]),
born 3-31-1750 and lived in Greenfield, MA with his
father until 1800. [MAVR-Greenfield][1790-1800
MAFC] **Jonathan**[5] married Elizabeth McClellan on 1-
10-1783. [MAVR] Elizabeth was born on July 21, 1752
and died 5-25-1825, the daughter of Robert
McClellan and Sarah Jane Williams. [Eldridge p107-
108]

    Jonathan[5], of Conway, on return of men drafted
from Hampshire Co. militia to march to Horse Neck
under command of Col. John Mosley but failed to
join Regiment, reported drafted from town of
Conway, drafted into Capt. French's Co. [MASS]

    He later moved to Truxton, NY. They settled and
raised their family on a farm at Truxton living
there until their deaths. **Jonathan**[5] died 5-15-1845
at the age of ninety-five years of age, called the
oldest person in the town if not in the county.
[Bowman]

    [JFS p18-19] describes **Jonathan**[5] as "a Man of
Medium height, straight, broad-shouldered, fine
physique, very supple, would turn a summersault at
the age of seventy-five years to the perfect
disgust of the boys".

Children: [JFS]
    i   **Jonathan**[6] b 10-17-1783 d 7-4-1788
    ii   **Hannah**[6] b 4-24-1785 m Charles Stewart 9-
           12-1805. Their son, (one of eight
           children) Robert M. Stewart, went on to
           become elected as the Governor of MO in
           1858.
    iii   **Elizabeth**[6] b 2-24-1787 d 7-4-1807 m
           Jonathan Squires 9-12-1805 of Fabius, NY
108 iv   **Jonathan**[6] b 10-23-1788 m Eunice Taggart
109 v   **John**[6] b 12-5-1791 Sabrina Smith

(47) Joseph[5], (Jonathan[4], Joseph[3], John[2], John[1]),
born in Greenfield, MA on 9-20-1760. He married

Mercy Allen on 9-28-1778. He lived in Greenfield
most of his life. [1790-1830 MAFC].

He served as a private under Capt. James
Walsworth's Co., Col. Elisha Porter's (Hampshire
Co.) Regt., enlisted 7-22-1779, discharged 8-27-
1779, service at New London, CT, sworn at
Deerfield, also descriptive list dated, Deerfield,
7-24-1780 of men detached from Hampshire Co.
militia, agreeable to resolve of 6-22-1780, and
returned by Maj. David Dickinson as mustered by him
by order of Lieut. Col. David Wells, 3d or 10th
Co., 5th Hampshire Co. Regt., age 17 yrs,
complexion dark, engaged for town of Greenfield,
also, private, under Capt. Isaac Newton's Co., Col.
S. Murray's Regt. enlisted 7-13-1780, discharged
10-10-1780. [MASS]

Joseph⁵ died on 11-24-1829 at Greenfield. Mercy
Allen died on 8-3-1801, at the age of 40, in
Greenfield, MA. [MAVR]

Children: [MAVR-Greenfield]
110   i   **Joseph⁶** b 2-1-1779 [MAVR]
     ii   **Christina⁶** b 3-9-1781 [MAVR] m Aaron
        White 7-5-1800
     iii   **Pliny⁶** b 5-27-1782 d 11-7-1783 **Pliny⁶** b
        2-2-1783 [MAVR] died young
111   iv   **Rodney⁶** b 11-7-1783 [MAVR] m Nancy
        Thompson
     v   **Mercy⁶** b 12-27-1785 d 5-8-1848
     vi   **Jemima⁶** b 4-2-1788 m Oliver Warner
        [Abbe-p308] Oliver's father was William
        Phelps Warner
     vii   **Susanna⁶** b 7-17-1791 [MAVR] m Elisha
        Munn 5-27-1811 Elisha was the son of
        Elisha Munn and Eunice Thayer, b 1-3-
        1789 and d 10-7-1824. [Suddaby p358]
112   viii   **Horace⁶** b 9-24-1793 [MAVR] d 9-11-1869 m
        Mary Fisk 8-31-1819 m Mary Ann Mc Carthy
     ix   **Marcy⁶** b 4-22-1795 [MAVR]
113   x   **Pliny⁶** b 7-24-1796 m Sophia Wrisley
     xi   **Henry⁶** b 7-27-1798
     xii   **Lovina⁶** b 7-27-1798 d 4-3-1866 at
        Greenfield, MA, unmarried. [MAVR]

(48) Solomon⁵, (Jonathan⁴, Joseph³, John², John¹),
born 9-20-1762 [MAVR] in Greenfield, MA and lived
there until about 1789 when he moved to Shelburn
and settled on a farm later called The Hanson Farm.
He advanced to Colonel in the military.

He remained a farmer and served as selectman for many years. He married Hannah Hoyt, daughter of Jonathan Hoyt and Experinece Childs. The marriage intentions were recorded on 11-21-1785. [MAVR] Hannah was born 7-27-1765 and died 5-18-1838. First two children born in Greenfield, the others in Shelburne, MA. [Sheldon p289] **Solomon**[5] died 11-12-1804 at Greenfield. [MAVR]

Children: [Sheldon p289]

114 i   **Robert Bruce**[6] b 10-1-1786 d 2-10-1830 m Diana Long 11-27-1810

115 ii   **Otis**[6] b 10-12-1788 m Abigail Stratton 2-8-1815

iii   **Harriet**[6] b 10-18-1790 d 8- -1857 m George Winslow M.D. 5-1-1822

iv   **Amanda**[6] b 1-28-1793 d 10-12-1802

v   **Miranda**[6] b 1-28-1793 d 8-15-1855 m Joel Allis 8-15-1855

vi   **Solomon**[6] b 7-26-1795 d 1-21-1797

vii   **Solomon**[6] b 11-1-1797 d 10-8-1802

viii   **Jonathan Hoyt**[6] b 10-5-1799 d 10-5-1802

ix   **Guy**[6] b 9-12-1801 d 10-5-1802

x   **Emily**[6] b 9-22-1803 in Shelburne, MA d 1-2-1871 m Joseph Sweet, son of Joshua and Mary Sweet of Shelburn, MA, 5-22-1862 at Greenfield, MA. [MAVR]

(49) Elihu[5], (Jonathan[4], Joseph[3], John[2], John[1]), born 11-3-1765 [MAVR] in Greenfield, MA. He remained in that area and led a very quiet life as a farmer and a hatter by trade. He only shows on the [1830 MA Census]. He married Martha Hitchcock, daughter of Luke Hitchcock and Lucy Merrick, on 11-26-1801 [MAVR]. Martha was born on 5-8-1772 and died 12-13-1836. [MAVR] Martha was a woman of cultured intellect, from a family well respected in the educational and scientific circles of MA. **Elihu**[5] died 11-24-1841 [MAVR].

I must include this note to illustrate some of the errors that have been made in recording this family. "**Elihu**[5] was the eighth son of **Jonathan**[4] Severance who came from England in 1755 (an officer in the Commissary Department of Gen. Braddock's Army) and became a pioneer settler of Greenfield, Massachusetts and afterward a soldier in the Revolution." [H&LCoOH] The vital records show that **Jonathan**[4] was born the son of **Joseph**[3] who came from Wales. And yet the lineage through the Massachusetts Vital Records make no mention of

50

this. It makes one wonder if perhaps more mistakes
were made in assigning these early families to
their rightful order.

Children: [MAVR-Greenfield]
116 i   **Ralph Abercrombie**[6] b 1-15-1803 m1 Mary
            Smith m2 Joanna Bailey
117 ii   **Ptolemy Philadelphus**[6] b 7-23-1805 d 1883
            m Margaret Caldwell on 12-28-1832 m2
            Harriet Converse 11-6-1855

(50) Rufus[5], (Jonathan[4], Joseph[3], John[2], John[1]), born
in Greenfield, MA on 3-20-1770 [MAVR] The [MAVR-
Greenfield] shows **Rufus**[5] died 9-10-1819
therefore he would have been born in 1779. He lived
his entire life there. He married Sarah Newton on
1-7-1802. [MAVR] She was born about 1772 and died
8-5-1806. He married second to Tirzah Root of
Montague on 1-1-1808 [MAVR-Montague]. Tirzah was
the daughter of Jonathan Root and Susanna Clapp of
Montague, MA. [Root p168] Tirzah died 6-28-1836.
[MAVR-Montague] **Rufus**[5] died 9-10-1819. [MAVR] He
never shows on the MA census records.

Children of **Rufus**[5] and Sarah Newton [MAVR-
Greenfield]
118 i   **Guy Carlton**[6] b 11-12-1802 bpt 9-24-1811
119 ii   **Solomon**[6] b 1-4-1805
    iii   **Rufus Newton**[6] b 8-3-1806 in Greenfield,
            MA [JFS p21] The [VTVR] shows him m to
            Ananda Hinsdill, daughter of Joseph and
            Hannah Bingham, on 9-8-1830. [Wallbridge
            p156] She d on 9-12-1874. [VTVR] **Rufus**[6]
            d on 5-5-1855. [VTVR] The [1850 VTFC-
            Bennington)] shows the family with a
            daughter **Margarit**[7] b 1840.

Children of **Rufus**[5] Severance and Tirzah Root
    iv   **Jonathan Root**[6] b 8-27-1811 and bpt 9-24-
            1811 [MAVR-Greenfield, Buckland,
            Colrain, and Montague][Sheldon p289]
120 v   **Franklin C.**[6] b circa 1813
121 vi   **George W.**[6] b circa 1815
    vii   **Sally**[6] bpt 5-11-1817
    viii   **William**[5] b 1-10-1819 d 7-29-1820 [MAVR]

(51) Moses[5], (Moses[4], Joseph[3], John[2], John[1]), born in
Montague, MA on 10-10-1763 and died 10-21-1823.
[MAVR] He remained on the family homestead. He is
listed in MA in 1810-1820. [MAFC] He was a Captain

51

of the militia, a farmer, and a member of the
Congregational Church. He married Abigail Austin of
Wilmington, VT on 12-25-1800. Abigail was born 1767
and died 8-24-1820. Marriage intentions for Capt.
Moses[4] of Montague, MA and Mrs. Clarissa Belknapp
were filed in E. Windsor, CT on 9-1-1821. He died
10-20-1823. [MAVR] [JFS p21-22]

Children: [MAVR-Montague]
  i   **Almira**[6] b 9-15-1801 d 12-25-1814 ae 13
        [MAVR]
  ii   **George**[6] b 4-20-1804 d 12-2-1813 [MAVR]
        Baby Son b 10-23-1805 d 10-27-1805
        [MAVR]
122 iii **Charles**[6] b 1-7-1807 m Melvina Hamilton
  iv   **Harriet**[6] b 3-5-1810 m Kendall Abbott 5-
        19-1827. Kendall B. was b 2-5-1803 in
        Montague, MA

(52) Elihu[5], (Moses[4], Joseph[3], John[2], John[1]), born 9-
6-1773 in Montague, MA and died 3-5-1834. He
married Tryphena Gunn on 7-6-1797. [MAVR] Tryphena,
was born 8-30-1773, died 4-17-1854, and was the
daughter of Israel Gunn and Mary Root of Montague,
MA. In 1799 they moved to Cazenovia, NY and settled
on a farm. At that time he had a Lieutenant's
commission. He was commissioner of highways and
school inspector and a supervisor of the town for
successive terms. [Tuttle p223] In 1820 he was
living at Cazenovia. [NYFC]

Children: [JFS p22]
123 i   **Luther**[6] b 10-29-1797 m Anna Hamlin
124 ii   **Moses**[6] b 9-1-1799 m Abigail M. Staples
125 iii **Apollos**[6] b 5-20-1802 d 1883 Cazenovia,
        NY
  iv   **Sophia**[6] b 6-10-1805 d 8-3-1879 m Daniel
        M. Fairchild. (Tryphena is shown on the
        1850 NY census with Sophia Fairchild)
126 v   **Henry**[6] b 1-30-1808 m Hannah Wooley
  vi   **Mary**[6] b 12-15-1810 d 10-27-1878 m Lewis
        Sears
127 vii **Charles**[6] b 8-29-1813 d 11-18-1837
        recorded as having one child in
        Cazenovia, NY

(53) James[5], (James[4], unconnected, Joseph[2], John[1]), b
circa 1750-1760. The 1790 MA census for Greenfield,
MA shows **James**[5] with 3 sons and 1 daughter. **Phillip**[6]
is listed with a daughter, and a **Joseph**[5] is listed

with 2 sons and 5 daughters. The 1800 Cheshire Co. NH census shows **Phillip⁵** with a daughter and **James⁵** with 2 daughters. These Severances could likely have moved into the state of NY.

Children: [1790 MAFC] conjecture based on research
	i	son, **James⁶** b circa 1785
129	ii	son, **Joseph⁶** b circa 1785
130	iii	son, **Phillip⁶** b circa 1785.
	iv	daughter

(54) Phillip Sr.⁵, (James⁴, unconnected, Joseph², John¹), born circa 1752 m Abigail Westcot 11-18-1795 in Scarboro, ME. This could have been a second or third marriage. He is likely from the Severance family of MA and NH but the correct lineage is still being worked out. **Phillip⁵** was at Parsonfield, York Co. ME with two sons ages 10-16 and himself age 26-45. By 1820 he had 3 daughters under 10 years, 1 daughter 16-26, and a wife age 26-45. [1810 MEFC] Perhaps he had a son named **Phillip⁶** born circa 1780.

Children of **Phillips Sr.⁵** Severance (conjecture)
	ii	daughter
131	iii	**Phillip Jr.⁶** m Susan Pendexter
132	iii	**Joseph⁶** b in June of 1800 in NH. His intentions marriage to Mary Foss were filed on 3-15-1826 at Parsonfield, York Co. ME.
	iv	daughter
	v	**Mary⁶** b circa 1805 m Enoch Hodsdon 2-7-1829 at Hollis, ME
	vi	**Lydia⁶** b circa 1808 **Lydia⁶** m James Hodsdon on 1-4-1834 at Hollis, ME.
	vii	daughter

(55) Joseph⁵, (James⁴, unconnected, Joseph², John¹), It is unclear at this point if **Joseph⁵** married or had any children.

(56) Ebenezer⁵, (James⁴, unconnected, Joseph², John¹), b circa 1750-1760. The intention of marriage on 2-3-1781 shows between **Ebenezer⁵** Severance and Experience Cahoon both of Harwich. [MAVR-Harwich-Kelly] There is an unconnected **Ebenezer⁵** on the 1790-1800 NH census.

Children: conjecture

133 i   **Ebenezer**[6], b circa 1785, settled in VT
             or NH.

(57) Joseph[5], (Joseph[4], unconnected, Joseph[2], John[1]),
b circa 1750-1760. He was married. [1790 MAFC] He
was indicated in New Bedford in 1810. [1810 MAFC]
The probate records show that he died in 1812. He
mentioned his son, **William**[6], in his Will.

Children:
134 i   **William**[6], b 11-12-1797 [MAVR], he
             married to Hannah Nye, who died 9-1-1852
             [MAVR] and **William**[6] remarried to Almira.
             The 1820 MA census shows him with 5
             sons. He died before 1841.
     ii   **Joseph**[6]
     iii   **John**[6], b 1813 d 10-12-1840,

(58) Thomas[5], (Joseph[4], unconnected, Joseph[2], John[1]),
b circa 1750-1760. He was married. [1790 MAFC] He
is indicated in New Bedford, MA in 1810 and 1820.
[MAFC] A **Thomas**[5] married to Rebecca Taber, 11-15-
1772 at Dartmouth, MA. [MAVR]

Children: [1790 MAFC] conjecture
     i   **Thomas**[6] ? the records don't seem to
             indicate that there was any lineage. It
             could be part of an unconnected family
             in MA, NH, VT, or NY. It is conjecture
             but this could be part of the New
             York Severance's of **Thomas** or **Nicholson**
             Severance families. In 1850 **Nicholas
             Jr.**[6] was a hotel keeper. In 1860 he was
             living with Phebe born 1797 in MA. [NYFC
             Castile, Wyoming Co]
     ii   daughter

(59) William[5], (Joseph[4], unconnected, Joseph[2],
John[1]), b circa 1750-1760. He is indicated in New
Bedford, MA in 1820. Since he appears to be a ship
Captain, and owner of several vessels through out
the world, it is very unclear, at this time, about
his ancestry. The children listed, seem to be
indicated at this time period in New Bedford. The
record seems to show that **William**[5] was the son of
William Sr.[4] of New Bedford, who was owner and
master of several ships of New Bedford including
the Reuben and Eliza registered 12-20-1806, the
Ophelia registered 1-7-1804, and Desdemona
registered 2-1-1806. [Ship Registers of New

Bedford, Massachusetts, Vol I 1796-1850, The
National Archives Project]

Children:
i   **Thomas⁶** b circa 1800, (married Betsey
        Stetson, 6-4-1822, Betsey died 3-31-1877
        at New Bedford.[MAVR] She was the
        daughter of Charles Stetson, a shipyard
        owner who had built 53 vessels before
        1815 in New Bedford. **Thomas⁶** was the
        Capt. and owner of several registered
        ships out of New Bedford. He died 6-3-
        1859 in Nevada County, CA. [NS New
        Bedford Mercury 1845-1874 P-Z]. They had
        a daughter, **Lucy N.⁷,** who died 9-3-1824
        age 6 yrs. Another daughter, **Jane Ann⁷** m
        Jireh B. Gifford of New Bedford, MA, 8-
        15-1852. [NS New Bedford Mercury] We
        know from street directories, census,
        and vital records, that **Capt. Thomas⁶**
        was a son of **William⁵** Severance. The
        1830-1840 MA census shows Olive, wife
        of **Thomas⁸** Severance living in
        Fairhaven, MA.

It is well known that New Bedford, was a great
shipping center and later became the whaling center
of the world and it is possible that these
Severance's are not part of the New England family
of **John¹** and Abigail Kimball.

(60) Joseph⁵ (Benjamin⁴, Ephraim³, Ephraim², John¹),
born in Kingston, NH on 7-21-1746. [Eastman] He
married in Chester, NH to Anna Currier, daughter of
Gideon Currier and Mary Brown, on 2-12-1771. Anna
was born 6-9-1747 [NHVR] died 10-20-1813 at
Salisbury, NH. [Currier p221]
    In his youth, **Joseph⁵** was bound out to a man by
the name of Stetson, at Dunbarton, where he
remained until he came of age. In 1769, moving from
Chester to Andover, he cleared land and built a log
cabin in Andover on the Andover side of Raccoon
Hill where he brought his family. By the following
year he acquired land in Salisbury and built the
first house on the Eliphalet Shaw place. A similar
account was given by Harvey L. Currier who was
author of Part One of [Currier p221-222]. He
settled there and lived out his life. He was chosen
one of the "Committee of Safety" and was active in
the welfare of the town during the Revolutionary

War. He served in the War as a commissioned officer in Col. Thomas Stickney's Regt. 13th NH., Militia, [NHPSP Vol 14.]

In 1790-1800 he was living in Salisbury, NH. [NHFC] He is also indicated on the military records with his brother **William**[5]. In 1810 he was living in New Chester, NH. [NHFC]

He was chosen as a delegate to the convention at Exeter to consider the Constitution. This was on 1-16-1788. He served as a Selectman in Salisbury in 1789. He d 3-16-1813 at Salisbury, NH at the Shaw Place. [Currier p222]

His later descendants can be found in and around Derby, VT.

Children: [Currier p221]

i   **Elizabeth**[6] b 10-5-1771 d 7- -1793 m Abner Hall (Tunbridge, VT) Elizabeth d July 1773.

136   ii   **Isaac**[6] b 10-4-1773 m Abigail Dean lived at Derby, VT and had eight children

137   iii   **David**[6] b 1-30-1775 m Mehitabel Meloon 5-17-1803, [IGI] she d 10-19-1819. He m2nd to Dolly Palmer, 2-17-1821 (Derby, VT)(Danbury, NH)

138   iv   **James**[6] b 12-19-1776 m Sarah True, Plainfield, VT. buried near Smith Corner in Salisbury, NH.

v   **Anna**[6] b 2-18-1779 d 5-28-1790

vi   **Lydia**[6] b 1-17-1781 d 6-16-1809 m Joseph Buswell

139   vii   **Joseph Jr.**[6] b 1-1-1783 d 10-10-1828 m Rillah Colby (Derby, VT)

140   viii   **Benjamin**[6] b 4-18-1785 m Hannah Ladd (Derby, VT) **Benjamin**[6] d 9-24-1863 at age 92. They had eight children

141   ix   **John**[6] b 5-30-1787 m Abigail True

x   **Richard**[6] b 5-2-1789 d 1-29-1813

[Sterns Vol I p996], says that **Joseph**[5] and Anna had a thirteenth child, **Emelia T.**[6], who m William Dunlap. This **Emelia**[6] was born 4-12-1826 and died 3-31-1855, however **Joseph**[5] Severance died in 1813 and therefore he could not be the father of **Emelia T.**[6] Severance. (See **Amelia T.**[8] as the daughter of **James**[7] Severns and Sarah True.

(61) Peter[5], (Benjamin[4], Ephraim[3], Ephraim[2], John[1]), probably born in Chester, NH circa 1754. Much of his life can be gleaned from the [NHPSP]. He was listed as being from Chester in 1775 at the age of 21. He was on the payroll with his brother, **William**[5], in May of 1775 which showed that he was with Capt. H. Hutchins, Lt. Emerson, and Col. James Reed's Regiment. He drew a blanket and payment for a regimental coat. [Hammond p76] He also served for nine months at Portsmouth, NH under Capt. Brown in 1776.

Peter[5] married Sarah Hall on 11-28-1780. [Chase p328] She was the daughter of Nathaniel and Mary (Wood) Hall. He shows on the 1790 NH census living at Salisbury and in 1800 in Rockingham Co. In 1810 he was living at Chester, NH. [NHFC]

In his pension records, [RWR #W19334] a letter of Sarah Severance recites that she left "nine children scattered all over the country from Maine to Arkansas, one of them living at Chester." In the same records it states that she has always believed that her husband enlisted first at Chester, in 1775, marched to Boston, was in the Battle of Bunker Hill and served at Portsmouth, New Hampshire, under Capt. Brown and was discharged in the fall or winter following.

In December of 1805, **Peter**[5] accidently killed Benjamin Whittier and he was convicted of man slaughter and sentenced to twelve month's imprisonment and costs. [Chase p167]

Sarah and her husband were distant cousins, both descended from Richard and Ursula (Scott) Kimball, [MBJ].

Peter[5] died 5-30-1817. Sarah Hall, widow of **Peter**[5] Severance, died 12-22-1839 [Chase p626] **Peter's**[5] death date was also indicated by his son **George W.**[6] Severance in a letter in his mother's pension file.

On 12-16-1817, Sarah and son, **James**[6], were bonded and named as administrators of the estate of **Peter**[5] who had died intestate. A letter dated 11-16-1827 in Hooksette, from **John**[6] Severance and his sister **Betsy**[6], asking for financial aid, says his mother put her hip out on the ice last March. She had not been able to do anything since and **John**[6] has had to care for her.

Children: [Johnsen p16]
    i   **Elizabeth**[6] b 1-24-1791 at Chester, NH d 7-4-1854 (Shipton, P.Q. Canada) m John C. Butler 12-31-1807. John was born 5-7-1783 at Haverhill, NH [Burleigh II]

57

	ii	**Sarah**[6] b 12-24-1782 d 1845 (Providence, RI) m Samuel Guild 12-1-1811 [Burleigh II]
142	iii	**George Washington**[6] b 2-6-1785 d 3-21-1864 m Mary Pike 8-19-1814 Chester, NH
	iv	**Josiah**[6] b 6-17-1787 d 7-12-1787 [NHVR]
	v	**Polly**[6] (Mary) b 12-29-1789
143	vi	**James M.**[6] b 2-1-1792 d 8-29-1863 m Dorothy Trefethan
144	vii	**Rufus**[6] b 9-15-1794 d 4-281874 m Susan Lance 1-19-1824 Auburn, NH, lived in VT and Auburn, NH
	viii	**Patty**[6] **(Martha)** b 1-3-1797 Auburn, NH
	ix	**Susanna**[6] b 2-18-1799
145	x	**John**[6] b 3-13-1801 m Lucinda Hazelton Hooksette, NH
	xi	**Frederick Jefferson**[6] b 12-13-1804 d 12-13-1885

(62) Joseph[5], (Joseph[4], Ephraim[3], Ephraim[2], John[1]), born 9-12-1750 at Nottingham West (later called Hudson, NH). Most of the research regarding this family has not been published before. Almost no family history was retained because **Joseph**[5] and his brothers traveled around so much and their mother remarried when they were young and her second husband died at a relatively young age. The hardships of the frontier were severe, leaving little time to worry about recording their lives.

The [RWR #S45145] for **Joseph**[5] Severance for MA service gives us a great deal of information regarding his life.

On April 14, 1818, **Joseph**[5] Severance of Lyndeborough, Hillsborough County, NH, but formerly of Scarborough, district of Maine, sixty-five years of age, enlisted in June, 1775 under Capt. Tyler, Col. Phinney, MA troops, and served until January 1776. He re-enlisted back into the same Regiment and served until 1-1-1777. He then enlisted in 1777 for three years under Col. Marshall, MA troops. He served out his time and was nonorably discharged.

On January 9, 1819, **Joseph**[5] Severance added that he was born in Nottingham West, NH. His father was taken and killed by the Indians when he was very young. The family was deprived for its main support and he (**Joseph**[5]) was bound out to a master, Samuel Marsh Esq. till he was twenty one. "a kind master he was to me"

At 21 he went with others to Scarborough and was a hired man there at the time of the war. He enlisted and went to Cambridge where he served out his term. That was when he signed up with Capt. Tyler.

At one time he was sick with the Small Pox and lost one eye from it. He was at Boston at the time this happened. He was later hired by a couple of gentlemen from Medford to perform a tour of Duty for them (about three months). On his way to New York they were halted at Watertown where an officer (Lieut Parks offered anyone who enlisted for three years would get a furlow so **Joseph**[5] took it and returned to Nottingham to see his "friends".

Next he rejoined his Regiment under Col. Marshall and marched to Ticonderoga, Stillwater, and after Burgoyne's surrender "we were ordered to the Southward for winter quarters, at Germantown I was, with about 40 others, taken prisoner by a party of Bristish, carried to Philadelphia, and from there to New York," he was imprisoned for 10 months, exchanged at Elizabethtown, NJ, rejoined his Regiment at White Plains and served out his term there, at West Point and at other places whose names he had forgotten. He received an honorable discharge and returned to his friends, for he had no home, almost worn out in his country's service."

A Sarah Cumings from Nottingham West stated on 10-13-1818 that **Joseph**[5] made his home at her father's house when he went to war and returned there when he was at Nottingham.

On 7-4-1830, **Joseph**[5] Severance of Lyndeborough, NH age 67, testified that he "never had any children, and that his wife lives separate from me." The Vital Records of NH shows that **Joseph**[5] Severance married Mary Harper on 11-22-1785 It appears that **Joseph**[5] died 2-16-1827.

(63) Caleb[5], (Joseph[4], Ephraim[3], Ephraim[2], John[1]), born 5-15-1753/55 at Nottingham West, NH (now called Hudson, NH). He later settled in Orrington, ME (formerly called Worcester, ME) and in Brewer, ME. He died on 6-30-1838. His wifes name is not known and little has been found about her. She was called the mother of Mrs. Olive (Ben) Need. Olive was born 1788. **Caleb**[5] reportedly enlisted from Newburyport, MA [House p42]

Caleb[5] deposed on 4-10-1818 at Brewer, Penobscot County, District of ME [RWR #S37379] for Continental service in NH and MA that about one week after the Lexington Battle in 1775 he enlisted

for eight months under Capt. Hugh Maxwell, Col.
William Prescott." He was 79 years old in 1818.

They were stationed part of the time in
Cambridge, and part on Sewall's Point. At the
expiration of this term he enlisted for one year in
the same Company and Regiment. "We marched on to
New York, were stationed on Governor's Island and
continued there till driven off by the British when
we went into NY to King Bridge and the White
Plains. I was in the Battle of White Plains."

He was discharged at Peekskill, NY, January 1,
1777. **Joshua**[5] Severance of Orrington, ME testified
on June 10, 1819 that he enlisted under Capt. Hugh
Maxwell in March of 1778 "at which time my brother
Caleb[5] Severance was a private in the same Company"

On June 27, 1820, **Caleb**[5] Severance of Brewer,
ME, sixty-seven years of age, testified that in
1802 his dwelling house was burned and his
discharge papers with it, and that his family
consists of a wife, sixty two years of age, and a
son seventeen years of age. It appears that the
pensioner d 6-30-1838 and that he lived in
Nottingham West during the Revolution.

Caleb[5] filed on June 29, 1818 warrant #17280,
Caleb[5] Severance (patentee) of Treat's 21st tract
SE 25 10 N 4 E, **Caleb**[5] Severance, Brewer, ME, 7-27-
1818. [Volkel, The National Archives]

Caleb[5] of Nottingham West, Hudson, NH, and
Brewer and Orrington, ME belonged to the New
Wrentham Religious Society in 1814. [MgBH]

Children:

147	i	**Samuel**[6] b 2-20-1781 m Hannah Godfrey
148	ii	**Reuben**[6] b 4-22-1783. He m **Sally**[5] Severance, daughter of **Joshua**[5] Severance and Elizabeth Snow, on 9-12-1805. **Sally**[6] remarried to Benomi Baker 5-21-1844
149	iii	**Joseph**[6] b 1788. He d 10-1-1874, 86 years old.
150	iv	**William**[6] m Polly Trafton?
	v	**Betsy**[6] **(Eliza)** m Christopher Taylor 10-30-1806 [MgBH Vol I No. III Bangor, ME September 1885] states that Christopher Jr. was b on 2-24-1785 at Chatham, MA. (MEVR)
	vi	**Polly**[6], possibley m to Thomas Kent, published 7-23-1809 [MgBH Vol 5]
	vii	**Lucy**[6] m Josiah Rogers 11-20-1811 in Brewer, Maine. [MEVR] [MgBH Vol I No. III Bangor, ME September 1885]

	viii	**Olive**[6] m Benjamin Ward of Brewer circa 1815
	ix	**Rachel**[6] b 6-17-1797. She m circa 1820 to Nathaniel Dennett of Brewer.
151	x	**Caleb**[6] b 1803 m Nancy (see Pension Records)
152	xi	**Thomas**[6], b 12-24-1803 m Lydia Lovell. The [RWR] applied for in 1820, shows that he had a son 14 years old living at home.

The 1790 ME census shows this family with 3 boys and 1 girl, the 180C ME census with 4 boys and 3 girls, and the 1820 ME census shows 2 boys at home.

(64) Joshua[5], (Joseph[4], Ephraim[3], Ephraim[2] John[1]), born in Nottingham West, NH on 12-22-1757 and died 8-29-1834. He was living there during the revolution. He disposed on April 1, 1818 at Orrington, Penobscot County, District of ME, age 60 years of age in regard to his Continental and New Hampshire Service that he enlisted in May, 1775 for eight months, under Capt. William Walker, Col. James Reed, being then of Nottingham West, NH and was in the Battle of Bunker Hill. On January 1, 1776 he re-enlisted under Capt. Hugh Maxwell, Col. William Prescott and served until January 1, 1777 when he was discharged at Peekskill. [RWR National Archives #W33174]

On June 10, 1819 **Caleb**[5] Severance of Brewer, ME testified to service with his "brother **Joshua**[5] Severance" under Capt. Maxwell, Col. Prescott for the year, 1776, both being discharged together at Peekskill, NY.

Additional service was with Capt. Cross and served at Rhode Island for six weeks in 1775 and 1776. In 1781 he served under Capt. Parson, Major Moulton for four months, in and near Castleton, Vermont. He was pensioned in 1818 but dropped from the roll on account of property. He was in the Battle on Breed's Hill and served under Capt. Peter Cross in 1778.

On February 9, 1839, Elizabeth Severance of Orrington, ME, seventy years of age, deposed that she is the widow of **Joshua**[5] Severance, Revolutionary Pensioner, to whom she was married 5-8-1787 and that her husband died August 29, 1834. "They were married May the 8 in the year of our Lord 1787, we moved upon the place we now live 12-5-1787." [MgBH Vol I No.III September 1885] [RWR National Archive #22174]

On 4-26-1839, Elizabeth Severance forwarded to the Department the private record of her marriage and also of the births of her children.

Elizabeth Snow was the daughter of Benjamin Snow and Mercy Paine. Benjamin was the son of Amasa Snow and Mary Collins, Amasa was the son of John Snow and Elizabeth Ridley, and John was the son of John Snow and Mary Smalley. This John was the son of Nicholas Snow and Constance Hopkins, daughter of Stephen Hopkins. [Machias Vol 14]

Joshua⁵ age 77 years died 8-29-1834 and Elizabeth age 81 died 12-15-1848 are buried in the Marston Cemetery at Orrington, ME

Children: [RWR #W22174)

	i	**Sally**⁶ b 8-15-1788 [MEVR says bpt 5-3-1790] She m first to **Reuben**⁶ Severance, son of **Caleb**⁵ Severance, on 9-12-1805. She m Benomi Baker on 5-21-1844 at Orrington, ME. [MEVR]
	ii	second child b 5-3-1790
153	iii	**Benjamin**⁶ b 4-20-1791
	iv	**Anna**⁶ b 3-23-1793 m William M. Verrill, son of Thomas Verrill and Susan Dolliver of Ipswich and Glousester, MA, on 2-1-1812 [Machias Vol 14 p7]
	v	**John**⁶ b 2-12-1795, hung himself in later life. He was unmarried [PRME-Orrington, Penobscot Co.]
	vi	**Jerusha/Jeremiah**⁶ b 6-18-1797 d 9-27-1797
154	vii	**Joshua**⁶ b 10-12-1798 m Almira Lunt
155	viii	**Cyprian**⁶ b 2-22-1801 m Mary Baker
	ix	**George**⁶ b 1800 may have died young
	x	**Joseph L.**⁶ b 7-22-1803, living in 1834-Probate for his fathers Will. The [PRME] show that he died young and unmarried. The 1860 ME census shows Sarah E. Eldridge, 29 years, (widow) and her daughter Ann Frances living with him.
	xi	**Rebecah**⁶ b 9-21-1807 m Dennis Ambrose of Orono, ME on 10-3-1833. **Rebecca**⁶ m secondly to John Perkins. (MEVR)
157	xii	**Ephraim**⁶ b 9-13-1808 went on board the Capt. Stoddard 4-21-1830 (evidently to sea) He married to Susanna Norris of Bangor, ME. He d 9-23-1868 ae 60 yrs [Waldo, Penobscot County]

xiii   **Massa⁶ (Mercy)** b 12-9-1810 married Capt. Cyrus Brown 3-2-1834 Bangor, ME. (MEVR)

xiv   **Elizabeth⁶** b 5-19-1813 m Nehemiah D. Sawtelle of Old Town, published 12-6-1835

Additional children were **Ruel⁶** and **Olive⁶** but they apparently died young as nothing can be found about them. The 1790 ME census shows him with 1 girl, the 1800 ME census shows 4 boys and 5 girls, and the 1810 ME census shows 6 boys and 2 girls.

When his Will was read in 8-6-1834, wife Elizabeth and children, **Joseph⁶**, **Benjamin⁶**, **Joshua Jr.⁶**, **Cyprian⁶**, **Ephraim⁶**, **Sally⁶**, **Anna⁶**, **Rebecca⁶**, **Mercy⁶**, **John⁶**, and **Eliza⁶** were named.

(65) John⁵, (Ephraim⁴, Ephraim³, Ephraim², John¹), born in Kingston, NH. He was bpt on 9-9-1750. [Tibbetts Vol 5 p159] He shows on the 1790 NH census at Kingston. His family later settled in Sandwich, NH as one of the first pioneer families. NOTE; Ezra Sterns, History of New Hampshire, indicated that **John⁵** married to Lydia Jewell. **This is incorrect**. His son, **John⁶**, married Lydia Jewell 12-9-1792. [NHVR] In 1800 he was living in Rockingham Co, NH and by 1810 he was settled at Sandwich, NH. [NHFC]

John⁵ Signed the Association Test in Kingston, NH, 1776. It was reported that to this **John⁵** was born an infant who died in Kingston, NH, 5-11-1778. [NHVR] [Hosier p361]

John⁵ married Susanna (Smith). The vital records for Sandwich, NH for this time period, were lost to fire and the family records for Susanna are unclear. Susanna's maiden name is not recorded but from the fact that her first son, **John⁶**, and her son **Nathaniel's⁶** middle names were Smith and **John⁶** was often called **Smith⁶** Severance it seem likely that Susanna's maiden name would be Smith. Lydia died on 12-30-1821 at the age of 73 years. They are buried at the Baptist Cemetery, at Center Sandwich, NH.

Children:

158   i   **John Smith⁶** b 12-7-1774 d 1-18-1845 m Lydia Jewell 12-9-1792 who was b 9-20-1777 and d 11-23-1857

159   ii   **Nathaniel Smith⁶** b 8-17-1776 m Betsy Fogg 4-17-1803

    iii   **Susannah⁶** b 9-7-1778 m William Vittum 9-27-1793 by Rev. Jermiah Shaw in

Moultonboro. They had two children. The
story is given in The Vittum Folks how
William Sr. enlisted in the U.S. Army
and was ordered to OH because of some
Indian outbreak. Learning that his wife
had died in NH, he obtained a discharge
and remained in OH. One of his sons,
William, back in NH was also dead and
his eldest son, Ephraim was of age and
so he remarried to Mrs. Clarinda Pratt
of Columbus, OH. He had another family
which remained unknown to his NH
relatives for almost 100 years. [Vittum
p55-56]

160 iv   **Ephraim**[6] b 7-16-1780 d 11-11-1836 m
Sally Leavitt 3-2-1800 who was b 9-18-
1779 and d 9-24-1838 [NHVR]

161 v   **Moses**[6] b 12-27-1782 d 2-20-1856 m Lydia
Thrasher 12-16-1807, Lydia b 3-3-1788 at
Sandwich, NH and d 7-2-1873 [NHVR-
Sandwich] was the daughter of Joseph
Thrasher and Joanna Quimby.

The cemetery yard behind the Baptist Church in
Sandwich is well kept but the age of some of the
first burials is quite evident. The Severance's
were by far the first to be buried in the yard.
Located in the South West corner, many of the
stones are worn away and almost unreadable. **Moses**[6],
Lydia, and their daughter have their three stones
enclosed in a double bar fence. [MDCD]

(66) Peter[5], (Ephraim[4], Ephraim[3], Ephraim[2], John[1]),
born in Kingston, NH on 3-6-1754. He later lived in
Deerfield, and Salisbury, NH. He served several
times in the military during the Revolutionary War.
In 1775 he served under Capt. Henry Dearfield. That
Company was engaged in the Battle of Bunker Hill.
He served again with Captain Dearborn, Col. Wyman's
Regiment. In the winter of 1777 he moved to
Salisbury, NH and enlisted with Captain Ebenezer
Webster, Col. Stickney's Regiment. This Company
took part in the Battle of Bennington, VT on August
16, 1777. As he put it "he was present at the
taking of General Burgoyne." He was discharged in
NY State in 1777. [RWR #S19077]
In the above record, Judith Clifford (wife of
Israel Clifford) of Corinth, VT, testified that her
"brother, **Peter**[5] Severance" came to "my mother in
Kingston, NH, and staid one night in the morning

started for Boston to join the American Army. At that time **Peter[5]** Severance lived in Deerfield, NH, and enlisted there in January 1776. My mother was sick of a fever of which she later died. While sick a letter was sent by some one in the family to the army to have my brother come home", but he did not return until after the mother's death.

Peter's[5] mother died in 1- -1776 at Kingston, NH. His sister Judith married Israel Clifford and in 1831 she was living at Corinth, Vermont. Thomas Watson made an aff'dt at Plainfield, NH and stated he was a relative of **Peter[5]** Severance. [Pension Records]

On 9-20-1779, [NHVR] **Peter[5]** married Abigail Pettengill. Abigail (Greeley) was first married to Andrew Pettengill. All of their children were born in NH. **Peter[5]** and his family moved to Bradford, Orange, Co., Vermont in 1796. **Peter[5]** died sometime after 7-31-1835 (VTVR) in Bradford. Abigail died 2-5-1819 in Bradford. (VTVR) [Greeley p101-102] They settled at Bradford, Orange Co. with four sons and 3 daughters. [VTFC].

Apparently **Peter[5]** married later to a Hannah as she is shown as his widow when the estate was settled in probate on 8-17-1835. "Hannah Severance, widow of **Peter[5]** Severance, late of Bradford, of said district, deceased, is appointed administratix". The whole inventory and note against **Reuben G.[6]** Severance was assigned to the widow, 8-17-1835 [PROVT p69 1835]

Children: [Greeley p 102]

   i   **Betty[6] (Betsey)** b 7-27-1780 in Salisbury, NH m1 ___Lyon m2 _____Hoit. No children.

   ii **Andrew Pettengill[6]** b 7-9-1782 d 4-6-1803 single, Salisbury, NH, [VTVR]

162 iii **Reuben Greeley[6]** b 6-6-1784 Salisbury, NH m Hadassah Esther Smith 6-22-1809 at Bradford, VT m2 to Anna Smith 12- -1829 a sister of Hadassah

   iv **Ruth[6]** b 8-8-1786 Salisbury, NH m Moses Smith 3-8-1806. He was the son of Aaron Smith and Abigail Kendrick (Hanover, NH)

   v   **Peter[6]** b 12-25-1788 d 4-6-1819 single

   vi **Moses[6]** b 9-30-1792 at Salisbury, NH m Lydia Stevens 9-11-1814 at Bradford, VT, she was b at Bradford 3-4-1791, daughter of Nicholas and ___Hunkins, she d 3-24-1860 (Bradford, VT) [Greeley p200] He

married second to Mary Jane Chadwick on
10-31-1861. [VTVR] Mary Jane Chadwick
was 69 years old at her 2nd marriage in
1861, [VTVR], she died 3-25-1902, the
daughter of John and Mary. [VTVR] **Moses**[6]
is living with his daughter, **Sarah Jane**[7]
Batchelder, on the 1860 ME census. He
died 5-10-1871. [VTVR] They had one
child, **Sarah Jane**[7] Severance b 11-3-1815
in Bradford, VT. [Greeley p200] m Hilas
Batchelder 4-18-1838, son of Samuel
Batchelder. Hilas d in Alabama in 1865.
She d in Bradford, VT, 4-8-1883. [VTVR]

(67) Jacob[5], (Jacob[4], Ephraim[3], Ephraim[2], John[1]),
born circa 1754 in Kingston, NH. He married Mary
Tucker on 3-12-1794. [NHVR] It was also reported
that **Benjamin**[5] married to Mary Tucker. [Tibbetts]
However, the [NHVR] shows **Jacob**[5] married to Mary
Tucker. One must keep in mind that it was custom to
name their first born son after the father.
Therefore it would seem probable that the [NHVR]
records are correct in this case. The vital records
show the parents of sons **Jacob**[6] and **Jonathan
Addison**[6] as **Jacob**[5] and Mary Severance.

Children:
163 i   **Jacob**[6] b 1795 d 4-24-1871
164 ii   **Jonathan Addison**[6] b 11-25-1800 at
            Kingston, NH. He d on 10-22-1888.
166 iv   **Martin**[6] b 1807 d 9-5-1864 Lowell, MA age
            57 yrs 2 days. He was married. Parents,
            Jacob and Polly of Kingston, NH and
            Boston, MA. [MAVR]

(68) Daniel[5], (Ephraim[4], Ebenezer[3], Ephraim[2], John[1]),
born circa 1750. He was born in Groton, MA or New
Ipswich, NH but moved to Washington as early as
1778. [HWNH p597] He lived a short while in
Topsham, VT but soon returned to Washington, where
he died on 3-10-1817. He shows on the 1790 NH
census at Washington and at Topsham, Orange Co in
1800 with 8 sons below the age of 26 years. [VTFC]
    It is said that **Daniel**[5] was a soldier in the
Revolution at Bunker Hill June 17, 1775, led by
Capt. Ezra Towne, in Col. Reed's Regiment. He
enlisted 4-23-1775 at the age of 23 years
(therefore he was born circa 1752). His occupation
was Blacksmith, height 5 ft 8 in. complexion brown,
eyes light. [Hammond][DAR Index] Near the year of

1796 he moved to Topsham, VT where he built a cabin. It was reported to have been taken from him by a neighbor in a land claim. He returned to New Ipswich by 1810 and then Washington, NH, where he died 3-10-1817.

He married Betsey Safford of New Ipswich, NH in 1778. Betsey was the daughter of Benjamin Safford and Prudence Melvin. She was born 1-31-1759 in New Ipswich and died circa 1826 in Washington, NH.

Children: [MAV]
167 i   **Daniel**[5] b in Washington m **Abigail**[5] Severance, daughter of **Rufus**[4] Severance 8-23-1815, settled in Wirt, Allegheny Co. NY State (1850)
168 ii   **Benjamin**[5] b in Washington 1782 d 9-29-1825 m Betsey Dodge
     iii   **Nathan**[5] b in Washington d in Claremont, NH
     iv   **Reuben**[5] b circa 1787 in Washington. He drowned near Cape Breton Island in May of 1818 at the age of 31 years old.
     v   unknown child
170 vi   **Jerimiah**[5], **Michael**[5] or **Micah**[5] b circa 1805. He shows on the 1860 NH census for Alstead. He d in Canada
172 viii   **Abijah**[5] b in Washington 6-15-1793 d 11-1-1865 m Hannah Searles 4-27-1819
     ix   **Joel**[5] b in Washington d in Claremont, NH
     x   **William**[5] b in Washington settled in NY where he died. The 1840 NY census shows **William**[5] living at Sandy Creek, Oswego County.
     xi   unknown child probably settled in the British Provinces
     xii   **Betsy**[5] b in Washington

(69) Ebenezer[5], (Ephraim[4], Ebenezer[3], Ephraim[2], John[1]), born 9-8-1752 in Temple, NH. He later settled in New Ipswich, and Charlestown, NH. He married Lucy Nutting of Hancock, NH on 4-9-1777. [IGI] In 1787 he moved to Windsor, VT. In 1818 he moved to Reading, VT, where he applied 7-30-1832 at the age of 80 years. **Ebenezer**[5] died after 1832 in Reading, VT.

The Muster Roll of the New Ipswich Company states that he enlisted from New Ipswich, age 22, lived at Temple, was a farmer, in 1787 he moved from Temple. NH to Windsor, VT, and then in 1818 to Reading VT. The 1790 VT census shows **Ebenezer**[5]

Severance living in Windsor with a family of 2 boys below the age of 16 and 3 females. In 1800-1810 he was living in Windsor. [VTFC]

Ebenezer[5] details his service to the country in the Revolutionary War. He deposed on July 30, 1832 at the age of 80 years old, that he enlisted at Temple, NH on 4-19-1775 where he was then living.

They first went to Cambridge, MA. Then about 5 weeks later he enlisted for eight months under Capt. (Ezra) Towne, and Col. James Reed. "A few days after he enlisted his Company was stationed on Charlestown Neck. On the day of the battle, which was June 17, 1775, his Company marched up on the hills, took its part in the action, later returned to Winter Hill and stayed there until the last of January 1776.

Other services included New York under Capt (Abijah) Smith of New Ipswich, NH, the Regiment was commanded by Col. (Nahum) Baldwin of Amherst, and Lieut. Col. Gordon Hutchins. Then he marched to Rindge, NH under Col. Hale. Then to Hartford, CT, New Haven, East Chester, NY and on to White Plains and were engaged in the battle there.

Then on May 1, 1777 he volunteered under Capt. Josiah Brown. They marched by way of Charlestown across Vermont to Ticonderoga, NY. "The Ti" was given up and they were released. He got the measles after he reached home but soon after he enlisted under Capt. Stephen Palmer of New Ipswich, NH and eventualy marched to Bennington, VT and fought in the battles there. While he was at Stillwater, he was stationed on Bemis Heights where he was engaged in a desperate fight on 10-7-1777 and received a musket ball wound in his leg which caused his discharge.

In 1787 he moved from Temple, NH to Windsor, VT and thence in 1818 to Reading, VT, where he has ever since resided." The [1800 VTFC-Windsor Co] shows Ebenezer with 2 males below 10 years and 2 females below 10 years of age. The [1810 VTFC] shows him living in Reading, VT.

On June 27, 1833, **Asa[6]** Severance (**Ebenezer's[5]** son) of Alstead, NH testified to personal knowledge of **Ebenezer's[5]** service in 1777 at Ticonderoga, the measles, and his later enlistment under Capt. Stephen Parker. [RWR #S22500]

Their childrens births are recorded as **Ebenezer[6]**, **Ruth[6]**, **Samuel[6]**, **Jacob[6]**, **Anna[6]**, and **Asa[6]**. That there were other children is quite probable as a grandson of **Samuel[6]** says his father (**Cyrus[7]**

Severance) had uncles **Isaac⁵** (probably the **Isaac⁵**
that married to Lucy Biglow and settled in WI) and
Stephen⁵ (who settled in VT) besides those named
above. [inquiry in NEHGR]

Children: born in Temple, Hillsboro County, NH
174 i   **Ebenezer⁶** b 11-8-1777 (son of **Ebenezer⁵**
          of Temple, Hillsboro Co., NH, d 1-15-
          1826 m Jerusha Kilby 5-12-1805. He
          probably m1 to Polly ___ and m2 to
          Jerusha Kilby/Kilbourne
     ii   **Ruth⁶** b 5-23-1779
175 iii **Samuel⁶** b 11-26-1780 m Susannah Warren
          1807 and settled in Essex, NY. The
          biography in the Leading Citizens of
          Clinton and Essex Counties, New York,
          was wrong in stating that **Samuel⁵**
          Severance and Azubah Smith were the
          parents of **Samuel⁶** Severance who m
          Susanah Warren.
     iv   **Jacob⁶** b 8-18-1782
     v   **Anna⁶** b 5-18-1784 d 9-30-1843 m Jonathan
          Bellows 8-26-1802 of Rockingham, VT.
     vi   **Asa⁶** b 1-24-1786. An **Asa** Severance from
          Temple or Claremont, NH. He d on board
          the ship Perserverance. [NSCC-
          Massachusetts, 7-4-1812]
176 vii **Levi⁶**, b 1792 m Hannah Bird of
          Dorchester, MA. Later settled in
          Pittsburg, PA. The [DARLR Vol 18] for
          Mrs. **Elizabeth Bird⁹** Severance Buchan
          #17816
177 viii **Stephen⁵**, circa 1796
178 ix   **Isaac⁶** b 1798 d 1877 at Waukesha, WI, m
          Lucia Bigelow 3-30-1823.

(70) Abel⁵, (Ephraim⁴, Ebenezer³, Ephraim², John¹),
born in New Ipswich, NH about 1754. He was a
resident of Washington in 1783. In 1790 he was
living in Washington, NH. [NHFC] He married Martha
Bruce at Stow, MA on 8-26-1779, [MAVR] and later
lived in Temple and then in Bradford, NH. In 1800
he was in Cheshire Co. [NHFC] Next he shows in
Alstead. By 1820 he was in Washington. [NHFC]
    He was a soldier in the Revolutionary War at
Bunker Hill and Winter Hill. He then went into NY
state and from there to Albany, then across the
Lakes to Montreal, returning to Mt. Independence
near Ticonderoga and stayed there until some time
in October when the regiment was ordered to the

Southern part of PA. [RWR #S45146]

Muster roll of the New Ipswich Company states that **Abel**[5] enlisted from Groton at age 21 and lived in New Ipswich, a farmer. Living with son **John**[6] in Bradford 6-1-1840.

He served from New Ipswich, birth place Groton, MA, from a descriptive list endorsed, 8-4-1775, under Capt. Ezra Town's Co., Col. James Reed's Regt., rank of Private, age 21 yrs, enlisted 4-23-1775, mustered 7-11-1775. [MASS]

Abel[5], son of **Ephraim Sr**[5]. was born about the year of 1754. He married Martha Bruce and resided at the east part of Washington, where Charles W.J. Fletcher now resides, near the school house. He was a resident of Washington in 1783, but it appears from the town record that he afterward, and for a short time, resided in Temple, NH.

He served as a deacon in his church. He died in Bradford, NH on 8-26-1842 at the age of 88 years old. Martha died 8-2-1836 age 76 [HWNH p604]

They are buried in Bradford Cemetery [Goss]

Children:
	i	**Patty**[6]
	ii	**Abigail**[6] b 9-1-1782/85 m Jesse B. Bailey, 9-8-1800 res. Groton, NH
179	iii	**Ephraim**[6] b 7-8-1785 settled in Bradford, ME [PRME Penobscot Co (2:28)] shows with Elijah[7], tanner of Dexter, Admr 11- - 1819 **Ephraim**[6] Severance.
	iv	**William**[6] b 1-11-1789 d in MA
	v	**Elijah**[6] b 9-17-1792 in Temple, NH, settled in Bradford, ME. He d in Dexter, ME at the age of 27 years. [MEVR 1785-1820 Vol 1 & 2] [NSG&B 10-11-1819/ 9-30-1819]
180	vi	**John**[6] b 6-3-1797 d 6-5-1883 m Maria Cheney 10-4-1818, [HWNH p604] **Abel**[5] was living with **John**[5] in 1810 on the New Hampshire Census of Pensioners

(71) Rufus[5], (Ephraim[4], Ebenezer[3], Ephraim[2], John[1]), born in New Ipswich, NH circa 1755 and settled in Washington. He married Martha Flagg, daughter of Nathaniel and Elizabeth Flagg. on April 20, 1785. [HWNH p599] He died in Washington, NH about 1835. [1790-1820 Washington, NHFC]

Children: [HWNH p599]
	i	**Sally**[6] b in Washington 3-12-1786 d age

```
                16 years
181  ii      Rufus⁶ b in Washington 11-29-1788 m
             Lydia Crane
182  iii     Joseph⁶ b in Washington 9-19-1790 m Mary
             Davis
183  iv      Ephraim⁶ b in Washington 4-19-1792 m
             Mary A. Rollins
     v       Abbie⁶ b in Washington 4-16-1794 m
             Daniel⁶ Severance Jr. 8-23-1815. Daniel⁶
             was the son of Daniel⁵ and Betsy
             Safford
     vi      Abel⁶ b in Washington 5-15-1796. Abel⁶ d
             in Washington, NH in 1846. m Persis
             Wheeler of Hillsborough, NH. Persis,
             daughter of Abraham Wheeler, was b 1-24-
             1807 at Bolton, Worcester Co., MA.
             [MBGD] The 1830 NH census shows him
             living in Hillsborough
184  vii     Joel⁶ b in Washington 4-15-1798 m Mrs.
             Jane (Weeks) Woodward
185  viii    Abijah⁶ b 4-14-1798 m Polly Spafford
     ix      Martha⁶ b 7-10-1799 m Benjamin Grandy
     x       Mary⁶ b 6-11-1801 m Ziba Colburn. One of
             their daughters, Martha Ann, m William
             Copp of Natick, MA. [Burleigh]
     xi      Emilla⁶ b 9-9-1805 m Tristram Collins 5-
             29-1831. She d in Wisconsin [HWNH]
186  xii     Asa⁶ b 2-3-1810 d 5-23-1885 m Sarah C.
             Bean 4-3-1842
     xiii    Rebecca⁶ b 2-3-1810
     xiv     Elzina⁶ b in Washington and d in
             childhood [HWNH p603]
```

(72) Ephraim⁵ *Sufferance*, (Ephraim⁴, Ebenezer³, Ephraim², John¹), born in Groton, MA, circa 1757/1759, before his family moved to Washington, NH. Although the [MAVR] would indicate that he was born in 1749, the Cemetery Records and Revolutionary War Records confirm the year as 1759. [CRRME]

Ephraim⁵ Severance deposed on April 10, 1818, [RWR #W25172] "of the plantation of Knox" in the District of Maine, "that in the fall of 1775 he enlisted for one year, was embodied at Cambridge, near Boston in a Company commanded by Capt. Gilman and Regiment commanded by Col. Nixon, Massachusetts Line", served out his term and was discharged at "Kingsbury, New York". He was living at Thorndike (Hancock) ME in 1827. [MEFC]

Receipt given to Benjamin Heywood, paymaster,

4th regt., dated Camp Mr. Washington, 9-29-1776, signed by said *Severens* and others belonging to Capt. Gilmans's Co., for wages, etc., due prior to 1-1-1776.

In April of 1777 he enlisted again for the war, "was embodied in a Company commanded by Capt. John Winslow, in a Regiment of Artillery commanded by Col. John Crane" and "served until peace except that I was at the Southward about one year in a Company of Artillery commanded by Col. Savage under the Marquis de La Fayette", was honorably discharged "at West Point in June, 1783 and received the Badge of Honor for good behavior." This was recorded on April 10, 1818 and **Ephraim**[5] was listed as being 61 years old (therefore he was born around 1757) and living in Thorndike, Maine.

The [TRNINH Vol 2 p327 (April 18, 1777)], states that "this may certify all whom it may concern that I, **Ephraim**[5] Severance, of New Ipswich am engaged and enlisted as a soldier in the Continental Service for and during the term of three years which service is to be reaconed and acconned for unto Ebenezer Champney, Francis Fletcher, John Cutter, and William Spear, the same as tho either of the said persons had served in person for said term and their proportion of said service. [[MASS p1009-1011][RWR W25172][House p42][NHPSP Vol 2 p193, 509, 709, 716, 742-3]

There was a tradition that **Ephraim**[5] was killed at the battle of White Plains, but by the best authority, Rev. **John F.**[6] Severance, the compiler of *The Severans Genealogy*, believed the statement to be erroneous. To substantiate his views he states that one **Ephraim**[5] Severance enlisted from New Ipswich, NH, 2-1-1777 was wounded 10-7-1777, and was with his regiment at Stillwater, New York 10-11-1777 a year after the battle at White Plains. [HWNH p597] He was uncertain whether this **Ephraim**[5] ever resided in Washington. However, **Ephraim**[5] is shown in Washington, NH as **Ephraim Jr**[5] *Severants* and his father **Ephraim Sr.**[4] *Severants* in 1771. It stated that **Ephraim Sr.**[4] was a resident for 3 years and six months and **Ephraim Jr.**[5], for 6 months. In 1773, they are shown along with **Daniel**[5]. [HWNH p404-412]

Next **Ephraim**[5] Severance was listed as a Hayward in Sanbornton, New Hampshire from 1789 to 1796. This **Ephraim**[5] appears to be the husband of Ruth Gould whom he married 10-30-1785 [PRNH-Rye] The 1800 Strafford Co., NH census shows **Ephraim**[5].

Ephraim⁵/Nathaniel⁵ Severance (usually written *Sufferance* on our town records) was the earliest settler on the Ede Taylor, now the Daniel R. Sanborn place, lived afterwards at the Woodman upper house, but removed to Belfast, Maine, soon after 1800. He was vividly remembered by the venerable Capt. John B. Perkins, from certain episodes of school-boy experience, as a citizen of the Centre School District, being the father of two sons and at least one daughter. The town records give only the former of the two following children." [Runnels Vol II p872]

The records show that this **Ephraim⁵** *Sufferance*, a Revolutionary Soldier, married to Ruth Gould, daughter of Christopher Gould and Elizabeth Waters, on 10-3-1785 at Rye, Rockingham County, NH, at the age of 26. They were both from Sanbornton, NH. [NHVR-Rye]

Christopher Gould married Elizabeth Waters on 12-31-1756, both of Durham, NH [PRNH Strafford Co p205] Apparently Christopher was a pauper as there was a town order in Hampton, NH referring to Christopher Gould, subjecting any person who should receive him into his family, to the fine specified in the former vote. [PRNH]

The records for Sanbornton, NH in the year of 1798 indicate **Benjamin⁶** and **Ephraim⁵** Severance living there. **Ephraim⁵** stated in a request to receive his pension from Bangor, ME, 7-26-1820, that "I am a farmer, but unable to labor, I have no children under my control except my son **Ephraim⁶** who is twenty years old, but labors for himself." Ruth "Sufferance" age 76 from Waldo, ME was listed on the census of pensioners for ME, June 1, 1840.

A document indicating that Ruth Sufferance, widow of **Ephraim⁵** Sufferance, had received her Semi-Annual Pension allowance dated 2-7-1839 shows on the back of the document, the names of **Lagrange⁵** Sufferance dated 7-10-1836 and **George⁵** Sufferance, believed to be their sons, dated 9-1-1838. This document also indicates that **Ephraim⁵** died on 3-6-1835 and the pension for Ruth commencing on March 4, 1836. Widow, Ruth Severance, was listed on the 1840 ME census at Mattawamkeag.

Although the Cemetery Records have been reported to give the deaths of **Ephraim⁵** at 3-4-1825 and Ruth as 4-18-1835, it appears that more realistic and accurate death dates would be 3-4-1835 and 4-18-1839 respectively. They both died at Knox, Waldo County, ME. They are buried in the East Knox

Cemetery, Knox, ME.

Children:

i   **a daughter**[6] m ___ Mulhoon [Hosier p361]

ii   **James**[6] b 3-18-1786 in Sanbornton, NH as shown on the [DARLR] for **Charles Edgar**[8] Severance. He was indicated as a son of **Ephraim**[5] and Ruth Gould. [Runnels p872] says a son of **Nathaniel**[5]. I am not sure if this **James**[6] had any children.

187 iii   **Jacob**[6] b 1788 d 1859 m (Susanna Haskell) Severance on 1-31-1839. **Jacob**[6] "Sufferance" of Knox, Maine, fifty years of age, (therefore b 1789) certified to the death of **Ephraim**[6] Severance as stated and to the continued widowhood of Ruth Severance

188 v   **Benjamin**[6] b 1792 m Lydia Sanborn in Maine. [Runnels] [LRME]

189 iv   **Ephraim**[6] b circa 1802 m Eliza Merriam. His father, **Ephraim**[5] "of Thorndike, but late of Knox" sixty one years of age, stated in 1820 that he had a son **Ephraim**[6] 20 years under his control.

190 vi   **George**[6] signed his name on the application for the continuation of Ruth's Pension. [PRME Book A Vol 1 p23]

vii   **Lagrange**[6] signed his name on the application for the continuation of Ruth's Pension. {PRME Book A Vol 1 p23]

(73) Asa[5], (Ebenezer[4], Ebenezer[3], Ephraim[2], John[1]), of Alstead, Cheshire Co., NH, was born 11- -1761 according to his Revolutionary War Records, he enlisted at Temple, NH in July of 1779. He supposedly married to Mary Dinsmore on 11-25-1788 at Temple, Hillsboro Co., NH. He shows as living in Temple. [1790/1800 NHFC-Temple] His pension records say that he first served 6 months under Capt. Daniel Emerson, Col. Hercules Mooney, New Hampshire Militia, went to Providence, Rhode Island, then to Tiverton, then over to Butts Hill and where he was stationed until December in the houses evacuated by the British and January 1, 1780 verbally discharged. In July of that year he enlisted at Temple for three months under Capt. Spaulding, Col. Nichols, went to West Point and was stationed first at Robinson's Farm, "was standing as a sentinel, at Arnold's door, when he went away..I stood at the North door and he went out the South door", then

went to West Point and was dicharged. [RWR S15636]
In 1810-1820 he was living at Alstead and in
1830 he was living in Swanzey. [NHFC]
On September 4, 1835 he applied for a transfer
to Lancaster, Erie Co., NY as "his son had
previously removed there and he wished to live with
or near them." On February 17 and June 22, 1848,
Asa[5] Severance applied again for a transfer to
Alstead, NH, where he "wishes to reside with his
children". [RWR S15636] The Census of Pensioners of
6-1-1840 shows **Asa**[5] age 78 with Corbin W. Powers in
Lancaster, Erie County, NY.
Asa[5] died 4-20-1854, age 93 years, at Alstead,
NH.

Children: [IGI]
i	**Asa**[6]	b 12-6-1789. The 1830 NYFC-Tioga Co shows **Asa**[6] living in Tioga.
191 ii	**Artemus**[6]	b 11-18-1791 m Caty Winch 10-27-1811
iii	**Polly**[6]	b 8-20-1793 m Jonathan Brown 9-2-1810
iv	**Lydia**[6]	b 12-22-1795
v	**Betsa**[6]	b 11-18-1797

192a   **John**[6] (unconnected) b 10-11-1800,
settled in KY. This is conjecture as to
the placement. We know that **John**[6], born
in NH, shows in Kentucky. He married to
Elizabeth Ham. This appears to be the
only family where he might fit. His
family will be continued as unconnected.
His childrens names seem to fit into a
pattern of similarity of other families
from the Kingston, NH area.

(74) Ebenezer[5], (Ebenezer[4], Ebenezer[3], Ephraim[2],
John[1]), born 9-8-1768 at Kingston, NH. [Tibbetts]
He shortly after moved with his family to Temple
and then Alstead, NH. It is possible that he
married first to Sarah or Sally Brown, daughter of
Elias and Rebecca Brown. [IGI] He was married to
Sally Coolidge. Sally was born 7-5-1779. Sally
Coolidge married **Ebenezer**[5] and had four children.
[Coolidge] The 1810 NH census for Alstead shows
only **Ebenezer**[5] and a wife.

Children: [Coolidge]
i	**Amanda**[5]	b 10-22-1810
ii	**Mary Addine**[6]	b 1-8-1813

192   iii   **Ariel Kendrick**[6] b 3-5-1815
      iv   **Phebe Ann Wood**[6] b 9-2-1817
      v   **Lucy Malanda**[6] b 9-17-1820 m Francis
            Coombs. (Frances R. Combs, first child
            of Barnabas Coombs, and Rebecca Willard,
            born in Rutland, MA 8-16-1821 m **Lucy**
            Malanda[6] Severance, daughter of **Ebenezer**[5]
            and Sarah Severance of Alstead. [NHVR]
            Lucy was born 9-17-1820.)
      vi   **Sarah Permela Carpenter**[6] b 1-13-1824 in
            Alstead, NH, daughter of **Ebenezer**[5] and
            Sarah Severance. [NHVR]

(75) Jonathan[5], (Jonathan[4], Jonathan[3], Ephraim[2],
John[1]), born in Kingston, NH on 7-31-1757. He grew
up in Kingston and married Mehitable Brown on 1-18-
1781. [NHVR] Mehitable was born 3-5-1761 in
Kingston and died 4-17-1846 in Tuftonboro, NH. He
lshows on the 1800-1810 NH census for Tuftonboro
next to his son, **Jonathan Jr.**[6]. There marriage was
recorded in Danville, NH and then again in Upper
Gilmanton (Belmont), NH. The family lived several
places. First at Kingston and then at Upper
Gilmanton. Next they lived at Chichester for a
short time and then Tuftonboro where **Jonathan**[5] died
on 2-15-1835. Mehitable was born 3-5-1761 at
Kingston and died 4-17-1846. Both **Jonathan**[5] and his
wife are buried in the Hersey Cemetery in
Tuftonboro.
    "From Upper Gilmanton, **Jonathan's**[5] family moved
to Tuftonboro where in 1804, **Jonathan**[5] purchased
from Mr. Page 100 acres for $590. [Strafford Co.
Deeds, Vol 45 p440] It was on this land that
Jonathan[5] constructed his home farm and began the
Severance families which still live in the
Tuftonboro-Lake Winnipesaukee area of New
Hampshire. Throughout the first part of the 1800's,
land was bought and sold by **Jonathan**[5] and his sons.
It appears that they were all successful farmers."
[MDW]
    Jonathan[5] spent some time during the
Revolutionary War [RWR #W16151, (New Hampshire
sevice) Vol 45]. On August 22, 1832 **Jonathan**[5]
Severance of Tuftonborough, Strafford County, NH
age 75 years deposed that in 1775 he served eight
months in NH Militia under Capt. Gilman, Col. Poor,
marched from Kingston, NH, where he then resided to
Winder Hill, where he served until January 1, 1776.
In the fall of 1777 he enlisted for three months at
Kingston under Capt. Ezra Currier, marched to

Bennington, then to Stillwater, NY where he
witnessed the Surrender of Burgoyne, "the battle
having been fought before my arrival.

On September 14, 1838, Mehitable Severance of
Tuftonborough, NH Age 73 years deposed that she is
the widow of **Jonathan**[5] Severance to whom she
married January 18, 1781 (certified October 11,
1838 by the Town Clerk of Kingston, NH) and that
her husband died 3-5-1835. [RWR #W16151]

Children: [MDW]
193   i   **Jonathan Jr.**[6] b 7-4-1781 m Marian Moyer
       ii   **Sarah**[6] b 9-10-1784
       iii   **Molly**[6] b 2-3-1788
194   iv   **Benjamin**[6] b 7-26-1790 m Elizabeth
              Burbank
       v   **Samuel**[6] b 5-1-1793. **Samuel**[6] moved to
              Moultonboro where he lived on the
              Richardson farm with his wife and her
              parents. They had a son, **Clarence**[7].
              [MDW]
195   vi   **Stephen**[6] b 7-26-1796 m Eliza King and
              settled in Brockton, MA
       vii   **Elizabeth**[6] b 7-26-1796
196   viii   **John**[6] b 7-14-1799 lived in Tuftonboro,
              NH and Lovell, ME.
197   ix   **Joseph**[6] b 1801. **Joseph**[6] married to Mary
              Moody and later settled in Lovell, ME.

(76) Benjamin[5], (Benjamin[4], Jonathan[3], Ephraim[2],
John[1]), born in Amesbury, MA on 2-10-1761. [MAVR]
He later lived in Kingston and Boscawen, NH. From
1790-1810 he was living at Boscawen. [NHFC] He
married Rebecca (Sweet) Holcomb 6-16-1784 in
Boscawen, NH. She was born 1-25-1758, the daughter
of Benjamin Sweat and Rebecca Pierce, at Newberry,
MA. [MAVR] Her maiden name was Sweet/Sweat but she
had married earlier to Mr. Holcomb.

Benjamin[5] was placed on the pension roll of
Morgan County, OH in 1832 for service 1778-79 in
Captain Spurr's Company, Colonel Nixon's
Massachusetts Regiment. He died in Brookfield
township, Morgan County, OH. [DARLR Vol 75 p169] He
died 6-8-1845.

Benjamin[5] Severance of Morgan County, OH deposed
on the [RWR #W9646 National Archives] for service
in MA 10-15-1832, age 72 that in May 1778 while a
resident of Boscawen, NH, enlisted under Capt.
Spurr, Col. Nixon, MA Line for nine months and then
honorable discharged at West Point, NY. and that in

July of 1780 he enlisted under Capt. Stoddart, Col.
Vose, MA Line for six months. The records further
show that on 11-11-1846, Rebecca Severance of
Brookfield, Morgan County, 88 years deposed that
she is the widow of **Benjamin⁵** Severance and they
were married 12-16-1784 at Boscawen, NH and her
husband died June 8, 1845, Morgan Coiunty, OH.
[DAR-Oregon State Roster of Ancestry, p323]
    In his Will, [PRMOH-1845] which was proved on 7-
28-1845, **Benjamin⁵** left to "my daughter, **Rebecca⁶**
Fowler, one dollar, I give and devise to my other
children, viz, **Hazen⁶**, **Benjamin⁶**, **Rodney⁶**, **Silas⁶** and
Sarah⁶ Burlingame and their heirs all my land or
farm whereon I now reside." He nominated Asa
Burlingame the executor of his last will and
testament.
    Benjamin⁵ shows on the OH census of pensioners,
June 1, 1840, in Brookfield, Morgan Co at 78 years,
head of the household.

Children: born in Boscowen, NH [MLSW]
    i   **Polly⁶** b 4-5-1790 m Michel Simon 10-13-
            1814 [NHVR-Boscawen]
    ii   **Sarah⁶** b 4-5-1791 d in September of 1859
            at Cole Co. MO. She m to Asa (Franklin)
            Burlingame in 10- -1822. He was b 2-28-
            1790 at Cranston, RI and d on 3-6-1864
            at Iberia, Cole County, MO. [DARLR,
            submitted by Mrs. Ardyce Stoddard
            Thompson, National #499353]
198 iii   **Benjamin⁶** b 4-2-1794 d 7-19-1847 m
            Rebecca Butler 2-21-1818 m2 Emma Jane
            Been
199 iv   **Rodney⁶** b 12- -1795 d 1870's m Jane
            Caldwell 3-31-1818
200 v   **Silas⁶** b 7-29-1797 d 1843-1850 m Mary
            Hupp circa 1820

The first 5 children were listed in *One Hundred and
fiftieth Anniversary of the Settlement of Boscawen
and Webster, Merrimack Co., N.H.*, printed by the
Republican Press Association, 1884

    vi   **Rebecca⁶** 1799-1872 m Royal Fowler 1-21-
            1821, he b 1798-1887 [DARLR Vol 123/75 &
            127]
201 vii   **Hazen⁶** b 1801 m Mary ___ circa 1830

(77) Nicols⁵, (Benjamin⁴, Jonathan³, Ephraim²,
John¹), born 10-15-1766 in Kingston, NH. He spent

much of his later life in Boscawan, NH. He married to Louise Swett, 9-21-1790 at Boscawen. [NHVR] He shows on the 1790 NH census for Boscawen, NH. The 1800 and 1810 VT census for Thetford, Orange Co VT shows **Nicholas⁵** Severance with his wife and 4 sons and 1 daughter.

Children:

	i	**Jemima⁶** b 12-12-1790 d 1833 [BWNH]
	ii	**Harrison⁶** b circa 1795
202	iii	**Nicholas⁶** b circa 1795 m Warner/Danforth
203	iv	**Thomas⁶** b circa 1798
	v	**Sapphina⁶** b circa 1800

(78) Samuel⁵, (Samuel⁴, Jonathan³, Ephraim², John¹), born 8-25-1775. He married to Judith Towle on 1-6-1802 at Kingston, NH. [NHVR]. Judith was from Hawke, New Hampshire, daughter of Jeremy Towle and Mary Sargent. He shows on the 1810 NH census for Kingston, NH.

Children: [Tibbetts Vol III p 171]

	i	**Mary (Polly)⁶** b 11-14-1805 d 9-13-1889 m William Winslow 2-26-1824 [Greely p615]
204	ii	**John⁶** b 11-14-1816 m Emily B. Hunt
205	iii	**Ora P.⁶** b 12-1828 m Ruth Ann (Smith) Stickney (Kingston, NH)

(79) John⁵, (John⁴, Jonathan³, Ephraim², John¹), born 7-23-1773 in Kingston, NH. During his life he lived in Hampstead and Pembroke, NH. He married Rachel Heath on 11-4-1807. She was born 1776 and died 10-9-1837. **John⁵** died 9-22-1847 in Pembroke, NH. The family lived at Kingston. [1810-1830 NHFC]

Children: They reportedly had 4 children. [MAM]

206	i	**Nathan⁶** b 9-9-1808 m Lydia Gould 9-19-1830 (Kingston, NH)

SIXTH GENERATION (80) John/Abba⁶, (Tabitha⁵, Daniel⁴, Ebenezer³, John², John¹), bpt 7-18-1762 [MAVR] at Springfield West, MA. Only his mother, **Tabitha⁶**, was listed as a parent. **John/Abba⁶** was the son of **Tabitha⁵**. **Tabitha⁵** Severance (her maiden name) married to Asa Miller, 12-12-1765, [MAVR-Springfield] three years after **John⁶** was baptized. She died relatively young and Asa Miller remarried to Eunice Shircoy (his second wife) [DARLR Vol 15 p74] Springfield, MA.

   Abbe⁶ Severance was mustered by Col. Enoch Hall

at Temple, NH on July 15, 1779 for Continental Service of one year. It also indicates that he later traveled back to Springfield, MA to visit. [RWR #W2643]) He d 1-23-1831 at Wallingford, VT.

John/Abbe[6] married Eunice Chase, both residents of Newbury, MA on 10-12-1781. [MAVR-Newbury] Eunice Chase, born 1-24-1760, was the daughter of Aquila Chase and Mary [MAVR]

John[6] and Eunice lived at Alstead, NH and later moved to Reading, VT. **John**[6] and Eunice died at Ludlow, VT. **Abby/John**[6] was living at Packersfield, Cheshire Co. with 4 boys and 1 girl in 1790. In 1810 he was at Alstead. [NHFC] Next, in 1820 he was found living at Ludlow, Windsor Co. VT. The last indication of him was in 1830 at Wallingford in Rutland Co. [VTFC]

The Revolutionary War Pension Records show that he filed from Windsor County on 4-9-1818, from Ludlow, VT in 1820, and Eunice applied from Orange Co. VT on 11-26-1838.

Children: probably all born at Alstead, NH

207	i	**John**[7] b 7-3-1782 m Lavina Dutton 11-8-1814
	ii	**Abner**[7] b 1-6-1784 d young
	iii	**Lucy**[7] b 3-11-1786
208	iv	**Abner**[7] b 3-11-1786 m Rebecca Hardy
	v	**Benjamin**[7] b 2-29-1788 d 6-23-1788
209	vi	**Nathan**[7] *Severens* b 3-7-1789 m Rhoda Thompson
210	vii	**Moses**[7] *Severens* b 10-19-1790 d 1871 m Anna Cooper b 9-17-1792 [MBB]
	viii	**Eunice**[7] b 6-6-1792
	ix	**Benjamin**[7] b 1-11-1795, I show this **Benjamin**[7] on the [1870 Bath, Clinton Co., MIFC] living with Jeffers family. **Eunice**[8] was the mother, the husband had died and apparently, **Benjamin**[7] was the father of **Eunice**[8].
	x	**Galen**[7] b circa 1803. [RWPR] he was living at home in 1820 at the age of 17 years. The 1830 NY census shows **Galen**[7] and **Benjamin**[7] living in Greenbush, Renesselaer Co.

(81) Samuel[6], (Ebenezer[5], Ebenezer[4], Ebenezer[3], John[2], John[1]), born in Northfield, MA on 2-2-1765. He married Mary Kirby of Litchfield, CT. in January of 1791. She was born 8-1-1771 and died 6-15-1861, (VTVR) the daughter of Abraham Kirby and Eunice

Starkweather. He settled in Middlebury, VT where he
died on February 11, 1851. [VTVR]
   They lived on Hyde's Pitch north of Kirby's farm
for at least six years. **Samuel⁶** Severance and John
S. Kirby exchanged Lands, and Kirby took possession
of Severance's farm. [Swift p209-210]
   "When a young man and before his father removed
from Northfield, (he) started out unmarried and
alone to make for himself a home in the wilderness.
His stock and store as he turned into the forest
consisted of a yoke of stags, an ox-sled, two log
chains, some harrow teeth, an ax, a chest of
clothing and provisions, a half barrel of whisky, a
half barrel of pork and a cow. Not a bad outfit for
those times."
   "He pitched his camp, after due time, in
Middlebury, Vermont, some twenty-five miles beyond
Pittsford, the nearest point, at which was a
gristmill. He settled on the east end of lot 55,
cleared lots 18 and 19, which were entirely wild."
[JFS p23] The 1810-1830 VT census for Middlebury
shows him living in that area.

Children: [JFS p23]
212 i   **Ebenezer⁷** b 11-3-1791 d 2-17-1880 [VTVR]
            m Corcina Jones 1-29-1817
     ii   **Eusebia⁷** b 4-24-1793, d 9-10-1794
     iii   **Patty⁷ (Miss)** b 3-9-1795 d 4-17-1889
            [VTVR] unmarried
     iv   **Hannah⁷** b 8-4-1797 d 4-30-1822 m Leonard
            Dakins 10-2-1821
     v   **Eusebia⁷** b 1-19-1800 m John Pomeroy
            Alvord 3-20-1821 near Middlebury, VT. He
            was b 3-24-1793 and d 3-15-1825.
            Eusebia⁷ remarried to ___ Rockwell. She d
            in Chicago, IL. 7-6-1890 [Alvord p257]
     vi   **Oliver⁷** b 4-27-1802 d 5-10-1826
     vii   **Eunice⁷** b 12-11-1804 m Clark Kirby 1-1-
            1827
     viii   **Azubia⁷** b 2-8-1807 m William S. Rockwell
            2-15-1838
214 ix   **Samuel Smith⁷** b 5-22-1809 m Maria Munger
     x   **Ann Barnum⁷** b 7-29-1811
215 xi   **Darius⁷** b 2-15-1814 d 7-27-1905 [VTVR] m
            Emeline S. Rockwell

(82) Daniel⁶, (Ebenezer⁵, Ebenezer⁴, Ebenezer³,
John², John¹), born in Northfield, MA on 11-19-1768.
He shows on the 1810-1830 MA census. **Daniel⁶** died
1-24-1859 at the age of 92 years. [MAVR] He married

Polly Starkweather on 8-12-1807. [MAVR] They
settled in Gill, MA. He is shown with Emiline
L.____ in later life whom he married 6-15-1828. She
died 9-20-1873.

Children: [JFS p23-24] born in Gill MA
216   i   **Nelson**[7] b 2-3-1808 [MAVR] m Emeline
            Park, m2 Elizabeth Plaistridge
      ii   **Alvah**[7] b 4-26-1809 at Gill, MA d 6-29-
            1864 at Northfield, age 55-3-7. [MAVR]
            They reportedly had a son, **Roswell**[8], b
            in VT, who m to Clara Fowler, 9-30-1871,
            as his second wife. She was the daughter
            of John and Abigail Fowler. [MAVR]
      iii   **Marilla**[7] b 12-20-1810
      iv   **Mary Parthena**[7] b 4-15-1814 [Gill, MAVR]
      v   **Lovina**[7] b 3-10-1815. She m to Addison
            Merrill, son of Riley and Anna Merrill,
            on 9-23-1850 at Northfield, MA. [MAVR]
      vi   **Charlotte**[7] b 6-27-1816 d 2-2-1848 age
            29-10-17 at Gill, MA [MAVR]
      vii   **Lucretia**[7] b 6-15-1818 [MAVR]
217   viii **Curtis D.**[7] b 7-6-1819 m Patience L.
            Scott on 11-5-1851 [VTVR] and Nancy
            Birge on 6-7-1876 [VTVR]
      ix   **Martha**[7] b 11-15-1823

(83) Enos[6], (Ebenezer[5], Ebenezer[4], Ebenezer[3], John[2],
John[1]), apparently born in Northfield, MA on 11-24-
1776. He died in Middlebury, VT on 7-26-1842.
[VTVR] He married three times. First to Lydia
Petty, daughter of Reuben and Lydia Petty, on 1-1-
1801, from which his first two children were born.
Lydia was born 11-5-1763. It was recorded that she
married to **Enos**[6] on 4-15-1794. [Johnson] She died
2-22-1813. [VTVR] He married second to Cloe Emerson
and they had their third child. **Enos**[6] married for a
third time to Mrs. Abigail Field. She died 8-29-
1851 at Greenfield, MA. [MAVR]
   According to [JFS p24], **Enos**[6] settled on a farm
in Northfield which was afterward set off to the
town of Gill. He was a successful honey bee farmer.
He settled on the west end of home lots 14 & 15
next north of his fathers and lived there until his
death in 1842. This is contrary to [Swift p210]
Enos[6] shows with his wife on the 1800-1830 VT
census, living in Middlebury, next to his father.
In 1820, he was living in Rochester, VT. [VTFC]

Children of **Enos**[6] Severance and Lydia Petty [JFS]

    i   **Philena**[7] b 3-25-1802 m Stillman Morgan
          12-12-1829
    ii   **Roxana**[7] b 9-9-1807 m E.P. Landon 6-21-
          1877?

Children of **Enos**[6] and Cloe Emerson [JFS]
    iii   **Lydia**[7] b 12-28-1815 m _____Hutchinson

(84) Moses[6], (Ebenezer[5], Ebenezer[4], Ebenezer[3], John[2],
John[1]), born on 2-2-1778 in Middlebury, VT. The
1830 VT census shows him living in Middlebury. He
died in Andrews, OH on 8-13-1851. He married Kezia
Andrews, daughter of James Andrews and Ruth Mills.
They settled in Andrews, (Cherry Valley, Astabula
County, OH). **Moses**[6] returned later to VT to care
for his father, **Ebenezer**[5]. Kezia died in
Painesville, OH on 10- -1874 when she was 91 years
old. She was to have had fourteen children [LCoOH
p221] [OHVR-Painesville]

Children: [JFS p24-25] born in Andrews, OH
    i   **Harriet A.**[7] b 1-1-1800 d 5-23-1882 m
          Julius Christopher Johnson
    ii   **Ruth Ann**[7] b 5-13-1802 d 12-27-1875 m
          Jedediah Darrow
    iii   **Eliza**[7] b 5-24-1805 d 7-5-1877 m Rodney
          Price 10-7-1830
    iv   **Sophia**[7] b 3-7-1807 d 3-16-1807
218 v   **Augustus N.**[7] b 2-16-1808 m Fanny
          Wainwright?
219 vi   **Lyman M.**[7] b 4-10-1810
    vii   **William**[7] b 8-19-1812 d October 1815
220 viii **James A.**[7] b 12-14-1814, the 1850 OH
          census shows **James**[7] with his parents,
          Mary b 1827 in Vermont, and **Viola**[8] b
          1841 in KY
    ix   **Lucretia M.**[7] b 3-10-1817 m Stephen S.
          McIntyre
    x   **Lucina M.**[7] b 2-26-1819 m Eli P. King
    xi   **Charry M.**[7] b 10-29-1821 m Luman C. Hyde
    xii   **William**[7] b 10-10-1824 d 11-15-1824
    xiii **William**[7] b 3-16-1827 d 8-17-1829
    xiv   **Mary**[7] b 3-16-1827 d 5-8-1870 m Eli P.
          King

(85) Elisha/Elijah[6], (Abner[5], Ebenezer[4], Ebenezer[3],
John[2], John[1]), born 2-6-1786 in Gill, MA. His
marriage intentions to Charlotte Starkweather were
recorded 9-14-1805. [MAVR] The 1820 MA census for
Gill shows him living in Franklin Co. **Elijah**[6] d 2-

2-1855, widowed, age 71, at Gill, MA, son of
Abner⁵. [MAVR]

Children: born in Gill, MA. [MAVR]

     i   **Mary Emilla⁷** b 7-28-1806

     ii   **Lewis⁷** b 1-11-1808. [MAVR]

     iii   **Charles Curtis⁷** b 2-18-1810 [Gill, MAVR]

221 iv   **Ebenezer⁷** b 6-5-1813 [MAVR] m Sophia

           Ferris

     v   **Harriet Charlotte⁷** b 10-4-1817 d 4-25-

           1843 [Gill, MAVR]

222 vi   **James Edwin⁷** b 8-27-1822

(86) Oren⁶, (Abner⁵, Ebenezer⁴, Ebenezer³, John²,
John¹), born 3-1-1786 and died 12-20-1825 [MAVR] He
lived in Gill, MA. [1820 MAFC-Gill] He married Cloe
Munn, daughter of Noah Munn and Desire Hitchcock,
on 6-23-1809. [MAVR] **Oren⁶** died at a young age on
12-20-1825.
Cloe Munn was born 3-28-1787 and d 9-8-1877 at
Gill, MA. [Suddaby]

Children: [JFS p25]

     i   **Samuel⁷** b 8-10-1810 [MAVR] d in Boston,

           MA, no other record of him

     ii   **Mary⁷** b 6-8-1813 d 8-1-1894, age 80-2-

           21, at Gill, MA, unmarried. [MAVR]

223 iii   **Avery⁷** b 9-15-1814 (b 6-7-1812) m Mary

           Ann Rix

     iv   **Ruth⁷** b 11-5-1816 (b 4-14-1816) d 9-12-

           1870 at Gill, MA m Lorenzo P. Munn 10-

           31-1838. He m second to Sarah Cleffin.

           [Suddaby p419-420]

     v   **Horace⁷** b 2-14-1818 at Lyman, NH, died

           9-21-1894.

     vi   **Harry⁷** b 2-7-1820 (b 11-28-1819) he was

           last heard from while in the U.S. Navy.

           It is recorded that **Henry⁷** m to Mary

           Berry of Kittery, ME. The [MAVR] shows

           dates, 3-21-1850, 11-8-1851 and 7-29-

           1852

224 vii   **Chandler⁷** b 11-12-1822 (b 11-21-1821) m

           Mary Ann Eaton

     viii **Rhoda⁷** b 11-7-1824 d 1841

(87) Obed⁶, (Abner⁵, Ebenezer⁴, Ebenezer³, John²,
John¹), was born 6-22-1792 died 4-13-1869. He lived
in Gill, MA. [1830 MAFC-Gill] He married to Nancy
Hale, daughter of Lieut. Samuel Hall and Anna Scott
of Bernardston, MA, [Jacobus p177] on 3-19-1817.

[MAVR] Nancy was born 9-19-1796. [Allen I p36] She died 11-11-1884 at Gill, MA at the age of 88-1-23. [MAVR] **Obed**[6] died on April 13, 1869.

Children: [JFS p25-26]
  i **Elvira**[7] b 7-31-1818 d 7-9-1857 m Adolphus Hosley
225 ii **Harris**[7] b 6-17-1820 m Betsey Williams
226 iii **Leonard**[7] b 7-25-1822 m Eunice Jamerson 3-31-1859
227 iv **Alvin**[7] b 7-29-1824 m Harriet Chapin
  v **Evaline**[7] b 2-19-1827 d 8-31-1864 m John H. Clark, son of John and Phebe Clark, 1-4-1854 at Gill, MA.
  vi **Sarah**[7] b 7-29-1829. She married Luke M. Hosley, son of Theron and Orilla Hosley, on 4-3-1865 at Gill, MA. [MAVR]
  vii **Adaline**[7] b 7-3-1831 d 11-3-1868. She m to Robert Alexander. son of James Alexander, on 11-18-1856 at Gill, MA. [MAVR]
228 viii **Charles**[7] b 9-16-1834

(88) Robert M.[6], (Thomas[5], John[4], John[3], John[2], John[1]), born in Christ Church Parish, Lynches Creek, SC in 1795 and died in 1840. He married Harriet ____. Harriet could have been a stepdaughter of John Huggins by a second marriage. [MWS] The 1860 SC census for Darlington Co shows Harriet Saverance age 65 living with her son **Paul S.**[7] and Clarissa Huggins who was age 85.

Children: [MWS]
229 i **Paul S.**[7] d 1867 m **Hester**[7] Severance
  ii **Samuel G.**[7] b 1821

(89) Paul[6], (Thomas[5], John[4], John[3], John[2], John[1]), born in 1770 [IGI] at Christ Church Parish, SC and died 5-10-1844 in SC.
 He married to Hannah Huggins on 2-23-1797. [MgSC Vol 34 p31] Hannah was born 1776 and died 1843. [MWR] He married secondly to Margaret Dixon but they did not have any children by that marriage. [MWS]
 Paul[6] Severance died at his residence in Darlington District on 5-10-1844 in the 74 year of his age and for more that 14 years an exemplary member of the Methodist E. Church. Father Severance was born in Christ Church Parish, where he lived until after he married. He then moved to Darlington

District where he spent the remainder of his life.
He left behind a widow and eleven children. [SCCR]
    Hannah was the daughter of Capt. John and
Clarissa Huggins. In the Will of Capt Huggins of
Darlington District, SC, which was written 10-20-
1820 and read 8-2-1825, [PRSC p123] states Hanna
Saverance and son in law **Paul**[6] Saverance, and in a
deed John Huggins to **Paul**[6] Saverance (Shoemaker),
Darlington District, SC 6-4-1804, 360 acres land he
purchased from Benjamin Dubose 5-15-1804 and sold
to **Paul**[6] Saverance for $450.00. John Huggins lived
on a plantation granted to him in 1705, which
appears from his will to have been in Christ Church
Parish in Berkley Co., fronting Santee Bay. Little
is known of the life and deeds of this man except
that which can be inferred from his Will, his real
estate transactions, and certain activites taken
part in by him, which are public record, and which
shed conflicting light on his background prior to
1705. The first of these grows out of the fact that
on 11-20-1706, he, John Whilden and Robert Murrell
executed a bond to Governor Johnson for John
Whilden Sr. late of Seawee, deceased. [MgSC Vol 13
p 56] This is of particular interest because it
appears from an article by Mrs. William Wilden
McIver, in the [MgSC Vol 43 p34] entitled "Wappetaw
Congregational Church" that the Whilden family
record states that the Whilden brothers came from
New England in 1695/6 that wrecked near Cape Fear,
they with some fifty others were brought to Sea Wee
Bay by Governor Archdale. John Huggins is shown to
have lived and died on Sea Wee Bay. His plantation
is shown on the map of a Henry Mouson in 1775 as
being on Sea Wee Bay (this being after his death
and in the possession of his son) She then shows in
a well documented article that the Whildens,
Whites, Murrells and others with whom John Huggins
was closely related friendship or marriage were the
founders of that church of which she wrote.
    The American Congregation Association Bulletin,
Vol 28 written 1977 No. 2 p6 states that on 12-5-
1695, a covenanted group of Congregationalist from
New England sailed from Boston and after a stormy
but rapid voyage arrived at Charles Town on the
20th. Part of this group were John Cotton who
located at Charles Town. Many of the others settled
inland and started what was known as the Dorchester
church.

Children: [MPN]

	i	**Sarah Susana**[7] b 1-2-1802 m Samuel King Jeffords
231	ii	**Robert Murrell**[7] b 2-4-1808 m Elizabeth Huggins
	iii	**Mary Margaret**[7] b 4-14-1809 m Dewitt Fields
	iv	**Frances**[7] b 2-11-1811 m Isreal Parnell
	v	**Martha Jane**[7] b 1814 m John Nims
232	vi	**Samuel G.**[7] b 1817
	vii	**Hester Hannah**[7] b 2-24-1819 m **Paul S.**[7] Saverance
	viii	**Clarissa Adeline**[7] b 3-15-1821 m Rev. Joseph Hendrix
	ix	**Elizabeth**[7] b circa 1819 m Tobias Lee
	x	**Eliza**[7] m Simpson Parnell
	xi	**Thomas**[7]
	xii	**George**[7]

(90) Matthew[6], (Matthew[5], Joseph[4], Joseph[3], John[2], John[1]), born 7-11-1765 at Greenfield, MA. [MAVR] He married to Mary Wells, daughter os Elisha Well and Abigail Brooks of Le Suer, MN, on 11-25-1784 [MAVR] and they settled at Leyden, MA. Mary died 10-22-1845 at Leyden, Ma. [MAVR] He is listed on the 1790-1830 MA census. He died on 10-29-1834. [MAVR]

Matthew[6] purchased a one hundred acre farm on the town of Leyden about 1793. His first vist to Leyden showed nothing of a town. It was in an unsettled natural state. He was guided by marked trees and only a log cabin to stay in. [Arms]

Children: [JFS p27]

	i	**Mehitable**[7] b 8-7-1787 d 4-6-1805
	ii	**Mary**[7] b 3-24-1790 d 7-20-1812 m Samuel Eason
	iii	**Matthew**[7] b 11-2-1793 d 9-21-1805
233	iv	**Cyrus**[7] b 11-15-1796 m Lephe Wells m2 Sarah Moore
234	v	**Chester**[7] b 4-20-1799 m Martha Smith Nash
	vi	**Miranda**[7] b 1-29-1802 d 12-5-1805
	vii	**Emerancy**[7] b 3-21-1804 d 11-23-1871 m Jonathan Bliss 6-1-1824 at Leyden, MA, Jonathan b 5-3-1801 d 5-9-1861. [MJJO]
235	viii	**Matthew**[7] b 8-9-1807 m Maria T. Stebbins
	ix	**Ross**[7] b 5-12-1810 d 5-28-1810
236	x	**Cephas Clesson**[7] b 4-23-1812 m Harriet Miner m2 Nancy Legate

(91) Zenas[6], (Matthew[5], Joseph[4], Joseph[3], John[2], John[1]), born on 7-26-1767. [Greenfield MAVR] He married Eunice Wood on 1-1-1790.

Children: [JFS p27]
237   i   **Ebenezer**[7] b 1-1-1792 m Roxalene Johnson.
            They lived in CT before moving to VT
238   ii   **Leonard**[7] b 11-6-1791 (1796) m Doraxa
            Frost [VTVR]
     iii   **Abigail**[7] 12-7-1793 m ___Parker
      iv   **Experience**[7] b 7-13-1795 m ___Slade

(92) Consider[6], (Matthew[5], Joseph[4], Joseph[3], John[2],
John[1]), born 12-21-1771. [MAVR] He married
Elizabeth Craige 8-16-1801 and they removed to and
settled in Burlington, VT. Elizabeth died on 3-8-
1851. [VTVR] **Consider**[6] died on 4-13-1840. [VTVR]
The 1820-1830 VT census for Caledonia Co shows
Consider[6] living in Burlington.

Children: [JFS p27]
      i   **Elizabeth**[7] b 7-9-1805 d 4-21-1812
239   ii   **Charles Consider**[7] b 10-17-1807 m Elisa
            Badgley, Sellena Ingales, Hannah Douglas
240 iii   **George**[7] b 8-4-1810, Mary Elizabeth
            Douglas
      iv   **Elizabeth**[7] b 7-9-1805 d 4-21-1812 [VTVR]
       v   **Mary**[7] b 2-20-1817 m Rev. A.B. Rich. Mary
            d April 1882
      vi   **Laura Ann**[7] b 4-12-1819 d 5-29-1839 at
            Burlington, VT, age 20, [VTVR]

(93) Ruel[6], (Matthew[5], Joseph[4], Joseph[3], John[2],
John[1]), born 12-29-1773. [MAVR] He married Nancy
Wilbur on 9-19-1797. [VTVR] They lived in
Greenfield, MA. Nancy was born 8-16-1779.

Children: [JFS p27]
241   i   **Ruel**[7] b 5-8-1798 d 2-3-1876 m Electa
            Rice
      ii   **Joseph**[7] b 6-10-1800 d 9-9-1805

(94) Aseph[6], (Matthew[5], Joseph[4], Joseph[3], John[2],
John[1]), born in Leyden, MA on 8-29-1781. He died on
2-13-1863 at Williamstown, MA. He married Amittai
Eason on 10-18-1801 [MAVR] and they settled in
Bristol, VT. He manufactured boots and shoes and he
was a stone mason. Later he moved to a farm and
farmed as well as cutting timber. He was a soldier
in the Battle of Plattsburg. [JFS p28] He died in
Bristol, VT on 2-12-1862. [VTVR]

```
Children:  [JFS p28]
242   i      Curtis⁷ b 10-7-1806 m Marcia Tuttle
      ii     Mehitable⁷ b 10-7-1806 [VTVR]
      iii    Electa E.⁷ b 3-4-1809 m Ransom Drake
      iv     Amittai⁷ b 3-20-1811
243   v      George W.⁷ b 7-4-1813 [Bristol VTVR] m
             Marietta Thurston 5-4-1836
      vi     Sarah L.⁷ b 11-15-181
244   vii    Luther N.⁷ b 1-28-1819 m Araminta Ann
             Baldwin
      viii   Aseph⁷ b 2-23-1822 d 2-6-1864
```

(95) Jesse⁶, (Jesse⁵, Joseph⁴, Joseph³, John²,
John¹), bpt in Deerfield, MA on 5-31-1778. [MAVR]
He married to Anna Sophia Abbott on 8-23-1800
[MAVR] in Conway, MA. He moved with his family to
Conway where he settled and learned the trade of
blacksmith. The 1810 MA census for Deerfield
indicates that he lived there. I have used only
vital statistics dates for Jesse⁶ and his family.
The dates listed in the History of Ontario County,
New York differs from the Vital Records for this
family.

   Jesse⁶ moved his family to Phelps, NY in 1815.
[HOCoNY p195] He lived in Phelps, Ontario County.
[1810-1840 NYFC] His son Charles⁷ was born in
Conway in 2- -1820 but the family is later listed
as residents of Phelps. Jesse⁶ died in 1865 in
Phelps, NY. All of his children were born in
Conway, MA.

   Sophia, age 55, wife of Jesse⁶ died 1-16-1832 in
Phelps, NY [Bowman p213]

```
Children:
246   i      William Sidney⁷ b 4-9-1802 m Arzelia
             Joslyn of Phelps, NY
      ii     Aurelia⁷ b 3-16-1804 [MAVR]
      iii    Edwin Cuthbert⁷ b 10-8-1806 in Conway,
             MA and later moved to Phelps, New York
             with his family. His name shows on the
             [1840 Phelps, Ontario Co. NYFC].
247   iv     Albert⁷ b 11-5-1808 [MAVR]
248   v      Joshua Abbott⁷ b 4-29-1811 m Mary A.
             [1850 NYFC]
      vi     Lucy⁷ b 3-7-1815 d 12-22-1815
      vii    Charles Allen⁷ b 2-10-1820
      viii   Sophia⁷ (indicated on the Ontario County
             History)
      ix     Asa⁷ b circa 1822 in Phelps, NY
             (indicated on the Ontario County
```

History)

x   **Porter**[7] b circa 1831 (indicated on the Ontario County History) A **Porter N.**[7] Severnace m Delara Phillips 3-25-1851 at De Kalb, IL

(96) Elihu[6], (Jesse[5], Joseph[4], Joseph[3], John[2], John[1]), was born 4-6-1782 in Conway, MA. [MAVR] Little is known of this family at this time. **Elihu**[6] would most likely be the one showing on the 1820-1830 Cazenovia and Sullivan, Madison Co NY census. It appears that he died before 1840 since only his widow is listed on the 1840 Cazenovia NY census.

Children:
249 i   **Frank (Benjamin Franklin)**[7] b circa 1820 m Elizabeth Britton in OH, they settled in NB.

(97) David[6], (Jesse[5], Joseph[4], Joseph[3], John[2], John[1]), born 2-22-1784. [MAVR] He married to Dolly (Mary) Beals, intentions were given 12-26-1807 [MAVR]. They lived in Conway, MA, the 1810 MA census shows them living at Ashfield, until about 1810 when they moved to, Sullivan, Madison Co, NY where the operated the French-Severance Hotel. His name shows on the 1820-1840 NY census living at Sullivan. In 1860, the daughter **Mary**[7] was living with Dolly in Sullivan, NY. [NYFC]

Children:
     i   **Clarissa Champion**[7] b 9-15-1808 in Conway MA [MAVR]
     ii   **David Jr.**[7] b circa 1815. The 1840 NYFC shows him living in Sullivan, Madison County, with his wife and 2 daughters below the age of 5
250 iii **Charles C.P.**[7] b 2-8-1820 m Sarah M. Wylie. [Bowman p213]
     iv   **Mary**[7] b circa 1823 [1860 NYFC]

(98) Asa[6], (Martin[5], Martin[4], Joseph[3], John[2], John[1]), born in Shelburne Falls, MA on 10-9-1802. [MAVR] He lived his entire life on the family homestead. On 11-18-1823, he married Calista Boyden, daughter of Joshua and Laura Boyden. He held several town offices, Board of County Commissioners, represented the district in the State Legislature for two years, and served as a colonel of the militia for three years. He was Congregational by religion and was elected deacon on 3-5-1841. [JFS p29] **Asa**[6] died 5-9-1851 at Shelburne, MA. Calista died on 7-10-1862. [MAVR]

Children: [JFS p29]
  i   **Amelia**[7] b circa 1825 d 8-28-1843 at Shelburne, MA aged 18 y 9 mons 28 dys [MAVR]
251 ii   **Martin Joan**[7] b 12-24-1826
  iii   **Tirzah C.**[7] b 8-3-1829 m 12-16-1852 J.R. Patch [MAVR]
  iv   **Sara L.**[7] b 10-20-1831. She m on 11-11-1857 to Samuel N. Gragg, son of Jacob and Cynthia Gragg. [MAVR]
252 v   **Melvin A**[7]. b 6-4-1833. The 1860 VTFC shows **Melvin A.**[7] age 26 born in MA with his wife Mary A. age 28, born in Ireland.
  vi   **Ellen R.**[7] b 5-27-1835 at Shelburn, MA. She m to William Gragg, son of Jacob and Cynthia Gragg, on 5-7-1857. [MAVR]
  vii   **Edward E.**[7] b 10-7-1837 killed 6-24-1863 in a battle during the Civil War at Port Hudson, LA
  viii **Henry C.**[7] b 3-14-1840. He was killed 5-31-1862 in battle during the Civil War at Fair Oaks, VA
  ix   **Amelia S.**[7] b 8-25-1844 m David E. Fulson, of Belding, MI, son of Samuel and June F. Fulson, on 5-25-1876 at Shelburne, MA.
253 x   **Alvan A.**[7] b 3-4-1848 [MAVR]

(99) Samuel[6], (Samuel[5], Martin[4], Joseph[3], John[2], John[1]), born on 3-22-1793. He reportedly married twice although his first wife is not known. He married second to Mary A. Parks on 1-12-1850. They settled in Springfield, PA. [JFS p29] It is questionable if the listed children actually belonged to this **Samuel**[6] and Mary Parks since **Samuel**[6] would have been 57 years old and Mary would have been 47. The 1850 PA census shows **Samuel**[6] living with a Sylvester Leonard family in Springfield, Bradford Co, PA. Also included were Sylvester's wife, Lydia, **Clarrisa**[7] Severance b 1835, Oliver and **Mary**[6] (Severance) Gates,

Children: Perhaps these children were for **Samuel**[7], a son of **Samuel**[6]
  i   **Belle**[7] b 10-27-1851 m T.L. Kinyon 9-13-

1874
ii   **Mary**[7] b 12-11-1853
iii   **Clarence**[7] b 2-21-1858. Although [JFS
      p29] says that **Clarence**[7] never m, the
      1900 PA census shows **Clarence**[7] b 2- -
      1858 living in Fox, Sullivan Co. with
      his wife Eliza b in 1863 with children,
      Mattie[8], b 4- -1888 and **Robert**[8] b 7- -
      1894 in PA. The 1920 PA census shows an
      additional son, **Charles W.**[8] b 1901 in
      PA.
iv   **Clara**[7] b 2-21-1858

(100) Elisha[6], (Samuel[5], Martin[4], Joseph[3], John[2],
John[1]), born on 1-31-1795. **Elisha**[6] was still young
when his parents moved to PA and lived there until
1819. Next they moved to and settled in Milan, Erie
Co, OH. Then in 1830, they moved to Clyde, Sandusky
Co, and in 1839 went to Peru Township, Huron Co,
and purchased a farm. **Elisha**[6] was a farmer and
learned a trade of cooper in MA. In 1853 he lived
in Greenfield township, MA and then in 1863 moved
to New Haven, OH to live with his son, **Warren**[7]. He
married first to Martha Bangs on 4-23-1823. She was
born on 2-25-1802 died 4-12-1829. He married
secondly to Phebe B. (Tracy) Morgan, daughter of
Abel Tracy and Melane Martin, of VT, on 5-7-1831 in
Monroesville, OH. Phebe was first married to
William Morgan, who died in Orleans Co., NY in
1828. **Elisha**[6] and Phebe settled in Chicago, OH.
Phebe died on 1-7-1879.
    Elisha[6] was a Whig before the war and after
became a Democrat. He died 10-13-1892 at the age of
98 years in New Haven, Huron Co, OH. [H&LCoOH]

Children of **Elisha**[6] Severance and Martha Bangs
i   **Charles F.**[7] b 7-26-1824 d 12-11-1824
ii   **Lucian**[7] b 11-15-1825 d 8-23-1826
iii   **Clarissa**[7] b 2-24-1828 d 4-1-1828
iv   **Samuel M.**[7] b 2-8-1829 d 1883 m Mary
      Brown on 10-14-1848. [OHVR] They lived
      in Huron Co, OH. **Samuel M.**[7] was called
      Melvin[7]. No children. [MHS]

Children of **Elisha**[6] and Phebe B. Morgan
254 v   **William M.**[7] b 2-12-1831 d 1883 in
          Illinois, m Mary T. Latimer
     vi   **Byron**[7] b 11-8-1833 d 7-28-1835
255 vii **Warren**[7] b 10-9-1836 m Philinda Shephard
256 viii **Byron**[7] b 2-2-1839 d 10-7-1892 a

carpenter and joiner of Fairfield Township, he m to Charlotte Arthur.

(101) Fairfield[6], (Selah[5], Martin[4], Joseph[3], John[2], John[1]), born in Heath, MA on 5-26-1799. He reportedly went with his parents to Shelburn where they settled on a farm. At age eighteen he went to Montague and later engaged in business in Boston and Taunton, MA. He returned to Shelburn Falls in 1828 and became a stone mason. [1830 MAFC] He married to Cynthia Davy Douglass, daughter of John Douglas of Plymouth, MA, on 11-29-1826. He was a member of the Congregational Church. [JFS p30] Fairfield died on 1?-4-1883 at Shelburne. Cynthia died 7-30-1893 at Shelburne, age 83-11-12. [MAVR]

Children: [JFS p30]
- i   **Emily William**[7] b 12-23-1827
- ii   **Hannah Jane**[7] b 9-20-1829 d 3-10-1877 at Shelburne, MA, single, of pneumonia. [MAVR]
- iii   **Harriet Augusta**[7] b 10-9-1831 at Shelburne, MA. She m to Joshua Williams, son of Ezra Williams and Anna Robinson, on 10-21-1879. [MAVR]
- 257 iv   **John Franklin**[7] b 1-24-1835 m Angeline Ware
- v   **Ellen D.**[7] b 10-13-1841 m Josiah Upton
- vi   **Amelia J.**[7] b 9-11-1843

(102) Luther[6], (Selah[5], Martin[4], Joseph[3], John[2], John[1]), born in Heath, MA on 1-22-1807. [MAVR] He went with his parents to Shelburn. He later traveled as a salesman through NY and OH. He returned to Ashland to farm. He married to Polly S. Eddy on 3-31-1831. Their children were born in Ashland but in 1853 the family moved to Chicago and then thirty miles south to the town of Crete in Will Co. IL. **Luther**[6] belonged to the Congregational Church. [JFS p31] He died 4-16-1883.

Children: [JFS p31]
- i   **Zebina Henderson**[7] b 10-20-1833 d 4-18-1841
- ii   **Almira M.**[7] b 11-11-1835 d 2-4-1853 at Buckland, MA [MAVR]
- iii   **Francelia G.**[7] b 11-28-1838 m Austin Hewes 2-13-1854 m David Bordwell 10-11-1866
- 258 iv   **Herbert Francis**[7] (known as **Francis H.**[7]) b

7-9-1848 in Shelburne, MA m Cornelia D. Ferguson. [MAVR]

(103) Lorenzo[6], (Selah[5], Martin[4], Joseph[3], John[2], John[1]), born in Shelburn, MA on 3-25-1813. He settled on a farm, became a prosperous farmer and a respected citizen. [1840 MAFC Shelburne] He was a member of the Congregational Church. [JFS p31] On 3-27-1834, he married to Amanda C. Stewart, daughter of John Stewart and Charlotte Flagg. She was born in 1810 and died on 2-23-1898 at age 88 years, in Shelburne, MA. **Lorenzo[6]** died on 9-22-1887 at Buckland, MA, age 76 yrs. [MAVR]

Children:
i	**Calvin Cuyler[7]** b 10-10-1835 d 3-27-1836
ii	**Mary Elizabeth[7]** b 5-3-1837 m Reuben W. Field 10-22-1872. Mary d 3-8-1890
iii	**May S.[7]** b 1838 (daughter of **Loren[6]** and Amanda) m John Kimball, son of Samuel and Electa Kimball, 8-23-1866 at Shelburne, MA. [MAVR]
iv	**Martha Ann[7]** b 5-3-1839 at Bernardston, MA. She m Henry O. Draper, son of Lyman and Mary Ann Draper, on 11-8-1877
v	**Benjamin Franklin[7]** b 3-2-1841, unm
vi	**James Hervey[7]** b 9-4-1844 d 2-15-1846 [MAVR]
vii	male b 11-12-1854 at Shelburne, MA [MAVR]
viii	**Herman Lorenzo[7]** b 11-4-1854 d 2-3-1855 [MAVR]

(104) John F.[6], (Selah[5], Martin[4], Joseph[3], John[2], John[1]), born on 3-12-1817 in MA. He married Hannah Maria Lindsley on 11-23-1848. She was born in NJ. As **John[6]** told of his own attributes in The Severans Genealogy, "he spent five years at the blacksmith trade; worked three years at the same, then fitted for Amherst College, and graduated from the same; spent a few years teaching, then graduated from Seminary and entered the ministry of the Presbyterian denomination, at which he spent most of the time. **John[6]** was living in Niagara, NY in 1860. He spent his later life in Chicago, IL. [JFS p33]

Children:
i	**Irving Lindsley[7]** b 5-5-1861 d 5-18-1861

(105) Seth W.[6], (David[5], John[4], Joseph[3], John[2], John[1]), born 8-8-1787. He married twice, first to Abigail Wells on 7-2?-1812 [MAVR] and secondly to Fanny Wells on 9-23-1861. **Seth**[6] settled in New Haven, Oswego County, NY. The 1820-1840 NY census shows him living at New Haven. He died on 3-7-1856.

An account of his life was printed in the *Oswego County History* and re-copied in The Severans Genealogy, "**Seth**[6] Severance was one of the earliest inhabitants of New Haven, township, having assisted in its organization, nearly three-fourths of a century ago, he came to this region, then an almost unbroken forest. Like all pioneers, he struggled with the inconveniences and trials incident to the settlement of a country. But he lived to see cultivated fields drive the forests to the swamps and the rock-crested hills, to see the beautiful farm-house, with its modern conveniences, dot every hill and valley around him, as well as villages with their stores, mills, churches, schools and comfortable residences."

"He maintained a character for unsullied integrity in his inter-coarse with his fellow-men. He enjoyed the implicit confidence of his neighbors, and for many years occupied, by their suffrages, the responsible offices of the township. He represented them in the board of supervisors of this county twenty-two years, took a deep interest in the temporal welfare of the entire region. Himself a model farmer, he sought, by example and precept, to induce thrift, good taste, and the highest success in that department. In this respect his death was a public loss, reaching far beyond his own neighborhood."

Children of **Seth**[6] Severance and Abigail Wells [JFS p33-34]

259	i	**Warren Decatur**[7] b 11-17-1812 m Sarah Bullak
	ii	**Abbie S.**[7] b 5-13-1814 m Albert Green 4-16-1840. He was b 10-6-1819
260	iii	**Joseph A.**[7] b 7-17-1816 m Caroline E. Wales
261	iv	**Avery W.**[7] b 2-23-1819 m Julia N. Marvin

Children of **Seth**[6] and Fanny Wells

	v	**Noble D.**[7] b 3-18-1823 d 4-29-1845
	vi	**Antoinette**[7] b 8-13-1825 m German Reynolds
	vii	**Camilla S.**[7] b 4-4-1826 m B.S. Mc Donald

5-9-1850, **Camilla⁷** d March of 1863

(106) Horace⁶, (David⁵, John⁴, Joseph³, John²,
John¹), born on 6-23-1796. He married twice. First
to Melinda Howard [MAVR] on 1-1-1827 and secondly
to Lucy Root on 2-24-1832. [VTVR] She was born 6-7-
1808 in Strafford, VT and died 1-7-1861 at
Brattleboro, daughter of William Brisco Root and
Edith Allen of Stafford, Vermont. Lucy married
secondly to Philander T. Clark of Brattleboro, VT.
She died 1-7-1861. [Root p213] **Horace⁶** settled in
Vernon, VT, where he died on 8-5-1841. He was a
shoemaker. [MAVR] The 1830 MA census shows him
living at Bernardston.

Children:
i   **David⁷** b 11-3-1828 d 12-8-1839
263 ii   **William⁷** b 12-7-1832 m Mary Ann Welch of
        South Hadley Falls in 1854. They lived
        in Ludlow, MA. He was in the U.S.
        service 1861-1863.
iii   **Sarah Zama⁷** b 8-31-1834. She m Giles
        Chapin, son of Giles S. Chapin of
        Chicopee Village, MA on 6-10-1857.
        [MAVR] They lived in Granby, MA. She m
        secondly to Marshall Pease.
iv   **Lovina⁷** b 5-16-1836 d 8-16-1838
        Bernardston, MA.
v   **David Allen⁷** b 7-5-1840 [Bernardston,
        MAVR] enlisted in U.S. service in 1861,
        d in fall of 1864 in hospital.

(107) Daniel Arms⁶, (Daniel⁵, John⁴, Joseph³, John²,
John¹), born 10-29-1802. He married Emily Willard
11-24-1831. She was born 9-12-1809, the daughter of
Benjamin Willard and Lydia Bennett. They settled in
Winchester, NH. He was living in Winchester [1820-
1830 NHFC] and later removed to Devenport, Scott
County, IA. [Willard] **Daniel** died on 1-6-1828.

Children: [Willard]
i   **Zama Sophia⁷** b 11-22-1832 m Cornelius
        Loring Newberry 10-26-1873
264 ii   **Daniel Healey⁷** b 12-25-1841 d 9-16-1871
        m in 1863 Melissa Lewis.
iii   **John Jenks⁷** was born 6-15-1837. He m
        first to Martha Bentley daughter of
        Geroge Bentley of Davenport, IA, on 12-
        31-1863. She d 9-23-1885. He m 2nd to
        Sophie Bowlin on 10-28-1889. They had no

children.

(108) Jonathan⁶, (Jonathan⁵, Jonathan⁴, Joseph³, John², John¹), born on 10-23-1788 in Greenfield, MA. A native of Sheldon, MA. He went to Truxton, Cortland Co., NY with his parents in 1801. On 2-2-1818 he married Eunice Taggart of Colerain, MA. She was born 8-17-1793 and died 4-26-1880. They settled on a farm near Wiscory or Hume, Alleghany Co., NY in March of 1829. [HACoNY] The 1820 NY census shows him living at Truxton. The 1830 NY census shows him living at Hume.

This family was highly esteemed by everyone in their circle of friends. **Jonathan⁶** died on 2-19-1845. Eunice died on 4-26-1880. [JFS p34]

Children:
i		**Hugh McClellan⁷** b on 11-26-1818. He m to Angelina Graves. He was a great reader of history and was active in politics. He was a good mathemitician and became surveyor of the county. He was a school teacher and was soon elected as town superintendent of schools. He then became superintendent for the common schools of Allegheny Co. In 1856, he was made resident engineer of the canals of New York. He m to Angelina Graves on 9-12-1862. During the Civil War he volunteered his support for the soldiers both in the camps and hospitals. After the death of his wife in 1879 he returned to the old homestead and lived with his sister, **Elizabeth⁷** and Elmira near Wiscoy, Allegheny Co., NY, where he d on 9-13-1880. He apparently left no children. [HACoNY]
	ii	**Jane⁷** b 10-23-1820 d 8-17-1846
	iii	**Elizabeth⁷** b 4-16-1823
265	iv	**James Taggart⁷** b 9-4-1824 m Marian Botsford
	v	**Elmira M.⁷** b 11-1-1826
266	vi	**John⁷** b 2-15-1830 m Elizabeth Westcott
	vii	**Mary Ann⁷** b 9-4-1832 m Wayne Young 8-5-1856

(109) John⁶, (Jonathan⁵, Jonathan⁴, Joseph³, John², John¹), born in Greenfield, MA on 12-5-1791. He also went with his parents to Truxton, NY in 1800. He married Sabrina Smith, of Colrain, MA. The

marriage intentions were recorded 2-26-1815.
[MAVR]. The family settled on a farm in Truxton
where **John**[6] established himself as a progressive
farmer. He accumulated land so that he could settle
his sons on each side of his land. He was a
Presbyterian by faith. The 1820-1840 NY census
shows him living at Truxton. **John**[6] died on 1-15-
1869 in Truxton, NY.

(Mrs. Whitmarsh (Esther Gazley) married secondly
on 8-28-1858 to **John**[6] Severance of Truxton (Deacon)
who died there 6-15-1869. In 1872 she was residing
at Franklin Village in Fabius, Onondaga Co. NY. In
1860 **John**[6], Esther, and **Octava**[7] living in Truxton,
NY. [1860 NYFC]

Children: [JFS p35-36]
	i	**John**[7] b 1-27-1813 d young
	ii	**Mariah**[7] b 2-27-1816 m Joel Gates
267	iii	**David Smith**[7] b 10-13-1819 m Harriet Newell Jeffrey
	iv	**John**[7] b 12-1-1821 d 7-10-1823
268	v	**Calvin**[7] b 5-15-1825 m Rosamond M. Fay
	vi	**Clarissa**[7] b 11-1-1829 m Timothy Brown. Timothy was the son of Timothy and Deborah (Morse) Brown. He m **Clarissa**[7] Severance b Truxton, 11-1-1829 d Wathena 9-1-1866 daughter of **John**[6] and Sabrina (Smith) Severance of Truxton, NY. He was Commissary Sergeant in the 14th KS Vol. Regt. in the War of the Rebellion. [Brown p493] **Clarissa**[7] d 9-1-1866.
	vii	**Octavia**[7] b 6-19-1832 unm

(110) Joseph[6], (Joseph[5], Jonathan[4], Joseph[3], John[2],
John[1]), born on 2-1-1779 [MAVR] in Greenfield, MA.
He married to Elizabeth Hubbard on 11-15-1808.
[MAVR] He was living in Greenfield in 1820 and
Shelburne in 1830. [MAFC] Elizabeth died 9-12-1838
at the age of 54. [MAVR] **Joseph**[6] remarried to
Abbie Hall Newton, daughter of Ozias H. Newton and
Hannah Smead, on 10-2-1839. [MAVR] Abbie H. died 6-
10-1869 at Greenfield, MA. He was a hatter! **Joseph**[6]
died on 2-8-1871. [MAVR]

Elizabeth supposedly was born 1780 and died 9-
12-1834 ae 54 according to the Greenfield MAVR.
There may be another marriage in this story as the
[MAVR] also show **Joseph**[6] m Elizabeth Hubbard 10-20-
1804 in Greenfield. (Was there an Elizabeth Howard
and an Elizabeth Hubbard?)

Children: [JFS p36]
269 i   **Ephraim Hubbard**[7] b 9-27-1805 m Maria H. Street

    ii   **Adaline**[7] b 2-23-1808 m _____ Tufts.
             Adaline[7] d on 12-17-1875. [MAVR

(111) Rodney[6], (Joseph[5], Jonathan[4], Joseph[3], John[2], John[1]), born in Greenfield, MA on 11-7-1783. He married Nancy Thompson on 8-28-1825. [VTVR] **Rodney**[6] died on 1-25-1826. [MAVR] As the records show, **Rodney**[6] died shortly after the birth of their daughter, **Nancy**[7]. [JFS p36]

Child:
    i   **Nancy**[7] b 9-15-1825. She married to John Hooper, son of John and Jane Hooper, 4-30-1848 at Lawrence, MA. [MAVR]

(112) Horace[6]. (Joseph[5], Jonathan[4], Joseph[3], John[2], John[1]), born in Greenfield, MA on 9-24-1793. [MAVR] He married first to Mary Fisk on 8-31-1819. [MAVR] She was born on 6-9-1798 and died on 5-9- 1848. He later married to Mary Ann Mc Carthy on 4-9-1853 at Greenfield, MA. **Horace**[7] died on 9-11-1869 at Greenfield. The 1840 MA census shows him living in Heath, MA.

Children: First eight born at Greenfield, MA., others born at Heath, MA. [MAVR]
    i   **Sarah**[7] b 4-2-1820 d infancy
    ii   **Mary**[7] b 4-2-1820 d infancy
    iii   **Mary**[7] b 6-17-1821 d 10-1-1844
    iv   **Elizabeth**[7] b 4-5-1823 m John F. Palmatier, son of Francis Palmatier, 1-15-1854 at Greenfield, MA. [MAVR]
    v   **Seth Washburn**[7] b 1-19-1825 m Abby Field, 5-16-1849 in Greenfield, MA. **Seth**[7] d 1-16-1853 at Greenfield [MAVR]
    vi   **Catharine Mercy**[7] b 4-13-1827 [MAVR] d 6-11-1861. She m to Chester Marsh, 5-31-1848, at Greenfield, MA.
    vii   **Eorace Henry**[7] b 1-2-1829 d 7-19-1848 at Greenfield, MA. [MAVR]
270 viii   **Joseph Fisk**[7] b 4-29-1831 m Flora Gilligan
    ix   **Hepzibah Fisk**[7] b 7-9-1833. She m to Samuel W. Lee, son of Samuel W. Lee, on 5-19-1856 at Northbridge, MA. [MAVR]
    x   **Adaline Melissa**[7] b 6-22-1836
    xi   **Angeline Theresa**[7] b 6-22-1836 d 6-1-1856

xii   **Lucy Ward**[7] b 3-24-1839 m Ephraim Clark, son of Michael D. Clark and Dorcas Fowler, 8-25-1875 at Northampton, MA. He was a stockraiser from NV. [MAVR]

(113) Pliny[6], (Joseph[5], Jonathan[4], Joseph[3], John[2], John[1]), born in Greenfield, MA on 7-24-1796. [MAVR] He married Sophia Wrisley on 1-1-1822. Sophia was born 9-25-1799 d 5-28-1871. **Pliny**[6] was a hatter by trade and followed that business until he was about thirty years old. At that time he began farming. In 1858, he moved his family to Grundy, IA and continued farming.

Children: [MAVR-Greenfield][JFS p37]
    i   **Henry**[7] b 1-25-1823 in Greenfield, MA. He m Lizzie M. Shattuck 1-5-1854. He mysteriously disappeared after 1856 and was never heard from again.
271 ii   **Edwin**[7] b 7-16-1825 m Caroline Agatha St. John
272 iii **George**[7] b 11-30-1827 m Eliza Elizabeth Bacchus
    iv **Sabra Sophia**[7] b 2-28-1830
    v   **Ellen Maria**[7] b 7-4-1835 d 1-25-1873
273 vi **Charles**[7] b 9-30-1838 m Elizabeth E. Robson
274 vii **Frederic Hollister**[7] b 9-24-1841, served three years in the First IA Calvary in the Civil War.

(114) Robert Bruce[6], (Solomon[5], Jonathan[4], Joseph[3], John[2], John[1]), born in Greenfield, MA on 10-1-1786. [MAVR] His parents moved to Shelburn, MA in 1790 to what was called the Hanson Farm. **Robert**[6] made the best of the rather poor public schools. He studied with Dr. John Long of Shelburn for the profession of medicine. He went to Brunswick, ME and graduated from Bowdoin College from the Medical Department. He returned to Shelburn, MA, opened a general store and practiced Medicine. He allowed others to manage the store and watch after his sons while he devoted full time to his medical practice. [JFS p37-38] His name shows on the 1840 MA census as living in Boston.

    He married Diana Long on 11-27-1810. This was Thanksgiving Day in 1810. Diana was born 10-12-1788. She died on July 22, 1830. [MAVR] **Robert Bruce**[6] was an active member of the Masonic fraternity and a philanthropist of public affairs but declined any public office. [JFS] He died on 2-10-1830. [MAVR]

Children: [JFS p38]
275 i   **Solomon Lewis**[7] b 4-9-1812 m Mary Long
          11-12-1833
276 ii   **Theodoric Cordenio**[7] b 3-1-1814 m
          Caroline M. Seymour
     iii **Erasmus Darwin**[7] b 3-14-1817 d 4-11-1840
     iv   **John Long**[7] b 4-4-1822 d 8-30-1859

(115) Otis[6], (Solomon[5], Jonathan[4], Joseph[3], John[2], John[1]), born in Greenfield, MA on 10-12-1788. [MAVR] He married first to Abigail Stratton on 2-8-1814. [MAVR] The vital records say that they were born in Hinsdale, NH. She died on 5-13-1842. He later married to Mary E. Smith in 1864. **Otis**[6] settled with his family in Clifford, PA where he died on 12-31-1874. [JFS p38]

Children: [JFS p38]
277 i   **Otis Cathestus**[7] b 11-13-1815 m Emeline
          Stevens
     ii   **Laura Mitilda**[7] b 2-22-1818 d 9-22-1866 m
          Ecrasny Mapes 1-15-1829
278 iii **Erasmus Cordenio**[7] b 10-12-1829 m Amanda
          Julia Arnold
     iv   **Carrie Ophelia**[7] b 10-23-1834

(116) Ralph Abercrombie[6], (Elihu[5], Jonathan[4], Joseph[3], John[2], John[1]), born in Greenfield, MA on 1-15-1803. [MAVR] After starting out early in life in the office of Dr. Amariah Brigham and Dr. Amasa Barrett of Greenfield, he went to Bowdoin College in ME and graduated from the Medical Department in 1831. He moved to Putney, VT where he stayed with his practice until February of 1833. He then spent a year at Saxton's River, VT. [JFS p38-39]
    In June of 1834, **Ralph**[6] moved to Bellevue, OH, where he spent the remainder of his life. In politics he was always the friend of the oppressed. An anti-slavery man by instinct, his house for many years was a station on the "Underground Railroad." [H&LCoOH] He married to Mary W. Smith on 9-5-1838. [VTVR] She was born 6-2-1817, died on 3-21, 1844. [VTVR] **Ralph**[6] remarried to Joanna Bailey on 6-11-1845. Joanna was born 9-4-1820. In 1880 they were living in York, Sandusky Co with their daughters and three of their Clark grand children. [OHFC] **Ralph**[6] died on April 23, 1893. [OHVR]

101

Children: [JFS p39]
279 i   **James Ralph**[7] b 4-5-1846 m Rosa S. Gridly
          in Oberlin, Ohio
     ii   **Mary Joanna**[7] b 3-19-1849 m Henry F.
          Clark 9-10-1872
     iii **Flora Irene**[7] b 5-18-1857 m Sumner C.
          Thompson 1-11-1882

(117) Ptolemy Philadelphus[6], (Elihu[5], Jonathan[4],
Joseph[3], John[2], John[1]), born in Greenfield, MA on 7-
23-1805. [MAVR] He married Margaret Caldwell on 12-
29-1833. [MAVR] She died on 5-8-1851 and he
remarried to Harriet Converse, daughter of James
and Charlotte, on 11-6- 1855. [MAVR] Harriet was
born in Weathersfield, VT on 8-30-1828.
    John F.[6] Severance illustrates this man in [JFS
p39-40] "He never engaged in any undertaking
without counting the cost, and it is not known that
he ever failed in the consummation of any of his
prominent plans. He lived for many years in the
'Old Homestead' on Main Street and carried on a
farm. He was one of those philantropic men who was
never satisfied with present attainments, he always
saw a point ahead to be reached, a public demand,
of this fact many of the highways of the county are
a verification. The Rocky Mountain road from
Greenfield to Turner's Falls one of his last
efforts for the public welfare is a standing
monument of his integrity and philantropy. In 1844
he was appointed superindendent of the locks and
canal at Montague, which position he occupied for
ten years. He was prominently identified in the
contract of the Glen Water Works which now supplies
the village with water. Held the office of
selectman and assessor for several years. He was
one of the oldest members of the Masonic Order in
the town, being a member of the Republican Lodge,
also a member of the Royal Arch Chapter at the time
of his death." [JFS p39]
    He was a member of the Congregational Church in
Greenfield. He died on 5-4-1883. [MEVR]

    Children of **Ptolemy Philadelphus**[6] Severance and
Margaret Caldwell [Sheldon p290]
     i   **Edward Hitchcock**[7] b 4-10-1835 m Ellen
          Barnes 5-3-1844, He lived in Toledo, OH.
          He left no family
280 ii   **Franklin C.**[7] b 12-24-1837 m Sallie J.
          Thurman
     iii **Elizabeth M.**[7] b 5-13-1844. She m William

Ambrose Ames, son of James M. and Eunice Ames, on 10-7-1876 [MAVR]

Children of **Ptolemy Philadelphus⁶** Severance and Harriet Converse [Sheldon p290]
    iv   **Charlotte Converse⁷** b 7-31-1860 in Greenfield, MA, m Herbert Collins Parsons 9-30-1891. [MAVR]

(118) Guy Carlton⁶, (Rufus⁵, Jonathan⁴, Joseph³, John², John¹), born 11-12-1802, [JFS], bpt 9-24-1811 [MAVR] The 1840 Bernardston MA census shows him. The 1850 MA census shows **Guy⁶**, born 1803 with his wife Rachel and their daughter's living in Springfield, Hampden County, MA. Guy was a carpenter. He died 3-1-1854 at Greenfield, MA. [MAVR]

Children: [1850 MAFC][Greenfield MAVR]
    i   **Lucy Maria⁷** b 1837 bpt 7-22-1849
    ii   **Mary Louisa⁷** b 1839 bpt 8-5-1849
    iii   **Angeline Melissa⁷** b 1841 bpt 7-22-1849
    iv   **Alexandria⁷** b 1842
    v   **Caroline⁷** b 1848 (daughter of **Guy C.⁶** and Rachell Severance, was adopted by a Haskell family). **Carrie W.⁷** Haskell m Charles H. French, son of Richard and Priscilla French, 1-29-1868 at Orange, MA. [MAVR]
    vi   **Julia Almeda⁷** bpt 8-5-1849

(119) Solomon⁶, (Rufus⁵, Jonathan⁴, Joseph³, John², John¹), was born 1-4-1805. He was bpt 9-24-1811. [MAVR] He married to Mary Guillon on 4-27-1832 [VTVR]. She was born 1805. [1850 MAFC]. He shows living in Greenfield, Franklin Co., MA. [MAFC]

Children:
    i   **Charles⁷** b circa 1835. He died on 5-2-1863 at Springfield, MA. He was a machinist and single. [MAVR]
    ii   **Mary⁷** b 1842
    iii   **Henry C.⁷** b 1845 in Greenfield, MA. **Henry⁷** m Nellie M. Landon, daughter of Henry and Harriet Landon, on 5-21-1866. Nellie M. d 3-2-1868 age 23-3-4. [MAVR] He d 8-17-1882, age 37-9-13, at Springfield, m, and a fireman from Greenfield. [MAVR] They had at least one daughter. **Addie⁸** b 1-24-1867 at

Spirngfield, MA d 1-25-1867, age 1 day,
at Springfield, MA [MAVR]

(120) Franklin C.[6], (Rufus[5], Jonathan[4], Joseph[3],
John[2], John[1]), born about 1813. He married to
Hannah-Lovina Winslow on 5-30-1837. [VTVR] She was
born 2-27-1815 and died 1848. [VTVR] [Winslow p799]
says Hannah was born in Coleraine, MA, the daughter
of George Winslow. **Franklin C.[6]** was a first or
second cousin of Harriet Severance, the third wife
of Dr. George Winslow. The VTVR shows the marriage
of **Franklin C.[6]** and Hannah L. Winslow at Charlemont
or Claremont, VT. The Official Army Register,
Volunteer Force of the U.S. Army 1861-1865, p226
shows **Franklin C.[6]** as 2nd Lieut. discharged 10-2-
1862 from the 52nd Regt. He settled at Hinckley, De
Kalb County, IL.

Children:
- i   **Henry Franklin[7]** b 3-11-1838 [MAVR] m
  Rhoda Ranney on 8-15-1858 [VTVR] **Henry
  Franklin[7]** probably went to De Kalb Co.
  IL with his parents. The [MAVR] shows
  the death of Charles E. F. Severance,
  age 6 months, on 12-6-1899 at Everett,
  MA. The parents were listed as Charles
  F.G., born in Wellesley and Fannie I.
  Ranney, born in Chicago. At this time I
  have nothing else but conjecture. It is
  possible that this **Henry Franklin[7]** was
  the father of **Wallace L.[8]** a publisher in
  Chicago. **Wallace's[8]** father married to
  Cedlia L. Henry in WI. **Wallace[8]** married
  Grace Ball of WI and they settled in WI.
- 281 ii   **George[7]** was married [Winslow p799]
- iii   **Mary[7]** graduated at Clark Seminary,
  Aurora, IL, where she had been a
  teacher, was unmarried in 1877 and
  engaged in teaching at Hinckley, IL.
- iv   **Ellen[7]** also graduated at Clark Seminary,
  and has been a teacher in that
  institution, was unmarried in 1877.
  [Winslow p799]]

(121) George W.[6], (Rufus[5], Jonathan[4], Joseph[3], John[2],
John[1]), born 4-10-1814 at Greenfield, MA. **George W.[6]**
was a farmer and tailor, a son of **Rufus[5]** Severance.
In 1840, he removed from Westfield, MA to Big Rock,
Kane Co., IL where they purchased a farm. He
married to Charlotte Nancy Newcomb on 10-17-1837 at

Greenfield, MA. She was born February of 1815 and died 1-18-1892 at Hinckley, IL. He died 3-14-1900 at Hinckley, IL. [Newcomb p272]

Children: [Newcomb p272]
   i   **Sarah C.** b 9-25-1839 d 5-28-1840 at Chicago
282 ii   **Charles W.**[7] b 3-28-1842 m Emma Nicholson 1-2-1870 (had 6 sons) resided at Clifton, IL and Sutherland, IA.
   iii   **Addie M.**[7] b 4-6-1845 resided Aurora, IL, m 5-2-1878 at Big Rock, IL, Joshua Rhodes who d 12-19-1910
   iv   **Maria H.**[7] b 12-9-1848 m1 Philo Slater 3-31-1885 m2 William Van Ohlen 8-30-1900 at Hinckley, IL

(122) Charles[6], (Moses[5], Moses[4], Joseph[3], John[2], John[1]), born in Montague, MA on 1-7-1807. [MAVR] The 1840 Montague, MA census shows him. He married to Melvina Hamilton on 6-20-1833. [Palmer, Hampden Co. MAVR] He shows on the 1860 NY census living in Pompey, Onondaga Co. NY with his wife, daughter **Mary**[7] and their last three children. **Charles**[6] died in Pompey, NY on 3-25-1895.

Children: [JFS p40]
   i   **Mary**[7] b 5-9-1834 b in MA
   ii   **Frank M.**[7] b 4-30-1835 in Pompey, NY. (He was actually b in MA) He m Zaide L. Cameron on 6-6-1878. They lived in Manilus, Onondaga Co, NY. [1900 NYFC] and Hamilton, NY. She was b on 7-18-1840. Zaide L. d sometime after 1920. She was shown living alone in Fayettesville, Onondaga Co, NY. [1920 NYFC]
   iii   **Henrietta**[7] b 5-1-1837 m James A. Tappan 3-3-1860
284 iv   **James H.**[7] b 6-20-1844 b in MA m Mary E. Barber
   v   **Helen**[7] b 11-21-1847 m H.D. Benjamin 11-4-1868
   vi   **Elva**[7] b 1-25-1850 m Wilfred M. Scoville 4-25-1870

(123) Luther[6], (Elihu[5], Moses[4], Joseph[3], John[2], John[1]), born in Montague, MA on 10-29-1797. Two years later the family moved to Cazenovia, NY and **Luther**[6] spent his early life on his father's farm.

Luther[6] led quite an interesting life. At seventeen he went to Peterborough to learn the printing trade under Jonathan Bunce. He stayed there for five years and then being of age he went to Philadelphia and found employment with William Duane who published the *"Aurora"*. It was here that Luther printed an article on the subject of the Missouri compromise which brought him credit from the President Monroe administration. He then worked in the office of the National Intelligencer where he continued to write political articles.

Luther[6] moved to Augusta, ME in 1824 and established the *Kennebec Journal*. He married Anna Hamlin on 10-12-1827. Ann was the daughter of Theophalius Hamlen of Augusta, ME. **Luther**[6] continued the Journal until 1854.

Rev. **John F.**[6] Severance includes this glowing description to **Luther**[6], "Mr. Severance was for five years the popular representative and senator of his state, and in 1835-1836 in the State Senate, in 1843-1847 a member of the National Congress. Here he distinguished himself by his able speeches favoring a protective tariff. He was one of the fourteen members who voted with John Quincy Adams against the bill for an appropriation to carry on the Mexican War, and which was urged through Congress without discussion."

"In 1847 he was again elected to the State Legislature, in 1848 a delegate and a vice-president of the National Convention which nominated General Taylor for the presidency."

"Upon the election of General Taylor, Mr. Severance was suffering much from ill health and he was appointed minister to the Hawaiian Islands in the hope that the salubrity of that climate might restore him. Accompanied by his family he sailed from Boston, Massachusetts in August of 1850 and arrived there in January of 1851."

"For three years he was the diplomatic representative of the United States and acquired great influence with King Kamehameha and his cabinet, besides winning the highest regard and esteem of the foreign consuls, the people of the Islands and his own countrymen. But the climate did not restore his failing health, and he returned to his home at Augusta, ME, 4-12-1854." [JFS p40-41] **Luther**[6] died on 1-5-1855. His name appears on the 1830-1840 ME census for Augusta, ME.

Children:

106

285 i   **Henry Weld**[7] b 7-12-1828 He served an
          apprenticeship to the druggist business
          with Eben Fuller in Augusta, removed to
          the Sandwich Island, and finally to San
          Francisco, CA. He m Hannah Swan Child,
          daughter of James L. Child of Augusta,
          ME, on 3-17-1857.

     ii   **Anna**[7] b 4-12-1832 m William G. Paile of
          Honolulu, Oahu, Sandwich Islands,
          January of 1856

286 iii **Luther**[7] b 6-1-1836 he removed to the
          Sandwich Island and purchased a
          plantation near Honolulu. He m Lucinda
          M. Clarke of Honolulu and they had one
          child, **(Helen**[8]**)** b 3-9-1867.

LUTHER[6] **SEVERANCE**

(124) Moses H.[6], (Elihu[5], Moses[4], Joseph[3], John[2], John[1]), born in Montague, MA, 9-1-1799, grew up in Cazenovia, NY, and later settled in Geneva, NY. He married Abigail Staples on 4-20- 1826.

He was an inspector of schools for many years and promoted the cause of education. He published school books, using his own press which was run by water power. This was an invention of his own. [JFS p42] **Moses**[6] died on 4-12-1835 (his last son was born in 1835) He apparently resettled in Waterloo, Iowa as the obituary shows him, "late of Waterloo, of the firm of R. Robbins and Co., Booksellers of Geneva, IA." In 1830 he was living at Waterloo, Seneca County. [NYFC]

Children: [JFS p42]
   i   **Mary**[7] b 3-28-1827 m Charles Jackson 10-9-1849
   ii   **Helen Miranda**[7] b 1-28-1829
   iii   **Elizabeth Grace**[7] b 10-20-1833
   iv   **Charles**[7] b 9-15-1835 d in early childhood

(125) Apollos[6], (Elihu[5], Moses[4], Joseph[3], John[2], John[1]), born in Cazenovia, NY on 5-20-1802. He settled on a farm in Cazenovia and married Rhoda E. Johnson on 2-4-1834. [JFS p42]

Rhoda Eveline Johnson, daughter of David Johnson and Rhoda Slade was born 12-9-1811 in Cazenovia, Madison Co., NY. The 1840 NY census shows **Apollos**[6] at Cazenovia. He died 12-29-1891 San Josa, Santa Clara, CA.

In 1860 he was living alone in Cazenovia. Eveline was living next door with her two daughters, **Sarah M.**[7] and **Frances**[7] next door. [NYFC]

Apollos[6] was a carpenter and joiner by trade with "somewhat eccentric characteristics". [JFS p42] He died on 1-16-1883.

Children: [JFS p42]
   i   **Sarah M.**[7] b 9-22-1835
   ii   **Francis A.**[7] b 7-20-1842 m J. Brainerd Johnson 7-17-1873
   iii   infant daughter b 4-7-1848 d 4-10-1848

(126) Henry[6], (Elihu[5], Moses[4], Joseph[3], John[2], John[1]), born in Cazenovia, NY on 1-30-1808. He married Helen J. Wooley on 5-23-1833 and they settled in Dunkirk, NY where **Henry**[6] died on January of 1892. [JFS p42-43]

Henry[6] moved to Dunkirk in 1851, and from that time to his death it was his home. He was not a well educated man in the formal sense but his knowledge of the workings of the government was below known. In his early life, Mr. Severance was a carpenter, but other business occupied his thoughts and attention for many years. He was thoroughly familiar with the doctrines and teachings of all political parties during the last three quarters of a century.

He was a clear and concise writer, and many of his productions were well known to readers over the well-known signature of *Dunkirk Farmer*. [NSDJ 3-8-1834] He was the author of *John Bull in America* and *Chautaugua*. [Edson p205]

Children:

i	**Helen[7]**	b 10-28-1834 d 7-11-1839
ii	**Harriet[7]**	b 5-29-1836 m E.M. Lucas 11-10-1864 [Edson p205]
iii	**Emma H.[7]**	b 9-20-1842 [Edson p205]
iv	**Flora Annette[7]**	b 3-17-1847 d 2-29-1864

(127) Charles[6], (Elihu[5], Moses[4], Joseph[3], John[2], John[1]), born in Cazenovia, NY on 8-29-1813. He spent his life there. He married Maria Farnham on 1-1-1837. **Charles[6]** died on 11-18-1837. Their only child, **Charles Jr[7]**, was born 2-15-1838, three months after his fathers death.

Charles[7], the son, enlisted in Co., A. 100 Regiment, New York, Vols, Infantry. He served in the Army of the Potomac in the Chickahominy Swamps; held the rank of 1st Lieutenant; died on the 11th day of May, 1862, at Nelson Hospital, Yorktown, VA. He was a graduate of Union College, NY; a good scholar, ambitious, and full of hope. [JFS p43]

(129) Joseph[6], (James[5], James[4], unconnected, Joseph[2], John[1]), b circa 1785. After probably living in NH, MA, and VT, he settled in NY. The town records for Colchester, VT (1797-1824) seem to indicate that Joseph lived there from around 1809 to 1815. He is listed as a voter, later asked to leave town, probably had children and took the freeman's oath in 1815. **Joseph[6]** was in living in Canton, St Lawrence Co, with a wife, a daughter and 2 sons under the age of 10 in 1820. Therefore the children were born circa 1810 and **Joseph[6]** was born about 1785. He was engaged in farming. [NYFC]

In 1850 **Joseph[6]** was with a family of children

born near this time period and later. A 10 year old
Sarah Crawford was living with them. [NYFC St.
Lawrence Co]

Children of **Joseph**[7] Severns and __, born in NY
State

	i	**George**[8] b 1819
	ii	**Lucy J.**[8] b 1829
291	iii	**Calvin L.**[8] b 1832 in NY m Martha M. who was b 1831 in NY

(130) Phillip[6], (James[5], James[4], unconnected,
Joseph[2], John[1]), b circa 1785. **Phillip**[6] was living
in Essex Co. with 4 sons and 4 daughters in 1800.
[1800 NYFC] It is likely that the birth date for
Phillip's[6] is wrong or the census records are for
another **Phillip** since it would be hard for him to
have 8 children by 1800 if he was born in 1785.
[NYFC] **Phillip**[6] was indicated on the 1830 Canton,
St. Lawrence Co. NY census with 2 boys and two
girls.
    St Lawrence Co. NY is the area where **Zacheus**[7]
was living. In 1830, **Benjamin** was with his brother
Galen and living in Greenbush, NY. **Moses** and
Phillip show in Edwards and Canton, St. Lawrence
Co. [NYFC]
    This could be the family that **Zacheus**[7] and
Luther[7] were born into although it is conjecture.

292	i	**Zacheus**[7], (unconnected)
293	ii	**Luther R.**[7], (unconnected)

(131) Phillip[6], (Phillip[5], unconnected, Joseph[2],
John[1]), b circa 1785, settled in Hollis, York Co,
ME, married to Susan Pendexter, daughter of Eliab
Pendexter and Mary Thomas. They were of Biddeford,
ME and settled in Cornish by 1826. Eliab
Pendexter's father, Henry, was from Portsmouth or
Newington, NH. Susan was born circa 1786. [Ridlon
II]

Children:

297	i	**Eliab**[7] b circa 1815 at Parsonfield, York Co. ME. He m to Sarah Wentworth. He died 4-1-1900, ae 85-11-8 [MEVR]
	ii	**Jacob**[7] b circa 1816 at Parsonfield. **Jacob**[7] and **Eliab**[7] could be the same person.
299	iii	**James**[7] b circa 1818 at Hollis. He m to Nancy Hodgdon on 10-12-1842.

300   iv   **William Darling**[7] b circa 1821 at Hollis, ME. He m to Arvilda Davis on 5-21-1853.

(132) Joseph[6], (Phillip[5], unconnected, Joseph[2], John[1]), b circa 1795/1800 in NH, settled in ME. He married to Mary Foss. Mary was born circa 1794. She died on 2-17-1883. He died on 11-25-1876 at East Parsonfield at the age of 76 years and 5 months. In 1860 **Joseph**[6] was living in Cornish, York Co. with his family. [MEFC]

Children: [1850 MEFC]
301   i   **David W.**[7] b 1- -1829 m Lydia Stanley.
302   ii   **Eben F.**[7] b 1832 m to Melissa Sarah Burnham on 11-7-1863. He d in 1886.
      iii   **Abigail**[7] b 1836
303   iv   **Joseph O.**[7] b 5-25-1824 at Cornish, ME. He m to Elizabeth J. Wesson.

(133) Ebenezer[6], (Ebenezer[5], unconnected, Joseph[2], John[1]), b circa 1777-1785, settled in NH, MA, or NY. Although it is conjecture, there are not many choices for the placement this **Ebenezer**[6]. He could be the one born 11-8-1777 at Temple, NH. He was probabaly from Alstead, NH at one time. Little is known of this family except from an eviction notice which was sent to the constable of Rockingham, Windham County, VT and stated, "You are hereby commanded to summon **Ebenezer**[6] Severance, Poley, **Polly**[7], **Eben Jr.**[7], **David**[7], **Ora**[7], **Alvira**[7], and **Rachel**[7], now residing in Rockingham to depart said town 4-26-1806. [PRNH]

Children: of **Ebenezer**[6] Severance and Polly
      i   **Polly**[7] m Jonathan Coolidge b 1-10-1791, justice of the peace, of Hinsdale, NH m first to **Polly** Severance. She d 4-5-1814 and he m secondly to **Betsey** Severance on 11-15-1815. [Coolidge]
      ii   **Ebenezer Jr.**[7] b circa 1792.
304   iii   **David**[7] b 4-12-1794/1795 m Esther Knapp circa 1815 and settled in OH.
      iv   **Ora**[7] circa 1798. **Ora**[7] m Charles Lyon on 8-9-1821. [VTVR]
      v   **Alvira**[7]
      vi   **Rachel**[7]

(134) William[6], (Joseph[5], William[4], unconnected, Joseph[2], John[1]), b 11-12-1797 [MAVR]. He married to Hannah Nye, who died 9-1-1852 [MAVR] and **William**[6] remarried to Almira. The 1820 MA census shows him with 5 sons. He died before 1841. They apparently lived in New Bedford and Dartmouth, MA, where their known children are recorded.

Children:
306 i   **James A**[7], b 6-3-1819, d 1-27-1878, son of William and Almira.
     ii   **William**[7]
    iii   **Jane A.**[7], who married to J.B. Gifford 8-15-1852. [MAVR] [NS New Bedford Mercury]

(136) Isaac[6], (Joseph[5], Benjamin[4], Ephraim[3], Ephraim[2], John[1]), born on 10-4-1773 probably in Salisbury, NH where his father had moved around 1770. He married Abigail Dean before 1796 and lived in Derby and Rockingham, VT for fifty years. He shows on the 1800 NH census for Cheshire Co. The 1810-1820 VT census for Derby, Orleans Co shows **Isaac**[6]. Isaac[6] married secondly to Sally (Weaver) Pulsipher. Sally Weaver, daughter of Daniel Weaver and Joanna Preston, born 3-13-1787 died 6-17-1863 who married first to Samuel W. Pulsipher. Samuel died 7-14-1817. [Weaver]

    Isaac[6] and Sally have **Eunice M.**[7] Severance, age 16, living with them. [1860 VTFC]

Children: all children of **Isaac**[6] and Abigail Dean
308 i   **James**[7] b 10-29-1796 m Sarah Goddard
    iii   **Annie**[7] never married
    iv   **Lydia**[7] never married
     v   **Betsey**[7] b 7-13-1802 m William Moon
    vi   **Hannah**[7] b 4-10-1804 m James Dane 7-4-1822
   vii   **Benjamin**[7] never married
309 viii **Elias J.**[7]
310 ix   **Franklin**[7] b 10- -1811 m Elizabeth (Wood) Pulsipher

(137) David[6] *Sevrens*, (Joseph[5], Benjamin[4], Ephraim[3], Ephraim[2], John[1]), born on 1-30-1775 in Salisbury, NH. He married to Mehitable Meloon on 5-17-1803. She died 10-19-1819. He remarried to Dolly Palmer 2-17-1821. They settled in Danbury, NH. They spelled their last name as *Sevrens*. [1810-1840 NHFC Danbury].

    David[6] *Sevrens* purchased 140 acres of land from Obidiah Judkins 5-28-1808. On August 20, 1808, the town records record a meeting where **David**[6] Severans and Obidia Judkins were "Taken to High preaching".

David[6] served Danbury as selectman, tax collector, and Highway agent among others. He died sometime after 1831 when he was last recorded at a town meeting. [TRDNH]

As **William G.**[10] *Sevrens*, great great grandson, noted, "there must have been alot of tragedy in the Severans house-hold, only eight of four children survived to adulthood. Mehitable d 10-19-1819. She left 4 young children. Mr. *Severans* remarried in 1821. [MWGS]

Children: born at Danbury, NH [MWGS]

	i	**Nancy**[7] b 8-6-1803 d 9-24-1804
311	ii	**Uriel**[7] b 4-30-1804 m Mary J. Hall 10-27-1842
	iii	**Nathan**[7] b 1805 killed by a falling tree 6-11-1819
312	iv	**Nathaniel**[7] b 11-10-1806. The [1850 VTFC Derby] shows **Nathaniel**[7] with wife, Alversa ____, b 1815 in VT. Children were **Nancy**[7] b 1837; **Laura**[7], b 1839; and **Martha**[7] b 1840.
	v	**David**[7] b 11-27-1808 at Danbury, NH He married Emily Bean, daughter of John Bean and Martha Deweir, on 9-22-1842 at Boston, MA. [MAVR] Emily was b in Danbury, NH and died 11-20-1894 ae 71-4-29 at Boston, MA. [MAVR] **David**[7] died 1-16-1892 of influenza-pneumonia, at Boston. [MAVR]
	vi	**John**[7] b 1-10-1812 d 1814
	vii	**Mehitable**[7] b 6-1-1813 d 4-5-1818
313	viii	**Jonathan Thompson**[7] b 7-12-1815 m Delia Caswell 4-18-1846

(138) James[6] *Severens*, (Joseph[5], Benjamin[4], Ephraim[3], Ephraim[2], John[1]), born on 12-19-1776 in Andover, NH. He moved while young and married to Sarah True in Plainfield, NH on 8-21-1803. The family lived for a time in Derby, VT, where their first five children were born. [1810/20 VTFC Derby, Orleans Co] After the death of **James'**[6] father, **Joseph**[5], he returned to Salisbury and carried on the farm for some years. [Eastman p222] The other children were born in Andover, NH. [1820-1840 Andover/Chester NHFC] **James**[7] was Deacon of the local church.

James[6] was born in Andover and inherited the excellent farm which he and his son, **Ziba**[7], made one of the noted farms in the town. "The deacon was a conscientious and stricly honest man, a good citizen and a consistent church member, sho took his religious spirit into his daily life." [Eastman p431]

Deacon **James**[6] died 3-10-1854 age 77 years [NHVR] and his wife died 2-12-1865 age 80 years. They spelled their last name as *Severens*. She died on 2-12-1865. They are buried at Smith's Corner in Salisbury, NH. [CRSNH]

Children: [Eastman p327-328 (except Ann)]
    i   **Abigail**[7] b 2-13-1806 m Enoch Rowe 2-25-1844 as his second wife
    ii   **Ann**[7] b 5-11-1806 m Marcus Sargent 12-27-1829 [Perley, Family 160] This **Ann**[7] is conjecture if her father was **James**[6] but they had a son named James Severance Sargent that moved to Kansas and died there on 7-2-1877.
314 iii **Ziba**[7] b 7-20-1807 m Sarah Ann Weare 10-27-1837 [Eastman p283]
    iv **James Royal**[7] b 2-5-1809 d 1-28-1814 [Eastman p304]
    v   **Salina**[7] b 10-6-1810 d 11-10-1810 [Eastman p311]
    vi **Pascal**[7] P. b 9-12-1811 d 1-1-1831 [Eastman p311]
    vii **Emily**[7] b 9-5-1813 d 7-20-1882 in Virginia, NV. She was the second wife of Aaron Cilley. Aaron was the son of Aaron Cilley and Lydia Currier. Aaron was b 2-3-1807 and d on 7-24-1870. He m first to Eliza Rolfe. [Eastman p86] Ezra Sterns wrongly placed **Emily**[7] as the daughter of **Joseph**[6] Severance and Ann Currier. [Sterns Vol I p996]see below **Aurelia T.**[7]
   viii **Salina**[7] b 11-12-1814 d 6-13-1893 [Eastman p316]] m Sanborn Shaw 11-23-1837 [Sterns Vol 1 p42]
    ix **Harriet Newell**[7] b 8-16-1816 d 2-21-1853 m A. J. Tucker 9-18-1838 m2 Samuel Morrill 6-18-1843. Samuel Morrill, son of Israel Morrill and Rosanna McPherson, married first to Miriam Cilley, daughter of Aaron and Lydia Currier. He m second to **Harriet Newell**[7] (Severance) Tucker, daughter of Deacon **James**[8] Severance. He m to Lucy Watson, daughter of Nicodemus Watson, daughter of Nicodemus Watson and Prudence Morrill. [Eastman p251]]

viii **Judith T.**[7] b 3-2-1818 m Charles Seamans
Sargent 12-24-1840. He was b 3-19-1817
d 12-30-1842. He was a merchant tailor
in New London, NH. They had no children.
[Perley, Family 160]

ix **Sarah T.**[7] b 12-24-1819 m John R. Brown
12-24-1840

x **Nancy Judson**[7] b 9-9-1821 d 3-3-1844 m
Andrew Jackson Cilley 3-24-1844. Andrew
was the son of Aaron Cilley and Lydia
Currier. Andrew was b in 7-16-1818 and
d in Kingston, NH on 5-21-1889. He
remarried to Susan G. Bowman and then
third to Mrs. Susan (Bartlett)
Marshall. [Eastman p87]

x **Ruth W.**[7] b 11-10-1823 d 1916 m Daniel C.
Stevens 4-20-1848

xi **Aurelia T.**[7] b 4-12-1826 d 3-31-1855 age
29 yrs [Eastman p328] She m to William
Dunlap 5-22-1851. [NHVR] [Sterns Vol 1
p996 said Emelia T.]

(The two Cilley brothers had another brother,
Benjamin Dodge Cilley, who m secondly on 10-28-1860
to **Emma J.**[7] Severance.) [Eastman p86]

(139) Joseph[6]. (Joseph[5], Benjamin[4], Ephraim[3],
Ephraim[2], John[1]), born on 1-1-1783 in Salisbury, NH.
He died on 10-10-1828 in Derby, Vermont. The 1820
VT census for Derby shows him living in that area.
He married to Rillah Colby. She was born at
Springfield, NH 9-23-1794 and died at Warner, NH in
1855. [Greeley p226]

Children: [Greeley p226]
315 i **Willard Colby**[7]
ii **Nancy Colby**[7] d at the age of 19 yrs old.

(140) Benjamin[6], (Joseph[5], Benjamin[4], Ephraim[3],
Ephraim[2], John[1]), born on 4-18-1785 in Salisbury,
NH. He was living in Salisbury in 1810. [1810 NHFC]
He married first to Edna Greenhough, 6-22-1808
[NHVR], who died on 7-21-1821 [VTVR]. He married
secondly to Hannah Ladd and they lived in Derby and
Rockingham VT. In 1820 he was living in Derby.
[1820 VTFC] Hannah died on 5-13-1855. [VTVR]
Benjamin[6] died in Rockingham, VT on 9-24-1863
[VTVR] The epitaph from his gravestone in the
cemetery at Derby Center reads, **"Benjamin**[6]
Severance died 9-24-1863 aged 77 years, came from

Salisbury, NH, 1815. One of the early settlers of
Derby, VT." [Currier p227] He Reportedly had 8
children. They lost one pair of twins and two other
children while young. [Eastman p224 additions]

Children: [Currier p226-228]
i   **Hannah Edna**[7] b 2-23-1825 d 12-24-1888 m
Charles B. West 3-18-1846 who was b 8-
29-1825.
ii   **George Washington**[7] b 9-23-1830 at Derby,
VT. He m 4-18-1857 to Josephine G.
Clough, [IGI] who was b in Lyman, NH, 6-
16-1834, and d 1-17-1900. They had one
daughter, **Alice Edna**[8] Severance b 1-27-
1868 at Beebe Junction, Province of
Quebec, m Charles E. Twombly 10-6-1887.
[Currier p228]
iii   **Elizabeth Hall**[7] b 9-25-1832 m Samuel
Benjamin Horton 5-15-1827, son of
Abraham Horton and Sarah C. Bingham. He
was b 5-15-1827 d 1-3-1904. [Currier
p227]
iv   **Roxanna Alpha**[7] b 11-29-1834 m1 James
Young Green. He was b 6-20-1833 son of
Ahirah Green and Roxanna Mears, and d 8-
4-1886 m2 Warren A. Himes 9-7-1887 son
of Alfred U. Himes. [Currier p227]

(141) John[6], (Joseph[5], Benjamin[4], Ephraim[3], Ephraim[2],
John[1]), born on 5-30-1787 in Salisbury, NH. He
married to Abigail True on 2-3-1811. She was born
3-29-1793. They settled and lived at Wilmot Flat in
Wilmot, NH. They are indicated on the 1810 NH
census for Kingston. The 1830 NH census shows him
in Andover. He shows on the 1840 NH census for
Wilmot. **John**[6] died on 8-31-1851. [Eastman p329]

Children: Wilmot, Merrimack Co, NH [Eastman p329]
316 i   **Ransom**[7] b 12-12-1811 d 7-26-1887 m
Lorinda Currier 5-3-1838
ii   **Emily**[7] b 9-5-1813 m Aaron Cilley 9-8-
1839. **Emily**[7] d 7-20-1882 [Eastman p86]
317 iii   **John**[7] b 8-1-1815 d 3-19-1892 m 2-11-1841
Camilla Mitchell
318 iv   **Newell**[7] b 3-19-1817 m Harriet S. Hall 3-
3-1847 at Lowell, Massachusetts.
319 v   **Hermon R.**[7] b 9-16-1818 d 7-27-1844
vi   **Roxey A.**[7] b 4-13-1820 m Samuel Durgin
11-17-1840; Roxey d 12-13-1875
320 vii   **Herod T.**[7] b 3-1-1822 m 11-5-1846 Sarah

Fowler, the [1880 MAFC] shows with
daughters **Ardela**[8] b 1857 and **Lulu**[8] b 1868
plus several other boarders. Lived at
Bristol, NH.

viii **Rhoda T.**[7] b 1-8-1824 d 10-24-1860 m
Ansel S. Dill 1-13-1851; Rhoda[7] died 10-
24-1860

ix **Lavinia**[7] b 9-11-1825 m ___ Fisher 9-11-
1851; **Lavinia**[7] d 1-23-1866

x **Sarah B.**[7] b 8-22-1827 m Jacob F. White
10-27-1850

xi **Abigail**[7] b 3-15-1829 d 8-6-1847 at
Lowell, MA [MAVR]

xii **Mary E.**[7] b 12-24-1832 m Robert Rowe 11-
18-1855; Mary d 12-25-1884

(142) George Washington[6], (Peter[5], Benjamin[4],
Ephraim[3], Ephraim[2], John[1]), born in Chester, NH on
2-6-1785. He married Mary Pike on 10-19-1814. They
settled in Chester, NH and then Auburn, NH. The
1820-1840 NH census shows them living in Chester.
In 1860 they were living in Auburn, NH with **Alfred**[7]
and **Fidelia**[7]. **George**[6] died on 3-21-1864. [MLWM Bible
Records of **Peter**[5] Severance, son of **Benjamin**[4] and
Ruth Long Severance]

Children: [MLWM]
i **Mary A.**[7] b 7-18-1818. She m to Sewell L.
Towne at Topsfield, MA on 12-24-1846.
[MAVR]

321 ii **Alfred P.**[7] b 2-5-1821

iii **Sarah J.**[7] b 4-3-1823

iv **Lenora**[7] b 2-22-1825

v **Melinda**[7] b 1828 [1850 NHFC]

vi **Fidelia**[7] b 2-24-1831 m George P.
Boynton, son of John Boynton and Sarah
Tilton of Stanstead, Canada, 8-7-1861 at
Charlestown, MA. [MAVR]

(143) James M.[6], (Peter[5], Benjamin[4], Ephraim[3],
Ephraim[2], John[1]), born on 2-1-1792 in Auburn, NH. He
married Dorothy Trefethan, daughter of Daniel
Trefethen and Dorothy Amazeen, of Kittery, ME. The
marriage intentions were in Kittery ME 12-2-1815
for **James**[6] Sevrence. [Gray Vol 3 p284] Dorothy was
born 11-5-1799. [BR **James M.**[6] Severance] They
lived in Chester between 1820-1840. [NHFC] In the
1850, they were living in Kingston, NH. [NHFC] By
1860 they were living in Auburn. **James**[6] died on 8-
29-1863 at Auburn, NH. [DARLR] Dorothy died on 5-

28-1898 at Manchester, NH. She is buried in Auburn, NH. [DAR Bennington, VT Chapter #589678]

Children: [BRJMS 1840]
     i   **Sophronia**[7] b 7-23-1816 m Robert Patten, **Sophronia**[7] d 3-31-1900
322 ii   **Charles**[7] b 1-23-1818 m Charlotte____
323 iii   **William**[7] b 11-6-1820 d 3-6-1891 [MLWM]
     iv   **Fanny**[7] b 9-14-1822 d 10-31-1834
323a v   **James Henry**[7] b 7-14-1825 at Boston d 3-31-1889 Lawrence, MA m Francis Ann Leer
     vi   **Elizabeth A.**[7] b 10-14-1828 d 1-5-1847
     vii   **Alzira**[7] b 10-5-1831 m ___Sawyer
     viii   **Fanny**[7] b 11-9-1834 m Joseph W. Merrill, 10-1-1860 [BRJMS] **Fanny**[7] died 8-14-1918
     ix   **Caroline**[7] b 10-12-1839 d 11-25-1839
     x   **Jane**[7] b 11-19-1843 m Charles A. Merrill, of Salem, New Hampshire. **Jane**[7] d 7-26-1931. [BRJMS]

(144) Rufus[6], (Peter[5], Benjamin[4], Ephraim[3], Ephraim[2], John[1]), born on 9-15-1794 in Auburn, NH. He married to Susan Lance on 1-19-1824. They settled in Cabot, VT where **Rufus**[6] died on 3-4-1877. Susan died on 4-28-1874. [VTVR] **Hannah**[7] and **Sarah**[7] were living with **Rufus**[6] and Sarah in Cabot VT in 1860. [VTFC]

Children:
324 i   **John Dow**[7] b 8-14-1824 [VTVR]
     ii   **Hannah**[7] b 1-29-1826
     iii   **Sally**[7] b 10-19-1827
     iv   **Sarah**[7] b 1831 d 6-25-1890

(145) John[6], (Peter[5], Benjamin[4], Ephraim[3], Ephraim[2], John[1]), born on 3-13-1801. He settled in Hooksette, NH where he married Lucinda Hazelton circa 1822. The 1830-1840 NH census shows him living at Bradford. Later found in Bristol, VT. **John**[6] does not show on the 1860 census with Lucinda and two of his children.

Children:
     i   **Mary I.**[7], possible daughter of **John**[6] Severance, b circa 1830 at Hooksette, NH, m Edmund D. Brown, son of David Brown, 10-29-1850 at Haverhill, MA. [MAVR]
324a ii   **Leonard H.**[7] b 2-19-1832
     iii   **Fredrick**[7] b 1841 as indicated on the 1860 NH census at Hooksett.

iv   **Charles**[7] b 9-29-1845 in Hooksette, NH d
        12-3-1921 in Bristol, NH. [NHVR] He was
        a railroad fireman. He m to Lucy P.
        Hobart, daughter of Daniel Hobart and
        May Frye. Lucy was b 9-19-1849 and d 7-
        19-1921. [NHVR] **Charles**[7] was a railroad
        fireman.

(147) Samuel[6], (Caleb[5], Joseph[4], Ephraim[3], Ephraim[2],
John[1]), born 2-20-1781 [MEVR] in Orrington, ME.
[HOPCoME pCXVIII] married Hannah Godfrey, daughter
of Joshua Godfrey and Naomi Kelley, on 9-28-1805.
She was born 5-24-1783 in Chatham, MA. [MgBH Vol 5]
Samuel's[6] name appears on the 1810-1830 ME census.
The 1860 ME census shows **Samuel**[6] born in NH, age
78, with Hannah, age 75, born in MA, living in
Bangor.

Children: 1820 ME census for Orrington
    i   **Cynthia**[7] b 3-19-1806
    ii   **Polly**[7] b 3-14-1809. She m to William P.
            Burr first and secondly to Orin Favor.
326 iii **Brewer Samuel**[7] b 1-12-1810 m Betsy W.
            Thompson b 12-17-1833
    iv   **Joshua Godfrey**[7] b 2-5-1812 perhaps
            married to Laurana B. Shattuck 1-16-1842
            at Boston, MA [MAVR] He died 3-10-1883
            at Andover, MA [MAVR]
327 v   **Hiram**[7] b 1-23-1814
    vi   **Hannah Godfrey**[7] b 3-16-1816
    vii **Caleb**[7] b 1819. It is conjecture that
            this **Caleb**[7] is the son of **Samuel**[8] and
            Hannah as a Caleb does not show on the
            [Town of Orrington, MEVR]. The [1850
            MEFC] shows **Caleb**[7] Severance, age 37
            (b 1813 in ME) living with Bradley
            Blackman.
    viii **Alphonso**[7] b 3-27-1822 in Orrington, ME.
            He d 9-26-1881 at Rollingsford, NH. He
            began his career as a school teacher.
            Then at age 19 he began to study
            dentistry. Four years later he opened
            his dental practice at South Berwick,
            ME, but in 1863 he opened an office at
            Salmon Falls village in the town of
            Rollingsford. He served on the
            Superintending School Committee number 1
            in the the village. [Catalfo] He m to
            Jane Moore, "about October 1846" in
            Boston, MA, [NHVR], daughter of Rev.

Forris Moore and Rebekah Smith. Sarah
Moore was b 11-28-1821. They were
divorced in September of 1872. [NHVR]
The [1870 NHFC Rollinsford] shows him
with his wife Rebecca J. and a son,
Alphonzo⁸ b 1851. The [1860 Bangor MEFC]
shows him with **Alphonzo⁸** b 1849 and
Leola⁸ b 1852.

   ix   **Thomas J.⁷** b 10-27-1824, He was the
first victim of cholera in Bangor, he
probably lived in Brewer, ME

   x   **Samuel⁷** b 1829

His son's, **Caleb⁷** and one of the **Samuel's⁷** do not
show on the Maine, Vital Records and therefore are
conjecture.

(148) Reuben⁶, (Caleb⁵, Joseph⁴, Ephraim³, Ephraim²,
John¹), born in Orrington, ME in 1785. He married
Sally⁶ (**Sarah**) Severance on 9-12-1805. She was the
daughter of **Joshua⁵** Severance. She married to
Benomi Wright after the death of **Rueben⁶**. [MgBH
Vol 5] **Reuben's⁶** name appears on the 1810 ME
census. It appears that he died before 1830.

Children: [MEVR]
   i   **Eliza⁷** b 12-22-1805 m to Calvin
Cleveland on 9-21-1827. [MEVR]

328 ii **Warren⁷** b 1-8-1809

   iii **William B.⁷** b 3-20-1811. He married Lucy
C. ___ . [MEVR] He died at Millbury, MA,
12-5-1881 age 70-7-15 of heart disease.
He was the Superintendant of the town
farm. I show that this **William⁷** had a
daughter named **Eunice A.⁸** born 1844. The
[1850 Abbott MEFC] shows **William⁷** born
1812, Asanath F., born 1826, and **Emma
A.⁸** born 1846.

329 iv **Reuben⁷** b 7-15-1813

   v   **George⁷** b 5-4-1816 d 11-16-1818

   vi **Sally⁷** b 7-16-1819. She m to Benoni
Baker

330 vii **Joshua⁷** b 3-15-1822. A **Joshua⁷** married to
Laurana B. Shattuck in January of 1842
in Boston, MA. [MAVR] There was a
Joshua⁷ who married to Martha A. Derby
on 8-20-1848 at Orrington, ME. [HOPCoME]
Joshua⁷ (invalid) who filed 8-3-1863 and
his widow filed 10-5-1888 for service 1
Co. Mass Sharp Shooter. [CWPR] It is

possible that these marriages were for
Joshua G.[7], son of **Samuel**[6] and Hannah
Godfrey.
viii   **Rebecca J.**[7] b 5-16-1827

(149) Joseph[6], (Caleb[5], Joseph[4], Ephraim[3], Ephraim[2],
John[1]), born 12-14-1785 in Orrington, ME. He died
10-11-1874 in Belfast, ME but formerly of Brewer.
[MEVR] He married Polly Lovell in 1813. Polly was
born 5-1-1789. [HOPCoME p36] His name appears on
the [1820/40 Brewer, MEFC]. The 1850 ME census
shows this family under the name of *Leverance*

Children: [MEVR]
i   infant d 1814
ii   **Eliza Pendleton**[7] b 5-18-1815
iii   infant d 1817
iv   **Joseph Franklin**[7] b 2-28-1819. The [1850
        MEFC] shows **Joseph Franklin**[7] living with
        his parents under the surname of
        Leverance. The census also shows a **Sarah
        F.**[7] age 19, probably his sister.
v   **George Washington**[7] b 1-7-1822 [IGI]
v   **Harrison Cushing**[7] b 2-7-1825
vi   **Sarah Isabel**[7] b 8-5-1831

(150) William[6], (Caleb[5], Joseph[4], Ephraim[3], Ephraim[2],
John[1]), born 1811-1812. He married circa 1844 to
Asenath Fogg Severance, who was born 1827-1828 died
3-6-1892, age 64-11-23, wife of **William**[6] Severance,
female, widow died at Oxford, Worcester County, MA.
[MAVR] She was born at Hebron, ME, daughter of
Samuel Fogg and Anna Merrill. Samuel was born at
Greene, Maine and Anna at Hebron. [Whitten Vol I
#1266] The family was living in Millbury, Worcester
Co MA in 1880. [MAFC]
   A pension was filed by the invalid 1-8-1866 and
by his widow 1-17-1883 for service C 2 ME., Inf.
[CWPR] He married to Polly Trafton with a question
mark. It is unclear if he indeed married to her.
[HOPCoME] **William's**[6] name appears on the 1830
Bangor ME census.

Children: [1870 MEFC-Abbot, ME]
i   **Emma A.**[7] b 1845/46 was a vest maker
ii   **Giles**[7] b 1851/52 was a machinist. He
        died 4-3-1876 at Oxford, MA, age 24-1-
        12, single, of typhoid pneumonia. [MAVR]
iii   **Frank W.**[7] b 1854/55
iv   **Flora A.**[7] b 1863/64

(151) Caleb[6], (Caleb[5], Joseph[4], Ephraim[3], Ephraim[2], John[1]), born in Brewer, ME circa 1803. He married Nancy ____. The 1820-1830 ME census shows him living in Brewer.

Children: [HOPCoME p77]
```
         i     Barbary Ann⁷ b 1-21-1825
        ii     Pilsbury⁷ b 7-3-1826 d 8-11-1826
333    iii     Russell Howard⁷ b 4-11-1828
        iv     Mary Jane⁷ b 9-10-1830
         v     Caroline Maria⁷ b 12-10-1833
        vi     Colinda Elizabeth⁷ b 4-10-1836
       vii     Hulda⁷ b 5-10-1840
      viii     Henry Lewis⁷ b 2-15-1842
```

(152) Thomas[6], (Caleb[5], Joseph[4], Ephraim[3], Ephraim[2], John[1]), was born 12-4-1803 in Orrington, ME, and later lived in Bangor, Penobscot Co, ME. He died 3-18-1858. [MEVR] He married to Lydia Lovell on 10-29-1826. [MEVR] She was born 4-24-1806. The 1830 ME census shows him living in Brewer.

Thomas[6] Severance of Dexter, ME, died 3-18-1858, his wife Lydia and minor children over 14 were listed as **Albert T.**[7], under 14, were **George A.**[7], and **Willis E.**[7] [39:23, 40:9, 485] The 1850 ME census shows **Charlotte S.**[7] b 1833, **Caroline T.**[7] b 1836, **Albert T.**[5] b 1843, **Willis E.**[5] b 1848, and **George A.**[7] b 1850. [PRPCoME p196]

The [IGI] shows **Willis Edgar**[7] b 9-2-1848 to **Thomas**[6] of Dexter, ME. Lydia Severence, mother of **Willis E.**[7] and **George A.**[7] Severence, minors under 14 years and heir of **Thomas**[6] Severence of Dexter, deceased-guardianship given to Lydia with $100 bond, April 27, 1858. [PRME]

Children:
```
         i     Martha Ann⁷ b 9-17-1827 Bangor, ME
        ii     Thomas Edwin⁷ b 2-24-1829 d 8-6-1829
       iii     Charles Edwin⁷ b 8-18-1830 d 7-22-1833
        iv     Charlotte Louisa⁷ b 5-22-1833 at Dexter,
               ME. She apparently m to a Hodgdon as
               that was her married name on the 1860
               ME census when she was living with her
               parents. However, the [MAVR] shows her
               marriage to Nelson W. Johnson, son of
               Benjamin and Elizabeth Johnson of
               Haverhill, MA., 9-10-1863 at Haverhill.
         v     Caroline Sarah⁷ b 9-19-1835
        vi     Harriet Augustus⁷ b 2-5-1838 d 10-7-1839
       vii     Albert Tefft⁷ b 9-17-1842, in Brewer,
```

Ma_ne. [MAVR] "Above the age of 14 years
and heir of **Thomas⁶** Severence of Dexter,
chooses John W. Sewell of Bangor for his
guardian." Dated April 27, 1858.
[PRPCoME] He m to Sarah Evans 12-10-1872
at Gill, MA, [MAVR] and divorced 4-27-
1876. [NHVR] He remarried to Sarah E.
Leavitt. She d 6-1-1922 in Exeter, NH.
[NHVR] **Albert⁷** d 1-13-1919 in Exeter,
NH. He was a dentist.

viii   **Frederick Henry⁷** b 7-26-1845 Dexter, ME,
       [IGI] d 4-3-1847
ix   **Willis Edgar⁷** b 9-2-1848 d 10-26-1861
x   **George Arthur⁷** b 4-26-1850 [IGI]

(153) Benjamin⁶, (Joshua⁵, Joseph⁴, Ephraim³,
Ephraim², John¹), born in Orrington, ME on 4-20-
1791. He was in the War of 1812 at the battle of
Hampden. He was one of the early settlers of
Orrington. [HOPCoME pCXVII] He married Kezia
(Baker) Pope, daughter of William Baker and Mary
Harding, on 1-28-1815. She was born 7-2-1798 and
died 5-29-1825. Kezia was of Chatham, MA. moving to
Orrington, ME with her mother and stepfather, John
Pope, after 1808. **Benjamin⁶** married secondly to
Anna Pope, daughter of John Pope and Mary Harding
4-15-1826. Anne was born 1-29-1805 and died 3-22-
1870. She and Kezia were half sisters. **Benjamin's⁶**
name appears on the 1820-1830 ME census for
Orrington.
   All of the Severance children were born in
Orrington, ME. Anna Harding Pope died 3-22-1879 at
the age of 65-1-23. Kezia born 7-2-1798 and died 5-
29-1825. The [CRME Orrington] show that **Benjamin⁶**
died 7-20-1860. [MDJS]

Children of **Benjamin⁵** Severance and Kezia Pope
Baker [PRPCoME p196] [IGI] and [PRME].
       i   **Sally⁷ (Sarah)** b 12-16-1817 m Foster
            Smith on 10-22-1838 at Orrington, ME.
            Foster was born on 2-1-1813 at
            Orrington. [MEVR]
335   ii   **Benjamin O.⁷** b 1-15-1820 m Mary A. Smith
336   iii **William B.⁷** b 3-24-1822 m Sophia B.
            Lancaster
       iv   **James⁷** b 5-10-1824 in MA. He shows on
            the [1870 MAFC] living in Chicopee,
            Hampden Co with his wife, Flora, who was
            b in 1828 in ME.
       v   **Kezia H.⁷** b 5-26-1825 d 12-17-1826

Children of **Benjamin**[6] Severance and Anna H. Pope
[1860 MEFC in part]

337 vi   **George N.**[7] b 7-27-1826 m Eliza A. ___

     vii   **Kezia**[7] b 12-18-1827 m John Jameson 5-27-
           1851

338 viii **Henry Albert**[7] b 10-12-1829 d after 6-22-
           1860 (listed on his fathers Will) This
           Henry A.[7] m to Eleanor M. Bowden.

339 ix   **Charles A.**[7] b 4-27-1831 m Lydia Bowden
           8- -1854

     x   **Hiram M.**[7] b 12- -1833 d 6-30-1834

     xi   **Cyrus B.**[7] b 4-14-1835 in Orrington, ME.
           He settled in Minneapolis, MN? This is
           conjecture. **Cyrus**[7] shows on the [1870
           MNFC] living with an Amos Jordan family
           and Charlotte Severance.

     xii   **Mary E.**[7] b 5-30-1836

340 xiii **Carlos (Harlow Erastus)**[7] b 1-27-1839 (1-
           27-1840 [MEVR] m Eunice Berry

     xiv   **Rosetta**[7] b 1-2-1841 d 6-2-1891 m James
           W. Harley

     xv   **Priscilla M.**[7] b 12-20-1842 d 2-10-1848

341 xvi   **Harvey A.**[7] b 11-16-1845 m to Louisa M.
           Bell and settled in MO.

     xvii **Francis Edwin**[7] b 3-6-1847 in ME. He m to
           Fanny Myrick on 4-18-1868 in ME. His
           death shows on the ME vital records as
           5-18-1905. Therefore he must have
           returned to ME before he died. He shows
           on the 1900 KS census with his wife
           Fanny Myrick who was b in September of
           1856 in ME and a nephew, James Merrick
           age 19 b in July of 1881 in CO. The
           Marston Cemetery records show **Francis
           E.**[7] Severance 1848-1905. It is not known
           if they had any children.

     xviii **Harriet**[7] b circa 1848 (of **Benjamin**[6] and
           Anna) 1m to Mr. Prebble. She 2m to
           William N. Burlingame, son of Franklin
           and Lucy Ann, 7-30-1888 at Amesbury,MA.
           She was b at Bangor, ME. [MAVR]

     xix   **Oscar**[7] b 1854 (son of **Benjamin**[6] and Annie
           P. of Orrington, ME m May A. Danforth,
           daughter of Nathaniel C. and Rosetta M.
           Danforth, on 6-13-1888 at Boston, MA. He
           was 34 and she was 26. He was a teamster
           and a mason. [MAVR] They had a daughter,
           Florence May[8] b 3-13-1890 at Boston, MA.
           [MAVR]

The Will of **Benjamin**[5] of Orrington, ME (6-22-1860) shows all of the children except for those that died young [PRPCoME 21:252]

(154) Joshua[6], (Joshua[5], Joseph[4], Ephraim[3], Ephraim[2], John[1]), born in Orrington, ME on 10-12-1798 and died 11-3-1881 [MEVR]. He married Elmira C. Lunt on 3-9-1834. [MEVR] Elmira born circa 1810 died 8-3-1789. [CRME] His name appears on the 1830 Orrington, ME census.

Children: [1860 MEFC] [Orrington MEVR]
    i   **Sarah A.**[7] b 8-5-1835 m Jeremiah Bowden
    ii   **Susan A.**[7] b 7-26-1837
    iii   **Laura S.**[7] b 7-7-1839 m possibly ___ Baker
    iv   **Ann M.**[7] b 7-7-1839
    v   **Olive L.**[7] n 3-26-1841
    vi   **Frances L.**[7] b 6-14-1843 at East Orrington, ME. She m to John C. Elms who was b in Lincolnville, ME. [MEVR] m2 James Duren
    vii   **Elmira[7] (Clarissa L.[7])** b 7-14-1846 m Elijah Lane
    viii   **John Smith[7]** b 6-18-1849 at Orrington, ME. He was living with his parents on the 1870 Orrington ME census. He m Sadie Atwood 9-12-1872. The [IGI] shows this **John S.**[7] as the son of **Joshua[6]** Severance and Elmira Lunt. The [MAVR] says **John S.**[7] of **Joshua[6]** and Elmira m Addie R. Wheelden, daughter of Benjamin Frank and Marion Wheelden, 9-20-1879 at Lowell, MA. He was 29 and a wood moulder and she 25. They had a daughter, **Marion C.**[8] b 10-30-1889 at Holyoke, MA. [MAVR]

(155) Cyprian[6], (Joshua[5], Joseph[4], Ephraim[3], Ephraim[2], John[1]), born at Orrington, ME on 2-22-1799. [MEVR] He married first to Mary Baker 3-5-1823 and secondly to Fran before 1850. They lived at Bucksport, Hampden, and Frankfort, ME. His name appears on the 1830 Orrington, ME census.

Children:
    i   **Mary A.**[7] b 8-13-1823 m Stillman H. Deane of Orrington, ME, on 5-20-1844. [MEVR]
    ii   **Caroline A.**[7] b 6-4-1825 m Horace T. Marston, son of William and Elizabeth Marston, 12-2-1842 at Orrington, ME.

    iii   **Hannah J.**[7] b 1-1-1828
342 iv   **Jerome P.**[7] b 6-30-1832
343 v   **George W.**[7] b 6-1-1832 m Sarah Jones who
           was b in Winterport, ME
    vi   **Elizabeth S.**[7] b 2-9-1834 m Alfred L.
           Colson 2-23-1854
    vii **Thankful N.**[7] b 3-21-1837
344 viii **John H.**[7] b 8-9-1840. He m 3 times.

Thankful[7] and **Hannah J.**[7] probably d young as they do
not show on the 1850 ME census.

The above children and birthdates show on the
[MEVR]. The children below show on the 1850 ME
census.
    ix   **Melville B.**[7] b 1842
    x   **Ellis V.**[7] b 1844
347 xi   **Winfield S.**[7] b 1847 m1 Lizzie H. Colson,
           m2 Florence E. Dollard

(157) Ephraim[6], (Joshua[5], Joseph[4], Ephraim[3],
Ephraim[2], John[1]), born 9-13-1808. There is record
that **Ephraim**[6] Severance went on board the Capt.
Stoddard on 4-21-1830 (evidently to sea). He
married to Susanna Morrill 6-18-1838. [Morsher p45]
Susanna is most likely the same as Susanna
Clark/Morrill/Norris. Susanna died 6-18-1884 ae 70-
5-14. Therefore born circa 1814. Susan Clark was
born circa 1814, and died 6-18-1884, at Hyde Park,
MA. [MAVR] [CRME] **Ephraim's**[6] name appears on the
1840 Bangor, ME census.

Children: [1860 MEFC] [MBGD]
    i   **William Henry**[7], **(Henry**[7]) b 6-18-1840 at
           Bangor, ME, the son of Ephraim and
           Susanna Morrill. [IGI] He m1 Sarah A.
           Gardner 9-10-1848 at Roxbury, MA, both
           of Boston. They had a son, **William H.**[8] d
           9-3-1851 ae 7 months. [MAVR] **William H.**[7]
           m2 to Carrie Crockett, daughter of Asa
           Crockett and Elvira Robbins, 11-22-1880.
           Carrie d 10-3-1884 ae 34-1-10 [MEVR] He
           d 11-18-1897 ae 58-8-4, at Hyde Park,
           MA. [MAVR] Buried at Rockland, ME.
    ii   **Emeline M.**[7] b 1841 in Bangor, ME, m
           Samuel Dickey, son of John and Sarah,
           10-6-1879 at Lowell, MA. [MAVR]
348 iii **Lorenzo G.**[7] **(Lonny)** b 1849 in Bangor,
           ME, d 8-7-1910 aged 62 yrs 11 mos 8 dys

at East Orrington, ME.

(158) John S.[6], (John[5], Ephraim[4], Ephraim[3], Ephraim[2], John[1]), born on 12-7-1774 in Sandwich, NH. It was this **John**[6] Severance who married Lydia Jewell, daughter of Jacob and Martha (Quimby) Jewell, on 12-9-1792 and not his father as was reported in History of New Hampshire, [Sterns Vol 2 p527-8]. **John**[6] grew to manhood on the family homestead and later inherited part of it. "He was by occupation a capable and prosperous farmer, and had considerable mechanical genius which served him well in various kinds of handicraft. He was a prominent and public-spirited citizen, and in politics a supporter of the Democratic party. He served his native town as tax collector for sixteen consecutive years. Both he and his wife were members of the Methodist Episcopal church." The family remained on the family homestead where **John**[6] died on 1-18-1845 and is buried in the Baptist Cemetery in Sandwich, NH. Lydia, who was born on 9-20-1777 and died on 11-23-1857. [GSNH] He is indicated on the 1810-1840 Sandwich, NH census.

John[6] owned and operated a saw mill on Weed Brook which was later sold to Nicholas Norris. [SHNE 14th Excursion p15]

Children: [MDCD]
349 i   **John Smith**[7] b 5-6-1793 m Dorothy French 3-14-1813. Dorothy French d 5-22-1842. He m2 to Abigail Hilton, daughter of David Hilton, who lived near Bear Camp River Bridge [SNHE 45th Excursion p24]

    ii   **Anne**[7] b 6-13-1795 m Jacob T. Mudgett 1-5-1813 in Sandwich, NH. Jacob was the son of Thomas b in Tamworth, NH on 2-8-1789 d in Winslow, ME on 5-10-1868. He was in Hanover, NH in 1818. [Mudgett p26]

350 iii   **Asa**[7] b 3-31-1798 d 2-29-1828 m Rhoda Webster 10-11-1821

351 iv   **Levi**[7] b 3-24-1800 m Ruth Skinner, **Levi**[7] signed the Will of **Moses**[6] Severance (**Levi's**[7] Uncle)

    v   **Lydia**[7] b 9-7-1802 m John Webster Jr. 12-27-1818

352 vi   **Jacob Jewell**[7] b 11-4-1804 d 1-9-1896 m Susanna Roberts, daughter of Joseph Roberts and Mary Davis of Meredith, NH.

    vii   **Sukey (Sarah)**[7] b 12-13-1806

353 viii **Sargeant Jewell**[7] b 3-20-1809 m Elizabeth Burton

ix **Martha F.**[7] b 5-31-1812 m John Gilman 11-14-1836 m2 Charles W. White 10-14-1845

354 x **James M.**[7] b 4-25-1814 d 12-15-1897 at 27 Belvidere St., Boston, MA m Adaline Randall 10-2-1834

xi **Polly M.**[7] b 5-14-1816 d 12-8-1844

xii **Eliza**[7] b 5-10-1822

(159) Nathaniel Smith[6], (John[5], Ephraim[4], Ephraim[3], Ephraim[2], John[1]), born in Sandwich, NH on 8-17-1776. [IGI] He died after 1840 when he was shown on the NH census. It is uncertain where **Nathaniel**[6] settled because he lived for several years in ME as well as living in NH for some time. The census records show him in Sandwich, NH and also living in Newport, ME. He married Betsey Fogg on 4-17-1803. [IGI] She was born circa 1785 and died 3-8-1817.

Betsey *Severns* 32 yrs, wife of **Nathaniel S.**[6] died on the 4th of March, 1817 at Starks, ME (from Sandwich, NH) and on the same day her brother William, age 20. Both of them died instantly. [NSAA 3-8-1817]

Nathaniel[6] showed on the 1840 Sandwich, NH census living alone. This could have been the son, **Nathaniel**[7], of **Nathaniel**[6] and Betsey. Some of the children remain a mystery because it is uncertain if **Nathaniel**[6] remarried after his wife Betsey died at a young age. The 1800 NH census does not show him. The 1810 Sandwich, NH census shows a male and 2 females. The 1820 NH census is absent. The 1830 Pittsfield, ME census shows **Nathaniel**[6] in ME. **Nathaniel**[6] Severance of Chandlersville and later of Palmyra and Pittsfield, ME, exchanged land with his son, **Jesse**[7], in the years 1833 thru 1855. [LRME]

Children:

355 i **Jesse**[7] b 1809 d 5-1-1885 ae 76 m Sarah Brown [NHVR] Sarah d 2-25-1880 ae 67-10-17

356 ii **Nathaniel**[7] b 1-28-1805. He m to Belinda Fogg. **Nathaniel**[7] d 6-30-1878 at Newport, ME. He was buried with sister **Mary Ann**[7], **Jesse**[7], (his brother) and Sarah, **Jesse's**[7] wife) and L.W. Gould (husband of Mary Ann). [CRME]

iii **Mary Ann**[7], Miss **Mary Ann**[7] Severance m Mr. Levi Gould on 1-31-1831 at New Sharon, ME. [MEVR] [CRME]

(160) Ephraim⁶, (John⁵, Ephraim⁴, Ephraim³, Ephriam², John¹), born in Sandwich, NH on 7-16-1780 (son of John and Susannah Severance [NHVR] He married Sally Leavitt on 3-2-1800. [IGI] She was born 9-18-1779 at Tuftonborough, NH and died at Sandwich on 9-24-1836 ae 59 yrs 6 days [GSNH]. They show on the 1810-1830 Sandwich, NH census. They were farmers and settled in Sandwich, NH. **Ephraim⁶** died on 11-11-1836. [Lighton]

Children:
357	i	**Peter⁷** b 7-8-1801, m Judith Glidden, Mary Roberts, and Lydia A. Goss Plumer.
358	ii	**Ephraim⁷** b 8-25-1804 d 9-18-1888 m Esther G. Currier
359	iii	**John Smith⁷** b 1806 m Rhoda (Webster) Severance 4-8-1830
	iv	**George Quimby⁷** lived in Sandwich, NH. Almost nothing is known of his life. He is buried in the Baptist Cemetery with the other Severances but even his wife's name is only known as W.L., and their daughter, **Idella J.⁸** b 1844 d 1-19-1851 age 7 years 10 months [GSNH]
	v	**Hannah L.⁷** b 18-- m Josiah T. Webster 6-3-1868
360	vi	**Enoch Quimby⁷** b 1808 m Hannah Currier
	vii	**Asa⁷** b 1814 d 9-26-1838 [NHVR]
361	viii	**Ira L.⁷** b 1815 d 5-14-1846 m Mary A. Currier

(161) Moses⁶, (John⁵, Ephraim⁴, Ephraim³, Ephraim², John¹), born in Sandwich, NH on 12-27-1782. He married Lydia Thrasher on 12-16-1807. Lydia, born 3-2-1788, was the daughter of Joseph Thrasher and Joanna Quinby (Joanna was the daughter of Joseph and Patience (Thompson) Quinby). [Quinby p117] **Moses⁶** and Lydia Severance lived on the family homestead and were farmers. They show on the 1810-1840 Sandwich NH census. **Moses⁶** died on 2-20-1856 and was buried in the Baptist Cemetery although he was a devoted Methodist his entire life. Lydia died on 7-2-1873 [Lighton] and was buried next to Moses.

"Center Sandwich is a picturesque village. The church spires of the Baptist and Methodist churches can be seen high above the white buildings of the town. Sandwich does not really show its age. However, the large cemetery behind the Baptist church and the plots scattered throughout the area indicate a town rich in history." [MDCD]

LYDIA THRASHER, wife of MOSES[6] SEVERANCE

CHARLES COLEMAN[8] SEVERANCE *CLARK* (grandson)

Children: Listed in **Moses**[6] Severance's Will and
Testament, dated 4-1-1856 [PRNH Carroll Co]
    i   **Sally M.**[7] b 5- -1808 d 2-13-1885 m
        Hanson Libby 12-3-1835. Hanson d 6-3-
        1892 age 83 yrs 10 months [Lighton
        p111]] Lydia was living with this couple
        on the [1860/1870 Sandwich NHFC]
   ii   **Lucy B.**[7] b 5- -1814 d 11-5-1880 ae 75y
        6m m late in life to Jason P. Marston,
        who was first m to Dolly Bean, 6-11-
        1833. She d 11-9-1844. [NHVR] Jason was
        the son of Shubael Marston of Tamworth
        Lucy[7] left legacies to **Atwood**[7] and
        Lagrange[7] Severance, cousins, and Albion
        Marston and Lizzie (Marston) Bennett,
        children of Jason's first marriage, in
        her Will. [PRNH Carroll Co, Vol 35 p109,
        Vol 38 p315, January 1890]
362 iii **Elbridge G.**[7] b 1820 m Olive Naomi
        Roberts 7-17-1845 [NHVR Belmont]

(162) Reuben Greeley[5], (Peter[5], Ephraim[4], Ephraim[3],
Ephraim[2], John[1]), born in Salisbury, NH on 6-6-1784
[IGI], died 2-11-1851. [VTVR] He married Hadassah
Esther Smith, daughter of Aaron Smith and Abigail
Kendrick, on 6-22-1809 in Hanover, NH [VTVR].
Hadassah died 7-9-1827 [VTVR]. **Rueben**[6] remarried to
Anna Smith, sister to Hadassah, on 1-18-1829.
[VTVR] They lived in Bradford, VT. **Rueben**[6] died 2-
11-1851 [VTVR]. Anna (Smith) Severance, daughter of
Aaron and Abigail Smith died 1-16-1882 age 85-9-25.
The 1830 Bradbury, Orange Co VT census shows Reuben
living along with his father **Peter**[5], and brother
Moses[6].

Children of **Reuben G.**[6] Severance and Hadassah
Esther Smith [Greeley p199]
    i   **Erastus Kendrick**[7] b 1-19-1810 d 7-30-
        1844 [VTVR] He had a son according to
        [VTVR] but his name or the mother's name
        is not known at this time.
   ii   Son b Bradford, VT
  iii Daughter b Bradford, VT
   iv   **Ephraim Carlton**[7] b 12-23-1814 d 2-6-1867
        Bradford, VT [VTVR] [buried on Wrights
        Mt., Vermont] The [1860 VTFC] shows
        him with his mother Anna, age 66 and a
        girl **Viena**[8] b 1834 in Vermont.
        Therefore, it is possible that **Ephraim
        Carlton**[7] married. I believe that

Erahaman, who shows on the [1850 VTFC] is actually **Ephraim**[7] or a son who died young. No other record can be found concerning **Erahaman.**

Children of **Rueben**[7] Greeley Severance and Anna Smith [Greeley p199]
    v   **Diantha Smith**[7] b 11-12-1820 m Caleb C. Fuller 11-9-1871

(163) Jacob[6], (Jacob[5], Jacob[4], Ephraim[3], Ephraim[2], John[1]), born in 10-7-1795 [IGI] and died 4-24-1871 in Kingston, NH. [NHVR] He married Jane Abbott 4-7-1819. [NHVR] The 1840-1860 Kingston NH census shows his with Jane. The 1870 Kingston NH census shows him with his wife Esther. Therefore, he may have married a second time.

Children:
	i	**Mary T.**[7] b 1819 d 5-1-1842
364	ii	**Benjamin**[7] b 8-10-1821 married to Patience Seaver.
	iii	**Junia L.**[7] b 1830
	iv	**Emily J.**[7] b 1835 at Kingston, NH m John B. Gilman, son of Nathan S. and Ruth B. Gilman, 8-8-1853 at Lowell, MA. [MAVR]
	v	**George P.**[7] b 11-6-1841 d 5-3-1909 single [NHVR] The [1900 NHFC] shows him as a boarder of Nancy B. Davis. He filed for Pension 6-23-1897 for service E. and A 1 MA Heavy Artillery from NH. [CWPR] [MGC]

(164) Jonathan Addison[6], (Jacob[5], Jacob[4], Ephraim[3], Ephraim[2], John[1]), born 11-25-1800 and died 10-22-1888 in Kingston, NH. He married Hannah Jane Judkins, [Judkins p24] daughter of Joel Judkins and Nancy Dudley, 7-23-1828. [NHVR] Hannah died on 11-6-1895 [NHVR] They are indicated on the [1840 Kingston, NHFC].

They are buried in the Plains Cemetery, Kingston, NH as **Benjamin,** Co. A 9th NH., Inf., Hannah J., wife of **Jonathan**[6] b 5-31-1809 d 11-6-1895. **Flora A.**[7] daughter, d 9-28-1857 ae 25-5, Doct. **Addison J.**[7] d 6-17-1864 ae 29-11-5. [CRPCNH]

Children:
	i	**Flora A.**[7] b 1832 d 9-28-1857
	ii	**Jonathan Addison**[7] b 7-2-1834 [IGI] Jonathan m to Rooxby Spafford, daughter of James and Martha Spofford. They had a

son, **Ralph**[8], born 4-19-1863 at Kingston, NH. However, **Jonathan**[7] d 6-17-1864 at the young age of 29-11-5 years. The 1870 NH census shows Rooxby and **Ralph**[8] living with her mother, Martha J. Spofford. Rooxby remarried to Orin F. Spofford, son of Henry and Hannah Spofford, on 8-24-1880. Ralph[8] d 5-11-1887 at North Andover, MA, age 23-11-30, from accidental drowning. [MAVR] **Jonathan**[7] is buried in Plains Cemetery. [CRPCNH]

  iii   **Bradley**[7] b 1835 d young [1860 NHFC]
  iv   **Hannah F.**[7] b 1837 [1870 NHFC]

(166) Martin[6], (Jacob[5], Jacob[4], Ephraim[3], Ephraim[2], John[1]), born 9-3-1807 in Union, ME died 9-5-1864 in Lowell, MA. [MAVR] He married to Elizabeth _____, who was born circa 1812 in NY. [1850 MAFC] The same census shows **Martin's**[6] mother, Mary, born 1768 in NH, living with them.

Children: [1850 MAFC]
  i   **William**[7] b 1843
  ii   **Mary Sophia**[7] b 7-12-1844 at Uxbridge [MAVR]
  iii **Sarah R.**[7] b 5-28-1847 at Uxbridge, MA d 3-12-1885, single, at Lowell, MA, at the age of 37-9-17. [MAVR]

(167) Daniel Jr.[6], (Daniel[5], Ephraim[4], Ebenezer[3], Ephraim[2], John[1]), was born in Washington, NH about 1780. [HWNH p597] He married **Abigail**[6] Severance, daughter of **Rufus**[5] Severance, [HWNH p602] on 8-23-1815. [IGI] It was reported that they settled in Allegheny Co NY. The 1830 NY census shows **Daniel**[6] living at Friendship, Allegheny County. The [1840 NYFC] shows him living at Wirts, NY.

Children:
     i   **Emily**[7] b 1820
     ii   **Mary**[7]
     iii **John**[7] b 1827
366 iv   **Samuel**[7] **S.J.** b 1831, the [1880 NYFC] shows him living in Allegheny Co. with a wife, Catherine, and several children.

(168) Benjamin[6], (Daniel[5], Ephraim[4], Ebenezer[3], Ephraim[2], John[1]), born in Washington, NH in 1782. He married Betsey Dodge of Andover, VT, 8-19-1805. She was born 5-17-1784 d 7-27-1858, age 74 years, [HWNH p597] the daughter of Joseph Dodge and Molly Ritter of Hancock, Hillsboro Co. NH. They are indicated on the 1810-1820 Washington, NH census. They lived in Washington for several years and then settled in Claremont, NH. [1840 NHFC Claremont] **Benjamin**[6] died on 9-29-1825. Betsey died 7-27- 1858. [HOS p11]

Children: born in Washington, NH [HWNH p597-598]

367   i   **Charles**[7] b 12-21-1805 settled in MI. He m Martha Lamb 7-15-1830. First moved to Geneva, NY in 1830 and then to Walled Lake, MI.

     ii   **Betsey**[7] b 1808 d 2-7-1863

368   iii   **Ezra**[7] b 6-24-1809 d 1-10-1879 settled near Plymouth, MI m Susan Lamb

     iv   **Joseph**[7] b 7-4-1810 d 2-18-1848 Enfield, NH

370   v   **Daniel**[7] b 2-16-1812 d 2-18-1848 m Martha Bradly

371   vi   **Nathan**[7] b 1813 d 4-21-1839 m Ruhamah Smith

372   vii   **Benjamin**[7] b 7-1-1814 d 1886 m Lois F. Osgood 10-15-1835 d 1886 in Claremont, NH.

373   viii   **Loammi**[7] b 9-20-1815 m Nancy Burnap 1-16-1837 settled in Claremont, NH., where he d about 1887.

     ix   **Lucinda**[7] b 2-6-1817 m William Redfield

     x   **Mary Jane**[7] b 4-10-1818 in Clarmont, NH m John Milton 3-19-1840 [Shurtleff p397] Mary Elizabeth Milton b in Claremont, NH, daughter of **Mary Jane**[7] Severance and John Milton, m Samuel Smith Shurtleff.

374   xi   **Lewis**[7] b 3-25-1822 m Almeda Nancy Green 10-9-1846

(170) Jeremiah[6]**/(Micha-Michael**[6]**)** (Daniel[5], Ephraim[4], Ebenezer[3], Ephraim[2], John[1]), born in Washington, NH circa 1788 and probably settled in the British Provinces. [HWNH p598]

   Jeremiah[6] Severance was born in Ipswich, MA 6-27-1788 d in Salmon River, Cape Breton. He married Ruth Holmes in 1810, who was born in Hartland, VT 7-30-1791. She died in Salmon River, Cape Breton N.S. 2-13-1838. [Shurtlett p172-173]

Children: The last four children were born in Salmon River, Cape Breton

     i   **Clorinda**[7] b 8-19-1811 in Cow Bay, Cape

Breton d unm in Fourchu, Cape Breton 10-30-1897

375 ii **William Daniel**[7] (note name, same as **Jeremiah's**[6] father) b 12-3-1812 in Cow Bay, m Hannah Murrant 1-16-1836 at Mira, Cape Breton, N.S. Canada

iii **Arnold**[7] (note name, same as her fathers name) b 2-13-1814 d unm. in Fourchu 7-29-1884

iv **Esther**[7] b 4-6-1817

376 v **Michael Benjamin**[7] b 11-15-1818 (note name Michael, same as fathers which is in the order of English tradition)

vi **Anna Jane**[7] b 3-29-1822

(172) Abijah[6], (Daniel[5], Ephraim[4], Ebenezer[3], Ephraim[2] John[1]), born in Washington, NH on 6-15-1793. [IGI][HWNH p598] he died 11-1-1865 in E. Bridgewater, Plymouth Co., MA, burial in Union Cemetery. He married Hannah L. Searles, daughter of Samuel Searles and Hannah Butterfield, of Townsend, MA, 4-27-1819 at Townsend. [MAVR] She was born 10-20-1788 and died 4-10-1875 at Brockton, MA. [MAVR] The 1820 NH census shows him living at Lempster. In 1830 and 1840 they were living in Claremont, Sullivan County. [NHFC] **Abijah**[6] was in the war of 1812 and was stationed at Portsmouth, NH, in Capt. Gregg's Co., enlisted 9-27-1814 for 60 days. He resided mostly in Lempster but later he lived in Claremont, NH, Newport, RI, and East Bridgewater, MA. The 1860 MA census shows him in East Bridgewater, Plymouth Co. He died at East Bridgewater, MA on 11-1-1865. [MAVR]

Children: [HWNH p598]

377 i **George**[7] b 2-12-1820 Lempster, NH, settled in VT as a clergyman. He m Huldah Julian Stone

ii **Mary A.**[7] b 8-3-1821 d 10-14-1884 Lempster, NH, m James T. Reed, son of Isaac and Sarah Reed, 10-25-1854 at East Bridgewater, MA. [MAVR]

378 iii **Walter Searles**[7] b 11-24-1822 m Sarah Forrest Mitchell in Lempster, NH

379 iv **James F.**[7] b 4-7-1827 in Lempster, NH d 3-27-1882 in Brockton, MA. He was a widower and a harness maker. [MAVR]

v **Sarah B.**[7] b 1835 Claremont, NH d 3-30-1869 in Bridgewater, MA, m Herman Hewitt, son of Joseph and Sarah Hewitt, on 5-24-1864. [MAVR]

(174) Ebenezer Jr.[6], (Ebenezer[5], Ephraim[4], Ebenezer[3], Ephraim[2], John[1]), born 11-8-1777 in Temple, Hillsboro Co. NH. (NHVR) He died 1-15-1826 aged 50 years at Colchester, VT. [VTVR]

In his early life he was in Weatherford, Hartford Co. CT. He married Jerusha Kilby (Kilbourne) in Hartford, CT on 5-12-1805. [IGI] She born in 1776 and died 8-15-1851 at Colchester, VT, age 75 years. [VTVR] She shows on the 1830 VT census in Colchester as head of the household. Their first son, **Samuel[7]**, was born in Hartford, CT [VTVR]. They undoubtedly had other children.

Ebenezer's father died in Reading, VT. The marriages of sons, **Samuel[7]**, **George[7]**, and **John[7]**, as sons of **Ebenezer[6]** and Jerusha are indicated on the [VTVR]. In 1850 Jerusha was living with **Samuel[7]**, she being 58 years old. [VTFC]

It is possible that **Ebenezer[6]** also had additional sons, **Gersham[7]** and **Nickerson[7]**. The Colchester, VT Town Records show **Nickerson[7]** along with **Ebenezer[6]** and **Gersham[7]**. The widow of this **Ebenezer[6]** shows in 1826 which would indicate that it is most likely Jerusha. **Nickerson[7]** died shortly before 1819. The Probate Records for Colchester, VT show that Hannah Severance, **Ebenezer[6]** Severance, **Joseph** Severance and Luther Brigham relinquish their right to administration for the estate of **Nickerson[7]** Severance, late of Colchester, Chittenden Co. [PRVT 10-1-1819]

Children:
	i	**Samuel[7]** b circa 1805 in Hartford, CT d 10-20-1876 (74 years), lived in Colchester, VT. The 1850 VT census shows **Samuel[7]** living with his mother, Jershua, in VT. She was 58 years old. It is possible that this is the same **Samuel[7]** showing on the 1860 VT census in which **Samuel[7]** was in the Poor House at age 60 years.
	ii	**Jane[7]**
	iii	**Mary[7]** (Polly)
380	iv	**John[7]** b 1813 d 6-11-1888 (75-2-2-) lived in Colchester, VT
381	v	**George[7]** b 1-10-1817 at Colchester, VT
	vi	**Angeline[7]**
	vii	**Nixon/Nickerson[7]** ?

(175) Samuel⁶, (Ebenezer⁵, Ephraim⁴, Ebenezer³, Ephraim², John¹), born 11-26-1780 at Temple, NH. [NHVR] His son's death record says that **Samuel⁶** was born in Groton, MA. He married Sussan Warren, daughter of Zenas Warren and Susanna Weston, 10-29-1807 [VTVR] [MWLS] They lived in Essex, NY. Susanna Warren was born 10-25-1785 and died at Essex, NY 7-14-1861 at Lewis. **Samuel⁶** died on 4-29-1842 at Lewis, NY.

Samuel⁶ and Susannah lived on the Connecticut River just south of White River Junction in VT. They later settled in the town of Essex, New York where he engaged in agriculture, owning a large and valuable farm. Samuel was gifted with great musical talent, and during the winter seasons taught singing school. [LCCEC]

The first three children were born at Windsor, VT and the others were born in Essex, Essex County, NY. **Samuel⁶** is listed on the 1820-1830 Essex, Essex Co NY census. The 1840 NY census shows him living at Lewis.

Children:

	i	**Lucy M.⁷** b 9-4-1808 m Jason North 9-22-1832
	ii	**Minerva B.⁷** b 1-12-1810 m William Frederick Sherman 6-3-1830
384	iii	**Levi A. Warren⁷** b 9-18-1811 m Catherine Ann Dods of Montgomery Co., NY 8-7-1838
	iv	**Melissa⁷** b 4-25-1814
385	v	**Benjamin W.⁷** b 9-26-1816 [MAVR death record says that he was b in Hillsboro, NH] m Lucy Allen
	vi	**Susan W.⁷** b 9-18-1818
386	vii	**Cyrus⁷** b 1-27-1822 d 7-9-1908
387	viii	**Lucius Warren⁷** b 12-30-1824 (settled in WI)
388	ix	**William⁷** b 10-19-1827 at Essex, NY

(176) Levi⁶, (Ebenezer⁵, Ephraim⁴, Ebenezer³, Ephraim², John¹), born in 1792 in VT. [DAR records for **Ebenezer⁵**] It appears that **Levi⁶**, married to Hannah Bird in 1817. She was born in Dorchester, MA. [Virkus]

He apparently moved to Pittsburgh in 1825 after learning the trade of blacksmith and nail maker in Vermont. After making his way over mountains and trecherous trails he settled where he invented and perfected the first spike and rivet-making machine and patented it. He used this machine in his first buisness in 1832. There was such a demand for the spikes that he soon built others. **Levi**[6] became ill during an epidemic of Asiatic cholera in 1854, which proved fatal for him. [HACoPA]

Children: there may have been more than one son
389   i   **Samuel Bird**[7] b 1831 d 1900 mfr, Pittsburgh. He m first, 1856 Eliza T. Miller (1833-1867). He m secondly, 1869 to Arabella Nelson Miller [Virkus]

(177) Stephen[6], (Ebenezer[5], Ephraim[4], Ebenezer[3], Ephraim[2], John[1]), born circa 1795 near Windsor, VT. **Stephen**[6] Severance and Harriet Nason were married first 12-18-1823 [VTVR] **Stephen**[6] married second to Sarah Mason 10-16-1849 [VTVR] The 1810 VT census for Sheldon, Franklin Co shows a **Stephen**[6]. In 1830 he was living at Cavendish, Windsor Co, and in 1840 he was living at Windsor, VT. If this is the same **Stephen**[6] and it appears that it is, then he would have been born before 1790. The Reading, VT records show **Stephen**[6] Severance appointed for highway supervision circa 1823.

Children:
    i   **Julia Eliza**[7] b 10-6-1824 at Windsor, VT d 5-23-1901 at Bridgewater, VT, m 3-14-1841 to Arnold Drake Stowell, who was b 9-9-1918 d 9-27-1852. She m 2nd at West Windsor, VT., 3-27-1853, Gaylon Davis who d 6-3-1878. [Stowell]
390   ii   **Stephen**[7] b circa 1827 in VT. [1860 NYFC] m Mary Jane Johnson 7-16-1857 [VTVR] She was b 1834. [1860 NYFC] **Stephen**[7] was a blacksmith. The VTVR shows Mary Jane Johnson, (age 29 b 1834) daughter of Elisha Johnson m to John Glassier on 12-12-1863. It was her third marriage. Therefore **Stephen**[7] may have died young.
  iii   **Sarah**[7] b circa 1834, she was living with **Stephen**[7] in 1850. [1850 NHFC]
  iv   **John L.**[7] b 4- -1846 at Windsor, VT (son of **Stephen**[6] and Harriet Severance, m Mary A. Dwinell, daughter of Jerome and Mary Dwinell, 3-7-1870 at Harvard, MA. [MAVR] She was b 3- -1850 [1880/1900 MAFC] They had at least one daughter, **Lillie M.**[8] b 3- -1871 at Lowell, MA. [1900 MAFC]

(178) Isaac⁶, (Ebenezer⁵, Ephraim⁴, Ebenezer³, Ephraim², John¹), born circa 1798 in Reading, VT. [DAR] This is most likely the uncle **Isaac⁶** which **Samuel⁸** Severance refers to in his account of his family. **Isaac⁶** would therefore be the son of **Ebenezer⁶** Severance and Lucy Nutter. The 1830 VT census shows him living in Reading, VT. **Isaac⁶** married Lucia Biglow, daughter of Elisha Bigelow and Rhoda Goddard of Colchester, CT, and Reading, Windsor Co VT, on 3-30-1823. [VTVR]

Isaac⁶ settled in Eagle, WI in the spring of 1838, where they lived on a farm. They later lived in Waukesha, WI where **Isaac⁶** died 1877 aged 80 years and Lucia died 12-11-1879 at the age of 77 years. [Howe p284]

Children: [Will and Testament of **Isaac⁷**, 10-18-1880 Waukesha Co. WI]
391   i   **Anson Biglow⁷** b 12-28-1823 m Mary Malcouson 6-24-1848
     ii   **Irvin J.⁷** b 1826 in VT m Mary Jane Vanderberg 12-9-1849 shows on the [1860 Steven's Point, Portage Co WIFC] with a daughter **Lillian E.⁸** b 1851 in WI
392   iv   **Collamer⁷** b 5-9-1829 Reading, VT d 10-11-1906 Milwaukee, WI
     iii   **Lucia Marion⁷** b circa 1836 in VT., only daughter in **Isaac's⁷** Will

(179) Ephraim⁶, (Abel⁵, Ephraim⁴, Ebenezer³, Ephraim², John¹), born 7-8-1785 in Bradford, ME. [IGI] He could have been born in Washington, NH. [MBGD] He sold his farm to James Ayer circa 1814. [HWNH p604] He later moved to and lived in Dexter, ME. He married Jamima Seeley in 1808. She was born on 2-10-1790 and died on 1-8-1866. The family is buried in Milo, ME. [MgBH Vol 5] **Ephraim⁶** died in Milo Piscatacuis, ME on 1-10-1870 age 85 years. His name shows on the 1320-1840 ME census for Dexter.

Children: born at Dexter, Penobscot County, ME
     i   **Sophrona⁷** b 3-14-1809 m James Pierce Jewell as his second wife.
     ii   **Martha⁷** b 12-13-1810
     iii   **Anna⁷** b 10-3-1812 d 10-23-1812
393   iv   **Isaac⁷** b 9-16-1813 m to Ann and they had a son **Enoch A.⁸**
     v   **Elijah⁷** b 6-6-1815 (IGI) b to **Ephraim⁶** and Jamima Seeley
     vi   **John⁷** b 4-27-1817 d 5-9-1817

395 vii **George Washington**[7] b 4-13-1818
   viii **Albert**[7] b 9-18-1821 d 3-16-1822
   ix **Jonathan Farrar**[7] b 1-20-1823 m Ruth T. (Long) Sturtevant on 3-22-1846, Penobscot Co. ME, [MEVR] and they had at least two daughters, **Emma**[8] b 1850, and **Eleanor**[8] b 1853
   x **Albion**[7] b 11-16-1825 at Dexter, ME [IGI]
   xi **Nabby Bailey**[7] b 1-10-1827
   xii **Ephraim**[7] b 1828 [MEVR] d 5-23-1914 ae 86-7 m Susan T. Bumps b 4- -1828. [1900 MEFC] The 1870 Milo, ME census shows them with two children, **George**[8] b 1861, and **Ardella**[8] b 1863 in ME.

(180) John[6], (Abel[5], Ephraim[4], Ebenezer[3], Ephraim[2], John[1]), born on 6-3-1797 in Washington, NH. [IGI] He married Maria Cheney, daughter of Samuel Cheney, on 10-4-1818. [IGI] they lived in Washington, NH. They are indicated on the 1870 NH census. She died in Tilton, NH on 8-3-1883. [NHVR] He died on June 5, 1883 in Tilton, NH Portsmouth, NH, where he was stationed duting the war of 1812. [HWNH p604-605]

Children:
   i **Mary A.**[7] b 1-22-1820 m Augustus Barnes in 1841. **Mary**[7] d 1867 in Tilton, NH. [HWNH p604]
   ii **John Jr.**[7] b 2-18-1822. **John**[7] d at Bradford, NH 7-28-1850. He m to Sarah Ann Goodale, [Williams] daughter of Levi Goodale and Mary Howlett, in 1844. Sarah Ann was b 12-21-1826 d 7-9-1889. [Williams] They had two children, **Mary M.**[8] b 1836 m William Colby and **Hannah J.**[8] b 1848. After **John Jr.**[7] died. Sarah Ann remarried to Charles P. Pike. There were three (Pike) children by her second marriage.

(181) Rufus[6], (Rufus[5], Ephraim[4], Ebenezer[3], Ephraim[2], John[1]), born in Washington, NH on 11-29-1788. [IGI] He married Lydia Crane, daughter of Joseph Crane and Deliverance Mills, on 3-22-1812. Lydia was born 6-8-1788. Except for a few years spent in Lempster, he lived in Washington, NH, where he died on 4-22-1851, age 63 years. The 1820-1840 NH census shows them living at Washington. Lydia was living with Hezekiah at Washington, NH in 1860. Lydia died 1-6-1877 in Washington, NH. [NHVR Washington]

Children: [HWNH p599-600]
   i   **Phidelia**[7] b 10-1-1812 m Moses H. Chase
         m2 Ebenezer M. Smith 2-8-1850
396 ii   **Joseph Crane**[7] b 5-9-1815 at Lempster, NH
         m Eliza J. Buswell
397 iii **Hezekiah M.**[7] b 10-5-1817 at Lempster, NH
         m Sarah J. Marshall 11- -1842
   iv   **Maria P.**[7] b 5-9-1823 m Daniel F. Carey
         7- -1844 m2 Moses H. Chase 2-17-1849

(182) Joseph[6], (Rufus Jr.[5], Ephraim[4], Ebenezer[3], Ephraim[2], John[1]), born in Washington, NH on 9-19-1790. [IGI] He married Mary Davis, daughter of Ephraim Davis and Sarah Farnsworth, on 8-22-1813 [IGI] who was born in 1788. He lived in Lempster and Washington but mostly in Washington, NH where he died on 3-11-1858. The 1830-1840 NH census shows him living in Washington. Mary d 9-13-1857. [HWNH p600-601] **Joseph**[6] died 3-11-1858 age 68 years. [GRWNH]

Children: [Nye p427]
   i   **Ephraim**[7] b 12-9-1813 in Washington, NH,
         d December 1839
   ii   **Sarah D.**[7] b 7-3-1815 d 1865 in
         Washington, NH m Nathaniel Friend Jr.
398 iii **William D.**[7] b 9-25-1816 in Washington,
         NH
   iv   **Rosina**[7] b 1818 d in infancy
399 v   **Joel**[7] b 4-13-1820 at Lempster, NH
   vi   **Lucy**[7] b 3-4-1823 d 2-4-1854 m Abel Davis
         9-18-1783 Lempster, NH, who was b 3-25-
         1820
400 vii **Joseph W.**[7] b 8-12-1825 m Adaline Putney

(183) Ephraim[6], (Rufus[5], Ephraim[4], Ebenezer[3], Ephraim[2], John[1]), born in Washington, NH on 4-19-1792. **Ephraim**[6] first married Mary A. Rollins of Hillsborough, NH on 5-24-1818 at Hillsboro, NH. The 1820 NH census shows them living in Washington. The 1830-1840 NH census shows them living in Dexter. They later resided in Hillsborough and Stockbridge, VT. His wife died in Hillsborough on 4-15-1854 at the age of 56 years. **Ephraim**[6] remarried to Martha Eastman, daughter of Jonathan Eastman and Mehitable Dole on 11-28-1854. She was born circa 1809 at Henniker, Merrimack County, NH and died 4-24-1888. He died in Hillsborough, NH on 7-24-1862. [MBGD]

Children: [HWNH p602]

    i   **Hiram J.**[7] b 8-1-1818 d 8-12-1848 in Hillsborough

    ii   **Lucinda J.**[7] b 11-7-1819 m Timothy W. Chase, Hopkinton, NH on 4-20-1848

401 iii   **Jonathan**[7] b 5-6-1824 m Harriet B. Copps on 11-27-1849 m2 Issa T. Davis 12-23-1886

    iv   **Holland**[7] b 5-1-1826 in Stockbridge, m Margaret Putnam of Hopkinton, **Holland**[7] d 10-12-1854 in Hillsborough, NH. It is unknown if they had a family.

    v   **Benjamin**[7] b 11-7-1827 in Stockbridge, VT d 9-6-1853 in Hillsborough, NH.

    vi   **Elzina**[7] b 2-7-1833 d 10-16-1852

    vii   **Lucy Anne**[7] b 5-14-1842 m Charles P. Wilder of Sterling, MA on 6-12-1863

(184) Joel[6], (Rufus[5], Ephraim[4], Ebenezer[3], Ephraim[2], John[1]), born on 4-15-1798 in Washington, NH. [IGI] He married Mrs. Jane (Weeks) Woodward, widow of Benjamin Woodward on 5-13-1828. (IGI) They lived in Washington, NH. [NHFC]. Jane Weeks died in 1872 and **Joel**[6] remarried to Jane Edes. **Joel**[6] died 1-20-1892 at the age of 93 years, 9 months. [NHVR]

Children: [HWNH p603]
    i   **Nancy J.**[7] b 2-8-1830 m Elbridge G. Benton 1-1-1856

    ii   **Diana H.**[7] b 8-12-1832 d 12-10-1879 m Alfred A. Tandy in 1853. They were living with her parents on the [1870 Washington, NHFC]

    iii   **George S.**[7] b 6-26-1834 in Washington, lived there until 1879 when he went to Unity and lived there (the [NHVR] says that the mother of George S. was Jane Edes). He m Ester E. Cram, daughter of Joseph Cram of Unity, 8-18-1860. They settled in Washington until 1870 and then in Unity. He was a farmer and had much experience in teaching being superintendant of schools in Washington and Unity. [HWNH p603] The 1900 NH census indicates that **George**[7] and Esther might have been a daughter **Minnie B.**[8] Severance, b 1- -1869 who m Samuel F. Reynolds. He died 11-8-1913 from an accidental fall from a scaffold, spinal damage after 6 days. [NHVR] She was born on 1-17-1834 and died 5-3-1901 age

(185) Abijah⁶, (Rufus⁵, Ephraim⁴, Ebenezer³, Ephraim², John¹), born in Washington, NH on 4-15-1798. [IGI] **Abijah⁶** was born on 11-1-1803 at Washington, NH. He died 3-30-1875. [GRWNH] He lived in Rutland, VT for one period of time and resided in Clarendon, VT. The 1830 VT census shows him living in Reading, Windsor Co. He m to Polly Spofford, daughter of Eliphalet Spofford and Sally Russell of Clarendon, VT. Polly was born 2-19-1807, died 9-15-1864. [VTVR], leaving sons **Alfred⁷** and **Rufus⁷** in Northfield, MN. [Spofford p130] The family shows on the 1860 Clarendon, Rutland, and Shrewsbury, VT census.

Children: [Hemenway]
403 i   **John Russell⁷** b on 4-9-1836 at Clarendon, VT and d at Pensacola, FL on 10-30-1908.
    ii   **Edward (Alfred)⁷** b 1836
    iii   **Rufus⁷** b 10- -1840 at Bridgewater, VT. He shows on the [1900 MNFC] living alone.
    iv   **Sally (Josephine)⁷** b 1840
    v   **Life A.⁷** b 1842 d 8-22-1862 of typhoid fever at Look-out Point, MD in the Civil War. Pension filed by father, **Abijah⁶**, for **Life A.⁷** 6-14-1868 for service F6 VT Inf. [CWPR]

(186) Asa⁶, (Rufus⁵, Ephraim⁴, Ebenezer³, Ephraim², John¹), born on 2-3- 1810 in Washington, NH [IGI], died 5-23-1885 age 75-3-20 at Townsend, MA. [MAVR] He married Sarah C. Bean on 4-2- 1843 in Charlestown, MA. [MAVR] Sarah was born circa 1821 in Canada and died in 1907. They settled in Townsend, MA. **Asa⁶** was a brewer.

Children: [1850 Townsend, MAFC]
    i   **Sarah Melvina⁷** b 12-6-1844 at Charlestown, MA. She m Adam S. Graham, son of Samuel Graham and Aseneth G. Adams, on 9-2-1862 at Townsend, MA. [MAVR]
    ii   **Julia H.⁷** (daughter of Asa and Sarah of Townsend) m Charles E. Case, son of John and Ann Case, 5-18-1867 at Melrose, MA. [MAVR]
405 iii   **George A.⁷** b 7-18-1848 [MAVR]

iv   **Hannah**[7] b 1847

v   **Nettie Jane**[7] b 2-16-1851 m Franklin Fowler, son of Adolphus Fowler and Lucinda Wadsworth, 7-21-1886 at Townsend, MA. [MAVR]

vi   **Abbie A.**[7] b 1856 m Vernal Barker, son of Elisha and Sarah Dix Barker, 9-8-1886 at Marlboro, MA. [MAVR] He (1840-1918) was a Priv. Co H, 4th Regt. Mass., Heavy Artillary. [Townsend MAVR]

vii   **Ella F.**[7] b 6-21-1858 at Townsend, MA [MAVR] d 1933 m Alvah J. Greenleaf (b 1860 d 1936), son of Thomas S. Greenleaf and Julia A. Collins. They were m at Townsend, MA

viii   **Lefy**[7] (female) b 6-15-1860 at Townsend, MA [MAVR]

ix   **Effie A.**[7] b 1861 m George A. Clark, son of Eben and Jennie A. Clark, on 11-15-1881 at Townsend, MA. [MAVR]

(186a) Christopher[6], (unconnected, Ephraim[4], Ebenezer[3], Ephraim[2], John[1]), b circa 1800. Although there is no factual evidence, I am putting **Christopher**[6] Severance as a close relative of **Ephraim**[5] Severance and Ruth Gould, because of the similarity of time and place. It is possible that this **Christopher**[6] was named after Ruth's father, Christopher Gould.

It is interesting to note the name **Ivory**[7] which would tend to place him in the same family as **Ivory**[7] of **Ephraim**[6] and Eliza Merriam.

Although the vital records show that he was the son of **Christopher**[5] and Susan, it appears more likely that this was a mistake and it should have said that he was the son of **Christopher**[5] and Nancy or the husband of Susan.

A **Christopher**[6] Severance shows on the 1860 Pattagumpus, ME census with his wife, Susan J. Crocker age 30 years. With them were children, **Alfred**[7] b 1851; **Henry A**[7]. b 1853; **Charles W.**[7] b 1856; **Loretta**[7] b 1859.

The 1870 Penobscot Co ME census shows **Christopher**[6], Susan, and their children, **Elly H.**[7] b 1851, **Henry A.**[7] b 1853, **Charles W.**[7] b 1856, **Laura E.**[7] b 1859, **Ivory E.**[7] b 1862, **Nellie A.**[7] b 1866, and **John Ellis**[7] b 2-14-1874. [MEVR]

Children of **Christopher**[6] and (Nancy Crocker)

i   **Christopher**[7] b 11-21-1829 [MEVR] m Susan

Crocker, who was b 1829 in ME died at age 66-4-23, (son of **Christopher**[6] and Susan Crocker)[MEVR]. He was therefore born 11-21-1829. **Christopher**[6] d 2-29-1895. [MEVR] They lived in Medway, Enfield, Winslow, and Greenbush, Penobscot, ME. The 1860 Maine census shows them with children, **Alfred**[7], **Henry**[7], **Charles**[7], and **Loretta**[7]. additional children were **Ivory**[7], **Nellie**[7], and **John E**[7].

(187) Jacob[6], (Ephraim[5] or Nathaniel[5], Ephraim[4], Ebenezer[3], Ephraim[2], John[1]), was born 10- -1789 [CRME] probably at Sanbornton, NH, he died 8-25-1859 age 70 at Knox, ME. [MEVR] [Robinson p328] The marriage intentions to Susanna Haskell were given on 8-9-1813 at Knox, ME. Susanna was born 7-27-1795, daughter of John Haskell and Mary Paine. She died on 4-8-1869 at Knox, ME. age 73-6-11. [Gray p130]

Middlesex County and Its People [Conklin], states that **Jacob**[6] Severance, great-grandfather of **George Oscar**[9] Severance, was a soldier in the Revolutionary War. This can not be true since **Jacob**[6] was born in October of 1789, after the war. His great great grandfather, **Ephraim**[5] did serve in the Revolutionary War.

Jacob's[6] name appears on the 1820-1840 ME census for Knox, ME. He certified to the death of **Ephraim**[5] and the continued widowhood of Ruth Severance. [DARLR]

Children: [MEFC and CRME]
	i	**Clementine**[7] b 1814 d 9-5-1819 [CRME] It appears that this child died from burns recieved when her cloths caught on fire. The daughter of **Jacob**[6] Severance of Knox, Maine. [Vital Records of Maine Newspapers 1785-1820 Vol 1 & 2, _Bangor Gazette_] died by fire, [_Bangor Weekly Register_][_Easter Argus_], cloths fire 9-16-1819 from burns in Knox, ME. [_American Advocate_]
408	ii	**James**[7] b 8-11-1815 at Knox, ME d 1-11-1892
	iii	**Susan**[7] b 1818 d 6-17-1837 [CRME]
	iv	**Clementine**[7] b 1822 d 9-25-1824 [CRME]
	v	**Mary S.**[7], b circa 1825 at Knox, ME, shown on the [1850/60/70 MEFC] as

```
                the wife of Nathan Hills
409  vi    Jacob Jr.⁷ b 1827/1830 at Knox, ME and d
           at Oka, MT on 3-1-1892.
410  v     Frederick⁷ b 1832 listed of Co. I 15 ME
           Inf [CWPR]
411  vi    Thomas Benton⁷ b 1835 m Lucinda
           Clements. They had a daughter, Edith⁸
           who d 12-1-1876 at Milton, MA at the age
           of 7 months. [MAVR] This is not the same
           Thomas B.⁷ b to Jesse⁶ Severance of
           Newport, ME.
     vii   Joseph⁷ b circa 1836 at Knox, ME, shown
           living with his sister Mary S.⁷ Hills on
           the [1860 MEFC]
     viii  Daniel⁷ b 1838
412  ix    William⁷ b 1840 or 1830 m Carrie R.
           Crockett, both of Rockland, ME, 11-22-
           1880. Carrie d at Rockland 10-3-1884
           aged 34-1-10, daughter of Asa Crockett
           and Elvira Robbins. [MEVR]
```

(188) Benjamin⁶, (Ephraim⁵, Ephraim⁴, Ebenezer³, Ephraim², John¹), born circa 1792 in Sanbornton, NH and died circa 1861 in Belmont, ME. He married Lydia Sanborn, who was born 3-23-1797, daughter of Peter Sanborn and Olive Thompson of Windsor, ME, on 11-19-1818. [Runnels Vol 2 p644] Olive was the daughter of William Thompson. Peter and Olive lived on the Joshua Lane place in Sanbornton, NH and afterwards removed to the vicinity of Bangor, ME.

Benjamin⁶ and Lydia moved to Windsor and then Belmont after their marriage where they settled and raised their family. The 1830-1840 and 1860 ME census shows him living in Windsor.

A land contract with **Ephraim⁵** links the two together. The property purchased from **Ephraim⁵** being in the Plantation of Knox and County of Hancock, ME was signed by **Ephraim⁵** Severance and sold to **Benjamin⁶** Severance, dated 4-15-1814. The other property purchased from Ezra Woodman to **Benjamin⁶** was originally of Benjamin Smith who sold that part to Ezra Woodman. The document is signed by **Ephraim⁵**, **Benjamin⁶** and Lydia (his wife) Severance, dated 5-21-1824. [LRME Hancock County]

The 1860 Windsor, ME census shows **Benjamin⁶** and Lydia living with some of their children, **Haskett⁷** and his wife Ann L., (and their children, **William F.⁸**, born 1851, **Frank⁸** b 1843 and **Mary E.⁸**,) and other children of **Benjamin⁶** and Lydia, **Deborah⁷**, **James A.⁷**, **Elizabeth⁷**, and **Emeline⁷**.

Children of **Benjamin**[6] Severance and Lydia Sanborn [Machias] The 1820 ME census shows **Benjamin**[6] with 2 males under the age of 16.

413 i   **Hasketta (Haskell)**[7] b 1820 Windsor, ME m Ann R. Clapp 6-6-1852 [IGI] He d in Mendocina, CA.

      ii   **Sophia M.**[7]

      iii **Lydia M.**[7]

      iv **Debora**[7] b 1831 Belmont, ME, d 1-9-1907 Augusta, ME, age 76 (daughter of **Benjamin**[7] Severance and Lydia Sanborn. [MEVR]

414 v   **Benjamin Jr.**[7] b 1832 m Augustus ____

415 vi **Franklin Sanborn**[7] b 8-12-1833 d 1-15-1884 Windsor, ME m Vandalia A. Clark 4-4-1866 [MEVR]

      vii **James D.**[7] b 1836. It is believed that he lived in CA with his brother. Little River, CA cemetery shows **James D.**[7] d 1883 buried with Mary Ella who d 1872 and **James'**[7] brother, **Haskett**[7] who d 1888 and his wife Ann R. Clapp d 1892.

      viii **Elizabeth C.**[7] b 1838

      ix   **Emeline L.**[7] b 1841

(189) Ephraim[6] *Sufferance*, (Ephraim[5], Ephraim[4], Ebenezer[3], Ephraim[2], John[1]), born 9-10-1802 in Sanbornton, NH. [NHVR] He married Eliza Merriam, [Easton Vol II p687-688] daughter of Matthew Thatcher Merriam and Abigail Smith, in 1826. Abigail Smith was the daughter of Benjamin Sr. and Elsie (Woodman) Smith of Sanbornton, NH. [Robinson p247] In early manhood went to Waldo County, ME. This area was later incorporated as the town of Morrill, ME. He died 3-21-1857. Keep in mind that **Nathaniel/Ephraim**[6] was living on the Woodman farm in Sanbornton, NH before moving to ME.

    Ephraim[6] and Eliza lived in Bangor, ME for a few years before moving to WI. Their children were born in ME. In 1850, **Ivory**[7] Severance, age 16 born 1834 in ME, was living with this family. He was not believed to be a son but perhaps a relative.

    Ephraim[6] died 12-9-1875 age 72 years 3 months, in Trimbelle, WI and is buried in Thurston Hill Cemetery, Pierce County, WI. [NSRFJ Monday 12-13-1875] Eliza Merriam, wife of **Ephraim**[6], died on 5-23-1888 aged 81 years and 9 months. She is buried in the Samuel Judkins Cemetery Lot, in Woodside Cemetery in Androscoggin County, Belgrade, ME. [CRME] Apparently Eliza returned to live with her daughter in ME after **Ephraim**[6] died in WI.

"In the year 1865, **Ephraim**[6] Severance, a native of Sanborntown, NH, but then residing at Bangor, ME, removed to Pierce County, WI and purchased a farm in the town of Trimbelle on what has been known as the Thurston Hill. He began the task of opening a farm in the dense forest. While in ME he had engaged in the lumbering business and was accustomed to the hard labor. He was a Republican and a consistent member in the Free Baptist Church." [Easton p687]

This family traveled and lived extensively. While living in ME, they left Belmont to go to Springfield, there they picked up a **Seth**[7] Severance, who shows on the Vital Records as living with them but probably not their son. Their son **Joseph**[7] was born in Old Town, ME, so they must have stopped there, after leaving Belmont, ME. They went further north on 12-16-1836. They stayed in Carroll until about 1849 having 4 children and **Fred A.**[7] was born near Bangor, ME, so they possibly went back to Old Town for awhile before going to Bangor, ME. **Orrin Frank**[7], **Joseph**[7], **Thatcher**[7], and **Daniel**[7] stayed in ME when the others went west to WI. Mrs. **Belle**[7] became Mrs. Judkins of Belgrade, ME, **Clara**[7] m Greenleaf Blethen of Old Foxcroft next to Sebec where **Daniel**[7] went, and **Elizabeth**[7] m a Mr. Hamlin. [MMS] The 1830 ME census shows him in Belmont and the 1840 ME census show him with not Township listed.

Children: [Pope II p118-119]
```
416   i    Thatcher⁷ b 9-10-1827 m Mary E. Berry on
           9-11-1850, d in the Civil War.
417   ii   Daniel⁷ b 6-27-1830 d 2-2-1913 m Laura
           A., settled in Dover, ME.
418   iii  Joseph⁷ b 10-8-1831 m Lydia F. Weston
           (Westers) Moved to N. Yakima, WA.
      iv   Elizabeth⁷ b 1838 m ___ Hamlin
      v    Delphina Arabelle⁷ b 7-11-1841 m Samuel
           Judkins, Lakeside, ME.
      vi   Delvia Clara Bell⁷ b 7-11-1841 m
           Greenlief Blethen on 8-15-1868. He d in
           1929.
419   vii  Franklin Orrin⁷ b 11-16-1844
420   viii Fred A.⁷ b 12-23-1850 m Etiole Chappel
```
There may have been another son named **Frank Edward**[7] (probably died young) The WI history says that they had 14 children. If they did have that many children then they must have died young.

(190) George[6], (Ephraim[5], Ephraim[4], Ebenezer[3], Ephraim[2], John[1]), born in NH in 1800. He later settled at Dexter and Bangor, ME. He married Sarah (Sally) Neal on 6-26-1828. [MEVR] He probably married secondly to Elizabeth Curtis, 1-4-1857 at Bangor, ME [MEVR] which shows on the 1860 ME census living in Dexter or Burlington, ME. **George[6]** was living along with **Ephraim[5]** and Eliza Merriam and some of **Ephraim's[5]** other sons in the same area of ME on the 1850 Bangor, ME census. The 1830 ME census shows him living in Waldo next to **Ephraim[6]** and **Jacob[6]** Severance and the 1840 ME census shows him in Bangor.

Children: [1860 MEFC]
i   **Persis A.[7]** b 1832. She was living with the Benjamin Millett family in Penobscot Co, ME in 1860
ii   **Solinda[7]** b 1837
iii   **Rosetta[7]** b 1841

(191) Artimus[6], (Asa[5], Ebenezer[4], Ebenezer[3], Ephraim[2], John[1]), born 11-18-1791 in VT [IGI] married Caty (Catherine) Winch 10-27-1811. The 1820 NY census shows him living in Richmond, Ontario Co. By 1830, he was living in Candice, Ontario Co, NY. The 1850, Union, Erie Co. PA census shows this family. **Artimus[6]** was 69 yrs and Catherine was 68 yrs, both born in VT.

Children:
421 i   **Artimus Jr.[7]** b 3-5-1830 NY State m Hannah S. Shattuck 2-18-1851.
ii   **Warden[7]** b 1832
iii   **Sarah[7]** b 1836

(192) Ariel Kendrick[6], (Ebenezer[5], Ebenezer[4], Ebenezer[3], Ebenezer[2], John[1]), born 3-5-1815 in Alstead, NH. [IGI] The 1840 NH census shows him living in Alstead. He died on 11-10-1851 in Alstead. He married to Mary Eliza Brown who was b on 12-3-1821 at Walpole, NH and died at Brattleboro, VT on 3-19-1857. [Elliot]

Child:
i   **Eliza K** b 3-24-1844 d 7-27-1854

(192a) John[7], (unconnected) was born 10-11-1800 in New Hampshire. He is first indicated in Kentucky on the 1840 Lincoln Co KY census. He married to

Elizabeth Ham on 10-24-1833. [KYVR] She was born in
1813. John died 10-7-1864 and he is buried at Crab
Orchard Cemetery Baptist Church.

Children: [1850 Lincoln Co KYFC]
422 i   **John**[8] b 1835 m Margaret A. Manuel 12-24-
          1857
423 ii   **William**[8] b 1837 m Mary E. Linsey.
424 iii   **Josiah/Joseph**[8] b b 1840 m Martha F.
          Warren 4-29-1864
    iv   **Daniel**[8] b 1842
    v   **George**[8] b 1844
    vi   **Sally Ann**[8] b 1846 m Perry T. Pollard 9-
          17-1867
    vii   **Samuel**[8] b 1846
    viii   **Ephraim**[8] b 1848
    ix   **Elizabeth**[8] b 1852 m David C. Paine on
          10-6-1870
    x   **Jane**[8] b 1854

(193) Jonathan[6], (Jonathan[5], Jonathan[4], Jonathan[3],
Ephraim[2], John[1]), born on 7-4-1781 in Kingston, NH.
He married Mariam Moyer on 1-10-1804 in Gilmanton
(Belmont), NH. She was born July 1786 and died 10-
21-1867 in Alton, NH. The 1830 NH census shows them
living at Tuftonboro. **Jonathan**[6] died before 1825
and Mariam remarried to William Mallard of
Tuftonboro, NH. By 1830, the family of **Jonathan**[6]
Severance was decimated. William Mallard died in
1833. **Jonathan**[6] probably served in the War of 1812.
[MDW]
    When **Jonathan Jr.**[6] died in 1814 his father
assumed guardianship of his children and according
to [PRNH Strafford Co] received compensation from
the estate for caretaking.

Children: [MDW]
    i   **Abigail**[7] b 1804 m Stephen Rollins 11-11-
          1824. **Abigail**[7] d in 1829. Stephen, son
          of Ichabod Rollins and Sarah Leighton,
          was b in Loudon, NH on 1-22-1804. He m
          2nd to **Mehitable**[7], **Abigail's**[7] sister.
          [Rollins p74]
    ii   **Jonathan**[7] b 1806 d (apparently young)
    iii   **Sally**[7] b before 1808
    iv   **Parker**[7] b circa 1808
    v   **Mehitable**[7] b 7-15-1810 m Stephen
          Rollins, as his second wife, in 1830
    iv   **Polly**[7] circa 1813 d young

(194) Benjamin[6], (Jonathan[5], Jonathan[4], Jonathan[3], Ephraim[2], John[1]), born 7-24-1790 in Gilmanton (Belmont), NH. He settled in Tuftonboro and married first to Elizabeth Burbank on 9-1-1813. She was born 9-13-1791, daughter of Jonathan Burbank and Ruth Gove. [Gove] Elizabeth died 11-24-1825 and **Benjamin[6]** remarried to Betsey Thompson in October of 1826. The 1830 NH census shows him living in Tuftonborough. He married 3rd to Lydia Tate on 11-10-1847. **Benjamin[6]** died in Tuftonboro, NH on 1-13-1866. [MDW]

"**Benjamin[6]** and his wife Elizabeth Burbank and infant son are buried with his parents in the Hersey Cemetery. The Burbanks had come from Rowley to Gilmanton, and then to Tuftonboro, and had, as the Severances, purchased 100 acres of the original Hersey Survey, a large tract of land owned by Woodbury Langdon of Portsmouth. Langdon was a member of the Mason Proprietors who were selling off sections of land to be developed as farmland in the interior of the state.

According to a **Samuel[7]** Severance descendant, **Benjamin's[6]** daughter **Hannah[7]** ran off with an Indian and was never heard of again" [MDW]

Known children of **Benjamin[6]** Severance and Elizabeth Burbank

425	i	**Samuel C.[7]** b 2-26-1814 m Ruth Grove Richardson
	ii	**Hannah[7]** b 8-17-1816 (supposedly ran away with a native American)
426	iii	**Jonathan Burbank[7]** b 5-7-1820 lived in Boston, MA, m Selina Wiggin
427	iv	**David[7]** b 5-7-1820 m Ruth Welch 2-1-1842
	v	**Benjamin** b 11-15-1825 d 12-6-1825

BENJAMIN[6] SEVERANCE 1790-1856

JONATHAN BURBANK[7] SEVERANCE 1820-1879

(195) Stephen[6], (Jonathan[5], Jonathan[4], Jonathan[3], Ephraim[2], John[1]), born in Chichester, NH on 7-28-1796. [NHVR] He married Eliza King of Tuftonborough in February of 1823 [Hayley] and they later settled in Ossipee, NH. He was a farmer and a member of the State Militia. For many years he officiated as deacon of the church. The 1830-1840 NH census indicates him living at Wolfeborough. The known children were from the 1850-1870 NH census for Ossippee, NH.

Children: [RMOFMA p1156]
428 i   **Newell Atchison[7]** b 1825 m Mary E. Brown of Wolfboro, NH
429 ii   **Lorenzo Fisk[7]** b 4-5-1827 Brockton, MA
430 iii   **Alonzo Clark[7]** b 4-5-1827 Brockton, MA
431 iv   **Ira O.**,[7] b 1829, He m first to Mary E. Bickford, Quincy, MA
     v   **James Horn[7]** b 1832. He m to Charlotte Kilgore on 7-13-1856 at Danvers, MA. [MAVR] He later settled in Chicago, IL and was a Hotel Manager.
     vi   **Jasper Nelson[7]** d age 14
     vii   **John Albert[7]** b 1839. He lived in Chicago, IL and worked as a Hotel Manager.
432 viii   **Stephen Nute[7]** b 1841 NY City, Central

433   viii   **Sylvester Edwin**[7] b 1845, probably m Abby
              F. Bean 12-25-1869 Lynn, MA

(196) John[6], (Jonathan[5], Jonathan[4], Jonathan[3],
Ephraim[2], John[1]), born on 7-14-1799 in Belmont, NH.
Later lived in Rochester, NH. He married Clara
Garland, daughter of Joseph Garland and Sarah Towle
of Ossipee, NH. [Garland p31] The 1830 NH census
shows him living in Tuftonborough.
    "**John**[6] Personally appeared before two men whom I
recognized as his neighbors in Tuftonboro and quit
claimed to brother **Benjamin**[6] any interest he had in
twelve acres of land which had belonged to father
Jonathan[5]. He appeared an signed 4-14-1835, and it
was recorded two days later on April 16. He signed
alone." [PRNH Strafford Co Book 164 p363]

Children: [Garland p31]
434   i   **Levi**[7] b 1822 m Sarah E. Hussey on 1-6-
            1850
      ii   **Jane**[7] m Mr. Bickford
      iii   **Emily**[7]

(197) Joseph Levi[6], (Jonathan[5], Benjamin[4], Jonathan[3],
Ephraim[2], John[1]), born about 1801 in Tuftonboro, NH.
[MEVR] Later lived in Hudson (Nottingham West), NH
and Lovell, Maine. He shows on the 1830 Tuftonboro,
NH census. He married Mary Moody on 1-15-1824.
[Tuftonboro, NHVR] Mary was born circa 1804 in NH
as is shown on the 1850 ME census.
    The sole entry for 1824, January, **Joseph**[6]
Severance of Tuftonboro and Mary Moody of
Wolfeboro, married by John Senter, J.P. [Hayley
p86]
    Joseph[6], of **Jonathan**[5] and Mehitable Brown, married
Mary Moody. **Jonathan**[5] was "of Chichester"
originally bought land in Tuftonboro in 1804, where
Joseph[6] was born circa 1801. A quitclaim by **Stephen**[6]
Severance of Ossippee and **Joseph**[6] Severance "of
Lovell in the County of Oxford in the state of ME."
[Carroll Co., N.H. deed dated 1-1-1846]. These were
the only living brothers of **Benjamin**[6] Severance who
were buying their rights in the land formerly owned
by their father **Jonathan**[5] now deceased and which
"has been occupied for several years by **John**[6]
Severance, now deceased."
    This certainly rules out son **John**[6] being
removed to KY. Since **John**[6] was in NH in 1835 when
the other **John** was in KY with a family.

As for **Joseph**[6], on 2-11-1830, he was of Tuftonboro when he bought from Francis Piper. By 5-4-1837 he was of Wolfeboro when he deeded to James W. Bryant. Wife Mary also signed. By 1846 he was of Lovell, ME. [1850 Lovell, MEFC]

MARY MOODY, wife of JOSEPH L.[6] SEVERANCE

EMMA[7] (SEVERANCE) MCINTYRE

Children: [Lovell MEVR][MWBM]
435　i　　**Charles M.**[7] b 3-17-1823
　　ii　　**Mary Jane** b 6-31-1828 m Eben McIntyre
　　　　　4-5-1848 Biddeford, ME
　　iii　　**Susan E.**[7] b 3-3-1825
436　iv　　**Sewell**[7] b 4-3-1831
　　v　　**Julia Ann** b 3-12-1833 m Southwell
　　　　　Farrington
437　vi　　**Joseph B.** (known as Bishop)b 6-9-1835
　　　　　at Wolfboro, NH
438　vii　　**Levi**[7] b 8-14-1837 d 11-12-1896 ae 59y 3m
　　　　　m Jennie Phoebe Ward m2 Mary E. Fogg
439　viii　**Asa Albion**[7]　b 11-16-1839
　　ix　　**Freeman**[7] b 9-5-1842 d 12-28-1849
　　x　　**Emma**[7] b 7-6-1845 Biddeford, ME m John
　　　　　McIntyre of Milan, NH 11-12-1861
　　xi　　**John M.**[7] b 11-6-1846 d 12-20-1849
　　xii　　**Thomas Freeman**[7] b 11-30-1850 at Lovell,
　　　　　ME [MEVR] m Carrie L. Dresser 12-16-
　　　　　1879. She was b 9- -1858. The family
　　　　　settled in Los Angeles, CA. They had a
　　　　　daughter, **Mabel L.**[8] b 6-3-1885 at
　　　　　Lowell, MA [MAVR] The [1920 CAFC] shows
　　　　　a son, **Harold**[8], b 1893 (with his wife
　　　　　Ruth b in CT,) and a daughter of Carrie,
　　　　　Sibil[8], b 1894

(198) Benjamin[6], (Benjamin[5], Benjamin[4], Jonathan[3],
Ephraim[2], John[1]), born in Boscawen, NH on 4-2-1796
[GWNH says b 4-2-1794] died 6-19-1847/1848 in
Kanawha Co., West VA. He married 1st to Rebecca
Butler 2-21-1818 in Knox County, OH. He married 2nd
to Emma Jane Been on 2-5-1833 in Meigs County, OH.
Emma Jane was born on 10-5-1812 in Kennebeck
County, ME. [BR of Benjamin Severance and Emma Jane
Been] The widow remarried to Tilly Rice. [DARLR Vol
127 p243][DAR #499353]
　　In an application for bounty land regarding
Benjamin Severance **Jr.**[6] 1858, Kanawha County, VA
for the children of the late **Benjamin**[6] Severance,
Tilly Rice and Martha Hagerman stated "they were
well acquainted with the family of **Benjamin**[6]
Severance, deceased, that the widow of said
Benjamin[6] having married on Tilly Rice and living
in the same village with afficants and have been so
acquainted for many years.
　　That **Leonora**[7] Severance, **Henry**[7] Severance,
Charles[7] Severance and **Alice**[7] Severance have always
been reputed and believed without any question
among their acquanintances to be the only lawful

and surviving children of the said Severance under 21 years of age on the 3rd day of March 1855."

This day personally came before me Tilly Rice and Martha Hagerman, credible witnesses residents of said county and made oasth that the ages of the children of **Benjamin**[6] Severance, late of said county, but since about the 10th day of July, 1847, deceased on the 3rd day of March 1855, was as following, **Leonora**[7] 19 years 9 months, **Henry**[7] 14 years 8 months, **Charles**[7] 11 years 9 months, and **Alice**[7] 9 years 7 months.

John Dryden, in behalf of and as next friend of the children of the late **Benjamin**[6] Severance, whose widow, Emma Jane remarried to Tilly Rice, states "**Benjamin**[6] Severance was a Private or Sargent in the company commanded by Captain Silas Call and Lieutenant Little, in the Regiment of NH militia, commanded by Colonel _____ in the War with Great Britain, declared by the United States in 1812, that he was draughted at the town of Bosquine (Boscawen), NH in August or September 1813 and was honorably discharged at Portsmouth, New Hampshire."

Benjamin[6], son of **Benjamin**[5] Severance and Rebecca Swett, daughter of Benjamin Swett and Rebecca Pierce, served in the NH military in 1813. His mionr children received bounty land for his service after he died. It is believed **Ben Jr.**[6] went with his family from New Hampshire to Ohio. He was a resident of Meigs County when he received land in 1817 at the Zanesville Land Office. A **Benjamin**[6] Severance married Rebecca Butler in Knox County, OH in 1818. We believe they had a baby girl, which was named **Rebecca**[7] after it's mother who failed to survive. We believe this little girl is the one with old **Benjamin**[6] and Rebecca in the 1830 and 1840 census. Rebecca raised this child and **Benjamin Jr.**[6] is never found with any family until fifteen years later when he married Emma Jane and moved to West Virginia. It is uncertain if the **Rebecca**[7] (daughter of **Benjamin**[6] and Rebecca Butler) or the **Rebecca**[7] (daughter of **Rodney**[6] and Jane Caldwell) was the one who married either Isaac Goodrich or Richard Swift. Lucile Swift White was a great grand daughter of the **Rebecca**[7] who married Richard Swift.

The birth, death, and marriage dates were given by Emma Jane (Been) Severance when she applied for the bounty land. [MLSW]

Children of **Benjamin**[6] Severance and Rebecca Butler
    i   **Rebecca**[7] b 1-2-1822 m 5-20-1841 either

156

Richard Swift or Isaac Goodrich

Children of **Benjamin**[6] Severance and Emma Jane Been
[Birth dates from The Family Bible records of
Benjamin[6] and Emma]

    ii   **Leonora**[7] b 5-22-1835, Kanawha County, VA
   iii   **Josephine**[7] b 1-24-1838 d 12-18-1838
          Morgan County, OH
    iv   **Henry**[7] b 6-30-1840 Kanawha County,
          West VA
     v   **Charles**[7] b 5-29-1843 Kanawha County,
          West VA
    vi   **Alice**[7] b 9-1-1845 Kanawha county, West
          VA

(199) Rodney[6], (Benjamin[5], Benjamin[4], Jonathan[3],
Ephraim[2], John[1]), born 12- -1795 in Boscowen, NH. He
died in the 1870's in Morgan Co OH. On 3-18-1818 he
married Jane Caldwell, daughter of Robert Caldwell
and Jane Fulton (niece of Robert Fulton).

Rodney[6] was a salt maker while living in OH. He
appeared to be quite prosperous as he sold several
pieces of land before he died, but he left no Will.
In 1870, **Rodney**[6] was found living with his daughter
Matilda Wallace McLaughlin. [MLSW]

Jane Caldwell's mother was a cousin to Robert
Fulton, the inventor of the steamboat.

Children: [MLSW]
440   i   **Rufus**[7] b 1819 m Elizabeth Gibson 12-9-
          1837 and Elizabeth Balderson
441 ii   **Robert**[7] b circa 1819 m Savilla Hedge 5-
          20-1841
442 iii   **Benjamin**[7] b 1820 m Mary Buchanon 10-9-
          1844
    iv   **Rebecca**[7] b 12-7-1822 m Isaac Goodrich 1-
          22-1843
     v   **Matilda**[7] b 1823 m Oliver Wallace 1-27-
          1847 and William McLaughlin
443 vi   **Arthur Rodney**[7] b 8-30-1826 m Margaret
          Shoemaker 10-9-1848

(200) Silas[6], (Benjamin[5], Benjamin[4], Jonathan[3],
Ephraim[2], John[1]), born 7-29-1797 in Boscowen, NH and
died 1843-1850 in Monroe County, OH. He married
circa 1820 to Mary Hupp, daughter of Philip Hupp
and Mary Buzzard.

A marriage record for **Silas**[6] was not found
however a lady doing research on the Hupp family
told about a military record regarding old Philip

Hupp. **Silas**[6] *Severenz* witnessed the document, signed as his son-in-law. [MLSW]

Children:
444   i   **Philip**[7] b circa 1821 m Rachel Chapman 1844
445   ii   **Benjamin**[7] b circa 1823 m Mary Hale 9-27-1851
       iii   **Sarah V.**[7] b circa 1830 m Perley J. Nott 9-16-1854
446   iv   **Arthur M.**[7] b circa 1832 m Mary Ann Dailey 4-15-1854
447   v   **Church**[7] b circa 1838 m Frances M. Nott 1859

(201) Hazen[6], (Benjamin[5], Benjamin[4], Jonathan[3], Ephraim[2], John[1]), born circa 1801 in Boscawen, NH. His death date is not known. He married Mary____. He is shown as being a Salt Boiler in Morgan County, OH. [1850/60 OHFC]

Children: [MLSW]
       i   **William**[7] b circa 1835
       ii   **Sarah**[7] b circa 1837
448   iii   **Hazen M.**[7] b 10-22-1839 d 1-6-1914 m Parmelia A. VanMeter
       iv   **Josiah W.**[7] b circa 1841 in OH. He was m to Priscilla on the [1920 Zanesville, Muskingum Co OHFC]
       v   **Isabella**[7] b circa 1846
       vi   **Mary**[7] b circa 1850

(202) Nicholas[6], (Nichols[5], Benjamin[4], Jonathan[3], Ephraim[2], John[1]), born circa 1795 married Polly Warner (Danforth) on 3-2-1815. [VTVR] They lived at Thetford, Orange Co VT. "7-2-1817 set off to Polly *Seaverance* her dower out of the real estate of **Nicholas** Seaverance late of Thetford, VT 8-22-1817." "November 25, 1823 appointed guardian to **Harrison**[6] and **Sapphina**[6] *Seaverance* minors under the age of 14 years of the estate of **Nichols**[6] *Seaverance* late of Thetford, VT." **Nicholas**[6] d circa 1817. [PRVT]

Children:
449   i   **Harrison**[7] b 1816 Thetford, VT. He d 4-8-1895 at Colebrook, NH. [VTVR] He had a daughter, **Clarissa Ann**[8] who m Henry Bradbury Gilkey in 1857. [Sterns Vol I p702]

(203) Thomas[6], (Nichols[5], Benjamin[4], Jonathan[3], Ephraim[2], John[1]), born circa 1798. The 1850-1860 NH census shows **Thomas[6]** and his son, **Thomas[7]**, and Nicholas Sweat born 1804 living with them. **Thomas Sr.[6]** is living alone in 1860 with his son, **Thomas[7]**, living nearby.

Children:
450   i   **Nickelson[7]** b circa 1823 in VT.
      ii   **Thomas[7]** b circa 1838
There were most likely other children.

(204) John[6], (Samuel[5], Samuel[4], Jonathan[3], Ephraim[2], John[1]), born 11-14-1816. He married Emily Hunt on 12-11-1841. [IGI] She was born 1819 and died 6-21-1886. **John[6]** died 5-17-1900. [NHVR] The 1840 NH census shows them living at Hooksett.

Children: [1850-1870 NHFC]
      i   **Mary[7]** b 1843
452   ii   **Mason Samuel (Samuel Mason)[7]** b 1847 m
             Nellie M. _____ [1880 NHFC]
      iii   **Nancy J.[7]** b 1850

(205) Ora P.[6], (Samuel[5], Samuel[4], Jonathan[3], Ephraim[2], John[1]), born 12-1-1828, he died 2-12-1914. [NHVR] He was a farmer and a brick-maker. His first marriage was to Ruth Ann (Stickney) Smith, daughter of John Stickney and Nancy Pearson. She was born 3-27-1830 and died at Plaistow, NH 7-3-1893 age 63. [NHVR] He married second to Elizabeth (Heath) Stickney, daughter of Samuel Heath and Abiah Gile, [NHVR] 11-27-1894 at Danville, Rockingham Co. NH. She was born in 1829 and died 10-4-1912 [NHVR]. The 1900 NH census shows **Ora P.[6]** born 12- -1828, and his wife, Elizabeth A. b 2- -1829. [MDS]

Children: [1870/1880 NHFC]
453   i   **George Washington[7]** b 12-9-1851 at
             Kingston, NH
      ii   **Sarah[7]** b 2-11-1860 at Plaistow, NH
      iii   **Daniel L.[7]** b 12-18-1862 at Plaistow
      iv   **Ora[7]** b 4-23-1876 at Plaistow

(206) Nathan[6], (John[5], John[4], Jonathan[3], Ephraim[2], John[1]), born 9-9-1808 in Kingston, NH died 12-7-1905, son of John and Rachel Heath, [NHVR] in Pembroke, NH. He married Lydia Gould 12-19-1830. [Tibbetts Vol VI p20] **Nathan[6]** was a shoemaker in East Kingston, NH. He died of cancer of the right foot and old age, at the age of 97. The 1840 NH census shows them living at Pembrook. His father **John**[5] Severance was a farmer in Kingston, NH.

Children: [MAM]

	i	**Rachel**[7] b 1-20-1838 at Pembroke, NH. She m1 William Garvin, m2 William Yeaton.
454	ii	**John**[7] b 7-4-1843 at Pembroke, NH, m Florence Jane Atwood.

SEVENTH GENERATION (207) John[7], (John/Abba[6], Tabitha[5], Daniel[4], Ebenezer[3], John[2], John[1]), born in Alstead, NH on 7-3-1782. [IGI] He married to Lavina Dutton on 11-8-1814, at Surry, NH. Lavina was born 1784. [IGI]

Children:

455	i	**Emery**[8] b 1817 m Arvilla Thrasher

(208) Abner[7], (John/Abba[6], Tabitha[5], Daniel[4], Ebenezer[3], John[2], John[1]), born in Alstead, NH on 3-11-1786 and died 7-5-1844. [VTVR] He married Rebecca Hardy. She was born 1789 and died 4-28-1866 at Cambridge, MA [MAVR] or at Windsor, VT. [VTVR] They are buried at Old South Cemetery, Windsor, VT. They lived at Windsor, VT. [1830-1840 VTFC Windsor, Windsor Co]

Children:

456	i	**Charles H.**[8] b 1810 m Abriah White 2-19-1846 at Newbury, VT [VTVR] In 1840 he was living in Windsor. [VTFC]
	ii	**Roswell**[8] b circa 1819, son of **Abner**[7] and Rebecca, at Windsor, VT. He was a printer and m Clarissa Fowler [MAVR] He d 12-2-1881 at Cambridge, MA age 62-3-13
457	iii	**Horace M.**[8] b circa 1822 at Woodstock, VT
458	iv	**Frederick**[8] b 1828 m Mary W. Bement, daughter of John Bement and Sylvia Thomas, 9-17-1890. [VTVR] Mary W. Bement was b 5-9-1829 d 4-2-1903. [NHVR] **Frederick**[7] was 62 years old when he m for the 2nd time. He was the son of **Abner**[7] and Rebecca Hardy. [VTVR]

(209) Nathan[7], (John/Abba[6], Tabitha[5], Daniel[4], Ebenezer[3], John[2], John[1]), born on 3-7-1789 in Alstead, NH. [IGI] The 1830 VT census shows him living in Ludlow, Windsor Co. He married to Rhoda Thompson, daughter of William Thompson and Martha

Hale of Alstead, NH. Rhoda d on 3-21-1872. [Hayward p401] They later settled in Shalerville, OH. The 1850 OH census shows the births of **William**[7] and **George**[7] in Vermont and the births of **Maudly**[7], **Maria**[7], and **Henry**[7] in OH. [Elliot p363]

Children: [Hayward p401]

	i	**Clarissa**[8] m Squire Marvin, son of Leland and Patty Thompson. [Elliot p365]
459	ii	**William T.**[8] b 1828 m Lavina Mitchell
460	iii	**Oscar**[8] b circa 1830 m Elizabeth Heriff
461	iv	**George**[8] b 1830 m Elizabeth Nichols
462	v	**Marvin**[8] b 6- -1832 m Laura Leonard
	vi	**Maudly**[8] b 1834
	vii	**Maria**[8] b 1837 m Clinton Nichols and settled in MI
463	viii	**Manly C.**[8] b circa 1835 m Juliett Harlow
	ix	**Augusta N.**[8] b 1839 Salem, NH m George Boynton, son of Richard and Polly Boynton, 1-4-1864 at Lowell, MA [MAVR]
463a	x	**Henry A.**[8] b 1840 m and resided in MI

(210) Moses[7] *Severns*, (John/Abba[6] (Abner), Tabitha[5], Daniel[4], Ebenezer[3], John[2], John[1]), was born on 10-8-1790 in Alstead, NH. or VT. He married Anna Cooper on 9-19-1813. They lived in VT, then moved to St. Lawrence Co, NY where **Moses**[7] died on 7-5-1834. Anna was born in NY 9-17-1792 and died 11-24-1871 at Grand Haven, MI. [Cooley p151] **Moses**[7] shows with 6 sons and 4 daughters and living at Edwards, NY. [1830 St. Lawrence Co. NYFC]

Some of his sons were known to have settled near Grand Haven, MI.

Children:

464	i	**Nelson Chase**[8] b 5-5-1816
464a	ii	**William**[8] b circa 1817. This child is conjecture as to his parents but the available research tends to verify **William**[8] as a son of **Moses**[7]
464b	iii	**Henry**[8] b circa 1818 in VT m Nancy Mary Hardy
	iv	son
465	v	**Charles**[8] b 3-5-1823 m Eliza Jane Pettricorn. They had a daughter, **Ida Estelle**[9] *Severns* b 11-11-1853 who m Ransom R. Goodrich 10-9-1879 Cass Co MI
	vi	son
	vii	**Olive Elvira**[8] b 6-16-1825 m ____ Pott?

```
viii    daughter
 ix     daughter
  x     daughter
```

(212) Ebenezer[7], (Samuel[6], Ebenezer[5], Ebenezer[4], Ebenezer[3], John[2], John[1]), born in Middlebury, VT on 11-3-1791. He married to Corcina Jones, daughter of Asahel and Catherine Jones, on 1-29-1817. [VTVR] She was born 1-29-1793 and died 1-27-1889. [VTVR] **Ebenezer[7]** was a farmer and a long standing member of the Congregational Church. He was always ready with a helping hand for others. They lived in Middlebury. [1830/1840 VTFC] He died in Middlebury on 2-17-1880. [JFS p44-45]

```
Children: [JFS p45]
        i       a son b 5-26-1819 [VTVR]
        ii      Mary Catharine8 b 8-11-1821 m W.W.
                Winchester 7-26-1848
466     iii     Edmund Kirby8 b 4-28-1823
        iv      Leonard8 b 1-25-1825 d 3-17-1825
467     v       Oliver8 b 2-14-1827 m Delia Cady
        vi      Asabel Jones8 b 12-1-1828. He m Martha
                W. Cady. He was early on a carpenter but
                later entered into the lumber business
                and opened a marble quarry. he then
                became involved with a diamond drill and
                left for CA. He returned to New York
                City dealing in mining interests. He
                left no family.
468     vii     Milton Leonard8 b 10-14-1830 [1860 NY.
                Census] m1 Emily A. Spencer m2 Ella
                Stewart
        viii    Frances Ann8 b 4-19-1832 d 8-12-1853
        ix      Emma Adelia8 b 4-19-1834 m Rev.
                S.L.Blake 8-16-1865. Emma8 d 8-31-1869
        x       Martha Agnes8 b 5-29-1837 m Col. L.E.
                Knapp 1-23-1865. Lyman Enos Knapp served
                as clerk in the VT Legislature 1886-1887
                and as Governor of Alaska 1889-1893.
                They later settled in Seattle, WA.
                [Howard]
```

(214) Samuel Smith[7], (Samuel[6], Ebenezer[5], Ebenezer[4], Ebenezer[3], John[2], John[1]), born in Middlebury, VT on 5-22-1809 and died on 1-21-1887. [VTVR] He spent his entire life in that area. On 11-7-1833, he married Maria L. Munger. [VTVR] She died 5-3-1880. **Samuel[7]** was a progressive farmer and never sought

office. He was a long time member of the
Congregational Church. [JFS p45]

Children:
469   i   **Philo Spencer**[8] b 2-28-1840 m Helen E.
            Atwood
470   ii   **Martin Egbert**[8] b 8-4-1843 m Mattie Van
            Slylie
     iii   **Jennie Ann Maria**[8] b 9-15-1856 d 3-18-
            1877 age 68 years 11 months (daughter of
            Samuel[7] and Lydia Munger) [VTVR]

(215) Darius[7], (Samuel[6], Ebenezer[5], Ebenezer[4],
Ebenezer[3], John[2], John[1]), born on 2-15-1814. He
married Emiline S. Rockwell on 3-11-1839. They
settled in Middlebury, VT.
     It was recorded that **Darius**[7] was a "farmer, and
efficient worker politically, a patriot and
philantrophist." [JFS p45] **Darius**[7] died 7-27-1905.
[VTVR]

Children: [JFS p45-46]
      i   **Edward Clark**[8] b 4-5-1840 m Ellen A.
            Perkins on 2-27-1872. [VTVR] Ellen was
            born in November of 1840. [1900 VTFC]
            They settled in Burlington, VT. The
            1900 VT census shows his father **Darius**[7]
            and a sister (**Rolla A.**[8] (Severance)
            Hallock) living with them.
     ii   **Edith**[8] b 4-16-1850 m John Avery, M.D.
            4-24-1875 at Middlebury, VT. [VTVR]

(216) Nelson[7], (Daniel[6], Ebenezer[5], Ebenezer[4],
Ebenezer[3], John[2], John[1]), born on 2-3-1808. [JFS
p46] He first married to Emeline L. Park on 10-21-
1837. She died 9-20-1873 [MAVR] He married second
to Elizabeth Woodbridge, daughter of Henry and
Elizabeth Woodbridge, on 3-31-1875 at Northfield,
MA. Elizabeth died 8-4-1888 at Reading, MA. [MAVR]
They lived in Gill, MA. **Nelson**[7] died 9-9-1890 at
Northfield, MA, age 82-7-25. [MAVR]

Children: [MAVR]
      i   **Elizabeth H.**[8] b circa 1839 at
            Northfield, MA m William D. Alexander,
            son of Josiah and Mira Alexander, 2-8-
            1864 at Northfield. [MAVR]
     ii   **Emma L.**[8] b circa 1841 at Northfield, d
            4-16-1869 age 27-7-9. [MAVR]

(217) Curtis D.[7], (Daniel[6], Ebenezer[5], Ebenezer[4], Ebenezer[3], John[2], John[1]), born in Gill, MA on 7-6-1819. [MAVR] He lived in Vernon and New Farm, VT. He married 1st to Patience L. Scott 11-5-1851 [VTVR]), married second to Nancy Birge 6-7-1876 [VTVR], and married third to Eunice L. Sargeant 3-14-1895, in Vernon, VT. [VTVR], Eunice was born 7--1827. [1900 VTFC].

Children:
  i   **Fred C.**[8] b 5-16-1853 at West Northfield. He m to Ada L. Hine, daughter of Martin L. and Lucretia Hine, 9-9-1889 at Springfield, MA. He apparently m a second time to Myra E. Mugridge, daughter of George L. Mugridge and Myra F. Fernald, on 11-9-1893 at Boston, MA. **Fred**[8] was a traveling salesman. [MAVR]
  ii   **Hattie E.**[8] b 1854 m Addino R. Baker, son of Loren and Cynthia Baker, 3-13-1886 at Greenfield, MA. He was 52 years old. [MAVR]
  iii   female b 1-24-1856 at Northfield, MA [MAVR]
  iv   Twin sons b 4-20-1859 at Northfield, MA [MAVR]
  v   **Frank S.**[8] b 1860 d 4-1-1862 at Northfield, MA of Scarlet Fever. [VTVR]

(218) Augustus N.[7], (Moses[6], Ebenezer[5], Ebenezer[4], Ebenezer[3], John[2], John[1]), born on 2-16-1808 in Salisbury, VT. He then moved to Ft. Ann, NY. He later married to Fannie Wainwright 3-13-1834 [VTVR] and they settled in Greeley, CO. **Augustus N.**[7] died 11-20-1884. [MDLB]

Children: [JFS p46]
471 i   **William N.**[8] b 2-21-1836,

There were most likely other children. The 1900 CO census shows an **Arthur J.** b 2- -1840 in VT and a **J.E.** b 3- -1852 in VT with wife Dora b 3- -1855 in VT.

(219) Lyman M.[7], (Moses[6], Ebenezer[5], Ebenezer[4], Ebenezer[3], John[2], John[1]), born in Middlebury, VT on 4-11-1810. He married Martha S. Bacon on 7-31-1840. She was the daughter of Benjamin and Sylvania L. Bacon of Bedford, MA. They lived in Middlebury, VT until 1854 when they moved to Dixon, IL and **Lyman**[7] continued his farming occupation. He invented the Victor Platform Scale and received patents for his invention. [JFS p46]

In 1869 he sold his property in IL and moved to Painesville, OH where he lived until his death on 1-25-1882. The 1880 OH census shows the family living in Painesville.

Children: [LCoOH p222]
    i   **Sylvia K.**[8] b 6-8-1843 m John T. Cheney 7-21-1866. The <u>History of Sanbornton, NH</u> lists John Tirrell Cheney, who was b 2-23-1830, as a proprietor of hotels at Dixon, IL and Grand Haven MI. He m first to Mary Briggs of Holderness, NH and secondly to **Sylvania**[8] Severance of OH. They had four children.

472 ii   **Edson J.**[8] b 3-17-1848
    iii   John Holland b 3-10-1859 (adopted) m Elizabeth R. Jenkins [OHVR] d 1934

(**Lyman**[7] had two more adopted daughters, Florence (*Severance*) Smith and Carrie (*Severance*) Davis (wife of G.C. Davis). [LCoOH p222] The quarterly also gives a detailed account of the **Lyman M.**[7] Severance family)

(220) James A.[7], (Moses[6], Ebenezer[5], Ebenezer[4], Ebenezer[3], John[2], John[1]), born on 12-14-1814 in Middlebury, VT. [JFS p47] He died on 8-24-1894, at Middlebury, VT ae 79-8-10. [VTVR] The 1850 VT census shows **James**[7] born 1817 and **Mary** born 1827 with **Viola** born 1841 living with **Moses**[6], Kezia and **Augustus**[6] in Ohio. I show him married to Elvira Baldwin on 9-12-1857. [VTVR] He married on 9-12-1874 to Mary ___. [IGI]

(221) Ebenezer[7], (Elisha/Elijah[6], Abner[5], Ebenezer[4], Ebenezer[3], John[2], John[1]), born on 6-5-1813 in Gill, MA. [MAVR] He married Sophia Ferris in Peru, Clinton Co. NY in May of 1835. **Ebenezer**[7] was a blacksmith.

Children: [MESS]
473 i   **Benton**[8] b 3-14-1835 m Julia Hodgson
    ii   **Albert**[8] b 2- -1840. He was a lodger in Denver, CO in 1920. [COFC]
    iii **Sarah**[8] b 1840
    iv **Harriet**[8] b 1844

The 1860 NY census also shows children, **Emma**[9] b 1855 and **William**[9] b 1858 in NY. They could have been children of **Benton**[8] or **Albert**[8]

(222) James Edwin[7], (Elisha/Elijah[6], Abner[5], Ebenezer[4], Ebenezer[3], John[2], John[1]), born in Gill, MA on 8-27-1822 [MAVR] and died 9-4-1902 in Hague, NY. He married to Maria Shattuck, the daughter of Austin Shattuck, on 3-1-1847 in Shoreham, VT, by the Rev. Kettridge Havens. She was born on 1-15-1823 in Hague, NY and died 2-18-1879 at Shoreham, VT. They are buried at the new Lake View Protestant Cemetery in Shoreham, VT

The Family Bible says **"James Edwin**[7] Severance" and his grave stone reads **"Edwin James**[7] Severance". [MESS]

With the help of **R. Scott**[10] Severance, this family line has been corrected. A history that detailed this family, A Genealogical Register of the Early Families of Shoreham, Vermont, 1761-1899, [MacIntire] errored in some of its research concerning the **James Edwin**[7] Severance lineage.

Children: born in Shoreham, VT [MESS]
- i **Augusta L.**[8] b 11-22-1847 d Hague, NY m Albert C. Clifton who was b 1-28-1842. [Smith I] She was b in Shoreham, VT. His family name was Graves but he changed it to Clifton after getting into some trouble during his service in the Civil War [MESS]
- ii **George G.**[8] b 2-1-1848. The 1920 WA census shows him b 2- -1850 in VT, m to Melissa b 3- -1847 in IN and living at Seattle, WA. They has a daughter, **Jennis L.**[9] b 4- -1880 in MN.
- iii **Charles C.**[8] b 6-18-1859 m Emma A. Decora on 11-20 1881, Shoreham, VT. [VTVR] Emma was b in August of 1862 in NY state. [MESS]
- iv **Mary E.**[8] b 9-13-1860 [VTVR]
- 475 v **Willie L.**[8] b 12-20-1861 [VTVR], **James Edwin**[7] was living with **Willie**[8] on the [1900 CTFC] at Bridgeport.
- vi **Henry**[8] b 1- -1862 d 8- -1862
- 476 vii **Scott Ellsworth**[8] b 7-31-1867/8 m Carrie Balcom

(223) Avery[7], Orin[6], Abner[5], Ebenezer[4], Ebenezer[3], John[1], John[1]), born at Gill, MA on 6-7-1812 and died

11-10-1881 at Gill, MA. [MAVR] He married to Mary
Jane (Rose) Rix, daughter of George and Mary Ross,
on 8-22-1854 at Brattleboro, VT [VTVR] She was born
1-31-1813 at Stanstead, Canada and died 1-19-1891
at Gill, MA. [MAVR]

Children: [Suddaby p411]
  i   **George Rose**[8] b 3-27-1855 d 3-15-1890 at
        Gill. [MAVR]
  ii   **Frank Rix**[8] b 5-19-1858 d 7-20-1887 at
        Gill, MA from shooting in the head as a
        suicide. Single. [MAVR]

(224) Chandler[7], (Orin[6], Abner[5], Ebenezer[4],
Ebenezer[3], John[2], John[1]), born on 11-12-1821. [MAVR]
He married to Mary Ann Eaton, daughter of Shepherd
and Ann (Kellogg) Eaton, on 11-9-1860, (OHVR)
[Suddaby p353 says 12-9-1860] She was b 9-5-1836.
[Sterling]. They lived first at Jefferson, OH and
later at Painsville, OH. [1900 OHFC] **Chandler**[7] d 2-
22-1901 in Painesville, OH. [NSPT 2-27-1901 p1, 4-
3-1901 p4]

Children: [JFS p47]
  i   **Mary Frankie**[8] b 2-9-1866 m Lewis E. Hill
        5-23-1889

(225) Harris[7], (Obed[5], Abner[5], Ebenezer[4], Ebenezer[3],
John[2], John[1]), born on 6-16-1820. [MAVR] He married
to Betsey Williams and they settled in Gill, MA.

Children:
  i   **Frank**[8]
  ii   **Alfred**[8]
  iii   **Edward**[8]
  iv   **Albert**[8] b 1851 d 5-23-1871 at Gill, MA.
        He hung himself in a suicide. He was
        single. [MAVR]
  v   **George F.**[8] b 5-18-1852 at Erving, MA
        [MAVR]
  vi   **Elvira Janette**[8] b 6-26-1854 at Gill, MA
        [MAVR] m Frederick H. Simonds, son of
        Nathan and Sarah H. Simonds, 3-12-1877
        at Erving, MA. [MAVR]
  vii   male b 7-5-1857 at Gill, MA [MAVR]
  viii **Isabell Annett**[8] b 3-29-1861 at Erving,
        MA. She m John William Delvey, son of
        John C. and Mary S. Delvey, 7-26-1886 at
        Northfield. [MAVR]

481　ix　　**Edson S.**[8] b 1868 m Lillie M. Morgan,
　　　　　Vernon, VT [VTVR]

(226) Leonard[7], (Obed[6], Abner[5], Ebenezer[4], Ebenezer[3],
John[2], John[1]), born 7-25-1822, died 8-2-1896 at
Gill, MA. He married Eunice S. Jamerson, daughter
of Winthrop and Caroline Fairbanks, 3-31-1859 at
Barre, MA. She was born 5-4-1836 died 3-3-1896 at
Gill, MA. [MAVR]

Children: [JFS p47]
　　　i　　**Evelyn C.**[8] b 4-2-1860 at Barre, MA
　　　　　　[MAVR]
　　　ii　　**John**[8] b 1-19-1862 in Gill, MA. [MAVR] He
　　　　　　m Ellen C. Hunt, daughter of Linus and
　　　　　　Emily Hunt, 10-15-1890 at North
　　　　　　Leverett, MA. [MAVR] She was b in
　　　　　　September of 1870 at Brattleboro, VT.
　　　　　　[1900 MAFC]
　　　iii　　**Luther S.**[8] b 10-31-1864 in Gill, MA
　　　iv　　**Clayton**[8] b 2-21-1868 d 7-3-1869 [MAVR]
　　　v　　**Clayton**[8] b 11-16-1870 d 5-30-1889 age
　　　　　　18-6-14 at Gill, MA. [MAVR]
　　　vi　　**Henry Orton.**[8] b 2-25-1873 in Gill, MA.
　　　　　　[MAVR] The 1900 MA census shows him m to
　　　　　　Mary S. ____ who was born in August of
　　　　　　1876.

(227) Alvin[7], (Obed[6], Abner[5], Ebenezer[4], Ebenezer[3],
John[2], John[1]), born on 6-29-1824 and died 8-8-1903
at Gill, MA. He married to Harriet A. Chapin,
daughter of Justin Chapin and Laurana Kenny, on 10-
4-1857 at Greenfield, MA. [MAVR] They settled in
Gill. Harriet was born 3-29-1836 and died 1-18-1903
in Gill, MA. [JFS p47]

Children: born in Greenfield, Franklin Co. MA
　　　i　　**Frederic Almon**[8] b 8-16-1858 at Gill, MA
　　　　　　[MAVR]
　　　ii　　**Mabel E.**[8] b 7-4-1860 at Gill, MA d 1-19-
　　　　　　1888 at Gill [MAVR]
　　　iii　　baby son b d 11-9-1862 at Gill, MA
　　　　　　[MAVR]
　　　iv　　**Alice M.**[8] b 6-22-1866 at Gill, MA [MAVR]
　　　　　　m Henry H. Tyler 9-23-1899
　　　v　　**Hattie A.**[8] b 1-9-1869 at Gill, MA [MAVR]

(228) Charles[7], (Obed[6], Abner[5], Ebenezer[4], Ebenezer[3],
John[2], John[1]), born 9-16-1834 at Gill, MA. He
married to Sarah E. Hayward, daughter of Charles

Hayward, on 7-29-1859 and they settled in Gill. [MAVR][JFS p48]

Children: [1880 MAFC]
    i   female b 12-15-1858 at Gill, MA [MAVR]
    ii   **Lizzie B.**[8] b 9-6-1860 d 12-15-1882
    iii   **Charles Herbert**[8] b 7-25-1861 at Gill, MA [MAVR] m Flora B. Williams, daughter of Samuel G. and Sarah Williams, 8-28-1890 at Bernardstown, MA [MAVR]
    iv   female b 12-15-1862 at Gill, MA [MAVR]
    v   **Jenny**[8] b 1-21-1864 d 8-26-1864 at Gill, MA [MAVR]
    vi   son b 9-29-1867 at Gill, MA [MAVR]
    vii   **Addie L.**[8] b 6-25-1872 at Gill, MA [MAVR] m George Cummings, son of Josiah Cummings, on 12-15-1892 at Montague, MA. [MAVR]
    viii **Gertie G.**[8] b 1874
    ix   **Ida P.**[8] 1879

(229) Paul S.[7], (Robert M.[6], Thomas[5], John[4], John[3], John[2], John[1]), born circa 1814 [1850 SCFC] in Berkely Co SC. He died in 1867. He married to **Hester**[7] Severance, daughter of **Paul**[6] Severance and Hannah Huggins , a cousin. She died in 1858 [MWS] He married secondly to Martha Langston Campbell. She was the widow of Rev. Campbell.

Children of **Paul S.**[7] Severance and Hester Severance
482 i   **Elias J.W.**[8] b 5-27-1839
     ii   **Hannah Angeline B.**[8] b 1-27-1842 [MWS][1850 SCFC]
     iii **Eliza Ann**[8] b 11-18-1843 (1845)
483 iv **Paul Elisha**[8] b 10-28-1847 m Emily
484 v   **Robert Elifers**[8] b 5-8-1849
     vi   **Harriet Susannah**[8] b 6-21-1853

Children of **Paul S.**[7] Saverance and Martha Langston Campbell
    vii   **Stephen Samuel**[8] b 8-20-1865 (by second marriage to Martha Langston Campbell)

(231) Robert Murrell Sr.[7], (Paul G.[6], Thomas[5], John[4], John[3], John[2], John[1]), born 2-24-1808 in Charleston, SC and died 9-30-1887. He married to Elizabeth Simmons Huggins. She was born on 9-13-1808 and died 12-30-1887 in SC. [MWS] They are buried in Fair Hope Cemetery in Darlington County, SC on Lynches River Road near Lamar, SC. The 1880 SC census

shows **Robert**[8] Savernace aged 72 and Elizabeth, his
wife aged 71 years. Living with them was their
grandson, **Thomas**[10] Saverance, age 16 (born 1864)

Robert Murrell Sr[7]. shared in his fathers' and
mothers' estate and was given land by **Paul**[6] before
his death. Along with brother **Samuel**[6], he bought
remaining 949 acres of **Paul**[6] Saverance Estate in
1847. He continued to buy land for several years.
As his children came of age he gave most or all of
them land. He lost three sons in the Civil War or a
result of the war. Namely **Thomas Glen**[8], **George W.**[8],
and **Joseph J.**[8] At least two other sons also served,
Paul A.[8] and **Robert M. Jr.**[8]

After the death of **Thomas Glen**[8], as a prisoner
of war in 1864, he raised his grandsons, **Robert
Calhoun**[9] and **Thomas Beauregard**[9] until they were
twenty or twenty-one years old. The last home of
Robert Murrell[7] Saverance and Elizabeth was located
on Old Creek Road in front of the Fair Hope Church.
The majority of the *Saverance's* in this area are
descendents of **Robert Murrell**[7] and Elizabeth.

Children:
	i	**Selena Emeline**[8] b 3-6-1830 d 7-7-1857
486	ii	**Thomas Glenn**[8] b 7-24-1831 d 12-27-1864 (in the Civil War) He married Martha Ham (They had 3 children, **Robert Calhoun**[9], **Elizabeth Bulah**[9], and **Thomas Beauregard**[9] raised up by **Robert Murrell Sr.**[6]
487	iii	**Robert M. Jr.**[9] The census indicates that he was born in 1836.
	iv	**Joseph**[9] b 1839. [1860 SCFC] He died in the Civil War
	v	**Paul A.**[9] b 1843 [1860 SCFC]
	vi	**George W.**[9] b 1-28-1844 d 1-27-1863, died in Civil War
	vii	**Elizabeth J.**[9] b 7-17-1846 d 4-6-1903 never married
	viii	**Hester S.**[9] b 1851 [1860 SCFC]
	ix	**William C.**[9] b 1853 [1860 SCFC]

(232) Samuel G.[7], (Paul[6], Thomas[5], John[4], John[3],
John[2], John[1]), born in 1817 in SC. He married Mary
Margaret ___, b 1836.

Children: [1860 SCFC]
	i	**Mary A.**[8] b 1836
490	ii	**Joseph J.**[8] b 1840
	iii	**Robert E.**[8] b 1842
	iv	**Clarrisa A.**[8] b 1847

| v | **Harriet S.**[8] b 1850 |
| vi | **Martha I.**[8] b 1856 |

Samuel G.[7] may have married a second time or this may be for the **Samuel**[7] that was born 1820.

vii	**Caroline**[8] b 1862
viii	**Joseph L.**[3] b 1865
ix	**Georgia A.**[8] b 1872 (dau)
x	**Robert L.**[3] b 1872
xi	**Frances J.**[8] b 1876

(233) Cyrus[7], (Matthew[6], Matthew[5], Joseph[4], Joseph[3], John[2], John[1]), born cn 11-15-1796. [MAVR] He married first to Lephe Louisa Wells on May 23, 1815. [MAVR] She was born 7-12-1798. He married secondly to Sarah Moore. **Cyrus**[7] died on 3-16-1862.

  Cyrus[7] was born at Leyden, MA. He purchased a lot in New Haven, Oswego Co NY in May of 1824. The deed lists[7] him as a farmer and shoemaker. **Cyrus**[7] was one of the leading members of the Baptist Church at New Haven. Both he and his second wife are buried in the New Haven Cemetery. [Oakes Vol I p633-634] The 1830-1840 NY census shows him living at New Haven.

Children: [JFS p48]
494	i	**Samuel Orton**[8] b 8-17-1816
	ii	**Mary**[8] b 2-27-1818
	iii	**Emily**[8] b 8-12-1820
	iv	**Amanthus**[3] b 3-13-1825
	v	**Theresa**[8] b 9-19-1827
495	vi	**Cyrus Wells**[8] b 8-11-1829/30 [Fieler]
	vii	**Harlow**[8] b 9-12-1831 d 2-3-1835
	viii	**Lephe Wells**[8] b 11-15-1833 d 1836
496	ix	**Anthony Peck**[8] b 10-8-1835
	x	**Harlow Wells**[8] b 1838
497	xi	**William Henry**[8] b 1840

The 1860 NY census shows **Cyrus**[7], age 63, Sarah b 1819 (his second wife), then it shows **Harlow**[8], **William H.**[8], and **Anthony P.**[8] with his wife, Frances b 1828, and three of their children, all born in New York, **Lafayette**[9] b 1857, **Charles N.**[9] b 1859, **baby**[9] 1/12 (b 1860), all b in NY.

(234) Chester[7], (Matthew[6], Matthew[5], Joseph[4], Joseph[3], John[2], John[1]), born on 4-20-1799 in Greenfield, MA. [MAVR] He died in 12-3-1884 at Leyden, MA. [MAVR] He married Martha (Smith) Nash on 1-19-1822. She was born 3-31-1793 died 10-29-1860. [MAVR] They settled in Leyden, MA. [1830/40 Leyden, MAFC] He reportedly married secondly to Elvira M. Nelson on 11-13-1861 at Leyden, MA. [MAVR] [Sheldon Vol 2 p290] **Chester**[7] was reported to have served as selectman, assessor, and collector for the town, and an overseer of the poor for many years. He was a farmer. He was also known as Leyden's first Historian.

Children: [Sheldon p290] born in Leyden, MA
- i **Adeliza**[8] b 5-8-1823 m John M. Thayer 8-16-1848 at Leyden, MA. [MAVR]
- ii **Mary Mehitable**[8] b 10-20-1824 m George W. Hastings, son of Rufus and Phoebe Hastings, 9-26-1852 at Leyden, MA [MAVR] Mary d on 9-30-1871
- iii **Martha**[8] b 10-7-1826 d 8-23-1828
- 499 iv **William Sidney**[8] b 3-24-1829 m Martha Elizabeth Lyman, dau of Thomas Lyman, 11-24-1853
- 500 v **Chester Wells**[8] b 2-27-1831 m Catherine Matilda Wilkins 11-25-1857
- 501 vi **Charles Earl**[8] b 8-7-1833, a doctor of Newark, NJ
- vii **Martha Ellen**[8] b 2-13-1840 m Hiram O. Smith 5-27-1863 at Shelburn, MA [MAVR] **Martha**[8] d 10-14-1863

(235) Matthew[7], (Matthew[6], Matthew[5], Joseph[4], Joseph[3], John[2], John[1]), born on 8-9-1807. He married to Marie Tharisa Stebbins on 11-3-1828. [MAVR] They settled in NY state where **Matthew**[7] died on 8-2-1867. **Matthew**[7] lived at Truxton, Cortland Co. [1830-1840 NYFC]

Children:
- i **Matthew Stebbins**[8] b circa 1828 m Harriet Belknap of Aldenville, PA. They had a daughter **Hattie Belknap**[8] b 5-24-1887 at Leyden, MA. [MAVR]
- ii **George**[8] b circa 1830 in NY State
- iii **Alice B.**[8]

(236) Cephas Clesson[7], (Matthew[6], Matthew[5], Joseph[4], Joseph[3], John[2], John[1]), born on 4-23-1812 in Leyden, MA. He married Harriet Miner on 10-24-1833. [MAVR] She died on 9-25-1853 at Leyden, MA [MAVR] and he married second to Nancy P. Leggett, daughter of John Leggett, 5-10-1855 at Colerain, MA. [MAVR] She was born 10-4-1813 at Charlemont, VT. They settled in Leyden, MA.

Children: [JFS p49]
503 i   **Samuel Clesson**[8] b 8-1-1836 m Angenette Dean 10-29-1872
     ii   **Harriet Ann**[8] b 10-5-1838 d 10-31-1892, age 54, at Leyden, MA, single. [MAVR]
     iii **Henry Harrison**[8] b 1-7-1841 d 7-28-1843 at Leyden, MA [MAVR]
     iv   **Mary Meroa**[8], b 8-4-1843 at Leyden [MAVR]
504 v   **Charles Francis**[8] b 7-11-1848 at Leyden, MA [MAVR]

(237) Ebenezer[7], (Zenas[6], Matthew[5], Joseph[4], Joseph[3], John[2], John[1]), born 1-1-1792 in Rockingham, VT. He died 7-21-1854 in St. Johnsbury, VT. [VTVR] He married to Roxalene Johnson on 7-23-1811. [VTVR] The family shows on the 1820 Waterford, Caledonia Co, VT census. She died 7-2-1829. He married secondly to Mrs. Rebecca (Chandler) Harlow, daughter of Arthur Chandler and widow of Levi Jr., of St. Johnsbury, VT, on 3-17-1830. [MAVR] She died 9-2-1855 in St. Johnsbury, VT. [VTVR]

Children of **Ebenezer**[7] Severance and Roxalene Johnson
505 i   **Quantus**[8] b 2-22-1812 [VTVR]

Children of **Ebenezer**[7] Severance and Rebecca (Chandler) Harlow
     ii   **Roxalana**[8] b 1831 d 9-2-1855 [VTVR] St. Johnsbury, VT
     iii **Mary C.**[8] b 1839 d 10-10-1863 [VTVR]
506 iv   **Chandler**[3] b 4- -1833

(238) Leonard[7], (Zenas[6], Matthew[5], Joseph[4], Joseph[3], John[2], John[1]), born in Greenfield, MA on 11-6-1791. [MDLB] He married Doraxa Frost on 11-15-1821. Doraxa was born 5-12-1798 and d 8-3-1879. They lived first in Greenfield, MA (Leyden) and later in Rockingham, VT. **Leonard**[7] died 1-5-1880 age 83-1-26. [VTVR].

Children: [JFS p49]
507 i   **Joseph Wood**[8] b 1-21-1823 m Mary A. Atcherson
     ii   **Phillip Smith**[8] b 11-10-1824 [VTVR] m Lydia W. Garland, daughter of Deacon John Garland, on 1-3-1853. They were

recorded in Newfield, ME, Lowell,MA, and Rockingham, VT. They left no children. She was b 10-17-1824 d 5-11-1873. [Garland p92]
- iii **Samuel White**[8] b 6-16-1827, m Adeline Keeler Hazen, on 4-11-1861. She was b on 2-22-1832 and d at Saxton's River, VT., 2-10-1897, no children [Hazen p153]
- iv **Martha J.**[8] b 12-13-1828 m William Kelly, son of Andrew and Mary Kelly, 9-20-1866 at Lowell, MA [MAVR]
- 509 v **Leonard S.**[8] b 5-3-1831 m Ophelia E. Geer
- vi **Laura A.**[8] b 6-18-1835 m Horatio W. Dutton 8-9-1866
- vii **Daniel D.**[8] b 4-20-1838 d May 1838
- 510 viii **Warren F.**[8] b 12-2-1840

(239) Charles Consider[7], (Consider[6], Matthew[5], Joseph[4], Joseph[3], John[2], John[1]), born on 10-17-1807 in Burlington, VT. He was graduated from the University of Vermont in August, 1827, and in the same year began in the office of Julius C. Hubbell, at Chazy, Clinton Co. New York. He closed his studies at Plattsburgh, NY in 1833, and was admitted to the bar at Albany, NY in October, 1833, and settled at Springville, Erie Co. NY. He was elected to the Legislature in 1848 and 1851. He held the office of Justice of the Peace for almost forty years. [JFS p50] The 1860 NY census shows him living at Concord, NY.

He married Elisa F. Badgley on 1-10-1842. She died 1-1-1848. ([MDLB] says 1848 and not 1840 as previously indicated) He married next to Sellena B. Ingalls on 2-21-1849. She died on 1-6-1857. He next married to Hannah M. Douglass on 4-6-1858. She died 6-2-1859.

Children:
- i **George Specer**[8] b 12-9-1848 d 7-26-1864
- 511 ii **Henry C.**[8] b 2-10-1852. The [1880 NYFC] shows **Henry C.**[8], his wife Ida and their son **Charles C.**[9] age 5 living with **Charles Sr.**[7]
- iii **Miranda E.**[8] b 11-25-1854 d 2-19-1855

(240) George[7], (Consider[6], Matthew[5], Joseph[4], Joseph[3], John[2], John[1]), born in Burlington, VT on 8-4-1810. He married Mary Elizabeth Douglass on 6-17-1836. She was born 6-17-1816. They settled in Chazy, NY. The 1840 NY census shows them living in

Chazy. They show on the 1860 NY census. **George**[7] was
a merchant, in business for himself. He was elected
Deacon of his Congregational Church. He died on 5-8-1875.

Children: [JFS p50-51]
  i   **Mary Lucretia**[8] b 4-6-1837
  ii   **Elizabeth Nancy**[8] b 8-12-1841
  iii **Charles Douglass**[8] b 3-6-1846 d 5-3-1865
512 iv **George Craige**[8] b 6-4-1853. The [1880
      NYFC] show **George**[8] living with his
      parents and family along with his wife
      Emma, age 26, and **Annie**[9] age 3, and
      Harold[9] age 11/12.
  v   **Frederic Henry**[8] b 11-20-1855 in Chazy,
      Clinton Co. NY. He is shown living with
      his family on the 1860 and 1880 NY
      census. He m to Cornelia Augusta
      Wheeler. [Wheeler] The 1900 NY census
      shows him with his wife, Cornelia who
      was born in October of 1859 in NY.

(241) Ruel[7], (Ruel[6], Matthew[5], Joseph[4], Joseph[3],
John[2], John[1]), born in Leyden, MA on 5-8-1798.
[MAVR] He married to Electa Rice, daughter of
Daniel Rice and Bethiah Newhall, [MAVR] on 4-10-
1826. [MAVR] Electa was born 8-30-1801 and she died
on 9-9-1874. [MAVR] They settled on a farm in
Shelburn Centre, MA, purchased of Moses Allen's
Heirs. [1830 Shelburne, MAFC] He was a progressive
farmer, a selectman for three years, and a member
with the First Congregational Church. **Ruel**[7] died on
2-3-1876. [MAVR]

Children: [JFS p51]
  i   **Nancy Wilbur**[8] b 5-7-1827 d 10-6-1876 m
      Charles S. Allen 2-8-1848 at Greenfield,
      MA [MAVR]
  ii   **Clarinda Arabella**[8] b 4-5-1829 at
      Shelburne, MA m Henry S. Shepardson, son
      of Stephen and L. Shephardson, 9-26-1852
      at Shelburne, MA [MAVR]
  iii **Diana Long**[8] b 11-25-1831 m William T.
      Peck, son of Peter Peck, 12-20-1856 at
      Shelburne, MA [MAVR]
  iv   **Lucia Ann**[8] b 7-18-1835 m Austin L. Peck
      9-17-1861 at Shelburne, MA [MAVR] Lucia
      d 2-10-1369
513 v   **Joseph Cordenio**[8] b 9-7-1841 Eliza
      Dinsmore 11-24-1861

(242) Curtis[7], (Asaph[6], Matthew[5], Joseph[4], Joseph[3], John[2], John[1]), born on 10-7-1806 in VT. [VTVR] He married Marcia M. Tuttle on 1-20-1838. They settled in Oswego, NY. Curtis was a store clerk. Marcia does not show on the 1850 NY census, therefore she had possibly died by then. The 1860 NY census shows **Curtis**[7] with his two sons, **Henry**[8] and **Albert**[8], living in Oswego, NY.

Children: [JFS p51]
       i   **Elvira Electa**[8] b 5-27-1839 d 1-5-1844
514   ii   **Henry Clay**[8] b 2-27-1841
      iii   **Albert Gallatin**[8] b 3-16-1843 in NY state
             and settled in IL.
      iv   **Jane Tuttle**[8]

(243) George W.[7], (Asaph[6], Matthew[5], Joseph[4], Joseph[3], John[2], John[1]), born 7-4-1813. [VTVR] He married to Charlotte on 5-18-1835. He apparently married second to Marietta Thurston, daughter of Gilman Thurston and Azybah Gillet, the intentions were filed at Greenfield, MA 8-1-1835. [MAVR] Marietta was born in Westminster, MA 4-1-1813 and married **George W.**[7] Severance 5-4-1836 of Detroit, MI. He died October 7, 1868 in Detroit, MI from wounds in the Civil War. Marietta died in Detroit 9-10-1885. [Thurston] The 1850 MI census shows **George**[7] living at Detroit. In 1860 he was living in Marquette, MI.

Children of **George W.**[7] Severance and Charlotte
Children of **George W.**[7] and Marietta Thurston
born in Detroit, MI
       i   **Sarah C.**[8] b 6- -1836 d 5-28-1840 [JFS
             p52] daughter of Charlotte. Not listed
             in the Thurston Genealogy
      ii   **Clarence L.**[8] b circa 1838 in CT, killed
             in the Civil War, Marrietta filed for
             his pension of L9 IL Cavalry. [CWPR]
      iii   **Helen Maria**[8] b 9-14-1837 [Chicopee Falls,
             MAVR]
      iv   **Adelaide**[8] b circa 1842
      v   **C. Oscar**[8] b 9-13-1846 [Hubbardston,
             MAVR]
      vi   **Eugene**[8] was b in March of 1849 in
             Hubbardston, MA
515   vii   **Emerson M**[8] b 5- -1849 in VT [1900 MOFC]
      viii   **Albert W.**[8] b 1854 in NY State [1860
             MIFC]

(244) Luther N.[7], (Asaph[6], Matthew[5], Joseph[4], Joseph[3], John[2], John[1], was born on 1-28-1819 at Bristol, VT. [MAVR] He married first to Araminta Ann Baldwin on 9-15-1830. She died on 9-28-1847 in Kingsbury VT. **Luther**[7] then married Zelia L. Landon 9-3-1848. Zelia L. was born 10-17-1824 at Hinesburg, VT and died 4-6-1886 at Williamstown. [MAVR] **Luther**[7] settled in Williamstown, MA. He died 9-28-1894 at Williamstown and burial was at Montague, MA. [MAVR]

Children: [JFS p52]
516 i   **Elmer D.**[8] b 5-12-1849
     ii   **Arthur Edwards**[8] b 12-19-1850
     iii   **Marion L.C.**[8] b 1-31-1853 m W.W. Gavitt, son of Ephraim Gavitt and Polly White, 5-21-1879 at Williamstown, MA. [MAVR]
518 iv   **Asaph C.**[8] b 4-25-1855
519 v   **Walter L.**[9] b 12-25-1857 m Carrie Briggs
     vi   **Minnie**[8] b 4-17-1860 [MAVR] d 5-9-1862 at Williamstown, MA. [MAVR]
     vii   **Fred C.**[8] b 6-1-1862 at Williamstown, MA. He m to Maggie L. Cleghorn, daughter of Andrew Cleghorn and Margaret Steel, 10-4-1887 at Fitchburg, MA. [JFS]
520 viii   **Frank E.**[8] b 12-7-1865 at Williamstown, MA [MAVR]

(246) William Sidney[7], (Jesse[6], Jesse[5], Joseph[4], Joseph[3], John[2], John-), was born in Conway, MA on 4-9-1800. [MAVR] There seems to be variance between the History of Ontario County [HOCoNY p195-196] and the vital records. I have used the vital records. **William**[7] went to Phelps, NY sometime after 1820 and located with his parents on Melvin Hill. He had a common school education and learned his fathers trade as black-smith and followed it all his active life. He married Arzelia Joslyn, daughter of Charles Joslyn, in Phelps. They spent their life in that area. He shows on the 1840 Phelps, Ontario Co. NY census. **William**[7] died in 1865 in Phelps, NY.

Children: [HOCoNY p196]
     i   **Ellen**[8] b m Jethro Sherborne
521 ii   **Oscar**[8] b settled in St. Louis, MO circa 1910
522 iii   **William Dwight**[8] b 5-11-1836 settled in Phelps, NY

(247) Albert G.[7], (Jesse[6], Jesse[5], Joseph[4], Joseph[3], John[2], John[1]), was born 11-5-1808. The 1860 NY census shows **Abert G.**[7] born 1808 in MA. He married to Mary I. ___, who was born in 1832 in NY. [1860 NYFC] They are shown living in Phelps, NY.

Children:
523   i   **Henry**[8] b 1839 he was a carriage maker
       ii   **Ada**[8] b 1842 d young
524   iii   **Charles**[8] b 1842
       iv   **Theodore**[8] b 1844 at Phelps, NY [1860 NYFC]
525   v   **Jesse P.**[8] b 1846
       vi   **Ada**[8] b 1851
      vii   **Minnie**[8] [1900 NYFC]

(248) Joshua Abbott[7], (Jesse[6], Jesse[5], Joseph[4], Joseph[3], John[2], John[1]), was born 4-29-1811 in Conway, MA. [MAVR] He married to Mary A. ___, who was born 1818. [1850 NYFC] They settled in Phelps, NY. [HOCoNY p195] His name shows on the 1840 Phelps, Ontario Co. NY census.

Children:
       i   **Theodore**[8] b 1844 as shown on the [1850 NYFC].
       ii   **Ann**[8] b 1846

(249) Benjamin Franklin[7], (Elihu[6], Jesse[5], Joseph[4], Joseph[3], John[2], John[1]), was born 1-6-1821 in NY state and died 1865. He married to Elizabeth (Betsy) Clark Britton, daughter of Alexander Britton and Amanda Quick. Betsy was born 1-7-1825 in OH and died 8-2-1908 in Barneston, Gage Co. NE. [1885 Barneston, NEFC] After the death of **Benjamin Franklin**[7], Betsy remarried (1869) to John Kiler in IA. [MPV]

Children: [MPV]
       i   **Clara**[8] b 2-20-1854 d 1937 m Isaac Kiler 7-24-187
       ii   **Emma**[8] m William Henry Smith 3-12-1867 in Porter, MI. She d 1929 in Mc Cook, NE
      iii   **Phimela**[8] b 12-27-1852 d 11-30-1933 Beatrice, NE, m Charles A. Smith 7-25-1869 at Mottville, MI
       iv   **Lucy M.**[8] m Sant Jones
526   v   **Edwin**[8] b 1861 m Clara Newman, They had one son, **Clarance**[9] Severance

(250) Charles C.P.[7], (David[6], Jesse[5], Joseph[4], Joseph[3], John[2], John[1], was born 2-8-1820 in Madison Co. NY. With his regular education he learned the trade of a blacksmith. In 1845 he went to New York city and worked in a general commission business. In 1848 he returned to Madison Co and kept a hotel. In March of 1852 he traveled to California via Nicaragua, arriving in San Francisco on April 10th. He mined for seven months in Tuolumne Co where he built a saw-mill and operated a lumber business. In 1858 he was elected for two years. In 1860 he moved to Virginia City, Nevada, where he prospected and mined in that district for two years. Then he returned to San Francisco and opened a pork-packing business. He did this for three years. Next he became a traveling salesman for Smith, Brown & Co. He remained with this company for four years. Until 1877 he speculated in mining stocks at which time he retired from business and settled at Saucelito. [HMCoCA p482]

Charles[7] married to Sarah M. Wylie in Madison, Sullivan Co. NY on 4-26-1843. [Bowman p213]

Children:

	i	**Clarissa H.**[8] b 1846 in Sullivan, NY
	ii	**Teresa**[8] b 1846 listed on the 1860 CA census
527	ii	**Charles W.**[8] b 1850 in Sullivan, NY [1860 CAFC]
528	iii	**Samuel Jerome**[8] was b May of 1858 in CA. The 1860-1900 CA census shows **Samuel J.**[8] Severance in San Francisco with his wife, Lillian S. b April 1864 in CA, and their children. The 1910 CA census shows the same **Samuel J.**[8] *Sevirmance* family living in San Anselmo, Marin Co. without the eldest son, **Frederick C.**[9] Severance
529	iv	**Frederick V.**[8] *Sevirance*, b in CA in February of 1863. He m to Lena, who was b April of 1871 in NJ, and a daughter, **Zella G.**[9] b September of 1896. **Frederick's**[8] mother, Sarah M. b March 1821 in NY, was living with them. [1900 CAFC] In the **Fred**[8] was living in San Francisco as a boarder with no family listed. **Zella G.**[9] was living as a lodger of Rasmus Rasmussen. [1910 CAFC]

(251) Martin Joan[7], (Asa[6], Martin[5], Martin[4], Joseph[3], John[2], John[1]), was born at Shelburn Falls, MA on 12-

24-1826. He was educated at the Shelburn Falls Academy and at Williamston Seminary at East Hampton. He studied law with John Wells, of Chickopee, and Beach and Bond, of Springfield, MA.

He moved to MN in 1856 and entered the law profession. He married Elizabeth P. Van Horn on 6-16-1858. She was born 5-7-1834 at Chicopee, MA and died on 3-18-1910. He was elected from the County of Sibley to the lower house of the Legislature in 1859 and 1862. In August of 1862 he enlisted as a private in Company I, 10th Regiment MN Volunteer Infantry, and served in the Indian War of 1862 in MN, and then 8 months in the Civil War.

He was mustered into his own Company as Captain and served until the end of the war. As a part of Gen. A.J. Smith's Sixteenth Army Corps, the Regiment participated in the battles about Tupelo, MS, July 13-15, 1864. Later in the same year it was on the "Oxford raid" when the town of Oxford, MS, was burned in retaliation for the destruction of the town of Chambersburg, PA, by the Confederates. In August he went to Devall's Bluff, AK, and from this post in September they started on the long and toilsome expedition of Gen. A.J. Smith after the Confederate raiding force under General Price that had invaded MO. The Tenth Regiment marched on this expedition from Devall's Bluff, through AK and MO almost to the KS line, near Kansas City, or until the Confederates had been overtaken by General Pleasanton's and General Curtis' Cavalry commands and defeated at the Little Blue, the Big Blue and Westport, all near the western line of MO, in the neighborhood of Kansas City. Then, with the main part of Smith's Corps, it was sent to TN, arriving at Nashville, November 30. It took part in the battles at Nashville, December 15 and 16, 1864, and on the latter day participated in the assault on General Hood's Confederate lines. After the victory it took part in the pursuit of Hood's broken army to the Tennessee river, going into camp for a month at Eastport, AL. In early spring of 1865 it was sent to the Gulf of Mexico and participated in the capture of Mobile, April 9. 1865.

After the war he returned to law pratice at LeSueur, MN. He later moved to Mankato and then St. Paul, MN. He was appointed Judge of the Sixth Judicial District by the Governor Pillsbury of MN in June of 1881. That appointment was to fill a vacancy. He was elected to that office in November of 1881 and again in 1888. [MBD p156-157] [Bryant p567] [DARGRC #259394][Flandrau]

Children: [MDLB]
   i   **Winthrop G.**[8] b 5-2-1859 and d in Mankato, MN at the age of 39. He m to Nettie Watkins on 8-20-1890. Nettie was from Racine, WI
   ii   **Frank G.**[8] b 4-15-1868 in Mankato, MN but later moved to NE and engaged in railroading.
   iii   **Nettie J.**[3] b 12-6-1871

(252) Melvin A.[7] **/Asa Melvin**[7], (Asa[6], Martin[5], Martin[4], Joseph[3], John[2], John[1]), was born 6-4-1833 at Shelburn Falls, MA. He married Mary Ann Early, daughter of John Lynch, 9-6-1854 at Buckland, MA. [MAVR] He married secondly to Mrs. Isabell Vroman on 6-18-1870. Isabell was born 11-2-1843. The 1860 VT census shows **Melvin**[7] and Mary A. living in Rockingham with no children. They settled in Belding, Ionia Co. MI. He served in the Civil War. [MISS] Pension was filed for by **Melvin**[7] on 6-18-1888 in Canada and by his widow on 3-26-1919 from NY. [CWPR] Isabell had been married before as the census shows the family with a step daughter born in 1875 (Alice Vroman). [1900 MIFC]

Children:
   i   **Mary L.**[8] born 8-31-1861
   ii   **Julia M.**[8] born 1-18-1863
   iii   **Elizabeth T.**[8] born 8-23-1867

(253) Alvin A.[7], (Asa[6], Martin[5], Martin[4], Joseph[3], John[2], John[1]), was born 3-7-1848 in Shelburne, MA. [MAVR] He apparently settled in CT. All of the children were born in that state. He was known as a lock shop worker. The family shows on the 1880-1920 CT census. He married Mary Evaline ____, who was born 11- -1854 in CT.

Children:
   i   **Mildred M.**[8] b 12- -1873 m Philly Stark of NY.
   ii   **Bertha (Beatrice E.)**[8] b 8- -1875, m ____Burchard. The 1920 CT census shows their two children who were b in NJ **Beatrice**[3], and the children show but no husband.

iii   **Howard O.**[8] b 1877. **Howard O.**[8], age 42 b
       CT (where his parents were from) and
       living in Bath, Sagadahoc Co. ME [1920
       MEFC]
iv   **Earl D.**[8] b in CT in July of 1881. [1900
       CTFC]. He is shown m to Violet A. ____.
       The 1920 CT census shows **Alvin A.**[7] and
       Mary E. Severance in Stamford, CT with
       Earl D.[8] and his wife Violet, and two of
       Alvin's sisters, **Mildred**[8] Stack and
       Beatrice[8] Buchard,

(254) William Morgan[7], (Elisha[6], Samuel[5], Martin[4],
Joseph[3], John[2], John[1]), born on 2-12-1832. He
married to Mary Turner Latimer on 6-8-1859. [OHVR]
They lived at Chicago Jct., Troy Mills, OH. They
settled in Calhoun, Richland Co. IL. Mary was b 11-
-1834. [1900 ILFC] Mary was the daughter of John
Mulford Latimer and Mary Emily Turner of Troy
Mills. **William Morgan**[7] d 8-3-1883 [MHS]

Children: [JFS p53]
     i   **Mary Latimer**[8] b 8-31-1861
     ii   **Julia M.**[8] b 1-18-1863
     iii   **Elizabeth Turner**[8] b 8-23-1867

(255) Warren[7], (Elisha[6], Samuel[5], Martin[4], Joseph[3],
John[2], John[1]), born on 10-9-1836 in Sandusky County,
OH. He married to Philinda Shepherd, daughter of
Israel Shepard of NY state, on 2-9-1860. Warren was
a school teacher and although he was also a farmer
he devoted full attention to his teaching duties.
In 1876, **Warren**[7] entered the legal profession and
on 3-28-1878, he was admitted to the bar at
Bucyrus, OH. By 6-3-1880 he was admitted to
practice in the United States Courts at Toledo, OH.
He was appointed as legal counsel for the Baltimore
and Ohio Railroad Company in 1891. He also assumed
full charge of an Insurance and Real Estate Company
in Chicago Juction, Huron Co. OH. **Warren**[7] was also
instrumental in the organization of the
Presbyterian Church at Chicago Junction. [H&LCoOH
p321]

Children:
530 i   **Elmer W.**[8] b 8-16-1861 [MHS]
     ii   **Clara May**[8] b 9-24-1868 m C.A.
           Weatherford of Chicago Junction [IGI]

Warren Severance

WARREN[7] SEVERANCE

ELMER[8] SEVERANCE

183

(256) **Byron**[7], (Elisha[6], Samuel[5], Martin[4], Joseph[3], John[2], John[1]), born on 2-2-1839. He married to Charlotte A. Arthur on 9-20-1859 [OHVR] in Chicago, Huron Co. OH. Charlotte was born 2-25-1840. They settled in that area.

Children: [JFS p53]
531 i   **Arthur Leason**[8] [Obituary Notice] b 7-14-1860 d 1935 m Mary E. West 1-7-1885 [MHS]
532 ii   **Ernest E.**[8] b 7-15-1868 d after 1935 (Obituary notice of **Arthur Leason**[7] Severance)

BYRON[7] SEVERANCE

ARTHUR L.[8] SEVERANCE

184

(257) John Franklin[7], (Fairfield[6], Selah[5], Martin[4], Joseph[3], John[2], John[1]), born on 1-26-1833 in Shelburn Falls, MA. (MAVR) He married Laura Angeline Ware on 1-1-1859. [VTVR] Laura A. Ware was born in April of 1841. The children were all born in MA but the family lived in Halifax, VT.

Children:
- i   **Clayton F.[8]** b 12-8-1859 in Shelburne Falls, MA. He m Amelia Koomry on 10-8-1884. The 1900 and 1920 MA census shows them without children
- ii   **Hattie Minetta[8]** b 6-24-1861 d 10-12-1863 at Buckland, MA. [MAVR]
- iii   **John Franklin[8]** b 11-16-1862 at Buckland, MA d 6-22-1889 at Shelburne, MA, unm. [MAVR]
- iv   **Jennie L.[3]** b 4-25-1865 at Shelburne, MA [MAVR]
- v   **Ethelyn Daisy[8]** b 11-2-1870 at Shelburne, MA [MAVR]
- vi   **Charles L.[8]** b 7-3-1878 possibly had a male twin. [MAVR]

(258) Herbert Francis[7] (**Francis H.[7]**), (Luther[6], Selah[5], Martin[4], Joseph[3], John[2], John[1]), born on 7-9-1848. [MAVR] He married to Cornelia D. Ferguson, who was born in 1848 in MI, and they settled in Jones, MI [JFS p54]

Children:
- i   **Nellie Maud[8]** b 2-7-1871
- ii   **Clara Belle[8]** b 9-14-1875

(259) Warren Decatur[7], (Seth[6], David[5], John[4], Joseph[3], John[2], John[1]), born on 11-17-1812. He married Sarah Bullock on 10-15-1837. Sarah was born 7-2-1814. They settled in Pulaski, MI. [JFS p54]

In May of 1835 he went to MI and located on a farm of 80 acres in Sec. 23. Ten years later he traded that land and bought a farm of 140 acres in Sec. 20. He returned to NY in 1835 and taught school for one winter. After his marriage in 1837 he returned to MI with his wife, where has remained ever since. [HJCoMI]

Children:
- i   **Helen[8]** b 4-7-1839
- ii   **Adalaide[8]** b 5-2-1848
- iii   **Joseph[3]** b 1849

iii   **Lovell Bullock**[8] b 1-31-1852 m May
          Gertrude Jacobs 10-6-1879 in Pulaski,
          Jackson, Co. MI. They lived in Albion,
          Calhoun Co. MI

(260) Joseph A.[7], (Seth[6], David[5], John[4], Joseph[3],
John[2], John[1]), born on 7-17-1816. He married to
Caroline E. Wales, who was born in 1827 in NY, on
2-11-1850. They settled in Mexico, NY. **Joseph**[7] died
on 4-23-1859. Caroline was with her young family as
a widow in 1860. [NYFC]

Children: [JFS p54]
533   i   **Seth**[8] b 2-10-1851 m Emma Steele
      ii   **George**[8] b 12-15-1853 d 10-10-1856
      iii **Wales Frank**[8] b 11-1-1855 had a law
           practice in Lincoln, NE
      iv   **George W.**[8] b 9-1-1857, He wrote articles
           for *Forrest and Stream* and *Angler,* d 3-
           12-1884 of an inherited lung disorder.
           At the early age of eleven, George made
           a profession of his faith with the
           Presbyterian church. He entered Hamilton
           College in 1876 and graduated from Law
           School in June of 1881. He was admitted
           as attorney and counselor at law and
           went to Lincoln, NE to enter with his
           brother, **W.F.**[8] Severance. [JFS p54-55]
      v   **John**[8] b 9-1-1857 d 11-25-1878

(261) Avery[7], (Seth[6], David[5], John[4], Joseph[3], John[2],
John[1]), born 2-2-1819 at New Haven, Oswego Co. NY.
He married to Julia Nichols Marvin, daughter of
Nathaniel Marvin and Julia Nichols, on 3-7-1844.
Julia was born 9-5-1823. They settled in New Haven,
NY [1860 NYFC] where **Avery**[7] died on 2-15-1874.
   Avery[7] was a highly respected citizen of Oswego
Co. NY. He was successful farmer of crops and
stock. He served on the Board of Advisors for the
county. In 1865, he represented the Third Assembly
District for the county in the Legislature. He went
by the name "Squire Severance". [JFS p56]

Children:
      i   **Noble D.**[8] b 6-18-1845 d 1-18-1875 m
           Harriet Matthews in 1868. They
           reportedly had one daughter, **Lena J.**[9]
           Severance who lived in Mexico, NY.
      ii   **Orla Avery**[8] b 8-19-1846 d 1-21-1869 unm

(263) William[7], (Horace[6], David[5], John[4], Joseph[3], John[2], John[1]), born on 12-7-1832 at Barnardstown, MA. He married Mary G. Welch, daughter of Benjamin F. and Mary F. Welch, 6-11-1854 at Hadley, MA. [MAVR] He served in the Civil War from 1861-1863 for the North. **William**[7] and Mary lived in Ludlow, MA. The family living in Ludlow, Hampden Co.in 1870. [1870 MAFC] **William**[7] was found dead in bed on 1-4-1892 at Ludlow, MA. [MAVR]

Children: [MAVR]
- i **Male** d 2-3-1855 at Shelburn, MA. He was b at South Hadley, MA [MAVR]
- ii **Female** b 4-27-1855 at South Hadley, MA [MAVR]
- iii **Male twins** b 4-14-1856 at South Hadley, MA [MAVR]
- iv **Female** b 7-13-1858 at South Hadley, MA [MAVR]
- v **Franklin E.**[8] d 5-4-1892, age 36 yrs 20 dys, at Ludlow of Bright's disease. He was single. [MAVR] The 1870 MA census shows Frank E. and Edwin F., both b in 1834. These are either the same person or they were twins.
- vi **Ada**[8] b 1860 at Ludlow. She m Elihu White, son of Loomis and Harriet White, on 6-11-1881 at Longmeadow, MA. [MAVR]
- vii **Eva E.**[8] b 1-18-1860 at Chicopee, MA [MAVR] m William A. Miller, son of Leonard and Mary Miller, on 12-10-1884 at Ludlow, MA. [MAVR]

(264) Daniel Healey[7], (Daniel[6], Daniel[5], John[4], Joseph[3], John[2], John[1]), born 9-25-1834 [JFS p57] (LSD Archive records says that **Daniel**[7] was born 12-25-1841) he died 9-16-1871. He married to Muraluisa (Melissa) Lewis on 1-1-1863. [JFS] They settled in Davenport, Scott Co. IA.

Children: born in Davenport, IA
- 535 i **Lewis Eggleston**[8] b 11-27-1863 m Mary E. Houghton 12-5-1888
- ii **Gertrude Iowa**[8] b 7-10-1866 m William Alan McCulloch 10-13-1887. He was b 11-6-1864
- iii **Sarah Ellen**[8] b 5-30-1869 m Jesse C. Wilson 5- -1888 settled in Denver, CO

(265) James Taggart[7], (Jonathan[6], Jonathan[5], Jonathan[4], Joseph[3], John[2], John[1]), born 9-4-1824 at Truxton, Courtland Co., NY. He married to Marian P. Botsford on 10-22-1856. She was born 5-9-1838 (grave stone says 1836) at Granger, NY died 12-11-1893 at Belfast, NY. He settled as a farmer in Canadea, Allegany Co., NY. [HACoNY] They moved to Hutchinson, KS in 1895. **James Taggart[7]** died on 10-20-1913 at Rural Halstead, Harvey Co. KS. He was buried at Burrton, KS.

As **Harold G.[10]** Severance wrote of his great grandfather, **"James Taggert[7]** Severance is buried in Burton, KS while his wife Marion Botsford Severance is buried in Belfast, NY. According to my late Uncle **Martin Elbert** Severance's information, after Marion d in 1893, **James[7]** just could not get along with relatives left in NY so he moved to KS to be near his sons Willard and Martin. Every now and then there was a spat and **James[7]** would move back to NY and live with the sister Elmira. When they could not get along he would move back to KS." [MHGS}

Children: [MHGS}
536	i	**John[8]** b 8-9-1859 m Lovilla Jane (Jennie) Markham 1-29-1885 d 9-16-1946 at Concordia, KS. The Severances of North Central KS are descendents of **John[8]** and Jennie of Belfast, Allegany Co. NY
537	ii	**Willard Lorenzo[8]** b 9-1-1862 d 2-26-1947 m Mary Rosetta Shank 12-24-1881 d at Newton, KS
538	iii	**Martin Harrison[8]** b 6-12-1875 d 1-22-1924 m Allia Grover C.A. Allbright 11-2-1911

(266) John[7], (Jonathan[6], Jonathan[5], Jonathan[4], Joseph[3], John[2], John[1]), born 2-25-1830. He married to Elizabeth Westcott on 5-25-1860. In 1853, **John[7]** left NY State and went to MO and became an engineer in the construction of the Hannibal and St. Joe and the St. Joe and Denver Railroad. He served as State Senator for that state in 1864 and was a colonel for the state militia in the Civil War. He was Mayor of St. Joseph (family records say he was mayor of Hutchinson, KS) for several years. In 1877 he moved to Axtell, Marshall Co. KS, then to Hutchinson, Reno Co. KS. Doniphan Co. KS, has a township named "Severance" after this **John[7]** Severance.

"*Severance*, one of the incorporated towns of Doniphan County, lies along the Wolf River. The town, named after **John**[6] Severance, was founded in 1869 and incorporated in 1877, **John**[6], with C.C. Clonch and Dr. Robert Gunn laid out the town. Some of the first settlers in the community were C.C. Clonch, Swintz and Waggoner. In 1855 Clonch was attacked in his cabin by Swintz and Waggoner, both of whom he killed. There is an account of a battle being fought on the site of Severance in 1844 between the Sacs and Foxes and the Pawnees." [Blackmar Vol II p671]

Children: [1880 KSFC]
- i **William O.**[8] b 3-12-1861 in MO, was living in Spring, KS in 1900 with his mother and brother, **Arthur**[8].
- ii **Jane Isabella**[8] b 2-28-1861 in NY
- iii **Clara**[8] b 12-7-1863 d 9-11-1864
- iv **Arthur**[8] b 8-4-1865 in MO, Lived in KS. He married to Katherine B. _____ who was born in 1873. [1880 OKFC] They show living in MO, KS, and Oklahoma City, OK. The 1920 OK census shows **Arthur**[8] living with his wife Kathrine B. and John Ballard, age 20, a nephew, and **William O.**[8], a brother. It states that **Arthur**[8] was born in MO. It also states that **William O.**[8] was born in MO. Elizabeth was age 60, born 9- -1839 in NY and with her sons **William**[8] age 39 born 3- -1861 in MO and **Arthur**[8] born 8- -1865 in MO in 1900. They were living in Spring, Harper Co KS. [KSFC]
- 540 v **John Elbert**[8] b 9-17-1869 in MO m Arminta _____, they later settled in CA

(267) David Smith[7], (John[6], Jonathan[5], Jonathan[4], Joseph[3], John[2], John[1]), born 10-13-1819 in Truxton, NY. He married Harriet Newell Jeffrey on 2-15-1842. They remained on the family farm and raised their family. **David**[7] had in his possession one of the wheels that carried his grandfathers family from Greenfield, MA in 1800. [JFS p59]

Children:
- i **John Jeffrey**[8] b 11-24-1848 d 3-12-1853
- ii **Jennie Harriet**[8] b 11-24-1852, the 1900 NY census shows a daughter **Harriet**[8] who m to Ray Woodward. Perhaps **Jennie** was also named **Harriet**[8]. The 1900 NY census

indicates that **Jennie**[8] is the only living daughter.
  iii   **David Allen**[8] b 12-19-1854 d 7-19-1855

(268) Calvin[7], (John[6], Jonathan[5], Jonathan[4], Joseph[3], John[2], John[1],) was born 5-15-1825. He married to Rosamond M. Fay on 3-21-1848. They began farming in Truxton, NY but moved to another farm near Cortland in 1863 and lived there the remaider of his life. [JFS p59] In 1860 he was living in Truxton, Cortland Co. [NYFC]

Children: [1860 NYFC]
  i   **George**[8] b 3-15-1850 m Lucy Electa Stillman, daughter of Linus Stillman and Rhoda Crampton Alvord, 2-22-1872. She b 12-1-1848 d 12-29-1888, Cortland, NY. He m second to Lizzie _____ who was b 5- -1865 according to the 1900 NY census. They lived at Cortland, NY. The 1900 NY census shows with **Arthur**[10] age 14 b 3- -1886 b in OH as a grandson.
  ii   **Louisa**[8] b 1856
  iii **Elizabeth**[8] b 1859

(269) Ephraim Hubbard[7], (Joseph[6], Joseph[5], Jonathan[4], Joseph[3], John[2], John[1]), born 9-27-1805 at Grafton, MA. He married Maria H. Street on 5-16-1843 at Grafton, MA. [MAVR] Maria Howe (Biscoe) daughter of Thomas and Bathsheba (Howe) Biscoe, born 6-27-1814 of Cambridge, MA, was first married to (3-22-1832) George Street. Maria's maternal great uncle kept the "Wayside Inn" of Sudbury, MA. [Street p135-136] **Ephraim Hubbard**[7] and Maria settled in Boston, MA. He died on 10-30-1879 at Worcester, MA age 74, a bookkeeper, resided at Newton. [MAVR]

Children: [JFS p58-59]
  i   **George L.**[8] b 3-14-1850
  ii   **Louisa M.**[8] b 5-7-1856
  iii **Lizzie Helen**[8] b 12-26-1859
  iv **John E.**[8] b 6-2-1867. **John E.**[8] was b 6- -1867, and living with Rose b 5- -1826, his mother, and others including Lois R. b 5- -1855 and Linda b 12- -1859. [1900 NYFC Cortland]
  v   **Arthur C.**[8] b 3-6-1869 d 8-22-1869
  vi **James Hubbard**[8] b 9-14-1844 d 2-10-1845
  vii **James Hubbard**[8] b 1-26-1845 d 2-26-1845
      [MAVR]

(270) Joseph Fisk[7], ¦Horace[6], Joseph[5], Jonathan[4], Joseph[3], John[2], John[1]¦, born 4-29-1831 at Greenfield, MA and settled in VT. He married to Flora Vinning/Gilligan 10-16-1859 [VTVR]

Children:
i   **Seth[8]**, There is a Seth b 8-15-1861 at Greenfield, MA to **Joseph F.[7]** Severance and Flora Vining [MAVR]
ii   **female** b 9-7-1862 at Chicopee, MA daughter of J.F. and Flora H. King. [MAVR]

(271) Edwin W.[7], (Pliny[6], Joseph[5], Jonathan[4], Joseph[3], John[2], John[1]), born 11-30-1825. He married to Caroline Agatha St. John on 4-29-1859. [OHVR Hamilton County, OH] They settled in Lincoln, IA. The family left IA after 1880 and settled in Jefferson Co. KY. Carrie was born in IN in April of 1839. [1900 KYFC]. She was widowed at that time. She had a total of 7 children but only 6 were living in 1900.

Children: [JFS p60]
i   **Edwin K.[8]** b 2-13-1860 in WI. He was living in KY in 1910 in Jefferson Co. with a wife Edith A., b 1866 in KY, and their son, **Murray[9]** b 1897, and daughter **Lou Virginia[9]** b 1899. Both of the children were b in KY.
ii   **Carlton Metcalf[8]** b 3-16-1861
iii   **William Mulholland[8]** b 8-11-1863 at Louisville, Jefferson Co. KY. He d 4-13-1895 in Los Angeles, CA. He m to Fearietta Weller, daughter of Zechariah Weller and Eliza Klingaman. Fear was b 6-27-1871 at Waterloo, Black Hawk Co. IA. Fear m second to Robert Gay Dupuy on 12-3-1898.
iv   **Lewis Howard[8]** b 3-13-1868 in IA
v   **Henry Wrisley[8]** b 12-11-1876 in IA. A **Henry W.[8]** Severance, b 1873, in IA but living in Elizabeth Town, Hardin Co. KY. [1920 KYFC]. He was m to Rose A. Zoeller, who was b 1878 in KY, and they had a son **Glenn L.[9]**, b 5-21-1912 in KY. [KYVR]
vi   **May Florence[8]** b 12-6-1877 in IA
vii   **Ellen Josephine[8]** b 6-13-1879 in IA

(272) George[7], (Pliny[6], Joseph[5], Jonathan[4], Joseph[3], John[2], John[1]), born 11-30-1827 in MA. (MAVR) He married to Eliza Elizabeth Bacchus in Guilford, VT on 11-24-1849. [VTVR]

Eliza was born on 3-12-1826 and she was from CT. Although **George[7]** was b in Greenfield, MA he moved to East Hartford, CT in 1854 and worked at his trade as burnisher until 1856, when he moved to and located in Grundy Co. IA and moved to Hudson in 1860. The 1900 IA census shows them at Black Hawk.

George[7] held offices of School Director one year, and Road Supervisor for three years. He was the first Road Supervisor elected in Grundy Co. There were only two houses in Grundy when **George[7]** first brought his family. He hauled the lumber from Dubuque, with an ox team, and built the first frame house built in Grundy Center. He came through from Chicago to Waterloo with team in 1856. He said "it rained every day but one while on the way." Mable Chambers, a grand daughter, age 12 who was born in 1888 and is living with **George[7]** and his wife. [1900 IA Census] [HBHCoIA p565]

Children: [JFS p60]
i	**Ann Elisabeth[8]**	b 2-18-1852 at Greenfield, MA [MAVR]
ii	**Isabel Maria[8]**	b 11-4-1854
iii	**Virginia Emma[8]**	b 5-14-1859
iv	**Carrie Josephine[8]**	b 10-24-1861
541 v	**Charles Frederic Malcom[8]**	b 7-4-1864

(273) Charles[7], (Pliny[6], Joseph[5], Jonathan[4], Joseph[3], John[2], John[1]), born in Greenfield, Franklin Co. MA on 9-5-1838. [MAVR] He died 9-5-1888 in Grundy, IA. In 1856, he moved to Grundy Center, IA with his mother and two sisters to where his father and the rest of the family had settled a short time earlier. At that time there were only three families living in Grundy. **Charles[7]** spent the rest of his life in that area. On 5-28-1880, **Charles[8]** married Miss Elizabeth E. Robson, a daughter of Thomson Robson of NY State.

Charles[7] was a Republican but never aspired to official office. He was held in high regard by all who knew him. He was interprising, public spirited and progressive.

He made a specialty of breeding thoroughbred short-horn cattle, keeping on hand registered stock. He was one of the leading farmers in Grundy

County with his 180 acres under a high state of cultivation. [P&BIA p386]

Children: [1900 IAFC]
        i   **Gertrude R.**[8] b 8- -1881 in Iowa
        ii   **Bertha R.**[8] b 8- -1882
542   iii   **Frank**[8] b 2- -1885

(274) Frederick Hollister[7], (Pliny[6], Joseph[5], Jonathan[4], Joseph[3], John[2], John[1]), born 9-24-1841 in Greenfield, MA. [MAVR] He served three years in the First IA Cavalry during the Civil War. **Frederick**[7] m Catherine L. Graves, daughter of William A. and Julia A. Graves, 10-11-1877. The 1880 IA census shows **F.H.**[7] Severance age 38 born in MA, living in Palermo, Grundy Co. It included Kate Graves, age 21, as his wife and born in Brattleboro, VT. Living with them were a daughter, **G.B.**[8] age 1, and Frederick's father **Pliny**[6] Severance. Kate's mother, J.A., age 64 and Kate's brother, W.A., age 23, were also living with them. The 1900 Meade, Merrick Co. NE census shows **Fred**[7] born 9- -1841 in MA with his wife, Catherine L. Graves, born 5- -1856 in VT. They were living in Omaha, Douglas Co. NE in 1920.

Children:
        i   **Grace B.**[3] b 8- -1878 in IA
543   ii   **Ralph S.**[3] b 9- -1882 in IA. [1900 NEFC]

(275) Solomon Lewis[7], (Robert Bruce[6], Solomon[5], Jonathan[4], Joseph[3], John[2], John[1]), born 4-8-1812. [MAVR] He married Mary H. Long on 11-12-1833. [OHVR] They settled in Cleveland, OH. **Solomon**[7] died on 7-13-1838, only five years after his marriage. Mary died on 10-1-1902.

Mary Long, the only child of Dr. David Long, was born and lived her life in Cleveland. Her father was a pioneer Doctor in Clevland. the distinguished pioneer physician of Cleveland. She was well educated and cultured.

She was active in the sanitary commission during the Civil War and assisted in the founding of the Protestant Orphan Asylum and the Lakeside Hospital. [Coates]

Children: [JFS]
544   i   **Solon Long**[8] b 9-8-1834 m Emily C. Allen
545   ii   **Louis Henry**[8] b 8-1-1838 m Fannie B.
                Benedict

(276) Theodoric Cordenio[7], (Robert[6], Solomon[5], Jonathan[4], Joseph[3], John[2], John[1]), born Shelburn Centre, MA on 3-1-1814. He lived there until he was fifteen years old. He then moved to Elyria, OH where he was a clerk. Next he went to Auburn, NY where he had a position in the Bank of Auburn. In 1836, he went to Cleveland, OH where he lived for the next twenty years while working as a banker. He married to Caroline M. Seymour, daughter of Orson and Caroline M. (Clarke) Seymour, on 8-27-1840. She was born 1-12-1820 died 11-10-1914. [JFS p61]

Theodoric[7] went to Boston, MA and engaged as cashier in the Bank of the Republic in 1855 and remained until 1862. Then because of his failing health he moved to South Carolina. He was appointed as Special Agent of the Treasury Department and Acting Collector of Customs for the District of Beaufort. He remained at this post for about four year he returned to Boston and then to Los Angeles CA where he lived until his death on 10-21-1892.

Caroline Maria was born in Canandaigua, NY, daughter of a banker. He died when Caroline was very young and she was under the guardinaship of an uncle with religious fervor and a mother who never recovered from the loss of her husband. Caroline was fifteen when she graduated from the Female Seminary at Geneva, NY, valedictorian of her class.

She was active in many Public affairs. In 1853 she was the first woman to read a paper before the Mercantile Library Association of Cleveland. The Ohio Woman's Rights Association asked her to submit a paper on woman's rights for circulation.

Caroline became known as "the mother of Clubs". The New England Women's Club in Boston. The Woman's club of Los Angeles, the Los Angeles Free Kindergarten Association, the Los Angeles Fellowship Club, the Severance Club, and the Ebell Club of Los Angeles are all credited to her. She also served as trustee of the public library and the Unitarian Church. [Malone]

Children:
- i **Orson Seymour[8]** b 7-5-1841 d 7-9-1841
- ii **James Seymour[8]** b 7-5-1842. Settled in San Francisco. Living alone on 1910 CA census
- iii **Julia Long[8]** b 3-8-1844 m Edward C. Burrage, son of Johnson C., and Emeline Burrage, 1-16-1866, at Newton, MA. [MAVR]

| 547 | iv | **Mark Sibley**[8] b 10-28-1846 settled in Los Angeles, CA. He married Anne Crittenden |
| 548 | v | **Pierre Clarke**[8] b 9-16-1849 settled in Boston, MA m 5-9-1883 to Isabel Morgan Rotch, daughter of William J. Rotch and Emily Morgan, of New Bedford, MA. [Jones p200] |

(277) Otis Cathestus[7], (Otis[6], Solomon[5], Jonathan[4], Joseph[3], John[2], John[1]), born in MA on 11-13-1816. [MAVR] He married to Emeline Stevens on 12-28-1837. Emeline was born 7-12-1824 and died 4-13-1889. The family settled in Dundaff, PA. **Otis**[7] died on 4-1-1877 in Dundaff. [JFS p61]

Children:

	i	**Eunice**[8] b 11-12-1838 d 9-24-1872 m Emery Harding
	ii	**Oresamus**[8] b 7-5-1840 d 4-11-1841
549	iii	**Oliver Cathestus**[8] b 10-24-1842 m Mary Harding, of PA, in 1863. She d in 1864 and he remarried to Sarah C. Bell on 3-16-1865.
550	iv	**Otis Cordenio**[8] b 10-25-1845 m Carrie Celestia Wetherby of PA
551	v	**Eugene Kincaid**[8] b 3-31-1848
	vi	**Emma Jane**[8] b 8-11-1851 m Luther Miller
552	vii	**Oscar Alphonso**[8] b 5-24-1854 m Matilda Bennett
	viii	**Emery**[8] b 2-18-1860. The 1900 PA census for Lenox, Susquehanna Co shows **Emery**[8] with his wife Annie Miller, daughter of Douglas S. Miller, and **Emery's**[8] daughter, **Orlie E.**[9] b in July 1886 in PA. They were all b in PA.

(278) Erasmus Cordenio[7], (Otis[6], Solomon[5], Jonathan[4], Joseph[3], John[2], John[1]), born in MA on 10-12-1829. He married to Amanda Julia Arnold on 9-28-1859. Amanda was born 6-29-1835. They moved first to Susquehanna Co. PA and then later settled in Manterville, MN.

Erasmus[7] was born in Susquehanna Co. PA and engaged in the mercantile business, lumbering and farming in PA and MN. He came to MN in 1855, and he resided here ever since. He was County Auditor of Dodge Co. in this State, for six years, and was about fifteen years ago, State Senator from that county. His wife, Amanda J. (Arnold) Severance, was born in CT and reared in MI. She d 3-6-1894. [Flandrau]

Children:
553 i   **Cordenio Arnold**[8] b 6-30-1862 m Mary
        Frances Harriman
   ii   **Carrie Ann**[8] b 9-14-1869

(279) James Ralph[7], (Ralph[6], Elihu[5], Jonathan[4],
Joseph[3], John[2], John[1]), born 4-5-1846 in VT. He
married to Rosa S. Gridley on 8-8-1871. [OHVR] They
settled in Bellevue, OH. The 1900-1910 OH census
shows them living at Oberlin, Lorain Co, OH.

Children:
   i   **Julia G.**[8] b 1-11-1877 [JFS p62]

(280) Franklin C.[7], (Ptolemy[6], Elihu[5], Jonathan[4],
Joseph[3], John[2], John[1]), born in Greenfield, MA on
12-24-1837. He married to Sallie J. Thurman on 5-
28-1828. He graduated from Amherst College in 1863.
At the start of the Civil War he enlisted as a
private in Company A. 52d Regt. of MA Vols., was
promoted to Lieutenant of his Company. After his
regular service he re-enlisted in the regular army
as hospital steward. His service as steward took
him to several hospitals where he served until
mustered out in November of 1866. At that time he
was employed as a clerk in the Treasury Department
at Washington, D.C. [JFS p62-63]

Children:
554 i   **Cassell**[8] b 3-18-1869
   ii   **Lizzie Barbes**[8] b 1-8-1873
  iii   **Frank Bidwell**[8] b 5-15-1875 He was shown
        on the 1880 WA D.C. census with his
        parents. He lived in NH.

(281) George[7], (Franklin C.[6], Rufus[5], Jonathan[4],
Joseph[3], John[2], John[1]), possibly born 5- -1844 in
IL. [1900 SDFC]. It seems probable that **George**[7] was
born in IL where his parents were living. The 1880
IA census for Union, Plymouth Co. IA, shows him
with his family and children who were b in IL. In
1900 he was with his with his wife, Mary A. ____,
who was born in August of 1847 in Pennsylvania, and
one of his daughters **Edith M.**[8], who was b in
September of 1875 in IL. [1900 SDFC]

Children: born in IL
   i   **Albert M.**[8] b 1871 in IL. The 1900 IA
        census shows him living alone in Union,
        Plymouth Co. In 1920 he was living in

Cavour, Beadle Co. without a family.
[SDFC]
ii   **Edith**[8] b 9- -1875
iii   **George W.**[9] b 1876 in IA. He m Nellie M.
        who was b in 1884 in SD. They had a son,
        Wales A.[10] b 1916 in SD. [CWPR] show that
        a claim was filed by **George W.**[9], the
        invalid 8-24-1892 from IA and by the
        widow 9-29-1919 from SD for service I
        141 IL Inf.
iv   **Bertha**[8] b 1877

(282) Charles W.[7], (George W.[6], Rufus[5], Jonathan[4],
Joseph[3], John[2], John[1]), born in Greenfield, MA on 3-
18-1842. He married Emma Nicholson, of PA, on 1-2-
1870. They settled sometime in Hinckley, IL, where
there first 4 children were born. Then they moved
to IA where there other children were born. The
1880 IL census gives the early times and the 1900
IA census shows the remainder of the children. They
were supposed to have had 6 sons but I could only
find 5 sons and 2 daughters.

Children:
        i   **John**[8] b 1871 and was living in Iowa in
                1900 and born in IL. [IAFC]
557   ii   **Walter I.**[9] b 1- -1875 in IL later lived
                in Waterman, O'brian Co. IA
558   iii   **Elmer**[8] b 1- -1877 in IL
559   iv   **Robert**[8] b 7- -1880 in IL
        v   **Ray C.**[8] b 6- -1883 in IA [1900 IAFC]
        vi   **Anna M.**[8] b 11- -1886 in IA
        vii   **Clara M.**[8] b 11- -1890 in IA

(284) James H.[7], (Charles[6], Moses[5], Moses[4], Joseph[3],
John[2], John[1]), born 6-20-1844 in Pompey, NY. He
married Mary E. Barber on 2-12-1868. She was born
on 2-18-1845. They settled in Hamilton, NY. [JFS
p63]
    The [1900 NYFC] says that **James**[7] was born in MA.
All the other members of the family were born in
NY.

Children:
        i   **Harry James**[8] b 3-18-1870. He m to
                Ida___, who was b 4- -1877. **Harry**[8]
                Severance age 29 b 3- -1879 in IN was
                living in San Antonia, Bexar Co. TX,
                with Ida, his wife, age 22 b 4- -1877 in
                TX. They were m one year. **Harry's**[8]

197

father and mother were both b in Boston, MA. [1900 TXFC]

ii **Charles Barber**[8] b 5-21-1876. He shows as living in NY

(285) Henry Weld[7], (Luther[6], Elihu[5], Moses[4], Joseph[3], John[2], John[1]), born 7-12-1828 in Augusta, ME. He attended school at Augusta and later at Cazenovia Seminary, Madison Co. NY. In 1848 he sailed from Boston, around Cape Horn to San Francisco and the Hawaiian Islands, where his father was stationed. He first settled in San Francisco in the mining regions. His father died in Hawaii in 1855. He m Hannah Swan Child, daughter of James Loring Child and Jane Hale of Kennebec, ME, 3-17-1857 and settled in HI. She was b 10-2-1836 in Augusta, ME. [MAVR] He established a large rice plantation (the first) and became a member of the Privy Council of State. In 1867 he visited CA and established business between HI and CA as a merchant, appointed by His Majesty, King Kamehameha V.. He lived in San Francisco while in CA. [JFS p63-64]

Henry Weld[7] died in Dover, NH on 2-12-1908 and was buried at Pine Hill but was later disintered by his wife and intered in Forest Grove Cemetery in Augusta, ME. [NHVR]

Children:
i **Alice May**[7] b 3-9-1867
ii **Gertrude Child**[7] b 1-26-1869 m Charles Francis Sawyer in Honolulu 1-26-1895. He was the son of Honorable Charles H. and Susan E. (Cowan) Sawyer of Dover, NH [Sterns Vol I p106]

(286) Luther[7], (Luther[6], Elihu[5], Moses[4], Joseph[3], John[2], John[1]), born Augusta, ME on 6-1-1836. He went to the Hawiian Islands with his parents in 1850. He married to Lucinda M. Clark on 1-1-1866 in Honolulu. He settled as a rice farmer. He was appointed by King Kamehameha V. to the Post of Collector of Customs and Port Masters at Hilo in 1870. [JFS]

Children:
i **Helen**[8] b 3-9-1867
ii **Ellen**[8] b 6-15-1872

(291) Calvin L.[8], (Joseph[7], James[6], unconnected) was b circa 1832. [NYFC] In 1850 he was living with his father, **Joseph**[8], who was born in MA circa 1788-1791. [1850 NYFC] He served under Orang. Newtons Co., F. enrolled 10-15-1861 at Potsdam, during the Civil War. He married to Martha Nichols. She was b circa 1831. [1860 NYFC] They lived at Stockholm, St. Laurence Co. NY. [NYFC]

Children:

i   **Marion**[9] b 1858

ii   **Charles**[9] b 1859 [1860-1880 Stockholm, St. Lawrence Co. NY]

iii   **George Elmer**[9] Severance b 1862 m Mary Jane Weegar, daughter of William and Sarah Pocrback Weegar, on 12-25-1893 at Canton. [NYVR] George and Mary had their first child, a daughter, 8-21-1891 at Canton, NY [NYVR]

iv   **William**[9] b 1876, (the [1920 NYFC] shows **William**[9] with out a wife but children, Luella b 1908, **Lewis**[9] b 1911, and **Leona**[9] b 1914, at Cranberry Lake, St. Lawrence Co.) and **Charles'**[9] wife Matilda and their daughter, **Marrian**[10] b 1880, all b in NY.

(292) Zacheus[7] *Severns/Siverence*, (Phillip[6], James[5], James[4], unconnected¡, born circa 1805, probably in Colchester, VT. He married Bernice Brouse, who was born circa 1804. The Colchester, VT town records show him on the Role of Militia of Colchester on June 1824 in the third Company, 1st Regiment, 2nd Brigade, 3rd Division. In 1830 he was living in Jackson, Washington Co. NY with 1 daughter. The Colchester records again show him in #2 school district in 1835 and 1836. The family then shows living at Pierpont and Russell, St. Lawrence Co. [1850 NYFC] Many of their children were indicated on the census. **Zacheus**[7] died 7-3-1875 age 70 years and Burnice died 5-31-1892 age 82 years. [CEMNY-Beech Plains, Pierrepont]

Children: born in NY State

i   **Samuel**[8] b 1829 may have d young since another **Samuel**[8] was b later

ii   **Harriet**[8] b 1831

iii   **Eunice**[8] b 1833

iv   **William**[8] b circa 1835. He lived in Washington Co. NY

561   v   **Charles H**[8] b circa 1836

vi   **Lisa/Louisa**[8] b 1839 m Edward Ellsworth, son of Lucian Ellsworth of Essex Co, VT. They had several children, including a daughter, Clara, b circa 1862 who married to Frank Eastman on 9-1-1894 at Russell, NY [NYVR]

vii   **Henry (Harry)**[8] b 1841. At age 20, he was living as a farm hand with the Joseph Matthews family. [1860 NYFC Pierrepont] He enrolled 10-15-1863 at Russell under Oliver B. Flaggs Co. [STL-NY] **Harry W.**[8] died 1879 at the age of 38 and is buried in the same cemetery as his parents and brother **Benjamin F.**[8] [CRNY-Beech Plains Cemetery]

viii   **Benjamin Franklin**[8] b 8- -1843 and d in 1911. He married to Arlina W. Frank. [Last Will and Testament] He enrolled for the Civil War 10-5-1863 at Russell under W.A. Treadwells Co. H. He filed for Civil War Pension on 8-20-1890 and his widow filed 5-1-1911 for service G/14 NY Hvy Art. They lived at Russell, St. Lawrence Co. [1900 NYFC] They are buried at Pierrepont, NY. [CEMNY-Beech Plains Cemetery] His last Will and Testament, St. Lawrence Co., 8-25-1911, listed his wife, brother, **Charles W.**[8], at Kent Michigan, sister, **Louisa**[8] Ellsworth at Russell, NY, and his brother, **Andrew G.**[8] at Hastings, MI. **Benjamin**[8] and Arlina probably had children. A grand daughter, **Jennie A.**[10] b 6- -1887, was listed on the 1900 NY census.

ix   **Gershom**[8] b 1846. Pension filed by his mother in 1880, for service in the Civil War, C 60 NY. **Gershom**[8], son of **Zacheus**[7], under Capt. John C.O. Reddington's Co., C. enrolled 9-25-1861 at Ogdensburg,

x   **Samuel**[8] b 1848

xi   **Nelson**[8] b 2-9-1849, son of **Zacheus**[7] and Burnice Severance. St Lawrence Co, NY

564 xii   **Andrew G.**[8] b circa 1851.

(293) Luther R.[7], (unconnected), b 1808. He married Jennette C. who was born in 1814.

Children: [NYFC 1850 Essex Co, 1870 Thurston, Steuben Co]

i	**Mary A.**[8] b 1838
ii	**Martha M.**[3] b 1840, died young
iii	**Charles E.**[8] b 1842. He settled in King Co., WA and married to Alla Wilda. She d 10-22-192⌐ age 69 in King Co., and **Charles**[8] d 2-14-1931 age 79. [WAVR]
iv	**David**[8] b 1843 settled in Bath, Steuben Co, NY and married Mary b 1857. He probably married twice. Children: **Harry**[9] b 1878, **Martha Mary**[9] b 1879, and **Earl J.**[9] b 1896. In 1920 **David**[8] was age 66, was with his wife Mary, and their son **Earl J.**[9] age 24 b in NY. [1920 NYFC Bath]
v	**James H.**[8] b 1845. He settled in Seattle where he d 9-2-1924 age 69 and his wife Annie d 7-2-1934 age 78 at Pierce, WA. [WAVR] A **James H.**[8], shows with his wife, Eva, sons **James P.**[9] b 1910, **Margaret**[9] b 1917, and **Edward E.**[9] b 1920 all born in NY. [1920 NYFC-Bath]
vi	**Martha**[8] b 1850
vii	**Adam W.**[8] b 1856. He settled in WA where he had m Susan, who was b 12- -1869 in MO. They had a son, **Darrow**[9] b 9- -1891 in WA. [1900 MOFC]
viii	**Luther Jr.**[8] b 12-18-1863 in NY. He married to Ida Gertrude Martin, daughter of William A. Martin and Phebe Minier of New Haven CT, 7-1-1881. They were m in Thurston, Steuben Co. NY. She was b 7-29-1862 in Addison NY. [1920 WAFC] **Luther Jr.**[8] later settled in Seattle, Washington where he died on 7-22-1932, age 70 and Ida G. d in October of 1940 age 77. [WAVR] They had a daughter, **Grace M.**[9], b 1-1-1887 in NY. [1920 WAFC] **Grace**[9] m Gilbert Hobbs 6-4-1908 at Seattle, WA. King Co.

(297) Eliab[7], Phillip Jr.[6], Phillip Sr.[5], unconnected), b circa 1815, he married to Sarah Wentworth in 1842 |IGI]. **Eliab**[7] and **Jacob**[7] could be the same person. She died 1-13-1909, age 85-11 b Limington, ME, daughter of Joseph Wentworth and Mary McKenney, widow of **Eliab**[7]. [MEVR] The marriage of **Eliab**[7] and Sarah Davis also shows on the Hollis records. **Eliab**[7] d cn 4-1-1900 at Hollis age 85 yrs 11 mon 8 dys. [MEVR]

(299) James[7], (Phillip Jr.[6], Phillip Sr.[5], unconnected) was born circa 1818 at Hollis, ME. He married to Nancy Hodgdon, daughter of Jacob Hodgdon, on 10-10-1842 at Hollis. She was born circa 1819 and died 3-14-1905 at Hollis, age 86 yrs 4 mons 17 dys.

Children of **James**[7] Severance and Nancy Hodgdon born at Hollis, York Co. ME

595	i	**Jacob H.**[8] b 2-26-1843
595a	ii	**William D.**[8] b 10- -1844 m Annie
595b	iii	**Charles H.**[8] b 1847/48 m Olive Chase 11-1-1874
	iv	**Nancy**[8] b circa 1849 m William H. Kimball on 9-9-1871
595c	v	**James**[8] b circa 1853 m2 Dell Lambert (Lumber)
	vi	**John A.**[8] conjecture

(300) William Darling[7], (Phillip Jr.[6], Phillip Sr.[5], unconnected) was born circa 1821. He married to Arvilda Davis, daughter of Theodore M. Davis and Margaret Wentworth, on 5-20-1852/53. {MEVR} She was born 1-16-1833 at Limington, ME and died at Hollis on 7-1-1903 aged 69-7-7. [MEVR] He died on 2-20-1905. He died at Hollis age 84 years.

Children:

	i	**Edwin**[8] b 3-5-1858 at Hollis, ME. He was unmarried.
596	ii	**John Henry**[8] b 3-14-1855 m Anna Guilford

(301) David W.[7], (Joseph[6], unconnected) was born in January of 1829. He married first to Sarah A. at East Parsonfield, ME. [MEVR] She was born circa 1845 and died on 1-3-1875 at the young age of 30 yrs 1 mon 8 dys. [MEVR] He perhaps married again to Harriet who was born in 1849 and died on 8-11-1879 at the age of 30 yrs 5 mons 9 dys. [MEVR] He later married to Lydia Stanley, daughter of Isaac Stanley and Susan Gould. She was born in February of 1842 at Porter, ME and died on 9-6-1904. He died on 10-14-1913 at the age of 85 yrs 9 mons 9 dys at Cornish, ME. [MEVR]

Children: of **David W.**[7] [1870 York Co MEFC]

	i	**Fred W.**[8] b 1862 in ME.
	ii	**Frank**[8] b 1866

(302) Eben F.[7], (Joseph[6], unconnected) was born circa 1832 at Cornish, ME. He married to Melissa Sarah Burnham, daughter of John Burnham and Lydia Burbank, on 11-7-1863. [MEVR] She was born on 2-14-1839 at Parsonfield, ME and died on 9-23-1905. **Eben**[7] died in 1886.

Children: born at Limerick, York Co. ME [1860 MEFC] [CRME]

	i	**infant** son b 1864 d 1864
	ii	**Florence W.**[8] b 1865 d 1935
	iii	**Lydia E.**[8] b 1866 m John B. Hill. She d in 1893
	iv	**Elma**[8] b 1867
601	v	**Walter H.**[8] b 5-6-1868 at Limerick, ME.
	vi	**John B.**[8] b 1870 d 1948. The 1900 CT census shows **John**[8] and his brother, **Louis R.**[9] as Officer at the State Farm.
	vii	**Louis R.**[8] b 1874 d 1936
	viii	**infant** son b 1875 d 1875
	ix	**infant** son b 1875 d 1875
	x	**Mable R.**[8] b 1879 d 1948

(303) Joseph O.[7], (Joseph[6], unconnected) born 5-25-1844 in Cornish, ME, [NHVR] He married Elizabeth J. (Wesson) Heywood, daughter of Charles H. Wesson and Sophia (Annie) Carney, on 1-1-1871 [MAVR] She was born 8-15-1847 in Boston, MA. [MAVR] Elizabeth J., formally of Boston, died in Grafton, NH, 4-14-1927, widow of **Joseph O.**[7] Severance. [NHVR] He died 5-21-1933 at Grafton, age 88 yrs 11 mons 26 dys. [NHVR] He was a teamster and an expressman. He could have had a son **Clarence**[9] b 1885?

Children: [1900 MAFC] [MAVR]

	i	**Mary Elizabeth**[8] b 6-15-1872 [MAVR]
	ii	**Annie M.**[8] b 7- -1874
	iii	**Joseph Osborn**[8] b 4-23-1879 at Boston
	iv	**Josephine W.**[8] b 6- -1885
	v	**Nellie Lorette**[8] b 10-30-1886 at Boston [MAVR]

(304) David[7], (Ebenezer[6], unconnected, John[1]), b 4-12-1794 in VT. [Cumming p23] Early in life he went with his family and lived in NY State. He moved to OH in 1819. The family settled, 12-31-1834, on the north side of section 36, town nine south, range one west of the meridian, in Mill Creek Township, Williams Co. OH. (that portion which is now in Gorham) **David's**[8] farm became part of Fulton Co.

Although he was the first settler in Mill Creek, he never became a resident of Fulton Co. because he died in 1843, before his farm became part of Fulton, Co. [Reighard Vol I p407]

David[8] married to Esther Knapp, daughter of Samuel Jr. and Deborah Knapp, 1815, in NY State. She was b 7-3-1797 in Jefferson, NY and she died in Williams Co. OH on 2-17-1887. She had lived in Fulton Co. for 37 years, making her home on the farm with her other children. **David**[8] died on 10-10-1843 in Williams Co. They are buried at the Olive Branch Cemetery, Millcreek, Williams Co. OH.

Two of their sons, **Waldron**[9] and **Alfred**[9] were in their teens when the family settled in Williams Co. They became the basic support of a large and growing family. [Reighard Vol I p407]

The 1810 NY census shows a **Joseph** living in Canton, St. Lawrence Co. The 1840 NY census shows **John** and Hannah Severance living in Clayton, Jefferson Co. It is uncertain if they were related to **David**[8].

Children: [MLM]
603b i   **Waldron M.**[8] b 12-28-1815 at Jefferson Co. NY.

    ii   **Cora E.**[8] b circa 1815 d 2-21-1899, buried at Olive Branch Cemetery.

    iii   **Hannah**[8] b circa 1818 at Jefferson Co. NY. m to Benoni L. Packard on 1-16-1838. She d in 1869 in IA.

603c iv   **Alfred**[9] b 1-11-1823 at Crawford Co. OH.

    v   **Mary Ann**[8] b circa 1825 m Joel Dow on 2-2-1841

    vi   **Elizabeth**[8] b 2-5-1826 in Crawford Co. OH. She m to Amos Calkins 11-27-1848. **Elizabeth**[8] d 10-20-1872 in Williams Co.

    vii   **Nancy**[8] b 9-7-1828 m John Jacoby 6-14-1846

    viii **Benjamin Samuel**[8] b circa 1833, m Jane Bates on 6-29-1859. [IGI] He d 5-3-1912. They had at least 2 children, **Williams**[9] and **Lanawee**[9].

    viii **Caroline**[8] b 9-11-1836 m William Ritter circa 1847 and she d 9-6-1919

    ix   **Lucinda**[8] b circa 1835/1840

(306) James[7], (William[6], Joseph[5], William[4], unconnected, Joseph[2], John[1]), was born 6-3-1819 and died 1-27-1878. [MAVR] He married to Mary P. Maxfield, daughter of Warren and Sarah Maxfield, 7-

31-1854. [MAVR] They lived in Fairhaven and
Acushnet, MA. **James**[7] was a mariner.

Children: born at Fairhaven, MA. [MAVR]
  i   **Henry Warren**[8] b 2-20-1858 d 9-13-1863
       [MAVR]
  ii   **Hannah E.**[8] b 10-4-1861
       Minnie L.[8] b 7-7-1864
  iii **Cora Leslie**[8] b 9-1-1866 d 2-20-1875 age
       8-5-15
  iv   **Harry**[8] b 3- -1869

(308) James[7], (Isaac[5], Joseph[5], Benjamin[4], Ephraim[3],
Ephraim[2], John[1]), born Springfield, NH on 10-29-
1796. He married to Sarah Goddard on 1-1-1817.
[VTVR] It was the third marriage for Sarah as she
had married first to Jonathan Frost and second to
Robert Kelsea. **James**[7] Severance and Sarah Goddard
settled first in Derby, VT where their first four
children were born. Then they moved to Holland, VT.
Around 1830 the family moved to Broome, Quebec,
Canada.

Children: [Currier]
  i   **Ann Maria**[8] b 1-28-1819 Derby, VT d 1868
       m1 Jonathan Frost 1- -1839 m2 Robert
       Kelsea. He d 9-10-1845.
  ii   **Rebecca Ward**[8] b 11-5-1820 at Derby, VT m
       Gideon Gay, Gideon was b 1807 at
       Tunbridge, VT [VTVR] and m1 Lucy Smith
       m2 to **Rebecca**[8] Severance 3-14-1861
  iii **Harriet**[8] b 7-3-1822 m George Pierce 9-
       22-1846. He b 5-4-1819 d 4-25-1898
  iv   **Susannah**[8] b 8-1-1824 d 2- -1842
  v   **George W.**[8] b 8-17-1827 in Holland, VT d
       6- -1832 in Broome, Quebec, Canada
604 vi **Elisha F.**[8] b 9-23-1831 in Broome,
       Quebec, Canada m 4- -1847
  vii **Abba Matilda**[8] b 4-20-1834, Farnham,
       Quebec d 2-14-1856
  viii **Lydia Lovisa**[8] b 9-27-1837, Broome,
       Quebec d 5-12-1899 m Charles R. Gay 4-4-
       1867. He was b 10-20-1841
This family shows on the 1850 VT census with the
last 4 living children at that time.

(309) Elias J.[7], (Isaac[6], Joseph[5], Benjamin[4],
Ephraim[3], Ephraim[2], John[1]), born circa 1810 at
Unity, NH and married Frances A. Huntoon 4-25-1838
[IGI] HE lived at Newport, NH. This may be the **Eli**

who shows on the 1830 Sandwich, NH census. It appears that **Elias James**[7] also married Julia Cole who was born in Lenoxville, Canada.

Children: of **Elias J.**[7] Frances Huntoon/Julia Cole
605　i　　**Frank G.**[8] b 8- -1840/42 (1848) Newport, NH m Bertha Rackliffe, 7-20-1868 at Glousester, MA. [MAVR]
　　ii　　**Proctor**[8] b 3-20-1850 Lenoxville, Canada [NHVR] son of Elias J. and Julia Cole
　　iii　　**Donald James**[8] b 1861 in Canada. He was a brakeman in Boston, MA. He m Annie of Prince Edward Island. They had a daughter, **Gertrude Elizabeth**[9] b 7-3-1889 at Boston. [MAVR]
　　iv　　**Carrie**[8] b 1864 at Lenoxville d 3-25-1880 of typhoid fever at Boston, MA, age 16 yrs 2 mons [MAVR]

(310) Franklin[7] (*Severens*), (Isaac[6], Joseph[5], Benjamin[4], Ephraim[3], Ephraim[2], John[1]), born in October of 1811 in Derby, VT. He married Elizabeth Stowell Pulsipher. Elizabeth, born 3-15-1816, died 9-28-1875, was the daughter of Samuel Wood and Sally Weaver. When Samuel Wood was drowned in 1817, Sally (Weaver) Wood remarried to Mr. Pulsipher. Therefore, Eliza was usually called Elizabeth Pulsipher. Her step father's surname was Pulsipher and she was called Elizabeth Pulsipher. **Franklin**[7] served as town representative for Rockingham, VT from 1859 to 1860. He was the father of **Henry F.**[8] Severance of Kalamazoo, MI, which was where **Franklin**[7] died. [Currier] [Weaver]

Children: born in Rockingham, Windham Co. VT
606　i　　**Henry Franklin**[8] b 5-11-1835 was a Judge in Kalamazoo, MI, m Sarah Clarissa (Whittlesey) Ryan 12-1-1863 at Medina, NY (her second marriage)
607　ii　　**Charles W.**[8] b 3- -1837 m Harriet Mc Quaide
608　iii　　**James M.**[8] b 8-25-1839
　　iv　　**Elma May**[8] b 3-26-1844 m George W. Perham 5-4-1870
　　v　　**Jefferson**[8] b 5-13-1849 d 2-3-1864
609　vi　　**Seymour B.**[8] b 7-26-1851 m Augustus Morse 1878
　　vii　　**Jessie F.**[8] b 4-25-1856 d 9-25-1890 m George Henry Smith 11-26-1876. He was b on 12-24-1854. They moved from

Rockingham to Pearl, MI in 1880. They lived in Holland, MI. [Weaver]

(311) Uriel[7] (*Sevrens*), (David[6], Joseph[5], Benjamin[4], Ephraim[3], Ephraim[2], John[1]), **"Uriel**[7] Severans, the oldest male resident of Woburn, passed away Thursday morning age 93 years 8 months and 17 days. He was born 4-30-1811 in North Danbury, NH, the son of **David**[6] and Mehitabel (Maloon) Severns, and his early life was passed upon the farm where he laid the foundation for a strong and healthy life."

"Almost 63 years ago he married Miss Mary Jane Hall (10-27-1842) (the [MAVR] says 2-3-1842 at Boston, MA) by whom he is survived. Soon after their marriage, Mr. and Mrs. Severns came to Woburn where a small farm was bought and here they have lived. Honored and respected by all." [NSW 8-19-1904]

Uriel's[7] great great grandson, **William**[10] Severance told "He was a truck farmer. He grew vegetables, carted them to Boston where they were wholesaled by push cart venders in the "Haymarket" area still famous today." **"Uriel**[7] was a scrappy little fellow, who walked every where. he would usually lead his horse drawn truck into Boston (15 miles)-His weightlessness being the more vegies he could retail," [MWGS]

The family shows on the 1860 MA census.

Uriel[7] *Sevrens* **and his Family**

Children: born at Woburn, MA [MAVR]
    i   **Mary Jane**[8] b 12-19-1842 [MAVR] d 10-27-
          1846 at Woburn, MA [MAVR]
    ii   **Hannah**[8] b 9-8-1844 [MAVR] m John I. Tay,
          son of Benjamin and Hannah, 6-21-1866 at
          Boston MA. [MAVR] No children
    iii   **Mehitable**[8] b 9-8-1844 [MAVR] m George
          King. They had children, Bertha, LeRoy,
          and adopted, Marie.
    iv   **Marrianne**[8] b 4-21-1848 m Thurston Ames
          [MAVR] No children
    v   **Marrietta**[8] b 4-21-1848 [MAVR] Never
          married
    vi   **Martha**[8] b 10-2-1852 [MAVR]
    vii   **Amanda**[8] b 11-25-1854 [MAVR] Never
          married
    viii **Amelia**[8] b 11-25-1854 [MAVR] m Frank H.
          Wendell, son of Henry and Julia A.
          Wendell, on 9-29-1873. [MAVR]
610 ix   **Oliver**[8] b circa 1858 m Annie B. Waite
    x   **Nathan**[8] b 2-12-1858 [MAVR] killed young
    xi   male b 10-9-1860 at Woburn, MA [MAVR]
611 xii   **William P.**[8] b 12-6-1863 at Woburn, MA
          [MAVR] m Elva Ward circa 1884

(312) Nathaniel[7] *Sevrens*, (David[6], Joseph[5],
Benjamin[4], Ephraim[3], Ephraim[2], John[1]), was born 11-
10-1806 at Danbury, NH. In 1850 **Nathaniel**[7] was
married to Alversa _____, who was born in 1815,
and with three daughters. [VTFC] He died 8-3-1886

Children:
    i   **Mary J.**[8] b 3-1-1834 d ae 1yr 7mons [IGI]
    ii   **Nancy Augusta**[8] b 10-7-1836 [VTVR] m ____
          Boynton
    iii   **Laura**[8] b 1839 [1850 VTFC] m ____Hunt
    iv   **Martha**[8] b 1840 [1850 VTFC]
    v   **George**[8]

(313) Jonathan Thompson[7] *Sevrens*, (David[6], Joseph[5],
Benjamin[4], Ephraim[3], Ephraim[2], John[1]), born 7-12-1815
in Grafton, NH [IGI] and later settled in Danbury,
NH with his parents. He married Delia Caswell on 4-
18-1846 [IGI]

Children: [1870 Grafton, NHFC]
612 i   **William**[8] b 10-19-1845 d 3-18-1906 in
          Grafton, NH. He was a farmer and the son
          of **Jonathan**[7] Severance and Dillia

Caswell. He m to Emily Amanda Peaslee 10-20-1869. [NHVR]

  ii **Hiram**[8] b July of 1847 in NH. [1900 NHFC] d 5-23-1924 age 78, b in Danbury NH and d in Franklin NH, the son of **Jonathan**[7] Severance and Delia Caswell [NHVR] He m Persis E. Huff 5-24-1894 at Derby, VT, aged 45. [VTVR] He was born in Franklin, NH. He was 78 years old when he died in 5-23-1924. [NHVR]

  iia **Horace**[8] b 1848

614 iii **Nathan**[8] b 1851 **Nathan**[8] married 2nd to Elizabeth S. Griffith 3-3-1892. [NHVR]

615 iv **George**[8] b circa 1856 d 8-6-1901 at the age of 45-11-18. He was a farmer and the son of **J.T.**[7] Severance and Dilly Caswell [NHVR] He was b in Grafton and d in Andover, NH

616 v **Frank P.**[8] (thought to be **Clyde Henry**[8]) b 5-18-1858 in Grafton, NH d 4-13-1912 in Manchester, NH, divorced. Son of **Jonathan T.**[7] Severance and Delia Caswell. His father was b in Danbury, NH. **Frank**[3] was a fireman. [NHVR] **Frank P.**[8] m Marion Wheeler as shown on their son's, **Henry C.**[9] Severance and Alice M. Rothwell's, marriage record. [NHVR] Family records say that **Clyde Henry**[8] had a son, **Henry Clyde**[9]

  vi **David**[8] b 1863 twin of Julia. [1870 NHFC]

  vii **Julia A.**[8] m John A. Wilkins 10-12-1890

  viii **Mary J.**[8] m George A. Chandler 11-29-1893 at Grafton, NH

  ix **Lucinda E.**[8] b 1865 m Joseph E. Harris, son of John and Eliza Harris, 2-7-1889 at Wilmot, NH [MAVR] The records says that she was b in 1861 although the census records indicate that she was b after **Mary**[8] or **David**[8]. [1870 NHFC]

(314) Ziba[7], (James[6], Joseph [5], Benjamin[4], Ephraim[3], Ephraim[2], John[1]), b 7-20-1807 at Derby, VT. He m to Sarah Ann Weare, daughter of Timothy and Sarah (Bachelder) Weare, on 10-27-1836. **Ziba**[7] d in Andover, New Hampshire, 11-14-1894. Sarah Ann died 2-3-1891 at Andover. [Eastman, Records from Lakeside Cemetery]

Children:

i   **Eliza Jane**[8] b 9-25-1837 m Scott J.
        Appleton 4-23-1872
ii   **Mary Weare**[8] b 11-13-1838
iii   **Sarah Adams**[8] b 2-29-1840 m Daniel B.
        Cummings 12-29-1880
iv   **Benjamin True**[8] was born 5-31-1843 d 9-
        17-1889 m Deborah Caroline Conner 1-29-
        1872 [NHVR] He is recorded at Manchester
        and Andover, NH. [Eastman] Benjamin d on
        9-17-1889 at the age of 46 years. [NHVR]
        He was living with his parents in 1860
        at age 17
v   **Laura Ann**[8] b 6-6-1851 m J. Henry Smith
        12-27-1876. She d 4-7-1891 age 39 years.

(315) Willard Colby[7], (Joseph[6], Joseph[5], Benjamin[4],
Ephraim[3], Ephraim[2], John[1]), of Springfield, NH,
married Art Ann Wormer of Springfield, NH. He
married at Claremont, NH, Susan Ellen (?Philbrook)
1-29-1868 or 1-19-1867 [NHVR] divorced 1-7-1876
[NHVR]. He lived in Grafton, NH where his son,
Joseph Colby[8] Severance was born.

Children:
617 i   **Joseph Colby**[8] b 1-2-1855 m Lucy J. Hardy
            11-25-1875

(316) Ransom[7], (John[6], Joseph[5], Benjamin[4], Ephraim[3],
Ephraim[2], John[1]), born 12-12-1811 at Wilmot Flat,
VT. He married Lorinda Currier, daughter of Abner
Currier and Ann C. Blodd, at Unity, NH on 5-2-1837.
He was in Acworth in 1832 but removed to Unity in
1857. [Merrill II p263] The 1840 NH census shows
him living in Acworth.
   He d on 7-26-1887 age 76 [NHVR] Lorinda was b 9-
28-1813 and d 4-7-1900.

Children: born in Unity, Sullivan Co. NH
i   **Flora J.**[8] b 1-16-1839 m William B.
        Johnson 1-26-1859, she d 1861
ii   **Burton D.**[8], (**B. Dean**) b 6-25-1841 at
        Unity, NH m Hattie B. Kendall, daughter
        of George Randall and Nancy Bisbee on 3-
        21-1867, resided in Wilmot, or Unity, NH
iii   **Louisa A.**[8] b 4-13-1846 m Dr. Jerry S.
        Elkins

(317) John[7] *Severns*, (John[6], Joseph[5], Benjamin[4],
Ephraim[3], Ephraim[2], John[1]), born at Wilmot Flat on
8-1-1815. **"Ransom's**[7] brother **John**[7] married Camilla

Mitchell, daughter of Thomas Mitchell and Mercy Slades." [Merrill II p263] This family shows on the 1850 NH census and had a son **William Hayward**[8] who married Catherine Miller. If this is true then Camilla must have died young, perhaps after the birth of **William H**[8]. **John**[7] married Ann___ on 2-11-1841. [NHVR-Andover] He died on 3-19-1892. [WIVR] **John**[7] was a blacksmith at Andover, NH for several years. **John G.**[7] was listed as a Lieutenant on 2-27-1840, and a Captain on 3-17-1841 of the Tenth Company. [Eastman]

John[7] and his family left for WI about 1852. They had two additional children born in Lenark, Portage Co. WI. [WIVR Portage Co]

Children of **John**[7] Severance and Camilla Mitchell [Eastman] [1850 NHFC] [1860 WIFC]

i	**George Elias**[8] b 4-26-1837 in Andover, NH. He reportedly later settled in MI. [Eastman]
ii	**Susan Frances**[8] b 3-23-1839 m George Hutchinson, Vilas Co. WI 3-25-1855 [WIVR]
iii	**William Hayward**[8] b circa 1842 m Catherine Miller. [Eastman p263] He was living with the George Houston family in 1860. He was 18 years old. [Acworth, NHFC] He perhaps settled in MN

Children of **John**[7] Severance and Ann____

	iv	**Adeline**[8] b 1841
619	v	**John**[8] b 1843 NH, settled in WI
620	vi	**Joseph Clinton**[8] b 1845 NH, settled in WI
	vii	**Ann**[8] (Abbe A.) b 1848 NH
621	viii	**Edward J.**[8] b 1850 in NH
621a	ix	**Albert**[8] b 1855 in WI, settled in IA and NB
	x	**Frank**[8] b 1857 in WI

(318) Newell (*Sevrens*)[7], (John[6], Joseph[5], Benjamin[4], Ephraim[3], Ephraim[2], John[1]), born 3-19-1817 in Danbury, NH, son of **John**[6] and Abigail, [MAVR] He married to Harriet S. Hall, daughter of Thomas and Mary Hall from ME, 3-3-1847. [Lowell, MAVR] Harriet was born in WI in 1824. [1860 WIFC] Their son was born in Lowell, MA. He was a shoemaker in Lowell (Natick) MA. The [Lowell, MAVR] shows Newell age 30 as a manufacturer. The 1870 WI census shows them living at Green Lake, Green Lake Co.

Children:
622   i   **Alonzo Miner**[8] b 1-2-1848 Lowell, MA and
                later settled in Green Lake, WI. [WIFC]

(319) Herod J.[7], (John[6], Joseph[5], Benjamin[4],
Ephraim[3], Ephraim[2], John[1]), was born 3-1-1822 in
Andover, NH. Lived in Lowell, MA. He married (Int.)
to Sarah Fowler, daughter of Stephen Fowler and
Sarah Mills, on 10-15-1846. [NHVR] Sarah was from
Freedom, NH, born in Andover, NH. [MAVR] The 1880
MA census for Lowell, shows Sarah born 1820 in NH
along with two daughters and 18 boarders. Sarah
died 12-19-1893 ae 72-10-24, at Boston, MA. [MAVR]

Children:
     i   **Abby O.**[8] b 1850 at Lowell, MA m Frederic
              P. Jacques, son of Nathan E. and
              Pamelia, 1-7-1869, at Lowell. [MAVR]
     ii   **George A.**[8] b 3-27-1852 at Bristol, NH
              but registered at Lowell, MA [MAVR] He d
              8-8-1853 at Lowell.
     iii   **Ardela K.**[8] b 1857 m George E. Griffin,
              son of George and Pamelia Griffin, on
              10-20-1881 at Lowell, MA. [MAVR]
     iv   **Lura**[8] b circa 1861 m Willard L. Cole,
              son of Morris and Elizabeth L. Cole, 9-
              21-1887 at Boston, MA. [MAVR]
     v   **Llewellen**[8] *Sevrens* b 6-3-1861 at Lowell,
              MA [MAVR]
     vi   **Lula**[8] b 1868

(321) Alfred P.[7], (George Washington[6], Peter[5],
Benjamin[4], Ephraim[3], Ephraim[2], John[1]), born 2-5-1821
at Chester, NH [IGI] and died 3-23-1893 in
Boscawen, NH. [IGI] He married to Sophronia
(Wheeler) Colby, 9-22-1864 [IGI] and they settled
in Allenston, NH. He married second to Mary C.
Ingalls on 6-3-1884. [IGI] This marriage ended in
divorce on 4-7-1891. [NHVR] **Alfred P.**[7] died 3-23-
1893.

Children:
     i   **Ida**[8] b 1868

(322) Charles[7], (James[6], Peter[5], Benjamin[4], Ephraim[3],
Ephraim[2], John[1]), born 1-23-1818 at Chester, NH. He
married first at Lowell, MA to Charlotte Thompson,
of Tyngsborough, on 7-23-1843. [MAVR] She was born
8-31-1816 and died 9-6-1856. He married second to
Clara (Clarrisa) H. Brown, daughter of David Brown

and Adeline Halbert, 9-21-1858. She was born 8-31-1834 and died 3-11-1899 at Chelsea. [MAVR] They settled in Auburn, NH. He was a carpenter. **Charles**[7] died 8-28-1897 at Chelsea, MA. [BRJMS]

Children of **Charles**[7] Severance and Charlotte Thompson
i   **Anna F.**[8] b 8-7-1846 at Chelsea, MA [MAVR]
ii   **Anna Frances**[8] b 8-16-1848 d 9-16-1848 at Chelsea, MA [MAVR]
iii   **Charles S.**[8] b 6-29-1850 at Chelsea, MA [MAVR] d 11-20-1856 [BRJMS]
iv   **Charlotte**[8] b 1856 d 9-6-1856
v   **Charlotte**[8] b 3-27-1856 at Chelsea, MA m Joseph C. Foster, son of Joel and Mary E. Foster, 7-19-1876 at Chelsea. She m Richard S. Merryman, son of Jacob and Susan Merryman, 6-27-1880 at Boston, MA. [MAVR]

Children of **Charles**[7] Severance and Clara H. Brown
vi   **Charles E.**[8] b 7-4-1860 at Chelsea, MA d 1-5-1899, single, age 38 years. [MAVR]

(323) William[7], (James[6], Peter[5], Benjamin[4], Ephraim[3], Ephraim[2], John[1]), born at Chester, NH on 11-6-1820. He married first to Sarah M. Whipple, daughter of James Whipple, of Chester, NH, on 4-12-1853 in Boston. [MAVR] She d 5-7- 1854 after the birth of their daughter **Sarah M.**[8]. He married secondly to Eliza Ricker (Reckord) on 4-2-1856 in Manchester, NH. [NHVR] She died on 5-7-1877. **William**[7] died on 3-31-1891 in Auburn, NH. [NHVR] [BRJMS]

Children of **William**[7] Severance and Sarah M. Whipple [1870 Auburn, NHFC]
i   **Sarah M.**[8] b 1854 d 6-15-1871

Children of **William**[7] Severance and Eliza Reckord
ii   **Lester H.**[8] b 1857 d 1858
iii   **Elizabeth Isabel**[8] b 7-11-1858 she m Joseph Waite Presby, son of Samuel Baker Presby, 7-29-1875. Joseph was b 3-9-1850 in Littleton. [Jackson Vol III p452]
623 iii   **Harvey**[8] b 5-4-1860 in Auburn, NH, he was the son of **William**[7] Severance and Elizabeth Reckard. **William**[7] was b in Auburn and Elizabeth was b in Chezey,

New York. He m to Hortensia N. Smith on
9-6-1881. At the age of 56, on 1-14-
1917, **Harvey**[8] Severance shot himself as
a suicide. He was a widower. [NHVR]

iv   **Elvira**[8] m to Story A. Smith, 4-8-1896.
She was the holder of the Bible records
which said that she was the daughter of
William[7], who d on 3-31-1891 and her
mother was Eliza Reckard. [BRJMS]

(323a) James Henry[7], (James[6], Peter[5], Benjamin[4],
Ephraim[3], Ephraim[2], John[1]), born Chester, NH [DAR
says Boston, MA] on 7-14-1825. He died on 3-31-1889
ae 63-8-17 at Lawrence, MA. **James**[7] married to
Frances Ann Lear, daughter of John and Clara Lear,
5-17-1857, she 23, he 30 and a carpenter [MAVR]
Frances was born on 12-6-1833 at New Market, NH and
died at Lawrence, MA on 9-14-1901 ae 67-9-8.
[DARLR] The Lear-Severance Lot [CRBMA] Additional
children which show in the lot are **Frances** d 2-26-
1907 ae 1 mon 27 27 days, **James E.** d 9-26-1898 ae
5-11-10 **Malcolm** d 4-15-1902 ae 7 mon 20 days, **John
M.** d 10-14-1934 ae 10 mons 28 days. They are
obviously children connected with this family.

Children:
i   **Emma J.**[8] b 6-30-1858 m John S. Porter,
son of John and Adeline A. Porter, on 4-
22-1874 at Lawrence, MA [MAVR]
ii   **Elma**[8] b 6-30-1858 at Lawrence, MA
624 iii   **John L.**[8] b 1859 d 5-3-1937 age 78-10-3,
[CRBMA Lear-Severance Lot] the census
records show him married to Grace ____
iv   **Minnie L.**[8] b 9-20-1860 at Lawrence, MA
[MAVR]
v   **Rose M.**[8] b 5-28-1866 at Lawrence, MA
[MAVR]

(324) John Dow[7], (Rufus[6], Peter[5], Benjamin[4], Ephraim[3],
Ephraim[2], John[1]), born 8-14-1824 in Cabot, VT.
[VTVR] He married to Janet/Jane A. Seales on 6-27-
1850. [VTVR] She was born 8- -1835. [1900 VT
Census] **John**[7] died on 4-5-1879 age 56-7-21. [VTVR]

Children:
i   **Ella**[8] b 1852
ii   **Clara**[8] b 1854
625 iii   **Henry E.**[8] b 1857
iv   **Female**[8] b 12-1-1860 [VTVR]

(324a) Leonard H.[7], ('John[6], Peter[5], Benjamin[4], Ephraim[3], Ephraim[2], John[1]), was born 2-19-1832 [NHVR] in Hooksette, NH and died 3-14-1911. [NHVR] He was the son of **John**[6] Severance and Lucinda Hazelton. [NHVR] He married Cynthia A. Harvey 4-9-1863. [NHVR] They were divorced on 4-9-1894 for "extreme cruelty". [NHVR] Cynthia A. Harvey, daughter of Gilman Harvey and Nancy Perry of Manchester, NH, died 11-7-1915 in Manchester, NH. [NHVR] The 1900 NH census shows **Leonard**[7] living alone.

Children:
	i	**Jennie B.**[8]
	ii	**Josie N.**[8] b 1874
627	iii	**Freddie G.**[8] b 1876 m 3-11-1903 to Myrtie E. Merrill of Manchester, NH. She was the daughter of Wesley Gile and Viola Foss of Hooksett, NH. [NHVR]
	iv	**John L.**[8] b 4-27-1882 d 9-19-1907 at the young age of 26-4-23. [NHVR] He m to Eleanor Bernadine Tate, daughter of Joseph Tate and Alice Abbott, 11-28-1906, at Manchester, NH. **John**[8] was a farmer and d at Allenstown, NH on 11-28-1906. [NHVR] He died on 9-19-1907 of TB. He was a clerk in a store when he died at the age of 26. [NHVR] The couple had a baby which died on 1-4-1908. [NHVR]

(326) Brewer Samuel[7], (Samuel[6], Caleb[5], Joseph[4], Ephraim[3], Ephraim[2], John[1]), born 1-12-1810 at Orrington, ME. [HOPCoME pCXVIII] He married to Betsy W. Thompson 12-17-1833. [MEVR] Betsey died 12-18-1882. **Brewer Samuel**[7] was a tin plater as indicated on the 1850 ME census.

Children:
	i	**Ella**[8] circa 1834
	ii	**Samuel**[8] circa 1836

(327) Hiram[7], (Samuel[6], Caleb[5], Joseph[4], Eprhaim[3], Ephraim[2], John[1]), born 1-23-1814 in Orrington. [HOPCoME pCXVIII] He married Julia E. Doane 9-28-1840 [IGI] of Orrington, Penobscot, ME. Julia was the daughter of Noah Doane of Bucksport, ME. She died circa 1862 at Brewer, ME. [Doane]

215

Children:
    i   **Jefferson**[8] b 1841, as shown on the [1870
            MEFC] He m to Elvira L. Lamb, 1-1-1864.
            [MEVR]

(328) William Warren[7], (Reuben[6], Caleb[5], Joseph[4],
Ephraim[3], Ephraim[2], John[1]), born 1-8-1809 in
Orrington, ME. [MEVR] He married Margaretta Darby
6-23-1839. [MEVR] [1860 MEFC]

Children:
628 i   **Ambrose Warren**[8] b 8-15-1840 [MEVR] He m
            first to Carrie. [1870 Old Town, MEFC].
            He m second to Ella Tewsbury on 9-10-
            1882 at Bangor, ME [MEVR]
629 ii   **Washington**[8] b 6-19-1843
     iii   **Mary**[8] b 1845
     iv   **Alice**[8] b 1848

(329) Reuben[7], (Rueben[6], Caleb[5], Joseph[4], Ephraim[3],
Ephraim[2], John[1]), born Orrington, ME on 7-15-1813.
[HOPCoME] He married to Mary Miller who was born
circa 1822 in NY. The 1860 ME census shows 10
children in the family. **Reuben**[7] died in
Passadumkeag, ME on 6-26-1894 age 80y 11m 21d son
of **Reuben**[7] and Sally. [MEVR] [CRME Mt. Hope
Cemetery, Bangor] Mary d 8-18-1910 at Bangor, ME.

Children:
630 i   **William H.**[8] b 6-30-1839 m Emily J.
            Thurlo and Eva M. Bickford
631 ii   **Walter F.**[8] b 1841 m1 Ellen A. Dennis m2
            Louisa D. Godfrey 1-30-1887
     iii   **Thersha**[8] b circa 1843 d 10-29-1922 ae
            79-6-7
     iv   **Rosetta**[8] b circa 1845
     v   **Reuben**[8] was born in 1847 in Orrington or
            Passadumkeag, ME.
     vi   **Rebecca**[8] b circa 1848
     vii   **Thomas J.**[8] b 4-22-1849 in Orrington, ME.
            He died on 5-11-1928 age 77-7-14. [MEVR]
            He had married to Sarah B. who died 3-
            26-1927. They were married for 37 years,
            having 2 children but only one living in
            1910. [1910 MEFC] The 1860 ME census
            shows **Thomas**[8] living alone.
     viii   Rebecca J., b 1849 (adopted as Jennie R.
            Perkins m Charles E. Johnson, son of
            Elisha and Elizabeth G. Johnson, 8-2-
            1879 at Lowell, MA. [MAVR]

        vix   **Martha W.**[8] b circa 1851
        x   **Charles K.**[8] b 1855 in Orrington, ME. The
               1900 ME census shows **Charles**[8] b 11-18-
               1856 at Winterport, ME with his wife,
               Maud E. b 3-18-1865. His mother was also
               living with them.
        xi   **Ava**[8] b circa 1858
        xii   **Georgia**[8] b circa 1860
632   xiii   **Evander O.**[8] b 6- -1863 m Etta M. Watson

(330) Joshua[7], (Reuben[6], Caleb[5], Joseph[4], Ephraim[3],
Ephraim[2], John[1]), born 3-15-1822 in Orrington, ME.
J.G.[7] m L.B. Shattuck on 1-16-1842 at Boston, MA.
[MAVR] It is possible that this **Joshua**[7] was the son
of **Samuel**[6] and Hannah Godfrey. A **Joshua**[7] also
married Martha A. Derby 8-20-1848. [MEVR] He was a
painter. He filed for his Civil War Pension on 8-3-
1863 and his widow filed 10-5-1888 for service 1 Co
MA Sharp Shooter. **Joshua**[7] died 3-10-1883 at
Andover, MA. [MAVR]

Children: of **Joshua** Severance and Martha Darby
        i   **Coresfelia**[8] b 11-25-1850 at Danvers, MA
               [MAVR]

(333) Russell Howard[7] **(Howard Russell)**, (Caleb[6],
Caleb[5], Joseph[4], Ephraim[3], Ephraim[2], John[1]), born 4-
11-1828 in Brewer, ME. [HOPCoME p77] He married to
Jennie Smith of Bangor, ME. **Russell Howard**[7]
Severance, fought in the Civil War for the Union
and supposedly died in the Civil War.

Children:
        i   **Nellie F.**[8] b 1852 in ME. She m Sewall
               Barrett, son of Abram and Mary E.
               Barrett, 5-15-1874 at Lynn, MA. [MAVR]
        ii   **Charles**[8] b 1855 in ME. [1860 MEFC]
636   iii   **William Henry**[8] b 1-12-1858 d 5-15-1933

(335) Benjamin Otis[7], (Benjamin[6], Joshua[5], Joseph[4],
Ephraim[3], Ephraim[2], John[1]), born 1-15-1820 in
Orrington, ME. He married to Mary A. Smith on 3-10-
1842. [MEVR] She died on 7-25-1897 in OR at the
home of her son in law, James D. Sutherland. [NSOR
The Oregonian] **Benjamin**[7] died 1-21-1897 age 77
years. They are buried in the Riverview Cemetery of
Portland, OR. [ORVR][MCoL] He reportedly had two
daughters. Mrs. **A.F.**[9] Learned and **J.D.**[9] Sutherland.
Benjamin[7] was reportedly a Postmaster. [HOPCoME]
The 1870 OR census shows him living at Powell's

Valley, Multnomah Co with his wife and children,
William[8] age 26 and **Fanny**[8] age 13.

Children: [MDJS with MCoL Portland, OR]
  i   **William M.**[8] b 3-1-1844. [MEVR] The 1870
       Powell's Valley, Multnomah Co. OR census
       shows him living with his cousin,
       Preston[8]. He later settled in St. John,
       OR. He is shown as the brother in law of
       R.F. Learned. [1900 ORFC]. He died 1-21-
       1897 at St. Johns, OR. [NSOR Portland,
       Oregon]
  ii   **Frances M.**[8] **(Fannie)** b 6-14-1846 [MEVR]
       d young d 8-15-1854 age 8-1-22 [CRME
       Orrington, ME
  iv   **Vienah A.**[8] b 1-14-1848 [MEVR]
  v   **Otis F.**[8] b 1850 d young 9-27-1850 age 2
       months [CRME Orrington, ME]
  vi   **Frances M.**[8] b 1856 d 1905. Shows on the
       1860 ME census

(336) William B.[7], (Benjamin[6], Joshua[5], Joseph[4],
Ephraim[3], Ephraim[2], John[1]), born 3-24-1822 at
Orrington, ME near Bangor. He later settled at
Abbot, ME. [HOPCoME] He married first to Sophia B.
Lancaster on 11-25-1847. [IGI] Sophia died on 12-
20-1854 ae 31 yrs 7 months. [MEVR] **William B.**[7]
married second to Lucy C. Lindsay on 1-11-1852.
William[7] shows on the 1870 Brewer ME census with
his second wife and their son, **Asel C.**[8], who was b
1859. The family later settled in Portland, OR.
   The 1860 ME census shows the family except for
their son **Preston Phillip**[8] who was later indicated
on the 1900 OR census. In 1880 **Preston P.**[8] was with
his wife and family and **William B.**[7] Severance and
his wife, Lucy C., the children of **Preston**[8] listed
as grandchildren of **William B.**[7] and Lucy. [ORFD]
The 1900 OR census shows **William B.**[7] living in
Multnoham Co. with his grandson, **William H.**[9] and
his wife, Daisy. She died 5-2-1882 age 50 years 3
months. [NSOR] **William B.**[7] Severance died 12-24-
1903. [ORVR]

Children of **William B.**[7] Severance and Sophia B.
Lancaster
637 i   **Preston Phillip**[8] b 9-21-1844 **Preston P.**[8]
        Severance d in Portland, 3-30-1896 age
        48 years, 6 months, and 10 days. He was
        b in Bangor, ME. [NSOR 4-2-1896]
  ii   **Russell**[8] b 1849

639   iii   **Edgar F.**[8] b 11-21-1850 [IGI]

Children of **William B.**[8] Severance and Lucy C. Lindsay
       iv   **Azel E.**[8] b 9-6-1859 [MEVR] He m to Mary
            E. Genthner on 7-4-1876. [MEVR] She was
            18 at her marriage and he was 19.

(337) George N.[7] (Benjamin[6], Joshua[5], Joseph[4], Ephraim[3], Ephraim[2], John[1]), born 7-27-1826 in Orrington, ME. He died on 8-14-1896. [MEVR] He married to Eliza Ann Goodwin, daughter of Stephen Goodwin and Rhoda Hinman, on 11-18-1849 in Hancock Co. ME. [MEVR Surrey] She was born circa 1831 in Surrey, ME and died at East Orrington on 4-11-1913 age 81-9-22. [MEVR] They lived in Surrey, Hancock, ME. The family shows on the 1860-1870 ME census.

Children:
       i   **Anna P.**[8] b 11-3-1851 at Orrington, ME
       ii   **George L.**[8] b 2-13-1864 at Orrington, ME

(338) Henry Albert[7], (Benjamin[6], Joshua[5], Joseph[4], Ephraim[3], Ephraim[2], John[1]), was born 10-12-1829 at Orrington, Penobscot Co. ME. He was listed in his fathers Will. He was probably the one who married to Eleanor Miranda Bowden on 10-14-1852. [IGI] Eleanor Bowden was born 6-27-1831. [MEVR] The 1870 ME census shows **Henry**[7] and Miranda with their children in orrington. **Henry A.**[7] filed 4-28-1865 for service in B 1 ME Heavy Art. [CWPR] **Henry A.**[7] d 10-9-1911. **Henry A.**[7] married Mary Crawford on 11-24-1900. He was 58 and she was 24. Both married for the second time. He was the son of **Benjamin**[6] Severance and Anne Pope. [MEVR]

Children: [MEVR]
       i   **Ida Augusta**[8] b 1-20-1854
       ii   **Alice N.**[E] b 6-7-1855
       iii **James B.**[E] b 10-17-1856 m Mary A. Hoxie
            at Orrington, ME on 10-7-1885. [MEVR]
       iv   **Lucy A.**[8] b 7-20-1860
       v   **Henry A. Jr.**[8] b 1-30-1864 m Fannie J.
            Harris 12-17-1882 at Orono, ME. [MEVR]

(339) Charles A.[7], (Benjamin[6], Joshua[5], Joseph[4], Ephraim[3], Ephraim[2], John[1]), born 4-27-1831 [MEVR] at Orrington, ME. He died 10-28-1880 age 67-6-1 [MEVR] His m Lydia Bowden on 8- -1854. [IGI] Lydia was born 6-27-1834 and died on 1-18-1903. [CRME

Orrington] Lydia was the daughter of Jeremiah
Bowden and Hannah Kilburn of Orrington, ME. The
family shows on the 1860-1870 ME census. **Charles**[7]
was at first a brick mason and then later engaged
in mercantile business and as Postmaster. He was a
selectman for four years. [HOPCoME]

Children:
  i   **Charles M.**[8] b 8-14-1860 d 1-30-1889
       [MEVR]
  ii   **Rose J.**[8] b 3-29-1862 [MEVR]

(340) Harlons Erastus[7], (Benjamin[6], Joshua[5], Joseph[4],
Ephraim[3], Ephraim[2], John[1]), born on 1-27-1840 in
Orrington, ME. [MEVR] He died on 2-4-1910 age 72
years and 8 days. [MEVR] He married to Eunice Berry
on 5-26-1867. [MEVR] He married to Emma L.___ in
1867 or shortly after. Emma Lizzie shows as his
wife on the 1870-1880 ME census. She was born 4-2-
1846. [MEVR] He married to Florence A. Chapman,
daughter of Lorenzo A. Chapman and Anna Bearce, on
1-24-1883 at Orrington, ME. [MEVR] She was born on
9-3-1852 and died at the age 67-7-15 on 18-1920.
[MEVR]

Children:
644 i   **Harry J.**[8] b 4-7-1872 [MEVR]

(341) Henry (Harvey) Albert[7], (Benjamin[6], Joshua[5],
Joseph[4], Ephraim[3], Ephraim[2], John[1]), born 11-16-1845
d 10-9-1911. He married to Louisa M. Bell on 4-13-
1870 in MO.
    Louisa was the daughter of Alfred Bell and
Hannah Emerine McHolland. (Hannah Bell, was living
with them in Meadville, Linn Co. MO in 1880). [1889
MOFC] Louisa died on 8-15-1929. This family was
from Orrington, ME, later lived in Meadville, MO,
and then settled in Los Angeles, CA. [MDJS] The
1880 MO census shows them living in Meadville, Linn
Co. with children, **Emma**[8] age 8 and **Charlie**[8] age 4,
both born in MO. The 1900 OR census shows them
living in Portland with 3 children, **Charles**[8],
Josie[8], **Fannie**[8], and Hannah E. Bell.
    Harvey[7], age 75, born in ME shows in Los
Angeles, Los Angeles Co. CA. Listed with him were
his wife Louisa, age 75, born in MO, Josie Hellman
age 38, daughter, (apparently her married name) and
Clarence Smith age 16 born in Oregon, his grand
son. [1920 CAFC]

Children: [1880 MOFC]
        i   **Mary⁸**
        ii   **Emma⁸** b 1872
645   iii   **Charlie Alfred⁸** b 4- -1876 m Clara Ester
                Bentz circa 1900/1901
        iv   **Josephine Bell⁸** b 1-3-1881 m Rollo
                Kellogg m2 to ___ Hellman
        v   **Frances E.⁸** b 11- -1884 m Willard
                Hellman

(342) Jerome P.⁷, (Cyprian⁶, Joshua⁵, Joseph⁴,
Ephraim³, Ephraim², John¹), born 6-30-1830 [IGI] at
Orrington, ME. He married Mary Jane Colson,
daughter of Anson Colson and Abigail Grant of
Frankfort, ME, on 10-1-1852 at Orrington, ME. Mary
died 9-4-1915 at the age of 84-10-4. [MEVR] The
1870 ME census for Waldo Co shows them living at
Winterport, ME.

Children:
        i   **Charles N.³** b 1856 at Winterport, ME, and
                later lived at Hermon, ME. He married
                first to Mrs. Emma E. Young on 2-28-1878
                at Hampden, Penobscot Co. ME. [MEVR] He
                married secondly to Maud E. Robinson on
                4-27-1897. [MEVR] Maude was the daughter
                of Rufus Robinson and Tempest Ellingwood.
                She died on 7-6-1908 at the age of 44
                years. She was born in Hermon, ME. Next
                he married to Alberta L. Curtis on 12-22-
                1909. [MEVR] The third marriage is
                conjecture but the MEVR says that **Charles
                N.⁸** and Alberta L. Curtis married on 12-
                22-1909 at Millinocket, ME. He was 54
                years and she was 38. He was born at
                Winterport and it was his third marriage.
                It was Alberta's second marriage. It is
                unclear if they had any children.

(343) George W.⁷ (Cyprian⁶, Joshua⁵, Joseph⁴,
Ephraim³, Ephraim², John¹), born 6-1-1832 in
Hampden, ME. He married to Sarah A. Jones (who may
have been his second wife). **George⁷** is shown living
in Mariaville, ME. Sarah was born circa 1858 in
Winterport, ME. The 1900 Orrington, ME census shows
Henry W.⁸, mother, Sarah, brother **Frank N.⁸**, and
sister, **Jean G.⁷** living together

Children: [1870-1880 MEFC]
647   i   **George M.⁸** b 7- -1859 m Emma F. Copeland

221

ii   **Mary E.**[8] **b** 1861
iii   **Frank Norman**[8] b 1- -1871. [1900 MEFC]
        I show a **Frank Norman**[8] m to Gertrude M.
        Wiley from ME. [MEVR]
648 iv   **Henry W.**[8] b 1871
     v   **Eugenia G.**[8] b 1880

(344) John H.[7], (Cyprian[6], Joshua[5], Joseph[4],
Ephraim[3], Ephraim[2], John[1]), born 8-9-1840 in
Newburgh, ME. He settled in Winterport, ME where he
married first to Melissa Cole 5-4-1864. They show
on the 1870 ME census with children, **Ida J.**[8] and
Melvin[8]. I also show the marriage of **John H.**[7]
Severance of Freedom and Isabel J. Lamson, married
4-19-1868 by Rev. T.E. Barstow. [MEVR] He married
next to Louisa Flinn, 12-11-1876, both of Newburgh,
ME. [MEVR] He married to Sarah V. Slack, daughter
of Isaac Slack and Harriet Martin of Providence,
RI, 9-1-1902. [MEVR] The 1880-1900 ME census shows
John H.[7] and Louisa F. born 1833 and the IGI shows
Ila[8], daughter of **John H.**[7] and Melissa Cole born 3-
26-1865. **John H.**[7] died 8-5-1907.

Children:
     i   **Ila M.**[8] b 3-26-1865
649 ii   **Melvin B.**[8] b 1868 in ME
     iii   **Percey E.**[8] b 1869/1871 in Newburgh, ME.
           He m to Mary J. Nealey on 6-1-1898.
           [MEVR] It is unknown if they had any
           children.
     iv   **Melissa Maude**[8] b 1874

(347) Winfield S.[7], (Cyprian[6], Joshua[5], Joseph[4],
Ephraim[3], Ephraim[2], John[1]), born 7- -1847. [1900
MEFC] He married first to Lizzie Hannah Colson on
1-18-1868. [MEVR] She died on 11-21-1886 at the age
of 34. He married second to Florence E. Dollard,
daughter of Leonard Higgins and Julia Ann Hooper,
on 12-21-1892. [MEVR] **Winfield S.**[7] died 5-7-1905
in Ellsworth, ME. [CWPR] Florence died in 1913.
They are found living in Winterport, Frankfort, and
Ellsworth, ME.

Children: [1870-1880 MEFC]
     i   **Walter**[8] b 7- -1869 in Maine.
     ii   **Varna**[8]
     iii   **Charles L.**[8] b 8-2-1871 d 8-30-1917 in ME
           m Zelma Hamor 5-8-1903 [MEVR] She was b
           circa 1873
     iv   **Lulie**[8] b 1874

(348) Lorenzo G.[7], **(Lonny)**, (Ephraim[6], Joshua[5], Joseph[4], Ephraim[3], Ephraim[2], John[1]), born on 8-29-1849 in Bangor, ME. [CRME] He married to Elizabeth E. Brastow/Barstow on 10-8-1875. [IGI] She was born 7-31-1857 and died on 1-8-1923. [CRME] He died 8-7-1910 aged 62 yrs 11 mos 8 dys at East Orrington, ME. [MBGD]

Children:
    i   **Carrie H.**[8] b 3- -1890

(349) John Smith[7], (John[6], John[5], Ephraim[4], Ephraim[3], Ephraim[2], John[1]), born in Sandwich, NH on 5-6-1793. [IGI] He was a farmer in Sandwich and married first to Dorothy French, "Dolly F.", on 3-14-1813. [IGI] She died on 11-22-1842. He married secondly to Abigail Hilton, [SNHE 55th p29] on 7-9-1845. [IGI] Abigail was the daughter of David Hilton of Sandwich, NH. The Hiltons lived directly north of the bridge across Bear Camp River. David Hilton had a large family. [SHNE 45th p29]

John[7] purchased the farm from Samuel M. Folsom. After a long and expensive litigation with his nearest neighbor, John Hunking Hilton, the farm equity was taken on an execution from a sheriffs sale on 10-3-1857 and sold to William M. Weed. John[7] had spent all he had to mortaged the farm to nearly its full value. [SHNE 45th p24] The article indicated that **John**[7] married Lydia Jewell as his first wife. **John's**[7] first wife was in reality Dorothy French. [NHVR] **John's**[7] name shows on the 1830-1840 NH census at Sandwich.

John S.[7] Severance, commonly known as **Smith**[7] Severance, "a near relative of Captain **Elbridge G.**[8] Severance■", was buried at Skinner Corner, Sandwich, NH. [Tasker]

John[7] Severance was born 5-6-1793 at Sandwich, NH. He died on 9-13-1867. His body was moved to Auburn, MA by train by Daniel Gramin after he died. [NHVR]

Many of the children settled or moved for a time to Maine. **Asa F.**[8] was from Nobleboro, ME, **Russell**[8] and **Andrew J.**[8] settled in Bradford, ME near the Randall family.

Children of **John**[7] Severance and Dorothy French
650 i   **Russell**[8] b 1813 m Hannah B. Randall
        (Hannah was the sister of Adaline (who
        married **James M.**[8] Severance, and Lewis
        B. (who m **Alvira**[8] Severance). Hannah B.

Randall was the daughter of William Randall and Betsey Burleigh, all b at Sandwich, NH.

ii   **John**[8] possibly b 1814/15 d young

iii   **Alvira**[8] b 4-15-1818 d 10-9-1891 m Lewis Burleigh Randall, (b 8-29-1820 d 6-29-1898), on 7-16-1844. Lewis was the son of William Randall and Betsey Burleigh of Sandwich, NH. They lived for several years in Boston, MA before moveing to Bradford, ME. [Burleigh I p64]

651 iv   **Sargeant French**[8], b 1822 d 12-6-1895 [MAVR] m Harriet Burleigh, daughter of Nathaniel and Phebe (French) Burleigh, on 4-22-1852. [Burleigh p122]. **Sargeant F.**[8] was a farmer at Sandwich, NH. He m a second time to Mary A. Baker on 2-9-1859 at Boston. The 1870 NH census shows him with Mary, age 43 and a daughter **Lizzie**[9] age 10.

v   **John N.**[8] b 1824 d 4-2-1840 [NHVR]

vi   **Lydia A.**[8] b 1827 at Sandwich, NH, daughter of **John**[7] Severance, m James B. Fellows, son of John Fellows of Pittsfield, NH, on 9-6-1855 at Boston, MA [MAVR]

652 vi   **Asa French**[8], b 7-29-1829 d 7-25-1913 m Mary Elizabeth Barstow (Nobleboro, ME)

653 vii   **Octavius Webster**[8] b 1832. **Octavius**[8], most likely the brother of **Russell**[8], was b 1832. He m Elizabeth Libbey, daughter of Isaac and Mary (Worster) Libbey. The [MEVR] show **Octavius W.**[8] Severance d 10-1-1864 age 33 years old at Bradford, ME. He was b at Sandwich, NH and his parents were **John**[7] and Dolly F. Severance both b in Sandwich, NH.

654 viii   **George A.**[8] b 1833 d 11-9-1905 [CRME] [MEVR] He m to Harriet and they had a son, **Octavus**[9] b 1865. The 1870 ME census shows them living in Alton. The 1860 Bradford, ME census shows **Russell**[8], Hannah B. (his wife), **Andrew J.**[8] (a brother of **Russell**[8]) and **George A.**[8] (a brother of **Russell**) Next door were (**O.W.**[8]) **Octavius Webster**[8] and Lizzie (Elizabeth Libby). **Octavius**[8] was b 1832 and Lizzie b 1841. **Russell**[8] was b 1814 and a physician and Hannah B. were both b in NH. [1870 MEFC]

655 ix   **Andrew J.**[3] b 1836 d 11-25-1904 [MEVR]
              Andrew J.[9] m Angeline C. Larrabee at E.
              Boston, MA. She was b 5-22-1844, the
              daughter of David Larrabee and Cynthia
              Chapman.

Children of **John**[7] Severance and Abigail Hilton
       x   **Francesa (Angela F.)**[8] b 1846 m Timothy
              Sly, son of Stephen and Lizzie Sly of
              Ryegate, VT, on 12-12-1891 at Worcester,
              MA. [MAVR]
656 xi   **John M.**[8] b b 1849/1851

The 1850 NH census shows **John**[7] with Abigail (wife)
and **Andrew**[8], **Francisa**[8], and **John**[8]. The 1860 NH
census shows **John**[7], Abigail, **(Angeley F.) Francisa**[8]
b 1846 and **John M.**[8] b 1851 (age 9).

(350) Asa[7], (John[6], John[5], Ephraim[4], Ephraim[3],
Ephraim[2], John[1]), born in Sandwich, NH on 3-31-1798.
[NHVR] When he was young he purchased a farm
adjoining the old homestead. He was a prosperous
farmer through his short life. He was a Free Will
Baptist and of the Democratic Party. [BioR] He
served as a Lieut. in the New Hampshire Military.
He married Rhoda Webster on 10-11-1821. [IGI]
Lieutenant **Asa**[7] died on 2-19-1828 at the age of 29
years 11 months. [Lighton] Rhoda remarried to **John**[7]
Severance. Rhoda died on 1-15-1879. **John**[7] was the
son of **Ephraim**[6] Severance.

Children:
657 i   **John Webster**[8] b 2-3-1822 [Sterns] d 5-
              19-1901 m 11-25-1841, Hannah J. Kaime,
              daughter of Benjamin Kaime and Sally
              Watson. [BioR] Although the genealogy is
              errored from Sterns errored history, it
              does mention **John Webster**[8], son of **Asa**[7]
              and Rhoda Webster.
     ii   **Jewell**[8] b 1826 d 5-4-1826 age 10 weeks
              [Lighton]
658 iii   **Asa**[8] b 2-3-1828 d 4-1-1901 m Hannah M.
              Webster 11-20-1850, Hannah b 10-10-1828
              d 9-29-1900. [Lighton] (They had a son
              John[9] **Webster** Severance)

(351) Levi[7], (John[6], John[5], Ephraim[4], Ephraim[3],
Ephraim[2], John[1]), was born 3-24-1800 [IGI] in
Sandwich, NH. He married Ruth Skinner of Brookline,
MA. Ruth, born circa 1795, was the daughter of

Jedediah Ingerson Skinner and Sarah Hurlbut.
[Fernald p128] They were born in Hebron and
Norwalk, CT, repectively. Jedediah Skinner came to
Sandwich about 1790. He was a noted singer and
taught many singing schools. Ruth Skinner died 7-4-
1889 at Malden, MA by accident, age 90 years.
[MAVR]
    Jedediah Skinner died in Sandwich, NH. [Fernald
p127] **Levi**[7] and Ruth (Skinner) Severance settled in
Boston, MA. The 1840 NH census shows him living in
Sandwich. **Levi**[7] was a Carpenter and died 5-7-1876
at Boston age 76-1-12. [MAVR]

Children:
659	i	**Elijah Charles**[8] b 11-11-1821 in Boston. He m Rhoda Hedges 10-14-1856
660	ii	**Charles W.**[8] b circa 1823
	iii	**Sarah/Harriet N.**[8] b 1827 Sandwich, NH m John E. Bubier, son of John and Eliza Bubier, 6-8-1864 at Boston, MA [MAVR]
	iv	**Clark**[8] b circa 1830, in 1860 he was living in Boston as a book keeper, living with Alden W. Titus and his brother **Nathan C.**[8] Severance.
	v	**Ursula**[8] b 1831 at Sandwich, NH m Francis Drake, son of Bradford Drake, 6-7-1856 at Boston, MA. [MAVR]
662	vi	**Nathan N.C.**[8] b circa 1835 m Lavina D. Keith
	vii	**Lydia J.**[8] b 1837 m John A. Hill, son of James and Milly Hill, at Stoughton, MA, 4-5-1855. He was a musician. [MAVR]
	viii	**Levi**[8] b circa 1837. He m to Caroline A. Mahan, daughter of John A. and Harriet Mahan, on 8-24-1880 in Boston. [MAVR] He worked in a resturant. He d of Brights Disease on 8-24-1889. [MAVR]
	ix	**Mary**[8] b 1839 at Sandwich, NH m Andrew L. Knight, son of Nathaniel and Sarah Knight, 3-8-1859 at Boston, MA. [MAVR]
663	x	**William H.**[8] b 7-27-1840 d 12-14-1915. He had been married. He was a Jeweller in Boston, MA.
	xi	**Harriet**[8] b 1840 was a dressmaker
	xii	**James H.**[8] b 1842. The 1860 MA census shows him m to Harriet ____, who was b in 1840 in MA. They were living in Boston in the 7th ward. Harriet was 20 years old and he was 18. Living next door was **Jacob Jewell**[8], who was a cousin

of **James M.**[8] Severance. The records show that **James**[8] m2 to Mary S. Sherman, daughter of Joseph and Cordelia Sherman, 1-7-1866 at Harwich, MA. [MAVR] **James**[8] m3 to Sarah P. Hanson, daughter of James L. and Amanda Hanson, on 6-8-1875. Sarah P. was b in 1853. [MAVR] **James**[8] d 2-12-1896 at Haverhill, MA. age 52 years, from accidental inhalation of gas. [MAVR] He was a restauranteur. They had a daughter, **Hattie Amanda**[9] b 4-16-1876 at Boston, MA [MAVR]

664   xiii   **Nathaniel C.**[8] b circa 1845 at Sandwich, NH. He married Olive Ann Gould of Livermore, ME. They lived in Boston, MA.

(352) Jacob Jewell[7], (John[6], John[5], Ephraim[4], Ephraim[3], Ephraim[2], John[1]), was born in Sandwich, NH the [TPNH 1895-1900] says that **Jacob**[7] was born in Deerfield, NH) on 11-4-1804, son of **John**[6] and Lydia Jewell. He was a farmer growing up on the family homestead in Sandwich. The 1840 NH census shows him living in Meredith. He married Susan R. Roberts 3-20-1842. The NH vital records for Meredith erroneously recorded Susan's maiden name as Robinson. She was the daughter of Joseph Roberts, born in Brentwood, NH, and Mary (Davis) Roberts of Meredith, NH. [TPNH] Susan died 5-12-1896. She was a sister of Olive Naomi Roberts who married **Elbridge G.**[7] Severance. **Jacob**[7] died on 1-9-1896. He is buried in the Old Smith Yard (Opeechee) in Meredith, NH.

"**Jacob Jewell**[7] Severance, age 91 years, died at his home on the Meredith Road in this city, Thursday night of last week. He was one of the oldest, if not the oldest citizens in Laconia having celebrated the ninety-first anniversary of his birth last November. He was enjoyed good health until within a comparitively short time and death was due to old age and a general breaking down of the system." [NSLD 1-17-1896]

His early life was spent on the farm in Sandwich, and he received his education at the district school until he was 18 years old, when he attended the Wolfeboro Academy one term. After finishing his education he taught school for several years in Sandwich, Tamworth, Meredith, Gilmanton and Belmont.

In 1829 he went to Bangor, ME, where he was for two years a clerk in a dry goods store, and was afterwards a traveling salesman in the same line of business through Maine, New Hampshire, and Vermont.

In March 1832 he was united in marriage to Susan Rosetta Roberts of Meredith, and since that time the couple have resided on the Roberts farm, now in the city of Laconia. The Roberts farm was settled by the wife's grandfather, Joseph Roberts, in 1771, when the locality was a wilderness. Since his marriage Mr. Severance followed the occupation of a farmer, with the exception of two or three years when he carried the U. S. mail between New Hampton and Alton.

He was survived by a wife, 83 years of age, a son, **William Jewell**[8] Severance, and a daughter, Miss **Mary Augusta**[8] Severance, both of this city, also one brother, **James Madison**[7] Severance, who was nearly 81 years old, resideing at Hotel Wyman, Boston. [NSLD 1-17-1896]

Children: [1870 Laconia, NHFC]
	i	**Mary Augusta**[8] b 3-26-1834 d 6-6-1913 single [NHVR]
665	ii	**William J.**[8] b 1839 m Mary Etta Wadleigh
	iii	**Alice**[8] b circa 1841

(353) Sargeant Jewell[7], (John[6], John[5], Ephraim[4], Ephraim[3], Ephraim[2], John[1]), was born 3-20-1809 in Sandwich, NH. He married there to Elizabeth Burton, of Philadelphia, PA on 11-25-1841. She was born 11-11-1814. They were the parents of six children, the first two of which were born in NH, the rest in PA. After the first two were born, they moved to Warren Co. PA. There he bought a farm of 300 acres, all timber, where the rest of his children were born, and where his wife died. About 1856, he moved to Dodge Center, MN, where he bought a farm about 7 miles south of the town, on what was called then, South Prairie.

The Dodge Center Seventh Day Baptist church was first started at South Prairie. **Sargent**[7] became one of the first members of that church, and remained a member the rest of his life.

Asa Walter[8] and **Rosanna**[8] stayed in the East when the rest of the family moved to MN, and nothing more is known of them. (They were little more than babies at that time) They were supposed to have been taken care of by other families, possibly relatives, and may have taken their names. The boys all came west and farmed with their father, and were all married in Dodge Center.

According to **Harland**[9] Severance, **Sargeant Jewell**[7] Severance did not remarry. [MHCS]

Children:
666 i   **William Norman**[8] b 12-27-1842 m1 Caroline m2 Elizabeth Franklin 4-25-1862
667 ii   **John Martin**[8] b 9-4-1845 m Ruth Haskins 1864
668 iii **Hector Calbreth**[8] b 7-19-1847 m Emma Ann Ellis 5-10-1876
669 iv **Thompson Burton**[8] b 12-8-1848 (of Warren City, PA), m Elnora Mills 1868 Dodge Center, MN)
     v   **Asa Walter**[8] stayed in PA
    vi   **Rosanna**[8] stayed in PA

(354) James Madison[7], (John[6], John[5], Ephraim[4], Ephraim[3], Ephraim[2], John[1]), born 4-25-1814 at Sandwich, NH. [IGI] He lived part of his life on the family homestead as a farmer. But he also lived in Bradford, ME and later in Boston, MA. He married Adaline Randall on 10-2-1834. [IGI] Adaline was the daughter of William Randall and Betsey Burleigh of Sandwich, NH. {MDS] In 1870 **James**[8] and Adaline were living in Bradford as a farmer with several of his relatives. [MEFC] Adaline was born 10-2-1834 and died 4-1-1883. [NHVR] **James**[8] died 12-15-1897 at 27 Belvidere St., Boston, MA. [MAVR]

The military records shows **James**[7] as 2nd Lieut. in 1836 and 1st Lieut of the Calvalry for 1840. [Mardecai]

In 1897, "the only survivor of the family is **James M.**[7] who resides in Boston. His wife, Adeline Randall, died leaving four children, **Eliza**[8], **Nancy**[8], **Alonzo**[8], and **Waldo**[8]." {BioR]

Children:
    i   **Eliza**[8] [BioR]
   ii   **Frank A.**[9] b 1835 d 5-6-1861 m Sarah Smart 7-2-1854, Tamworth NH., **Frank**[8] shows on the 1860 NH census at Center Harbor, NH with a wife, Mary. **Frank**[8] probably never had any children.
  iii **Nancy**[8] b 1837 married a _____ Webster
670 iv **Alonzo**[8] b 10-13-1842 d 1-24-1924 m Louisa E. Vittum 3-24-1864 [MDS]
    v   **James Martin**[8] b 1844 d 3-18-1856
671 vi **Asa Waldo**[8] b 11-3-1847 d 9-26-1909 Bradford, ME.

The 1870 ME census shows **James**[7] Severance and
Adaline with **Waldo**[8] age 22, **Lizzie**[8] age 29 and
Isaac[9] Severance age 1. Lizzie was the wife of **Asa
W.**[8] and **Octavus**[8] Severance.

(355) Jesse[7], (Nathaniel[6], John[5], Ephraim[4], Ephraim[3],
Ephraim[2], John[1]), was born circa 1809 in Sandwich,
NH. He died on 5-1-1885 at Newport, Penobscot
County, ME. His life and family are not well known.
He was settled in Newport, ME in his adult life. He
may have married twice as his child **Atwood**[8] was
born in 1832, five years before he married to Sarah
Brown. She was born about 1814 and died on 2-25-
1880 at Newport, ME. The marriage intentions were
recorded for 2-10-1837, then the marriage
certificate for 2-26-1837. [Clinton, MEVR] The
records also show for a Civil Marriage on Kennebec,
[MEVR] as 3-21-1837. He married late in life to a
cousin, **Lucy B.**[7] (Severance) Marston, sister of
Elbridge G.[7] Severance of Sandwich and Laconia, NH.
She had been married previously to Jason Marston.
Lucy B.[7] Severance left legacies to **Atwood**[8] and
Lagrange[8] (studying to become doctors) in her Will
when she died. [PRNH-Carroll Co]
   The 1840 ME census shows **Jesse**[7] living at
Newport. The ME Cemetery Records show **Jesse**[7] buried
with **Mary Ann**[8], L.W. Gould (Levi Gould?) (a
marriage between Levi Gould and **Mary Ann**[8] Severance
1-31-1832 shows for New Sharon, ME), **Nathaniel**[7],
and **Jesse's**[7] sister, **Mary**[8].

Children:
672	i	**Atwood**[8] b 11- -1832 [1900 MEFC] m to Sarah A._____ and Nancy A._____
673	ii	**Lagrange**[8] b 12-28-1839 in ME, he became a doctor, m Henrietta Drummond and settled in Huntington, IE.
	iii	**Thomas B.**[8] b 1842 The 1860-1870 ME census shows him living with his parents

(356) Nathaniel[7], (Nathaniel Smith[6], John[5], Ephraim[4],
Ephraim[3], Ephraim[2], John[1]), born on 1-28-1805 at
Sandwich, NH. [CRME] He married to Belinda Fogg on
11-29-1828. [IGI], She was born on 2-25-1809 as the
daughter of Samuel and Dorothy Fogg. The [MEVR
Starks] shows this Fogg Family who entered that
town and recorded their family late in life. Maine
Land Records show transactions between **Jesse**[7] and
Nathaniel[7] 9-16-1833 and at that time they were
living at Chandlersville, Somerset Co. ME. His name

shows on the |1840 MEFC] for Palmyra. The 1850 ME
census shows him as a Tin Peddler. The 1870 ME
census shows them living in Stetson, ME. **Nathaniel**[7]
died 6-30-1878 at Newport, ME. [CRME]

Children:
674 i   **Samuel F.**[3] b 1830 m Christina, who was b
         1830
675 ii **Joshua/Josiah Gould**[8] b 9-30-1832 m Mary
         J. Tiel in the autumn of 1862. He went
         in search of gold and settled in CA
   iv **Mary E.**[8] b 1837
   v   **Emma R.**[8] b 1845. The 1850-1860 Newport,
         ME census shows Emma living with her
         parents
The above family was researched from Archive
Records, Land Records, and Vital Records. [MBGD]

(357) Peter[7], (Ephraim[6], John[5], Ephraim[4], Ephraim[3],
Ephraim[2], John[1]), born on 7-8-1801 in Sandwich, NH.
He died 10-21-1871 age 72 yrs, at Greenfield or
Gilford, NH. |NHVR] His birth and parents were
rather elusive. However, on the vital records for
his third marriage his parents were listed as **E.**[6]
and Sally Severance. This is undoubtly for **Ephraim**[6]
Severance and Sally Leavitt. He shows living at
Meredith, NH. [1840-1850 NHFC]
    Peter[7] was married first to Judith Glidden on 3-
11-1821. [VTVF] She was born on 9-30-1798 and died
on 9-22-1855. He married secondly to Mary Roberts
in April of 1859. She was born in 1802 and died 6-
14-1864. And he married third to Lydia A. Plumer on
1-1-1865. [1870 NHFC] She was born on 5-8-1811.
[BRRF] This is indicated in the various census
records where he is listed with his wives.
    It appears that either **Peter**[7] was living in VT
when he married to Judith or perhaps she was from
VT and they married there and then removed back to
NH.
    Jesse Plumer born 7-23-1802 married Lydia Goss
of New Hampton and he died 6-18-1854. She married
2nd to **Peter**[7] Severance of Meredith, NH. Jesse
Plumer and Lydia had 2 sons, one, **Aaron**[8], was
reported to be alive in 1877. [Runnels]

Children: [BRRF]
   i   **Ursula M.W.**[8] b 2-11-1823 d 1909 m Eben
        Leavitt on 1-6-1846. [NHVR]
   ii **Eliphalet G.**[8] b 1-21-1826 d 12-23-1850
        age 24-9-2

iii   **Lucinda**[8] b 8-7-1829 d 2-19-1909 m John
M. Robinson on 3-26-1856. He was b 8-14-
1828 d 7-12-1903

676 iv   **Charles R.**[8] b 12-22-1831 d 5-30-1864 m
Sarah Mansfield on 12-30-1855

v   **Mary S.**[8] b 9-4-1834 d 12-28-1903 m John
S. Lee on 7-13-1856

vi   **Priscilla Ann**[8] b 1-18-1837 d 12-27-1851
age 14 years

vii   **Ephraim F.**[8] b 8-4-1841

(358) Ephraim[7], (Ephraim[6], John[5], Ephraim[4], Ephraim[3],
Ephraim[2], John[1]), born in Sandwich, NH on 8-25-1804.
He married Esther G. Currier, daughter of John and
Hannah Currier. [Currier p498]] She was born 4-12-
1804 and died 10-9-1873. The 1830-1840 NH census
shows him living at Sandwich. In 1880 they are
found living in Tamworth, NH. [NHFC]. The 1860 NH
census shows **Ephraim**[7] and Esther, **Ira G.**[9] born 1853
as their grandson, along with Huldah Folsom, mother
in law. **Ephraim**[7] died on 9-18-1888. [NHVR]

Children:

i   **Dorothy**[8] m Stephen Andrews 10-30-1842 at
Lowell, MA. [MAVR]

678 ii   **Ira E.**[8] b 1834, an **Ira**[9], b 1853, was
listed as a grandson of **Ephraim**[7] on the
1860-1870 NH census. **Ira**[8] Severance m
Elma A. Folsom, 2-3-1879 at Sandwich,
NH. [IGI] She was b 12-27-1843,

(359) John Smith[7], (Ephraim[6], John[5], Ephraim[4],
Ephraim[3], Ephraim[2], John[1]), born in 1806. [NHVR] He
lived in Sandwich, NH. He married to Rhoda
(Webster) Severance on 4-8-1830. [IGI] His name
shows on the 1830-1840 Sandwich, NH census. Rhoda,
the former wife of **Asa**[7] Severance, was born 1803
and died 1-15-1879. **John**[7] died on 7-27-1886. [NHVR]

Rhoda was the first wife of **Asa**[7] Severance. In
1880 **John S.**[7], age 74 was living with **Asa**[8] 52,
Hannah 51, (she would be Hannah Webster), daughter
Alice[9], and **John W.**[9], 28, and Helen M., **John's**[9]
wife, daughters **Mary**[10] and **Alice**[10]. [NHFC] The 1870
NH census shows **John S.**[7], living with Rhoda,
Ephraim[7] (b 1805), Ester, wife of Ephraim, and **Ira**[9]
age 16 (grandson of **Ephraim**[7]), **Asa**, Hannah, and
sons, **John W.** age 17, and **Frank** age 13, **Alonzo** age
27 and Louisa age 24, Sargent age 48, Mary, and dau
Lizzie age 10. The 1850 NH census shows **John S.**[7]
with Rhoda 48, Betsy 16, and Sally 11, apparently

children from Rhoda's first marriage to **Asa**[7] Severance. Their was another daughter (**Sally**[8]) of **John S.**[7] and Rhoda.

John S.[7], son of **Ephraim**[6] and Sally Leavitt died in Sandwich, NH at the age of 80 years.

Children:
i   **Betsey**[8] b 3-5/6-1834 d 4-24-1914 m Harrison Marston Quimby, son of J. Smith Quimby, on 9-30-1857 at Sandwich, NH. He was b 6-22-d 4-10-1898 [Quinby p299]
ii   **Sarah**[8] b 1838 d 11-7-1850 [Lighton]
iii **Sally**[8] b

(360) Enoch Quimby[7], (Ephraim[6], John[5], Ephraim[4], Ephraim[3], Ephraim[2], John[1]), born about 1808 and died 7-13-1867. He lived in Sandwich, NH. **Enoch Q.**[7] married to Hannah Currier, on 11-13-1832, [Currier p498] a sister of Esther G. Currier, (who married **Ephraim**[7] Severance). Hannah died in December of 1842. He married next to Mary Currier 6-25-1843. [MAVR] **Enoch Q.**[7] died on 7-13-1867 at the age of 59 years. It is possible that some of their children settled in ME. Lydia (Brackett) Hill was born 5-21-1823) married first to **Enoch**[7] Severance. She married 3rd to ____ Burbank. She had two children by her first marriage. **Enoch**[7] shows on the 1840 NH census in Tamworth.

Children of **Enoch Q**[7] Severance and Hannah Currier
i   **Asa C.**[8] b 1839 in Sandwich, NH. He d 5-30-1861 age 22 years. [NHVR]

Children of **Enoch Q.**[7] Severance and Mary Currier
ii   **Daniel H.**[8] b circa 1840 in Sandwich, NH. He d 7-11-1851 age 11 yrs
iii **Mary Josephine**[8] b 10-23-1844 [MAVR] d 7-3-1846 of Scarlet Fever age 1-5-12 [MAVR]

Children of **Enoch Q.**[7] Severance and Lydia (Brackett) Hill
iv   son d 8-25-1854 [NHVR]
v   **Frank W.**[8] b 6-9-1856 [NHVR] d 2-4-1877 age 20-8-4 of heart disease, at Somerville, MA. He was listed as the son of **Enoch Q.**[9] Severance and Lydia. [MAVR]

(361) Ira Leavitt[7], (Ephraim[6], John[5], Ephraim[4], Ephraim[3], Ephraim[2], John[1]), was born 1815 and died

5-14-1846 age 31 years. He married Mary A. Currier
on 9-5-1841. Mary, born 5-16-1821, was the daughter
of Benjamin Currier and Ruhama B. Jewell, of
Sandwich, NH. [Currier p499]

Mary married second to Benjamin F. Griffin, 3-
28-1852 at Lowell, MA, [MAVR] and lived in Concord,
NH. [Greeley p549]

Children:
    i   **Sarah**[8] b 1844 d 1-19-1851

(362) Elbridge G.[7], (Moses[6], John[5], Ephraim[4],
Ephraim[3], Ephraim[2], John[1]), born in Sandwich, NH
circa 1821. The exposition of the facts for this
family show a picture of intrigue, mystery,
cunning, and deceit. The exact birth date for
Elbridge[7] is not known. The Sandwich, NH vital
records for the time period were lost to fire.
However, from the 1850-1860 NH census, his birth is
indicated to be around 1820.

The former home of **Elbridge G.**[7] Severance was
commonly called the Hall Pasture or Lot. **Elbridge**[7]
was the brother-in-law of Hanson Libbey. It was
said that the buildings were taken down and used by
John M. Quimby in building his new ones at what is
now the summer home of John McGowan. Butternuts in
the yard and a willow growing in the cellar mark
the site of the old house which stood on the right
hand side of the road. The barn was across the
road, and a little lower on the hill as shown by
the "wharfing" which led up to the big barn door.

It should be pointed out here that Hanson
Libbey, brother in law of **Elbridge**[7], and husband to
Sally[7] Severance, was the most skillful basket
maker in the region, as it is said, whose baskets
would hold water. [SNHE 15th Annual Excursion p27]

Elbridge G.[7] Severance married Olive Naomi
Roberts on 7-17-1845 in Belmont, NH. [NHVR] Olive
was a daughter of Joseph and Mary (Davis) Roberts
of Meredith, NH.

The Severance's were farmers. **Moses**[6] had
inherited the family homestead of his father, **John**[5]
Severance. **Elbridge**[7] lived on the farm for awhile
even after he married. During this period, NH had a
large military force which included most of the
young men. Most of the Severance's of Sandwich
enjoyed active rolls in this service. **Elbridge**[7]
advanced to Captain of his Cavalry Unit in 1846.
[Mardecai]

The family lived on the Severance homestead until 1853 when **Elbridge**[7] sold his share of the farm. He purchased part of the Roberts estate in Laconia, NH in 1856. In 1866 **Elbridge**[7] and Olive bought another farm in Gilmanton, NH. Then in 1867 they used their farm as collateral for the Nathaniel Veazey farm of Gilmanton.

Harrison[8] Severance had marred Ella J. Blaisdell on 11-1-1866. However he did not live with her and later he was found living with another women. In fact he had apparently lived with several other women. This promted the divorce by Ella from **Harrison**[8] on grounds of adultry in December of 1870. [CRBCoNH]

On 3-18-1866, **Elbridge**[7] Severance was put before a Grand Jury. He was accused of using said Oliver R. Woodman to steal money and then receiving this money through an elaborate scheme with **Harrison**[8] and a friend even when he (**Elbridge**[7]) knew that the money was stolen.

Elbridge[7] was to be put before another Grand Jury on November 1, 1867. **Elbridge**[7] and his son, **Harrison**[8], were accussed of assualt and attempted murder of said Plummer M. Davis. No sentences were issued due to the fact that **Elbridge G.**[7] Severance's and his son **Harrison's**[8] legal problems led them to "leave the state for parts unknown." [CRBCoNH]

Family history tells that the Severance's went west in 1868 and stayed a few months in Downer's Grove, IL. After leaving Downer's Grove they moved to Marquette Co. WI where **Elbridge**[7] bought a parcel of land in what is now Westfield, WI.

Apparently **Elbridge G.**[7] Severance was trying to relieve himself of the past. He sold his property to **Charles** *Clark* (his youngest son) and Olive N. *Clark* (his wife) (note the apparent name change of his son and wife)

On 3-16-1868, **Elbridge**[7] Severance purchased from William Young, the NE1/4 of section 12 T14N R8-9E (Moundville, Marquette Co. WI. **Elbridge**[7] still maintained his surname, Severance, on July 11, 1872 when he satisfied a nortage with S.G. Churchill on this same parcel of land.

During the years of 1870 to 1872, **Charles**[8] was envolved in land transactions dealing with the SW1/4 of section 12 T14N R8-9E (Moundville, Marquette Co. WI). The Severance's (*Clark's*) cleared the land and built a frame house and buildings on this land.

When the farm was sold to Enoch Nixon (grandfather of Charles Dewsnap) on 1-19-1874, **Charles**[8] (Severance) *Clark*, Olive N. *Clark*, and Edwin *Clark* signed the transaction. (note the complete surname change to Clark)

On 3-14-1877, Edwin *Clark* (**Elbridge**[7]), bought from George M. Chase and wife, one hundred and sixty acres in Ft. Winnebago, Columbia Co. WI. (W1/2 of NE1/4 and E1/2 of NE1/4 of sect. 23 in T13N R9E)

In partnership with his wife and two sons, Edwin (**Elbridge**[7]) built a fine home and developed a progressive farm. This farm was recorded on the Plat Book for Columbia County in 1880. **Harrison R.**[8] later left the partnership and moved to Madison, Lake Co. OH. He married Eliza Cross, of Moundville, WI, in 1869 and they had at least one daughter, **Myrtle**[9]. This family was living in Ft. Winnebago, WI in 1880. In 1910, **Harrison**[8] and his family were living in Madison, OH. [OHFC]

Olive Naomi *Clark* (Severance) died 7-26-1892 and was buried in the Old Fuller Cemetery in Ft. Winnebago. Family records say that Edwin (**Elbridge**[7]) moved to Cleveland, OH at this time and lived with his son **Harrison**[8].

There is record that on 8-12-1893, Edwin (**Elbridge**[7]) sold his remaining ownership in the farm in Ft. Winnebago (E1/2 of NW1/4 and W1/2 of NE1/4 S23 T13 R9E) to his son **Charles**[8]. At that time Edwin (**Elbridge**[7]) was living in Madison-on-the-Lake in Lake Co. OH. [Record of Deeds, Columbia County, WI]

Elbridge G.[7] Severance (using his birth name) died on 1-23-1895 at the age of 75 years and is buried in Madison, Ohio. [Madison, Lake Co. OHVR]

Children: [MDCD]
679 i   **Harrison Roberts**[8] b 8- -1847 m Ella J. Blaisdell [NHVR] m2 Eliza Cross [WIVR]
680 ii   **Charles Coleman**[8] b 7-29-1855 m Agnes E. Rodgers 12-27-1882 [WIVR]

ELBRIDGE G.[7] SEVERANCE *CLARK*

OLIVE NAOMI (ROBERTS) SEVERANCE *CLARK*

(364) Benjamin[7], (Jacob[6], Jacob[5], Jacob[4], Ephraim[3], Ephraim [2], John[1]), born on 8-10-1821. [IGI] Little is known about **Benjamin[7]**. It is noted that he married Patience Seaver on 9-3-1848. Patience was born 1-21-1824 and died 4-1-1910 in Kingston, NH. She was the daughter of Stephen and Hannah Seaver. [NHVR] Patience's husband was shown as **Benjamin[7]**. He was a blacksmith. They resided in Kingston, NH. [Greeley p384] **Benjamin[7]** died 10-11-1885. [NHVR]

Children:
- i **Benjamin[8]** b circa 1851. [1860-1870 Kingston, NHFC]
- ii **Frank[8]** b 1856 [1860 NHFC]
- iii **Arthur[8]** b circa 1859/1865 in Kingston, NH. [1880 NHFC] He was a shoemaker. He m to Alice O. Dow. They had a daughter, **Alice May[9]** b 4-30-1887 at Haverhill, MA., **male** d 8-21-1889 [MAVR] **Elsie Helen[9]** b 5-8-1892, [MAVR] **Arthur G.[9]** b 4-9-1894 at Haverhill, MA d 7-20-1895 age 1 yr 3 mons of Acute Meningitis [MAVR]
- iv **Anthony[8]** b 9- -1863 m Ethel M. Pratt 2-22-1913, at Kingston, NH. He was 45 and she was 19. She was the daughter of Horace L. and Minnie Pratt of Haverhill, MA. [NHVR] **Anthony[8]** was a shoemaker and Ethel was a shoe stitcher. In 1900 he was shown living only with his mother, Patience, **Anthony[8]** d on 12-21-1944, age 78-3-13. [MGC]
- v **Mary J.[8]** b 1869 m John P. Davis Jr., son of John P. and Mary A. Davis, on 7-3-1894 at Haverhill MA [MAVR]
- vi **George E.[8]** b 1873 d 6-29-1927 (widowed). He m Sarah (West) Hoyt 10-30-1907 at Kingston, NH [NHVR]. The bride had been m a 1st time. George m only once. George was a shoemaker. Sarah was the daughter of Josiah West and Hannah Glover. The [NHVR] says that he was b in Canada and d at Brentwood, NH. He was a resident of Kingston, NH.

(366) Samuel S.J.[7], (Daniel[6], Daniel[5], Ephraim[4], Ebenezer[3], Ephraim[2], John[1]), was born circa 1831. In 1880 he was living in Allegheny Co. NY married to Catherine _____. [NYFC] A pension was filed by the

invalid 12-8-1881 and by his widow 9-1-1890 from NY
for service B 189 NY., Inf. [CRPR]

Children:
<table>
<tr><td></td><td>i</td><td>Lulyn[8] b 1862</td></tr>
<tr><td></td><td>ii</td><td>Albert[8] b 1864</td></tr>
<tr><td>684</td><td>iii</td><td>Reuben[8] b 12- -1868 in Allegheny Co. NY.
[1920 NYPR] He married to Florence, who
was born in January of 1866. They had a
daughter, May L.[9] b 5- -1890 in NY</td></tr>
<tr><td></td><td>iv</td><td>Myrtic[8] b 1871</td></tr>
<tr><td></td><td>v</td><td>Eva[8] b 1874</td></tr>
</table>

(367) Charles[7], (Benjamin[6], Daniel[5], Ephraim[4],
Ebenezer[3], Ephraim[2], John[1]), born in Washington, NH
on 12-21-1805. He married Martha Lamb 7-15-1830 at
Geneva, NY. [Bowman p213] Martha Lamb, b 3-9-1812,
was the daughter of Nehemiah Lamb and Hannah
Palmer.
Four of her brothers were Baptist ministers in
Michigan. **Charles**[7] and Martha moved to Geneva, NY
around 1830 and then to a farm at Northville, MI
about four miles from Walled Lake, MI in 1835. They
built a log house and often accommodated travelers
and at one occasion had 16 overnight guests. He was
a poor man when he moved to MI but he accumulated
considerable property. Martha was a member of the
Baptist Church and **Charles**[7] was affiliated with the
Deocratice Party. [HOS p11]
The 1830 NY census shows him living at Seneca,
Ontario Co. The 1840-1850 MI census shows them
living at Commerce in Oakland Co.

Children: [HOS]
<table>
<tr><td></td><td>i</td><td>Lewis D.[8] b 1831 d 1846</td></tr>
<tr><td>685</td><td>ii</td><td>Charles Lamb[8] b 12-14-1833 d 4-30-1907 m
Louisa Forbush 6-13-1856</td></tr>
<tr><td>686</td><td>iii</td><td>Thomas Chalkley[8] b 12-18-1835 d 6-6-1914
Walled Lake, MI</td></tr>
<tr><td></td><td>iv</td><td>Adelia Diana[8] b 11-8-1837 m Glover
Williams</td></tr>
<tr><td>687</td><td>v</td><td>Nathan Ezra[8] b 4-22-1840 d 2-22-1920</td></tr>
<tr><td>688</td><td>vi</td><td>John[8] b 3-23-1843 d 4-28-1894</td></tr>
<tr><td>689</td><td>vii</td><td>King Jotham[8] b 7-7-1844 d 2-11-1927</td></tr>
<tr><td></td><td>viii</td><td>Elmira[8] b 5-14-1850 d 1-8-1892 m Frank
Sherman</td></tr>
</table>

(368) Ezra[7], (Benjamin[6], Daniel[5], Ephraim[4],
Ebenezer[3], Ephraim[2], John[1]), born in Washington, NH
on 6-24-1809. [HWNH p597] He married to Susan Lamb

and they settled near Plymouth, MI. His name shows
on the 1840-1850 Plymouth, Wayne Co. MI census.
Ezra[7] died on 1-10-1879.

Children: [HOS p11]
The 1850 MI census shows the earlier children
    i   **Elizabeth**[8] b 1834 in NY State
    ii   **Rozina**[8] b 1837 in MI
    iii   **Ann M.**[8] b 1839
    iv   **Orwell/Roswell**[8] b 1841
    v   **Emma**[8] b 1843
    vi   **Daniel N.**[8] b near Plymouth, MI in 1846
            [HOS p11] The 1900 MI census shows
            Daniel[8] b 6- -1845 and living alone at
            Ithica, MI. He is shown on the 1920 CA
            census living with his brother, **Horace
            B.**[8], in Los Angeles, CA
690 vii   **Frank/Francis**[8] b circa 9- -1848
691 viii **Horace B.**[8] b 1852 living with his
            brother **Daniel N.**[8] in Los Angeles, CA
            [1920 CAFC]
692 ix   **Lucien**[8] b circa 5- -1855

(370) Daniel[7], (Benjamin[6], Daniel[5], Ephraim[4],
Ebenezer[3], Ephraim[2], John[1]), born in Washington, NH
on 2-26-1812 and died on 5-23-1878 at Goshen,
Sullivan Co. NH. [HWNH p598] He married first to
Martha Bradley, daughter of Jonathan Bradley Jr.
and Araminta Blodgett. [GSNH Claremont] Martha was
born 7-2-1810 at Wheelock, VT and died 1858.
Daniel[7] remarried to Lucy [Wheeler p407] Latimer,
daughter of Jonathan Wheeler and Thankful Cutting,
(former wife of Amos Latimer) on 2-20-1859 [NHVR]
[Wheeler] He married third to Sarah M. Chamberlain,
daughter of Simeon Chamberlain and Rhoda Dunham, on
1-26-1870 at Newport, NH. **Daniel**[7] had settled at
Claremont, NH. [HOS p11] The 1840 NH census shows
him living at Claremont.

Children:
    i   Daughter b 1839 d 5-2-1839
    ii   **Adeline B.**[8] b 11-20-1840 d 10-31-1869
693 iii **Orren J.**[8] b 10-3-1846 m1 Lucy Chase m2
            Sarah M.P. Messer

(371) Nathan[7], (Benjamin[6], Daniel[5], Ephraim[4],
Ebenezer[3], Ephraim[2], John[1]), born circa 1813 and
married Ruhamah Smith circa 1835. She was born 8-
25-1817 and died 9-2-1896 in Claremont, NH. **Nathan**[7]
died in Claremont, NH on 4-21-1839. [HWNH p98]

Children:
694 i   **Charles Ezra**[8] b 5-28-1836 m Martha J. Downing, 11-21-1860 [IGI]

(372) Benjamin Jr.[7], (Benjamin[6], Daniel[5], Ephraim[4], Ebenezer[3], Ephraim[2], John[1]), born in Washington, NH on 7-1-1814. He married Lois F. Osgood on 10-15-1835. She was born circa 1816. **Benjamin**[7] died in Claremont, NH on 10-16-1885 age 71 years and 4 months. [NHVR]

Children: [1870 Claremont, NHFC][HOS]
     i   **Emily L.**[8] b 8-27-1836 d 3-12-1837
695 ii   **Charles Lucien**[8] b 1-25-1839 d 11-13-1901 m Laura H. Blake 10-10-1871
     iii   **Elizabeth L.**[8] B 12-12-1842 d 3-23-1846
696 iv   **George Henry**[8] b 4-5-1845 d 9-11-1924
     v   **Lucinda E.**[8] b 1-24-1848 d 8-17-1850
     vi   **John L.**[8] b 8-20-1850 d 10-10-1853
697 vii   **Benjamin F.**[8] b 3-8-1853 d 11-13-1926

(373) Loammie[7]. (Benjamin[6], Daniel[5], Ephraim[4], Ebenezer[3], Ephraim[2], John[1]), born in Washington, NH on 9-20-1815. [HOS p11] He is also recorded at Claremont, NH. [1870 NHFC] He married Nancy Burnap of Ludlow, VT on 1-16-1837. [VTVR] **Loammie**[7] died about 1887.

Children:
     i   **Joseph**[8] b 2-22-1839 d 7-24-1841
     ii   **John**[8] b 12-13-1842 d 8-18-1843
     iii   **Lydia A.**[8] b 4-25-1845 d 1923 m Charles F. Webster, son of Horace H. and Nancy E., 11-9-1869 at New Bedford, MA [MAVR]
     iv   **Maria**[8]

(374) Lewis[7], (Benjamin[6], Daniel[5], Ephraim[4], Ebenezer[3], Ephraim[2], John[1]), born in Claremont, NH on 3-25-1822. He married Nancy Almeda Green on 10-9-1846. She was born on 10-9-1830 and died 6-9-1892 in Commerce, MI. Nancy was the daughter of Ripley Green, born in Livonia, Livingston Co., NY. In July of 1832 her family moved to West Bloomfield, Oakland Co. MI, where they settled. The 1840 MI census shows him living in Oakland Co. In 1850 they were living in Huron, Wayne Co. MI. [MIFC]
    Lewis[7] and Nancy purchase a farm on the Wyandotte Reservation near the village of Flat Rock, MI and lived there for five years. After moving to Fenton, MI. they cleared and developed a

farm along the banks of Long Lake. **Lewis**[7] died in January of 1870. Nancy assumed the work and responsibilities until her sons were older
  She passed away on 6-9-1892 at her home at Long Lake, near Fenton, Genesee Co., MI. [Green II]

Children:

  i **Ellen Sophronia**[8] b 2-26-1847 in Flat Rock, MI, d 4-15-1922 m Edgar Hiram Moore. [Kennedy] He was the son of Andrew Brown Moore and Lydia Ann Mead 9-16-1865. Hiram was b 1-18-1846 d 4-27-1914. Both are buried in the Oak Hill Cemetery, Pontaic, MI.

  ii **Emma Sophia**[8] b 4-27-1850 in Flat Rock, MI, d 5-9-1926 m 12-26-1871 to Joseph L. Seaton, son of Richard Seaton. Joseph d 3-27-1919.

  iii **Charlotte Emily**[8] b 6-8-1853 d 3-11-1936 m Frederick C. Beeman 1-23-1879. He was the son of David Beeman and Caroline Cook. Frederick d 4-27-1931.

  698 iv **Edgar Carlos**[8] b 4-18-1856 farmer in Fenton, MI m Hettie A. Sullivan

  v **Bessie Eva**[8] b 9-3-1858 trained nurse, Pontiac MI. She d 3-20-1935 At Fenton, MI.

  vi **Frederick Lewis**[8] b 1-23-1863 Fenton, MI d 3-7-1865 d 3-7-1866

  699 vii **Morris Ripley**[8] b 8-19-1868 Fenton, MI m Anna L. Stannard 4-2-1890 settled in Portland, OR

(375) William Daniel[7], (Jeremiah[6], Daniel[5], Ephraim[4], Ebenezer[3], Ephraim[2], John[1]), born 12-3-1812 at Cow Bay, Cape Breton, Nova Scotia, Canada. He died 12-22-1899 at Fourchu. On 1-16-1836 he married Hannah Murrant of Mira, Cape Breton, Nova Scotia, Canada. She was born 3-14-1816 and died 2-4-1900. [Shurtleff Vol I]
  The reasoning behind placing this family into this line was the fact that others of **Jeremiah's**[7] family did go to this same area and one of **Jeremiah's**[7] brothers was drowned off the Cape in a fierce storm.

Children: born at Grand Mira, Cape Breton, Canada

  i **Arnold**[8] b 2-3-1838 d 8-8-1854

  ii **James**[8] b on 6-28-1841 in Canada. He m to Christiana Campbell 7-24-1865.

iii   **Thomas**[8] b 10-21-1843 d 12-9-1843

iv   **Ruth**[8] b 10-31-1844 m Charles William Hardy 2-6-1866

v   **William**[8] b 8-8-1847 m Mary Jane Nichol 12-16-1873, she was b 11-20-1863 at Cape Briton, N.S. Canada

vi   **Henry**[8] b on 7-14-1850 in Canada. He m to Sarah Frances Nicol on 10-11-1881. She was b on 11-20-1863.

vii   **Louisa Maria**[8] b 3-12-1853 m **John**[8] Severance 12-9-1873

viii   **Mary Ann**[8] b 1-25-1856 m Enos Henry Cann 12-15-1873

ix   **Sarah Jane**[8] b 4-2-1859 m John Rafuse 1-3-1876

(376) Michael Benjamin[7], (Jeremiah[6], Daniel[5], Ephraim[4], Ebenezer[3], Ephraim[2], John[1]), was born 11-15-1818 at Salmon River, Cape Breton, Nova Scotia, Canada. He died 4-30-1892 at Fourchu, Cape Breton. He married Phebe Jane Hardy, daughter of John Hardy and Ruth Bagnell, on 2-14-1852, at Gabarouse, Cape Breton. Phebe was b 9-19-1829. [Shurtleff Vol I]

Children:

700   i   **John**[8] b 11-21-1852 at Gabarouse, Cape Breton m **Louisa Maria**[9] Severance, daughter of **William Daniel**[8] Severance and Hannah Murrant, on 12-9-1873

ii   **Ruth Maria**[3] b 7-10-1855 d 9-1-1863

701   iii   **Arnold Holmes**[8] b 1-28-1859 d 12-18-1935 m Flora Margaret Ferguson 10-11-1881

iv   **William Henry**[8] b 5-26-1864 m Annie McQueen 2-16-1886

v   **Alice Eliza**[8] b 5-8-1867 d 4-25-1899 m Edmund Joshua Bagnell 8-10-1881

(377) George[7], (Abijah[6], Daniel[5], Ephraim[4], Ebenezer[3], Ephraim[2], John[1]), born 2-12-1820 at Lempster, VT. He was a clergyman, a Universalist Minister, and resided in VT. He married Huldah J. Stone, daughter of Mathias and Judith Stone, on 5-30-1850 at Duxbury, MA. [MAVR] Huldah was the daughter of Matthias Stone and Judith Fox Bangs. She was born 11-30-1815. She died 2-25-1889 in Royalton, VT. [Stone p352] **George**[7] died 3-9-1899 at Northfield, MA. [MAVR]

"He Studied for the ministry with Rev. Samuel C. Loveland of Weston, VT. He began to preach at Sherburne, VT 10-11-1846. Received to the

fellowship of the Green Mt. Association 6-10-1847.
Ordained at Washington 10-1-1848. Itinerating in NH
and VT 1847/8. Pastor, Surry 1849, Washington 1850,
Duxbury, MA 1851-2, East Bridgewater, MA 1853,
Cabot, VT 1855, Gover, VT 1857-70, Essex, VT 1871-
2, Essex Junction, VT 1873, Tunbridge, VT 1874-83,
South Royalton, VT 1884-91, Barnard, VT 1892,
Royalton, VT 1893-9. **George**[7] represented Glover in
the Legislature 1868-9." [MAV]

George[7] married second to Clara Ann (Holmes)
Chamberlin, daughter of Benjamin Holmes and Ursula
Stetson on 5-13-1891 in Montpelier, VT.

A letter provided by Avis Munro, a descendant of
George[7] and Huldah Severance which was sent from
South Royalton, VT on 1-8-1884 to **George's**[7] sister
Mary[7], gives a lively account of the family and
Northern VT at that time period. **George**[7] tells of
his correspondence with the Rev. **John F.**[6] Severance
who was writing the The Severans Genealogy at that
time. He mentioned **Daniel**[5], "our grandfather and
Uncle **Able**[6] were at the battle of Bunker Hill and
there were two Severances who fought at the battle
of Bennington under Gen. Starke." [MAM]

Children:
703 i   **Mazzini**[8] b 6-7-1853 m1 Ellen L. Bickford
            on 2-21-1876 m2 Maud Callow on 6-7-1883
            and m3 Florence Louise Smith on 1-1-1895
     ii   **Georgiana**[8] m Alvin C. Bean 10-10-1888
            in Hartford, Windsor Co. VT.

It is possible that another child **Channing**[7]
Severance, b 6- -1855 should be here or somehow
related as they were living in CA. [1900 CAFC].
Annette O. (wife of **Channing**[7]) being a sister of
Matthias Stone (this could be Matthias Stone Jr.,
Huldah Stone was a daughter of Matthias Stone Sr.

(378) Walter Searles[7], (Abijah[6], Daniel[5], Eprhaim[4],
Ebenezer[3], Ephraim[2], John[1]), born in Lempster, NH in
11-24-1822. **Walter Searles**[7] married to Sarah
Forrest Mitchell, daughter of William Mitchell and
Susanna Forrest, 4-23-1851 in E. Bridgewater, MA.
[MAVR] She was born 8-21-1829 [MAVR] and died 4-15-
1907. He died 6-23-1896 in E. Bridgewater, MA.
[MAVR] He was born in Union Cemetery in E.
Bridgewater. **Walter**[7] was a Delegate to Union Church
of E. and W. Bridgewater, MA in 1880 to vote in
Ministry of Rev. John T. Blades, South
Congregational Church, Brockton, MA. The family

shows on the 1860 MA census in East Bridgewater, MA.

Children:
704   i   **George Walter**[8] b 9-1-1852 at East Bridgewwater m Celia Phillips Washburn
705   ii   **Minot Forrest**[8] b 8-19-1855 in E. Bridgewater. [MAVR] He m Loretta C. (Lyon) Chandler 5-26-1894. He painted a portrait of Mary Baker Eddy in 1888 which hangs in the Historical Home of Chirstian Scientists in Swampscott, MA.
   iii   **Susi Augusta**[8] b 10-31-1857 East Bridgewater, MA. [MAVR] m Charles Everett Cole, son of Ornan M. and Abby W. Cole, 9-17-1878 at East Bridgewater. [MAVR] Charles was b 7-24-1858.

(379) James F.[7], (Abijah[6], Daniel[5], Ephraim[4], Ebenezer[3], Ephraim[2], John[1]), was born 4-7-1827 Keene, Cheshire Co. NH. He married to Sarah H. Holt, daughter of William and Susan A. Holt of ME, 9-8-1850. [MAVR] **James**[7] was a harness maker and the family shows on the 1860 MA census in East Bridgewater, MA. **James**[7] d 3-27-1827 at Brockton, MA. [MAVR] Sarah d 10-15-1880 at Brockton, MA age 54-3-15. [MAVR]

Children:
   i   **Charles Frederick**[8] b 6-20-1851 at E. Bridgewater, MA [MAVR] m Ida M. Cushing 9-15-1881 at Hingham, MA. [MAVR] They had a daughter, **Florence H.**[9] b 11-7-1882 at Brockton, MA. [MAVR]

(380) John[7], (Ebenezer[6], Ebenezer[5], Ephraim[4], Ebenezer[3], Ephraim[2], John[1]), born circa 1813 and died 6-11-1888 Colchester, VT. **John**[7] of Colchester, VT, born circa 1813 m Harriet Fowler, daughter of Joshua Fowler, on 1-1-1840. [VTVR] Harriet died on 11-29-1897 at Colchester, VT. [VTVR] Harriet was 75 years old.

Children: [1860 VTFC-Colchester]
   i   **Caroline**[8] b 1844 [1850/60 VTFC]
706   ii   **John Martin**[8] b 7- -1845. [1850/60 VTFC] m Celia Fisher 12-25-1866 [VTVR] **John Martin**[8] m Celia Ellen Percy. [MBGD]
   iii   **William B.**[8] b 1851. [1860 VTFC] m Clara Fisher at Colchester, VT. [VTVR] m2 to

Mary Hine 9-5-1885. [VTVR] The [VTVR]
records show **William**[8] was 22 at his m1
and 33 at his 2nd marriage. The [1900
VTFC] shows Sidney A. Beardsley b 4- -
1885 in VT living with them. (perhaps a
son of Mary Hine?)

iv   **Mary**[8] b 1854 [1860 VTFC] m Frank Smith.
[VTVR]

v   **Ellen Marie**[8] b 1859 [1860 VTFC] m Frank
Smith 4-9-1876. **Ellen Maria**[8] was the
daughter of **John**[7]. [VTVR]

(381) George[7], (Ebenezer[6], Ebenezer[5], Ephraim[4],
Ebenezer[3], Ephraim[2], John[1]), born 1-10-1817 at
Colchester, Chittenden Co. VT, died 12-22-1892.
[VTVR] He was the son of **Ebenezer**[6] and Jerusha
Kilbourn (Kilby) formerly of Hartford, CT. **George**[7]
married first to Betsey Cook, he married second to
Eveline Sager, daughter of Frederick Sager and
Lyddy. Eveline was b circa 1823, she died 7-23-1875
at Colchester, VT, age 52 yrs and 2 months. He
married third to Eunice Goddard 2-21-1881 at
Berkshire, MA. Eunice was 63 years old at the time
of the marriage. [VTVR] [HCCoVT] **George**[7] was made
highway Surveyor in 1845 at Colchester and he is
indicated along with his brothers, **John**[7] and **Henry**[7],
in regard to school matters. [Colchester, VT Town
Records, 1797-1824]

Children: born at Colchester, VT

i   **Clarence L.**[8] b 1850 d 10-6-1876

ii   **Mary Emelia**[8] b 1850 d 3-20-1861

iii   **Jane Eliza**[8] b 1856 d 3-20-1861

iv   **Lillian**[8] b 5-12-1857 m Charles McMath of
Kansas

v   **Charles W.**[8] b 3-5-1863 m Julia E. in
March of 1864 in WI. The 1920 IL census
shows them in Chicago with no children
although it indicated that Julie had 5
children but none living.

708   vi   **Bertrand Ernest**[8] b 5-19-1864 m Lillie E.
Bombard 4-15-1885

       Ettie C.[8] b 7-28-1867 (may not be a
child of **George**[7])

vii   **Angie L.**[8] b 1-9-1867

viii   **Jennie N.**[8] b 12-2-1868

ix   **Eddie**[8] b 6-29-1870 (may not be a child
of **George**[7])

x   **George**[8] d 11-7-1870

(384) Levi A. Warren[7], (Samuel[6], Ebenezer[5], Epraim[4], Ebenezer[3], Ephraim[2], John[1]), born 9-18-1811 and married Catherine Ann Dodds of Montgomery Co. NY 8-7-1838. The 1850 NY census says that he was born on the Atlantic Ocean.

Children: [1850 NYFC]
709   i   **Alanson**[8] b 1839
     ii   **Mary**[8] b 1840
   iii   **Hester**[8] b 1847
    iv   **Robert**[8] b circa 1850

(385) Benjamin Warren[7], (Samuel[6], Ebenezer[5], Ephraim[4], Ebenezer[3], Ephraim[2], John[1]), born 9-26-1816, at Hillsboro, NH or Lewis, NY. [MAVR] He married Lucy R. Allen, daughter of Jacob and Lucy G. Allen. He was recorded in Essex Co. NY, then NH, NJ, and Boston, MA. [MRS] [LCCEC] **Benjamin W.**[7], son of **Samuel**[6] and Susanna, died 10-8-1882 at Boston, MA of pneumonia. He was a widower. Lucy had died at Boston of ovarian cancer on 5-15-1880. [MAVR]

Children:
    i   **Samuel Augustus**[8] b 5-28-1844 in Elizabethtown, NJ and d 9-25-1891 in NH. [NHVR] **Samuel**[8] **Augustus**[8] m to Rosie A. Fullerton, daughter of Ezekiel and Adaline E. Fullerton of Raymond, NH. [MAVR] **Samuel**[8] and Rosie had a son, **Eugene E.**[9] who d 2-15-1873 at Charlestown, MA, five days after his mother, Rosie died. [MAVR] He m next to Mary Abbie Miller, daughter of Lewis G. and Abigail Miller, on 6-26-1879 in Waltham, MA. She was b 11-13-1853. He settled as pastor of the Baptist church in Turner, ME, 7-1-1881 to 5-1-1883, in Maplewood, MA, 5-1-1883 to 10-1-1889 in Keene, NH. They had no children. [Thurston]
   ii   **Eveline Matilda**[8] b 3-4-1849 at Manchester, MA [MAVR] m Oscar R. Skillings, son of Samuel and Elvira B. Skillings, 11-13-1873 at Charlestown, MA. [MAVR] In 1880 the Severance family was living with the Skillings family. [MAFC]

(386) Cyrus[7], (Samuel[6], Ebenezer[5], Ephraim[4], Ebenezer[3], Ephraim[2], John[1]), was born 1-27-1822 and died 7-9-1908, 2 daughters by first wife, (Phebe Wardner), who was born 1824 in NY and had 2 sons by 2nd wife (Amey E. (Reynolds) Angier) who was born 1- -1825 in NY. The 1860 NY census shows **Cyrus**[7], Amy, **Elvira M.**[8], **William**[8], and **Christopher**[8]. His mother, Susanna, born in NH, was living with them.

Children of **Cyrus**[7] Severance and Phebe Wardner
The 1850 NY census shows **Cyrus**[7], Phebe, **Emma**[8] age 2, and **Minerva**[8] age 0 living with the Wardner family.
- i **Emma S.**[8] b 1848
- ii **Elvira Minerva**[8] b 1850
- iii **Marguerite Fredal**[8] m Johnson

Children of **Cyrus**[7] Severance and Amey E. (Reynolds) Angier [1860 Lewis, Essex Co. NYFC]
- iv **William**[8] b 1855 in Essex, NY, settled in Lowell, MA was a piano tuner or player
- v **Charles I.**[8] b circa 1859 in Essex, NY. He shows on the 1860 NY census at age 1 with his parents.

(387) Lucius Warren[7], (Samuel[6], Ebenezer[5], Ephraim[4], Ebenezer[3], Ephraim[2], John[1]), was born 12-23-1824 at Essex, NY. He was a marble monuments dealer, first with Mr. S.D. Wright, then went into business with S.C. Haskell and in 1882 the firm became Severance and Steel, manufacturing the finest of monuments from the best foreign and American marble, and of Scotch and native granite.

When he was only 20 years old, he went to Manchester, MA, where he learned the machinist's trade. He worked as an operator of machinery, being employed in one mill at Manchester seventeen years. He married at Willsboro, Essex Co. NY on 5-22-1851 to Lucretia Maria Hayward. Lucretia, daughter of David Hayward, was born 4-30-1828 at Essex, NY and died 10-20-1918 at Buffalo, NY. [HWCoWI]

He died at Whitewater, WI 4-14-1885. The 1870 WI census shows the family living at Whitewater, Walworth Co.

Children:
- i **Charles Lucius**[8] b 4-28-1852 at Manchester, MA. [MAVR] Educated at Beloit College, WI, studied medicine, and attended two courses of lectures at the Hahnemann Medical College of Chicago. He d 1872 unm at Whitewater, WI.

710 ii   **Frank Hayward**[8] b 11-28-1856 at
                Manchester, MA m 8-19-1885 to Lena
                Lilian Hill at Isle La Motte, VT.
                Settled at Ithaca, NY. He was editor of
                the *Buffallo Express* [Stratton]

(388) William[7], (Samuel[6], Ebenezer[5], Ephraim[4],
Ebenezer[3], Ephraim[2], John[1]), born 10-19-1827 in
Essex, NY. He married to Eunice Maria Hayes,
daughter of Philo Hayes and Deborah Moore, on 6-15-
1852. She was born 7-26-1831 at Willsborough and
died at Keesville, NY on 1-4-1922. **William**[7] was a
farmer and Insurance Agent (assessor). [Smith III
p736] He also made shoes according to the census
records.
    He was a member of the Methodist Episcopal
Church. **William**[7] died on 6-22-1902. [MRS]

Children: [LCCEC] [NYFC]
711 i   **Benjamin Warren**[8] b 7-31-1855 m Lena
                Woodruff
     ii   **Eugene H.**[8] was b on 8-7-1857 [JFS]. He
                married to Carrie E. Helms of Willsboro,
                NY. She was born in July of 1858 in NY.
                [1900 NYFC] **Eugene**[8] Severance was a
                farmer in Willsboro, NY. He died 11-29-
                1930. Carrie died in 1936. [LCCEC]
     iii   **Clara**[8] (Cora) was the wife of Dr. G.W.
                Bond, of Ticonderoga, NY
712 iv   **Robert D. (Bert)**[8] was senior member of
                the large dry-goods firm of Severance
                Brothers in Willsboro, m Nellie E.
                Smith, daughter of Edward Smith. Also
                called **Elbert DeLoyd**[8]
713 v   **Karl Jerome**[8] was a physician at
                Keeseville, he m Kate M. Foss, of
                Vergennes, VT, 3-18-1891
714 vi   **Rolland Augustus**[8] was the junior member
                of the enterprising firm of Severance
                Brothers.
     vii   **Peaslie**[8] (Pearl)

(389) Samuel Bird[7], (Levi[6], Ebenezer[5], Ephraim[4],
Ebenezer[3], Ephraim[2], John[1]), born in 10-28-1831 at
Pittsburg, PA. When he was only eight years old he
began to work in his father's factory, where he
soon learned all the practical business details in
order to assume the management of his father's
business. He was asked many times to take office in
the operation of the city of Pittsburg but declined

to spend full time to his business. From the very
beginning of the Penn Bank of Pittsburgh, **Samuel**[7]
was one of its directors and later became the
President.

He was instrumental in developing the idea of
the contruction of a railroad from Pittsburgh, PA
to Youngstown, OH, call the *Pittsburgh and
Northwestern Railroad.* [HACoPA p191-192]

Samuel[7] married to Eliza T. Miller in 1868 in
Pittsburg. She was born in 1831 and died in 1867.
Samuel m secondly to Arabella Nelson Miller in
1869. [Virkus p154]

Children of **Samuel Bird**[7] Severance and Eliza T.
Miller
  i   **Elizabeth Bird**[8] b 10-7-1857 d 6-7-1920 m
       George R. Buchan. Mrs. **Elizabeth**[8]
       Severance Buchan of Sewickley, PA was
       elected a Prilgrim Tercentenary Member
       in 1920. [NEHGR Vol 75]
  ii   **Charles Sands**[8] b 1856 d 1883
715 iii **Samuel**[8] b 1861 m Eleanor Schmertz
  iv   **Laura Belle**[8] b 1865 m V. Mott Pierce
  v   **George Edgar**[8] b and d 1867

Children of **Samuel Bird**[7] Severance and Arabella
Nelson Miller
716 vi   **Frank Ward**[8] b 11-30-1870 Allegheny, PA.
       Pres. of S. Severance Mfg. Co.,
       Pittsburgh, PA. Member of S.A.R. Resided
       at Glassport, PA. **Frank**[8] m Florence
       (Walker) Wallace, daughter of John
       Walker, 7-22-1913. They had a son **Frank
       Ward Jr.**[9] b 4-1-1916 in Sewickley, PA.
  vii **Lyde Miller**[8] b 1873 d 1921 m Oliver
       William Rafferty

(390) Stephen[7], (Stephen[6], Ebenezer[5], Ephraim[4],
Ebenezer[3], Ephraim[2], John[1]), born in 1827 in VT,
[1860 NYFC] married Mary Jane Johnson, daughter of
Elisha Johnson, 7-16-1857. [VTVR] She was born in
1834 [NYFC] They settled in White Creek, Washington
Co. NY. **Stephen**[7] was a blacksmith. **Stephen**[7] could
have died young.

It appears that Mary Jane m John Glassier on 12-
12-1863, she was 29 years old and it was her third
marriage. [VTVR]

Children: [1860 NYFC]
  i   **Henry**[8] b 1851 in VT

        ii   **Freeman**[8] b 1853 in VT
        iii   **Emma**[8] b 1855 in NH
        iv   **Abby**[8] b 1859 in VT

(391) Anson Biglow[7] *Severans*, (Isaac[6], Ebenezer[5], Ephraim[4], Ebenezer[3], Ephraim[2], John[1]), born in Reading, Windsor Co, VT in 12-28-1823 [VTVR] but moved to Eagle, Waukesha Co. WI with his parents in 1837. From around 1837 to 1847, he lived in Eagle, WI and then moved to Palmyra, Jefferson Co where he worked in the hotel business. He married Mary Malcouson (J.H.) on 6-24-1848 in Milwaukee, WI. [WIVR] Mary was born in 1829. [1850-1860 WIFC]
    Mary was known as Mrs. J.H. Severance, M.D. She was a graduate in 1838 of the Hygeo Therapeutic College in New York City. Since that time she has been a regualr practicing physician in Milwaukee.
    Anson Bigelow[7] Severance was also a phychometrist and reportedly had the power of describing character, by personal observation, from a letter, a lock of hair, or a photograph. He was sonsulted daily from all parts of the country.
    Anson[7] and his brother, **Collamer**[7], owned and played in the Severance and William's Band organized at Whitewater, WI in 1850 by the Severance and William's brothers. **Anson**[7] was second violinist and assistant manager of the Band. [Conrad]

Children: [WIVR]
719 i   **Otto**[8] b 1852 m Hattie
    ii   **Detta**[8] b 1856 m Hattie The 1870 WI
            census also shows **Eloi**[8] b 1862 and
            Ernest[8] b 1868 living with Mary. It
            appears that **Anson**[7] had died.

(392) Collamer G.[7] *Severans*, (Isaac[6], Ebenezer[5], Ephraim[4], Ebenezer[3], Ephraim[2], John[1]), was born 5-9-1829 in Reading, VT, died 10-11-1906 in Milwaukee, WI. He married Helen Bunker who was born 4-25-1834 and died 1-6-1854. He married secondly to her sister Sarah J. Bunker who was born 3-2-1831 in NY [1900 WIFC] and died 2-15-1910. Helen and Sarah J. were daughters of Alexander Francis Bunker and Sarah Mead. [Moran Vol 2 p78] The family shows on the 1860 WI census.
    Professor **C.G.**[7] Severance was born in Windsor Co. VT. At the age of 8 years he moved with his parents to WI and settled near Whitewater, WI on a farm. He lived there until 1860. He started his

study of music at the age of 18 years, under a
private teacher in that vicinity. In 1850, he
became connected with a professional dancing master
in Wasukesha Co. with whom he studied and was
engaged in teaching the art in that area for 10
years. He moved to Milwaukee in 1860, he was
connected with the musical profession until October
1865 when he established his dancing academy, with
himself and wife as teachers. [The History of
Milwaukee, Wisconsin, 1881]
    The 1880 WI census shows a **Marion**[7] (his sister)
b 1837 in VT along with the Severance children.

Children:
721   i   **Coello B.**[8] b 1858 m Frances
     ii   **James**[8] b 1862 and married Frances _____
          in WI
    iii   **Myrtle**[8] b 1870

(393) Isaac[7], (Ephraim[6], Ebenezer[5], Ephraim[4],
Ebenezer[3], Ephraim[2], John[1]), born 9-16-1813. [MEVR]
The census records says that he was born in NH. In
1860 he was living in Garland, ME. He married Ann
and lived in Dexter, ME. The 1840 ME census shows
them living in Harmony. The 1870 ME census shows
them living in Buxton, ME with a Hollis, ME Post
Office. **Isaac**[7] died on 9-19-1873 [CRME Mt. Hope]

Children:
    i   **Enoch A.**[8] b 1838

(395) George Washington[7], (Ephraim[6], Ebenezer[5],
Ephraim[4], Ebenezer[3], Ephraim[2], John[1]), born on 4-13-
1818 in Dexter, ME. [IGI] He married first to
Dulcena Lindsay, daughter of James Lindsay, 10-30-
1843 [IGI] She died on 12-29-1860 in Lincoln, ME.
George[7] went to Lincoln in 1845 and work on the road
between Bangor and Mattawamkeag, ME. He was
recorded as being in the Arrostock War. [Fellows
p406]
    He married second to Jane Helen Evans in 11- -
1861 at Foxcroft, ME. [IGI says 1854] **George W.**[7]
died on 12-21-1883 in Medford, ME. He is buried in
Lincoln, ME.

Children: **George Washington**[7] Severance and Dulcena
Lindsay [1850-1880 MEFC]
    i   **William Albion**[8] b 7-8-1844 at Bangor, ME
    ii   **Frances Ellen**[8] b 2-6-1847 at Lincoln, ME
          m Alfred Grout Wetherbee, son of Henry

and Prudence, at Worcester, MA, on 10-12-1869. [MAVR]

iii **George Albert**[8] b 1-1-1849 d 4-29-1855 at Lincoln, ME. [Fellows p406]

iv **Lucy J.**[8] b 1850 d 3-23-1894, age 43-1-13, single, at Worcester, MA. She was b in Lincoln, ME [MAVR]

v **Georgiana**[8] b 1851 d 8-27-1854 at Lincoln, ME

vi **Lydia Ella**[8] b 1853 d 2-9-1859 at Lincoln.

vii **George Arnold**[8] b 6-10-1857 d after 1920 at Lincoln, ME. He m Elizabeth J. Burnip. **George**[8] was an engineer from Milo, ME. [IGI] **Ardelle**[9], daughter of **George A.**[8] m Fred Merrow [NHVR] The 1900-1920 ME census shows **Georges'**[8] family with daughters, **Madaline**[9] b 8- -1991, **Mande**[9] b 11- -1894, and **Adelie**[9] b 7- -1899.

Children of **George Washington**[7] Severance and Jane Helen Evans

viii **Ella**[8] b 9-6-1862 [IGI]

ix **Charles Elijah**[8] b 8-5-1863 [IGI]

x **Lydia Dulcinia**[8] b 12-14-1864 [IGI]

xi **Milton G.**[8] b 1870 [1880 MEFC] d at Lincoln, ME

(396) Joseph Crane[7], (Rufus Jr.[6], Rufus Sr.[5], Ephraim[4], Ebenezer[3], Ephraim[2], John[1]), born in Lempster, NH on 5-9-1815. He married Eliza J. Buswell, daughter of Edward Buzzell and Betsey Gove, of Wilmot, NH on 3-19-1846. He was a farmer and spent his married life in Washington, NH. [HWNH p599] **Joseph**[7] died on 5-10-1892. Eliza was born 10-19-1826 at Springfield, NH, and died 5-27-1909 [NHVR]

Children: [NHVR]

i **Lydia C.**[8] b 2-22-1847 in Washington, NH d 3-10-1847

ii **Hiram J.**[8] b 7-10-1848 in Washington m Savallah E. Chase 11-25-1878, settled in Loudon, NH. She was b 7-31-1855 and d at Bradford, NH, 1-8-1917. [NHVR]

iii **Alberto D.**[8] b 7-19-1850 in Washington d 8-10-1858

iv **Addie C.**[8] b 4-26-1853 in Washington d 8-10-1858

    v   **Oralin S.**[8] b 3-23-1857 in Washington d
              9-1-1858
722 vi   **George W.**[8] b 11-16-1859 in Washington
              resided in Washington, NH. He m 1-1-1895
              in Hillsboro, NH to Gertrude J.
              Mcilvain, daughter of John and Abbie
              Mcilvain. Gertrude was born circa 1874.
    vii   **Kate B.**[8] b 5-6-1863 in Washington d 3-6-
              1864

(397) Hezekiah M.[7], (Rufus[6], Rufus[5], Ephraim[4],
Ebenezer[3], Ephraim[2], John[1]), born in Lempster, NH on
10-5-1817. He married Sarah J. Marshall in 12-22-
1842. (IGI) They lived in Washington, NH. **Hezekiah**[7]
died 5-17-1895. He is shown living with his entire
family on the 1850 NH census but on the 1860-1870
NH census he is only living with his mother, Lydia.

Children: [1850 NHFC]
    i   **Lovica A.**[8] b 1843 d 9-17-1863 age 19 in
            Washington, NH. [GRWNH]
    ii   **Miranda**[8] b 1846
    iii   **Harriet**[8] b 1848
    iv   **Georgie**[8] (female) b 1850

(398) William D.[7], (Joseph[6], Rufus[5], Ephraim[4],
Ebenezer[3], Ephraim[2], John[1]), born in Washington, NH
on 9-25-1816 and died 9-18-1905 [NHVR] He married
Clarissa Edes, who was a native of Greenfield, NH,
on 12-18-1842. **William**[7] was a farmer. They lived in
Washington, NH. Clarissa was born 1812 and died
1894. [NYE]

Children: [HWNH p600-601]
    i   Franklin W. (step son of **William D.**[7]
            Severance) b 6-11-1842, a soldier in the
            Civil War, d 9-16-1862 in VA
    ii   **Mary R.**[8] b 7-30-1844 (lived in
            Washington, NH) d 1-21-1923 single
            [NHVR]
    iii   **Edward Woodman**[8] was b 3-9-1847 at
            Washington, NH [NHVR] d 9-25-1927 at E.
            Washington, NH [NHVR] He was a farmer
            and m on 10-9-1876 to Melissa Ann
            [HWNH p600], daughter of Nelson Wellman
            and Laura Ann Frances Brown. Melissa Ann
            was b at Seekonk, MA, 8-26-1845. Melissa
            d 8-29-1925 at Washington, NH [NHVR]
            [Wellman p310] He served in Co. I 16th
            Regt. N.H.V. for the Civil War. [CWPR]

Edward Woodman[8] Severance served in Co., I 16th Regt. NH., as a volunteer during the Civil War. They reportedly had no children.

723 iv **Hiram Abel**[8] b 5-28-1850 m Ellen D. Tandy in 1872 (lived in Washington) **Hiram A.**[8] of East Washington, NH (b 5-28-1850) d 1-7-1929 widower of Melissa Severance [NHVR]

The 1880 NH census shows the grand children, **Hatch C.**[9] b 1873, **Hattie M.**[9] b 1875, and **Etta M.**[9] b 1879 living with **William**[7] and his son **Hiram C.**[8] and Ellen D. Tandy.

v **Sarah J.**[8] b 3-6-1853 d 10-6-1855

(399) Joel[7], (Joseph[6], Rufus[5], Ephraim[4], Ebenezer[3], Ephraim[2], John[1]), born in Lempster, NH on 4-13-1820. [IGI] He married Lucy Fletcher, daughter of Jeremiah Fletcher and Lucy Davis of Washington, NH, in April of 1846. She died on 3-7-1852. He married again to Eliza J. Dole, daughter of David Dole and Annis Rideout of Washington, on 6-6-1852. He settled in Washington. He was an industrious and successful farmer. He represented the town in the legislature. [HWNH p601] He died on 11-4-1879. Eliza died on 3-15-1886. **Joel**[7] was a grocery Man [NHVR]

Children:
724 i **Arthur F.**[8] b 3-6-1852 in Washington, NH. The [NHVR] says that **Arthur**[8] was b on 3-6-1843, He d 7-24-1929 [NHVR] m Mary A. Gove 6-7-1876 and settled in Washington, NH. They had 3 children. [HWNH p601]

(400) Joseph W.[7], (Joseph[6], Rufus[5], Ephraim[4], Ebenezer[3], Ephraim[2], John[1]), was born in Washington, NH on 8-12-1825. He married to Adaline Putney of Bradford, NH on 9-6-1857. Adaline was born 5-1-1838 and died on 4-18-1892. They settled in Washington after living in Marlow, Stoddard, and Hillsborough. **Joseph**[7] died on 4-24-1899 [MAM]

Children: [HWNH]
i **Aluira G.**[8] b 9-10-1858 in Stoddard, m Albert N. Cooledge 12-25-1875
ii Frank H. b 1859
725 iii **Herbert D.**[8] b 3-10-1860 in Stoddard

iv   **Fred R.**[8] b 6-10-1861 in Stoddard d in 1864

v   **Della M.**[8] b 11-24-1864 in Marlow m Charles C. Strickland 5-7-1882. She m 2nd to Isaac F. Wilkins, son of Iva and Dorcas Flint of Hillsboro on 3-3-1911. He was 80 and she was 40. The third marriage for both of them. [NHVR]

vi   **Clarence E.**[8] was b 5-2-1869 [NHVR] at Marlow, NH. He d 1-5-1909. [GRWNH] He was a silver plater and farmer and lived some time in Antrim, NH where he d on 1-5-1909. [NHVR], unmarried

727 vii   **William Joel**[8] b 11-22-1870 in Washington

viii   **Lizzie J.**[8] b 2-22-1873 in Washington

728 ix   **Ernest Bertrand**[8] b 8-8-1879 in Washington

(401) Jonathan[7], (Ephraim[6], Rufus[5], Ephraim[4], Ebenezer[3], Ephraim[1], John[1]), born in Stockbridge, VT on 5-6-1824. He married Harriet B. Copps, daughter of Moses Copp and Mary George, of Hopkinton on 11-27-1849. [NYGBR p138-139] She was born 9-15-1821. They settled in Washington. He was a prosperous farmer and an esteemed citizen. He represented the town in the legislature in 1881 and 1882. Harriet d on 1-9-1883. [GRWNH] Jonathan apparently m a second time on 6-13-1868 as the [NHVR] shows the death of Issa L. Davis of Walpole, NH, daughter of Alva Davis and ____ Danforth, d 1-21-1928. She was b on 6-13-1868. She was the widow of **Jonathan**[7] Severance. **Jonathan**[7] d on 10-2-1909 at Hillsborough, NH. [NHVR]

Children:

i   **Harriet Lovilla**[8] b 3-22-1851 in Washington d 5-16-1853

ii   **Loren P.**[8] b 4-10-1858 d 4-14-1858

729 iii   **Melvin J.**[8] b 3-9-1889 Hillsboro, NH, son of **Jonathan**[7] Severance and Issa Davis [NHVR]. **Jonathan**[7] b at Stockbridge, VT. and Issa b at Deering, NH. If this is true then **Jonathan**[7] was 65 years old when **Melvin J.**[8] was born. When **Melvin J.**[8] m Georgianna M. Russell, his father, **Jonathan**[7], was listed as being 85 years old and his mother, Issa Davis was 44.

(403) John Russell[7], (Abijah[6], Rufus[5], Ephraim[4], Ebenezer[3], Ephraim[2], John[1]), born on 4-9-1836 at Clarendon, VT. He died on 10-30-1908 at Pensacola,

FL. **John Russell**[7] married to Mary Ann McCormick on
7-9-1866. She was born on 7-4-1844 at Montreal,
Canada and died at Chicago, IL on 3-4-1932. [DARGR]
The 1880 IA census shows **John**[7] and his wife,
Mary, and their four children, **Grace**[8], **Kate**[8], born
in IL, and **Ernest**[8], and **Martha**[8], born in IA.
In 1900 **John**[7] was with his wife and family. They
were living at Rt. #6, Escambia Co. FL. **Ernest**[8] was
living in Pensacola as a boarder of Steven M.
Besford. [FLFC]

Children: [1900 FLFC]
	i	**Grace**[8] b 1869 in IL
	ii	**Kathrine**[8] b 10- -1871 in Chicago, IL
730	iii	**Ernest**[8] b 8- -1876 in IA, settled in Chicago, IL with his wife Blanche Smith.
	iv	**Martha**[8] b 2- -1880 in IA
	v	**Rose**[8] b 9- -1885 in IA

(405) George A.[7], (Asa[6], Rufus[5], Ephraim[4], Ebenezer[3],
Ephraim[2], John[1]), born in Townsend, MA in 1848.
[1850 MAFC] In 1900 he was in Port Huron, St. Clair
Co. MI, married to Caroline ____, who was born 6- -
1849 in Canada. [MIFC]

Children:
	i	**Hattie**[8] b 9- -1871 in MI
	ii	**Ethel M.**[8] b 5- -1879 in Canada

(406) Christopher[7], (Christopher[6], unconnected
Ebenezer[3], Ephraim[2], John[1]), was born 11-21-1829
[MEVR] He married to Susan or Nancy Crocker,
daughter of Avrill Crocker and Nancy Glidden, who
was born 1829 at Winslow or Lincoln, ME. She died
9-27-1917 at Greenbush, ME, age 91-3-22. The 1860
ME census for Pattagumpus] shows this family with
four of their children. **Christopher**[7] died 2-29-1895
at the age of 66-4-23. [MEVR]

Children; [1860/1870 MEFC-Pattagumpus]
731	i	**Alfred**[8] b 1851 living at Medway, ME. m Martha J. b 1- -1861 ME. [1900 MEFC]
732	ii	**Henry A.**[8] b 1853 m Nora E. Mercier 7-26-1916 [MEVR] She was b 1873 [MEVR] Lived at E. Millinocket, ME.
	iii	**Charles W.**[8] b 1856
	iv	**Loretta**[8] b 1859
	v	**Ivory E.**[8] b 1862
	vi	**Nellie A.**[8] b 1866
	vii	**John E.**[8] b 1870

733　viii　**Christopher**[8] b 2-14-1874 (Son of
　　　　　　Christopher[7] and Susan) [MEVR] This
　　　　　　is the same date as **John Ellis**[8]
　　　　　　Severance. It is possble that this
　　　　　　Christopher[8] was adopted or perhaps the
　　　　　　son of a **Christopher Jr.**[7]

(407) Ivory[8], (Nathaniel[7], unconnected, John[5],
Ephraim[4], Ephraim[3], Ephraim[2], John[1]), probably born
6-27-1834 at Bangor, ME. He married to Ellen A.
Sargent on 11-7-1858 [IGI]. She was born 10-29-1838
at Milo, ME and died 2-3-1922 at Portsmouth, NH.
She was the daughter of Hector Sargent and Mary
Currier of Milo, ME. [NHVR] **Ivory**[8] died on 3-27-
1917 at the age of 83. [MEVR] They are shown living
at Bangor, Penobscot Co. ME, and Parkman and Milo,
Piscataquis Co. ME. A request was filed by the
invalid 6-7-1893 and from the widow 8-24-1917 from
NH for service in B 20 ME Inf and D 2 ME Inf.
[CWPR] **Ivory**[8] died at the Nathional Soldiers Home
in ME.

Children:
　　　　i　　**Ardith M.**[9] (Addie M.) b 8-5-1858 at
　　　　　　Sebec, ME [IGI]
735　ii　　**Frank L.**[9] b 3-21-1861 at Sebec, ME d 9-
　　　　　　13-1908
　　　　iii　**Nellie J.**[9] b 11-4-1864
　　　　iv　**Sarah M.**[9] b 5-1-1867
　　　　v　　**Lennie J.**[9] b 3-11-1869 at Lincoln, ME
　　　　　　[IGI]
　　　　vi　**Merton L.**[9] b 3-4-1870 at Guilford, ME
　　　　　　[IGI]
　　　　vii　**Kate E.**[9] b 9-11-1873 at Parkman

The 1910 Sangervill, ME census shows **Ivory**[8] born
1833 with wife, Ellen A. born 1837 and daughter
Addie M.[9] Tucker born 1860 and Doris S. Pingrees
born 1896.

(408) James[7], (Jacob[6], Ephraim[5], Ephraim[4], Ebenezer[3],
Ephraim[2], John[1]), born 8-11-1815 at Knox, ME. He
died at Searsmont, ME on 1-11-1892 age 76 yrs, 5
mos. [Searsmont MEVR] He married first to Hannah C.
who was born on 9-22-1822 and died 4-7-1860. [CRME]
James[7] and Hannah are buried together with **F.E.**[8]
Severance (Civil War Veteran) Co. I 15 ME Infantry.
[Robinson]
　　　James[7] married secondly to Mary Sanborn,
daughter of Peter Sanborn and Phebe Elwell of

Waldo, ME, on 4-7-1861 [MEVR] both from Searsmont, ME. Mary (Sanborn) Severance married secondly to Alvin B. Brown, 7-1-1896. [MEVR] The 1850 ME census shows that **James**[7] had children **Frank**[8], **Fred**[8], and **Eva**[8]. No wife was indicated for **James**[7] but Mary Sanborn was living with them. The family with **James**[7] and Mary Sanborn shows on the 1870-1880 ME census.

Children of **James**[7] Severance and Hannah C. _____ [1870 Searsmont MEFC]

736   i   **Frank E.**[8] b 1842/46 in Knox, ME m Maragaret Hitchcock d 12-4-1888 [Searsmont, MEVR]

737   ii   **Fred A.**[8] b 1853 [1860 MEFC] m Miss Clara Wing of Searsmont, 4-20-1881. [marriage int] **Fred**[8] was from Oka, MT Territory. [Searsmont, MEVR]

      iii   **Eva P.**[8] was b 1858 m Fred C. Alden of Camden, ME, 12-31-1878 [Searsmont, MEVR marriage int]

Children of **James**[7] Severance and Mary Sanborn

      iv   **Mariette**[3] b 1862 [1870 MEFC] m int. to Frank Barlow of Searsmont on 9-22-1890

      v   **George H.**[8] could have been another son as the cemetery records show a Caroline E. died 10-12-1856 age 30 years and 2 months and the wife of **George H.**[8]

(409) Jacob Jr.[7], (Jacob[6], Ephraim[5], Ephraim[4], Ebenezer[3], Ephraim[2], John[1]), born 1827 at Knox, ME, and died at Oka, MT on 3-1-1892. The DAR records for the lineage of **Charles Edgar**[8] Severance shows his father as **Jacob Jr.**[7], who married to Eliza Jane Lawry on 9-12-1853. She was born on 11-11-1831 at Friendship, ME and died at Oka, MT on 3-1-1883. [DARGR-**Jacob**[7] Severance Jr.] **Jacob**[7] and Eliza Jane came to MT in the early 1880's. Eliza Jane was the first postmaster of Oka, MT but she must have died shortly after getting that postition. [Deal p587]

Children: [1870 Unity, MEFC]

738   i   **Charles Edgar**[8] b 8-6-1855 at Knox, ME and d at Spokane, WA on 2-9-1913. He m to Helen Hussey on 8-11-1883. Helen was b on 11-25-1857 at Unity, ME. [DARLR-**Charles Edgar**[8] Severance] The 1880 MT census shows him living with his parents

in Mussellshell Valley, Meagher Co. MT. [Sanders p1291]

(410) Frederick Mortimer[7], (Jacob[6], Ephraim[5], Ephraim[4], Ebenezer[3], Ephraim[2], John[1]), born 7- -1833 at Knox, ME. [1900 MTFC] He married Sarah Ann Beale, daughter of Joseph S. Beale and Susanna Holbrook, on 12-29-1859 at Quincy, MA. He was of Stoughton and a carpenter, age 25, in Quincy, MA [MAVR] Sarah was born 10-28-1837. The couple resided in Bercial, MT. [Sanders p220]

Children:
    i   **Carrie H.**[8] b 5-2-1862 at Dorchester, MA. She m to Samuel A. Shaw, son of John A. Shaw and Lucretia R. Adams, on 9-3-1885 at Milton. [MAVR]
    ii   **Mable**[8] b 6- -1867
    iii   **Clara Anna**[8] b 1-18-1873 at Boston, MA [MAVR] m Samuel Brown Chase Jr. 12-27-1893 at Oka, Meagher Co. MT. He was b in Chicago, IL and d at Great Falls, MT on 3-23-1955. [Sanders p220]
    iv   **Russell**[8] b 12-13-1874 at Milton, MA [MAVR]

(411) Thomas Benton[7], (Jacob[6], Ephraim[5], Ephraim[4], Ebenezer[3], Ephraim[2], John[1]), born 4-20-1835 in Knox, ME. He died on 1-8-1908 in Rockland, ME, age 72-8-19, the son of **Jacob[6]** and Susan Haskell. [MEVR] His father, **Jacob[6]**, was born in Charleston, NH. He is buried in ME. [CRME] He married to Lucinda Frances Clements, daughter of Enoch Clements and Joanna Hall, on 11-20-1865. [Mosher Vol II p328] [MEVR] She died 7-27-1875 age 34 at Taunton, MA or Knox, ME. [MAVR][MEVR] The birth and death records show on [PRPCoME]

Thomas[7] was living in Rogers, Sebastian Co. AR as a boarder of Mark H. Wilbiforce. **Thomas[7]** was 66 years and born in April of 1834 in Maine. [1900 ARFC]

Children:
    i   **Edith**[8] b 1-9-1869 at Quincy, MA [MAVR] d 12-1-1877 at the age of 7 years and 10 mons, Knox ME [MEVR]
    ii   possibly a son **Haskell**[8]?

(412) William Wallace[7], (Jacob[6], Ephraim[5], Ephraim[4], Ebenezer[3], Ephraim[2], John[1]), born circa 3-4-1835.

[DAR grand children Lineage Records] The actual records were lost to the San Franscico, CA fire of 1906 and the available information was passed down from family members. Since **Thomas B.**[8] was recorded as born 4-20-1835, it is certain that **William's** birth date is wrong, unless they were twins and the dates were slightly mixed up.

William[7] married Matilda Irdall Sullivan, daughter of William Sullivan, of Mokelumne Hill, CA. She was born around 1-25-1846 in Chicago, IL. Her father died as a result of illness during his service in the Mexican War. **William**[7] died on 4-13-1903 at San Francisco, CA.

"The old family home of the Severance family still stands in ME. **William Wallace**[7] Severance went to Boston when quite a young man and from there to CA. He went by boat to Nicaragua, then on mule back across the mountains to the Pacific coast. After landing in San Francisco he went to the goldfields in Calaveras Co. He became the owner of the first water supply to miners in famous Red Hill, Rich Gulch. He was also interested in mines in Chile Gulch, CA, and White Pine, NV. He became quite wealthy."

"Mrs. Severance tells of seeing colors of gold in the streets of Rich Gulch and Mokelumne Hill after every rain, also of finding gold dust hidden away in cracks on miner's cabins which were considered too insignificant to bother with." [DARLR Vol 12]

This family shows on the 1870-1900 CA census. Although there are conflicts of dates and ages, the records clearly show **William**[7], Matilda, and their two children, **Fred E.**[8] and **Alice Eva**[8].

Children:
  i   **Fred Ellsworth**[8] b 6-11-1861 in Rich Gulch, Calaveras Co. CA. **Fred**[8] shows on the 1910-1920 CA census with no family
  ii   **Alice Eva**[8] b 12- -1876 [1900 CAFC Penryn, Placer Co] m Herman Schieck, son of Johann Gottfried Schieck and Margarethe Hemesvord Frederick, of Glenn Ellen, CA on 9-21-1905.

(413) Hasketta[7], (Benjamin[6], Ephraim[5], Ephraim[4], Ebenezer[3], Ephraim[2], John[1]), born circa 1820 in Orrington, ME and died 1888 in Ukiah, Endocina Co. CA. He married to Ann R. Clapp, daughter of Billins

Clapp and Emily Whitney, on 6-6-1852 at Orrington,
ME. [MEVR] Ann was born 1835 at Eddington, ME. and
she died on 7-24-1892 at Boston, MA. [MAVR] He was
living with another lumberman on the 1850 census.
[MEFC] In 1860 he was living with his parents and
other members of his family in Windsor, ME. The
1860 Big River, Mendocina Co. CA census shows
Haskell[7] age 38 born ME as a contractor. The 1870
CA census shows **Haskett**[8], age 18, living with his
mother Ann R. Severance. Also shown are **Haskett
Jr.'s**[8] brother and sister.

The Little River Cemetery in Mendocino Co. CA
shows the burial of **Haskett**[7], 1888 and his wife,
Ann R., died 1892. [Historical Society Records of
Endocina County, California]

Children:
    i   **Haskett**[8] b 1852 It is possible that he m
         to Mary ___. They had **Lillie**[9] and **Emma**[9]
         in the late 1860's or early 1870's.
    ii   **Franklin W.**[8] b 4- -1853, with his wife,
         Jennie P. b 11- -1860 and **Carrie**[9] b 2- -
         1885 all in CA. [1900 Mendocina, CAFC]
         The 1910 CA census shows **Frank**[8] living
         alone.
    iii **Mary Ellen**[8] b 1857

(414) Benjamin[7], (Benjamin[6], Ephraim[5], Ephraim[4],
Ebenezer[3], Ephraim[2], John[1]), born circa 1832 in
Orrington, ME. He later settled in Mendocina Co.
CA. He married to Augustus M. Spinger, both of Old
Town, ME. They show on the 1900 CA census in Arena,
Mendocina Co. as **Benjamin**[7] *Seberance* born 6- -1831
in ME and A.M. *Seberance* born 4- -1835 in M*E.*

Children:
    i   **Frederick**[8] b 1858 in ME. In 1910 he was
         age 52 with wife Flora, age 35 b in CA.
         [1910 CAFC]
    ii   **Carrie**[8] b 1861 in ME. She shows on the
         1920 CA census age 55 b in ME and living
         in Los Angeles with her daughter Sibyl
         age 26 who was b in MA.
    iii **Walter**[8] b 8- -1869 ME. [1910 Ten Mile
         River, Mendocino Co. CAFC] The Fort
         Bragg, CA cemetery shows the death and
         burial of **Walter B.**[8] Severance, 4-16-
         1932 and his wife, Anna Severance, who d
         8-8-1927.

(415) Franklin Sanborn[7], (Benjamin[6], Ephraim[5], Ephraim[4], Ebenezer[3], Ephraim[2], John[1]), was born 8-12-1833 [MEVR] died 1-15-1884. He is shown in Windsor, Bangor, and Pittston, ME. He married Vandalia A. Clark on 4-4-1866. [IGI] **Frank S.**[7] died 1-15-1884 age 49, at Augusta, ME [MEVR]

(416) Thatcher[7], (Ephraim[6], Ephraim[5], Ephraim[4], Ebenezer[3], Ephraim[2], John[1]), born on 7-16-1827 in Carroll, ME [Belmont, MEVR] the son of **Ephriam[6]** and Eliza Merriam. He was apparently named after someone in the Merriam family as there were **Thatcher's[7]** in that family. He married Mary E. Berry, daughter of ___ Berry and Olive Shurburn, [MEVR] on 9-10-1850, both of Old Town, ME. [MEVR] She was born 1830 and died 9-10-1906. **Thatcher[7]** and Mary were married in Bangor, ME before going to WI where his father had settled. He died during the Civil War. Ira L Gould, among others, appointed to asses the value of **Thatcher's[7]** estate. The estate was paid to Mary C. Severance and she was appointed legal guardian. [PRME Piscataquis Co 2-22-1866]

Mary E. Severance remarried 8-1-1871 to a Mr. Towne. The 1870 Sebec, ME census shows them living with Luke Towne.

Children: [PRME 10-3-1869 giving Mary guardianship]
	i	**Sarah S.**[8] b circa 1851
	ii	**Mary E.**[8] b circa 1853
740	iii	**Frank**[8] b circa 1854
	iv	**Eliza E.**[8] b circa 1856
	v	**Marcella**[8] b circa 1858
741	vi	**Orrin P.**[8] b 4-9-1859 in Dover Foxcroft, ME and he stayed there although others of his family moved to WI. He m to Della Perham and had a son **Orman**[9]. **Orrin P.**[8] d 12-20-1934. Buried in Barnard, ME.
742	vii	**Joseph**[8] b 3- -1861
	viii	**Clara B.**[8] b 1864

(417) Daniel[7], (Ephraim[6], Ephraim[5], Ephraim[4], Ebenezer[3], Ephraim[2], John[1]), born 6-27-1830 at Belmont, Waldo Co. ME and died 2-2-1913 age 82 yrs 7 months and 24 days at Sebec, ME (The Cemetery Records say 2-21-1913). [Belmont, MEVR]. He married Laura A. Simonds, daughter of William Simonds and Almira Stacy. She was born 5-5-1835 in NY and died 4-28-1910 age 74-11-22 at Sover-Foxcroft, ME [MEVR] They are buried in the Rural Grove Cemetery, Dover-Foxcroft, ME.

Daniel[7] can be found in the records at Belmont, Foxcroft, Dover, and Sebec, ME. The 1870 Sebec, ME census shows the family with his mother, Eliza, living with them. The 1900 ME census shows a grandson, Daniel A. Hubbard living with the family.

Children:
743 i   **Delbert**[8] b 3-25-1866
744 ii   **Chester L.**[8] b 1- -1868. The 1900 ME census shows him living at home. He m to Clara E. McNaughton 8-12-1902.
     iii **Elmira**[8] b 1874 m Wendell P. Hubbard 4-5-1893 [MEVR]

(418) Joseph[7], (Ephraim[6], Ephraim[5], Ephraim[4], Ebenezer[3], Ephraim[2], John[1]), was born 10-8-1831 and died 2-22-1914. He was recorded as living in Bangor and Carroll, ME and Beldenville and Trime Belle, WI, and N. Yakima, WA. He was in the Civil War, Co., A. 12th WI Inf. He married to Lydia Frances Weston on 11-4-1858. She died 2-11-1913. They were living in Trimbelle, Pierce Co. WI in 1860.

The 1900 OR census shows that **Joseph**[7] and Lydia were born in ME but Etta, their 9th child, was born in OR.

"**Joseph**[7] Severance passed away at his home at 1020 N. First St. this city 2-22-1914 after an illness of two weeks, death resulting from pneumonia. Mr. Severance was born at Old Town, Maine on 10-8-1831 and at the time of his death was in his 83rd year. He was a veteran of the Civil War, enlisting in Co. A. 12th WI. Inf. and at the time of his death was a member of the Meade Post of this place. He is survived by four children, Attorney **A.W.**[8] Severance now residing on his farm at Donald, Washington. **E.W.**[8] Severance, a farmer at Parker, Mrs. **Abbie**[8] Maier, who had resided here and taken care of her father during the past year, and Ella Severance, a teacher in the schools at Sunnyside, also a sister, Mrs. **Belle**[8] Judkins of Belgrade, Maine and two brothers, **F.A.**[7] Severance of Beldenville, Wisconsin and **Frank**[7] Severance of Tillamook, Oregon." [NSYDR] Reprinted in the [*River Falls Journal*, 3-5-1914]

Children: [1880/1900 Portland, ORFC]
     i   **Joseph Frank**[8] b circa 1860 in Trimbelle, WI. lived at Donald, WA. He married to Mable Carr in Pierce Co. WI on 7-4-1885.

[WIVR]. His family later settled in
Tillamock, OR.
745 ii **Abel W.**[8] b 1862
iii **Emily**[8] b 1863 d 8-3-1880 age 18 yrs 3
days. [CR Thurston Hill, Pierce Co. WI]
iv **Horace**[8] b 1864
v **Mabel**[8] b 1870
vi **Lizzie**[8] b 1872
747 vii **Edward W.**[8] b 8- -1874 lived at Parker,
WA
viii **Abbn**[8] b circa 1876 in Trimbelle, WI. She
m to a ____ Maier. It is uncertain where
they settled. She most likely moved to
Portland, OR with her parents.
ix **Etta**[8] b 12-31-1878. She m to a Mc
Spadden on 7-24-1917 of Los Angeles.
[WIVR] They lived at Sunnyside, WA
x **DeForest**[8] b 10- -1879 [1900 WIFC] in
Trimbelle, WI. He shows on the 1900 WA
census living with his brother, **Edward**[8]
living in Yakima, WA.

(419) Franklin Orrin[7], (Ephraim[6], Ephraim[5], Ephraim[4],
Ebenezer[3], Ephraim[2], John[1]), was born 11-16-1844 in
Belmont, ME. He married to Sophia R. Thurston on 8-
25-1873. [WIVR] He was recorded at Bangor, ME,
Carroll, ME, Beldenview, WI and Tillamook, OR. The
1900 OR census shows them living at Fairview,
Tillamook Co.

Children:
i **Egbert D.**[8] b 7- -1875 in WI [1900 ORFC]
A notice in the *Oregonian*, shows "Auto
Victim Dies, Death of Mrs. **Egbert**[8]
Severance 65, Kellogg Park, at good
Samaritan hospital Monday, of injuries
suffered in an auto accident, was
reported to the coroner's office. Mrs.
Severance, a pedestrian, was struck by
an automobile at S.E. McLoughlin
Boulevard and Ochoco Street, outside
the city on October 10." [NSOR 11-20-
1945]

(420) Fred A.[7], (Ephraim[6], Ephraim[5], Ephraim[4],
Ebenezer[3], Ephraim[2], John[1]), was born 12-23-1850 in
Belmont, ME. He later moved to Beldenville, and
Ellsworth, WI where he died 3-10-1941. [NSEWI 3-13-
1941]

He married first to Etiole Ann Chappel, daughter of William H. Chappel and Elizabeth Phillips, 12-25-1875. [WIVR] Etiole A. was born 8- -1857. [1900 WIFC] She died in 1912. He married secondly to Willabelle Goldsmith in 1914. **Fred**[7] became a Judge.

"He was a son of **Ephraim**[7] and Eliza Severance and he was born in Bangor, Maine on 12-23-1850. When about 18 years he removed to Pennsylvania, where he resided for about 2 years, and then emigrated to the town of Trimbelle, where he purchased a farm near that of his father. To the first purchase he has added others until now he owns one of the finest farms in the valley comprising about 320 acres and where he makes his home."

In 1890 he gave up the active work of farming and devoted his time to mercantile pursuits. He was appointed postmaster of Beldenville in 1897. In 1890 he was chosen as one of the presidential electors and cast his vote for William McKinley. He held several other civic offices. [Easton p688]

Children:
- i   **William L.**[8] b 1877 graduated from the University of MN and became a lawer at St. Louis Park in Mineapolis, MN. He m Marie Thompson of Minneapolis.
- 749 ii   **Delbert A.**[8] b 5- -1880 He graduated from the University of MN and was a salesman for the Fleming Mill Company of Hastings, MN. He d 1934 [CRBWI]

(420a) Seth Lawrence[6] Severance, (unconnected) born 1-1-1813, came to Carroll, ME in April of 1836. **Seth**[6] was with **Ephraim**[6] Severance and wife Eliza Merrian, and family. Therefore **Seth**[6] could be a brother, nephew, or son of **Ephraim**[6]. I am placing **Seth**[6] here so that his lineage can be carried forward.

"The family moved in 1849, I believe to Bangor, ME. The records of Carroll, ME were burned, and I found **Seth's**[6] birthday from an old paper that a woman in Carroll had. This **Ephraim**[6] and Eliza came to Carroll, ME from Belmont, ME. **Seth's**[6] parentage is unknown. **Seth Lawrence**[6] Severance Sr. had a son **George**[7] and **George**[7] had a son **Seth Lawrence Jr.**[8] who married Mary Severance.

His descendants know nothing about him. He married first, at the age of 40, to Sarah June Munday and had three children and secondly to

Mariah Sweet, 11-28-1865 in Carroll, ME, and they had five children." [MMS]
   Seth[6] died circa 1916/17 at Kossuth, Washington Co ME.

Children of **Seth**[6] Severance and Sarah Jane Munday
750 i   **Fred Leon**[7] b 2-11-1853 d 1939 Topsfield, ME m Albina L. Powell 5-1-1884. [MEVR]
751 ii   **Charles**[7] b 1855 d in Brockton on visit to his brother **Fred**[7]. **Charles**[7] lived in Erie, PA
    iii   **Flora**[7] b 1859

Children of **Seth**[6] Severance and Mariah Sweet
752 iv   **George**[7] b in March of 1866 in Carroll d 1942 in Mattawamkeag. Father of **Seth Lawrence**[6] Severance Jr. m Flora Lois Chubbuck
    v   **Roxa**[7] b 1868 Carroll, ME m George Briggsbur, South Springfield, ME
753 vi   **Artemus Cushman**[7] b 1-21-1868/70 m Elizabeth Bryant buried in Carroll, ME
    vii   **Ethell**[7] b circa 1880
    viii **Avesta**[7] b circa 1880 d 3-15-1894
    ix   **Jennie**[7] b 1883 m Cornelius Day buried in Marshfield, ME
754 x   **Frank Edward**[7] b 10-2-1885 buried in Kingman, ME. His first wife was Mina Aldrich. His 2nd wife was Annie Linscott.

(421) Artimus F.[7], (Artimus[6], Asa[5], Ebenezer[4], Ebenezer[3], Ephraim[2], John[1],) There is an **Artimus** who shows in Ackley, IN born 1830 which might be of this family. The IN **Artimus F.**[7] was born 3-5-1830, married to Hannah S. Shattuck, daughter of Chauncey Shattuck and Sally M. Rowley, on 2-18-1851. Hannah was born on 4-26-1831. This family is shown in IN, NY, IL, and IA. [Dunham][BR Smith-Nye (IAPA Vol 4 p123)] The family shows on the 1900 IA census.

Children:
    i   **Ida E.**[8] b 12-22-1854 m Joseph S. Nye
    ii   **Burt Rowley**[8] b 11-11-1861 in IL m Berenice Smith on 4-20-1887. Berenice was b 6-20-1864. They had a son, **Artemus**[8] b 4-28-1889.

(422) John[7], (John[6], unconnected) was born in 1835 in KY. He married Margaret Manuel on 12-24-1857.

[KYVR] In 1866, he was elected to the position of Lincoln County Clerk and again in 1870, 1874, 1878, 1882, and 1886. **John**[7] died during this last term and his son, **William**[8] was appointed to fill out the unexpired term. He died on 4-25-1897. [KYVR]

Children: [1880 Marion Co KYFC]
    i   **Mary Alice**[8] b 11-3-1863 d 1-22-1883 [KYVR]
    ii   **William**[8] b 1866 living with his mother in 1900 at South Lebanon, Marion County, Kentucky. **William**[8] Severance d 5-16-1921 in Jefferson County, Kentucky. The 1920 KY census shows **William**[8] b 1866 as a patient at Central State Hospital, Jefferson Co.
    iii **Mary**[8] b 1868
    iv **Linette**[8] b 1870
    v   **Laura**[9] b 1872 living with her mother in 1900 in Marion County.
    vi **John**[8] b 6-9-1875 in Marion County, Kentucky. [KYVR] The 1900 Pine Tavern-Lebanon Junction, Bullitt Co KY census shows **John**[8] as a boarder and a R.R. Fireman.
    vii **Joseph**[8] b 1877

(423) William[7], (John[6], unconnected) was born in 1837 in KY. He married to Mary Linsey on 9-17-1867. Sgt. **William**[7] Severance Co. B. 8th KY., Cav. Section B.O.C. Cemetery. Mary E. Linsey, wife of **William**[7] Severance, was born 2-8-1844 and died on 8-19-1891. **William**[7] took over the term of County Clerk when his father died unexpectedly in 1884. He was elected in again 1890 but then resigned in 1894.

Children:
    i   **Mary**[8] b 1869 in Kentucky
    ii   **Elizabeth**[8] b 1872
    iii **William Jr.**[8] b 1875 m Mary Pickett. He shows with Mary and part of her family on the 1900 Stanford, Lincoln Co KY census. They were married 6 years but no children.
    iv **Jennie**[8] b 1877 living with **Hiram**[9] in 1920. [Lincoln Co KYFC]
759 v   **George**[8] b 1879 m Elizabeth (Bettie) Taylor

vi   **Hiram**[8] b 1885. Living with his sister in
         1920. [Lincoln Co KYFC]

(424) Joseph[7], (John[6], unconnected) was born in 1840
in Lincoln County, KY. He married to Martha F.
Warren, on 4-29-1864. [KYVR] She was born in 1842.
His father was born in New Hampshire and his mother
was born in Rockcastle Co KY. He was a dry goods
merchant.

Children: born in Kentucky
    i   **James**[8] b 1865
    ii   **William**[8] b 1867 m Mary Pritchett and
             they had no children as of 1900. He was
             living in Stanford, Lincoln County in
             1920 with his wife and mother in law,
             Alice Pritchett.
761 iii   **Joseph B.**[3] b 1- -1869.
    iv   **Albert**[8] b 1871. In 1920 he was with his
             wife Florrie b 1871 in Kentucky.
             [Stanford, Lincoln Co KYFC]
763 v   **Samuel W.**[8] b 1- -1881.

(425) Samuel C.[7], (Benjamin[6], Jonathan[5], Jonathan[4],
Jonathan[3], Ephraim[2], John[1]), born 2-26-1814 in
Tuftonboro, NH. He died 3-31-1875 in Moultonboro,
NH. He was most likely a farmer. **Samuel C.**[7]
Severance shows as an Ensign in 1844 on the
military record of Sandwich, Carroll County, NH.
[Mardecai] He married to Ruth Gove Richardson,
daughter of Josiah Richardson and Mary Burbank, on
2- -1839 in Moultonboro, NH. She was born 6-23-1815
and died 5-4-1890 in Moultonboro. The 1840 NH
census shows him living at Moultonboro.

Children: [MDW]
764 i   **Julian Edgar**[8] b 11-30-1840
    ii   **Hollis Eugene**[8] b 11-30-1844 m Mary E.
             Brown, daughter of Charles and Margaret
             Brown, 10-18-1870 in Salem, MA. [MAVR]
766 iii   **Charles Almon**[8] b 10-25-1847 m Matilda
             Ladd 9-28-1870

(426) Jonathan Burbank[7], (Benjamin[6], Jonathan[5],
Jonathan[4], Jonathan[3], Ephraim[2], John[1]), born 5-7-1820
in Tuftonboro, NH and died 2-13-1879 in Malden, MA.
[MAVR] He is buried in Stratham, NH. [MDW] He
married to Selina Wiggin, daughter of Zebulon
Wiggin and Mary Odell, 9-7-1845 in Stratham. She
was born 1-16-1823 and died 12-2-1897. Burial in

Everett, MA. [MDW] This was Debbie Wilson's great great grandfather.

As Debbie Wilson says, "**Jonathan**[7] was well-educated and came to Stratham, NH to teach school. There he married Selina Wiggin in 1845, daughter of the postmaster, Zebulon Wiggin.

After a wedding trip to Boston, they returned to live in Tuftonboro. Daughter **Emma**[8] born in 1850 is erroneously listed in the 1850 NH census as Julia."

"In the 1850's, **Jonathan**[7] and his family moved to Boston where he opened a meat business at Fanieul Hall Market. He became very wealthy, eventually supplying all of the government installations around Boston. They maintained homes in Malden, West Cedar St. on Beacon Hill in Boston, a beautiful farm in Stratham, New Hampshire, and property for a while in Tuftonboro. Their daughter **Emma**[8] attended a school for young ladies in Boston, and the sons both attended private military schools for boys. **Jonathan**[8] increased his wealth by purchasing bounty lands in the west." "**Jonathan**[8] was generous, lending money to family and friends, not always getting it back. After his father's death, there is record of his supporting his step mother Lydia back in Tuftonboro."

Another note-as Debbie points out, "When **Jonathan**[7] died in Boston in 1879 from diabetes, he was buried in Woodlawn Cemetery in Everett, MA, with his daughter, **Emma**[8]. In 1884, wife Selina had him exhumed and brought to Stratham near her to be buried. Yet when she died in 1896, she was sent back to Woodlawn in Everett to be buried." [MDW]

Children:

i   **Elizabeth Adelaide**[8] b 2-17-1846 in Stratham, NH. She d 9-3-1846 at Stratham, NH. [NHVR]

ii **Emma**[8] b 6-23-1850 in Boston, MA. [MAVR] She m to William H. Dodge, son of Addison and Mary B. Dodge, on 1-1-1873 at Boston.

iii **Frank Burbank**[8] b 8-17-1859 in Boston, MA d 6-21-1944 in Boston. Burial in Everett, MA. [MDW] The [MAVR] states that **Frank B.**[8] m Florence M. Beazley, daughter of Richard T. and Jennie J. Beazley, on 9-11-1881 at Boston. Florence was b in Waterville, ME. The couple lived in Boston, MA.

767   iv   **Fred Wiggin**[8] b 3-23-1867 at Boston, MA
               [MAVR] m Annie Odell Smart

(427) David[7], (Benjamin[6], Jonathan[5], Jonathan[4],
Jonathan[3], Ephraim[2], John[1]), born in Tuftonboro, NH
on 5-7-1820, a twin brother of **Jonathan B.**[7]
Severance. The Severance brothers inherited
extensive holdings and money from their parents,
Benjamin[6] and Elizabeth Severance. **Benjamin**[6] had
married secondly to Mrs. Betsey Thompson and
thirdly to Lydia Tate, However, Elizabeth Burbank
was the twins mother
    David[7] Severance, was born 5-7-1820, lived on
the family homestead and married Ruth Welch of
Ossipee on 2-1-1842. Ruth was born on 12-15-1819.
[MBG]
    They had ten children but only one, **Charles**[8],
lived to maturity. Most of the children died of
diphtheria.
    On September 1869, **David**[7] Severance wrote his
Will leaving the bulk of the estate to his wife,
Ruth and son **Charles**[8]. **David**[7] died the following
day, 9-12-1869, of diphtheria. He is buried in the
Hersey Cemetery along with his wife, Ruth, who died
on 5-4-1896. Seven of their young children are also
buried with them.
    David[7] left to his wife, Ruth, and his son,
Charles[8], the homestead farm, the Coffin Place, the
Fry Place and meadow, the Canning Place and other
property. However, the Will of **David**[7] was
challenged by his twin brother, **Jonathan B.**[7]
Severance on grounds of his alleged unsound mind.
After a lengthy legal battle, the Will was up-held
and Ruth and **Charles**[8] became sole owners of the
Severance Farm. They lived on this farm, which is
on Rt 109A for fourteen more years. [MDW]

Children: born in Tuftonboro, NH
    i   **Jonathan B.**[8] b circa 1843 in Tuftonboro,
           NH. He m to Anna S. Tibbitts, daughter
           of Francis S. and Margaret P. Tibbetts,
           1-29-1865 at Boston, MA [MAVR] The vital
           records show Georgie A. (female) b 2-22-
           1870 at Charlestown, MA. He was of
           Charlestown, MA when he quit claimed any
           interest he had in his father's estate
           to brother **David E.**[9] Severance on 12-17-
           1869. His wife, Anna C., signed it also.
           [MDW] The [MAVR] shows the death of a
           son **Jonathan B.**[9] on 5-4-1898 at Reading,

271

MA, age 4 months. His parents were **Jonathan B.**[8] of Tuftonboro, NH and Mary E. Collins of London, England. **Jonathan B.**[8] m Mary E. (Collins) Franklin, daughter of Joseph Collins and Mary Payne, 11-29-1896. [MAVR]

  ii   **Hannah**[8] b 3-21-1844 d 12-25-1844

  iii   **Bradley W.**[8] b 1846 m Marietta Edgerly 6-12-1868 divorced 4-19-1878 in NH [NHVR] They lived in Boston, MA. He d 5-20-1889 at Boston, MA. He was living in Moultonboro, NH. He was listed as a widower. [MAVR]

768 iv   **David Edwin**[8] b 5- -1848 m Mary A. Milliken 4-16-1871 in Tuftonboro, NH

  v   **William M.**[8] b 11-16-1850 d 5-9-1864

  vi   **Lizzie**[8] b 12-19-1853 d 9-21-1856

  vii   **Ruth**[8] b 7-3-1857 d 2-17-1864

  viii **Charles Walter**[8] b 6-15-1859 d 1897 in Malden, MA. He m Addie A. Neal 4-29-1886, [Birgham p97] daughter of Tyler R. Neal and Mary Elizabeth Keniston. [MAVR] Addie was b 12-18-1864 d 1897. They are buried in the Forestdale Cemetery, Malden, MA. They had no children.

  ix   **Freddie**[8] b 7-25-1861 d 8-2-1865

  x   **Vernon**[8] b 10-15-1863 d 1-31-1864

  xi   **Cora**[8] b 1-5-1867 d 8-27-1869 at Charlestown, MA. [MAVR]

(428) Newell Atchison[7], (Stephen[6], Jonathan[5], Jonathan[4] Jonathan[3], Ephraim[2], John[1]), was born circa 1825 and died 5-28-1887. [NHVR] He was "a farmer who died in Wolfboro". **Newell**[7] married to Mary E. Brown. She was born 1828 and died 10-2-1894 aged 66-8-12 [CRWNH]

Children:

  i   **Porter A.**[8] b 1856 d 11-12-1880 ae 24, single [NHVR]

  ii   **John A.**[8] b 1858 d young [1860 NHFC]

769 iii   **Everett N.**[8] b 10 - -1863 Wolfboro,

(429) Lorenzo Fisk[7], (Stephen[6], Jonathan[5], Jonathan[4], Jonathan[3], Ephraim[2], John[1]), was born 4-5-1827 at Wolfboro, NH and died 12-1-1902. He lived in Ossipee, NH, and died in N. Bridgewater, MA. He married to Mary Miranda Perry 1-16-1853 at Holliston, MA. He was 25 and she was 19. [MAVR] She was the duaghter of Edwin Perry and Sallie Johnson Masson.

Lorenzo Fisk[7] Severance was educated at Ossipee, NH where his parents had settled. He was a farmer with his father in his younger years. Then he went to Natick, MA, where he began shoemaking. He return to Wolfboro and followed the trade of shoemaking for three years. His brothers, **Ira**[7] and **Alonzo**[7], offered him a position in their meat and provision store at North Bridgewater, MA in 1856. He bought into partnership with his brothers and the firm becames known as **L.F.**[7] & **A.C.**[7] Severance. Their first location was at the corner of Main and High Streets and later in the Enterprise Building, on Main Street, and then across the street moved to what was later called Bickford's Market. The family kept the market until shortly after 1881 when **Lorenzo F.**[7] left it to his son **Harry C.**[8] Severance who shortly after discontinued it. [RMOFMA p1157]

Children:

  i   **Harry C.**[8] b 4-22-1858 at North Bridgewater MA [MAVR] d 7-9-1891 unm. [MAVR]

  ii   **Annie K.**[8] b 6-11-1861 m Frederick A. Hoyt, son of George A. and Sophia J. Hoyt, 11-24-1880 at Brockton, MA. [MAVR] The MA vital records show an **Annie K.**[8] born 6-11-1861 at North Bridgewater, MA, daughter of **Alonzo F.**[7], of Wolfboro, NH and Margaret M. Severance of Brunswick, VT.

  iii **Edwin Percy**[8] b 5-20-1869 at North Bridgewater, MA [MAVR] unm

  iv   **Ralph Nelson**[8] b 4-22-1873 at North Bridgewater, MA [MAVR] d 2-26-1904 unm

(430) Alonzo Clark[7], (Stephen[6], Jonathan[5], Jonathan[4], Jonathan[3], Ephraim[2], John[1]), was born 4-5-1827 at Wolfboro, NH. He settled in N. Bridgewater, MA, in partnership with his brothers in the **L.F.**[7] & **A.C.**[7] Severance Company. He married to Elizabeth P. Wade, daughter of Daniel C. and Betsy Wade, 10-5-1856 at North Bridgewater, both for the first time. Elizabeth died 7-12-1884 at Brockton, MA. Alonzo died 1-18-1879 at Brockton. He was a provision dealer. [MAVR]

Children:

273

       i   **Frank N.**[8] b 7-18-1857 d 2-6-1858 at
               North Bridgewater, MA. [MAVR]
      ii   **Willie H.**[8] b 8-13-1858 at North
               Bridgewater, MA [MAVR]

(431) Ira O.[7], (Stephen[6], Jonathan[5], Jonathan[4],
Jonathan[3], Ephraim[2], John[1]), born 2-25-1829 [MAVR]
He married first to Mary E. Bickford. "Mary E.
Bickford, wife of I.O. Severance died 10-30-1867 ae
36y 6m 13d". Also in the same lot, "Cora May
Severance, daughter of Mary E. Severance died 3-18-
1859 ae 4y 5m. [CRWNH p199, Nute's Ridge Graveyard]
His second wife was known as J.S. (Julia A.) Morse,
daughter of Otis and Lucy Morse, whom he married on
2-7-1869 at North Bridgewater, MA. [MAVR] (At the
time of **Ira's**[7] father, **Stephen's**[6], death, **Ira's**[7]
wife signed as J.S. The family shows on the 1860 MA
census living in North Bridgewater, MA. [MDW] [IGI]
He died in Quincy, MA in 1898. [MAVR]
    Pension filed by invalid 1-19-1894 from MA, and
by widow (Julia A.) on 11-18-1899 for service 29
Co. untch'ed Mass H.A. [CWPR]

Children: [Johnson II]
       i   **Cora M.**[8] b 10-18-1854 d 3-18-1855
      ii   **Cora**[8] b 11-7-1855 at North Bridgewater,
               MA [MAVR]
     iii   **Ela Eliza**[8] b 8-21-1857 at North
               Bridgewater, MA [MAVR]
      iv   **Carrie C.**[8] b 7-4-1859 at North
               Bridgewater, MA [MAVR] m Walter Shute,
               son of James M. and Mary E. Shute, 3-14-
               1888 at Boston, MA. [MAVR]
       v   **Charles O.**[8] b 1-8-1861 at North
               Bridgewater, MA [MAVR]
      vi   **Horace J.**[8] b 11-6-1862 at North
               Bridgewater, MA [MAVR] He was reportedly
               married
     vii   **Mary A.**[8] b 9-29-1864 (the [MAVR] shows
               the birth of **Abbie May**[8] b 10-25-1864 at
               North Bridgewater, MA to **Ira O.**[7]
               Severance

(432) Stephen Nute[7], (Stephen[6], Jonathan[5], Jonathan[4],
Jonathan[3], Ephraim[2], John[1]), born 6- -1841 [1900
NYFC], settled in NYC, Central Park as a Hotel
Manager. Married to Martha R.____, who was born 4-
-1844 in New York. [1900 NYFC] **Stephen**[7] was the
proprietor of the "Severance Hotel" near Central

Park, NY City, where he died. (The census records showed him with 32 servants and 21 boarders)

Children: [1900 NJFC]
    i   **William W**.[8] b 7- -1872 in NY. He m Lena
             ___ who was b 3- -1873 NY

(433) Sylvester Edwin [7], (Stephen[6], Jonathan[5], Jonathan[4], Jonathan[3], Ephraim[2], John[1]), born in Tuftonboro, NH in 1845, a twin to **Elizabeth**[7] Severance. He married Abby F. (Emily F.) Bean, daughter of Nehemiah and Rosanna Bean, on 12-25-1869 in Wolfeboro, NH. She was born 1- -1858. [1900 MAFC] (the [1880 NHFC] says born 1848). She died 2-14-1893 at Lynn, MA. [MAVR] Not much is known of this family except that they later lived in Ossippee, NH. They were recorded as owning and operating a market business in Lynn, MA.

Children:
    i   **Horace**[8] b 1863 [1870 NHFC]
    ii   **Walter E**.[8] b 1871 [1880 MAFC]

(434) Levi[7], (John[5], Jonathan[5], Jonathan[4], Jonathan[3], Ephraim[2], John[1]), born circa 1822, he married to Sarah E. Hussey on 1-6-1850, [IGI] and lived in Rochester. [Garland p31] The 1850 NH census show **Levi**[7] of Rochester, Strafford Co. born 1822 and Sarah was born 1829. The 1860 NH census shows **Levi**[7] with Sarah, **Lucy**[8] born 1851 and **Lillian**[8] born 1858 all of Strafford Co.

Children: [1870 Rochester, NHFC]
    i   **Lucie J.**[8] b 5-24-1850 d 2-22-1888 m
            Eugene Augustus Hayes, son of Capt.
            Lorenzo Dow Hayes and Martha Augusta
            Leighton. Eugene was b 11-18-1850 d 6-
            17-1924. He m second to Adelia Lois
            Teague in 1891. [Leighton Vol I p421]
    ii   **Lillian**[8] b 1858
    iii   **James Anslie**[8] b 1860 d 10-10-1883 [NHVR]
773 iv   **George V.**[8] b 5-15-1862 d 11-14-1904 was
            m and lived in Rochester, NH.

(435) Charles M.[7], (Joseph Levi[6], Jonathan[5], Benjamin[4], Jonathan[3], Ephraim[2], John[1]), born in Lovell, ME on 3-17-1823. [Lovell, MEVR] He married to Achsah Watson. **Charles**[7] died 8-30-1890. The family shows on the 1860 Lovell, ME census.

Children: [MEVR-Lovell]
774 i **Thomas Freeman**[8] b 11-30-1850
    ii **Mary Ellen**[8] b 1-12-1852 m Duane Rose
775 iii **Henry Butler**[8] b 12-18-1853 (named after Henry Butler Watson)
    iv **Adelphia**[8] b 5-14-1856 m James Martin
776 v **Joseph Granville**[8] b 10-6-1864 m Miranda W. Pike 11-26-1885 [IGI] and had a son, **George Freeman**[9] b 6-15-1886.

(436) Sewell[7], (Joseph L.[6], Jonathan[5], Benjamin[6], Jonathan[7], Ephraim[8], John[1]), was born 4-3-1831 at Tuftonboro, NH. [MEVR] [1850 MEFC] He married to Miss Mary (Sarah) Jane Tate on 1-28-1854. "Married by Justice of the Peace agreeable to the statute in such cases". [MEVR]

Children:
    i **Sarah T.**[8] b 11-24-1854 at Rockport, MA [MAVR]

(437) Joseph Bishop[7], (Joseph Levi[6], Jonathan[5], Benjamin[4], Jonathan[3], Ephraim[2], John[1]), was born 6-9-1835 in Wolfboro, NH. [NHVR] He was also known as **Bishop**[7] [MEVR-Lovell]. The [PRPCoME] show **Joseph**[7] born at Wolfboro, NH and died 8-14-1906 at Dover, NH. His first wife Elizabeth J. [1870 MEFC] was born 4-8-1840 and died 11-26-1892, previous residence was Biddeford, ME. [1860-1870 Biddeford, MEFC] He married secondly to Bertha Crediford, daughter of Israel and Sarah Crediford, 1-20-1894 who was born 1870 in Sandwich, NH. [NHVR] **Joseph**[7] was 57 years old at his second marriage and this wife (Bertha was 23 years old. **Joseph Bishop**[7] was later living in Biddeford, ME where his children were born.
    The 1900 ME census shows Bertha's mother, Sarah B. Crediford, was living with them as well as her sister, Elmina E. Crediford.
    Joseph B.[7] died 8-14-1906 [CRME] in Dover, NH the son of **Joseph**[6] Severance and Mary Moody of Tuftonboro, NH. His previous residence was Biddeford, ME. [NHVR]
    The marriage of **Bishop C.**[8] Severance to Gladys E. Plummer was in Dover, NH. The bride was from Sandwich, NH. The parents of **Bishop**[8] were **Joseph B.**[7] and Bertha Crediford. **Joseph**[7] was b in Wolboro, NH and aged 71 and Bertha was 44 years old.

Children:

i		**Elizabeth**[3] b 12-1-1894 (marriage age 18, [NHVR] m Leland D. Stevens 10-9-1912 of Dover, NH. (**Elizabeth**[8] was listed as the daughter of **Joseph B.**[7] deceased and Bertha [NHVR])
777	ii	**Bishop Clayton**[8] b 9-10-1896 in Biddeford, ME m Gladys E. Plummer 1-15-1929 in N. Sandwich, NH. Gladys was from Sandwich, NH, the daughter of Hattie M. Plummer. They were later found in Dover, NH. The [NHVH] shows a **Marion A.**[9] Severance b 3-8-1930 d 3-15-1930, daughter of **Clayton B.**[8] Severance and Gladys Plummer of Rochester, NH. **Bishop**[8] was a lumber maker.
	iii	**Mildred (Frances)**[8] b 3-20-1898 m Chester Hardy of Rochester, NH on 2-26-1914. He was the son of Demick Hardy and Lucinda Wentzell of Nova Scotia, Canada. **Mildred**[8] was the daughter of **Joseph Bishop**[7] Severance and Bertha Crediford [NHVR] (it is possible that **Mildred**[8] was b in 1897. She was 17 at her marriage in 1914. [NHVR]

(438) Levi[7], (Joseph Levi[6], Jonathan[5], Benjamin[4], Jonathan[3], Ephraim[2], John[1]), born in Lovell, ME, on 8-14-1837 [Lovell MEVR] He died on 11-12-1896, age 59 years and 3 months. (MEVR) He married first to Mary E. Fogg on 4-29-1865. She died 2-16-1871. [MEVR] He married to Jennie Phoebe Ward. She died 12-1-1896. [MEVR]

Children:

i		**Annie J.**[8] b 3-17-1872 [MEVR]
ii		**Clarenda L.**[8] b 5-1-1874 [MEVR]
iii		**Clarence L.**[8] was b on 5-1-1874 at Lovell, ME. [MEVR] He m to Mabel L. Stetson, daughter of Leonard A. Stetson and Ella A. Scott, on 10-10-1901. [MEVR] **Clarence L.**[8] settled at Durham, Androscoggin, ME but d at Wolfboro, NH, on 3-12-1922. [MEVR]

(439) Asa Albion[7], (Joseph Levi[6], Jonathan[5], Benjamin[4], Jonathan[3], Ephraim[2], John[1]), born 11-16-1839. [MEVR-Lovell] **Albion**[7] married to Fanny ____. She was born in 1844 in NH. He lived in the states of ME, NH, PA, MI, and CA.

Children:
 i   **Harry**[8] b 1866 PA. He settled in CA circa
      1870. [1870 CAFC]
 ii   **Frank**[8] b 1869 ME. He settled in CA. circa
      1870. [1870 CAFC] They had a daughter,
      Emma M.[8] b 2-15-1880 [MEVR]

(440) Rufus[7], (Rodney[6], Benjamin[5], Benjamin[4],
Jonathan[3], Ephraim[2], John[1]), born circa 1819 in
Morgan Co. OH. He married Elizabeth Gibson on 12-9-
1837. [OHVR] The 1870 WI census shows them living
at Summit, Juneau Co.

Children: [MLSW]
 i   **Marinda**[8] b 1848 m _____ Higgins [WIVR]
 ii   **Lavina**[8] b 1849 in OH m John Nesbitt 5-
      12-1879 in Necedah, WI
778 iii **Lafayette**[8] b 1851 in OH, he was in WI by
      1880, m to Ellen C. Driscoll 4-24-1881,
      Juneau Co. WI. Ellen was the daughter of
      John Driscoll and Sarah Jane Walker.
      Ellen was b 12-28-1859 d 12-25-1932
      [WIVR]
779 iv **Fayette**[8] b 1853 in OH, he was in WI by
      1880, m Frances Elizabeth Finn 9-28-1880
      (Juneau Co. WIVR)
 v   **Robert**[8] b 1855 d young ??

(441) Robert C.[7], (Rodney[6], Benjamin[5], Benjamin[4],
Jonathan[3], Ephraim[2], John[1]), born circa 1819 in
Morgan Co. OH. He married to Savilla Hedge on 5-20-
1841 in Morgan Co. OH. **Robert**[7] died circa 1858, at
the age of 39 years.
     At the estate settlement in Morgan Co. OH in
1858, his widow was appointed guardian of their
minor children. The only daughter had married to
Samuel Wilson before that time.
     After **Robert**[7] died Savilla and some of her sons
went to WI. The 1880 OH census shows Savilla living
with son, **Robert**[8], who was unmarried. **George**[8] had a
1 year old son **Rodney**[9]; **Rufus**[8] had 9 month old
Arthur[9]; **Silas**[8] had 2 year old **Sidney**[9] and 7 month
old **Charles**[9]; and **Lewis**[8] had **Elnora**[9] 2 years and
Norman[9] 2 months. The 1870 WI census shows the
family living in Summit, Juneau Co. with out
Robert[7].

Children: born in Morgan Co. OH
780 i   **Rufus**[8] b 1841? m Clara D. Stillson,
         daughter of Sylvester Stillson and Lucy

278

Arvilus, 12-2-1875. Clara b 4-4-1855 d
9-11-1938 [Juneau Co. WIVR]

781 ii **Silas**[8] b 1842 m Phebe Huntley [WIVR]
iii **Leonora**[8] b 1843 m L.A. Wilson 5-19-1859
782 iv **Lewis**[8] b 1845 m Mary E. Cattle 7-13-1876
[WIVR]
v **Rodney**[8] b 12-4-1845 in OH, settled in
Juneau Co. WI and died on 6-18-1885, m
Mary C. Briggs, daughter of Ervin Briggs
and Anna Torey of NY, NY, on 2-18-1885.
[WIVR] Mary was b 11-1-1857 She was born
on 11-1-1857 in Jefferson Co. WI d 3-16-
1938 [Juneau Co. WIVR] There were no
children per Probate settlement of the
estate. [PRJWI]
783 vi **Robert**[8] b 1846 m Emma Spaulding 11-16-
1888 [WIVR]
784 vii **George R.**[8] b 1848 m Lizzie Wilson 8-17-
1879 [WIVR]

(442) Benjamin[7], (Rodney[6], Benjamin[5], Benjamin[4],
Jonathan[3], Ephraim[2], John[1]), born circa 1822 in
Morgan Co. OH. [1850 OHFC] He married Mary Buchanon
on 10-9-1844 at Muskingum, OH. Mary was born 7-15-
1824 and died on 9-3-1907 in OH. The 1900 OH census
shows them living in Pennsville. **Benjamin**[7] died 5-
14-1903 in Morgan Co.

Children:
i **Clarissa**[3] b 1845 969
ii **Silas**[8] b 12- -1848 in Ohio. [1900 OHFC]
He married to Ellen ___. She was born in
W. VA in 1- -1856. They settled in
Cleveland, Cuyahoga Co OH. [1900 OHFC]
iii **Matilda**[8] b 1850
iv **Elizabeth**[8] b 1855

(443) Arthur Rodney[7], (Rodney[6], Benjamin[5], Benjamin[4],
Jonathan[3], Ephraim[2], John[1]), born 8-30-1826 at
Morgan Co. OH, and died after 1880 in Chariton Co.
MO. He married Margaret Shoemaker on 10-9-1848 in
OH. **Arthur**[7] and Margaret moved to Chariton Co. MO
in 1870. [MLSW]
"He was the youngest of a family consisting of
four sons and two daughters, the children of Rodney
Severance originally of New Hampshire, and wife
previously Miss Jane Caldwell, who was born and
reared in Morgan county, Ohio."
"In 1869 he sold out in Ohio and removed to
Missouri, to Cunningham township where he bought a

large farm and settled as a farmer of choice stock
and grains." [HHCCoMO p901-902]

Children:
    i   **Elizabeth J.**[8] b 1851 m Fred Erb
785 ii   **Oliver S.**[8] b 3-30-1853 m Ada E. Marshall
    iii   **Hiram**[8] b 1857
787 iv   **Arthur E.**[8] b 2- -1862 m Ednonia ____
788 v   **Benjamin F.**[8] b 10- -1864
    vi   **Pauline**[8] m H.F. Hart
    vii   **Cinderilla**[8]
    viii **Flora**[8] m O.J. Davis

(444) Phillip[7], (Silas[6], Benjamin[5], Benjamin[4],
Jonathan[3], Ephraim[2], John[1]), was born 4-4-1823 and
died 9-23-1894 in OH. He married to Rachel Chapman
on 10-7-1844. **Phillip**[7] was of Monroe Co. OH and
Rachel was of Washington, Co. They were married at
Lowell, OH. She was born 8-16-1823 and died 2-12-
1905.

Children: [BRPS]
    i   **Augusta J.**[8] b 8-20-1845 d 12-14-1893 m
             Amos Wright 12-19-1863
    ii   **Sarah V.**[8] b 2-3-1847 d 5-29-1911 m
             Purdey Nott 4- -1864
789 iii   **Silas O.**[8] b 12-19-1848 d 6-7-1909 m
             Nellie Phelan 1- -1880
    iv   **Ammarilla J.**[8] b 12-31-1850 d 9-9-1859
    v   **Mary F.**[8] b 12-20-1853 m H.N. Smott 5-27-
             1874
    vi   **Alfred E.**[8] b 12-21-1856 d 12-23-1856
    vii   **Nettie L.**[8] b 10-27-1863 d 12-27-1948 m
             M.C. Seeley 1-4-1896

(446) Arthur M.[7], (Silas[6], Benjamin[5], Benjamin[4],
Jonathan[3], Ephraim[2], John[1]), born circa 1832. He
married to Mary Ann Dailey on 4-15-1854.

Children:
    i   Baby b 12-15-1867 [OHVR]

(447) Church B.[7], (Silas[6], Benjamin[5], Benjamin[4],
Jonathan[3], Ephraim[2], John[1]), born circa 1838. He
married to Frances M. Nott in 1859. He apparently
married a second time as his pension records for
the Civil War show his widow to be Margaret F.
Nott. The 1880 W. VA census shows the family.

Children:

i   **Sadie May**[E] b 1-31-1876 [OHVR]
ii   **Nellie**[8] b 1879 in West VA

(448) Hazen M.[7], (Hazen[6], Benjamin[5], Benjamin[4], Jonathan[3], Ephraim[2], John[1]), born 10-22-1839 in Morgan Co. OH. **Hazen**[7] married Parmelia A. VanMeter who was born 1846 in VA. The 1900 Perry Co. OH census shows the family living in Salt Lick. He is living alone on the 1910 Perry Co. OH census She died 1903 in OH. **Hazen**[7] died on 1-6-1914 in Shawnee, Wayne Co. OH. [MLSW]

Children:
791 i   **Charles F.**[8] b 1860 d 1949 m Harriet Jones
    ii   **Laurae**[8] b 1864 d 1946 m John Post
792 iii **Fred**[8] b 11-9-1876 d 6-18-1958 m Ruth Thomas
    iv   **Jacob H.**[8] b 10-14-1877 d 8-4-1964 m Cecilia Gaver
    v   **Louis (Lewis C.)**[8] b 3- -1881 m Emma Barton
    vi   **John L.**[8] b 11- -1883
    vii **Anna**[8] m Ulyssus Hazelton
    viii **Dorothy**[8] m ___Woodruff

(449) Harrison[7], (Nicholas[6], Nichols[5], Benjamin[4], Jonathan[3], Ephraim[2], John[1]), born in Thetford, VT circa 1816. His death date is recorded as 4-8-1895. [VTVR] The 1860 VT census shows that he was married to Laura/Lovina, who was born in 1823. The 1870 Colebrook NH census shows him living with Clarissa York, age 28, with her two small children.

Children:
    i   **Clarissa Ann**[8] b 1841 m in 1857 to Henry Bardbuy Gilkey, son of Merritt and Lucy Blodgett Gilkey. [Sterns]
    ii   **Albion**[8] b 1845
    iii **Byron**[8] b circa 1845 in Colebrook, NH m Flora E. French, daughter of David and Sophronia of Mt Vernon, ME. **Byron**[8] was 29 and a baggagemaster and she was 28. [MAVR] They lived in Lowell, MA. [1900 and 1920 MAFC] They had daughters, **Myrtle L.**[8] b 2-24-1881 and **Nellie Allice**[8] b 4-26-1886 at Lowell, MA [MAVR]
    iv   **Mary Ann**[8] b 1849 [1860 NHFC]

(450) Nicholas[7], (Thomas[6], Nichols[5], Benjamin[4], Jonathan[3], Ephraim[2], John[1]), born 1820 in NY. He shows on the 1850 MI census with his wife Jane R. born 1826 in VT and children, **Frank[8]** born 1849 and **Albert[8]** born 1850, both born in MI. Harriet Sweat born 1819 in NH was living with them. **Nicholas[7]** born 1820 in NY state shows living with his wife, Mary, born 1824 in NY State. In 1860 he was living in Leroy, Calhoun Co. MI with his wife Mary and their sons. [Leroy, Calhoun Co. MIFC] **John[8]** born 1847 in MI and **George[8]** born 1851 in MI. It appears that this is the same family but it is conjecture.

Children:
  i   **John[8]** b 1847 in MI
  ii   **Frank[8]** b 1849
  iii **Albert[8]**
  iv   **George[8]** b 1851 in MI

(452) Mason Samuel (Samuel Mason)[7], (John S.[6], Samuel[5], Samuel[4], Jonathan[3], Ephraim[2], John[1]), was born circa 1848. He married first to Lettie O. Sawyer, daughter of Leonard and Rachael Sawyer, on 6-3-1871 at Haverhill, MA [MAVR] He married secondly to Nellie Colford, daughter of John and Eliza Colford, 5-25-1876 at Lawrence, MA. [MAVR] He was 67 years old in 1914 when his son **Jason S.[8]** married and when their daughter **Ellen B.[8]** was married in 1916, His wife, Nellie Colford, was 65. **Mason Samuel[7]** was a shoemaker at Kingston, NH.

Children:
  i   **Minnie[8]**
  ii   **Hattie[8]** b 1880 m Frank J. Gilman on 12-28-1901 [NHVR], Frank was the son of Eusebe Gilman and Elbena Jaques of Canada [NHVR]
796 iii **John S.[8]** b 4- -1881 Exeter, NH m Antionette Forcier 10-10-1914 at Manchester, NH. Antionette was the daughter of Michel Forcier and Mary Jane Landry. [NHVR] **John[8]** was the son of **Mason[7]** Severance and Nellie Colford of E. Kingston, NH [NHVR]
  iv   **Ellen B.[7]** b 1897 m Joseph H. Greenleaf 5-31-1916 [NHVR] at Kingston, NH, Joseph was the son of Joseph H. Greenleaf and Grace L. Nickerson of NY City.

(453) George Washington[7], (Ora P.[6], Samuel[5], Samuel[4], Jonathan[3], Ephraim[2], John[1]), was born 12-9-1851 at Kingston, NH. He married Ella May Osgood, daughter of George and Roxie Osgood, 12-3-1881 at Haverhill, MA. [MAVR] Ella was born 1855 at Holyoke, MA and died in 1927. **George W.**[7] died 11-7-1891 at Plaistow, NH. [MDS]

Children: born at Plaistow, NH
	i	**Willie B.**[8] b 5- -1883 d 10-7-1883
797	ii	**Herbert Winfred**[8] b 7-26-1884 at Plaistow, NH. Settled at Haverhill, MA. She m to Lilla Belle Price of Lowell, MA.
	iii	**Ruth A.**[8] b 8- -1889 m George W. Tuttle 4-14-1902. She d 1958
	iv	**Geneva May**[8] b 6-26-1891 d 1912

(454) John[7], (Nathan[6], John[5], John[4], Jonathan[3], Ephraim[2], John[1]), was born 7-4-1843 at Pembroke, NH [NHVR] (one report says that he was born in England which was obviously wrong)

He died at Pembroke on 5-22-1926. [NHVR] He married to Florence Jane Atwood, daughter of Alba Atwood and Marguerite Cleasby. Florence was born 9-13-1854 at Andover and died 8-2-1933 at Manchester, NH. [NHVR] **John**[7] was a farmer.

Children: born at Pembroke, NH
	i	**Lydia Estelle**[8] **(Estelle L.)** b 7-16-1873 at Pembroke, NH, d 1950 Concord, NH, m Rossini E.W. Osgood who was b 12-9-1874 at Allenstown, NH.
	ii	**Everett**[8] b 10- -1879 lived in CA
799	iii	**Earl L.**[8] b 6-30-1888 d 5-15-1967 Concord, NH., m Sylva Worth b 2-9-1883 d 11-24-1962 at Concord, NH.,
800	iv	**Frank**[8] b 1893 d 1966 m Ethel Dyer, daughter of Charles Frank Dyer and Nettie B. Crane, 4-29-1915 at Concord, NH (NHVR) He was a farmer. Ethel was b 1891 d 1975.

EIGHTH GENERATION (455) Emery[8], (John[7], John/Abba[6], Tabitha[5], Daniel[4], Ebenezer[3], John[2], John[1]), born circa 1817 in VT. He married to Arvilla Thrasher, daughter of Daniel and Safronna Thrasher, on 8-1-1844. Arvilla was born in 1826 and died 10-30-1883 age 56-9-0 at Brookfield, VT. In 1860 they were

living at Tunbridge, Orange Co. [VTFC] **Emery**[8] died
11-6-1884 at Granville, VT. [VTVR]

Children: [VTVR] and [1850/1880 VTFC]
- i **Isabella**[9] b 1849 in VT
- ii **Charles Marcellan**[9] b 1853 d 3-8-1908 ae
  54-8-11 at Londonderry, VT. [VTVR] m
  Elva M. Cady 12-28-1879 ae 26 at
  Rochester, NY.
- iii **Emma R.**[9] b 1860 of Granville, VT m
  Orrison C. Briggs 2-14-1884. She was 24.
  [VTVR]
- iv male child b 12-14-1862 [VTVR]
- v **Corneily**[9] b 1863 [1880 VTFC]
- vi **Ella**[9] b 1864 [1880 VTFC]
- vii **Nellie**[9] b 1868 m William Reed 9-23-1893
  at St Albans, VT

(456) Charles H.[8], (Abner[7], John[6], Tabitha[5], Daniel[4],
Ebenezer[3], John[2], John[1]) born circa 1809/11 in
Windsor, VT. He was 72 years old on 10-15-1881.
[Hemenway] He married Abriah White, daughter of
Samuel White and Sarah Brock on 2-19-1846. [VTVR]
She died 12-9-1882 age 69-7-0. **Charles**[8] died on 4-
10-1885 age 76. [VTVR] In 1860 the family was
living at Montpelier. [VTFC] **Charles**[8] was a master
printer or painter. [VTVR]

Children: born in VT
- i **Hettie**[9] b 1841
- ii **George L.**[9] b 1842
- iii **Mary**[9] b 1845
- iv **John W.**[9] b 1853 [VTVR]
- v **Julia W.**[9] b 1855 m John Hines [VTVR]

(457) Horace M.[8], (Abner[7], John[6], Tabitha[5], Daniel[4],
Ebenezer[3], John[2], John[1]), born 12-27-1818 at
Woodstock, VT and married Ruby Y. Titus on 7-1-1851
at Ipswich, MA. [MAVR] Ruby was the daughter of
John Smith Titus and Sarah/Sally Boynton. She was
born in Lyman, NH 9-25-1822. [Cambridge, MAVR] He
was of Boston and died 12-29-1897 at Cambridge, MA.
He was a printer. [MAVR]

Children: [Titus]
- i **Emily**[8] b 5-10-1852 at Cambridge, MA
  [MAVR] d 9-11-1941
- 801 ii **Horace**[8] b 2-14-1854 in Cambridge, MA.
  [MAVR] The 1900 MA census shows him
  with his mother, Ruby, and sister.

iii		**Louis H.**[8] b 2-28-1856
iv		**Lois F.**[8] b 2-28-1856 at Cambridge, MA [MAVR]
802	v	**George E.**[8] b 8-18-1859 at Cambridge, MA m Addie A. Grout, daughter of Elbridge and Sarah W. Grout, on 9-10-1884 at Cambridge, MA. [MAVR]

(458) Frederick[8], (Abner[7], John[6], Tabitha[5], Daniel[4], Ebenezer[3], John[2], John[1]), born circa 1825. [1860 VTFC] He probably married first to Cassandana Dinsmore, 6-19-1851. **Frederick**[8], Cassandana (Carrie) and their children were living at Windsor, VT in 1860. [VTFC] He married to Mary W. Bement on 9-17-1890. [VTVR] **Frederick**[8] was 62 at his 2nd marriage. [VTVR] Mary died on 4-2-1903. Mary W., daughter of John Bement and Sylvia Thomas was born 5-9-1829. [NHVR]

Children:
i	**Florance A.**[9] b 1854
ii	**Leigh Pearson**[9] b 10-11-1858 at Windsor, Vermont. He d 9-30-1913 at Boston, MA. [NHVR] He m Josephine M. Saunders, 12-26-1881, in Manchester, NH. [IGI]. Josephine was b 9- -1863. [MEFC] They did not have any children living with them in 1900. [MEFC]

(459) William T.[8], (Nathan[7], John[6], Tabitha[5], Daniel[4], Ebenezer[3], John[2], John[1]), was born circa 1825. He settled in OH. He married to Lavina (Louisa) Mitchell, 10-14-1850. [OHVR] He was shown living in Rutland, VT, KS, Shallersville, OH, and Brooklyn, MI. They reportedly had 6 children, however in 1902 the only living child was **Lucille**[9] who married to George Barstow in MI. [Radasch] He died in Brooklyn, MI in 1917 and she died 1929, both are buried in Highland Cemetery.

William T.[8] Severance served in the 104th Ohio Volunteer Infantry during the War of the Rebellion, and at its cloe he removed to Brooklyn, MI. He was a member of the G.A.R. and one of the oldest Masons of Brooklyn. [MIPH Vol 32]

Pension filed by invalid 6-8-1888 from KS and by widow 2-20-1902 from MI for service D 104 OH., Inf. [CWPR]

Children: six children were born.

i   **Lucille**[9] b 1854 d 1929 m George Barstow
         b 1853 d 1917, son of Samuel and Polly
         Barstow.

(460) Oscar F.[8], (Nathan[7], John[6], Tabitha[5], Daniel[4],
Ebenezer[3], John[2], John[1]), born circa 1830. He
married to Elizabeth B. (Heriff) Moses 7-4-1849.
[OHVR] [Hayward p401]

Children:
803 i   **Charles**[9] b 1889, m Viola E. ___. Settled
              in Williams Co and Defiance Co OH. [1920
              OHFC]

(461) George[8], (Nathan[7], John[6], Tabitha[5], Daniel[4],
Ebenezer[3], John[2], John[1]), was born 4- -1830. **George**[8]
married to Elizabeth Nichols, [Hayward p401] who
was born 12- -1825. They were living in Ravenna,
Portage Co. OH. The 1880-1900 OH census, also shows
a grandson, **Norman E.**[10] Severance born 7- -1899 in
OH.

Children: [1880 OHFC]
     i   **William**[9] d unm
804 ii   **Clinton**[9] b 10- -1856 m Flora Wilson
805 iii   **Clarence**[9] m Ella Baldwin
806 iv   **Frank L.**[9] b 8- -1861
     v   **Ella R.**[9] b 1863
     vi   **George E**[9]. b 2- -1868 m Ella/Ida N. and
              they had a son **Norman E.**[9] b 7- -1899.
              [1900 OHFC]

(462) Marvin[8], (Nathan[7], John[6], Tabitha[5], Daniel[4],
Ebenezer[3], John[2], John[1]), was born 6- -1832 in OH.
He married to Laura Leonard [Hayward p401] who was
born 1- -1838 in NY state. They lived at Ravenna,
Portage Co. OH. [1880/1900 OHFC]

Children: born in OH.
808 i   **Marcus**[9] b 1858 m Mary A., and settled in
              MN with children
     ii   **Eva**[9] b 1862
     iii   **Maud**[9] b 1877

(463) Manly C.[8], (Nathan[7], John[6], Tabitha[5], Daniel[4],
Ebenezer[3], John[2], John[1]), born 1835 and married to
Julia _____, they are shown living at Ravenna and
Alliance, OH. The children were listed in the
[Hayward p401] They had at least two grandchildren,

Pearl[10] born 2- -1885 and **Henry**[10] born 8- -1887.
[1900 OHFC]

Children: born in OH
	i	**Eugene**[9] b 1862
810	ii	**Clifford**[9] b 1864
	iii	**Flora**[9]
	v	**Clara**[9] b 1867 in Ohio [1880 OHFC]
	iv	**Eva**[9]
	vii	**Millie**[9] b 1874 in Ohio [1880 OHFC]

(463a) Henry A.[8], (Nathan[7], John[6], Tabitha[5], Daniel[4], Ebenezer[3], John[2], John[1]), was born 1840 in OH. Indicated in the [Haryward p401]

Children: born Mill Creek, Williams Co. [OHFC]
	i	**George**[9] b 6- -1869
	ii	**Daniel**[9] b 5-30-1872 [OHVR] Later showed in Fulton Co. OH.
	iii	**James A.**[9] b 11- -1881
	iv	**Sylvia**[9] b 10- -1884
	v	**Joseph**[9] b 11- -1887
	vi	**Eliza**[9] b 11- -1891

(464) Nelson Chase[8], (Moses[7], John[6], Tabitha[5], Daniel[4], Ebenezer[3], John[2], John[1]), born 5-5-1816 probably in VT and later settled with his parents at St. Lawrence, NY. He married Elizabeth Waters, daughter of Sylvanus Waters, 2-1-1839 and they were recorded at Battle Creek, MI. His name shows on the 1840-1850 MI census at Battle Creek. He was living in Polkton, Ottawa Co. [1870 MIFC] Elizabeth was born 5-18-1818 and died 5-27-1874. **Nelson**[8] died on 11-8-1895. [MDH]

Children: [1850/1870 MIFC]
	i	**Mahala**[9] b 1839 in MI
	ii	**Franklin**[9] b 1841 in MI
	iii	**Sarah J.**[9] b 1845 in MI
812	iv	**Sylvester Chase**[9] b 5-22-1854/55 m Emma L. Ross who was b 11-12-1865
	v	**Ida A.**[9] b 1856
	vi	**Frances M.**[9] b 1859

(464a) William[8], (Moses[7], John/Abba[6], Tabitha[5], Daniel[4], Ebenezer[3], John[2], John[1]), was born circa 1817 in Colchester, VT. He married to Anna Fifield. She died 1-20-1897. age 54, at Potsdam, NY. She was born at Pierrepont. [NYVR] In 1870, **William**[8] was listed with Fannie b 1821 in NY and a son, **William A.**[9] b 1852 in NY. [NYFC]

Children:
812a i   **Sylvester**[9] b circa 3- -1834 in Canada
            and married Louisa Fifield
812b ii   **Ambrose**[9] b circa 1839 and married to
            Hannah Crossman.
812c iii   **Unrico**[9] b circa 1847

(464b) Henry[8], (Moses[7], John/Abba[6], Tabitha[5], Daniel[4], Ebenezer[3], John[2], John[1]), was born circa 1817 at Colchester, VT. [1850 VTFC] He later settled about 1864 in Pierrepont, St Lawrence Co, NY. **Henry**[8] married to Nancy/Mary Hardy, daughter of John and Sally Hardie. Nancy/Mary was b circa 1822 in VT and died 3-13-1895 at Pierrepont, age 75-3-10. [NYVR]. **Henry**[8] died in 1898. They are buried in NY. [CEMNY-White Church/Martin Ridge Cemetery, Pierrepont/Canton]

Children:
        i   **Edwin C.**[9] b 1843 d 1868 buried at Martin
              Ridge Cemetery, Pierrepont, NY
       ii   **Lucia**[9] b 1847
       ii   **Alice Margaret**[9] b 1849 d 6-1-1889 age 39
              yrs at Pierpont [NYVR] m Alonzo Wood.
              They had a daughter, Bessie Wood b in MI
              and later m to Charles B. Bailey of
              Potsdam, NY, on 6-12-1896
      iii   **Lovina/Louisa B.**[9] b 8-19-1852 at
              Colchester, VT, daughter of Henry and
              Nancy Hardy, m George E. Healy of
              Potsdam, 10-17-1872. They are buried in
              Fairview Cemetery, Canton, NY. George
              E., 1855-1943 and Louisa/Lovina 1852-
              1936
812d v   **Leslie P.**[9] b 10-12-1853 at Colchester
              VT. He moved to Canton, NY in 1864
812e vi   **Henry Rollin**[9], b 5-12-1857 Colchester,
              VT. [VTVR] He m to Mary (Marion)
              Elizabeth Brown
        v   **Ellen Maria**[9] b 3-22-1859 at Colchester,
              VT. [VTVR] An **Ellen** Severance m Alvin
              Corbin. They had a son, Elmer Corbin who
              m Mary Trumbley 5-7-1903 at Colton.
              Elmer was 23 years old in 1903,
              therefore born circa 1880.
       iv   **Frank W/H.**[9] b 6-6-1861 in VT, d 11-14-
              1892 age 32 yrs at Canton, NY. [NYVR] He

had a son, **Frank Jr.**[10] b 1891 d 1920, both are buried in Martin Ridge Cemeter, Pierrepont, NY.

(465) Charles[8] *Severns*, (Moses[7], John/Abba[6], Tabitha[5], Daniel[4], Ebenezer[3], John[2], John[1]), was born 3-5-1823 in Edwards, St. Lawrence Co. NY and died 7-13-1894 in Daily, Cass Co. MI. He married to Eliza Jane Petticron, daughter of James Petticron, on 3-19-1848. She was born 11-5-1825 at Warren Co. NY and died 10-3-1882.

Children:
    i   **Ida Estelle**[9] b 11-11-1853 in Cass Co. MI m Ransom R. Goodrich, who was b 5-29-1854. [Cooley p151]

(466) Edmund Kirby[8], (Ebenezer[7], Samuel[6], Ebenezer[5], Ebenezer[4], Ebenezer[3], John[2], John[1]), born in Middlebury, VT on 4-28-1823. He settled in that town and filled the office of Selectman and Lister for several years. He married first to Emma Perkins 12-30-1847 and married second to Mary A. Landon on 12-14-1869. [JFS p64] **Edmund**[8] died on 8-9-1906 at Middlebury, VT. [VTVR]

Children: [JFS p65]
        i   Charles K. d 3-13-1878 ae 18-4-3, Middlebury, VT the adopted son of E. Kirby and Emma Perkins. [VTVR]
        i   **Nellie M.**[9] b 9-22-1871
813 ii   **Frank Edmund**[9] b 9-4-1872 VTVR d 5-1-1960 at Burlington, VT m Lena Adelia Kelsey, daughter of Ansel Wallace Kelsey and Celestia Matilda Billings, b 7-14-1874 d 7-8-1953 at Middlebury, VT [Kelsey Vol IV]
814 iii   **George M.**[9] b 1-2-1876
     iv   **Jennie A.**[9] b 7-10-1878
     v   **Martha A.**[9] b 8-17-1880 [VTVR]
     vi   **William M.**[9] b 10- -1883 [1900 VTFC]

(467) Oliver[8], (Ebenezer[7], Samuel[6], Ebenezer[5], Ebenezer[4], Ebenezer[3], John[2], John[1]), born in Middlebury, VT on 2-14-1827. He married Delia Helen Cady on 3-18-1849. She was born on 4-16-1832.
    Oliver[8] was a carpenter and builder but became interested in water power. He started in motion the impetus to provide Middlebury with grist mills, machine shops, wollen factories, and two large

paper mills, both which later burned. He showed
good judgement in estimating the value of property.
He had a large ranch in Texas which he used in the
sheep trade. His sons were involved in business
with him. [JFS p65]
   He is also recorded as living in Windsor, VT and
Lenox, NY. The 1900 VT census shows him living
alone. **Oliver**[8] died 5-15-1907. [VTVR]

Children: {JFS p65]
   i   **Julia Adalaide**[9] b 7-10-1850 d 12-11-1860
          [VTVR]
   ii   **Junius Eugene**[9] b 9-7-1851 m Dora D.
          Biggart 11-18-1873, he was
          superintendent of the Barcelona Silver
          Mine in NV which positon he resigned and
          engaged in a quartz mill in Candelaria,
          NV. [JFS] The 1920 CO census shows them
          living in Co with out any children.
   iii   **James**[9] b 1852, shows on the 1880 VT
          census with Dora (his wife)
816 iv   **Charles Carlton**[9] b 9-17-1853 [JFS] He m1
          Ida L. Latimer. She d in 1891. He m2
          Lena Woodruff 7-4-1879. They lived in
          Middlebury, VT. They had a son **Guy
          Carlton**[10] b 5-9-1880
   v   **Florence Lillian**[9] b 1-30-1856 m Charles
          B. Warren 1-5-1881
   vi   **Willie Frank**[9] b 4-15-1860 d 6-2-1861
   vii   **Fred Wilmot**[9] b 2-2-1862 d 6-17-1878
          [VTVR]
817 viii   **Frank Oliver**[9] b 8-28-1864 [JFS] m
          Carrie L. Tyrel 6-28-1887 in Burlington,
          VT.
   viii   **Lizzie Ethel Daisy**[9] b 11-12-1873 d 2-11-
          1896 ae 22-11-30 in Middlebury, VT.
          [VTVR]

(468) Milton Leonard[8], (Ebenezer[7], Samuel[6],
Ebenezer[5], Ebenezer[4], Ebenezer[3], John[2], John[1]), born
in Middleburry, VT on 10-14-1830. [DAR application
for Milton Leonard Jr. 4-13-1892] He married Emily
Augusta Spencer on 8-16-1859 [VTVR] and they
settled in Bennington, VT. She died 5-24-1898.
[Carleton] He worked on his fathers farm until he
was 21 years old. Working his way through several
colleges, he attended the final year at the Andover
Theological Seminary in Andover, New Hampshire. He
served in several positions through-out New
Hampshire, showing excellence in every-one of them.

During interim from one position, he toured Europe, going through England, Scotland, Belgium, Ireland, Germany, Switzerland, Italy, and France. His last church was in Bennington, VT. [JFS p66]

He prepared for College in Burr and Burton Seminary. Teacher, Ticonderoga, NY 1859-1860. Union Theological Seminary, 1861-1862. Andover Theological Seminary 1863. Ordained 1864. Pastor, Congregational church, Boscawen, NH 1863-1868; Orwell, VT 1869-1880. Financial agent, Middlebury College 1881-1882. Principal, Burr and Burton Seminary, 1882-1888. Pastor, Bennington Center, 1888-1899. [Howard p154]

Milton[8] married a second time to Ella Barkley Stewart on 11-12-1900. [VTVR] **Milton**[8] was living with his nephew, **Charles C.**[9], in 1900 in Middlebury, VT.

Children:

i   **Claude Milton**[9] (minister) b 11-3-1861 at West Salisbury, VT, d 6-15-1939 in Jersey City, NJ, m1 Almona Gill, daughter of Edward Gill and Esther Young, on 7-12-1892 m2 to Minnehaha Schnabel 7-8-1901. Left no children. "He graduated at Middlebury College, class of 1883, taught school two years. In 1885 he went to Germany studied one year, accepted a professorship in Oahu College at Honolulu, graduated in 1890 from Yale Theological Seminary, was ordained at Newton, MA, and sailed for Japan under the auspeces of the A.B.C.F.M. He graduated at Cooper Institute, NY, taught two years in Oberlin, OH. In 1887 went as missionary for the A.B.C.F.M. They now take charge of the work at Tsu-Japan." [JFS] He was an author of several articles on Japanese subjects. He later settled in Brooklyn, New York. [Howard p195]

ii   **Wilburt Nathaniel**[9] b 8-18-1863 in Salisbury, VT. He prepared for College in Middlebury High School, Jeweler, Manchester, VT 1885-1887, with the New Haven, Connecticut Clock Co., 1887-1889. Jeweler, Atlantic City, NJ, 1889-1891 Bennington, VT 1892-1900. Settled in Burlington, VT. [Howard p197] The 1920

VT census shows him as a patient at the VT State Hospital.

818 iii **Carlton Spencer**[9] b 8-15-1867
    iv **Maude Emily**[9] b 11-28-1879 [VTVR]
819 v **Herbert Allen**[9] b 12-2-1873

Children of **Milton Leonard**[8] Severance and Ella Barkley Stewart
    vi **Milton Leonard**[9] b 12-13-1902, Burlington, VT. [VTVR] (from second marriage) [Carleton] **Milton**[8] (the father) would have been 71 years old. [DAR application for Milton Leonard Jr. 4-13-1892]

(469) Philo Spencer[8], (Samuel[7], Samuel[6], Ebenezer[5], Ebenezer[4], Ebenezer[3], John[2], John[1]), born in Middlebury, VT on 2-28-1840. He graduated from Middlebury College. He entered into the Civil War as a private, heavy artillery, battery B, 11th Regt., VT Vols., and was mustered out as Lieutenant. On 6-24-1865 he was discharged from the 1st Regt. as a 2nd Lieut. [Official Army Register Volunteer Force of the U.S. Army]. He married to Helen E. Atwood on 2-2-1867 and they settled as farmers dealing in registered sheep. [JFS p67] **Philo**[8] died 3-4-1897. [VTVR]
    The 1880 VT census shows **Emma**[9] and **Ernest**[9] as granchildren of **Samuel Smith**[7] Severance. Also living with them were **Philo S.**[8] age 40, and Helen age 34.

Children:
    i **Emma**[9] b 9-12-1871 (IGI) m Homer Baine 3-5-1890 He was 18 years old. [VTVR]
    ii **Ernest**[9] b 1-9-1880. He married to Emma Moore on 10-3-1906, age 26. [VTVR] The [1900 VTFC] shows **Ernest**[9] living with his mother, Helen E. Atwood, and a couple of other people in Middlebury, VT.

(470) Martin Egbert[8], (Samuel[7], Samuel[6], Ebenezer[5], Ebenezer[4], Ebenezer[3], John[2], John[1]), born in Middlebury, VT on 8-4-1843. He graduated from Middlebury College in 1870. He married Mattie Van Slyke on 11-26-1878. [WIVR] Mattie was born in December of 1849. [1900 WIFC] He was a teacher and surveyor in the west and later worked in trade in the Dakota's. They settled in Lisbon, ND.

He prepared for College in Oneida, NY, Middlebury and New Haven, VT. Surveyor in MN, 1871-1872. In mercantile business, MN 1873. Principal of Afton Academy, MN and River Falls Instituate, WI 1874-1877. Mercantile business, Fargo and Lisbon, ND, fifteen years. U.S. Deputy Surveyor, 1891-1893. City Engineer, Lisbon, thirteen years. [Howard p176]

He is recorded in Pierce Co. WI before settling in Dakota. The 1880 Dakota census shows him living in Fargo, Cass Co. In 1900 he was living with his family in Liston, Ransom Co. [NDFC]

Children:

	i	**Jennie**[9] probably d young as not listed in 1880.
	ii	**Florence M.**[9] b 1876 in MN, m Roy R. Johnson.
820	iii	**Edwin S.**[9] b 4- -1879 in MN
821	iv	**Leroy**[9] b 2- -1882 in ND

(471) William N.[8], (Augustus[7], Moses[6], Ebenezer[5], Ebenezer[4], Ebenezer[3], John[2], John[1]), born 2-21-1836 in VT. **William**[8] went with his father and settled in CO. This may the **William N.**[8] that shows in 1900 CA census with wife Matilda and children **Fred E.**[9] and **Alice**[9]. He is not on the 1920 CO census.

Children: [1900 CAFC]

	i	**Fred E.**[9] b 6- -1861 in CA. The 1920 CA census shows him living alone in PA Grove, Sanoma Co. CA.
	ii	**Alice**[9] b 12- -1876 in CA

(472) Edson J.[8], (Lyman[7], Moses[6], Ebenezer[5], Ebenezer[4], Ebenezer[3], John[2], John[1]), born in Painesville, OH on 3-17-1848. He married Mahala Kate Smith on 7-25-1869. She was born 7-25-1849, the daughter of Phineas and Hannah W. Smith of PA.

He learned the trade of a jeweler and he began a business in Moline, IL. Then he moved to Henry, IL and manufactured jewelry. During the Civil War he served in the 140th Regt. of IL Vol. Inf.

Apparently **Edson J.**[8] remarried because the [1900 ILFC] shows him with a wife, Hattie, born February of 1862 in IL and a daughter, **Martha**[9], who was born in April of 1900. It also shows two of his first children, **Victor**[9], and **Jonnie**[9], both born in IL.

Children of **Edson J.**[8] Severance and Mahala Kate Smith

   i   **Victor Lyman**[9] b 2-21-1870
   ii   **Emma Viola Jane**[9] b 6-17-1871
   iii   **Victoria Jennie C.**[9] b 8-17-1874, she m to Ernest Eugene Hannum (his second marriage) 9-3-1892 in Moline, IL. He was b 7-24-1856. [Hannum p474]
   iv   **Johnie Smith**[9] b 2-29-1876. He is shown living in Moline, Rock Island, IL. The [1900 ILFC] shows him living with his father, **Edson J.**[8] Severance.
   v   **Arthur Edson**[9] b 3-19-1878, he is shown on the 1900 KS census, living in Owl Creek, Woodson Co., as Nephew of Calvin W. Griffin. He was born in IL.

Child of **Edson J.**[8] Severance and Hattie _____
   vi   **Martha**[9] b 4- -1900

(473) Benton[8], (Ebenezer[7], Elijah[6], Abner[5], Ebenezer[4], Ebenezer[3], John[2], John[1]), born 3-14-1835 in Clinton Co. NY. He traveled around in his younger years. He spent three years and graduated from a Massachusetts Academy and then worked in machine shops and with his father in blacksmithing. In 1857, he went to Belgrade, MN and stayed for two years. In 1859 he went to Haughton Co. MI and three years later to Clinton Co. NY, where he stayed one year. After living about eighteen months in WI and two years more in the state of NY, he returned to Belgrade and worked in farming and blacksmithing. **Benton**[8] served as justice of the peace for eleven years and held the office of Town Clerk. He married Julia Hodgson on 2-17-1862. [Bryant p675]

Children:
822 i   **Charles A.**[9] b in December of 1861 in WI. The 1900 MN census shows **Charles A.**[9] in Belgrade, Nicollet Co. with his wife Mary, b 10- -1873 in MN and a son, **William J.**[9] b in June of 1895. His mother, Julia A. (Hodgson) Severance, b 9- -1835 in VT, was also living with them.
    ii   **Anna E.**[9]
823 iii **David J.**[9] b in October of 1866 in NY state. He shows on the 1900 MN census with his wife Camelia A. b 11- -1866 in

MN and a daughter, **Annie A.**[10] b 2- -1892
in MN.

(475) Willie L.[8], (James Edwin[7], Elijah[6], Abner[5],
Ebenezer[4], Ebenezer[3], John[2], John[1]), born 12-21-1861
in VT. The 1900 NY census shows that he married to
Lizzie ____, who was born in January of 1866 in NY
state. They settled in CT where his children were
born. The children show on the 1900 CT census as
well as **William's**[8] father **Edwin J.**[7] Severance who
was born in Gill, MA and later lived in Hague, NY.

Children: [1900 NYFC]
    i   **Maud E.**[9] b 5- -1888
    ii   **Madeline A.**[9] b 10- -1890
824 iii   **Ellsworth W.**[9] b 7- -1894 m Louise
          E.____. Shows on the 1920 CT census

(476) Scott Ellsworth[8], (James Edwin[7], Abner[5],
Ebenezer[4], Ebenezer[3], John[2], John[1]), was born 7-31-
1868 in Shoreham, VT, died 10-9-1936 in Granville,
NY, married Carrie Balcom 9-26-1886. [VTVR] Carrie,
daughter of Myron Balcolm and Lucina Ackerman, was
born 5-29-1866 in Hague, NY and died 6-23-1938 in
Granville, NY. It is believed that **Scott**[8] traveled
alone out west and as far as Alaska in his early
life but there is no data to support this. He was
employed by a paper mill in Ticonderoga, NY and
around 1890 moved to Graphite (West Hague) where he
was employed by Frank Hooper, who was
superintendent of the Graphite Mine, to design and
construct the 1891 "new mill". The original mill of
1888 was destroyed by fire. This "new mill" was
destroyed by fire in 1900 and **Scott**[8] was again
employed by Hooper to construct the 'modern mill".
After the mill closed in 1920 the family moved
first to North River, then North Creek and finally
to Granville, NY, a slate mining town.
    The Severance's were residents of Granville for
only a few years, but during that time they
operated a bakery shop in the Pember Opera House
Building, which they owned, as well as operating
the Opera House [MESS]
    E. Scott[11] Severance told some interesting
anecdotes about his great grandfather. **"Scott**[8] was
particularly fussy about the cleanliness of his
bakery shop and he never placed anything on sale
unless it was of the best and finest quality. One
day when a local woman entered the bakery shop
while Severance was in attendance, he watched the

woman as she walked about the store, going from
counter to counter, poking her fingers into the
fresh baked bread, warm donuts, and fancy cakes
displayed on the counters. His jaw snapped, his
eyes blazed with anger, trying hard to withhold his
comment. but after the woman made her rounds of the
counters containing freshly baked foods and
fingered about everything on the counters, she
inquired if these were fresh? Severance could no
longer retain his temper and in a gruff, loud voice
said, "What in Hell do you think we are running
here, an antique shop?". The would be customer
threw up her hands and ran out of the bakery shop
at breakneck speed."

    "**Scott E.**[8] was a tall, raw boned individual
whose word was as good as his bond. He had a walrus
mustache and preferred a tight fitting cap to a
hat. Carrie was a kindly, motherly woman who
everyone liked and respected." [MESS]

Children:
825	i	**Milton Balcom**[9] b 7-1-1887 m Anne Mallory, settled in Buffalo and Syracuse, NY
	ii	**Sadie Maria**[9] b 8-1-1888 in Shoreham, VT d 5-2-1981 m Tom Rider in 1920
826	iii	**Raymond Clarence**[9] b 5-10-1890 in Ticonderoga, NY d 5-1-1952 in Mechanicville, NY.
	iv	**Denzil**[9] d young at 4 years of age.
827	v	**Haswell Gordon**[9] b 1895 in Hague, NY d May of 1947 m Sarah "Sadie" Church on 7-4-1911.

(481) Edson S.[8], (Harris[7], Obed[6], Abner[5], Ebenezer[4],
Ebenezer[3], John[2], John[1]), born in October of 1864,
Irving, MA. [NHVR] He married Lila M. Morgan of
Irving, MA on 8-13-1893. [VTVR] She was born in
January of 1870. [1900 NHFC] They are shown on the
[NHVR] where their baby son was born on 10-1-1904
and died the same day at Manchester, NH. **Edson**[8] was
a farmer and miller.

Children:
	i	**Leta May**[9] b 1-11-1894 at Northfield, MA [MAVR]
	ii	**Otis R.**[9] b 9-28-1895 at Northfield, MA [MAVR]
	iii	**baby son** b 1904 d 1904 [NHVR]

(482) Elias James W.[8], (Paul S.[7], Robert M.[6], Thomas[5], John[5], John[3], John[2], John[1]), born 5-27-1839 in SC. He married to Ellisa Adeline Mims who was born circa 1844. He was a Confederate Soldier in the Civil War. [MWS]

Children:
828 i   **William Joseph**[9] b in September of 1861 m Mary Elizabeth Julia Gatlin

(483) Paul Elisha[8], (Paul S.[7], Robert M.[6], Thomas[5], John[4], John[3], John[2], John[1]), born 10-28-1847 in SC. He married first to Emily Elizabeth McKenzie Law. [MWS] The 1870 SC census shows his second wife as Angeline. He was a merchant in Leesville, Williamsburg Co. SC.

Children of **Paul Elisha**[8] and Angeline _____
    i   **Joseph**[9] b 1870. The 1870 SC census shows **Joseph Jr.**[9] born 3- -1871, married to Ottie who was born 11- -1880. They had daughters, **Angeline**[10] born 4- -1889 and **Mamie**[10] born 4- -1900 in SC.
829 ii   **Robert James**[9] b 12-6-1873
    iii   **Hester Irvin**[9] b 5-16-1878 m George James Brothers. He was b 7-6-1872 and d 3-21-1925 [MWS]
    iv   **Harriet Susannah**[9] b 6-22-1880 m John Wesley Floyd
    v   **Cecil Elizabeth**[9] b 10-17-1881
831 vi   **Martin Luther**[9] b 11-10-1885 m Maggie Atwood Whitaker
    vii   **Lena**[9] b 11-25-1885?? m _____ Parks
    viii   **Curtis**[9] b 10-31-1887 d 9-18-1888
    ix   **Willard Murry**[9] b 1-2-1891
    x   **Hattie Ruby**[9] b 9-10-1893 m James Edwards Stokes
    xi   **Paul**[9] b 6-18-1896 d 8-12-1977. The 1920 SC census shows him as a soldier at Camp Jackson.

This may indicate children of two families as there were two **Paul Elisha's**[8].

(484) Robert Elifers[8], (Paul S[7]. Robert M.[6], Thomas[5], John[4], John[3], John[2], John[1]), born 5-8-1849 in SC. He married to Margaret McKenzie who was born in 1860. [1880 SCFC] They Lived in Florence, Carlington Co. SC.

Children: [1880 SCFC]
    i   **Walter**[9] b 1868
    ii   **Thomas**[9] b 1869
836 iii   **William Elias**[9] b 9-7-1870

The 1870 SC census shows **Walter**[9] and **Thomas**[9] and yet
the **William**[10] Saverance Manuscript shows them with
only the son **William Elias**[9]. It is probable that
the first two boys died young.

(486) Thomas Glenn[8], (Robert M. Sr.[7], Paul S.[6],
Thomas[5], John[4], John[3], John[2], John[1]), born 7-24-1831
in SC. He married Martha Ham, daughter of Ferney
Ham. They lived in Darlington Co. SC. In 1862
Thomas[8] sold his farm to his brother, **Joseph**[8], when
he was drafted or enlisted into Co. C 3rd Palmetto
Battalion, SC Light Artillery. In March of 1862 he
was captured at Fort Gainey, AL during the battle
of Mobile Bay. On 8-8-1864 he was a prisoner of war
on Ship Island, MS where he died on 12-27-1864.
After the death of **Thomas Glen**[8], his father, **Robert
Murrell**[7] raised the two boys until they were 21
years old. [MWS]
    Martha remarried to a Blackwell. Her daughter
Elizabeth Bulah[9] was living with her during the
final settlement of the estate of **Joseph H.**[8]
Saverance in 1887. Martha died during the 1890's.
[MWS]

Children:
837 i   **Robert Calhoun**[9] b 11-4-1861 [1900 SCFC].
          [MWS]
    ii   **Elizabeth Bulah**[9]
838 iii   **Thomas Beauregard**[9] b 10-8-1864 m Ella
          Parnell

(487) Robert M. Jr.[8], (Robert Murrell[7], Paul S.[6],
Thomas[5], John[4], John[3], John[2], John[1]), born 1- -1836
he married to Sarah S. Commander. [MWS]

Children: [1860 SCFC]
    i   **Jason F.**[9] b 1859

(490) Joseph J.[8], (Samuel G.[7], Robert[6], Thomas[5],
John[4], John[3], John[2], John[1]), born 1840. He married to
Merab Abigail Dewitt who was born 3-5-1838 and died
12-14-1918. They lived in Mr. Pleasant, SC.

Children:
    i   **John C.**[9] b 2- -1861 d 1930

          ii   **Columbus Robert**[9] b 9-16-1863 d 1932
          iii   **Maggie**[9] b m John Clements

(494) Samuel Orton[8], (Cyrus[7], Matthew[6], Matthew[5],
Joseph[4], Joseph[3], John[2], John[1]), born in Leyden, MA
on 2-27-1818. [JFS p67] (An inquiry in [New England
Historic Genealogical Society] says born 8-7-1816)
and died on 12-27-1877, age 59 yrs and 10 months,
in Chili, NY. He married Susan Lewis on 9-12-1842.
She was born 8-28-1824.
     Samuel[8] and Susan settled in Scottsville, NY and
he was in the saddle and harness business for
several years. he later purchased a farm and became
a farmer. They were later recorded in Chili, NY.
They were also recorded at Wheatland, Montgomery
Co. NY.

Children: [JFS p68] [1860 NYFC]
842   i   **Horace Wells**[9] b 5-13-1844 m Eleanor
            Ballantine on 12-22-1869. She was b 7-
            28-1848 Scottsville, NY
843   ii   **Homer R.**[9] b 6-15-1846 m Jeanette D.
            Warren 2-6-1873, Scottsville, NY
      iii   **Mary Emma**[9] b 10-23-1850 d 11-27-1861
      iv   **Ella Maud**[9] b 8-24-1856 m John Y. Reed 3-
            26-1879

(495) Cyrus Wells[8], (Cyrus[7], Matthew[6], Matthew[5],
Joseph[4], Joseph[3], John[2], John[1]), born at New Haven,
NY on 8-11-1830. [BR] He married to Mary Hafner on
2-4-1867 [BR] in North Chili, NY. Mary was born 1-
12-1842 in Germany. She was a widow and had a son,
Frank, who later took the name of Severance. [JFS
p68] has only **George W.**[9] listed as their child.
     Sometime before 1890, this family moved to
Lawndale, IL, then in 1892 they moved to a farm
east of Hobart, Porter Co. IN. **Cyrus Wells**[8] died 1-
9-1907 (the DAR says 4-18-1892). Mary died 4-18-
1907. [BR-**George W.**[10] Severance Jr.] They are buried
in the Crown Hill Cemetery in Hobart. [Fieler]

Children:
844   i   **George W.**[9] b 1-15-1870 at North Chili,
            NY. He m to Agnes Jane Burns.

(496) Anthony Peck[8], (Cyrus[7], Matthew[6], Matthew[5],
Joseph[4], Joseph[3], John[2], John[1]), born in New Haven,
Oswego Co. NY on 10-8-1835. He was a farmer.

He married Frances Arabelle Rathburn on 3-13-1856. She was born on 1-18-1837 in New Haven, Oswego Co. NY. [Cooley p241]

Children: [Oakes Vol I p633-634]
845 i   **Fayette George**[9] b 1-4-1857, Parish, NY m Anna Bonnett 1-24-1876. Their children were, **Anna Maud**[10], **Cyrus William**[10], **Fayette Bonnett**[10], and **Edna Frances**[10]. He was pastor of the Methodist Church at Bemus Corners, Jefferson Co., NY. (1890)
846 ii **Charles Nicholas**[9], b 10-25-1858 in New Haven, NY m Gertrude A Calkins, daughter of Jesse W. and Lydia A. Calkins, 8-7-1884. Their children were **Gertrude Jean**[10] b 8-23-1886 and **Ruth**[10] b 1-1-1889. **Charles**[9] became a Congregational minister and located at Garden City, KS.
847 iii **Frank B.**[9] b 7-3-1860 at Trenton, NY m Charlotte Loretta Scott 8-4-1890. She d 5-1-1892. **Frank**[9] was a Methodist Clergyman and located at Frankfort, NY.
848 iv **Cyrus Job**[9] b 7-16-1863 m Hattie E. Davis 2-11-1883. He was a doctor
      v **Cynthia Electa**[9] b 10-22-1867 and became the wife of Edward E. Samuel of Remsen, NY.
     vi **Helen Lydia**[9] b 9-18-1875 and becames the wife of William Pritchard of Remsen.

(498) William Henry[8], (Cyrus[7], Matthew[6], Matthew[5], Joseph[4], Joseph[3], John[2], John[1]), born 9- -1840 m Nancy _____ who was born 2- -1846 in NY. [1900 MIFC] **William H.**[8] died 6-19-1909 [CWPR] They later settled in Thornapple, Barry Co. MI. [MISS]

Children:
      i **William A.**[9] b 7- -1875 in MI m Maude ___, who was b 10- -1875 in MI [1900 MIFC]

(499) William Sidney[8], (Chester[7], Matthew[6], Matthew[5], Joseph[4], Joseph[3], John[2], John[1]), born in Leyden, MA on 3-24-1829. **William**[8] became a Medical Doctor. He married Martha Elizabeth Lyman on 11-23-1853. [VTVR] Martha was born 10-17-1931, daughter of Thomas Lyman and Zama Johnson. [Coleman L p233] The marriage took place in VT. [Hemenway] They lived first in Shelburne Falls and later settled in Greenfield, MA.

Children: [JFS p68]
The [MAVR] indicated that Martha Elizabeth Lyman
married to **William *Chester*[8]** Severance. I think that
they errored and it should have been written as
William Sidney[8] Severance.

i   **William Lyman[9]** b 9-17-1858 at Shelburne,
     MA [MAVR]

ii   **Wilhelmina[9]** b 3-1-1866

850   iii   **Charles Dori[9]** b 12-18-1868 at
     Greenfield, MA [MAVR] m Henrietta E. and
     lived in Greenfield, MA. The 1920 MA
     census shows them with a son **Charles
     Sidney[10]** b 1915.

(500) Chester Wells[3], (Chester[7], Matthew[6], Matthew[5],
Joseph[4], Joseph[3], John[2], John[1]), born in Leyden, MA
on 2-27-1831. He married Catherine Matilda Wilkins,
daughter of Dr. Willard A. Wilkins, on 11-25-1857
at Leyden, MA. [MAVR] She was born 2-10-1840. They
remained and settled in Leyden. **Chester[8]** was a
farmer. He also taught school and served as school
commissioner and selectman for the town.

     Chester Wells[8] was an organizer of the Leyden,
MA Library. He was a musician of voice and violin.
He gave the Leyden Centennial Address, which
appeared in the *Franklin Gazette* [NSFG 8-14-1909
Philadelphia PA] [Arms p199-200]

     The family shows on the 1900 MA census and in
1920 **Chester S.[8]** (**W.**), age 88, was with Kate A.,
age 80, **Lillian E.[9]** age 59, and **Chester C.[9]** (**G.**) age
50. [MAFC]

Children:

i   **Kate Florabel[9]** b 10-17-1858 at Leyden,
     MA d 8-28-1878, single, at Leyden, MA.
     [MAVR]

ii   **Lillian Louise[9]** b 9-20-1860 at Leyden,
     MA [MAVR]

iii   **Willard Wilkens[9]** b 7-30-1862 at Leyden,
     MA [MAVR] m Harriette who was b 10- -
     1870 in NH

iv   **Etta May[9]** b 5-17-1865 at Leyden, MA
     [MAVR] m Allen Sylvester Newcomb, son of
     Charles W. Newcomb, 5-20-1886 at Leyden,
     MA. [MAVR][Newcomb p696]

v   **Ulysses Grant[9]** b 12-15-1867 at Leyden,
     MA d 3-10-1868 [MAVR]

vi   **Chester Gilbert[9]** b 9-29-1869 at Leyden,
     MA [MAVR] He shows on the [1900 MAFC]

with his parents and sister **Lillian L.**[9] Severance.
vii   **George Henry**[9] b 2-2-1873 at Leyden, MA [MAVR] d 1-21-1876 at Leyden, MA. [MAVR]

(501) Charles Earl[8], (Chester[7], Matthew[6], Matthew[5], Joseph[4], Joseph[3], John[2], John[1]), born 8-7-1833 in Leyden, MA [MAVR] He died 6-20-1907. [VTVR] He married Mary Ellen Wilson, daughter of Dr. Milo Wilson, on 5-14-1862 at Greenfield, MA. [MAVR] She was born 8-14-1840 at Fayettsville, VT died 11-19-1872 at Shelburne, MA. [MAVR] He married secondly to Mary Evelyn Sawyer on 6-17-1875. [VTVR] The [MAVR] shows that they married on 5-14-1875 at Shelburne, MA.

    Charles[8] studied medicine and graduated from the University of Vermont at Brattleboro, VT. He then settled at Shelburn Falls and practiced for several years. He was appointed surgeon of the 73rd Regt. of the New York Vol. Infantry. He was acting surgeon at Seamen's Retreat Hospital, and visiting surgeon of Eastern Dispensary, New York City. In 1886 he left Shelburn Falls and located in Newark, NJ. [Cabot Vol II p938-939]

Children of **Charles Earl**[8] Severance and Mary Ellen Wilson
i   **Earl Clarendon**[9] b 2-7-1864 at Shelburne, MA [MAVR] drowned 5-17-1877 at Shelburne, MA [MAVR]
ii   **Martha Helen**[9] b 10-12-1868 at Shelburne, MA [MAVR]

Children of **Charles Earl**[8] Severance and Mary Evelyn Sawyer
iii **Franklin Sawyer**[9] b 1-3-1880 d 4-18-1880. [MAVR]
iv   **Evelyn Kendall**[9] b 12-30-1881 at Shelburne [MAVR]
v   **Kendall Earl**[9] b 12- -1881. He lived MA, NJ, and VT. He later showed as a Rev. in Pyramid Lake, NV.

(503) Samuel Clesson[8], (Cephas C.[7], Matthew[6], Matthew[5], Joseph[4], Joseph[3], John[2], John[1]), born on 8-1-1836 in Leyden, MA. **Samuel**[8] was a farmer. He married to Angenette Dean on 12-10-1872 at Gill, MA. Angenette was born 6-11-1843. [MAVR]

Children:

	i	**Edith Leila**[9] b 11-26-1873 at Leyden, MA [MAVR]
	ii	**Leon Henry**[9] b 2-15-1875 at Leyden, MA [MAVR] The 1920 MA census shows him m to Mildred who was b in 1884 in MA
	iii	**Harriet Gertrude**[9] b 12-2-1876 at Leyden, MA [MAVR]. She had a daughter, **Hope**[10], b 12-25-1893 at Leyden, MA [MAVR]
853	iv	**Herman Waldo**[9] b 11-22-1881
	v	**Mildred E.**[9] b 2- -1883 [1900 MAFC]
	vi	**Guy Raymond**[9] b 11-2-1889 at Leyden, MA [MAVR] In 1920 **Guy R.**[9] was with his wife Flora F. born in VT age 38 and a stepson Verne A. Dean age 12 born in MA. [MAFC]

(504) Charles Francis[8], (Cephas C.[7], Matthew[6], Matthew[5], Joseph[4], Joseph[3], John[2], John[1]), born on 7-11-1848 in Leyden, MA. He married Ella S. Vining, daughter of Nancy J. Vining, on 11-24-1871 at Greenfield, MA. [MAVR] Ella was born 1-7-1852. They settled in Leyden. He was a farmer.

Children:
	i	**Gratia Ethel**[9] b 7-6-1874 at Shelburne, MA [MAVR]. She was an early promoter for the Leyden, MA Library, m _____ Campbell
	ii	**Frances Agnes**[9] b 5-26-1876 d 5-22-1892 age 15-11-26 at Leyden, MA [MAVR]

(505) Quantus[8], (Ebenezer[7], Zenas[6], Matthew[5], Joseph[4], Joseph[3], John[2], John[1]), was born 2-22-1812 in VT. [VTVR] He married to Diana Ducan on 9-19-1834. [VTVR] **Quantus**[8] died 3-22-1872. [VTVR] The 1860 VT census shows them living at St. Johnsbury, Caledonia Co.

Children: born in VT
	i	**Franklin**[9] b 1837 d 10-14-1857 [VTVR] of Thyphoid Fever.
	ii	**Henry V.**[9] b 1839 m Laura Strickney 6-4-1863. [VTVR] A pension was filed for by the invalid 6-22-1889 from VT and by the widow 7-29-1919 from CA for Service S.M. and 68 VT Inf. [CWPR]
	iii	**Osman**[9] b 1841 m Sarah Banfield 7-17-1864 He d 8-23-1881 ae 40-4-23 [VTVR]
	iv	**Eliza J.**[9] b 1846

(506) Chandler[8], (Ebenezer[7], Zenas[6], Matthew[5], Joseph[4], Joseph[3], John[2], John[1]), was born 4- -1833.

[1900 VTFC]. He married to Sophronia M. Chapman, of East St. Johnsbury, in April of 1857 [VTVR] She was born 2- -1840. **Chandler**[8] died 4-18-1907 age 73-11-18. [VTVR]

Children:
    i   **Carrie R.**[9] m Charles H. Olcott 2-1-1879 at Littleton, VT
    ii   **George I.**[9] b
    iii   **Charlie D.**[9]
    iv   **Nellie C.**[9]

(507) Joseph Wood[8], (Leonard[7], Zenas[6], Matthew[5], Joseph[4], Joseph[3], John[2], John[1]), was born on 1-21-1823. [JFS p70]
    He married Mary Angeline Atcherson, daughter of Thomas and Charlotte Atcherson, on 8-4-1846. [VTVR] She was born 10-30-1827 and died on 1-24-1899. [VTVR] They settled in Rockingham, VT. **Joseph**[8] died on 12-31-1895. [VTVR]

Children: [JFS]
    i   **Joseph W.**[9] b 1-12-1848
    ii   **Clariot P.**[9] b 11-20-1849

(509) Leonard S.[8], (Leonard[7], Zenas[6], Matthew[5], Joseph[4], Joseph[3], John[2], John[1]), born on 5-3-1832 in VT. He married Ophelia E. Geer on 1-1-1857. Ophelia was born on 11-24-1838 in CT. Her parents are unknown. The 1860 NH census shows them living in Manchester, 4th ward. **Leonard**[8] and Ophelia later settled in New Buda, IA. They show on the 1900 IA census with **Leonard**[8] age 68 and Ophelia age 62.

Children: [JFS 71]
    i   **Ida D.**[9] b 8-12-1858 m 4-9-1874

(510) Warren F.[8], (Leonard[7], Zenas[6], Matthew[5], Joseph[4], Joseph[3], John[2], John[1]), born on 12-2-1840. He was still living in 1900. He married Ancy C. Dutton on 8-20-1861. [VTVR] She was born 9-10-1841. They were recorded in Chester, Rockingham, and Saxton's River City, VT. [Stowell] In 1860 he was living with the George Wiley family in Charlestown, NH. **Warren's**[8] family shows on the 1880 VT census. [JFS p71]

Children:
    i   **Elsie C.**[9] b 9-4-1865 m Lewis O. McQuaid, son of Lewis O. and Olive Emeline

Stowall, b 1- -1868 m at Rockingham, VT
[Stowell]

ii   **Joseph W.**[9] b 6-24-1867 in VT. He married
to Mabel Henry, of IL, on 11-28-1901.
[VTVR] [Stowell]

iii   **William S.**[9] b 7-29-1869 m Laura E.
McQuaid b 11- -1873

857 iv   **Derrick Dutton**[9] b 4-13-1871 at
Rockingham, Windham, VT, m Olive M.
Cutler, daughter of Silas Cutler and
Maria Woodward. Olive was b in
Springfield, VT in 1867. They had two
children; **Miriam Elsie**[10] b 5-29-1901 and
Cutler Frost[10] b 7-10-1904. [VTVR]

v   **Leonard S.**[9] b 2-8-1873 d 9-3-1874

vi   **Lemira D.**[9] b 4-24-1875 m John Jacobs 9-
10-1902 [VTVR]

(511) Henry C.[8], (Charles C.[7], Consider[6], Matthew[5],
Joseph[4], Joseph[3], John[2], John[1]), born on 2-10-1852.
He married Ida Wilson on 5-6-1874. She was born 11-
25-1852. They settled in Springville, NY. [JFS p71]

Children:

858 i   **Charles C.**[9] b 4-28-1875. **Charles**[9] shows
on the 1880 NY census with his parents
Henry[8] and Ida and **Henry's**[8] father
Charles C. Sr.[7]

(512) George Craige[8], (George[7], Consider[6], Matthew[5],
Joseph[4], Joseph[3], John[2], John[1]), born on 6-4-1853. He
married Emma Alida Gilbert on 12-1-1875. She was
born 8-21-1853 in NY. They settled in Chazy, NY and
later in Asbury Park, NJ. [JFS p70]
The family shows on the 1880 NY and 1900 NJ
census. In 1900 his sister, **Elizabeth N.**[8] who was
born 8- -1842 in NY was living with them. [NYFC]

Children:

i   **Annie Douglas**[9] b 5-27-1877

859 ii   **Harold Craige**[9] b 7-1-1879

iii   **George Malcom**[9] b 8-5-1882

iv   **Helen**[9] b 12-1886[9] in PA

v   **Frederick**[5] b 1- -1892 in NY State. The
1920 NY census shows him living in NY
City with his wife Louise born 1892 and
Anna Douglas[9] Severance.

(513) Joseph Cordenio[3], (Ruel[7], Ruel[6], Matthew[5],
Joseph[4], Joseph[3], John[2], John[1]), born on 9-7-1841 in

305

Shelburn, MA. [MAVR] He married Eliza J. Dinsmore on 11-24-1861. They settled in Shelburn Centre on the old homestead farm. **Joseph**[8] was a farmer, producing good crops and raising fine animal stock. [JFS p70] This family shows on the 1880 MA census

Children:
  i   **Alice Maria**[9] b 5-3-1861 at Shelburne, MA [MAVR] m Taylor S. Trusdale, son of Gardner and Melissa Trusdale, 12-13-1886 at Shelburne, MA. [MAVR]
  ii   **Mary Electa**[9] b 5-23-1868 at Shelburne, MA [MAVR] m George A. Chesbro, son of Charles A. and Martha J. Chesbro, 8-29-1888 at Shelburne, MA. [MAVR]
860 iii **George Alvin**[9] b 7-22-1871 at Shelburne, MA [MAVR]
  iv   **Lucia Jane**[9] b 3-25-1874 at Shelburne, MA [MAVR] m Herbert J. Moore, son of James Moore and Elizabeth Thayer, in November 1893, at Shelburne, MA. [MAVR]
  v   **Joseph Ruel**[9] b 6-7-1880 d 4-4-1885, age 4 yrs 9 mons 27 dys, at Shelburne, MA. [MAVR]

(514) Henry Clay[8], (Curtis[7], Asaph[6], Matthew[5], Joseph[4], Joseph[3], John[2], John[1]), born on 2-27-1841 in MA. He married Emily E. Townsend on 10-28- 1863. She was born 12-25-1840. They settled in Chicago, IL.

Children: [JFS p71]
  i   **Frederic A.**[9] b 8-2-1864. He lived in IL

(515) George Emerson[8], (George W.[7], Asaph[6], Matthew[5], Joseph[4], Joseph[3], John[2], John[1]), was born in May of 1849 in MA. [1900 MOFC]. He married to Florence who was born in March of 1861 in PA. They lived in Kansas City, MO. [1900-1910 MOFC] **Emerson**[8] was called **George**[8].

Children:
  i   **Leslie**[9] b 8- -1892/10- -1896 in MA. There is a **Leslie T.**[9] born circa 1892 in Cambridge, MA and married to Emma B. Korman in Portland, ME. [MEVR] She was born circa 1895. [MEVR]
  ii   **Ray**[9] b 1- -1899 in MO
  iii   **Roy**[9] b 1- -1899 in MO

(516) Elmer D.[8], (Luther N.[7], Asaph[6], Matthew[5], Joseph[4], Joseph[3], John[2], John[1]), born on 5-12-1849 at Hinesburg, VT. [MAVR] and lived at Williamstown, Berkshire Co. MA. He married Alice Lester, daughter of Edward and Olive Lester, on 10-30-1879. Alice died 4-1-1886, age 30 dys 5 mons 23 dys at Montague, MA. [MAVR] They settled in Miller's Falls, MA. He married secondly to Mary Sophia Graves, daughter of Jotham Franklin Graves and Eliza A. Smith, on 1-4-1887 at South Hadley, MA. [MAVR] She was born 4-2-1859 and died 3-21-1936. **Elmer**[8] was a silver plater and died on 5-29-1932.

Children:
	i	**Ruth Lester**[9] b 2-16-1883 at Montague, MA [MAVR]
	ii	male b 2-10-1885 at Montague, MA [MAVR]
861	iii	**Robert Graves**[9] b 10-26-1891 at Montague, MA [MAVR] [SAR application of **Robert Graves**[9] Severance at Buffalo, NY, 8-19-1936, he was 44 years old]

(518) Asaph C.[8], (Luther N.[7], Asaph[6], Matthew[5], Joseph[4], Joseph[3], John[2], John[1]), was born 4-25-1855. He married to Grace E. Warner. She was born in December of 1869. They show on the 1900 MA census as **Asaph**[8] or **Asa C.**[8] Severance. He was a silver plater and born in Charlotte, VT. [MAVR]

Children:
	i	**Warner E.**[9] b 4-1-1894 at Montague, MA [MAVR]
	ii	**Mildred E.**[9] b 6- -1897

(519) Walter L.[8], (Luther N.[7], Asaph[6], Matthew[5], Joseph[4], Joseph[3], John[2], John[1]), born on 12-25-1857 at Charlotte, VT. [VTVR] He was a silver plater. He married Carrie Briggs, daughter of Colburn and Orra Briggs, on 11-3-1878. [MAVR] She died on 5-6-1885. He married secondly to Celia E. Briggs, daughter of Colburn and Orianna Briggs, 1-3-1887 at Montague, MA. Celia was born at Shutesbury. [MAVR] They settled in Williamstown, MA. They were recorded at Gill, Montague and Williamstown, MA and Charlotte, VT. [JFS p72]

Children of **Walter L.**[8] Severance and Carrie Briggs
	i	**Marion**[9] b 4-24-1879 at Montague, MA [MAVR]

ii   female child d 11-9-1883 at Montague,
        MA. [MAVR]
iii   **Carrie E.**[9] b 4-6-1885 at Montague, MA
        [MAVR] d 8-31-1885 age 4 mons, at
        Williamstown, MA. [MAVR]

Children of **Walter L.**[8] Severacne and Celia E.
Briggs
iv   **Walter M.**[9] b 6-14-1889 d 8-10-1893 age 4
        yrs at Montague, MA. [MAVR]
v   **Harold E.**[9] b 7-16-1891 at Montague, MA
        [MAVR][1900 MAFC]

(520) Frank E.[8], (Luther N.[7], Asaph[6], Matthew[5],
Joseph[4], Joseph[3], John[2], John[1]), born 12-7-1865 in VT
(MAVR says Williamstown, MA). He married Maria
O'Hara on 7-15-1888. [VTVR] The 1920 MA census
shows a **Frank E.**[8] Severance age 52, born 1867 in MA
and now living in Boston with his wife Marie and
daughter **Hazel L.**[9] age 27, all born in MA.

Children:
i   **Roy**[9] b 11- -1888 in MA
ii   **Hazel L.**[9] b 1/2-26-1891 at Montague, MA
        [MAVR]

(521) Oscar[8], (William Sidney[7], Jesse[6], Elihu[5],
Joseph[4] Joseph[3], John[2], John[1]), was born circa 1829
and married Janet, of Phelps and Buffalo, NY.
Oscar[8] was shown as a Tabacconist on the 1850 NY
census. He settled in St. Louis, MO circa 1910?

Children:
i   **Harriet**[9] b 1846
ii   **Frances**[9] b 1848 [1850 NYFC]

(522) William Dwight[8], (William Sidney[7], Jesse[6],
Elihu[5], Joseph[4], Joseph[3], John[2], John[1]), was born 5-
11-1836 in Phelps, Ontario Co. NY on the homestead
at Melvin Hill. He was educated in the union
schools and learned of his father's blacksmith
trade. In 1857, he left home and located at Terra
Haute, IN where he was a blacksmith. In 1862 he
returned to Phelps and went into farming, dealing
with horses, sheep, and cattle. He was a member of
the Methodist Episcopal Church and a Republican. He
married to Caroline A. Warner, daughter of Chester
Warner. She was born 10-10-1839. [HOCoNY] The
family shows on the 1880-1900 NY census.

Children: [HOCoNY]
    i   **Zella**[9] b 12-25-1859
865 ii   **Ralph**[9] b 2-27-1870 d 2-9-1899 m Augusta
              Hyna and had one child named **Marion**[10] b
              12- -189ī.

(523) Henry[8], (Albert G.[7], Jesse[6], Elihu[5], Joseph[4],
Joseph[3], John[2], John[1]), born in 1839 in Phelps, NY
[1860 NYFC]. He was listed as a carriage maker. He
married to Laura A. Strickny 6-4-1868. [VTVR] She
was born 3- -1851. The 1920 CA census shows Laura,
born in VT age 68, with **Perly B.**[9] age 39, born in
VT in Samardino, CA.

Children:
    i   **Lena A.**[8] b 11- -1872 in VT
   ii   **Perley V.**[8] b 9- -1881 in VT

(524) Charles[8], (Albert[7], Jesse[6], Elihu[5], Joseph[4],
Joseph[3], John[2], John[1]), born in 1842 in Phelps, NY.
[1860 NYFC]. The 1900 Phelps, Ontario Co. NY census
shows **Charles**[8] born 1841 with wife, Frances born
10- -1845 in NY.

Children:
    i   **Fred**[9] b 1- -1873. The 1920 NY census
            shows **Frederic C.**[9] b 1873 with his
            wife, Helen W. b 1877 in NY

(525) Jesse P.[8], (Albert[7], Jesse[6], Elihu[5], Joseph[4],
Joseph[3], John[2], John[1]), born in May of 1846 in
Phelps, NY. [1860 NYFC] He married Julia ___ who
was born in September of 1856. His sister **Minnie**[8]
(Severance) Edgecomb was living with them in 1900.
[NYFC].

Children: [1900 NYFC]
    i   **Ada**[9] b 8- -1883
   ii   **Grace**[9] b 3- -1890
  iii   **Helen**[9] b 8- -1891

(526) Edwin[8], (Benjamin Franklin[7], Elihu[6], Elihu[5],
Joseph[4], Joseph[3], John[2], John[1]), born in 1861 and
married to Clara Newman. **Edwin**[8] age 58, born 1862
in MI, was living in Beatrice, Gage County, NE with
his wife Mary, who was born 1861 in IA. [1920 NEFC]

Children: [MPV]
    i   **Clarence**[9]

(527) Charles W.[8], (Charles C.P.[7], David[6], Jesse[5], Joseph[4], Joseph[3], John[2], John[1]), born 10- -1851 in Sullivan, NY state, with his wife Allie born 12- - 1852 in NY state. [1900-1920 WAFC]

Children: [1900 WAFC]
    i   **Howard**[9] b 8- -1878 in NY state. The 1920 WA census shows him with his wife Ethel b 1883 in MA.
    ii   **Florence**[9] b 11- -1883 in NY state

(528) Samuel Jerome[8], (Charles C.P.[7], David[6], Jesse[5], Joseph[4], Joseph[3], John[2], John[1]), was born in May of 1858 in CA. The 1900 CA census shows **Samuel J.**[8] Severance in San Francisco with his wife, Lillian S. born 4- -1864 in CA and their children. The 1910 CA census shows the same **Samuel J.**[8] *Sevirmance* family living in San Anselmo, Marin Co. without the eldest son.

Children:[1900 CAFC]
866 i   **Frederick C.**[9] b 11- -1882. The 1920 CA census for Alameda, Alameda Co. shows **Fred C.**[9] with wife Kate E. age 35 b in CA and their children.
      ii   **Clarissa T.**[9] b 8- -1889
867 iii **Alfred D.**[9] b 5- -1893. [1920 CAFC San Francisco]
      iv   **Sible J.**[9] b 4- -1895

(529) Frederick V.[8] *Sevirance*, (Charles C.P.[7], David[6], Jesse[5], Joseph[4], Joseph[3], John[2], John[1]), born in February of 1863 in CA. The 1900 CA census shows him married to Lena ____, who was born 4- -1871 in NJ. **Frederick's**[8] mother, Sarah M., born 3- -1821 in NY state was living with them. The 1910 CA census shows **Fred**[8] living alone with no family in San Francisco. **Zella G.**[9], his daughter was living alone as a lodger.

Children:
    i   **Zella G.**[9] b 9- -1896 in CA

(530) Elmer Warren[8], (Warren[7], Elisha[6], Samuel[5], Martin[4], Joseph[3], John[2], John[1]), was born 8-16-1861 and died 9-24-1913 at Willard, Huron Co. OH. He married Hattie Eliza Young, daughter of James Lewis Young and Julia A. Warren. Hattie was born 11-25-1862 and died 5-11-1949. [Young p84] [OHVR] **Elmer**[8]

and Hattie settled near Chicago Junction, Huron Co.
OH. [1900 OHFC]

Children:
    i   **Florence J.**[9] b 5-11-1892 d 11-2-1892

(531) Arthur Leason[8], (Byron[7], Elisha[6], Samuel[5],
Martin[4], Joseph[3], John[2], John[1]), born 7-14-1860,
Peru, OH. He married to Mary E. West on 1-7-1885.
[OHVR]

    Arthur Leason[8] was born at what is known as the
Western Reserve District of OH. He received a good
education in the common schools of his native state
and at Oberlin College. He then lived at Wakeman,
OH for five years.

    After his marriage he moved from OH to Hope, AR
in 1888 where he worked in the lumber business for
about 12 years. In 1900, he moved to Durant
(Oklahoma) and organized the **A.L.**[8] Severance
Hardware Co. He was a director in the Durant
National Bank, a founder of the Durant Building and
Loan Association, a member of the first board of
directors, a member of the first school board,
played an important part in the building of the
Oklahoma Presbyterian College for girls and a
liberal contributor of that project, and a member
of the Woodmen of the World. [OKCR Vol 18 March
1940] The family shows on the 1900 AR and 1910 OK
census.

    He died in May 10, 1935. He was a member of the
Sons of the American Revolution. [DAR applied for
11-23-1918]

Children:
    i   **Alma**[9] d young
    ii   **Beulah**[9] d young
    iii   **Mary**[9] d young
    iv   **Marion**[9] b 10- -1897 in AR and later
          moved to OK with her parents. [DAR
          #163637]

(532) Ernest Elton[8], (Byron[7], Elisha[6], Samuel[5],
Martin[4], Joseph[3], John[2], John[1]), born 7-15-1868,
Peru, Greenfield Twp., Huron Co. OH. [OHVR] He
married to Helen E. Newcomb in 1891. [DAR #163635]
She was born 7- -1879. They lived in Chicago
Junction, OH. [1900 OHFC]

Children:
    i   **Gladys E.**[9] b 9- -1896 [1900 OHFC]

ii   **Harry Lu**[9] b 9-20-1900 at Chicago
       Junction, OH [DAR Family Records]

(533) Seth[8], (Joseph A.[7], Seth[6], David[5], John[4],
Joseph[3], John[2], John[1]), born 2-10-1851 in NY. He
married to Ella Steele, daughter of Edwin Steele
and Caroline Stewart, on 7-22-1875 in Manchester,
IA. She was born on 5-11-1852. The couple lived in
Deleware, Scott Co. IA. [JFS p72]

Children: [1900 IAFC]
869 i   **George W.**[9] b 2-6-1876 in IA. He shows on
            the 1920 SD census with wife, Nellie M.
            age 36 b in SD, and a son, **Wales A.**[10],
            age 3 4/12 b in SD.
     ii   **Eva**[9] b 4- -1878 in IA
     iii   **Jessie R.**[9] b 2-14-1880

(535) Lewis Eggleston[8], (Daniel Healey[7], Daniel
Arms[6], Daniel[5], John[4], Joseph[3], John[2], John[1]), born
11-27-1863 in IA. He married Mary E. Houghton on
12-5-1888. She ("Minne E.") was born in November of
1865. They lived in Davenport, Scott Co. IA. [Pope
III] The family shows on the 1920 IA census and her
mother, Frances Houghton, age 78 and born in
England, is living with them. In 1900 the family
was living with her parents, James R. and Frances
Houghton. [IAFC]

Children: born in IA
     i   **James H.**[9] b 1892
     ii   **Jeanette**[9] b 1894
     iii   **Frances**[9] b 1897
     iv   **John D.**[9] b 1898

(536) John[8], (James T.[7], Jonathan[6], Jonathan[5],
Jonathan[4], Joseph[3], John[2], John[1]), was born 8-9-1859
at Wiscoy, Allegheny Co. NY and died 9-16-1946 at
Concordia, Cloud Co. KS. Buried at Concordia, KS.
He married to Lovill Jane (Jennie) Markham,
daughter of Ransom Markham and Elizabeth Bundy of
Calendonia, NY, on 1-29-1885 at Hemlock Lake, NY.
     She was born 2-22-1862 at Caledonia, Livingston
Co. NY and died 9-21-1951. They settled in Belfast,
NY and later at Concordia, KS.
     The Severances of North Central KS are
descendents of **John**[8] and Jennie Severance of
Belfast, Allegany Co. NY. **John**[8], along with his
brothers, **Willard Lorenzo**[8] and **Martin Harrison**[8],
moved to Hutchinson, KS in 1895. Their mother,

Marion (Botsford) Severance, died 12-11-1893 and is buried in Belfast, NY. The father, **James Taggart**[7] Severance, later moved to KS. He died 10-20-1913 and is buried at Burrton, KS.

John[8], as a boy lived on a farm in the Genesee Valley in Western NY. He worked with his father, a contractor, on construction and maintenance work on the Genesee Valley Canal. He also worked in the oil fields of PA and on the construction of wooden bridges for the Pennsylvania Railroad. He moved, with his new wife and his brothers, to Hutchinson, KS in 1895. **John**[8], **Willard**[8], and **Martin**[8] operated the Queen City Meat Market. **John**[8] later left and accepted a position with the E.W. Biggs and Co., of Kansas City, MO where he was a dealer in hides and pelts. This position moved to Concordia, Kansas where he was employed until his retirement. [MHGS]

John[8] and Jennie show on the 1900 KS census with their children, **Elbert**[9], born in NY, **Robert J.**[9], born in KS and **Ella M.**[9], born in KS.

Children: [MHGS]
870   i   **Martin Elbert**[9] b 6-2-1893 in Belfast, NY.
871 ' ii   **Robert James**[9] b 11-17-1895 in Hutchinson, KS.
     iii   **Ella Marguerite**[9] b 1-14-1900 in Hutchinson, KS. After her education, which included the Pratts Business School of New York City during the 1920's, she worked for various businesses in Concordia. For almost 20 years she worked in the Cloud County Probate Judge's office. She m Fredrick A. Young on 10-3-1954. She was a member of the First Methodist Church of Concordia. **Ella**[9] d 12-10-1987. They had no children. [MHGS]

(537) Willard Lorenzo[8], (James T.[7], Jonathan[6], Jonathan[5], Jonathan[4], Joseph[3], John[2], John[1]), was born 9-1-1862 at Caneadea, Allegany Co. NY and died 2-26-1947 at Newton, Harvey Co. KS. He married to Mary Rosetta Shank on 12-24-1881 at Oramel, NY. She was born 2-13-1861 at Rushford, NY and died 11-1-1951 at Halstead, Harvery Co. KS. **Willard**[8] and Mary show on the 1920 KS census. The 1900 KS census also shows this family and **Willard's**[8] brother, **Martin**[8] age 24 was living with them. Both **Willard**[8] and Mary are buried at Burrton, KS.

313

Children:
i   **Elizabeth (Lizzie) Belle**[9] b 5-14-1883 at
Caneadea, Allegheny Co., NY, d 5-29-1972
at Halstead, Harvery Co. KS. She m to
Alton Russell Challender, who was b 2-
26-1879 at Neponset, Bureau County, IL
and d 12-17-1973 at Halstead. They had 2
children, Willard Alton Challender, and
Mary Maxine Challender.

(538) Martin Harrison[8], (James T.[7], Jonathan[6],
Jonathan[5], Jonathan[4], Joseph[3], John[2], John[1]), was
born 6-12-1895 at Caneadea, Alleheny Co. NY died on
1-22-1924 at Hutchinson, Reno Co. KS. He married
Allia Grover C.A. Allbright 11-2-1911 at
Kingfisher, OK. She was born 8-9-1885 at Round
Stone, KY died 6-1-1976 at Colorado Springs, CO.
[MHGS}
In 1920 the family was with their daughter
Virginia[9] and a niece, Ruth Runyon, age 18, born in
CO. [KSFC]

Children:
i   **Mary Catherine**[9] b 6-7-1914 at
Hutchinson, Reno Co. KS, d 6-10-1914
ii   **Virginia Lu Etta**[9] b 12-29-1915 at
Hutchinson, Reno Co. KS d 5-10-1982 at
Eads, CO. She m 9-28-1941 to James
Alfred Sollars at Sheridan Lake, CO.

(540) John Elbert[8], (John[7], Jonathan[6], Jonathan[5],
Jonathan[4], Joseph[3], John[2], John[1]), born 9-17-1869,
Hutchinson, KS. He married to Arminta ____. She was
born 11- -1874. [1900 KSFC]. Minta Severance, age
45 and born in MO, was living in Santa Monica with
sons **Wilbert**[9], **Joseph**[9], and **Arthur**[9]. [1920 CAFC] In
1920 this family shows with all the children.
[IDFC]

Children: [MHGS}
i   **Clara Belle**[9] b 7- -1899 in KS or MO
ii   **Fred**[9] b 1902 in KS [1920 IDFC].
iii   **Wilbert**[9] b 1904 in OK
iv   **Owen**[9] b 1906 in OK
v   **Joseph**[9] b 1908 in KS
vi   **Robert Arthur**[9] b 1912 in ID

(541) Charles Frederic Malcom[8], (George[7], Pliny[6],
Joseph[5], Jonathan[4], Joseph[3], John[2], John[1]), born 7-4-
1864 in IA. He most likely was told the story of

how his father, **George**[7], hauled lumber from
Dubuque, IA and built the first frame house in
Grundy Center, IA. He was living in Cedar Fall,
Black Hawk Co. with his wife Luela T. age 31 born
12- -1868 in IA and their daughter, **Mildred**[9] born
6- -1899 in IA. [1900 IAFC]

Children:
    i   **Mildred**[9] b June of 1899 in IA

(542) Frank B.[8], (Charles[7], Pliny[6], Joseph[5],
Jonathan[4], Joseph[3], John[2], John[1]), born circa 1886.
In 1920 he was age 34, born in IA, and living in
Grundy, Grundy Co. IA with his wife, Iris, age 27 b
OH. [IAFC]

Children:
    i   **Harold Judson**[9] b 1917 in Grundy, IA

(543) Ralph S.[8], (Frederick Hollister[7], Pliny[6],
Joseph[5], Jonathan[4], Joseph[3], John[2], John[1],) born 9- -
1882 in IA. In 1920 he was living in Merrick Co.
with his wife, Ella b 1884 in NE. [NEFC]

Children: born in NE [1920 NEFC]
    i   **Helen**[9] b 1906
    ii   **Ralph H.**[9] b 1909
    iii   **Donna P.**[9] b 1916
    iv   **Phil H.**[9] b 1918

(544) Solon Long[8], (Solomon Lewis[7], Robert Bruce[6],
Solomon[5], Jonathan[4], Joseph[3], John[2], John[1]), born 9-
8-1834 and married Emily C. Allen 10-10-1860.
[OHVR] She was born 6-9-1840, the daughter of Peter
Allen and Charity Dudley. They were found living in
Trumbull Co. OH. (Peter Allen was born in Norwich,
CT and served as a physician and surgeon in
Kinsman, OH for over 40 years)
  He was one of the pioneering families of Ohio.
After completing his schooling he started in the
banking business as an office boy. He used his
experience from several advancements and became one
of the organizers of the Euclid Avenue National
Bank, and president at the time of the Euclid Park
Bank, which later became merged with the First
National Bank of Cleveland. This made him the
director of the largest bank in Ohio. His
memberships included the Chamber of Commerce, the
Union Club, and a charter member of the Woodland

Avenue Presbyterian Church. [Coates Vol III p152-153]

In 1910, the children, **Allen**[9] and **Mary**[9], were still living at home. [OHFC]

Children: [JFS p72]
  i   **Julia Walworth**[9] b 11-23-1862 m 12-1-1891, Dr. Benjamin Millikin
  ii   **Allen Dudley**[9] b 3-12-1865. He became an educator and professor and held a chair in Western Reserve University.
  iii   **Mary Helen**[9] b 3-12-1865
  iv   **Paul Frame**[9] b 12-18-1871 d 7-27-1872

(545) Louis (Lewis) Henry[8], (Solomon Lewis[7], Robert Bruce[6], Solomon[5], Jonathan[4], Joseph[3], John[2], John[1]), was born 8-1-1838 [OHVR] and died 6-25-1913. He married Fannie Buckingham Benedict of Cleveland, OH, 8-13-1862. [OHVR] Fannie was born on 8-14-1839 and died in 1874. **Louis**[8] remarried to Florence Harkness, daughter of Stephen D. Harkness, in 1894. Florence died in 1895.

Solomon Lewis[7] Severance, the father, died about a month before **Louis Henry**[8] was born. The widowed mother returned with her small family to her father's home, where the boys grew to manhood. **Louis Henry**[8] attended Cleveland public schools and in his eighteenth year found employment in the Commercial National Bank.

Louis[8] served in the Union Army during the Civil War for 100 days. After the War he became envolved in oil production in Titusville, PA. In 1875 he became a major stockholder in the Standard Oil Company and served as first treasurer.

He spent most of retirement life in New York City, but he died in Cleveland. [Malone Vol XVI]

Children: [JFS p73]
872 i   **John Long**[9] b 5-8-1863 d 1-16-1936 m Elizabeth Huntington DeWitt 11-3-1891, Cleveland, OH, she d at Pasadena, CA on 1-25-1929.
873 ii   **Bessie Lill**[9], b 11-16-1865 d 1944 m1 Dr. Dudley P. Allen 1852-1915 m2 Francis F. Prentiss 1858-1937, she was benifactor to Severance Hall at Wellesley College, MA. She had been a student of Wellesley College from 1883 to 1886. She gave the largest individual donation for the completion of the Hall.

iii   **Annie Belle**[9] b 4-24-1868
iv   **Robert Bruce**[9] b 4-28-1872 d 7-29-1872

(547) Mark Sibley[8], (Theodore C.[7], Robert Bruce[6], Solomon[5], Jonathan[4], Joseph[3], John[2], John[1]), was born 10-28-1846 in OH. He married Anne Crittenden 11-1-1879. Anne was born 8-26-1859. They lived in Los Angeles, CA. The 1910 CA census shows **Mark**[8] living as a boarder of Albert S. Bilicke. The 1920 CA census shows him age 73 in Pasadena, CA with a daughter, **Marjorie S.**[9] (Severance) McPherson, wife of Walter S. McPherson, and their two children, Marjorie Ann age 5 b CA., and Harriet S. age 4 3/12 b CA., and his mother in law Adella Fulton age 55 born in Canada. **Marjorie**[9] was born in UT.

Apparently **Mark Sibley**[8] had married a second time as Adella Fulton was his mother in law.

Children:
i   **Hattie Ivison**[9] b 9-8-1884
ii   **Marjorie S.**[9] b 1887 [1920 CAFC]. She m to Walters S. McPherson. They had two daughters, Marjorie Ann and Harriet S. McPherson.

(548) Pierre Clarke.[8], (Theodore C.[7], Robert Bruce[6], Solomon[5], Jonathan[4], Joseph[3], John[2], John[1]), was born 9-16-1849 in Cleveland, OH. [MAVR] He died 4-20-1890 at Bourne Street, Boston, MA, age 40-8-4. [MAVR] **Pierre Clarke**[8] married to Isabel Morgan Rotch, daughter of William J. and Emily Morgan Rotch, 5-9-1883 at New Bedford, MA. [MAVR] She was born 5-30-1850. They lived in Boston and New Bedford, MA. He was in the glass trade. [Jones] Isabel M. is shown as a widow of **Pierre C.**[8] in the New Bedford, City Directories in 1896. **Pierre**[8] is buried in the Oak Grove Cemetery at New Bedford, MA.

Children:
i   **Emily Morgan Rotch**[9] b 10-11-1884 at Boston, MA [MAVR] m Lawrence Grinnell, son of Frederick Grinnell and Mary B. Page, 10-3-1907. Lawrence was b 6-18-1885 and graduated from Harvard College in 1908. [Emery]
874 ii   **William Rotch**[9] b 10-17-1886 at Boston, MA [MAVR] m Susan Williams Grinnell 2-18-1911. Settled in San Bernardino, CA.

(549) Oliver Cathestes.[8], (Otis C.[7], Otis[6], Solomon[5], Jonathan[4], Joseph[3], John[2], John[1]), was born 10-24-1842 in MN. He married on 2-18-1863 to Mary Harding who was born 2-18-1843 and died 2-22-1864. He married secondly to Sarah C. Bell on 3-16-1865. They settled in Clifford, PA. The census says that Sarah C. was born in February of 1847 in PA. [PAFC]

Children: [1900 PAFC]
	i	**Arthur**[9] b 3-9-1864
875	ii	**Lyman Cathestes**[9] b 11-9-1866
	iii	**Kirk Eugene**[9] b 11-29-1869
	iv	**Eleanor May**[9] b 10-28-1877
	v	**Martin Oliver**[9] b 12-28-1880 d 9-19-1881

(550) Otis Cordenio[8], (Otis C.[7], Otis[6], Solomon[5], Jonathan[4], Joseph[3], John[2], John[1]), was born 10-25-1845 and married Carrie Celestia Wetherby 3-17-1867. She was born 4-21-1848. They lived in Lenox, PA. The 1900 PA census shows a grand daughter, **Cora L.**[10] born 9- -1894 living with them.

Children: [1900 PAFC]
| 876 | i | **Burton Cordenio**[9] b 2-8-1870 |
| | ii | **Addie Alverna**[9] b 1-11-1880 |

(551) Eugene Kincaid[8], (Otis C.[7], Otis[6], Solomon[5], Jonathan[4], Joseph[3], John[2], John[1]), was born 3-31-1848 and married Sarah Ann Miller 12-15-1869. They settled in Lenox, PA

Child:
| i | **Ella May**[9] b 8-18-1871 |

(552) Oscar Alphonso.[8], (Otis C.[7], Otis[6], Solomon[5], Jonathan[4], Joseph[3], John[2], John[1]), was born 5-24-1854 in MN. He married Matilda Bennett 7-3-1874. She was born in 1858 in PA. They settled in Lenoxville, PA. **Oscar**[8] does not show on the 1900 PA census and perhaps he had died before that time.

Children:
877	i	**Worden Oscar**[9] b 12-1-1875. He was most likely later called **Ward O.**[9] b 1876
	ii	**Viola Emeline**[9] b 7-21-1877 d 11-25-1879
	iii	**Walter Henry**[9] b 8-15-1880 d 9-27-1884
	iv	**Charles H.**[9] b 10- -1884 in PA [1900 PAFC]
	v	**Burnice M.**[9] b 11- -1891 in PA

(553) Cordenio Arnold[8], (Erasmus C.[7], Otis[6], Solomon[5], Jonathan[4], Joseph[3], John[2], John[1]), was born 6-30-1862 at Mantorville, Dodge Co. MN. He married Mary Frances Harriman, daughter of Gen. Samuel Harriman and Fidelia Holbrook Fawning, of WI, on 6-26-1889. General Samuel Harriman was a prominent veteran of the Civil War. She died on 3-6-1894. They settled in Mantorville, out side of St. Paul, MN.

Cordenio Arnold[8] was born at Mantorville, Dodge Co. MN 6-30-1862. He attended the public and high schools in that village. After attending Carleton College at Northfield, he studied law with Hon. Robert Taylor, of Kasson, MN, and was admitted to the bar in 1882. He entered the office of Senator Davis in St Paul in 1885 and in January of 1887 he became his partner. The firm of Davis, Kellogg and Severance was formed the first of October, 1887. [Flandrau Vol I p410-411]

Cedarhurst, the stately mansion or country estate of Mr. and Mrs. **Cordenio[8]** Severance is listed in the National Register of Historic Sites. The original part of the house was built about 1860 by Mrs. Severance's maternal grandfather, Charles O. Fanning. In 1888 the house was remodeled and in 1917 a ballroom wing was added.

When Mr. Kellogg became a U.S. Senator in 1916, **Cordenio[8]** offered his country estate as a meeting place of high governmental officials. House guests included Presidents Theodore Roosevelt, William Taft, and Warren B. Harding. Queen Marie of Romania was also a guest. It has been said that it was in this house that the historic Kellogg-Briand Peace Pact of 1928 was drafted.

Child:

  i   **Alexandria[9]** b 1894 d 1895, initially Mary Harriman Severance "Class of 1885" provided a few hundred dollars in memory of her little daughter **Alexandria[9]** for beds of flowers. In 1906 she and her husband, **Cordenio A.[8]** decided to expand the planting within the quadrangle and gave ten thousand dollars to endow the quadrangle at Wellesley College, in Wellesley, Massachusetts.

(554) Cassell[8], (Franklin C.[7], Ptolemy Philadelphus[6], Elihu[5], Jonathan[4], Joseph[3], John[2],

John[1]), born 3-18-1869 in KY. His parents were from NH and later MD. He married Jessie L. Lewis. **Cassell**[8] and Jessie show on the 1900 MD census which says that **Cassell**[8] was b in KY. **Cassell**[8] is shows on the 1910 CA census in Los Angeles with his wife Jessie L. Lewis and children, **Vance L.**[9] and **Cassell Jr.**[9], all b in Washington, D.C. Jessie was born in MD in January of 1872. [1900 MDFC] In 1920 Jessie L. was living with her mother Delle Lewis of NY and Jessie's son **Cassell**[9] age 19 and **Hattie S.**[9] Severance age 18 born in MO listed as a daughter in law. [CAFC Los Angeles]

Children:
- i **Vance L.**[9] b in March of 1899 in Washington, D.C. He shows on the 1920 CA census as a son in law of Minnie Moore and living in Los Angeles, CA. No one else was living with them.
- ii **Cassell**[9] b 1901 in Washington, D.C.

(557) Walter I.[8], (Charles W.[7], George W.[6], Rufus[5], Jonathan[4], Joseph[3], John[2], John[1]), was born in January of 1875 in IL. In 1900 he was living in Waterman with his wife Josephine F. who was age 25, born in March of 1875 in IA. [IAFC]

Children:
- i **Merl L.**[9] b March of 1900 in IA

(558) Elmer[8], (Charles W.[7], George W.[6], Rufus[5], Jonathan[4], Joseph[3], John[2], John[1]), born 11- -1877 in IL. [1900 IAFC]. He married to Helen. [1920 MNFC]

Children:
- i **Roy**[9] b 1914 in IA
- ii **Bernice**[9] b 1916 in SD
- iii **Louisa**[9] b 1918 in SD

(559) Robert W.[8], (Charles W.[7], George W.[6], Rufus[5], Jonathan[4], Joseph[3], John[2], John[1]), was born in Iroqouis, IL on 7-10-1880. He later settled in IA. He married to Eleanor Irene Trask on 9-30-1920 at Pipestone, MN. It was her second marriage. She was born 3-8-1892 at Renwick, IA. **Robert W.**[8] died 1-23-1947 at Eagle Grow, IA. He is buried at Waterman Cemetery, Sutherland, IA. [Trask]

Children: [1920 MNFC Pipestone Co]
- i **Cecil**[9] (son) b 1914 in IA

          ii   **Marion**[9] b 1919 in MN

(561) Calvin L.[8], (Joseph[7], James[6], unconnected) was
b circa 1832. [NYFC] In 1850 he was living with his
father, **Joseph**[7], who was born in MA circa 1788-
1791. [1850 NYFC] He served under Orang. Newtons
Co., F. enrolled 10-15-1861 at Potsdam, during the
Civil War. He married to Martha Nichols. She was b
circa 1831. [1860 NYFC] They lived at Stockholm,
St. Laurence Co. NY. [NYFC]

Children:
    i   **Marion**[9] b 1858
    ii   **Charles**[9] b 1859 [1860-1880 Stockholm,
           St. Lawrence Co. NY]
    iii   **George Elmer**[9] Severance b 1862 m Mary
           Jane Weegar, daughter of William and
           Sarah Poorback Weegar, on 12-25-1893 at
           Canton. [NYVR] George and Mary had their
           first child, a daughter, 8-21-1891 at
           Canton, NY [NYVR]
    iv   **William**[9] b 1876, (the 1920 NY census
           shows **William**[9] with out a wife but
           children, **Luella**[9] b 1908, **Lewis**[9] b 1911,
           and **Leona**[9] b 1914, at Cranberry Lake,
           St. Lawrence Co.) and **Charles'**[9] wife
           Matilda and their daughter, **Marrian**[10] b
           1880, all b in NY.

(561) Charles H.[8], (Zacheus[7], Phillip[6], James[5],
James[4], unconnected) was born circa 1836. He was
listed as a son of **Zacheus**[7] when he enrolled on 9-
9-1861 at Canton, NY for service in the Civil War
under William B. Goodrich's Co A. He was later
living in Kent, MI as indicated in his brother's
Will and Testament.
    In 1870 **Charles**[8], his wife, Verleda, and a
daughter **Ellie**[9] b 1869 were living with the Lucian
Ellsworth family. [NYFC Pierpont] His sister,
Louisa[8] had married Edward Ellsworth.

Children: conjecture
878 i   **Charles**[9] b circa 1859 m Matilda Ladison
     ii   **Ellie**[9] b circa 1869

(564) Andrew G.[8], (Zacheus[7], Phillip[6], James[5],
James[4], unconnected) was born circa 1851. He lived
in Pierrepont, NY and later in Hastings, MI. In
1900 he was living in Hastings, Barry Co. MI with
his wife Mary and their children. [MIFC]

Children: [1900 MIFC]
    i   **Gershom E.**[9] b 1880 in NY. In 1920 he was
            living in Royal Oak, Oakland Co, with
            his wife, Della E. age 38 and b in MI.
            [MIFC]
    ii   **Lizzie**[9] b 4- -1883 in NY
    iii   **Jerry**[9] b 9- -1884 in MI
    iv   **Leo**[9] b 6- -1886 in MI
    v   **Rosie**[9] b 9- -1888 in MI
    vi   **William**[9] b 10- -1892 in MI

(595) Jacob H.[8], (James[7], Phillip[6], Phillip[5],
unconnected) was born 2-26-1843 at Hollis, ME.
[MEVR] He married first to Sarah C. Smith at
Dayton, ME on 9-24-1866. [MEVR] He married secondly
to Elizabeth C. Holden at Biddeford, ME on 3-31-
1875. [IGI] Elizabeth was born in August of 1849.
Jacob[8] died 10-6-1915 at Hollis. [MEVR]

(595a) William D.[8], (James[7], Phillip Jr.[6], Phillip
Sr.[5], unconnected) was born in October of 1843 at
Hollis, ME. He married first to Sarah A. (Clay)
Maddox, daughter of Jonathan Clay and Jane Young of
Standish, Cumberland, ME, on 1-22-1871. She was
born 4-18-1835 and died 3-18-1917 at Hollis. He
reportedly married second to Lucinda. He died on 1-
22-1871 at Hollis.

Children: [MEVR]
    i   **Matilda**[9] b 1872
    ii   **Ellie**[9] b 1874

(595b) Charles H.[8] (James Sr.[7], Phillip Jr.[6],
Phillip Sr.[5], unconnected) was born 1847/48 at
Hollis, ME. He married to Rebecca W. Bean on 6-9-
1867. She died in March 1870 of child birth. He
married secondly to Olive A. Chase on 11-1-1874.
She was born in 1848.

Children:
    i   **Anna**[9] b 1875
    ii   **Charles C.**[9] b circa 1879 at Saco,
            York Co. ME. He married to Hattie Jones,
            daughter of Laura E., of Danvers, Essex
            Co. MA. **Charles C.**[9], died on 2-2-1899 at
            Watertown, ME. Children of **Charles C.**[9]
            Severance and Hattie Jones included **Otis
            C.**[10] b 10-6-1897 at Sanford, ME. [MEVR]

(595c) James Jr.[8], (James Sr.[7], Phillip Jr.[6], Phillip Sr.[5], unconnected) born in March of 1853 at Hollis, ME, son of **James[7]** and Nancy A. Hodgdon. **James Jr.[8]** married first to Jane Parks. He married secondly to Lucy Irvins on 2-16-1888 and third to Dell Lambert, daughter of Lewis and Delvine Lambert, on 8-23-1891 at Lowell, MA. [MAVR] Dell was born in December of 1857. The 1880 ME census shows **James Sr.**, and Mary (Nancy) with **James Jr.**, and two of **James Sr.'s**[7] grand children, **Billings E.**[9] b 1876 and **John A.**[9] b 1878, living in Hollis, ME.

Children: [MEVR]
- i **Billings E.**[9] b 1876 at Hollis, ME m Flora Chamberlin, 6-27-1896. [MAVR] He d circa 1896 at Lowell, MA. [MAVR]
- ii **John A.**[9] b 5- -1875 [1900 MAFC]
- iii **Jennie M.**[9] b 5-15-1892 at Lowell, MA [MAVR]
- iv **Della**[9] b 5-5-1894 at Amesbury, MA [MAVR]
- v **James L.**[9] b 9-14-1895
- vi **Joseph L.**[9] b 1-21-1897

(596) John Henry[8], (William Darling[7], Phillip Jr.[6], Phillip Sr.[5], unconnected) born 3-14-1856 at Hollis, ME. [MEVR] He married Annie Guilford, daughter of Ellison and Hannah Guilford on 12-18-1873. [IGI] She was born in 1856 and died on 2-5-1886 at Hollis. He died in 1934. [MEVR]
Elsie L.[9] b 1- -1883 and **Greenleaf**[9] b 1- -1886 are living with **William**[8] and Arvilda as grandchildren in 1900. [MEFC]

Children: born at Hollis, ME.
- i **Sarah Elizabeth**[9] b 4-26-1875
- ii **Ethel Estelle**[9] b 9-26-1877
- iii **Ethel Estelle**[9] b 11-26-1878
- iv **Hannah Alberta**[9] b 7-2-1880
- v **Elsie Aline**[9] b 6-4-1882 m to William S. Dow 3-28-1902. He was an overseer of dyeing in the Old Town Woolen Co. [Dow]
- vi **Greenleaf Frank**[9] b 12-10-1885 at Hollis. He m to Margaret Theresa (Maloney) Arey on 6-20-1917 at Rockport, ME. She was born in 1893. [MEVR] It was her second marriage. She m first at age 21 years and then m **Greenleaf**[9] at 24 years old. **Greenleaf Frank**[9] had children, **Lloyd Francis**[10] b 5-22-1919, **Lowell**[10] b 1919, Anna **Guilford**[10] b 10-19-1920, **Ida Belle**[10]

b 3-26-1922, Wesley D. b 1914 (may have been Margaret's son from a previous marriage.

(601) Walter H.[8], (Eben F.[7], Joseph[6], unconnected) was born 5-6-1868 [CRME] He married to Calista B. Brady/Boody, daughter of Edmund T. Brady/Boody and Lucinda Emery, on 8-29-1893. [MEVR] She died 5-26-1914. [CRME] They were found living at Limerick and Limington, York Co. ME. He died 4-30-1920. [CRME] She was b on 10-10-1859 at Limington, ME and d on 5-26-1914 at Portland, aged 54 yrs 7 mons 16 days. [MEVR] **Walter**[9] d on 4-30-1920 at Limerick.

Children:
    i   **Belle G.**[9]

(603b) Waldron[8], (David[7], Ebenezer[6], unconnected, Ebenezer[3], Ephraim[2], John[1]), born 12-28-1815 in Jefferson Co. NY. He married to Elizabeth Forman on 2-18-1839. **Waldron**[8] d 4-7-1902 at Millcreek, OH. The [1880 Williams Co. OHFC] shows **Waldron**[8] with his wife, Elizabeth and a son **Jessie**[9] b 1866. Their son **David**[9] b 1856 and his wife, Sarah, were living next door. He moved with his family to Williams Co. OH when he was young. Elizabeth Forman, was the daughter of Sarah Sloat Forman Griffin. Elizabeth was born circa 1820 and died in 1899. They are buried in Olive Branch Cemetery, Millcreek, OH.

Children: [MLM]
	i	**John K.**[9] b 1840 d 7-24-1907. Burried in Olive Branch Cemetery.
904	ii	**William Henry**[9] b 10-16-1841 in Crawford Co. OH. He m to Rosannah Rhoades on 6-9-1867 and d 7-24-1907 at Millcreek.
	iii	**Adelia Caroline**[9] b 8-25-1843 d 6-27-1885 at Millcreek.
	iv	**Sarah E.**[9] b 10-25-1845 d 10-7-1865
	v	**Annice A.**[9] b 1848 d 1908
905	vi	**James**[9] b 10-1-1850 m Lydia J. Esterline
	vii	**Phebe E.**[9] b 1-18-1852 d 9-24-1887
906	viii	**David W.**[9] b 2-4-1855 m Sarah I Bachman. He d 4-27-1940 at Olvordton, OH. They are buried at Olive Branch Cemetery.
	ix	**Luther U.**[9] b 5-14-1856 d 6-5-1862
	x	**George E.**[9] b 1858 d 1860/1870

(603c) Alfred[8] (David[7], Ebenezer[6], unconnected, Ebenezer[3], Ephraim[2], John[1]), He married to Gertrude (Beilharz) Stucker on 4-7-1853. He died in Williams Co. on 2-28-1897. They had a son **George**[9] born 1855 and died 1929 near Waldron, Michigan. **George**[9] married Lealine Ebaugh. Their son, **Earl Ernest**[10] Severence was born 10-11-1887 near Waldron, MI, and married Amber Mary Van Arsdalen 1-30-1912 at Wauseon, OH

(604) Elisha F.[8] *Sevrens*, (James[7], Isaac[6], Joseph[5], Benjamin[4], Ephraim[3], Ephraim[2], John[1]), born 9-23-1831 in Canada. [Eastman] The WI vital records Vol 1 p440 says that he was born 9-23-1825 in NH. He married to Helen ____, who was born 2- -1843 in NY. [1900 WIFC] Although they were from Canada, they later settled in VT and then onto Ashland, (Lemouirier) Langlade Co. WI where they lived. [1870 WIFC Juneau Co.] They were married in April of 1847. In 1920 **Henry**[10] Sevrens, age 40 born 10- - 1875 in WI, (their son) was living in Antigo, Langlade Co. with Emma Severance age 62 born in VT as his mother, and **Elisha**[8] *Sevrens* age 93 born in VT as his grandfather. [WIFC]

Children:
- i **Eunice**[9] b 1-28-1858 [VTVR]
- ii **Emma**[9] b 1- -1859 in WI
- iii **George Franklin**[9] b 9-28-1860 d 9-25-1861 [WIVR]
- iv **Ella**[9] b 1867 in WI
- v **William**[9] b ? m Emma b 1858. The WIVR show **Henry G.**[10] (son of **William**[9]) b 10-27-1883 d 6-15-1935 ae 57-7-17. **Henry**[10] m to Nora, daughter of Herman Kaven. She was b 6-4-1884 and d 5-18-1977 ae 79. [WIVR Vol 8 p620] They were living in Antigo, Langlade Co. WI.

(605) Frank G.[8], (Elias J.[7], Isaac[6], Joseph[5], Benjamin[4], Ephraim[3], Ephraim[2], John[1]), b 8- -1840/42 at Newport, NH m Bertha E. Rackliff 7-20-1868. **Frank**[8] was a carpenter.

Children:
- i **Claud F.**[9] b 1-28-1873 d 10-24-1888 at Gloucester, MA [MAVR]
- ii **Estella Bertha**[9] b 2-25-1876 at Gloucester, MA [MAVR]

iii   **Margie T.**[9] b 8-6-1884 at Gloucester, MA
        [MAVR]
iv   **Hugh**[9] b 1-2-1886 d 3-10-1886 at
        Gloucester, MA [MAVR]

(606) Henry Franklin[8] *Severens*, (Franklin[7], Isaac[6],
Joseph[5], Benjamin[4], Ephraim[3], Ephraim[2], John[1]), was
born 5-11-1835 in Middlebury, VT. He settled in
Kalamazo, MI where he served as Judge. He married
first to Rhoda Ranney on 8-6-1858. He married to
Carrie Ryan* on 12-1-1863. She was born on 10-3-
1838 and died in 1925.

He prepared for College in Saxtons River
Seminary and Chester Academy, entered 1854. He was
principal, Bellevue, IA 1857-1858, Saxtons River,
VT 1858-1859, admitted to the bar 1859, Lawyer,
Centerville, MI 1860-1865, Kalamazoo 1865-1886.
State's Attorney for St. Joseph Co. 1862-1865,
United States Judge, Western District of MI 1886-
1900, and United States Circuit Judge, Sixth
Judical Circuit, 1900. [Howard p150]

*Sarah Clarissa Whittlesey, daughter of Austin
Whittlesey was born 10-3-1838 at Cayuga, NY. She
married first to Charles Ryan, who was born 5-3-
1836 and died 8-27-1860 at Medina, NY. They had two
children, John Austin Ryan and Kate Lee Ryan. Sarah
(Carrie) married secondly to **Henry Franklin**[8]
Sevrens who was U.S. Judge of the Western District
of MI, Kalamazoo, MI. He d in 1910 and she in 1925.
[Whittelsey p381]

Children of **Henry F.**[8] Severens and Rhoda Ranney
    i   **Franklin Grant**[9], apparently died young
            [Howard p150]

Children of **Henry F.**[8] *Severens* and Carrie Ryan
    ii   **Mabel**[9] b 11-19-1868 at Kalamazoo, MI m
            James Bird Balch 9-7-1897. They had a
            son named Severens Balch.
    iii   **Carrie**[9] b 10-22-1872 at Kalamazoo, MI

(607) Charles Weaver Pulsipher[8] *Severens*,
(Franklin[7], Isaac[6], Joseph[5], Benjamin[4], Ephraim[3],
Ephraim[2], John[1]), born in Rockingham, VT in March of
1837. He married to Harriet Ann McQuaide on 11-28-
1860. [VTVR] She was born 11-21-1838 and died 6-9-
1911. **Charles**[8] died on 10-16-1876 in VT. [VTVR]
[Weaver] He was a farmer at Rockingham, VT.

Children: [Lovell p735]

907   i   **Martin Ellsworth**[9] b 8-12-1861 d 6-19-1923 ml Dora A. Woolley (1883) of Grafton, VT, (1 child) m2 Abbie Susan Davis 12-24-1889 of Athens, VT (5 children)

       ii   **Ida May**[9] b 1-14-1863 d 5-30-1925 ml Cyrus Buss m2 Charles Kellam

908   iii **Jefferson F.**[9] b 10-26-1864 d 3-27-1899 m Elizabeth Walsh

(608) James M.[8] *Severens*, (Franklin[7], Isaac[6], Joseph[5], Benjamin[4], Ephraim[3], Ephraim[2], John[1]), was born 8-25-1839 in Derby, VT.

James[8] moved to IL when he was about 16. In 1863 and 1864 he was in the Law Office of his brother, **Henry F.**[8] who became a Judge of the U.S. Court of Appeals for MI, OH, KY and TN, residing at Kalamazoo, MI. **James**[8] attended the Law Department of the University of MI in 1865. He was graduated in 1867, and at once admitted to the MI Bar. He married to Mary Ann Billings in 1868. She was born in 1846 in PA. That same year he came to MN, and lived in Rice and Waseca Co. until 1871, when he moved to Montevideo. He worked in the nursery business.

He served as auditor, being elected to 6 consecutive terms. He also served as cashier in the Citizens State Bank and the Bellingham State Bank. He was the village recorder and in 1896 he was elected Judge of Probate for at least 3 terms. He also served as postmaster of Montevideo from 1872 to 1882. **James**[8] belonged to the Independent Order of Odd Fellows and was a member of the Knights of Pythias. [BMN p397-398]

Children: [1870-1880 MNFC]
       i   **Jessie M.**[9] b 1869
       ii   **J. Frank**[9] b 1871 in MN. The 1900 MN census shows him living in Adrian, Nobles Co. with his wife Mollie who was born 1- -1876 in WI.
909   iii **Charles H.**[9] b 1873
910   iv   **George M.**[9] b 1875
       v   **J. Fred**[9] b 1879
       vi   **Roy L.**[9] b circa 1881

(609) Seymour B[8]. *Severens*, (Franklin[7], Isaac[6], Joseph[5], Benjamin[4], Ephraim[3], Ephraim[2], John[1]), born 7-26-1851. He married first to Augustus Morse in 11-28-1878. [VTVR] This is recorded in Springfield,

VT. Apparently **Seymour**[8] remarried as he is indicated with his wife, Jennie L. *Severens*. [1900 MIFC] They lived in Clyde, Allegan County, MI.

Children:
  i   **Elva**[9]

(610) Oliver P.[8] *Sevrens*, (Uriel[7], David[6], Joseph[5], Benjamin[4], Ephraim[3], Ephraim[2], John[1]), was born 8- - 1858 at Woburn, MA. [1900 NHFC] [MWGS] He married first to Alice M. Fisk, daughter of John and Judith Fisk, on 11-26-1885 at Woburn. [MAVR] She died on 3-28-1887 at Woburn, MA, age 26-7-20. [MAVR] He married secondly to Phebe C. Foote, daughter of Henry and Mary J. Foote of Newfoundland, 1-7-1891 at Woburn, MA. [MAVR] Phebe was born in New Foundland. Oliver was a butcher. He married third to Annie G. Waite who was born in 1868 in Mansfield, CT. [NHVR marriage of their son]

Children of **Oliver**[8] *Sevrens* and Alice M. Fisk [Notes from an unpublished, A New England Legend, by Arlene Wendell Dewey and C. Mina Wendell Ertelt, 1985, a family history]
  i   **Oliver F.**[9] b 3-16-1887 at Woburn, MA [MAVR]

Children of **Oliver**[8] *Sevrens* and Phebe C. Foote
  ii   **Marion Irene**[9] b 7-31-1893 at Woburn, MA, daughter of Oliver and Phebe C. Foote. [MAVR]
  iii   **Linton Garfield**[9] b 6-10-1895 at Worburn, MA [MAVR]

Children of **Oliver**[9] Sevrens and Annie G. Waite
  iv   **Guy Eugene**[9] b 1896 m Ellen Cora Carey, daughter of Caleb Carey and Nancy Black of Wendall, MA, on 9-21-1921. Ellen was b in 1901. [NHVR] **Guy**[9] and Ellen were from Richmond, NH. [NHVR]

(611) William P[8]. *Sevrens*, (Uriel[7], David[6], Joseph[5], Benjamin[4], Ephraim[3], Ephraim[2], John[1]), was born 12-6-1863. He was a resident of Woburn, MA. He married Alva Ward, daughter of Charles and Sarah Ward, 2-24-1884 at Woburn, MA. [MAVR] She was born in September of 1864 according to the census records.

He was the great grandfather of **William G.**[11] Sevrens who gave the following reflections on his family. **"William P.**[8] was very close to his grandson, **Palmer Earl**[10], and much of what he taught **Palmer**[10] was passed on to **William**[11], **Palmer's**[10] son. **William P.**[8] worked for the Boston and Maine Railway and was instrumental in operating the famous "Ski Trains". These were special week-end trains that traveled through town to the ski trails of New Hampshire. My father, his friends and sisters used to board the box cars and head for the trails, **William P.**[8] conducting. He would often have several rows of saftey pins and shoe laces stuck to the inside of his parka. "You never know when some one may need one." He would procure old snowshoes and ski equipment from the local Salvation Army, fix them up and loan them to needy skiers. He was known as Old Man Ski Train. he was a gentle sort. **Palmer Earl**[10] tells that, when angry, he would 'blow a wind storm through his mustache' and declare 'no good will come of that. **William P.**[8] probably should have lived longer than his 75th years as his father was 93 and his son was 98.

However, he developed complications after gallbladder surgery and died. For reasons unknown **William**[8] was the only one of his eight siblings who did not become Seventh Day Adventist. [MWGS]

Children: [1900 MAFC]
    i   **Palmer W.**[9] b 10- -1884 in MA
    ii   **Charles V.**[9] b 5-6-1886 d 5-6-1886 at
           Woburn, MA. [MAVR]
911 iii   **Clinton Earle**[9] b 8-2-1889 at Woburn, MA
           [MAVR] d 10-4-1987 m Helen Poole who d
           in November of 1986. They were married
           for 74 years. [*Daily Times Chronicle*,
           Woburn, MA, 10-5-1987]
912 iv   **Chester S.**[9] b 11- -1891 in MA
    v   **Lorrimer R.**[9] b 6- -1897 in MA

(612) William[8], (Jonathan Thompson[7], David[6], Joseph[5], Benjamin[4], Ephraim[3], Ephraim[2], John[1]), born on 10-19-1845 at Grafton, NH. [NHVR] He died on 3-18-1906. [NHVR] He married to Emily Amanda Peaslee, daughter of Daniel H. Peaslee and Emily A. Churchill, 10-20-1869 at Grantham, Sullivan Co. NH. She was born 12-13-1849 at Monmouth, ME and died 1-27-1917 at Grafton, aged 67 yrs 2 mon-8 days. [NHVR] **William**[8] was a teamster and he was married at the time of his death. [NHVR] This family was listed on the 1880 NH census with two sons. There may have been other children.

Children:
        a male child b 9-19-1870 at Newport, NH
    i   **John N.**[9] b 1871
913 ii **George W.**[9] b 1874 m Annie E. Graham 4-4-1897

(614) Nathan[8], (Jonathan Thompson[7], David[6], Joseph[5], Benjamin[4], Ephraim[3], Ephraim[2], John[1]), was born in Danbury, NH in September of 1850, son of Jonathan T. Severance and Julie Caswell. [VTVR] **Nathan**[8] of Danbury, NH married to Martha A. Braley on 11-19-1876. [IGI] They lived in MA for a period of time. He married secondly to Eliza S. Griffith, daughter of Jonathan P. Griffith and Semantha S. Russell, on 3-3-1892 in Manchester, VT. **Nathan**[8] was 41 yrs old. [VTVR] Eliza was born in June of 1852. **Nathan**[8] died on 3-22-1900. [VTVR]

(615) George[8], (Jonathan Thompson[7], David[6], Joseph[5], Benjamin[4], Ephriam[3], Ephraim[2], John[1]), born in October of 1855 in Grafton, NH. [NHVR] He married to Anna M. Bean on 3-30-1884. She was born in April of 1860. [1900 NHFC] **George**[8] died in Andover on 8-6-1901 [Eastman] **George**[8] is shown living in Wilmot, Andover, and Hillsboro, NH.
    Anna M. married a second time to Fred E. Putney. [1910 NHFC] Anna had one son with Fred Putney.

Children:
914 i   **Leon O.**[9] b 2- -1885 m Florence M. Sanborn in Andover on 8-19-1895 [Eastman]
    ii   **Clifford L.**[9] b 8- -1887 d 9-10-1887. [Eastman p334]
    iii   **Maud (Manda) E.**[9] b 8- -1889 m Leon M. Mills, son of Fred W. Mills and Isabella M. Brown, 11-27-1910.
    iv   **Edith L.**[9] b 8- -1891
    v   **Florence E.**[9] b 1- -1893, m Gardner W. Hazen, son of Charles W. Hazen and Alice M. Young 6-30-1916 at Andover, NH.
    vi   **John B.** b 1901

(616) Frank P.[8] **(Clyde Henry**[8]), (Jonathan Thompson[7], David[6], Joseph[5], Benjamin[4], Ephraim[3], Ephraim[2], John[1]), born 5-18-1858 and died 4-13-1912. He married to Marion (Mary S.) Wheeler, 11-24-1890. [IGI] She was born 10- -1878. [1900 NHFC] **Franklin**

P.[8] resided in Grafton and Manchester, NH. He was a fireman [NHVR]

The census for Dunbarton, Merrimack Co. NH show **Franklin P.**[8] Severans, age 52, (b 1858) 1st marriage living with brother in law Charles N. Blackman. [1910 NHFC] That would make **E.**[8] (Severance) Blackman (wife of Charles) a sister of **Franklin P.**[8]. **E.**[8], (Severans) Blackman was married first to a Severans and had children, **David C.**[9] b 1892, **Henry C.**[9] b 1894, and **William W.**[9] b 1896. It appears that **Clyde Henry**[8] died young and his wife remarried to Charles N. Blackman.

A letter in possession from **Henry Clyde's**[9] son says that his father, **Clyde Henry**[8], and his brothers, were born on a farm in Danbury, NH. **Henry Clyde**[9], who was the youngest, moved to Concord, NH. The oldest was named **David**[9] who settled in Lowell, MA, and the third was **William**[9]."

Children: [1900 NHFC]
i   **David C.**[9] b 1- -1893, lived in Manchester, NH. [1900 NHFC] **David**[9] supposedly settled in Lowell, MA.

ii   **Henry Clyde**[9] b 1894 Danbury, NH and settled in Concord, NH. He m1 to Luella E. Powell, of Concord, 11-19-1922. The [NHVR] shows a stillborn 9-1-1922, son of **Henry C.**[9], and Luella E. Powell. They were divorced on 6-28-1929. [NHVR] m2 to Alice M. Rothwell of Concord, NH, daughter of George E. Rothwell and Zella Tyler, on 1-15-1930. [NHVR] Alice was b circa 1910 in Concord. At the time of Henry's m2 he was a truck driver. He was living in Concord in 1920 as a laborer of Warren J. Shine. [1920 NHFC]

iii   **William W.**[9] b 9- -1896, he was living with a Blackman family on the [1910 NHFC]. He settled in West Fairlie, VT. In 1920 he was living in Orange Co. VT with his wife Marietta who was born in 1898 in VT and their son **William H.**[10] Severance was born in 1916. [1920 VTFC]

(617) Joseph C.[8], (Willard C.[7], Joseph[6], Joseph[5], Benjamin[4], Ephraim[3], Ephraim[2], John[1]), born 1-2-1855 at Toronto, Ontario, Canada [NHVR] died 10-26-1928 at Springfield, NH. [NHVR] It appears that he married first to Mary Bedsome. They show with a son **Joseph**[9], born 3-23-1870 at Springfield, MA. He was a carpenter and born in Canada. [MAVR] He married secondly to Lucy J. Hardy 11-25-1875. She was born in 1854. Lucy was the daughter of Hiram Warren Hardy and Elcy Tucket, born in 1854. [Hardy] This Hardy family first lived in Pepperell, MA, then Springfield, NH. In 1870 they went to Guelph, Ontario, Canada, and then to Uxbridge, Ontario in 1874. I mention this only to correspond with the fact that **Joseph C.**[8] is recorded as being born in Ontario, Canada but afterward of Springfield, NH. [NHVR] He was a farmer.

This family was living with Sophia Colby in 1880. [NHFC] The 1910 NH census shows **Joseph C.**[8] and Lucy J. with their son **Henry S.**[9] and his family. **Joseph C.**[8] died on 10-26-1928 [NHVR]

Children:

i   **Clara S.**[9] b 1877

915   ii   **Willard William**[9] (his name was recorded as **William Warren**[9] on the death certificate for Blance. [NHVR 6-7-1923] was b circa 1879, probably at Grantham, NH. He m1 Blanche Emma Tenney, daughter of Kirk Tenney and Emma Heath, 10-19-1901. Blance d on 6-7-1923. [NHVR] **Willard**[9] was a mail carrier and stage driver. [NHVR] Blance was b 8-20-1883 d 2-26-1924. **Willard**[9] m2 Angie B. Beyer (Grace) 8-20-1927. They were divorced in Union, ME. [MEVR]

iii   **Abbie M.**[9] b 1882 m Henry E. Young, son of George D. Young and Nellie T. Horton, 10-22-1902. [NHVR Springfield]

916   iv   **Henry S.**[9] b 7- -1886. He m to Amelia M. and had at least one daughter, **Bessie C.**[9] b 1910. [1910 NHFC]

(619) John[8], (John[7], John[6], Joseph[5], Benjamin[4], Ephraim[3], Ephraim[2], John[1]), born 7- -1843. He married to Arabelle M., who was born 11- -1849 in New York. [1900 WIFC] He was born in Andover, NH. [Eastman p453] After leaving NH, he settled in Medford and then Waupaca, WI. **John**[8] was in the Civil War and filed for pension on 5-24-1886 for service A & H Wis. Cav. [CWPR]

Children:

i   **William**[9] b 1870 in WI [1880 WIFC]
He apparently d young as the 1900 WI
census only shows **John**[8] and Arabella
with their grandchildren, **Melvin**[10] b 12-
-1892, **Holly**[10] b 9- -1894, and **Clara**[10] b
9- -1896 all in WI.

(620) Joseph Clinton[8], (John[7], John[6], Joseph[5],
Benjamin[4], Ephraim[3], Ephraim[2], John[1]), born 11-2-1845
in Andover, NH [Eastman p453] and died 9-21-1920
Eagle River, Vilas Co. WI. [WIVR] The records show
that he married first to Elizabeth Wall on 4-11-
1869 and married secondly to Anna McRea McCullon,
daughter of William and Flora McCullon of Thersen,
Quebec, Canada, 5-1-1896. [WIVR] The 1870-1880 WI
census shows **Joseph**[3] with his wife Elizabeth and a
daughter, **Burnice**[9] born 1870 from his first
marriage. The 1900-1920 WI census shows **Joseph**[8]
living alone. He lived first in Amherst, Waupaca
Co. WI and then in Eagle River. **Joseph**[9] was a
farmer.

(621) Edward[8], (John[7], John[6], Joseph[5], Benjamin[4],
Ephraim[3], Ephraim[2], John[1]), was born in December of
1850. He married Ella Ray. [VTVR] Ella was born in
December of 1855 in VT.

Children:
i   **Ray (Sydney)**[9] b 10-31-1883 [VTVR]
ii   **Ethel**[9] b 6-18-1885 [VTVR]
iii   **Ella**[9] b 9- -1891 [1900 VTFC]
iv   **Marion L.**[9] b 8-14-1898 [VTVR]

(621a) Albert M.[8], (John[7], John[6], Joseph[5], Benjamin[4],
Ephraim[3], Ephraim[2], John[1]), was born 4- -1855 in WI.
He later settled in NE where he is found on the
1900 NE census with his wife Winifred M., born 9- -
1864 in IA.

Children: [1920 NEFC]
i   **Mary E.**[9] b 5- -1889 in IA
ii   **Effa K.**[9] b 6- -1891 in IA
iii   **John L.**[9] b 3- -1894 in NE
iv   **Paul W.**[9] b 10- -1898 in NE. **Paul W.**[9], age
21 b in NE shows living in Mackell,
Dixon Cc.in 1920 as a boarder. [NEFC]
v   **Maud**[9] b 1902 in NE
vi   **Sylvia**[9] b 1909 in NE

(622) Alonzo Miner[8] *Sevrens*, (Newell[7], John[6], Joseph[5], Benjamin[4], Ephraim[3], Ephraim[2], John[1]), was born in Lowell, MA on 1-2-1848. [MAVR] He later settled in Green Lake, WI. The 1860-1880 WI census indicates that he married Emma ___ who was born in 1852.

Children:
i   **Henrietta**[9] b in ME, shows with her parents. [1860 WIFC]
918   ii   **Percy E.**[9] b 1875, shows on the 1920 SD census with wife Cora M and children **Fred E.**[9] and **Earl L.**[9] *Sevrens*.
iii   **Young**[9] (female) b 1876
919   iv   **Ernest**[9] b 8- -1878 in WI, m to Jessie who was b 10- -1878 in NY
v   **Eugene H.**[9] b 7- -1880 in WI, shows living with his brother **Ernest**[9] [1900 SDFC]

(623) Harvey[8] **(Lester)**, (William[7], James[6], Peter[5], Benjamin[4], Ephraim[3], Ephraim[2], John[1]). **Harvey**[8] shot himself on 1-14-1917. His wife Hortensia M. Smith was born 5-26-1856 and died 9-10-1916. She was the daughter of Daniel D. Smith and Sarah Ballou of Londonderry, NH.

Children:
i   **William Bernard**[9] (Hubbard) b 1882 at Auburn, NH. [NHVR] He m to May Gertrude Adams, daughter of James B. Benson and Sarah Fox, on 7-1-1914 **William**[9] was a master plumber. [NHVR]

(624) John L.[8], (James H.[7], James[6], Peter[5], Benjamin[4], Ephraim[3], Ephraim[2], John[1]), born in July of 1858 at Lawrence, MA. He married to Grace Butler, who was born in February of 1871. [1900 MAFC] **John**[9] died 5-3-1937 ae 78-10-3. [CRMA Bellevue Cemetery, Lawrence]

Children:
i   **Malcolm B.**[9] b 8-26-1891 at Lawrence, MA [MAVR]
ii   **James Echard**[9] b 10-28-1892 at Haverhill, MA d 9-26-1898 ae 5-11-0 at Lawrence, MA
iii   **Malcolm B.**[9] b 4- -1898 in MA, d 4-15-1902 ae 7 months 20 days. [MAVR]
iv   **John L.**[9] b 1905
v   **Frances**[9] d 2-26-1907 ae 1 month 27 days

vi   **Margorie**[9] b 1914 in MA
There were most likely other children

(625) Henry E.[8], (John Dow[7], Rufus[6], Peter[5], Benjamin[4], Ephraim[3], Ephraim[2], John[1]), born circa 1857 at Cabot, VT. He settled in Orange, Orange Co. VT. [1880 VTFC] **Henry**[8] married to Clara Morse on 2-24-1875. [VTVR]

Children:
   i   **Max Elwin**[9] b 12-18-1877 at Marshfield, VT. [VTVR] He only shows on the [1880 VTFC]
   ii   **Maebelle**[9] b 1881 in VT, m Eugene Dutton 2- -1908 [VTVR]
   iii   **Pansy Maud**[9] b circa 1881 in VT, m to William Jones 9-25-1907, she was 26. [VTVR]

(627) Freddie G.[8], (Leonard H.[7], John[6], Peter[5], Benjamin[4], Ephraim[3], Ephraim[2], John[1]), born in Hooksett or Hillsboro, NH in September of 1876. [1900-1920 NHFC] He married to Myrtilla E. Gile on 3-11-1903 [NHVR] She was born in 1875. [NHFC] Myrtilla married as her second husband, **Fred G.**[8] Severance. The listed children were by her marriage to **Fred**[8].

Children:
       baby (**Fred D.**[9]) b 4-28-1904 d 5-1-1904 [NHVR]
   i   **Charles L.**[9] b 1906 at Manchester, NH. He married to Marguerite E. Palmer, daughter of Mr. Palmer and Mabel Crockett. Marguerite died 3-20-1926 at the age of 18. [NHVR]
920 ii   **John W.**[9] b 1907
   iii   **Ellen S.**[9] b 1908
   iv   **Nancy B.**[9] b 1909
   v   **William W.**[9] b circa 1911 at Hooksett, NH m Virginia M. Davis, daughter of Charles F. Davis and Edna Cotten, of Pittsfield, NH on 12-2-1934 at Hooksett, NH. [NHVR] He was the son of **Fred G.**[8] Severance and Mytilla E. Gale of Londonderry, NH. Virginia was born in Tewksbury, MA circa 1904.
   vi   **Esther May**[9] b 3-13-1912 d 3-1-1913 of measles. [NHVR]
   vii **Dean R.**[9] b 1915

(628) Ambrose W.[8], (Warren[7], Reuben[6], Caleb[5], Joseph[4], Ephraim[3], Ephraim[2], John[1]), was born 8-15-1840 in Orrington, ME, the son of **Warren**[7] and Margaret Lunt. [MEVR] He married to Ella Tewsbury on 9-10-1892. [IGI] **Ambrose**[8] died on 3-16-1914 in Bangor, ME. [MEVR] **Ambrose**[8] served in the Civil War as the [CWPR] indicate. He filed for pension on 7-9-1890 and his widow filed on 3-25-1914 for service in D 2 Battn 17 U.S. Inf. from ME.

Children:
    i   **Jessie**[9] b 1879 in ME

(629) Washington Bainbridge[8], (Warren[7], Reuben[6], Caleb[5], Joseph[4], Ephraim[3], Ephraim[2], John[1]), was born 6-19-1843 in ME. He died 9-24-1917. [MEVR] He married Ida May Page who was born 11- -1856 in ME.

Child:
    i   **Virginia**[9] b 12- -1888

(630) William H.[8], (Reuben[7], Reuben[6], Caleb[5], Joseph[4], Ephraim[3], Ephraim[2], John[1]), born 6-30-1839 at Orrington, ME and died on 10-14-1917. [MEVR] He lived in Orrington and Bangor, ME. He married to Sarah E. (Beal) Pike, daughter of Matthew W. Beal and Elizabeth A. Perry, who was born 6- -1842 and died 2-23-1908 from Hingham, MA. [MAVR] He also married to Emily J. Thurlo at Woodstock, ME. [MEVR] He married Eva M. Bickford on 1-17-1911 (he was 71 years old and she was 30 years). The 1910 ME census shows **William**[8] living with an adopted daughter.

Children of **William H.**[8] Severance and Sarah _____
    i   **Ella F.**[9] d 8-25-1891 and was buried in
         Mt. Hope Cemetery, Bangor, ME.

Children of **William H.**[8] Severance and Eva M. Bickford
    ii   **Gladis**[9] b 5-10-1913 at Bangor, ME

(631) Walter F.[8], (Reuben[7], Reuben[6], Caleb[5], Joseph[4], Ephraim[3], Ephraim[2], John[1]), born in 1841 although the census says 1845. He died on 3-29-1906 at the age of 65 years. He is buried at Mr. Hope Cemetery, Bangor, ME. He lived at Old Town and Bangor, ME. **Walter F.**[8] Severance married to Nettie/Ellen A. Dennis on 11-28-1872 at Passadumkeag, ME. [MEVR] Miss Dennis died on 8-28-1880. [CRME] The 1900 ME census shows him as the husband of Louisa D.

Godfrey whom he married 1-20-1887. [MEVR] She was
born 3- -1840. He filed for his Civil War Pension
6-30-1889 and his widow filed 5-16-1906 for service
A 1 ME Cav. [CWPR]

Children:
   i   **Ernest Walter**[9] b 6- -1873 m Lena Ellen
       O'Niel on 7-8-1903. Both of them were b
       at Passadumkeag, ME. [MEVR]

(632) Evander O.[8], (Reuben[7], Reuben[6], Caleb[5],
Joseph[4], Ephraim[3], Ephraim[2], John[1]), was born 6- -
1863 in Old Town, ME. He married to Etta M. Watson
on 11-27-1888. [IGI] She was born 7- -1866. [1900
MEFC]

Children:
   i   **Howard Laurence**[9] b 6- -1890 [1900 MEFC]
       He m to Gertrude Arvilla Poaler on 6-7-
       1912. [MEVR] She was b in 1892. Their
       children included **Irene Laura**[10] b 4-19-
       1913 at Milo, ME [MEVR] **Laurence Pooler**[10]
       b 11-24-1916 at Old Town. He was a
       fireman and m Ruth as his second wife.
   ii female[3] b 1-19-1901 2nd child [MEVR]

(636) William Henry[8], (Russell Howard[7], Caleb[6],
Joshua[5], Joseph[4], Ephraim[3], Ephraim[2], John[1]), born 1-
12-1857 in Bangor, ME (NHVR) died 5-15-1933 at
Brentwood, NH. [NHVR] His father and mother were
also born in ME before him. He married first to
Lizzie Meade 8-8-1883 at Lynn, MA. [MAVR] He was a
butcher. She died in Brentwood, NH at the age of 74
years, 4 months, and 3 days. [NHVR] He married
secondly to Bessie (Eaton) Chase on 9-22-1926, the
second marriage for both. Bessie was the daughter
of Emery G. Eaton and Martha E. Morse of Hampstead,
NH. [NHVR]
   William Henry[8] Severance of Lynn, MA, who
represented the 12th Essex District in the State
Legislature of 1897 started life with the early
loss of his father in the Cival War and a mother
who was broken with grief. Before he was 11 years
old, he attended the district schools of Bradford,
ME. He worked his way and attended school only part
of the day. This took him to Cambridge, MA. In 1880
he went to Lynn and opened a meat and provision
market on Pratt Street. In 1895, He started a
steamboat express business between Lynn and Boston.
[MFES] **William H.**[8] was buried in Lynn, MA. [MAVR]

Children:
 i   **Alice Amidon**[9] b 4-12-1884 at Lynn, MA d
        7-14-1896 at Lynn. [MAVR]
 ii   **Victorine W.**[9] b 9-16-1887 at Lynn, MA
        [MAVR]
 iii   **Clara Mable**[9] b 11-18-1888 at Lynn, MA
        [MAVR]
922 iv **Frederick Earle Sr.**[9] b 11-8-1891 at Lynn
        MA [MAVR] m Catherine Carney
 v   **William Mead**[9] b 11-17-1893 at Lynn, MA.
        [MAVR] The 1920 MA census shows a
        William M.[9] Severance, born 1894 living
        in Lynn, Essex Co. as a brother in law
        of Benjamin F. Allen.

(637) Preston Phillip[8], (William B.[7], Benjamin[6],
Joshua[5], Joseph[4], Ephraim[3], Ephraim[2], John[1]), died on
3-30-1896 at the age of 47 years [NSPCA Portland 4-
1-1896] from injuries he received from a fall from
a log slip. He fell over the edge, striking on the
logs below, fracturing several ribs, so that the
ends pressed against his heart. He had been a boom
man at the Willamette Lumber Mills for 20 years.
[NSOR Portland 4-2-1896] **Preston P.**[8] Severance
married Juliette Harlow 1-1-1874 at St. Johns,
Oregon. [ORVR]
    The family lived at Portland, OR. Juliette was
born in IL. They were living with his father
William B.[7] Severance. [1880 ORFC]

Children: [1880 ORFC]
 i   **Asel F. (Azel)**[9] b 1875
924 ii **William H.**[9] b June of 1877 in OR.
 iii   **Elizabeth**[9] b 1879

(639) Edgar F.[8], (William B.[7], Rueben[6], Caleb[5],
Joseph[4], Ephraim[3], Ephraim[2], John[1]), born 11-21-1850
in Orrington, ME. [IGI] He is later indicated in
Portland, OR. He married to Anna ____. She was
born in July of 1866. [1900-1920 ORFC]

Children:
 i   **Cliff B.**[9] b 3- -1884
 ii   **Hazel M.**[9] b 2- -1890

(644) Harry J.[8], (Carlos Erastus[7], Benjamin[6],
Joshua[5], Joseph[4], Ephraim[3], Ephraim[2], John[1]), was
born 4-7-1872 at Orrington, ME. [MEVR] He married
Lulu Ethel Lancaster, daughter of Frank Lancaster
and Hattie Lyshow of Hudson, ME, on 11-26-1896.

[MEVR] Lulu Ethel was born 11- -1872. [1900 MEFC] The 1910 ME census shows **Harry J.**[8], age 38, Ethel L. age 35, with **Harold E.**[9], **Charles F.**[9], and **Aileen E.**[9], all born in ME.

Children:
926 i   **Harold E.**[9] b 12-2-1897 [MEVR]
     ii   **Charles Francis**[9] b 6-22-1902
     iii   **Ailene Eunice**[9] b 11-14-1902

(645) Charles Alfred[8], (Harvey A.[7](Henry Albert), Benjamin[6], Joshua[5], Joseph[4], Ephraim[3], Ephraim[2], John[1]), born in April of 1876. He married to Clara Ester (Bentz) Steurer, daughter of John Henry Bentz and Nancy Adeline Smith. Clara was born on 11-16-1882 at Colusa, CA and died on 10-13-1960 in CA. **Charles**[8] died on 12-9-1931 at Whittier, CA.

Children:
928 i   **Raymond Gerald**[9] b 8-23-1909 m Dorothy Alyce Bouvier on 12-19-1936
     ii   **Charles Harvey**[9] b 6-11-1902 in CA and d 9-8-1964. It is unknown if he married or had children. [MDJS]

(647) George M.[8], (George W.[7], Cyprian[6], Joshua[5], Joseph[4], Ephraim[3], Ephraim[2], John[1]), born in July of 1859 in Holden, Penobscot Co. ME. [1900 MEFC] He died in 1921 in Hanson, MA. [MAM] **George**[8] married to Emma F. Copeland who was born in October of 1864. She died in 1940.

Children:
    i   **Verne C.**[9] b 10- -1891 [1900 MEFC]

(648) Henry W.[8], (George W.[7], Cyprian[6], Joshua[5], Joseph[4], Ephraim[3], Ephraim[2], John[1]), born around 1871. He married to Mini Grace Bickford, daughter of Sumner H. Bickford and Emma M. Vincent, on 10-26-1904 [MEVR] She was born 1882 in ME. [1920 MEFC] **Henry**[8] was a Rural Delivery Carrier.

Children:
    i   **Mini Katherine**[9] b 4-18-1906
    ii   **Ralph H.**[9] b 11-15-1907
    iii   **Olive June**[9] b 3-17-1911
    iv   **Quentin Roosevelt**[9] b 10-12-1919 at Ellsworth/Brewer, ME. [MEVR] He married to Ethelyn Maud Dunbar.

          v   **Barbara Lois**[9] b 1-3-1922 at Brewer, ME
                  [MEVR]

(649) Melvin B[8]., (John H.[7], Cyprain[6], Joshua[5],
Joseph[4], Ephraim[3], Ephraim[2], John[1]), born in December
of 1868. [1900 MEFC] He was of Newburgh, ME. He
married to Effie E. Lewis on 7-14-1897. [MEVR] She
was born in November of 1871. [1900 MEFC] **Melvin**[8]
died in 1956. Effie died in 1940
     Cemetery records show **Carroll Harold**[9] Severance
as the owner. Gladys, daughter of George Lewis and
Devin Grow, is buried in the cemetery. She is most
likely the wife of one of the sons. **Melvin**[8], Effie,
Maud[9], **Carroll**[9], **Harold**[9], and **Gladys**[9], are buried in
the Chapman Cemetery, Newburg, ME.

Children:
     i   **Agnes G.**[9] b 5-22-1898 in ME [MEVR]
     ii   **Maude M.**[9] b 8-8-1899 d 2-16-1900
     iii   **Percy H.**[9] b 2-3-1901. [MEVR] He married
            to Rose E. Carleton. Percy was listed as
            living in Newburgh and Bradford, ME.
     iv   **Beatrice May**[9] b 12-23-1902. The 4th born
            child at Newburgh, ME [MEVR]
     v   **Lloyd M.**[9] b 8-2-1905
     vi   **Carroll G.**[9] b 12-10-1907 d 6-13-1908
            [MEVR]
     vii   **Harold J.**[9] b 12-10-1907 d 1-13-1908
     viii   **Gladys E.**[9] b 5-27-1909 at Newburg, ME
            [MEVR]
     ix   **Morris A.**[9] b 8-29-1911 at Newburgh, ME
            [MEVR]
     x   **Ruth Evelyn**[9] b 12-26-1912 [MEVR]
The family shows on the 1920 Newburgh, Penobscot Co
ME census minus the children who died young

(650) Russell French[8], (John[7], John[6], John[5],
Ephraim[4], Ephraim[3], Ephraim[2], John[1]), was born 8-1-
1813 in Sandwich, NH. He died on 10-23-1873 in
Bradford, ME. [CRME Bradford] He married Hannah B.
Randall, daughter of William Randall and Adaline
Severance, on 2-8-1842. **Russell**[8] was a physician.
Hannah died on 5-20-1898. [MEVR] [CRME] They are
buried in the Williams Cemetery in Bradford, ME.
     Andrew J.[8] age 34 and **George A.**[8], age 27, were
living with **Russell**[8] and his wife. [1860 MEFC]

Children:

i   **Albert F.**[9] b 1846 shows on the 1850 ME census but may not be of **Russell**[8] and Hannah.

ii   **Charles**[9] b 1847 shows on the 1850 ME census but may not be of **Russell**[8] and Hannah.

(651) Sargeant French[8], (John[7], John[6], John[5], Ephraim[4], Ephraim[3], Ephraim[2], John[1]), was born 1822 and died 12-6-1895 in Sandwich, NH. [MAVR] His first marriage was to Harriet L. Burleigh, daughter of Nathaniel Burleigh and Phebe French. She died 5-11-1854 at Boston, MA aged 31 yrs 3 mons [MAVR] He married secondly to Mary A. ____, [1860 MAFC] who was born in 1825. [MAVR] **Sargeant**[8] is later found living in Boston, Chelsea, and Malden, MA. He left the Sandwich, NH area for a few years and had accumulated some wealth. When he returned he bought his father's farm which was about to be sold at auction.

In 1860, **S.F.**[8] Severance living in the 10th ward of Boston. He was born in 1822 in NH and he is a messenger, living with his wife Mary A. who was born in Pittston, ME in 1826 and their daughter **Elizabeth**[9], age 6/12 born in MA. [1860 MAFC] The 1870-1880 NH census for Sandwich, Carroll Co] shows **Sargeant**[8] Severance, his wife Mary and their daughter, **Lizzie**[9] age 20.

Children: [1870 NHFC]
    i   **Lizzie Munroe**[9] b 11-15-1850 at Boston, MA [MAVR]

(652) Asa French[8] (John[7], John[6], John[5], Ephraim[4], Ephraim[3], Ephraim[2], John[1]), was born 7-29-1829 and died 7-25-1913. [MEVR)] **Asa F.**[8] was born in Sandwich, NH, a mechanic, son of **John**[7] and Dorothy French, of old Revolutionary stock, his great grandfather, Jacob Jewel of Calvinist faith, was the first minister to preach and settle in Sandwich, NH. [Dodge] He married Mary Elizabeth Barstow on 7-26-1856. She was born 4-22-1833 and died 9-1-1901. [MEVR]

Mary was the daughter of Lot Barstow and Betsey Hammond of Nobleboro, ME. [Radasch]

It appears that **Asa**[8] was a piano maker as was indicated on the [MEVR]. They are recorded in Nobleboro, ME, and Sandwich and Concord, NH.

Children: [MEVR]

    i   **Harry F.**[9] b 1861 d 1869
    ii   **Fred N.**[9] b 1866 d 1869
    iii   **Lewis J.**[9] b 1869 d 1869
There could have been other children

(653) Octavius Webster[8], (John[7], John[6], John[5],
Ephraim[4], Ephraim[3], Ephraim[2], John[1]), born 1-8-1832
and died on 10-1-1864. [CRME] **Octavus**[8] was living
with his brother, **Russell**[8] Severance. [1850 MEFC]
Octavus[8] lived in Bradford and Burlington Alton,
ME.
    His first marriage was to Elizabeth (Lizzie)
Libby on 5-1-1859 at Bradford, ME. [MEVR] She was
the daughter of Joseph Libby and Myra Jones of
Biddeford, ME. [MEVR]
    The Probate shows **Octavus W.**[8] of Bradford, ME,
Will on 9-13-1864, [PRME 21:482 November of 1864]
with Elizabeth as the executer, signed by Isaac
Libby, **Russell** and Hannah B. Severance, and **George
W.** Severance. **Octavus W.**[8] Severance is buried in
the Mills Cemetery, Bradford, ME. It indicates that
he died 10-1-1864 age 32-9-8. [CRME]
    This is the cemetery where **Isaac L.**[8] Severance
and his family are buried. Elizabeth (Libby)
Severance, wife of **Asa W.**[8] Severance is also buried
there. (She died 11-26-1892 age 52-7-18) Elizabeth
m on 11-28-1867 (IGI) to **Asa Waldo**[8] Severance, son
of James and Adaline Randall, after the death of
Octavus[8] who had died on 10-1-1864.
    It is unknown if they had any children.

(654) George A.[8], (John[7], John[6], John[5], Ephraim[4],
Ephraim[3], Ephraim[2], John[1]), was born 1-20-1823 and
died 11-9-1905. [MEVR] **George**[8] was born in
Sandwich, NH and later settled in Bradford, ME. He
married first to Amanda A. Bailey who died in 1866
in Bradford, ME. He married secondly to Harriette
Miller on 5-1-1870, daughter of Alfred Miller and
Roxanna Clark, who died on 9-2-1904 at the age of
75 years. [MEVR] Harriette was born in Burlington,
ME and died in Bradford, ME.

Children:
933 i   **Octavius**[9] b 6-30-1865 in Bradford, ME, m
           Leah Osgood Miller 1-5-1887

(655) Andrew J.[8], (John[7], John[6], John[5], Ephraim[4],
Ephraim[3], Ephraim[2], John[1]), was born on 9-18-1836
[MEVR] in Sandwich, NH. He died 11-25-1904 at
Bradford, ME, burial in Williams Cemetery. He

married to Angeline J. Larrabee, daughter of David Larrabee and Cynthia Chapman, on 10-20-1872. [MEVR] Angie was born in Boston, MA on 5-22-1844. She died 11-29-1918. [MEVR] They lived at Bradford, ME for some time with the other Severances of Sandwich, NH. He later married to Mary D. Bradbury, daughter of William F. Bradbury and Sophia Ripley, of Dover, NH. [MEVR] Mary died on 8-5-1907 at the age of 67 in Portland, ME.

Andrew J.[8] living with **Russell**[8] and Hannah B. Severance and a **George A.**[8] Severance. **George**[8] and **Andrew**[8] were both 24 years old. All of them were born in NH. [1860 MEFC]

Children: born at Bradford, ME [MBGD]
i	**Russell**[9] b 4-14-1879 at Bradford, ME d 9-20-1838
ii	**Lillian M.**[9] b 8-31-1880 d 10-4-1897 ae 17-1-4 [MEVR]
iii	**Angie**[9]
iv	**Hannah**[9] b 4-12-1882 [1900 MEFC]. She m to Merton E. Bartlett circa 1903.

(656) John N.[8], (John[7], John[6], John[5], Ephraim[4], Ephraim[3], Ephraim[2], John[1]), born circa 1850. The 1860 NH census shows **John Sr.**[8] and Abigail (Hilton) with Angeley F. and **John N.**[9] age 9 years.

John N.[8] of Hyde Park, MA, married to Maria Norris, daughter of Bradford S. and Elizabeth Norris, on 12-26-1887 at Springfield, MA. He was born at Sandwich, NH and she at Hyannis, MA. [MAVR]

(657) John Webster[8], (Asa[7], John[6], John[5], Ephraim[4], Ephraim[3], Ephraim[2], John[1]), was born 2-3-1822 and died 5-19-1901. [NHVR] He married Hannah J. Kaime 11-25-1841. Hannah J. Kaime, daughter of Benjamin Kaime and Sally Watson, was born 8-25-1823 [Stearns Vol I p672] and died 8-24-1908. [NHVR] **John W.**[8] Severance attended school until he was about 10 years old in Sandwich, NH. After moving to Chichester, NH he learned the trade of an edge-tool maker, and followed if for a short time. He worked in Lowell, MA and Manchester, NH being as a practical machinist. He then moved to Hannah's parents farm where they lived out their lives. They were members of the Free Will Baptist Church. **John**[8] represented Manchester, NH in the legislature during 1855, 1856 and 1876-1877. He was with the Mechanics' Lodge No. 13, Patrons of Husbandry, and

was one of the organizers of Catamount Grange, of
Pittsfield. [BioR p316]

Children: [1870 Chichester, NHFC]
    i   **Walter A.**[9] b 1850 in PA. [1860
          Manchester NHFC]
    ii   **Alice L.**[9] b 1862
    iii   **George**[9] b 1868 in NH

(658) Asa[8], (Asa[7], John[6], John[5], Ephraim[4], Ephraim[3],
Ephraim[2], John[1]), was born 2-3-1828 and died 4-1-
1901 Sandwich, NH, son of Lieut. **Asa**[7] and Rhoda
Webster. [NHVR] He married Hannah M. Webster 11-20-
1850 [Tasker] who was born 10-10-1828 and died on
9-29-1900. **Asa**[8] and Hannah M. were baptized on 7-
25-1858 at Sandwich, NH. Deacon Severance was the
son of Lieut **Asa**[7] and Rhoda Webster Severance.
Lieut **Asa**[7] was the son of **John Jr.**[6] Severance and
John[6] was the son of **John**[5] and Susanna Severance.
[Tasker]
    Asa[8] was a Deacon in his church. An arrow back
rocker, a Sheraton Windsor type, which belonged to
Deacon **Asa**[8] Severance sits in the Sandwich, NH
Museum. In 1880 Hannah was living with her daughter
Alice[9]. [NHFC]

Children:
933a i   **John W.**[9] b 1853 [1870 NHFC](age 17)
    ii   **Frank A.**[9] b 1858 d 9-17-1873 age 16
          years 11 months [Lighton]
    iii   **Josiah Hermie**[9] b 1863 d 1-16-1869 age 5
          yrs 6 mons [Lighton]
    iv   **Alice M.**[9] b 1871 d 9-29-1894 age 23 yrs
          8 mons. [Lighton]
There were possibly other children

(659) Elijah Charles[8], (Levi[7], John[6], John[5],
Ephraim[4], Ephraim[3], Ephraim[2], John[1]), born 11-11-1821
[VTVR] in Boston, MA. He died on 9-21-1866 at the
age of 44-10-10. [VTVR] He married to Rhoda Hedges,
daughter of Richard and Julia Hedges, Northfield,
VT, on 10-14-1856. Rhoda died 11-27-1901. [VTVR]
Elijah[8] and Rhoda are buried in the Edmund Cemetery
in Northfield VT.

Children:
    i   **Julia**[9] d 8-5-1860 at Northfield, VT
         [VTVR]

(660) Charles W.[8], (Levi[7], John[6], John[5], Ephraim[4], Ephraim[3], Ephraim[2], John[1]), born circa 1823. [Mardecai] He is indicated as the son of **Levi[7]** and Ruth Severance in Boston, MA. He was a restorator. and **Charles[8]** died on 6-15-1884 at Sandwich, NH, age 60-2-10 years.

Charles[8] married to Sarah H. Donavan. She was born on 4-15-1825 and died on 8-1890 in Sandwich, NH. They are buried in Little's Pond Cemetery, Hill Cemetery, Sandwich, NH.

Children:

i   **Charles Wesley[9]** b 5-24-1851 at Boston, MA d 11-2-1852 age 1-7-9 years [Tasker]

ii   **George E.[9]** d 1-31-1854 age 10 months [Tasker]

(662) Nathan N.C.[8], Levi[7], John[6], John[5], Ephraim[4], Ephraim[3], Ephraim[2], John[1]), born circa 1835. He married to Lavina Delia Keith, daughter of Isaac Keith, on 8-20-1857 at Sandwich, NH. [MAVR] He operated an eating house and later was a depot master. [MAVR]

Children:

i   **Frederick Sawyer[9]** b 2-16-1858 at Boston, MA [MAVR]

ii   **Alice E.[9]** b 6-13-1859 at Sandwich, NH

(663) William H.[8], (Levi[7], John[6], John[5], Ephraim[4], Ephraim[3], Ephraim[2], John[1]), was born circa 1843 [1880 MNFC] at Sandwich, NH. [NHVR] He was a Jeweller at Boston, MA where he lived for about ten years of his adult life. The 1860 MA census shows him living with his brother, **Levi[8]**, and they were waiters at a resturant. **William[8]** married to Ann Augusta Chapman, daughter of Roswell S. and Augusta Chapman, 6-24-1867 at Haverhill, MA. [MAVR] He probably married first to a Martha.

Children of **William H.[8]** Severance and Martha _____ [1880 MNFC]

i   **Herbert[9]** b 1864 in NH. The 1900 NH census shows him living in Laconia, NH as a boarder of Albert H. Davis. He moved to MN in 1900. The 1920 MN census shows **Herbert[9]** b 1865 in NH and living alone in Wyanett, Isanti Co. MN. His father, **William H.[8]** had settled in MN earlier.

345

 ii **John**[9] b 1864 in NH but later settled in MN when his parents moved there about 1871.

 iii **William**[9] b 1866 in NH. The 1880 MN census shows him with his parents.

 iv **Flora**[9] b 1866 in NH

Children of **William H.**[8] Severance and Ann Augusta Chapman

 v **Frank**[9] b 1868 in MN [1880 MNFC Spencer, Isanti Co] He was living with his parents who were born in NH.

 vi **Clarissa Chapman**[9] b 10-6-1871 at Haverhill, MA daughter of **William H.**[8] Severance and Augusta Chapman. [MAVR]

 vii **Lila**[9] b 1872 in MN

933b viii **Clarke**[9] b 1877 in MN

 ix **Harry H.**[9], born 1885 and died 2-5-1896 at Haverhill, MA, age 21 years, single. [MAVR]

(664) Nathaniel C.[8], (Levi[7], John[6], John[5], Ephraim[4], Ephraim[3], Ephraim[2], John[1]), born in Sandwich, NH circa 1845. He married to Olive Ann Gould who was born in Livermore, ME. [MAVR]

Children:

 i **Fred Clark**[9] b 1-15-1872 in Boston, MA. He m to Isabelle Arkett, daughter of John Arkett and Mary J. Swan, on 9-5-1893. They had children, **Carroll Clark**[10] b 3-28-1894, **Myron Albert**[10] d age 2 mons, **Ethel May**[10] b 5-3-1897 d 5-4-1897. [MEVR] **Fred**[9] d 5-18-1920 in Auburn, MA at age 48-4-3. [MAVR]

(665) William J.[8], (Jacob Jewell[7], John[6], John[5], Ephraim[4], Ephraim[3], Ephraim[2], John[1]), born 8-27-1840 in Laconia, NH and married Mary Etta Wadleigh, daughter of Joseph Neal Wadleigh and Myron A. Moore, on 2-2-1867. [Moore I][Hanaford p577]] Mary Etta was born 9-28-1846 and died 2-5-1897. [NHVR] William was a farmer at Laconia, NH. He died on 12-14-1915 at Meredith, NH. They were living in Johnstown, NH in 1928. [NHVR-marriage record of **Leroy**[9] Severance]

 The 1880 NH census had the name spelled as Leverance.

Children:

934   i   **Fred Merserve**[9] b 4-2-1860 in Laconia, NH
            d 12-24-1920 Lakeport, NH, machinist, m
            at the time of his death [NHVR] m to
            Dora B. Noble, daughter of Scamon F.
            Noble and Lucrecia Jane. Dora was b 11-
            26-1864 Meredith Bridge (Laconia), NH d
            10-5-1936 Laconia. [NHVR]
935   ii   **Leroy J.**[9] b 12-17-1870 m1 Ilsa M.
            Sanborn 6-28-1891 Laconia, divorced 4-
            26-1921 [NHVR] m2 to Mary E. Robinson,
            daughter of Charles F. Swain and Della
            M. Goodwin, 1-10-1928, divorced 5-15-
            1929 [NHVR]

(666) William Norman[8], (Sargeant Jewell[7], John[6],
John[5], Ephraim[4], Ephraim[3], Ephraim[2], John[1]), born 12-
27-1843 [MNVR] in Sandwich, NH. **William**[8] died on 1-
24-1914 in Dodge County, MN. [MNVR]

William[8] moved to PA with his father when he was
very young. **Sargeant**[9] took his entire family. The
family then went and settled in Wasioja, Dodge
Center. **William**[8] married Caroline Elizabeth
Franklin 4-25-1862 at Dodge Center, MN. She was b
on 8-30-1846 and d 11-2-1914. [MNVR]

The 1910 MN census shows **William N.**[8] Severance
and Elizabeth living at Wasioja, MN.

William[8] and Elizabeth are buried at Reiverside
Cemetery at Dodge Center, MN. [MDCD]

Children: [MHCS]
      i   **Emmie**[9] **(Elizabeth)** b 8- -1863
936   ii   **William Hector**[9] b 8- -1868 m Lillian
            Perkins
      iii   **Annetie Bell (Nettie)**[9] b 4-29-1870
            [MNVR]
      iv   **Gertrude Ann**[9] b 8-4-1872 [MNVR]
      v   **Lavica**[9] b 1874 d 1875
      vi   **John**[9] b 3-5-1876 d age 4 [MNVR]
937   vii   **Lester Floyd**[9] b 2-20-1881 m Marietta
            Dibble
      viii **Sadie May**[9] b 12- -1883
      ix   **Gladys**[9]

(667) John Martin[8], (Sargeant Jewell[7], John[6], John[5],
Ephraim[4], Ephraim[3], Ephraim[2], John[1]), born 9-4-1845
in Sandwich, NH. He lived first in PA with his
parents and then moved and settled with them to
Wasioja, MN. He married Ruth Haskins in 1864. They
lived in Moody Co. Dakota's in the 1880's. They
later remove to Milton, WI. The 1900 IA census

347

shows **John**[8] and his daughter, **Angie L.**[9] age 21, born
9- -1878 living in Larchwood, Taylor Co. The [1920
IAFC] shows **John**[8] and Phoebe? (his mother) living
with **Edward**[9] (their son) and his family in Garwin,
Tama County, IA.

"**John Martin**[8] was a farmer all of his life. In
his later years he ran a grocery store in the
Milton House and gardened and carred for his
chickens."

"He died in 1946 at almost 101 years of age. He
might have lived longer but he fell and broke his
hip on slippery, icy steps while taking feed to his
chickens. Both **John Martin**[8] Severance and Ruth
Haskins are buried in the Milton Cemetery, Milton,
WI." [MHCS]

This family seemed to move about. The 1870 MN
census indicated that they were in that state. The
1880 Dakota census shows them in that state.

Children:

	i	**Eva**[9] b 12-23-1865 d 1866 at 5 months of age
	ii	**Ida Lutiske**[9] b 10-2-1867 in MN m William Jones and d a young lady. William remarried to Martha Grow.
938	iii	**Arthur B.**[9] b 4-16-1870 in MN m Emma Grow
	iv	**Agnes**[9] b d 6 years
939	v	**Edward Clifford**[9] b 10-5-1876 in MN [MNVR] **Edward**[9] shows on the 1920 IA census with his wife Grace, and their children, **Mildred**[10], **Leonard**[10], **Elda**[10], and **Illo**[10]. His father, **John**[8], and mother, Phoebe, who were both b in PA, are living with them.
	vi	**Angie Leona**[9] b 9- -1878 in MN d age 20 years
	vii	**Sargeant**[9] b 9-11-1878 (to **John M.**[9] and Ida) He must have d young as nothing else is known about him.
	viii	**James Leonard**[9] b 7-17-1881 [MNVR] He died on 8-4-1956. He married to Lydia Blanche Rinehart who was born on 2-15-1895. James and Lydia lived at Waterville, MN. He was a painter and candy maker. They did not leave any children. [MHCS]
	ix	**Herbert Giles**[9] b 2-26-1883 [MNVR] He died on 3-31-1963. He married Myrtle ____ after retirement. He lived first in Sioux Falls, SD as a chicken farmer and

then in Fresno, CA. **Herbert**[9] and Myrtle
did not leave any children. [MHCS]

(668) Hector Calbreth[8], (Sargeant Jewell[7], John[6],
John[5], Ephraim[4], Ephraim[3], Ephraim[2], John[1]), born 7-
19-1847 in Warren City, PA, where his father
Sargeant Jewell[7] Severance had a timber farm of 300
acres. He later settled in Dodge Center, MN where
both he and his father had farms. **Hector**[8] married
to Emma Ann Ellis on 5-10-1876. She was born on 2-
28-1858 in Peoria Co. IL. She died on 4-23-1942 at
Tipton, IA where she had remarried to a Mr. Griffis
a few years previously. **Hector Calbreth**[8] Severance
died on 2-15-1907 at Gantry, AR.

Hector Calbreth[3] came west with his father and
three brothers around 1856-1857. They were supposed
to have come, part way at least, by stage coach,
and partly by river steamer. At nearly 29 years of
age, after bachelor farming for several years he
married Emma Ellis who was just 18 years old. He
was a pioneer at heart and when homestead land
became available in Indian Territory, in what is
now South Dakota he moved there with his young
family. (His first two children were born on the
farm near Dodge Center) He took up a homestead of
160 acres near Glandreau, South Dakota.

After proving up on the homestead, and when
grasshoppers, drouth, hail and low prices drove him
from the farm which he sold, he moved to Milton,
WI. There he operated a feed store as well as
operating a farm. About 1900, a group from that
church investigated the country around Gentry, AR
and liked it so well that they persuaded a number
from the Milton and other churches, to move there.

That is where **Earland Claude**[9] Severance was born
and where **Hector**[8] died in 1907. [MHCS]

Children: [1900 WIFC].
940 i **Louette Carl**[9] b 11-23-1879 [MNVR] in
        Dodge Co. MN
     ii **Winnie Floss**[9] b 4-5-1882 in MN
    iii **Marion Alton**[9] (son) b 4-21-1885 in MN
     iv **Mabel Clair**[9] b 8-25-1888 in SD d after
        1987
      v **Clara Maude**[9] b 4-26-1893 in SD, m
        Charles A. Nelson, son of N.P. Nelson
        and Caroline Olson of Denmark, 8-19-1909
        Antigo, Langlade Co. WI. [WIVR Vol 2, p
        316] She d after 1987

vi   **Myra Evangeline**[9] b 6-7-1898 in WI d
        after 1987
941 vii   **Harland Claude**[9] b 8-3-1904 m Vesta 8-8-
        1922 in Montague, CA. **Harland**[9] d after
        1987.

(669) Thomas Burton[8], (Sargeant Jewell[7], John[6],
John[5], Ephraim[4], Ephraim[3], Ephraim[2], John[1]), born 12-
8-1848 in Warren City, PA. Later settled in
Wasioja, Dodge Center, MN. He married to Elnora
Mills in 1868. **Thomas**[9] died on 11-25-1872, [MNVR]
at the young age of 23 years 11 months 16 days.
[MHCS]

Children:
    i   **Walter**[9] b 4-5-1869, living alone in 1900
        [NDFC]
943 ii   **Rollo**[9] (male) b 4-5-1870
944 iii   **Frank**[9] b 9- -1871
945 iv   **Bert**[9] b 1-21-1873. **Bert**[9] would have been
        born after his fathers death. **Lorna**[10] b
        4-13-1899 was a daughter of **Bert**[9]
        Severance. **Mabel**[9] Severance, b 1880, m
        O. Deforest Crandall who was b 1875 in
        IL. They were living with **Berton**[9] in
        1920. [MNFC]

(670) Alonzo[8], (James M.[7], John[6], John[5], Ephraim[4],
Ephraim[3], Ephraim[2], John[1]), born 10-13-1842 and died
1-24-1924 at Laconia, NH. [NHVR] **Alonzo**[8] was a
farmer after living in Boston where he was a
shoemaker. He married to Louisa Evelyn Vittum,
daughter of Stephen Jr. Vittum and Ruth Ann Tappan
of Sandwich, NH, on 3-24-1864. She was born 10-31-
1845 and died 11-1-1894. They later lived next to
her parents in Sandwich on the farm which was later
called the Tappan-Severance Place. It was sold to
Samuel Hill about 1910. She was a school teacher.
[SNHE 45th Excursion] The 1880 NH census shows
James M.[7] Severance and Adeline (his wife) living
with **Alonzo**[8] and Louisa. Louisa d in Laconia, NH.
The 1910 NH census shows **Alonzo**[8] living alone in
Sandwich. **Alonzo**[8] and Louisa are buried in the
North Sandwich, Skinner Corners Cemetery
    Donald[10] Severance (a grandson of **Alonzo**[8]) was
told as a child that he had been seiously injured
when a tree fell on him. About 1916 he moved to
Laconia to live with his daughter, **Ruth**[9], and her
husband Frederick W. Fowler. Mr. Fowler was Judge
of Probate in Laconia for many years. **Alonzo**[8] was

an avid reader and could be found seated with a cane. "He actually died with a book in his hands." [MDS]

Children:
i   **Ruth Ann**[9] b 9-12-1870 m Fred W. Fowler 1-18-1839, he was b 10-10-1859 at Laconia. NH. [Greeley]

946 ii   **Walter Edmund**[9] b 4-12-1883 d 7-14-1936, [NHVR] from a train accident in Charlemont (Greenfield), MA. He was a locamotive engineer. He m 1st to Florence Bessie Porter 5-18-1912. She was the daughter of Dennis Porter and Mary Ann Longever, Florence was b 5-15-1875 d 3-23-1923. **Walter**[9] m2 to Muriel Helen Shea of West Lebanon, NH, 12-1-1923. Muriel was the daughter of William H. Shea and Celia Freeman of VT.

(671) Asa Waldo[8], (James M.[7], John[6], John[5], Ephraim[4], Ephraim[3], Ephraim[2], John[1]), born 11-3-1847 at Sandwich, NH and died 9-26-1909 at Lowell, Middlesex, MA. Burial was in the Mills Cemetery, Bradford, Penobscot, MA. He married to Lizzie Libby on 11-28-1867 at Bradford, ME. [MEVR] She was born 1-27-1841, the daughter of Isaac Libbey and Mary Worster, at North Berwick, York, ME. Elizabeth Libby died 9-19-1919 at Milo, Piscataquis, ME. [MEVR] She is also buried at the Mills Cemetery, Bradford, ME. [CRME]

    Asa Waldo[8] Severance, was removed from Lowell, MA where he had lived for the past 12 years and died there as a result of injuries received by a runaway horse, and buried in Bradford, ME. Mr. George Hall, a brother-in-law, accompanied the remains. **Waldo**[8] left his wife, one son, **I.L.**[9] Severance, and daughter, Mrs. Josiah Goodwin of Corinth. The funeral was held from the home of his son, September 27. [NSME 9-30-1909 Funeral Notice]

    Asa Waldo[8] was living with his parents, **James**[7] and Adaline in 1870 along with Eliza, wife of **Asa W.**[8], and their son **Isaac L.**[9] Severance who was born in 1869. [MEFC] In 1880 the family of **Asa W.**[8], Lizzie, **Isaac L.**[9] and **Louise**[9] was living with Isaac Libby. [MEFC]

    Elizabeth (Libbey) Severance was a widow when she married **Asa**[8], having first married his cousin **Octavius**[8], the son of **James**[7] Severance's brother **John**[7] and his wife Dolly French. **Octavius's**[8] older brother **Russell**[8] was also in Bradford by 1850, probably he and **Octavius**[8] came together. Before 1860, their brothers **George**[8] and **Andrew**[8] had also moved to ME and were in the household of **Russell**[8] and Hannah Severance.

Asa[8] went to Lowell, MA around 1897 to work as a teamster for the City of Lowell Locks and Canals. He died there in 1907 and was returned to Bradford for burial. Lizzie apparently never went to Lowell with him but lived with her son **Isaac**[9], moving also when he moved to Milo, ME around 1918. Upon her death in Milo in 1919, she was also taken to Bradford for burial. **Octavius**[8] Severance is buried with her and **Asa**[8] in one of the Libbey family lots." [MINB]

Children:
947 i **Isaac Libby**[9] b 8-22-1868 [CRME] m Flora E. Barter
     ii **Carrie F.**[9] b 12-21-1870 in Bradford, ME d 5-7-1871 age 4 months 16 days at Bradford. Burial in the Mills Cemetery, Bradford.
     iii **Louise**[9] b 10-8-1875 d 3-17-1953 m Josiah Goodwin 11-28-1901. She is buried in the Mills Cemetery Bradford.

(672) Atwood[8], (Jesse[7], Nathaniel[6], John[5], Ephraim[4], Ephraim[3], Ephraim[2], John[1]), born in 11- -1832 probably in Pittsfield, ME. [1900 LAFC] [1860 MEFC] He apparently married twice, since a Nancy A. _____, wife, born 1851, and all the children were listed in 1880. [LAFC] Sarah A. _____, born 9- - 1835, is indicated in 1900. [LAFC].

Atwood[8] moved many times. He is shown living in ME, TN, KY, and Lake Charles, LA. **Atwood**[8] was a school teacher and his parents were born in ME.

Children: [1880-1900 LAFC]
     i   **Abbie D.**[9] b 1868 in TN
     ii **Loana**[9] b 11- -1870 in TN
     iii **Vesty**[9] b 1873 in TN
     iv **Verra**[9] b 1873 in TN
     v   **Jessie**[9] b 10- -1878 in KY. The [1910 LAFC] shows **Jesse**[9], age 30, and his sister, **Lona**[9], age 39 born in TN, living in Vernon County, LA.

(673) Lagrange[8], (Jesse[7], Nathaniel[6], John[5], Ephraim[4], Ephraim[3], Ephraim[2], John[1]), born on 12-28-

1839 in Newport, ME. He died on 1-26-1893 in
Huntington, IN. [NSHMW 1-31-1893 p3 col 3][NSHI]
The History of Huntington [Brant] incorrectly
reported that **Lagrange[8]** died 2-18-1928. He married
to Henrietta Eliza Drummond on 2-17-1870. [Slevin
Vol 1 Book E] She was the daughter of Jared
Drummond and Philura Austine. Henrietta was born on
6-27-1842 in Maumee, OH and died at Winfield, KS on
2-6-1906.

He left the public schools and academy at the
age of fourteen, and entered the office of the
Bangor Daily Whig and Courier, in Bangor, ME. He
worked there until he was 21 years old. He served
in the Civil War as a private in Co., H. 12 Regt.
ME Vols.

He began to study medicine and graduated from
the Eclectic Medical Institute, Cincinnati, Ohio in
May of 1868. He then practiced medicine in South
Whitley, IN and in October of 1869, he went to
Huntington Co. He was a member of the Masonic
Order, having attained the rank of Knight Templar.
[Brant p533-534]

"He received a gun shot at Ponchatoula, LA on 9-
15-1862, which hit in the right left leg just below
the knee. Then at Port Hudson, Louisiana in May of
1863, he received another shot also on the right
leg below the knee." [CWPR filed 12-7-1864]

Lagrange[8] died 1-26-1893. [CRPR #403184 filed by
Henrietta E. Severance] **Lagrange[8]** does not show
with the family on the 1900 census. [INFC]

Children: born in IN
  i   **Harriet[9]** b 4-2-1873 in Huntington, IN,
        m to Edward C. Putman on 6-8-1906. He d
        in February of 1916. **Harriet[9]** d on 4-20-
        1941 in Huntington, IN. They had two
        daughters that settled in Wichita, KS.
 ii   **Frances F.[9]** was b on 6-16-1875 at
        Huntington, IN. She m to Bert James
        Bartlett on 10-8-1896. [INVR] Bert was b
        on 6-16-1875 in Claremont, NH. He d 3-
        22-1931. **Frances[9]** d on 3-26-1953 at
        Huntington, IN.
iii   **Arthur L.[9]** b 5- -1877 lived at
        Coffeyville, KS were he was employed in
        "Indian Territory". The 1920 KS census
        shows him with his wife Florence O. ___
        age 41 b in MO.
 iv   **Jessie[9]** b 10- -1879 m Mr. Stacey E.
        Graham [CWPR]

> v   **Henriett E.**[9] b 1-7-1881, the youngest
> daughter of **Lagrange**[8], d 8-21-1934, m
> Clyde B. Mendenhall, a dendist in
> Wellington, KS on 6-3-1910. [CWPR]
>
> vi   **Howard G.**[9] b 5-11-1883 in Huntington,
> IN. He later worked for the Santa Fe
> Railroad. [CWPR] He married to Mary
> ____. [1900 INFC] She was born in 1884
> in KS. He supposedly lived in Winfield,
> KS. however **Howard**[9] was living in
> Monterey, Monterey Co. CA with his wife
> in 1910. [CAFC] **Howard**[9] d 1908.

(674) Samuel F.[8], (Nathaniel[7], Nathaniel Smith[6],
John[5], Ephraim[4], Ephraim[3], Ephraim[2], John[1]), born
circa 1830 probably near Palmyra, ME. [LRME] He
married to Christina ____. **Samuel**[8] and Christina
were living in Huntington, IN near **Lagrange**[8]
Severance. (A newpaper article indicates that
Lagrange[8] and **Samuel**[8] were cousins) [NSHMW 1893] and
Christina died in Oregon but was returned to IN for
burial.

The Will for **Samuel F.**[8] Severance of Newport,
County of Penobscot and State of Maine, [PRME Will
"D" pages 561-2], wife Christena E. Severance.
Probated 2-16-1898, Executrix, Christena E.
Severance, Witnesses, George W. Whitney, Kingman
Gurney, and Philip A. Coller all of Newport.

The 1850-1860 ME census shows that he was born
in NH and settled in Bangor, ME. In 1860 he was
living at Newport, ME. His wife was Christina
____. He was listed as a tin plater. The 1870 ME
census shows them living in Newport, ME with two
children, not their own. Christina Severance, born
11- -1829 in ME was living in Los Angeles with her
son in law, William R. Ream Sr. [1900 CAFC] She
therefore must have had a daughter. Christina died
in Portland, OR. She was born in 1829 in ME and
died 11-9-1907 at the age of 78 years. [NSOR] The
[ORVR] shows that she was born in ME and was
removed for burial in Huntington, IN.

(675) J.G. (Joshua G./Josiah Gould)[8], (Nathaniel[7],
Nathaniel Smith[6], John[5], Ephraim[4], Ephraim[3],
Ephraim[2], John[1]), was born on 9-30-1832. He married
to Mary J. Tiel in the Fall of 1862. Mary was born
in 1836. **J.G.**[8] was an Attorney at Law and living
with M.J. [1870 CAFC] The 1850 ME census shows
J.G.[8] as the son of **Nathaniel**[7] and living in Bangor,

ME. After 1860, he is only found living in CA. 1870-1920 CAFC

Joshua Gould[8] Severance prepared for college at Hampden Academy and entered at Bowdoin (ME) in 1852. Before graduating he entered the study of the law in the office of Hon. Hannibal Hamlin at Hampden, (ME) where he remained for about a year, when he entered the law office of Hon. John E. Godfrey for years and now Probate Judge of Penobscot County at Bangor. **Joshua**[8] was admitted to the Supreme Judicial Court of the state of ME in 1855 and arrived in San Francisco on the first day of January of 1356 and settled at Lancha Plana, Amador County. [SFSC]

He was elected a member of the Board of Supervisors in the Fall of 1856 and in 1858 District Attorney by the Douglas Democracy and was made chairman of its first County Central Committee. In 1862 he was elected District Attorney for Calaveras County. He edited the *Amador Ledger* and was the proprietor and editory of the *San Andreas Register*. [HACoCA p292]

In 1900 he was living as a boarder in San Francisco. [CAFC]

(676) Charles Robinson[8], (Peter[7], Ephraim[6], John[5], Ephraim[4], Ephriam[3], Ephraim[2], John[1]), born 12-22-1831 at Meredith, NH and died 5-30-1864. He married to Sarah Mansfield, daughter of Robert and Prudence Mansfield, on 12-30-1855 at Needham, MA. [MAVR] [BRRF] Apparently **Charles**[8] died in the Civil War as pension was applied for by Sarah from MA on 10-10-1864 for service of **Charles R.**[8] Severance in A 56 Mass Inf. [CWPR] The [MAVR] says that he was born in Canada and a painter at the time his son was born.

Children: born at Needham, MA [MAVR]
950　i　　**Charles F.G.**[9] b 9-30-1858
　　ii　　**Emily M.**[9] b 7-17-1860
　　ii　　**William Edgar**[9] b 1-24-1862
　　iii　 **Helen L.**[9] b 8-7-1864

(678) Ira G.[8], (Ephraim[7], Ephraim[6], John[5], Ephraim[4], Ephraim[3], Ephraim[2], John[1]), born 1853 in Sandwich, NH. He married to Elma A. Folsom, daughter of Josiah P. Folsom and Huldah Downs of Tamworth, NH, on 2-3-1879. [IGI] She was born 12-27-1843 The Folsom's were from Tamworth and Lowell, NH. She was born in 1850. [Folsom Vol I p375-376] The 1880 NHF

census shows this family and **Ephraim⁶, Ira's⁸**
grandfather and Huldah Folsom, his mother in law.

Children:
    i   **Esther G.⁹** b 1879

(679) Harrison R.⁸, (Elbridge G.⁷, Moses⁶, John⁵,
Ephraim⁴, Ephraim³, Ephraim², John¹), born in August
of 1847 in Sandwich, NH. He married Ella Blaisdell
on 11-15-1866 in Laconia, NH, [CRBCoNH] They were
divorced in December of 1870. [NHVR] He moved to
Donners Grove, IL and then Westfield, WI with his
parents. He married secondly to Eliza Cross in
Marquette Co. WI [WIVR] around 1869. She was born
in NY State in September of 1852. **Harrison⁸** went
into partnership with his parents and brother for
farming in Columbia Co. WI.
    Harrison⁸ moved to Madison on the Lake, OH in
the late 1880's and lived the rest of his life
there with his wife Eliza and their daughter. The
1900-1910 OH census shows them in Madison, Lake Co.
OH. [MDCD]

Children:
    i   **Myrtle⁹** b 4- -1878 in WI. She was living
           with her parents in Madison, OH in 1910.
           [OHFC]

(680) Charles Coleman⁸, (Elbridge G.⁷, Moses⁶, John⁵,
Ephraim⁴, Ephraim³, Ephraim², John¹), born on 7-29-
1855 at Sandwich, NH. In early manhood he traveled
to Donners Grove, IL and then to Westfield, WI with
his parents. He later settled in Fort Winnebago,
Columbia Co. WI where he went into farming
partnership with his father and brother. He married
Agnes Elizabeth Rodgers, daughter of Alexander
Rodgers and Margaret Gregg of Merritts Landing
(Endeavor), WI. [WIVR] The Rodgers were immigrants
arriving from Scotland in 1850. Agnes was born 8-
25-1860 at Merritts Landing, WI.
    Charles⁸ used the surname of *Clark* after
difficulties with his father. His family retained
the *Clark* surname. He died on 12-7-1930 at Madison,
WI and Agnes died at Portage, WI on 9-13-1941.
[WIVR] They are buried in the North Marcellon
Cemetery, Pardeeville, WI. [MDCD]

```
Children:  [MDCD]
        i       Pearl Naomi⁹ (Clark) born 10-15-1885 d
                6-5-1947 m  Walter Billington on 9-13-
                1905
951    ii       Ivy Coleman⁹ (Clark) born 10-21-1888 d
                1-6-1976 m Emma Turner on 8-25-1920
952    iii      Earold Roberts⁹ (Clark) born 8-9-1892 d
                5-16-1961 m Lela Eldora Peckham 6-23-
                1915
        iv      Grace Olive⁹ (Clark) b 7-21-1895 d 6-15-
                1973 unm
```

CHARLES C.⁸ SEVERANCE *CLARK* **AND AGNES RODGERS**

HAROLD ROBERTS[9] SEVERANCE *CLARK*

(685) Charles Lamb[8], (Charles[7], Benjamin[6], Daniel[5], Ephraim[4], Ebenezer[3], Ephraim[2], John[1]), was born 12-14-1833 and died 4-30-1907 in Flint, MI. He married Louisa Forbush, daughter of Nehemiah Lamb and Hanna Palmer, on 6-12-1856. Four of the Lamb's sons were Baptist ministers in MI. Louisa was born 3-4-1834 and died 12-26-1909. The family is recorded in Walled Lake, MI, St. Johns, MI, South Lyon, MI and Andalusia, IL. Charles Lamb was a farmer and Merchant. [HOS] In 1860 they were living at West Bloomfield, Oakland Co. [MIFC]

Children: [HOS]

	i	**Perry[9]** b 6-2-1857 d 10-9-1863 Walled Lake
953	ii	**Arthur[9]** b 9-19-1860 Walled Lake, MI
954	iii	**Eugene[9]** b 7-16-1862 Walled Lake
955	iv	**Palmer[9]** b 7-30-1864 Walled Lake
956	v	**Henry Ormal[9]** b 2-19-1867 St. Johns Michigan, m Anna M. Lane
	vi	**Clara Catherine[9]** b 3-17-1871 Andalusia, IL m Albert George Weatherhead 6-30-1896, he was b 12-14-1869 d 3-18-1920 at Flint, MI.
957	vii	**Charles[9]** b 11-4-1873 Andalusia, IL m Carrie E. English 4-28-1896, she d 5-

358

1896, m2 Gertrude Emily Patch 3-21-1900,
she was b 4-19-1876.

(686) Thomas Chalkley[8], (Charles[7], Benjamin[6],
Daniel[5], Ephraim[4], Ebenezer[3], Ephraim[2], John[1]), born
12-18-1835 at Northville, MI and died 6-6-1914 at
Pullman, WA, He married Martha McCall, daughter of
Clarke McCall of NY State, in June of 1858. She was
born 4-20-1838 and died 1-8-1884. All of the
children were born on the farm in Walled Lake, MI.
   The maternal grandfather, Rev. Nehemiah Lamb,
was one of the first settlers in Farmington
Township, coming here as a missionary. The parents
of **Thomas[8]** came to Northville, MI in 1835. They
then removed to this farm where the son now
resides.
   Thomas[8] was an active member of the Baptist
Church at Walled Lake. He served as Treasurer,
Clerk, and Deacon. He has been a member of the
Grange and also of the School Board, serving on the
School Board with positions of Director, Assessor
and moderator. [P&BOMI p691]
   In 1860 the newly married couple was living with
others from Prussia, NY State, and MI. [MIFC]

Children: [HOS p16-17]
	i	**Martha[9]** b 9-26-1861 d 2-21-1925
958	ii	**Thomas Chalkley Jr.[9]** b 7-26-1863 m Julia Frances Mason.
	iii	**Mary[9]** b 8-16-1864 d 6-30-1878
959	iv	**Lewis[9]** b 1867 m Lillie Holton 11-2-1891, she was b 11-2-1874.
960	v	**Ira[9]** b 1-18-1869 m Blanche M. Lewis 4-27-1899 settled in Minneapolis, MN
	vi	**Irene[9]** settled in Spokane, WA She was b 10-29-1871 m Warren E. Waste 10-1-1916 who was b 7-16-1868
961	vii	**George[9]** b 2-4-1874 m Ethel E. Espy 8-28-1907 She was b 4-9-1883.
	viii	**Howard[9]** b 4-7-1876 d 8-17-1910 at Wixom, MI. He was a student at MI State College
	ix	**Mabel Connelly[9]** b 11-4-1879 settled in Puyallup, WA d 2-20-1913 she was a teacher

(687) Nathan Ezra[8], (Charles[7], Benjamin[6], Daniel[5],
Ephraim[4], Ebenezer[3], Ephraim[2], John[1]), born 4-22-1840
Walled Lake, MI. He was a farmer at Mason, MI.
Nathan[8] died 2-22-1920. He married Janette Thoburn,

12-16-1868. She was born 7-23-1845 in Lanarkshire, Scotland. [HOS]

Nathan E.[8] Severance was in Co. C., 16th MI., Inf. Vol 16, [MISS p144]

Children: [HOS p18]
    i   **Walter E.**[9] b 7-18-1870 at Walled Lake, m Alice Fay 10-3-1894. She was born 9- - 1873 in MI. They lived at Lansing, MI. They left no children.
962 ii   **Frank J.**[9] b 9-4-1873 at Mason, MI, he was a farmer m Amy V. Bullen 5-1-1907
     iii   **Agnes May**[9] b 8-27-1876 at Mason, MI
     iv   **Minnie E.**[9] b 6-15-1882 at Mason, MI. She was a teacher.

(688) John[8], (Charles[7], Benjamin[6], Daniel[5], Ephraim[4], Ebenezer[3], Ephraim[2], John[1]), was born 3-23-1843 at Walled Lake, MI. He was a shoemaker. He died 4-28-1894. **John**[8] married Marian McCall 11-19-1862. She was born 3-7-1841 and died 6-24-1916. They lived at Walled Lake, MI where all the children were born. The 1870 MI census shows the family living in Bingham, Linton Co. [HOS p18]

Children:
    i   **Betsey**[9] b 9-17-1863 d 10-7-1863
963 ii   **Melvin**[9] b 9-18-1865 at St. Johns, MI. He was a farmer, m Minnie Murdock on 4-9-1887
964 iii   **Lemuel**[9] b 1-24-1868 at St. Johns, MI, m Laura May Chappell on 6-15-1898
     iv   **John Wesley**[9] b 10-29-1869 at St. Johns, MI, m Henrietta Strudwick 7-3-1871, she d 5-29-1927, they lived at Bad Axe, MI He was usually called **Wesley**[9]. He was an accountant with the aid of a colleague he established a uniform system of accounting in the counties of MI.
     v   **Adelaide**[9] b 7-21-1871, Walled Lake, MI, m Fred Miles 5-2-1888
     vi   **Sophronia**[9] b 11-13-1872 at Walled Lake, MI, m Ray Sibley Drew 9-6-1892
     vii   **Jeanette**[9] b 3-20-1874 d 1-1-1876
     viii   **Martin L.W.**[9] b 6-2-1875 d 2-11-1880
965 ix   **Chester Cole**[9] b 2-12-1879 at Walled Lake, MI, m Bessie Mabel Bone 8-20-1898
     x   **Nellie**[9] b 8-2-1879 at Walled Lake, MI, removed to St Louis, MO

966 xi **Miraon**[9] b 10-7-1881 m May Allen 11-19-1902

xii **Marian**[9] b 10-7-1881 at Walled Lake, MI m John Bandt 10-6-1902, settled at St. Johns, MI

967 xiii **Earl Lewis**[9] b 8-3-1883 m 11-19-1903 Grace DeGroot

xiv **Laura Mae**[9] b 5-1-1885 d 5-1-1885

(689) King Jotham[3], (Charles[7], Benjamin[6], Daniel[5], Ephraim[4], Ebenezer[3], Ephraim[2], John[1]), born 7-7-1844 at Walled Lake, MI and died 2-11-1927 at St. Johns, MI. He was a farmer. He married first to Sarah Cantwell 1-1-1866 who was born 6-2-1850 and died 3-3-1877. He married second to Sophia Cornell 4-9-1878 at Ypsilanti, Washtenaw Co. [Kennedy] Sophia was born 2-22-___ in Windsor, Canada. [HOS p21-22]

Children of **King Jotham**[8] and Sarah Cantwell

i **Cora Ann**[9] b 4-28-1868 at Walled Lake, MI m Ephraim Jennings Ford 11-3-1891, who was b 11-14-1859 at Howell, MI, they settled at Los Angeles, CA

ii **Lucy**[9] b 9-10-1870 at Walled Lake, MI m Edgar M. Moore 1913, he was b 6-29-1867, settled in Mason, MI. "On October 29, 1913, at Cheboygan, MI, Mr. Moore married a cousin of the first Mrs. Moore, namely, **Lucy**[9] Severance, daughter of **King Jotham**[8] and Sarah (Cantwell) Severance, who was born at Commerce, Michigan, September 10, 1870." [Green II p220-221]

968 iii **Charles Jotham**[9] b 10-9-1872 at Walled Lake, MI m 9-1-1906, Cora E. Slaybough who was b 12-10-1878

iv **Emma Jane**[9] b 8-24-1875 at Walled Lake, d 2-20-1927 m Addison Darwin Stile 10-12-1898, he was b 6-24-1861

Children of **King Jotham**[8] Severance and Sophia Cornell [HOS p22]

969 v **Edgar M.**[9] b 4-22-1879 at Walled Lake, MI

vi **Naomi**[9] b 6-11-1881 at East Jordan, MI m B.C. Butler, Lansing, MI

vii **Ruth**[9] b 4-11-1883 at East Jordan, MI m Frank Mankey, St. Johns, MI

viii **Agnes**[9] b 1-18-1885 East Jordan, MI m C.H. Lyon, Lansing, MI

(690) Frank[8], (Ezra[7], Benjamin[6], Daniel[5], Ephraim[4], Ebenezer[3], Ephraim[2], John[1]), born 9- -1848 near Plymouth, MI. The 1910/1920 Jordan, MI census shows this family. He married to Harriet L. who was born 12- -1854.

Children:
969a	i	**Benjamin[9]** b 8- -1877
	ii	**Emma[9]** b 11- -1878
	iii	**Howard D.[9]** b 11- -1892
	iv	**Myrtle H.[9]** b 2- -1855
969b	v	**William[9]** b 5- -1891

(691) Horace B.[8], (Ezra[7], Benjamin[6], Daniel[5], Ephraim[4], Ebenezer[3], Ephraim[2], John[1]), born circa 1852 [1920 CAFC] near Plymouth, MI. The 1900 MI census shows **Horace[8]** in Lansing, MI with his wife Elizabeth who was born 9- -1863 in Scotland.

Children:
i	**Douglas[9]** b 5- -1891 in MI. In 1910 he was a roomer of Ray H. Babcock.

(692) Lucius E.[8], (Ezra[7], Benjamin[6], Daniel[5], Eprhaim[4], Ebenezer[3], Ephraim[2], John[1]), born 5- -1855 near Plymouth, MI. He married to Rosa M. ___ who was born 8- -1865 in MI.

Children:
i	**Clyde T.[9]** b 7- -1876 in MI
ii	**Lyle E.[9]** b 6- -1891 in MI

(693) Orren J.[8], (Daniel[7], Benjamin[6], Daniel[5], Ephraim[4], Ebenezer[3], Ephraim[2], John[1]), was born 10-3-1846 at Claremont or Sunapee, Sullivan County, NH, and died 11-6-1912 at Newton, NH. [NHVR] In 1870, at the age of 23, he was living with his parents at the age of 23. [Newport, NHFC]

    Orren J.[8] married first to Lucia Chase, daughter of Charles and Mary Ann Chase. Lucia was born 12-27-1847 and died 10-23-1869 at Wheelock, Caledonia Co. VT. He married secondly to Sarah Messer, daughter of Samuel Messer and Thirza Battles of Newton Junction, NH, 1-12-1873. [IGI] Sarah was born 6-27-1847 and died 2- -1887. **Orren[8]** married third to Mary A. Lane 10-15-1890 at Newton, NH, she was born 5- -1848, daughter of Frank Lane.

    Orren J.'s[8] occupation was teaming. [1880-1910 NHFC]. **Orrin J.[8]** lived in Sunapee (at age 26) and

he was a teamster, born in Claremont. [NHVR]
Orren's[8] father was **Daniel**[7], a stonecutter.

Children:
i   male b 3-28-1869
ii   **Lucia M.**[9] b 1874 to **Orren J.**[8] and Sarah
         M.P. Messer. She d young
iii   **Lucy Ann**[9] b 7-26-1875 died young.
969c iv **Albert Henry**[9] b 8-31-1876 at Sunapee, NH
         d 7-31-1924, m1 Florence Adelaide Green
         5-18-1905 [NHVR] m2 Elizabeth Perkins
v   **Myron D.**[9] b 8-22-1879 in New London. The
         1920 MA census shows him and his wife
         Signe with their daughter, **Signe I.**[9],
         was born 1916 in at Peabody, MA.

(694) Charles Ezra[3], (Nathan[7], Benjamin[6], Daniel[5],
Ephraim[4], Ebenezer[3], Ephraim[2], John[1]), born 5-28-1836
in Claremont, NH, where he lived until 1866 and
then after living at Lawrence, MA for 4 years, he
settled in Boston, MA. He died 4-2-1915 at Danvers,
MA. [Grow p433]
   He married to Martha Jenette Downing, daughter
of Joshua Downing and Sarah Jane Brown, 11-21-1860
in Hopkington, NH. [IGI] She was born 2-24-1845 in
Boscawen, NH and died 6-24-1866 in Claremont. He
married a second time to Esther (Gambell) Smith, 9-
22-1902 in Boston, MA. [MBFS] In 1900 he was living
in Lawrence as a boarder of Anne M. Fowler. [MAFC]
   Charles[8] served in the Civil War, Co G, 5th
Regt, under Colonel Edward E. Cross, 10-12-1861 to
7-1-1863. He was wounded at Fair Oaks. [CWPR
#25041]

Children: [MBFS]
970 i   **Birney Charles**[9] b 5-1-1862 at Claremont
         d 11-23-1918 at Chester, Vermont m
         Florence Nightingale Grow in 3-17-1880.
         They lived in Chester, VT

(695) Charles Lucien[8], (Benjamin[7], Benjamin[6],
Daniel[5], Ephraim[4], Ebenezer[3], Ephraim[2], John[1]), born
1-25-1839 at Claremont, NH. He died 11-13-1901.
[NHVR] He married to Laura H. (Blake) Hancock,
daughter of William F. Blake and Betsey A. George,
10-10-1871 at Claremont. Laura was born 12-7-1848
and died on 10-19-1922. [NHVR]
   He was mustered into Co. G, 5th NH Vols. on 10-
12-1861. **Charles**[8] was wounded at the battle of
Antietam, 9-17-1862 and carried a ball in his thigh

for the rest of his life. He was mustered out of service on 10- -1864. He participated in the siege of Yorktown, Battle of Fair Oaks and the Seven Days Fight. He also served as Corporal, as Post Commander, and Grand Army of the Republic and on the staff of State Department Commander. [HOS]

He did much to help build up the part of Claremont, NH, known as Severanceville in earlier times.

Child:
971   i   **Harry Lucien Don**[9] b 6-17-1880, m Marion Doe, 6-28-1906, [NHVR] daughter of Warren W. Doe and Isabel C. Stevens of Salem MA. Marion was b 10-26-1881. [Doe] **Harry**[9] was a postal clerk and Marion was a school teacher at the time of their marriage. [NHVR]

(696) George Henry[8], (Benjamin[7], Benjamin[6], Daniel[5], Ephraim[4], Ebenezer[3], Ephraim[2], John[1]), born on 4-5-1845 and died 9-11-1924 at Claremont, NH. [NHVR] He married to Mrs. Vietta (Stockwell) Smith, on 11-21-1877. [IGI] Vietta was the daughter of George Stockwell and Sophronia Carroll of Croydon, NH. Vietta was born 7-3-1851 and died 6-11-1933. [NHVR] He was a carpenter and builder and spent most of his active years in the development of the south part of Claremont. He was a member of the Trinity Lutheran Church.

The family shows on the 1880 NH census with the last name spelled Leverance. The children included **Anna**[9], **Ida**[9], and Albert Smith (Vietta's son by her first marriage). The 1910 NHFC census shows **George H.**[8] and Etta A. as well as **Ida S.**[9] age 30 and single and **Ethel N.**[9] age 21 and single. It indicated that Etta had been married twice with a total of 5 children and 5 living.

Children:
  i   **Anna Lois**[9] b 9-3-1878 at Claremont, NH, was a Postal Clerk 1899-1901 m James H. Carroll, 6-12-1901. He was a horse dealer and son of James Carroll and Helen Burnes of Walpole and Boston, MA. [NHVR]
  ii   **Ida Sophronia**[9] b 4-7-1880 gradate of Fitchburg Normal School 1906
972   iii   **George Henry Jr.**[9] b 4-8-1884, he was a minister in Detroit, MI. received his

A.B. at Middlebury College 1908 B.D. Gen
Theolog. Sem., New York City, A.M.
Columbia University 1913. Ordained to
Episcopal ministry 12-21-1911,
missionary in charge of Okanogan Co. WA,
1914. He m to Liela Parson on 6-22-1921.
iv   **Ethel M.**[9] b 5-29-1888, Graduate of
Fitchburg Normal School 1911. She was a
teacher in MA and CT.

(697) Benjamin F.[8], (Benjamin[7], Benjamin[6], Daniel[5],
Ephraim[4], Ebenezer[3], Ephraim[2], John[1]), born 3-8-1852
[NHVR] and died 11-13-1926 at Claremont, NH. He
married first to Lucinda L. Locke. He married
secondly to Mary A. Cram on 11-20-1885 at Newport,
Sullivan Co. NH. She was born in 1820 and died in
1885. In 1900 the family was living with B. Cram,
mother in law, age 73 born in April of 1827. [1900
NHFC] **Benjamin**[8] was a farmer. [NHVR]

Children:
i   **Annie Etta**[9] b 1878 NH d 11-13-1883 at
Lawrence, MA. [MAVR]
ii   **Jesse W.**[9] b 1879 [1880 NHFC] d 3-1-1900
at Newton, NH and is buried at
Willowdale Cemetery. He was 20 years 13
days old.

(698) Edgar Carlos[8], (Lewis[7], Benjamin[6], Daniel[5],
Ephraim[4], Ebenezer[3], Ephraim[2], John[1]), was born 4-18-
1856 at Fenton, Genessee Co. MI. After his father's
death, he attended school and assisted his mother
on the farm, where he spent his entire life and
where he died on 1-29-1935. He married Hettie A.
Sullivan, daughter of Charles Sullivan and Sarah
Grinell, on 10-15-1884. **Edgar**[8] and Hettie were
members of the M.E. Church at Fenton, MI. [Green II
p106]

Child: [Green II]
i   **Clare Sullivan**[9] (male) b 10-22-1887. He
lived in Ellis, MI.

(699) Morris Ripley[8], (Lewis[7], Benjamin[6], Daniel[5],
Ephraim[4], Ebenezer[3], Ephraim[2], John[1]), born 8-19-1868
at Fenton, MI. After completing his High School
education and some work in a business college, he
became a farmer. [HOS]
    He married to Anna Louise Stannard on 4-2-1890,
the daughter of Marcus Cooley Stanard and Statira

Sheldon of Mundy Township, Genesee Co. MI. She was
b 12-20-1870. She was born in MI but had lived in
Portland for 35 years. She taught at the Fenton
(MI) Normal School until her marriage. She was also
a member of the Methodist Deaconess Board and
Treasurer for several years of the former Methodist
Deaconess Auxiliary and member of Mount Hood
Chapter, O.E.S. She died 8-13-1946 [NSOR 8-14-1946]

Morris[8] became Principal of the high school at
Gains, MI in 1892. Two years later he entered the
Methodist College at Albion, MI, receiving his
degree of B.S. in 1898. He then taught in the
Albion, MI High School. In 1911 they moved to
Portland, OR where **Morris**[8] d on 7-24-1929. [Green
II p107]

Children:
i   **Ruby Lucile**[9] b 12-24-1891 graduate of
         University of MI, m Ray Burk Gripmen,
         Banker at Detroit, MI 1906
973 ii   **Laverne Stanard**[9] b 10-28-1902, graduate
         of Oregon A.C. 1926 [HOS]

(700) John[8], (Michael Benjamin[7], Jeremiah[6], Daniel[5],
Ephraim[4], Ebenezer[3], Ephraim[2], John[1]), born 11-21-
1852 at Gabarouse, Cape Breton, Novia Scotia,
Canada. He married to **Louisa Maria**[8] Severance,
daughter of **William Daniel**[7] Severance and Hannah
Murrant, on 12-9-1873. She was born 3-12-1853 at
Grant Mira, Cape Breton. [Shurtleff Vol I]

Children: born at Fourchu, Cape Breton, Nova Scotia
i   **Annie Maria**[9] b 3-16-1875
ii   **Ruth Delila**[9] b 11-9-1876 m James Cann
       12-15-1897
iii   **Marian Jane**[9] b 2-23-1880
iv   **John William**[9] b 6-29-1890 d 3-27-1891
v   **John Wilbert**[9] b 4-11-1892
vi   **Bessie Louisa**[9] b 5-8-1896

(701) Arnold Holmes[8], (Michael Benjamin[7], Jeremiah[6],
Daniel[5], Ephraim[4], Ebenezer[3], Ephraim[2], John[1]), was
born on 1-28-1859 in Fourchu, Cape Breton, Nova
Scotia, Canada. He died 12-18-1935 at Louisburg,
Nova Scotia. On 10-11-1881 he married Flora
Margaret Ferguson, daughter of Donald and Sarah
Ferguson. Flora was born 9-23-1858 Frambois,
Richmond and died 1-21-1950 at Louisbury, Nova
Scotia. [Shurtleff II]

Children: born at Fourchu, Cape Breton, Nova Scotia [MBGD-MSJSM]
i   **William (Wesley) Hardy**[9] b 7-19-1882/3 d 12-30-1945 unm
ii   **John Edward**[9] b 11-6-1884/5 d 5-15-1911 unm
iii   **Frances Matilda**[9] b 1-2-1887 m Hardy Alfred Daye 11-27-1905 d 1-1-1937
iv   **Sarah Jane**[9] b 7-22-1896 m Peter Mac Donald 11-3-1915 d 6-22-1956
v   **Florence Maude**[9] b 7-20-1896 m John Raymond Martell 1-7-1914

(703) Mazzini[8], (George[7], Abijah L.[6], Daniel[5], Ephraim[4], Ebenezer[3], Ephraim[2], John[1]), born 6-7-1854 at Cabot, VT and died 3-21-1928 at Unity, NH. He was a railroad conductor. [NHVR] He married Ellen L. Bickford on 2-21-1876 at Glover, VT. [VTVR] He married Maud Callow on 6-7-1883 in Londonderry, VT. [VTVR] **Mazzini**[8] married a third time to Louise Florence (Farwell) Smith, daughter of George G. Smith, on 1-1-1895. [VTVR] Lastly he married to Gertrude A. Baker (he was 52 and she 35) on 5-10-1905 [NHVR] at Winchester, NH. She was the daughter of Stephen W. Bishop and Lizzie M. Cook. They were divorced in 1913. [NHVR]

    In 1910 **Mazzini**[8] was living alone. He had been married four times. [NHFC]

Children of **Mazzini**[8] Severance and Ella Bickford
i   **Arthur**[9] b 8-19-1878 at Glover, VT

Children of **Mazzini**[9] Severance and Maud Callow
ii   **Harry L.**[9] b 12-12-1885 at Brattleboro, VT [VTVR]

(704) George Walter[8], (Walter Searles[7], Abijah L.[6], Daniel[5], Ephraim[4], Ebenezer[3], Ephraim[2], John[1]), born 9-1-1852 at E. Bridgewater, MA. He died 9-1-1943 at E. Bridgewater. **George Walter**[8] married Celia Phillips Washburn, daughter of Allen Washburn and Sophie Moore Beals, on 9-1-1873 at East Bridgewater, MA. [MAVR] [NSNBMA] She was born 12-10-1852 at E. Bridgewater, MA, and died 5-3-1931 in Hanson, MA and is buried in E. Bridgewater. **George**[8] was a book-keeper. **Minot F.**[8], who was born in 1855 and brother of **George**[8], was living with this family in 1880. [MAFC].

    George[8] and Celia are the grand parents of Avis Munro. [MAM]

Children: [MAM]
 i   **George**[9] b 7-20-1875 at Plymouth, MA
       [MAVR]
 ii   **Walter Allen**[9] b 7- -1875 Plymouth, MA d
       3-6-1876 at East Bridgewater, MA. [MAVR]
 iii   **Lottie Louise**[9] b 8-13-1876 at East
       Bridgewater, MA [MAVR]
975 iv **Fred Allen**[9] b 1881 m Elsie M. Leslie
       [NHVR]
 v   **Wesley Forrest**[9] b 2-1-1882 at South
       Abington, MA [MAVR] m Edith Mildred Ells
       6-22-1912, she b 9-22-1893 he d 9-16-
       1918. They had no children. [Briggs Vol
       III p985] The 1920 MA census shows
       Wesley[9], age 37, living with the
       parents.
 vi   **Walter Harris**[9] b 2-1-1887 d 12-5-1889 E.
       Bridgewater, MA. [MAVR]
976 vii **Lester Washburn**[9] b 10-26-1888 at East
       Bridgewater, MA [MAVR]
 viii **Evelyn Searles**[9] b 10-11-1891 at Hanson,
       MA [MAVR] m Winfield S. Hammond [NHVR]

(705) Minot Forrest[8], (Walter Searles[7], Abijah L[6].
Daniel[5], Ephraim[4], Ebenezer[3], Ephraim[2], John[1]), born
8-19-1855. He shows living with **George**[8] and Celia
in 1880. [MAFC]. He married to Loretta C. (Lyon)
Chandler, daughter of Isaac Keith Lyon and Sarah
Leach, on 5-26-1894. [MAVR] He died on 3-4-1906.
    "**Minot Forrest**[8] Severance was a crayon artist.
He painted a portrait of Mary Baker Eddy in 1888,
which hangs in the Historical Home of the Christian
Scientists in Swampscott, MA." [MAM] The 1900 MA
census shows him with his wife and mother in law,
Sarah Lyon, and a sister in law, Lucy A. Lyon.

(706) John Martin[8], (John[7], Ebenezer[6], Ebenezer[5],
Ephraim[4], Ebenezer[3], Ephraim[2], John[1]), born in July
of 1845. He married to Celia E. Alice Fisher (the
[IGI] says Celia Frechette) on 12-25-1866. [VTVR]
She was born in July of 1845 in Canada. The 1860 VT
census shows two *Sevin* children, **Joseph**[9], born 1850
and **Peter**[9] born 1853, living with a Frechette
family in Milton, VT. Neither **John**[8] nor Celia were
listed. **John M.**[8] Severance died on 9-2-1906. [VTVR]

Children:
 i   **Jennie H.**[9] b 12-2-1868 in Colchester, VT
       [VTVR]
 ii   **Etta C.**[9] b 7-2-1867 [VTVR]

977 iii   **Edwin J.**[9] b 6-29-1870 in VT. [VTVR] They
                had children, **Caroline M.**[9] b 3- -1894
                and **Herbert J.**[9] b 6- -1895, shown as
                grandchildren of **John**[8] and Celia
                Severance.
978 iv   **Percy W.L.**[9], (son of **John**[8] and Celia
                Fisher) who was b in 1-26-1882 in VT
                [VTVR] and shows with **Edwin**[9] on the
                [1900 VTFC]. He m to Josephine Etta
                Boyden on 2-21-1903. [VTVR] They had a
                child **Maurice Marvin**[10] b 4-22-1903.
                [VTVR]

(708) Bertrand Ernest[8], (George[7], Ebenezer[6],
Ebenezer[5], Ephraim[4], Ebenezer[3], Ephraim[2], John[1]),
born 5-19-1864 at Colchester, VT. He married Lillie
E. Bombard 4-15-1885 who was born in December of
1886 at Colchester.

Children:
i   **Mary Eveline**[9] b 4-29-1887 m Edward S.
            Gilmore 6-11-1907
ii   **George Bertrand**[9] b 11-5-1889 at
            Colchester, VT, m Blanche Heywood,
            daughter of Charles Heywood and Julia
            Cross, at Saranac, NY, 6-5-1912. He was
            22 and she was 18. It was the first
            marriage for both of them. [NYVR]
iii   **Charles Leland**[9] b 4-28-1892 at
            Colchester, VT. [VTVR] m Laura Mae
            Plante, daughter of Henry Plante and
            Adeal Richards, 6-25-1914 at Mooers
            Forks, NY. [NYVR]
iv   **Carroll Ernest**[9] b 2-1-1905
v   **Clarence A.**[9] b 8-27-1907 [VTVR]

(709) Alanson[8], (Levi A. Warren[7], Samuel[6], Ebenezer[5],
Ephraim[4], Ebenezer[3], Ephraim[2], John[1]), born in 1839.
[1850 NYFC] He was with Amanda, his wife, who was
born in 1850. They lived in Fulton Co. NY.

Children:
i   **Dewitt**[9] b 5- -1868 m Margarett ____, who
            was born 2- -1868. [1900 NYFC] The
            1920 NY census also shows themn with no
            children
ii   **Estelle**[9] b 1870
iii   **Myrtie**[9] b 1874

(710) Frank Hayward[8], (Lucius Warren[7], Samuel[6], Ebenezer[5], Ephraim[4], Ebenezer[3], Ephraim[2], John[1]), born 11-28-1856 at Manchester, MA [MAVR]. He died on 1-26-1931. **Frank**[8] married Lena L. Hill on 8-19-1885 at Isle Lamotte, VT. [VTVR] [MBS-Ancestry of **Frank H.**[8] Severance sent to his cousin **Bert**[8] Severance, 9-23-1926] Lena L. Hill was born on 11-21-1855, the daughter of Andrews Hill of North Hero, VT. Lena died on 9-25-1942 at Buffalo, NY. **Frank**[8] and Lena are buried at North Cemetery, Isle La Motte, VT.

In 1900, the mother, Lucretia M. Severance, age 72, was living with **Frank**[8] and Lena Severance. [NYFC]

Lena had been a classmate of **Frank's**[8] when he studied at Cornell University, NY. She attended Oswego State Normal School, and received a B.A. degree from Cornell University and studied at the University of Strasbourg. She was co-author of the *History of the Niagara Frontier*. [Stratton p322] [HWCoWI p641]

After the Civil War **Frank**[8] moved to Whitewater, WI. with his family. **Frank**[8] entered Knox College in 1874 and Cornell University in NY State 1875. He was an assistant in microscopic Botany and editor of the *Cornell Review* and the *Cornell Era* during the last two years of school and in 1879 he became a reporter on the *Gazette* at Erie, PA. In 1880 he went to Buffalo, NY as marine editor on the *Buffalo Express*. In 1886 he became the managing editor of the *Illustrated Sunday Express*, where he was able to report on the funeral of President Garfield and the 1889 Johnstown flood.

The Seneca Indians adopted him into their tribe for stories which he did on the Niagara frontier. This information he had collected while as editor of the *Illustrated Sunday Express*. When he became Secretary of the Buffalo Historical Society in 1901 he was able to utilize his collected information.

He was well traveled and in botanical hunts went to Burham, India and Japan. He served as President of the NY State Historical Association for 1923/25 and served as a member of the fine arts commission of New York State.

He is credited as the author of *Old Trails on the Niagara Frontier* (1899), *The Story of Joncaire* (1906), *Studies of the Niagara Frontier* (1911), *The Picture Book of Earlier Buffalo* (1912), *Peace Episodes on the Niagara* (1914), and *An Old Frontier of France* (2 vols., 1917). He edited William

Walton's *The Captivity and Sufferings of Benjamin Gilbert and his Family* (1784) and the publications of the *Buffalo Historical Society* from 1896 to 1930. [Malone Vol XVI]

Children:
    i   **Hayward Merriam**[9] b 1-19-1887, Buffalo, NY
    ii   **Mildred**[9] b 9-10-1892, Plattsbury, NY
    iii   **Edith Lilian**[9] b 8-14-1900, Buffalo, NY

(711) Benjamin Warren[8], (William[7], Samuel[6], Ebenezer[5], Ephraim[4], Ebenezer[3], Ephraim[2], John[1]), was born 7-31-1855 in Willsboro, NY. On May 10, 1882 he married to Lena Woodruff, daughter of Samuel H. Woodruff, of Moriah. Lena was born in November of 1858. [NYFC]

After completing his schooling at Sherman Collegiate Institue at Moriah, he started teaching at Moriah Centre and then at the Union School in Witherbee. He graduated in 1882 from the Homoeopathic Hospital College at Cleveland, Ohio. and on March 22, 1882 he opened his practice in Mineville.

He served as Coroner of the County, a member of the Board of Regent's Examiners, and as Supervisor of the town of Mineville. **Benjamin**[8] was also a ardent lover of horses and kept some well-bred roadsters. [LCCEC p47]

Children:
    i   **Glen W.**[9] b 1-28-1883. The 1900 NY census shows **Glen W.**[9] living in Gouveneur, St. Laurence Co. NY as a farm laborer.
985 ii   **Spencer W.**[9] b 12-16-1887 m Ivy Ashley. She was born in 1874. They lived at Pittsfield, Berkshire Co MA. The 1920 MF census shows them with two children, **Velma**[10] b 1913 and **Glen**[10] b 1914. Her mother, Katherine Ashley was also living with them.
986 iii   **Karl W.**[9] b 8-15-1894 m Pearl

(712) Bert D.[8] (**Elbert Deloyd**), (William[7], Samuel[6], Ebenezer[5], Ephraim[4], Ebenezer[3], Ephraim[2], John[1]), born on 10-15-1863. [MWLS] He married to Nellie E. Smith, daughter of Edward Smith, on 9-30-1891. **Bert**[8] died on 1-11-1929. Nellie was born in September of 1862.

They lived in Willsboro, Essex Co. NY. **Bert**[8] was a senior member of the large dry-goods firm of Severance Brothers in Willsboro, NY. [LCCEC p46]

Children: born in NY state
987   i   **Frank Rolland**[9] b 12-7-1892
988   ii   **Raymond William**[9] b 12-1-1897
      iii   **Bert Vernon**[9] b 1-16-1900 in Willsboro, NY. He married to Gladys Coburn on 6-10-1926. She was born on 11-18-1899 at Lewiston, ID. **Vernon**[9] (as he was called) went to the University of MI, with his brother **Raymon**[9]. They both traveled west in 1922 and found jobs with the telephone company. **Vernon**[9] was an excellent wood worker and his speciality was to cane the seats of chairs. **Bert**[9] died after 1992. They did not leave any children.
989 iv   **Leroy E.**[9] b 8-21-1904

(713) Karl Jerome[8], (William[7], Samuel[6], Ebenezer[5], Ephraim[4], Ebenezer[3], Ephraim[2], John[1]), born on 10-3-1865 in Chesterfield, NY. He married Kate M. Foss on 3-18-1891 in Keeseville, VT. [VTVR] She was born in June of 1869 in Vergennes, VT. [NYFC] **Karl**[8] was a physician. He died on 7-28-1920.

Children:
     i   **Marian**[9] b 2- -1899 [1900 NYFC]

(714) Rolland Augustus[8], (William[7], Samuel[6], Ebenezer[5], Ephraim[4], Ebenezer[3], Ephraim[2], John[1]), born on 8-6-1868 at Willsborough, NY and died there on 1-2-1948. He married to Flora Elizabeth Smith on 11-13-1895. She was born on 5-16-1869. She died on 12-12-1964 at Willsborough, NY. **Rolland**[8] and Flora lived in Willsboro, Essex Co, NY.

   Rolland[8] was the junior member of the enterprising firm of Severance Brother's Store, with his Brother **Bert**[8], in Willsboro, NY. [LCCEC p46]

Children:
     i   **Emily Aileen**[9] b 5-24-1899
     ii   **Lucile Norma**[9] b 12-10-1904 at Willsborough NY. She m Charles Francis Nettleship on 10-7-1902 at Newark, NJ.
     iii   **Kathryn Elizabeth**[9] b 2-10-1907

(715) Samuel[8], (Samuel Bird[7], Levi[6], Ebenezer[5], Ephraim[4], Ebenezer[3], Ephraim[2], John[1]), was born 10- -1861 in Pittsburg, PA. He married to Eleanor Schmertz.

Children:
- i **Samuel[9]** b 11- -1890 in Pittsburg [1900 PAFC]
- ii **Eleanor S.[9]** b 1890. [1920 PAFC] She was living with her husband, Clarence L. Saxton, and her parents.

(716) Frank Ward[8], (Samuel Bird[7], Levi[6], Ebenezer[5], Ephraim[4], Ebenezer[3], Ephraim[2], John[1]), was born 11-30-1870. **Frank Ward's[8]** application for membership to the Son of the American Revolution indicated that his line of descent was **Samuel[7]** Severance and Arabella Nelson Miller, **Levi[6]** and Hannah Bird, and **Ebenezer[5]** and Lucy Nutting. **Ebenezer[5]**, husband of Lucy Nutting, was born in Temple, NH on 9-8-1752. He continues to give the account of **Ebenezer's[5]** service in the Revolution from 4-19-1775 at Temple until his discharge at Saratoga on 10-17-1777.

Frank[8] married Florance Wallace on 7-22-1913. She was born 1878 in PA. [Virkus] Florance had a son, Daniel H. Wallace, born 1908 before she married to **Frank[8]**.

Children:
- i **Frank W.[9]** b 4-7-1915 in Sewickley, PA

(719) Otto R.[8], (Anson Bigelow[7], Issac[6], Ebenezer[5], Ephraim[4], Ebenezer[3], Ephraim[2], John[1]), born in June of 1852 in WI. [1900 WIFC] He married to Hattie J. Walbridge, daughter of Guy and Sophronia Walbridge, 10-29-1877 at Webster, MA. [MAVR] She was born in May of 1852 in CT. They show living in Whitewater, Walworth Co. WI. In 1900 Sophronia Walbridge age 77, born 11- -1822 in ME, (mother) was living with them. [WIFC]

Children:
- i **Pearl W.[10]** b 4- -1879 in MA [1900 WIFC]

(721) Coello B.[8], (Collamer[7], Issac[6], Ebenezer[5], Ephraim[4], Ebenezer[3], Ephraim[2], John[1]), born in March of 1857. [1900 WIFC]. He married to Fannie B. Keimbach on 6-17-1896. [WIVR] She was born in July of 1870/71. [1900 WIFC]. They first lived in

Milwaukee, WI but later moved to CA. He died on 10-12-1906, at the age of 83, in Fresno, CA.

He was a widely known dancing Master. He was a descendant of a long line of dancing masters and musicians and proprietor with his father of a dancing school at Fresno. Surviving were the professor's widow, Frances, a sister, Mrs. **Merite**[9] Steele, Milwaukee, and four daughters, **Helen**[10], Evanston, IL, **Phyllis**[10], **Harriet**[10], and **Jane**[10], all of CA. [NSMWI 9-14-1939]

Children:

  i   **Phillis J.**[10] b 4- -1897 in WI
  ii   **Helen L.**[10] b 1898 in WI
  iii **Harriet**[10]
  iv   **Jane**[10]

(722) George Washington[8], (Joseph C[7], Ephraim[6], Abel[5], Ephraim[4], Ebenezer[3], Ephraim[2], John[1]), born 11-16-1859 in Washington, NH. [IGI] He died on 2-10-1921. [NHVR] The death records shows that he was married and the 1900 NH census shows his wife as Gertrude J. McIlvain, born April of 1873.

Children:

  i   **Abbie A.**[9](or **E.**) b 4- -1895 [1900 NHFC]
  ii   **Harry J.**[9] b 1908 [1910 NHFC]

(723) Hiram Abel[8], (William D[7], Joseph[6], Rufus[5], Ephraim[4], Ebenezer[3], Ephraim[2], John[1]), born 5-28-1850 in Washington, NH. [IGI] He married Ellen (Elinor) D. Tandy, daughter of Alfred Tandy and **Diana H.**[7] Severance, on 12-18-1872. [NHVR] **Diana H.**[7] was the daughter of **Joel**[6] Severance (son of **Rufus**[5]) and Jane (Weeks) Woodward. Elinor was born 3-18-1857 and died 2-12-1923 (wife of **Hiram A.**[8] Severance). [NHVR] They are living with Alfred A. Tandy, age 32 and **William D.**[7] Severns, age 41 and Severns children, **Edward D.**[8], born 1855, **Ellenor**[8], born 1858, and **Delia A.**[8], born 1859 all in NH. [1860 NHFC]

Children: born in Washington, NH

  i   **Hatch C.**[9] b 3-28-1873. The 1910 NH census shows him with his wife Frances C. and living in Washington, NH, without children.
  ii   **Hattie M.**[9] b 3-28-1875, m Charles R. Peaslee at Washington, NH on 12-12-1906

374

[NHVR] He was the son of Humphrey Peaslee and Elizabeth B. Brown.

iii   **Mabel E.**[9] b 7-4-1879

(724) Arthur F.[8], (Joel[7], Joseph[6], Rufus[5], Ephraim[4], Ebenezer[3], Ephraim[2], John[1]), born 3-6-1852 [NHVR] in Washington, NH, and died 7-24-1929 [NHVR] in Washington. He was a farmer. He married to Mary A. Gove, daughter of Enoch Page Gove and Lucy Ann Cram, on 6-7-1876 in Unity, NH. They were divorced on 11-11-1904 [NHVR]. Mary Ann was born 7-9-1858 at Washington, NH and died in 1908 at Concord. [Gove p313]

The [NHVR] says that **Arthur**[8] was born 3-6-1843 although his parents were not married until 1846 and the second marriage was 6-6-1852.

The 1880 NH census shows Eliza J. age 55, living with **Arthur**[8] and Mary A. and indicates that she was his mother although it would be his step mother since **Arthur's**[8] actual mother died 2 months after he was born.

Children:

991 i   **Fred Barton**[9] b 3-17-1880 in Washington, NH, worked in a shoe shop, m1 9-30-1903 Margaret E. Clark, daughter of George L. Clark and Karen C. Lockwood, at Claremont, NH. Divorced 11- -1905 [NHVR] m2 Christina May Smith, 7-2-1906, daughter of Richard Smith and Ellen Hart.

ii   **Willis E.**[9] b 2-28-1882 in Washington, NH, electrician and lived in Orange, MA, m Mary L Hunter, 9-1-1908, daughter of Harvey M. Hunter and Lucy Pierce. [NHVR]

iii   **Enoch A.**[9] b 8-12-1884 in Washington. In 1900 he was a boarder of Clark S. Spaulding. [1900 NHFC]

iv   **Tracy P.**[9] b 6- -1888 [Gove p313] He married to Ethel A. ____, who was born 1884 in NY state. In 1910 he was living alone with no wife. In 1920 he was living with his wife and no children. [NHFC]

(725) Herbert D[8], (Joseph W.[7], Joseph[6], Rufus[5], Ephraim[4], Ebenezer[3], Ephraim[2], John[1]), born 3-10-1860 at Stoddard, NH and died 11-3-1933 at Hopkinton, NH. [NHVR] He married Lena M. Colby on 8-24-1909 at

Concord, NH. [NHVR] She was the daughter of Abram Putnam Colby and Christina A. Richards. **Herbert D.**[8] was a farmer and paper maker. The 1920 Hopkinton, Merrimack Co. NH census shows **Herbert D.**[8], his wife Lena M., her mother, Christina A. Colby, and **Herbert's**[8] son, **Harry A.**[9] b 1911 in NH.

Children:
i   **Harry A.**[9] b circa 1911 d 5-2-1989. He was b in Contoocook and lived in the area most of his life before moving to Franklin several years ago. He attended Hopkinton High School. He was a former member of the Contoocook Baptist Church and a member of the Franklin Baptist Church, where he was a former member of the choir. [NSUL 5-3-1989 obituary] At the time of his death, the only living relative was recorded as a second cousin, Josephine Kryzaniak, of Contoocook.

(727) William Joel.[8], (Joseph W.[7], Joseph[6], Rufus[5], Ephraim[4], Ebenezer[3], Ephraim[2], John[1]), born 11-22-1870 at Washington, NH. He married to Florence E. Fowler who was born 10-1-1872 at Washington. **Willie**[8] was a teamster at Washington, NH.

Children:
i   **Effie E.**[9] b 1894, Hopkinton, NH m Charles S. Hoyt, son of Edward F. Hoyt and Charlotte M. Buttrick, 9-10-1914. [NHVR]

ii   **Howard C.**[9] b 11-7-1896 at Washington, NH, d 3-6-1923 at Hopkinton, NH, a farmer, m Mary Blanchette, daughter of Joseph and Jennie Blanchette, on 9-9-1918 at Henniker, NH. [NHVR] She was born in 1902. **Howard C.**[9] died on 3-6-1923. [NHVR] He was a young farmer and died of the flu.

iii   **Isabel D.**[9] b 1899 at Hopkinton, NH, m Leslie C. Barton, son of Robert Barton and Mabel Thompson, 5-10-1916. [NHVR]

993 iv   **Archie William**[9] b 1903, Hopkinton, NH. He m Ardis M. Cilley, daughter of Leonard W. Cilley and Lina M. Flanders of Orange, NH [NHVR] He divorced Ardis M. 1-25-1928. They were m 10-7-1923. [NHVR] He m Odena I. Gagnon, daughter of

Honore Gagnon and Rose Priere of Canada,
4-30-1932. She was b 1903 at Pembroke,
NH [NHVR]

v   **Alfred P.**[9] b 1904 m Ethel A. Cooper,
daughter of Clarence C. and Slanor M.
Cooper, on 11-23-1924. [NHVR] **Alfred**[9]
was a Teamster. The NH vital records
show that a female was born in 1924 and
died the same day.

vi   **Dorothy H.**[9] b 1907 m Moses D. Clark, son
of Frank Clark and Georgianna McDole,
11-20-1926

(728) Ernest Bertrand[8], (Joseph[7], Joseph[6], Rufus[5],
Ephraim[4], Ebenezer[3], Ephraim[2], John[1]), born 8-8-1879,
at Marlow, NH. [NHVR] He married first to Annie
Wiggin circa 1899/1900. [Ellison p501] He married
secondly to Cora Swett, daughter of Luman A. Swett
and Alma E. Swett, on 11-25-1903 at Atrim, NH.
[NHVR] **Ernest**[8] divorced Cora at Antrim, NH on 10-
15-1910. [NHVR] He next married to Mabel Davis,
daughter of Harry H. Bailey and Abbie Noris, at
Hillsborough, NH. (his third-her 2nd) on 6-3-1913
[NHVR] He was widowed. **Ernest B.**[8] was a Livery man,
conducting a livery business in Antrim. He later
moved to Hillsboro, NH. [Browne]

Children:

i   **Ernest**[9] b 3-28-1900

ii   **Etta Alma**[9] b 3-25-1903 m Roy C. Knapton,
son of Walter E. Knapton and Anna May
Huff, 9-20-1924 at Henniker, NH. He was
a painter. [NHVR]

(729) Melvin J.[8], (Jonathan[7], Ephraim[6], Rufus[5],
Ephraim[4], Ebenezer[3], Ephraim[2], John[1]), born 3-9-1889
at Hillsboro, NH. (NHVR) He died on 10-26-1918.
[NHVR] According to the records, when **Melvin J.**[8]
Severance was born his father, **Jonathan**[7], was 65
years old. When **Melvin**[8] married, to Georgianna M.
Russell in 7-29-1912 (NHVR), his father, **Jonathan**[7],
was listed as being 85 years old and his mother,
Issa Davis, was 44. It is possible that **Melvin**[8] was
the son of Issa (Elizabeth) before she married to
Jonathan[7].

Children:

i   **Charlotte Jane**[9] b 1913 m Frank Joseph
O'Conner on 7-4-1932 at Hillsboro, NH

ii   **Janet**[9] b 4-28-1917 d 7-18-1931 single at Hillsborough, NH

iii   **Melvin J.**[9] **II** b 1919 in East Washington. He was employed for 25 years at the A&P Stores which he managed in Penacook and Pittsfield. He d 11-5-1990. His family included his wife, Rowena (Chadwick) Severance of Concords, two sons, **Melvin J. III**[10] of Concord and **Donald C.**[10] of Epsom, a daughter, **Donna North**[10] of Easton and two sisters, **Claudia**[9] Simcock and **Barbara**[9] Murphy." [NSUL Manchester 11-8-1990]

(730) Ernest[8], (John Russell[7], Abijah[6], Rufus[5], Ephraim[4], Ebenezer[3], Ephraim[2], John[1]), born in IA in August of 1876. His parents later settled in Escambia Co. FL, where **Ernest**[8] can be found living in 1900 as a boarder in Pensacola.

In 1920 **Ernest**[8] was living in Chicago with his wife Blanche Smith. She was born circa 1889 in Illinois. [ILFC]

Children:
i   **Ernest**[9] b 1915 in Chicago, IL

(731) Alfred H.[8], (Christopher[7], unconnected, Ephraim[5], Ephraim[4], Ebenezer[3], Ephraim[2], John[1]), was born 1- -1848, living at Medway, ME. He married to Martha J. who was born 1- -1861 in ME. [1900 MEFC]

Children:
i   **Frank Roy**[9] b 5- -1879

(732) Henry A.[8], (Christopher[7], unconnected, Ephraim[5], Ephraim[4], Ebenezer[3], Ephraim[2], John[1]), was born circa 1853. He married Nora E. Mercier 7-26-1916. She was born 1873. [MEVR] This was probably his second marriage since the 1900 ME census shows **Harry A.**[8] born 7- -1854 and Sadie F. born 11- -1856 as his wife. They lived at E. Millinocket, ME.

(733) Christopher/John Ellis[8], (Christopher[7], unconnected, Ephraim[5], Ephraim[4], Ebenezer[3], Ephraim[2], John[1]), was born 2-14-1874 (son of **Christopher**[7] and Susan) [MEVR] I also show a **John Ellis**[8] born the same day at Medway, ME. He married first to Mary E. (Maud) Littlefield, daughter of Fred Littlefield and Martha Trask, 5-5-1895 at Monroe, ME. [MEVR] He married second to Ezzie (Lizzie) Adams, daughter of

Justus Adams and Lucinda Smith, 6-16-1898. She died in 1958. [MEVR] In 1920 **John E.**[8], age 49, was living at Greenbush with Ezie age 37 and their children, (all born in ME) {MEFC] **John**[8] died in 1956 at Cardville, Penobscot Co. ME [CRME]

Children: [1910 MEFC-Greenbush, 7 ch born 4 living][1920 MEFC]
    i   **Myrtle E.**[9] b 7-1-1898 1st ch [MEVR] d 2-10-1899. [MEVR]
    ii
    iii
    iv   **Archie M.**[9] b 2-23-1903 4th ch [MEVR]
    v   **Alice W.**[9] b 1905
    vii   **Ellis W.**[9] b 1906
    vi   **Hattie E.**[9] b 9-10-1906
    vii   **Albion J.**[9] b 1911
    viii   **Bernice A.**[9] b 1914

(735) Frank L[8], (Ivory[7], unconnected), was born 3-21-1861. (IGI) He married to Lizzie M. Shaw, daughter of Joseph Shaw and Julia Brown of Exeter, on 4-16-1892. [MEVR] She was b 10- -1864. [1900 MEFC] **Frank**[8] died 9-13-1908 at Kittery ME. [MEVR]

Children:
    i   **C.E.**[9] b 1891
    ii   **Clifford B.**[9] b 1892 d 4-10-1900 [MEVR]
    iii   **Joseph R.**[9] b 1903 [1910 MEFC]

(736) Frank E.[8], (James[7], Jacob[6], Ephraim /Nathaniel[5], Ephraim[4], Ebenezer[3], Ephraim[2], John[1]), was born in Knox, ME in 1842/1846 and died 12-4-1888 at Searsmont, ME. [MEVR] He was employed in the Bates Mill in Lewiston, ME, for a number of years, and during the Civil War served with the Fifteenth Maine Regiment, remaining in service throughout the entire period of the conflict. He married to Martha Hitchcock. She was born in Strong, ME, and died in Butte, MT in 1882. [Conklin Vol IV p444]

Children:
    i   **Elizabeth**[9]
994 ii   **George Oscar**[9] b circa 1876 [1880 MEFC]

(737) Fred A.[8], (James[7], Jacob[6], Ephraim/Nathaniel[5], Ephraim[4], Ebenezer[3], Ephraim[2], John[1]), born 10- -1855. [1900 MTFC] Although he was born in Knox, ME, his family soon after found themselves as sheep

ranchers in the high plains of MT. He apparently
traveled back to ME to marry Clara Wing, daughter
of Peleg S. Wing and Zanna McFarland, of Searsmont,
ME on 4-20-1881. The marriage records show that
Fred[8] was from Oka, MT Territory. However they must
have soon returned to MT. The 1900 MT census for
Big Timber, Sweet Grass Co. shows the family as
Fred A.[8] born in ME, his wife Clara M. born 6- -
1860 in ME, and their children. **Fred**[8] was living
with his uncle, **Jacob**[7], on the 1880 MT census.

Children: [Searsmont MEVR]
  i   **Eva Mable**[9] b 4-24-1882 in ME [MEVR] m
         ___ Shipton
  ii   **Millie Wing**[9] b 5-7-1883 in ME [MEVR] m
         ___ Snyder
  iii **Paul Frederick**[9] b 7-4-1887 in ME [1900
         MTFC]
  iv   **Ernest Sprague**[9] b 9- -1892 in MT [1900
         MTFC] The 1920 MT census shows him with
         his wife Clara, age 20, living at Big
         Timber, MT.
  v   **Lloyd Dewey**[9] b 10- -1898 in MT [1900
         MTFC]

(738) Charles Edgar[8], (Jacob, Jr.[7], Jacob[6], Ephraim[5],
Ephraim[4], Ebenezer[3], Ephraim[2], John[1],) was born 8-6-
1855 in ME and married Helen Hussey 8-11-1883 in
Unity, ME. [MEVR] He was in San Jose, CA when his
daughter, Helen Hussey Severance, was born. **Charles
Edgar**[8] died 2-9-1913 in Walla Walla, WA. He spent
much of his younger life in Montana as a sheep
rancher on the C.E. Severance Sheep Company. [1880
MTFC Musselshell Valley, Meager Co] [Stout p112,
1159] The [DARLR #180905+166, Walla Walla WA]

Children:
  i   **Helen**[9] m Ralph Reser 2-15-1914 [MEVR]
         at Spokane, WA. Ralph was b 7-21-1891.
         The genealogy of the family of **Helen**[9]
         Severance Reser and of the Reser
         branch, was compiled by her mother,
         Helen Hussey[8] Severance. [Pioneers of
         Washington State]

(740) Frank[8], (Thatcher[7], Ephraim[6], Ephraim[5],
Ephraim[4], Ebenezer[3], Ephraim[2], John[1]), born circa
1854. **Frank**[8] married to Annie J. Walker, daughter
of Joshua Walker, on 12-31-1880. [MEVR] She died on
9-21-1912 at the age of 55. [MEVR] **Frank**[8] died on 3-

22-1927. They are shown living at Orrevill and
Foxcroft, ME. In 1900 **Frank P.**[8] *Severns* born 6- -
1855, was with his wife Annie J. born 1- -1857 and
children, **Eva M.**[9] born 6- -1884 and **Mollie M.**[9] born
4- -1895. They were living in Lewiston,
Androscoggin Co. ME. He was of Foxcroft, ME with
wife Annie and a grand-daughter in 1910, [MEFC]

(741) Orrin T.[8], (Thatcher[7], Ephraim[6], Ephraim[5],
Ephraim[4], Ebenezer[3], Ephraim[2], John[1]), born 4-9-1859
in Bangor, ME. [MEVR] He died on 12-20-1934. [MEVR]
He married Della Perham who died in 1898. [CRME] He
was recorded as living in Dover-Foxcroft, Bangor,
Sebec, and Barnard, ME. The cemetery records show
Orrin[8] and Della buried together. The census
records do not show Della but they do show a Mary,
born 9- -1830 as the mother of **Thatcher**[7]. This
would have been Mary E. Berry.

Children: [1900 MEFC] and [MEVR]
997 i   **Orman J.**[9] b 8- -1885
   ii   **Gertrude M.**[9] b 7- -1887
   iii **Maud B.**[9] b 9- -1889
   iv
   v   **Clara F.**[9] b 1892
   vi
   vii **Clarence T.(O)**[9] b 1897 d 9-22-1899 age 2
        years
   viii Male, the [MEVR] shows this male as the
        eight child

(742) Joseph[8], (Thatcher[7], Ephraim[6], Ephraim[5],
Ephraim[4], Ebenezer[3], Ephraim[2], John[1]), born in March
of 1861 at Sebec, ME. [1900 MEFC] He married to
Mary Loomer, duaghter of John and Annie Loomer, 10-
16-1886 at Boston, MA. He married Mary E. Roche on
8-15-1894 and Esther Moore, daughter of Joseph and
Elizabeth Moore, on 12-1-1896. [MEVR] Esther was
born in December of 1869. The 1900 ME census shows
two of Esther's sisters, Sarah J. and Edith M.
Moore, 18 and 12 years old respectively, living
with them. The Severance family lived in Foxcroft,
Saco, and Lewiston, ME.

Children:
   i   **Silvia E.**[9] b 1- -1897. [1900 MEFC]
   ii   **Ethel Pearl**[9] b 3-15-1900 at Lewiston,
       ME. Listed as the second child [MEVR]

(743) Delbert A.[8], (Daniel[7], Ephraim[6], Ephraim[5], Ephraim[4], Ebenezer[3], Ephraim[2], John[1]), born 3-25-1866 in Sebec, ME. **Delbert A.**[8] married to Emma G. Curtis on 10-4-1885. She was born in 1867 in ME. While in ME, **Adelbert**[8] was a foreman at a pulp mill.

They are buried in the Rural Grove Cemetery, Dover-Foxcroft, ME. Gravestone markers indicate that **Delbert**[8] was born 3-25-1886 and died 8-1-1943. His wife Helen Sprague, no dates, and a daughter, **Ola A.**[9], of **Della**[8] and Emma G. died 1-17-1893 ae 1-9-15.

Children:
<table>
<tr><td>i</td><td></td><td>Ola A.[9] d at Foxcroft, ME 1-17-1893 ae 1-10-15 [MEVR]</td></tr>
<tr><td>998</td><td>ii</td><td>Delbert A.[9] the 1920 PA census shows Delbert[9] b 1892 in ME with his wife Jemima age 28, Dorothy[10] age 9, Lucille[10] age 7, Raymond[10] age 5, Glenn[10] age 3 1/2 and Arlene[10] (baby), all b in PA except for Delbert[8]</td></tr>
<tr><td></td><td>iii</td><td>William L.[9] b circa 1895 at Foxcroft, ME. [MEVR]</td></tr>
<tr><td></td><td>iv</td><td>Leon E.[9] b 1896. He married first to Edith May Blizzard, daughter of Lemuel Blizzard and Ada Nichols, on 11-22-1916. They had a daughter, Pauline M.[10] born 12-6-1917 in Bangor, ME. Pauline[10] married to Sidney H. Lovering on 6-3-1946. [MEVR] Edith died 12-12-1919. She was b in Frederickton, N.B., Canada. She is buried in Mt Hope Cemetery, Bangor, ME. Leon[9] married secondly to Rose M, Prue on 7-28-1920. Leon[9] d on 2-25-1923 age 29-4-9 They are all buried at Mt Hope Cemetery in Bangor, ME.</td></tr>
</table>

(744) Chester L.[8], (Daniel[7], Ephraim[6], Ephraim[5], Ephraim[4], Ebenezer[3], Ephraim[2], John[1]), born circa 1868/1870 in Sebec, ME. He married to Clara E. (McNaughton) Berce, daughter of James McNaughton and Lois A. Hutchins, on 8-12-1902 in NH. [MEVR] It was indicated that this was his first marriage but her third. The [MEVR] show the marriage for **Chester**[8] to Clara E. Berce as his first and her third, he was 32 years old and she was 35.

Children: [1920 MEFC]
<table>
<tr><td>i</td><td>Everett W.[9] b 1905 in ME</td></tr>
</table>

(745) Abel W.[8], (Joseph[7], Ephraim[6], Ephraim[5], Ephraim[4], Ebenezer[3], Ephraim[2], John[1]), born 4- -1861, [1900 ORFC] in Trimbelle, WI. After leaving WI, they first lived in Tillamook, OR. He married to Eliza ____, who was born in 1- -1865 in WI. The [1920 WAFC] shows his second wife, Dora___, born 1874 in Iowa. His parents later moved to and settled in WA State and Portland, OR. [NWI Vol 14 p10-11 **Joseph[7]** Severance-River Falls, WI 1831-1914] **A.W.[8]** Severance a farmer at Parker, WA. [NSYDR]
"Tillamook, Oregon, July 18, 1900. The wife of Postmaster **A.W.[8]** Severance died yesterday. She had acted as assistant Postmaster until a few months ago when she was taken down with consumption. She was a member of the Degree of honor, A.O.U.W." [NSOR 7-19-1900]

Children: [1900 ORFC][1920 WAFC]
i   **Warren[9]** b 9- -1893 in OR
ii   **Logan[9]** b 2- -1896 in OR. The 1920 OR census shows **Logan[9]** living with his parents and family in Donald, Yakima Co. WA.
iii **Mary[9]** b 5- -1898 in OR
iv   **Ruth B.[9]** b 1909 in OR
v   **Mildred F.[9]** b 1912 in WA

(747) Edward W.[8], (Joseph[7], Ephraim[6], Ephraim[5], Ephraim[4], Ebenezer[3], Ephraim[2], John[1]), born in August of 1874 in Trimbelle, WI. His wife was indicated as Belle, b 1880 in WI. [1920 WAFC] He later lived in Parker, WA. The 1900 WA census shows **Edward[8]** living with his brother, **DeForest[8]**, in Yakima, WA.

Children: [1900 WAFC]
i   **Ralph J.[9]** b 1912 in WA

(749) Delbert A.[8], (Fred A.[7], Ephraim[6], Ephraim[5], Ephraim[4], Ephraim[3], Ebenezer[2], John[1]), born in May of 1880 in Pierce Co. WI. He married to Nellie R. ____, who was born in 1886 in MN. The 1910 PA census shows them living in Philadelphia. He died in 1934 in Minneapolis, MN.

Children:
i   **Delbert A.[9]** b 1910 in PA
ii   **William L.[9]** b 1914 in MN
     [NWI-*Elsworth Herald* 3-13-1941, Vol 44 p155-156]

(750) Fred Leon[8], (Seth[7], unconnected, Ephraim[5], Ephraim[4], Ebenezer[3], Ephraim[2], John[1]), was born 2-11-1853 and died 3-12-1939 after a brief illness of influenza at Topsfield, ME. He was married to Albina Louise (Powell) Bailey, daughter of Even and Louise (Loran) Powell, on 5-1-1884. Albina died just 6 days after **Fred[8]** passed away. The obituary from Topsfield, ME indicates that **Fred[8]** was born in the town of Carroll, a son of the late **Seth[7]** and Jane (Munday) Severance. He was survived by five children, one great grandchild and several grandchildren. He had reached the advanced age of 86 years and had resided practically all his life in Topsfield. Good health had permitted him to attend to his farm duties until only a few days before his death. [MMS]

The funeral service were conducted by Rev. Angus Lyons on 5-15-1939. Interment was in the family lot in Topsfield, ME.

In 1880 he was living in Washington Co. ME, age 27 and living with the still complete family of **Seth[7]** and Mariah Severance. [MEFC] In 1900 he was living at Topsfield, Washington Co. [MEFC]

Children:
- i   Mrs. **Edith M.[9]** Bowker of Augusta, ME. b 4-25-1885
- ii   Mrs. **Nola[9]** Mallory
- iii   Mrs. **Inez Ethel[9]** Stevens, b 4-26-1887
- iv   Mrs. **Flora[9]** Wright, b 2- -1890
- v   **Fred Jr.[9]** b 6-7-1892 d 10-16-1918
- vi   **Leon[9]** b 5-1-1895
- vii **Lloyd Elbert[9]** b 8-19-1897 m Angie M. Cochran, daughter of Fred Cochran and Mary A. Bailey, 1-19-1921. Angie was b 6-3-1902 at Codyville Pt., ME. They had a daughter, **Irene Velma[10]** b 9-30-1921 at Codyville.

(751) Charles[8], (Seth[7], unconnected) was born 8- - 1856. **Charles[8]** was living in Jones, Elk Co, PA with his wife Annie between 1900-1910. [PAFC] She was born in December of 1860 in ME.

Children: The first 3 children born in ME, the last 3 in PA.
- i   **Ethel[9]** b 4- -1886
- ii   **Helen[9]** b 10- -1888
- iii   **Delbert[9]** b 4- -1891
- iv   **Dora[9]** b 9- -1891

v   **Joseph Jerome**[9] b 8- -1895
vi   **Raymond**[9] b 3- -1898
vii   **Maurice**[9] b 1902

(752) George Edward[8], (Seth[7], unconnected) b 3- -
1866. He was of Springfield, ME in 1939. The 1880
Kossuth, Washington Co. ME census shows him with
his parents and family. He married Flora Lois
Chubbuck on 1-3-1888 at Carroll, ME. [MEVR] She was
born 11- -1868. The 1900 ME census Topsfield,
Washington Co. shows the family of **George**[8] and
Flora Severance.

Children:
i   **Carrie**[9] b 9-12-1888 Carroll, Penobscot
         Co. ME.
ii   **Solomon**[9] b 4-24-1890 m Carrie Glidden 4-
         19-1911.
iii   **Charles**[9] b 2- -1892
iv   **Clarence**[9] b 3-21-1894 Topsfield,
         Washington Co. ME. He married first to
         Phoebe E. Chase, daughter of John G.
         Chase and Rachel Aldana Holden, on 6-26-
         1917 at Madison, ME. She was born at
         Bingham, ME on 6-26-1885 and died 10-21-
         1917 at Norridgewock, Somerset Co. ME.
         He married secondly to Gladys Price of
         New Brunswick.
v   **Earl Lee**[9] b 6-2-1896
vi   **James Henry**[9] b 4-20-1898 m Lillian P.
         Smith 7-27-1918
vii   **George Harold**[9] b 3-22-1900 m Hazel S.
         Burton 12-22-1920
viii   **Frank Leslie**[9] b 3-28-1902
ix   **Laura May**[9] b 4-30-1903
x   **Albion**[9] b 8-9-1905 d 8-18-1905
xi   **Allison Augustus**[9] b 1907
xii   **Everett L.**[9] b 6-6-1909
xiii
xiv
xv   **Ruth**[9] b 9-9-1914 Kossuth, ME. Stillborn.

(753) Artemus Cushman[8], (Seth[7], unconnected) was
born 1- -1872 in ME. He must have married early and
then he married to Elizabeth Ann Bryant on 6-21-
1908 at Topsfield, ME. [MEVR] She was born 1872
[1920 ME Census Records] They lived in Carroll and
Kossuth, ME. In 1900 **Artimus (Artie)**[8] was living
with Elizabeth McLaughlin and two McLaughlin
children and the daughter **Delvina**[9] born 1- -1893 in

ME, son, **Joseph**[9] born 5- -1895, daughter, **Victoria**[9] born 6- -1898 and **Frank**[8] born 12- -1885. [MEFC] Elizabeth was the daughter of Isaac Bryant and Margaret Scott. Elizabeth died 7-28-1932.

There is record that **Jesse Forest** Severance, born in Carroll or Prentiss, ME circa 1921, married to Ruth Bertha Hurd on 7-18-1945 at Lincoln, ME. **Jesse** was the son of **Joseph L.** Severance, born in Prentiss, ME (circa 1921) and Ethyl McLaughlin. [Candage p899]

Children: [1920 MEFC]
i	**Delvina**[9] b 1- -1893
ii	**Forest/Joseph**[9] b 5- -1895
iii	**Victoria**[9] b 6- -1898/1900
iv	**Grace**[9] b 1902
v	**Merle**[9] b 1904
vi	**Rubin**[9] b 1906
vii	**Rachael**[9] b 1908
viii	**Clara**[9] b 1911
ix	
x	**Gerald A.**[9] b 4-18-1912
xi	**Orland Lane**[9] (Allen) b 12-20-1912 at Kossuth, ME, the 11th child of **Artimus**[8] and Elizabeth Bryant [MEVR]

[The last two entries are from queries of Geneva G. McLaughlin of Togus, ME]

(754) Frank Edward[8], (Seth[7], Unconnected) was born 10-2-1885 at Carroll, ME and died 10-7-1973. He married to Mina A. Aldrich, daughter of Everett F. Aldrich and Hattie E. Bowker 12-31-1905 at Carroll, ME. He married secondly to Anna M. Linscott on 5-10-1913 at Kingsman, Washington Co. ME.

Children of **Frank Edward**[7] Severance and Mina A. Aldrich
i	**female**[9] b 3-25-1906 at Carroll, ME
ii	**Kenneth E.**[9] b 4-21-1908 at Springfield, ME

Children of **Frank Edward**[8] Severance and Anna M. Linscott
iii	**Beverly Isaac**[9] at Kingman, ME
iv	**Truth E.**[9] b 4-4-1915 at Kingman m Philip M. Eldrige 3-23-1935
v	**male**[9] b 5-1-1916
vi	**Theo Clyden**[9] b 1-15-1919 at Kingman m Richard A. York 3-12-1938

vii   **Earl Franklin**[9] b 4-16-1920 at Kingman m Thelma V. Little 8-18-1940

viii   **Nettie Maria**[9] b 9-16-1922 at Kingman m Leroy A. Stimpson

ix   **Evon M.**[9] b 7-28-1925 at Passadumkeag, ME

x   **Hope A.**[9] b 4-5-1927

xi   **William**[9] b 2-17-1930 at Passadumkeag

xii   **Helen Alfreda**[9] b 5-28-1932 at Passadumkeag m Donald W. Davis 6-1-1952

xiii   **Durward Lawrence**[9] b 2-24-1934 at Passacumkeag

xiv   **Frank Edward**[9] b 2-7-1939 at Passadumkeag

(759) George[8], (William[7], John[6], unconnected) was born 1875 and died 1943. He married to Elizabeth (Bettie) Taylor (1881-1960). [MNY Ohio]

Children: [1920 Crab Orchard, Lincoln Co KYFC]

i   **Georgia Ann**[9] b 1-20-1905 d 1979 m Brogan Roberts

ii   **Jennie**[9] b 1908 m Eugene Pruitt m Marvin Morgan

iii   **Della**[9] b 1909 m Robert Wilson m ___? m William Mucheng

iv   **Walter**[9] b 1912 in IL

v   **James David**[9] b 3-23-1914 [KYVR] m Della

vi   **Homer A.**[9] b 1917 m Opal

(761) Joseph[8], (Joseph[7], John[6], unconnected) was born in January of 1869. He shows on the [1900 KYFC] living in Mays Lick, Mason County as a pastor of the Christian Church with his wife Margaret b 6--1879. Margaret was born in MS. The 1910 KY census shows them living in Frankfort, Franklin Co. By 1920, they were living in Louisville, Jefferson Co. [KYFC] **Joseph**[8] had a newphew, **Heath**[9], b 1899, living with him.

Children:

i   **Lucy**[9] b 1- -1898 in MS or TN

ii   **Josephine**[9] b 1901 in KY

iii   **Margaret**[9] b 1902

iv   **Margaret**[9] b 1910

v   **Frances Carroll**[9] b 2-11-1912 [KYVR]

vi   **Joseph Jr.**[9] b 1919 in KY

(763) Samuel W.[8], (Jospeh[7], John[6], unconnected), born in Stanford KY 1- -1881, attended University of Chicago, 1901, Transylvania University, Lexington, 1902. He began newspaper work on the

Lexington Herald, reporter, *Louisville Herald* 1905-
07, *The Courier* Journal 1908, managing ed., The
Market Growers' Journal until 1918, state ed., The
Courier-Journal until 1923. Advt. Mgr. Hillerich
and Bradshy Co., since 1923. KY State Golf Assn.
secy. [Who's Who In Kentucky, published Standard
Printing co., Louisville, KY. 1936] The 1910
Louisville, Jefferson Co KY census shows him with
his wife Ollie R., born 1883, in Kentucky

Children: [1920 Louisville, Jefferson Co KYFC]
All born in Kentucky [KYVR]
   i   **William Warren**[9] b 7-15-1911 in Jefferson
        Co
   ii   **Martha H.**[9] b 1-5-1913
   iii **Samuel Walton Jr.**[9] b 1-4-1914
   iv   **Humphrey Wilson**[9] b 1-2-1915

(764) Julian Edgar[8], (Samuel[7], Benjamin[6], Jonathan[5],
Benjamin[4], Jonathan[3], Ephraim[2], John[1]), was born 11-
30-1840. He married Alice A. Morrison, who was born
in Quebec, Canada. [NHVR] Alice A. was born in
1850. She died 4-26-1896 at Everett, MA. The [1880
MAFC] shows them living in Chelsea, MA dealing in
Real Estate. Both of them lived in Boston and
Chelsea, MA. They were married in Sommersworth, NH.
[NHVR] **Julian E.**[8] was a laundry man.
   Julian E.[8] Severance, son of Samuel and Ruth G.
Severance, and E. Margaret Morrison, were married
8-2-1861 at Boston, MA. He was born in Moultonboro,
NH and she was born in Fenwick, Canada, daughter of
Alexander and Margaret Morrison. [MAVR]
   Nellie Severance, daughter of Alex and Margaret
Morrison, died 5-28-1873 at Somerville, MA, age 34-
9-28, born in Canada. [MAVR]

Children:
   i   **Maud Annie**[9] b 10-26-1871 at Charlestown,
        MA [MAVR]
   ii   **John A.**[9] b 1878 in Chelsea, MA m Helen
        M. Harmon, daughter of William F. Harmon
        and Lizzie Bray, 7-3-1906 [NHVR]
   iii **Eva Florence**[9] b 3-6-1882 at Chelsea, MA
        [MAVR] d 3-20-1888 age 6 yrs 14 days at
        Chelsea [MAVR]
   iv   **Reginald E.**[9] b 4-18-1887 at Chelsea, MA
        [MAVR]
   v   **Ida V.**[9] b 11-17-1889 at Chelsea, MA
        [MAVR] d 1-14-1895 age 5-1-27 at Chelsea
        [MAVR]

(766) Charles Almon[8], (Samuel[7], Benjamin[6], Jonathan[5], Benjamin[4], Jonathan[3], Ephraim[2], John[1]), was born 10-25-1847 in Moultonboro, NH. He married to Matilda Ladd, daughter of Samuel Ladd and May Moulton, on 9-28-1870. [IGI] She was born 4-8-1848 in Tuftonboro, NH and died 3-20-1919 in Moultonboro. She died of Brights Disease of which she suffered about 12 years. She had formerly lived in Stoneham, MA. [NHVR]

Apparently **Charles[8]** ran a boarding house in Stoneham as the 1900 census shows him with 12 boarders and 1 servant living with his family.

Children: [MDW]
- i   Child b 7-10-1877 in Moultonboro, NH
- 1004 ii   **William R.[9]** born 1878 in Moultonboro, NH. He m1 Edna W. Tyler 1-11-1900 in Stoneham, MA. She was b 9-13-1876 d 9-29-1910 in Moultonboro, NH. [NHVR] She was the daughter of Fred M. Tyler and Laura Keyser of Benton, NH. [NHVR] He m2 to Grace Cropley, daughter of Solomon F. Cropley and Elizabeth H. Demeritt on 11-5-1916. [NHVR]
- iii   **Charles H.[9]** b 6-2-1879 in Moultonboro, NH. [1880-1900 NHFC]

(767) Fred Wiggin[8], (Jonathan Burbank[7], Benjamin[6], Jonathan[5], Benjamin[4], Jonathan[3], Ephraim[2], John[1]), born 3-23-1867 in Boston, MA. He died 11-14-1950 in Stratham, NH. He married Annie Odell Smart, daughter of Joseph Taylor Smart and Sarah Elizabeth Prior, 5-18-1887 in Stratham. Annie was born 6-4-1869 and died 6-20-1949. Both of them are buried in Stratham, NH.

When his father, **Jonathan Burbank[7]** died, **Fred[8]** Severance and mother Selina Wiggin Severance returned to Stratham to their farm to live with her brother Andrew Wiggin. **Fred[8]** married Annie Odell there and began to farm. With his wealthy mother's help, he imported the best beef cattle from the west for his farm. He also had two livery stables, one in Exeter, NH and one in York Beach, ME. He was generous to a fault and not good with money management but loved by everyone. His investments proved not lucrative, and the money he inherited from his mother who died in 1896 was soon gone. After farming, he worked on the trolley cars, and later at the Portsmouth Naval Shipyard. He died in

1950, living out his retirement years on his
beloved farm in Stratham. [MDW]

Children: born in Stratham, NH
    i   baby b 5-3-1888 d same day
1005 ii   **Fred Burbank**[9] was b 9-28-1889 in
             Stratham, NH, d 8-3-1967 in Portsmouth,
             NH. He m Eva May Swett, daughter of
             Frank Osgood Swett and Grace Mac Kenzie
             on 11-27-1919 in Amesbury, MA. She was b
             2-8-1898 in Amesbury, MA and d 12-21-
             1974 in Portsmouth. [NHVR] **Fred**[9] worked
             on the trollies in Stratham and on the
             Portsmouth Naval Shipyard. He served as
             a private in the Army medical corps in
             WW I. He enjoyed talking about his
             family and childhood days in Stratham.
   iii   **Pauline Smart**[9] died less than a month
             short of her 100th birthday. She was b
             11-1-1891 in Stratham, NH and d 9-7-1991
             in Rye, NH. She m to John Mac Donald on
             9-7-1921. [MDW]

(768) David Edwin[8], (David[7], Benjamin[6], Jonathan[5],
Benjamin[4], Jonathan[3], Ephraim[2], John[1]), born in May
of 1848. [COFC] He married Mary Milliken, daughter
of Ivory Milliken and Lois Rogers, on 4-16-1871.
She was born 2-8-1848 in Newton, MA. **David**[8] and
Mary lived in Greely, CO. [Rodlon III p185] [1920
Windsor-COFC]

Children: [Ridlon III p185] [Glavinick p342]
    i   **Augusta**[9] b 5-13-1872 (5-6-1873) in
         Tuftonboro, NH, d 5-3-1884 in Greeley,
         CO
   ii   **Dora**[9] b 5-6-1873 in Tuftonboro, NH
   iii   **David**[9] b 11-15-1877 in Tuftonboro. The
         1920 CO census shows **David E.**[9] age 41,
         born in New Hampshire and living in Weld
         Co. with a housekeeper.
   iv   **Fred**[9] b 7-18-1879
   v   **Mary A.**[9] b 5-16-1886 in Greeley, CO

(769) Everett N.[8], (Newell Atchison[7], Stephen[6],
Jonathan[5], Jonathan[4], Jonathan[3], Ephraim[2], John[1]), b
10- -1863 in Alton, NH. [1900 NHFC] He married
Juliet L. Sougee 11-27-1890 [IGI] She was b 10- -
1868. [1900 NHFC] They lived at Wolfboro, Carroll
Co. NH. He died in 1941.

Children:
    i   **Vernon P.**[9] b 2- -1895 [1900 NHFC]

(773) George V.[8], (Levi[7], John[6], Jonathan[5], Jonathan[4], Jonathan[3], Ephraim[2], John[1]), born 5-15-1862 [NHVR] and lived in Rochester, NH, son of **Levi**[7] and Sarah Hussey. [NHVR] **George V.**[8] died on 11-14-1904 at the age of 42 years at Rochester. He married to Ada B. Conant. **George**[8] was a Superintendant in a shoe manufacturing company at Rochester.

Children:
    i   **Charles C.**[9] b March of 1885 in Sliapleigh, ME. and shown m to Florence M. Burnham on 9-18-1912. Florence was the daughter of R. De Witt Burnham and Maryetta Twombly of Rochester, NH. **Charles**[9] was a resident of Amarilla, TX. His parents were from Rochester, NH. [NHVR]

(774) Thomas Freeman[8], (Charles M.[7], Joseph Levi[6], Jonathan[5], Benjamin[4], Jonathan[3], Ephraim[2], John[1]), born 11-30-1850 in Lovell, ME. [MEVR Lovell] He was a baker. He married to Carrie L. Dresser, 12-16-1879, [MEVR] who was born on 9- -1858 in Lovell, ME. [1900 MEFC] The family later moved to CA and settled in Los Angeles.

Children:
    i   **Arthur F.**[9] b 2- -1887 in MA, moved to Los Angeles where he m to Byrd J.____, b 1880 in PA. [1920 CAFC]
    ii   **Harold Henry**[9] b 6-28-1891 in MA [MAVR] but moved to CA and married Ruth ____, b 1894 in CT. [1920 CAFC]
    iii   **Mabel L.**[9] b 6- -1884
    iv   **Sybil**[9] b 9-24-1893 in Chelmsford, MA [MAVR], living with her mother in CA in 1920

(775) Henry Butler[8], (Charles M.[7], Joseph Levi[6], Jonathan[5], Benjamin[4], Jonathan[3], Ephraim[2], John[1]), born 12-18-1853. [MEVR Lovell] He married to Cora B. Jackman at Lowell, MA on 1-19-1887. [MAVR] She was born in July of 1861 in ME, [1900 MEFC] the daughter of Eli and Hannah Jackman. [MAVR] **Henry B.**[8] died on 5-14-1921. [MEVR] **Henry Butler**[8] was

named after Henry Butler Watson, probably the
father of Ashsah Watson, mother of **Henry Butler**[8].

Children:
  i   **Lewis Harry/Louis H.**[9] b 6-17-1893.
       [MEVR] He m Marion R. Jennes, daughter
       of William H. and Mrs. Elizabeth Jennes,
       12-26-1925 at Dover, NH. [NHVR] [MEVR] I
       show them living at various times in
       Lovell, ME, Providence, RI, and Dover,
       NH. The 1920 ME census shows them living
       at Dover, ME without any children.
  ii   **Perley C.**[9] b 7- -1893 [1900 MEFC]

(776) Joseph Granville[8], (Charles M.[7], Joseph Levi[6],
Jonathan[5], Benjamin[4], Jonathan[3], Ephraim[2], John[1]),
was born 10-6-1864. [MEVR] **Joseph Granville**[8]
Severance of Lovell, ME, married Miranda W. Pike,
of Fryeburg, ME, at Chatham, NH on 11-26-1885.
[MEVR] Miranda was born 4- -1865 in MA. [1900 MEFC]

Children:
  i   **George Freeman**[9] b 6-15-1886. [MEVR]

(777) Clayton Bishop or **Bishop Clayton**[8], (Joseph
Bishop[7], Joseph Levi[6], Jonathan[5], Benjamin[4],
Jonathan[3], Ephraim[2], John[1]), born in 9-10-1896
[MEVR] at Dover, NH and later lived in Biddeford,
ME. He married to Gladys E. Plummer, daughter of
Hattie M. Plummer, on 1-15-1929. **Bishop**[8] was a
lumber maker.

Children:
  i   **Mildred**[9] b 1897 [NHVR]

(778) Lafayette[8], (Rufus[7], Rodney[6], Benjamin[5],
Jonathan[4], Jonathan[3], Ephraim[2], John[1]), born 6- -
1851. [1900 WIFC] He was born in Summit, Morgan Co.
OH. He married to Ella C. Driscoll, daughter of
John Driscoll and Sarah Jane Walker, on 4-24-1881.
Ella was born on 12-28-1859 in WI and died on 12-
25-1932. [WIVR Juneau Co] [MLSW]

Children: born in WI [1900 WIFC]
1011 i   **Earl Longley**[9] **(Volney)** b 4-6-1883 m
          Louise Weiler
  ii   **Iva L.**[9] b 1- -1886
  iii **Fern E.**[9] b 1- -1887
  iv   **Crotia L.**[9] b 8- -1890
  v   **Lucretia**[9]

vi   **Lloyd Earl**[9] b 9- -1892
vii **Velma L.**[9] b 12- -1893
viii **Elwood L.**[9] b 10-28-1895
ix   **Lynn Earl**[9] b 10- -1896

(779) Fayette[8], (Rufus[7], Rodney[6], Benjamin[5], Jonathan[4], Jonathan[3], Ephraim[2], John[1]), born in February of 1852 in OH but settled in WI near Mauston. [1900 WIFC]. He married to Frances Elizabeth Finn on 9-28-1880. [WIVR] She was born in February of 1862. All of their children were born in WI.

Children: [1900 WIFC]
i   **Cora Ann**[9] b 7- -1881
ii   **Mary Elizabeth**[9] b 1- -1882
iii **Fayette**[9] b 7- -1884
iv   **Martin LaFayette**[9] b 3- -1886 in WI, He shows in Tulare, Spink Co. with his wife, Merle A., age 19, born in SD, and mother in law, Myrtle Avery. [1920 SDFC]
1345 v **Robert Cowill**[9] b 10- -1887 m Hazel M. of ND.

(780) Rufus[8], (Robert C.[7], Rodney[6], Benjamin[5], Jonathan[4], Jonathan[3], Ephraim[2], John[1]), born in February of 1852. He was born in OH. [1900 WIFC] He settled in Galesville, Trempealeau Co. WI and married to Clara D. Stillson who was born in April of 1855.

Children: born in WI
1016 i **Arthur**[9] b 9- -1879
ii   **Lynn**[9] (male) b 11- -1885

(781) Silas[8], (Robert C.[7], Rodney[6], Benjamin[5], Jonathan[4], Jonathan[3], Ephraim[2], John[1]), born in July of 1853 in OH. He married to Phoebe C. Huntley in Mauston, Juneau Co. WI, She was born in September of 1852 in NY state. The family later settled in NE where their son **Robert L.**[9] was born. In 1910 Phoebe C. was divorced and living at Horse Creek, Crook Co. WY, with her son **Robert L.**[9] Severance. [WYFC]

Children: [MLSW]
1018 i **Sydney Semour**[9] b 9-23-1877 in WI
ii   **Charles W.**[9] b 9- -1879 in WI, he shows on the [1920 KSFC] with his wife Augusta L. age 30 b in KS and their son, **Charlie R.**[10], age 3 2/12 and b in WY

        iii   **Julia S.**[9] b 10- -1883 in WI
1020 iv   **Robert L.**[9] b 2-25-1889 in NE. He d on 9-
                23-1941.

(782) Lewis Cap[8], (Robert C.[7], Rodney[6], Benjamin[5],
Jonathan[4], Jonathan[3], Ephraim[2], John[1]), born in 1856
in OH. He married to Mary Esther Cattle on 7-13-
1876. [WIVR] Mary was born in 1857 in WI.

Children: [1900 WIFC][WIVR Juneau Co]
        i   **Lewis A.**[9] b 8-27-1877
        ii   **Elnora**[9] b 1878
        iii   **Norman**[9] b 4- -1881 in WI. [1900 SDFC]
                He was living alone as a boarder of
                James P. Turner in Faulkton, Faulk Co.
                SD

(783) Robert[8], (Robert C[7], Rodney[6], Benjamin[5],
Jonathan[4], Jonathan[3], Ephraim[2], John[1]), born in May
of 1858 in OH. [1900 WIFC] He married to Emma R.
Spaulding on 11-16-1888. [WIVR]
    Emma Spaulding, daughter of Harrison Spaulding
and Elizabeth Little, married to **Robert C.**[8]
Severance in 1889. Emma was born in WI on 10-19-
1870. [Spalding p795]
    They settled near Mauston, Juneau Co. WI.

Children:
        i   **Leona**[9] b 11-16-1889, apparently died
                young
1021 ii   **Ernest Stillman**[9] b 2-7-1893
        iii   **Lewis B.**[9] b 1-8-1898
        iv   **Leona C.**[9] b 2- -1896
        v   **Robert C.**[9] b 5-11-1902

(784) George R.[8], (Robert C.[7], Rodney[6], Benjamin[5],
Jonathan[4], Jonathan[3], Ephraim[2], John[1]), born in 1848
in OH. He married to Lizzie Nilson on 8-17-1879 in
WI. [WIVR] Lizzie was born in 1855. [MLSW]

Children:
        i   **Rodney**[9] b 1879 in WI

(785) Oliver S.[8], (Arthur Rodney[7], Rodney[6],
Benjamin[5], Jonathan[4], Jonathan[3], Ephraim[2], John[1]),
born on 3-30-1853 in McConnelsville, Morgan Co.
OH. He married to Ada E. Marshall, daughter of T.J.
Marshall, 11-16-1881. [MLSW]
    Oliver[8] came to Missouri in 1870 and taught
school during the winter and farmed in the summer.

In 1876 he worked for the McCormick Harvesting Machine Co. as a salesman. He later bought out the interest of his partner, Mr. Hart.

He was appointed township clerk and ex-officio assessor in 1881 and became the assessor for the township. [HHCCoMO p901-902]

Children:
i   **Harold Clyde**[9] settled in MO

(787) Arthur E.[8] *Suverance*, (Arthur Rodney[7], Rodney[6], Benjamin[5], Jonathan[4], Jonathan[3], Ephraim[2], John[1]), born 2- -1862 in Morgan Co. OH. He married to Edmonia ____. She was born in VA in 1864. [1900-1910 MOFC] They lived in Chariton Co. MO. [MLSW]

Children: born in Chariton Co. MO
i	**Erwin L.**[9]	b 11- -1885
ii	**Ethel C.**[9]	b 2- -1887
1023 iii	**Fred C.**[9]	b 10- -1888 m Mabel K. ____. Lived in Parson, Labette Co. KS
iv	**Charles W.**[9]	b 10- -1890
v	**Ollie E.**[9]	b 3- -1899

(788) Benjamin F.[8], (Arthur Rodney[7], Rodney[6], Benjamin[5], Jonathan[4], Jonathan[3], Ephraim[2], John[1]), born in October of 1864 in OH. He was living in Oak, Mills Co. as **Benjamin F.**[8] age 35 and born in OH. His wife Louisa, age 30, was born in IN in June of 1870. [1900 IAFC]

Children: born in MO
i	**Clarence R.**[9]	b 6- -1889
ii	**Garnett O.**[9]	b 7- -1894
iii	**Edith F.**[9]	b 8- -1899

(789) Silas O.[8], (Phillip[7], Silas[6], Benjamin[5], Benjamin[4], Jonathan[3], Ephraim[2], John[1]), was born 12-19-1848 and died 6-7-1909. He married to Nettie Phelan on 1-19-1880 [OHVR] She was born 9- -1856 in West Virginia. [1900 OHFC Cleveland].

Children:
1026 i   **Phillip**[9] b 10- -1880 in VA

(791) Charles F.[8], (Hazen[7], Hazen[6], Benjamin[5], Jonathan[4], Jonathan[3], Ephraim[2], John[1]), born in September of 1865. He married Harriet Jones. She was born in July of 1870. [1900 OHFC]. They lived

in Somerset, Perry Co. OH. **Charles[8]** died in 1949.
[MLSW]

Children: born in OH [1900-1920 OHFC]
        i   **Naomi[9]** b 6- -1889
1027   ii   **Bert V.[9]** b 1- -1890
       iii   **Cecil[9]** b 12- -1896
       iv   **Ruth[9]** b 1900
       iv   **Anna P.[9]** b 1903
        v   **Theodore R.[9]** b 1905
       vi   **Norman[9]** b 1909
       vii   **Russell[9]** b 1911
       viii   **Harold[9]** b 1915

(792) Fred[8], (Hazen[7], Hazen,[6] Benjamin[5], Jonathan,[4]
Jonathan[3], Ephraim[2], John[1]), born on 11-9-1876.
[OHVR] Recorded in Zanesville, Muskingum Co. OH.
[IGI] He married to Ruth Thomas, who was born in
1881 in OH. [1910 OHFC] **Fred[8]** died 6-18-1958. At
various times they were found in McCunneville,
Shawnee, Zanesville, and Columbus, OH.

Children: [1910 OHFC]
        i   **Hattie L.[9]** b 1893
       ii   **Mattie Lois[9]** b 9-4-1897 [OHVR]
       iii   **Ruth L.[9]** b 10-18-1901 [OHVR]

(793) Jacob A.[8], (Hazen[7], Hazen[6], Benjamin[5],
Jonathan[4], Jonathan[3], Ephraim[2], John[1]), born on 10-
14-1877. He married to Cecilia Gaver. She was born
in 1881 in OH. [1920 OHFC] They lived in Muskigum
and Perry, Co. OH. **Jacob[8]** died on 8-4-1964 [MLSW]

Children: born in OH [1910/1920 OHFC]
        i   **Bertha[9]** b 1903
       ii   **John W.[9]** b 1906
       iii   **Edith I.[9]** b 1912
       iv   **Beatrice C.[9]** b 1915

(796) John[8], (Hazen[7], Hazen[6], Benjamin[5], Jonathan[4],
Jonathan[3], Ephraim[2], John[1]), born in OH in 1884.
[1920 OHFC] He married to Mary ___ who was born in
1884 in OH. They lived in Guernsey Co. OH. [MLSW]

Children: [1920 OHFC]
        i   ?
       ii   **Margaret[9]** b 1906
       iii   **Lewis[9]** b 1908

(797) Herbert Winfred[8], (George Washington[7], Ora P.[6], Samuel[5], Samuel[4], Jonathan[3], Ephraim[2], John[1]), born on 7-26-1884 in Plaistow, NH. He married Lilla Belle Price, of Lowell, MA.

She was b on 11-23-1884. They lived in Haverhill, MA. **Herbert**[8] was an Express Agent. [MDBS]

Children:
	i	**Geneva B.**[9] b 1905 at Haverhill, MA, m Oscar E. Page, son of Charles G. Page and Hattie J. Newcomb, 7-10-1920, at Brentwood, NH [NHVR]
1029	ii	**Arthur W.**[9] b 1906 m2 Caroline Hopkins, daughter of Oscar Hopkins and Fannie Laferty, 8-5-1928. The groom was widowed [NHVR]
1030	iii	**Roland L.**[9] b 1908 m Dorothy Burnham. Lived in Haverhill, MA
	iv	**Helen Pauline**[9] b 1910

(799) Earle Leroy[8], (John[7], Nathan[6], John[5], John[4], Jonathan[3], Ephraim[2], John[1]), born 6-30-1888 at Pembroke, NH and died 5-15-1967 in Concord, NH. He married to Sylva Estella (Worth) Warren, daughter of George D. Worth and Emily Watson, on 5-29-1911. [NHVR] She was born 2-9-1883 and died 11-24-1962 at Concord, NH. [NHVR]

Children:
1031	i	**Leroy Warren**[9] b 1-23-1910 Cambridge, MA d 6-27-1975 at Concord, NH. He m first to Thelma Heath, daughter of George Heath and Effie Charles, on 11-5-1931. [NHVR] He divorced Thelma on 7-6-1934. [NHVR] He m second to Margaret Wilson Kent, daughter of Arthur Stevens Kent and Mary Wilson, 8-19-1934. Margaret was b 11-1-1908 in Saco, ME. [NHVR]
	ii	**Ella Jane**[9] b 7-13-1925 m Anthony Tawa b 8-22-1922
	iii	**Ida Mildred**[9] b 4-3-1912 d 9-26-1915 [NHVR]

(800) Frank[8], (John[7], Nathan[6], John[5], John[4], Jonathan[3], Ephraim[2], John[1]), was born in 1893 at Pembroke, NH. He died in 1966 at Concord, NH. He married to Ethel Mary Dyer on 4-29-1915. [NHVR] She was born 1891 in Newport, NH and died 1975 at Concord, NH.

Children:
    i   **Stanley**[9] b 6-23-1917, Concord, NH
    ii   **Lloyd**[9] b 4-30-1924

NINTH GENERATION (801) Baxter Horace[9], (Horace M.[8], Abner[7], John/Abba[6], Tabitha[5], Daniel[4], Ebenezer[3], John[2], John[1]), born 2-14-1854 at Cambridge, MA. He married Ella F. Curtis, daughter of Horace T. and Caroline M. Curtis, 10-26-1876 at Cambridge. [MAVR] In 1880 **Horace**[8] was with his wife, Ella F. Curtis, born in 1856 in Freeport, ME. Cora A. Curtis, sister in law of **Horace**[8], was living with them in 1920. [MAFC]

Children:
    i   **Grace Ella**[10] b 1877 m Heber Augustus Hopkins, son of Albert B. Hopkins and Martha C. Hatch, 4-25-1900 at Cambridge, MA. [MAVR]
    ii   male b 10-28-1878 at Cambridge MA [MAVR]
    iii   **Herbert C.**[10] b 1879 in MA. The 1900 MA census shows **Herbert C.**[10] born 10- -1878 with sister Louise F. born 8- -1881. **Herbert**[10] was the son of **Baxter H. (Horace)**[9] and Ella F. _____. **Baxter**[9] was born 2-14-1854 [MAVR] and Ella F. was born 11- -1855.
    iv   female b 8-16-1881 at Cambridge, MA [MAVR]

(802) George E.[9], (Horace M.[8], Abner[7], John/Abba[4], Tabitha[5], Daniel[4], Ebenezer[3], John[2], John[1]), born 8-13-1859 in MA. **George**[9] was a book keeper at Cambridge. His wife, Maritta /Addie was born in August of 1868 in ME. [1900 MAFC]

Children:
    i   **Walter E.**[9] b 10-24-1885 at Pittsfield, lived in Cambridge, MA. [MAVR] Inducted 5-24-1918 at Chelsea ae 23 a/2 discharged 9-15-1919. [WWI] In 1920 **Walter E.**[9], Elsie M. born 1887 in England (his wife), and a daughter, **Dorothy**[10], b 1911 in MA. were living in Boston. [MAFC]
    ii   **Leon Morse**[9] b 9-28-1891 at Cambridge, MA [MAVR] The 1920 Watertown, Middlesex Co MA census shows **Leon**[9], his wife, Elsa, b 1894 in MA and children, **Robert**[10] b 1915 and **Muriel**[10], b 1918 in MA
    iii   **Leslie T.**[9] b 10- -1896
    iv   **Ruth**[9] b 1904 [1920 NHFC]

(803) Charles⁹, (Oscar⁸, Nathan⁷, John/Abba⁶, Tabitha⁵, Daniel⁴, Ebenezer³, John², John¹) born 1889 and married Viola E._____ . He settled in Williams and Definace Co. OH. [1910/1920 OHFC]

Children: born in OH.
i   **Hazel Alice¹⁰** b 1906
ii   **B. Russell¹⁰** b 1908
iii **Hershel Dale¹⁰** b 1910
iv   **Marvel Louisa¹⁰** b 1913
v   **Arlo J.¹⁰** b 1915
vi   **Artiss Eveline¹⁰** b 1918

(804) Clinton⁹, (George⁸, Nathan⁷, John⁶, Tabitha⁵, Daniel⁴, Ebenezer³, John², John¹), born 10- -1856 in Shalersville, OH. [1880/1900 OHFC] He married to Florance A. Wilson who was born 2- -1861. They were living in Shalerville, OH in 1880. They later settled in Detroit, MI. [Hayward p401] Florance's mother, Polly A. Wilson, was living with them on the 1910 MI census.
     The census film shows **Clinton's⁹** father was born in VT and his mother was born in OH. **Clinton⁹** was a farmer and was married for 20 years. Florance had had 6 children and 6 were living.

Children: [1880/1900 MIFC]
i   **Mercy¹⁰** b 1880
ii   **George W.¹⁰** b 2- -1881
iii **Howard A.¹⁰** b 4- -1885 m Olivia b 1880,
     lived in Ravenna, Portage Co. OH, one
     daughter, **Hilda¹¹** b 1913 [1920 OHFC]
iv   **Arthur E.¹⁰** b 6- -1887
v   **Joe E.¹⁰** b 11- -1889
vi   **Wilson V.¹⁰** b 10- -1898
vii **Mercy¹⁰** b 1899

(805) Clarence⁹, (George⁸, Nathan⁷, John⁶, Tabitha⁵, Daniel⁴, Ebenezer³, John², John¹), born in January of 1858 in OH. He married Ella Baldwin [Hayward p401] In 1900 **Clarence⁸** was living in Atwater, Portage Co. OH as a carriage trimer, his father was born in VT and his mother was born in OH. In 1920 he was living in Youngstown, OH. His wife was indicated as Emma G., therefore he probably married a second time. [OHFC]

Children:

i   **Raymond Clarence**[10] b 3- -1884 in OH [1900 OHFC]

(806) Frank L. (Francis Lewis)[9], (George[8], Nathan[7], John[6], Tabitha[5], Daniel[4], Ebenezer[3], John[2], John[1]), born 4- -1861 and is shown living in OH. [1900 OHFC] He married Jennie M. Bosh, 7-4-1885. [OHVR] She was born 12- -1861. [1900-1910 OHFC] They are shown living in Farmer Town, Defiance Co. OH.

Children: born in OH
i   **Charles F.**[10] b 4- -1882
ii   **Walter L.**[10] b 6- -1890. m Della b 1894, children: **Francis**[11] b 1914, **Berniece**[11] b 1916. [1920 OHFC Defiance Co]
iii **Sarah M.**[10] b 9- -1892
iv   **R.L.**[10] b 1- -1894
v   **Emma**[10] b 2- -1896

(807) George E.[9], (George[8], Nathan[7], John[6], Tabitha[5], Daniel[4], Ebenezer[3], John[2], John[1]), born 2- -1868 and is shown living in OH. He married to Ida N. ____. She was born 1866 in PA. [1920 OHFC] The 1920 OH census shows **Frank L.**[9] age 56 born 1864 in OH as a brother living with **George E.**[9] and his wife Ida N.

Children:
i   **Norman**[10] b 1900 in OH

(808) Marcus M.[9], (Marvin[8], Nathan[7], John[6], Tabitha[5], Daniel[4], Ebenezer[3], John[2], John[1]), was born 5- -1859 in OH. [1900 MNFC] He married Mary A. who was born 2- -1858. [1900 MNFC]

Children: [1900 MNFC-Minneapolis, Hennepin Co]
i   **Blanche M.**[10] b 5- -1884 in OH
ii   **Fredrick W.**[10] b 2- -1886 in MN. He later settled in TN with his wife, Ida, and son **Donald M.**[11] b 1909. [1920 TNFC]
iii **Raymond C.**[10] b 10- -1892 in MN
iv   **Chester M.**[10] b 1- -1898 in MN

(810) Clifford H.[9], (Manly C.[8], Nathan[7], John[6], Tabitha[5], Daniel[4], Ebenezer[3], John[2], John[1]), born 1865 in OH. He was living in Alliance, Stark Co. [1910-1920 OHFC] He married to Elizabeth ____ who was born in 1865. [1910 OHFC] The 1920 OH census shows the absence of **Clifford**[9] and only shows Elizabeth with **Clifton Eugene**[10] and **J. Arthur**[10] as her sons.

Children: born in OH
i   **Dorance H.**[10] b 7- -1885. He m to Maud B. and had a son, **Clarence B.**[11], b 1911 in OH
ii   **Zua A.**[10] b 12- -1886
iii **Iva**[10] b 1887 m a Hoffman b 1887
iv **Charles M.**[10] b 1- -1891
iii **Clinton D.**[10] b 4- -1892. The children were **Lawrence C.**[11] b 1915, **George B.**[11] b 1915, and **Eugene L.**[11] b 1919. [1920 OHFC] There were probably more children.
iv **Irene M.**[10] b 5- -1897
v   **Clifton Eugene**[10] b 1900
vi **J. Arthur**[10] b 1904

(811) James A.[9] *Severnce*, (Henry[8], Nathan[7], John[6], Tabitha[5], Daniel[4], Ebenezer[3], John[2], John[1]), born 11- -1881 Mills Creek, Williams Co. OH. The 1920 MD census shows him (Jack A. born 1881 in OH) living there with his wife Ruth E. Devore, daughter of Rosella Devore born 1855 in OH, who was born 1894 in PA.

Children:
i   **Esther R.**[10] b 1918 in OH
ii   **Hilda P.**[10] b 1920 in MD

(812) Sylvester Chase[9], (Nelson Chase[8], Moses[7], John/Abba[6], Tabitha[5], Daniel[4], Ebenezer[3], John[2], John[1]), born 5-22-1855 in MI. He married to Emma L. Rose on 3-31-1880 in Westville, Montcalm Co. MI. She was born 11-12-1865 and died on 3-13-1903 at Presque Isle Co. MI. In 1920 he was living alone in Cheboygan Co. MI. **Sylvester Chase**[9] died on 1-30-1936 in Prineville, Crook Co. OR.

Children:
i   **Charles Nelson**[10] b 11-11-1880 in Douglas twp, Montcalm Co. MI. He m to Maud E. MacDermaid, daughter of John and Isabel Scott, on 5-4-1904. Maud was b 2-17-1884 d 7-28-1956. **Charles**[10] d on 3-1-1946. They had a daughter, **Marion Isabel**[11] Severance of Flint, MI, buried, Elmwood Cemetery, Onaway, MI. [MDH] This family shows on the 1920 MI census in Presque Isle Co, with children, **Marguerite**[11] b 1906, **Harry**[11] b 1911, **Marion**[11] b 1913, **Emma**[11] b 1915, and **Robert**[11] b 1917

(812a) Sylvester[9], (William[8], Moses[7], John/Abba[6], Tabitha[5], Daniel[4], Ebenezer[3], John[2], John[1]), was born 3- -1834 in Canada. At age 20, he was living with a Starks family in 1850. [NYFC] He married to Louisa Fifield. She died 9-29-1909, age 77, at Colton, NY. They had lived at Colton for 40 years. [NYVR]

Children: [1860-1880 NYFC]
- i **Mary S.[10]** b 1853/1854
- ii **Imogene[10]** b 1855
- iii **Adelia[10]** b 1857
- iv **James M.[10]** b 5- -1858 in NY. In 1900 he was living with his wife, Rena L. b 6- -1861 and children: **Blance M.[11]** b 7- -1887, **Floyd D.[11]** b 3- -1893, and **Abbie R.[11]** b 6- -1896. [NYFC]
- v **Ira[10]** b 1860/1861 m Emily Bean 8-9-1890 at Pierpont. [NYVR] They had a son, **Ira[11]**, who d 12-17-1894, age 2 years, at Colton, NY, [NYVR] and a daughter, **Lettie[11]**, who m Louis H. Bigwarf 9-22-1898 at Potsdam, NY. [NYVR]
- vi **Julia[10]** b 1863 m Peter Foster
- vii **George[10]** b 6- -1865 in Pierrepont, NY. He m Eva Corbin, daughter of Sylvanus and Diantha Corbin, were married 3-6-1886 at Potsdam, NY. [NYVR] In 1900 he is with his wife Eva, who was b 12- -1868 and their children: **Grace M.[11]** b 2- -1887, **George E.[11]** b 11- -1889, **Della M.[11]** b 8- -1892, and **Leo[11]** b 8- -1899. [NYFC] The NYVR show **George Stanley[11]**, son of **George[10]** and Mary d 6-6-1892, age 10 mons.
- viii **Eugene[10]** b 1869
- ix **Viola[10]** b 1871 m Peter Haven, son of Peter Haven and Louisa Stone, 7-17-1888 at Peirrepont. [NYVR] She m Hiram Dennis and they had a child on 10-25-1901. [NYVR]
- x **Nora[10]** b 1874
- xi **Henry[10]** b 1876 at High Falls, m Clara Sellus, daughter of William Sellus and Tripena Wheeler, 5-7-1903 at Parishville, NY. [NYVR]

(812b) Ambrose[9], (William[8], Moses[7], John/Abba[6], Tabitha[5], Daniel[4], Ebenezer[3], John[2], John[1]), was born circa 1839. He married to Hannah Crossman, daughter of William Crossman. **Ambrose[9]** died 12-7-1904 at Fine, NY. [NYVR]

Children:
 i **Charles Ryland**[10] b 1866 m Hannah or Emma
   Bump, (her third marriage) daughter of
   Richard Corbin and Sarah Wells, 10-16-1890,
   at Pierrepont, NY. [NYVR] They had a son,
   Jimmi Edwin[11] b 6-10-1892 at Pierrepont to
   Charles R.[10] and Emma Corbin. [NYVR]
 ii **Emma/Lovisa**[10] b 1870 at St. Lawrence Co. She
   m Charles McCoy, son of John McCoy and Mary
   Johnson, 9-15-1893, at Pierrepont. [NYVR]
 iii **William**[10] b 1880 at Peirrepont. He m Maud
   (adopted) Severance, daughter of **Unrico**[9]
   and Arvilla (Comstock) Severance, 9-8-1906.
   There is a **William**[10] Severance 1881-1934
   buried in Pleasant Mound Cemetery in
   Colton, NY.

(812c) Unrico[9], (William[8], Moses[7], John/Abba[6],
Tabitha[5], Daniel[4], Ebenezer[3], John[2], John[1]), was born
4- -1848 at Canton, NY. He married to Maria. This
first family shows on the 1880 NY census. He
married secondly to Ida Arillie Comstock, daughter
of David Comstock and Malissa Fifield, 5-24-1890,
at Edwards, NY. [NYVR] His second family shows on
the 1900 NY census. He filed for his Civil War
Pension 10-8-1889 and his wife filed 3-4-1914 for
service in G 193 NY Inf. [CWPR] **Unrico**[9] is buried in
Jerusalem Cemetery, Canton, NY.

Children: [1880 NYFC]
 i **Irene**[10] b 1861
 ii **Henry**[10] b 1875, son of **Unrico**[9] and Mary,
   died 4-20-1897, age 22, laborer, born at
   Canton and died at Colton, NY. [NYVR]
 iii **Laura**[10] b 1879
 iv **Maud**[10] b 9- -1892 (daughter of **Unrico**[9] and
   Ida)

(812d) Leslie P.[9] *Severana*, (Henry[8], Moses[7],
John/Abba[6], Tabitha[5], Daniel[4], Ebenezer[3], John[2],
John[1]), born 10-12-1853 at Colchester, VT. He
married 1-1-1879 to Eva Higley, daughter of Julian
Higley, (descendants of Capt. John Higley of CT in
1650), and Sylvina Currier, at or near Crary Mills,
NY. Eva was born 11-8-1853 at Fredonia, OH, **Leslie
P.**,[9] came to Pierpont, NY at age 11. He shows on
the 1900-1920 NY census with wife Eva, and two
children, **Mary P.**[10] and **Herbert**[10]. **Leslie**[9] and Eva
celebrated their 60th wedding anniversary 1-3-1939.
Eva died 8-5-1944 at Canton. They are buried in

Martin Ridge Cemetery, Pierrepont, NY.
[Genealogical Records of St. Lawrence Co, NY]

Children: all born in NY
>   i   **Hubert/Herbert**[10] b 1879 d 3-14-1893 age
>   13-6 b Potsdam. [NYVR]
>   ii   **Fred Henry**[10], son of **Leslie P.**[9] and Eva
>   Higley, b 6-6-1881 at Potsdam, m Olgie
>   Wires who d 8-29-1930. His second wife
>   was Mrs. Mabel Miles Ayers of Potsdam
>   who died 11-1-1948. His third wife was
>   Mrs. Ada Miles Russell, sister of his
>   2nd wife, whom he married 10-1-1949.
>   **Fred Henry**[10] d 11-28-1950.
> iii   **Wilmer**, son of Leslie, b 1- -1886 in NY
>   [1920 Ogdensburg, St. Lawrence Co. NYFC]
>   with wife, Hazel B. b 1889 in NY. **Wilmer**
>   **L.** Severance 1886-1959 and his wife
>   Hazel Runions b 1889 are buried in
>   [CEMNY Crary Mills Cemetery] Canton and
>   Pierrepont NY.
>   iv   **Mary P.** b 3-5-1891
>   v   **Frank** b 1- -1892

(812e) Henry Rollin[9], (Henry[8], Moses[7], John/Abba[6],
Tabitha[5], Daniel[4], Ebenezer[3], John[2], John[1]) b 5-12-
1857 Colchester, VT. [VTVR] He married to Mary
(Marion) Elizabeth Brown. [1880 NYFC] **Rollin H.**[9]
1857-1915 and wife Marion E b 1857-1932 are buried
in Peirrepont Hill Cemeter, NY. **Rolland**[10] was at
Pierrepont, St. Laurence Co. with wife Marion b 3-
-1857, and son in law Ernest Crary b 2- -1879 and
daughter **Alice** (Severance) Crary b 4- -1879 all in
NY. Alice M. Crary, Ernest H. Crary. [1900 NYFC]

Children:
>   i   **Anna**[10] b 1876, m Clayton Crossman, son
>   of Edgar Crossman and Kitty Hackett, 8-
>   26-1897 at Colton
>   ii   **Mildred May**[10] b 2-11-1877 in Pierrepont,
>   NY [IGI] **Millie**[10] m Arthur Shipman, son
>   of Albert and Maria Searles Shipman, 9-
>   13-1895 at Colton, NY [NYVR]
> iii   **Alice**[10] b 1879 m Ernest H. Crary, son of
>   Leslie Crary and Philena Montague, 3-7-
>   1897 at Colton

(813) Frank Edmund[9], (Edmund[8], Ebenezer[7], Samuel[6],
Ebenezer[5], Ebenezer[4], Ebenezer[3], John[2], John[1]), born
on 9-4-1872 in Middlebury, VT, the son of **Edmund**

Kirby[8] and Mary A. Landon. [VTVR] He married Lena Adelia Kelsey on 11-13-1901. [VTVR] She was the eldest daughter and child of Ansel Wallace Kelsey and Celestia Matilda Billings. Lena was born on 7-14-1874 at Salisbury, VT and died on 7-8-1953 at Middlebury, VT. They lived in Burlington, VT. In 1900 **Edmund**[9] was living alone. [VTFC] [Kelsey Vol IV p416-417]

Children:
  i   **Ruth Beatrice**[10] b 8-22-1902 at Salisbury, VT [VTVR]
  ii **Mabel Kelsey**[10] b 12-1-1905 at Middlebury, VT [VTVR] She m Allison Burton Ellsworth at Glenn Falls, NY on 9-4-1932.

(814) George M.[9], (Edmund[8], Ebenezer[7], Samuel[6], Ebenezer[5], Ebenezer[4], Ebenezer[3], John[2], John[1]), born on 1-2-1876. [VTVR] He married to Grace D. Amidon on 12-6-1899. [VTVR] She was born in May of 1879. [1900 VTFC]

Children: [VTVR]
  i   **Milton George**[10] b 5-15-1900 d 7-9-1900
  ii   **Earl Ross**[10] b 5-6-1902
  iii **Mabel Grace**[10] b 12-2-1904
  iv   **Doris Amidon**[10] b 11-6-1906

(816) Charles Carlton[9], (Oliver[8], Ebenezer[7], Samuel[6], Ebenezer[5], Ebenezer[4], Ebenezer[3], John[2], John[1]), born 9-17-1853. [VTVR] He married first to Lena Woodruff who was born in April of 1853. [1880 VTFC] He married secondly to Ida L. Latimer on 7-4-1879. [Middlebury, VTVR] Ida died in 1892.
  Guy[10] was listed as a grandson of William Latimer. [1800 VTFC] **Guy**[10] was a baby at one month old. His uncle, **Milton L.**[8] Severance, living with them in 1900. [VTFC]

Children:
  i   **Guy Carlton**[10] b 5-9-1880

(817) Frank Oliver[9], (Oliver[8], Ebenezer[7], Samuel[6], Ebenezer[5], Ebenezer[4], Ebenezer[3], John[2], John[1]), born on 8-28-1864 in Burlington, VT.
  He married Carrie L. Tyrel on 6-28-1887. [VTVR] Carrie was born in November of 1861 in VT. The 1900 VT census shows with Mary L Tyrel as the mother of **Carrie**[11] and **Frank T.**[11], born 8-1891 as a grandson of Mary L. Tyrel of Brandon, VT.

Children:
i   **Carri**[10] was indicated on the 1900 VT census
ii   **Frank Tyrel**[10] b 8-18-1891 at Middlebury, VT
       (VTVR)

(818) Carlton Spencer[9], (Milton Leonard[8], Ebenezer[7], Samuel[6], Ebenezer[5], Ebenezer[4], Ebenezer[3], John[2], John[1]), born 8-15-1867 in VT. The census shows his birth date as March of 1868 but everything else is the same. [1900 ILFC] He was a boarder of Eva S. Miller, and living in Chicago, Cook Co. IL. I believe this same **Carlton**[9] shows on the 1920 AZFC. He was born in 1869 and although the census says he was from NH, the simalarity is too real. He is shown with wife Jan who was born in Turkey, 35 years old.
     A women wrote concerning **Carlton Spencer**[9]. She said, "my husband is **Carlton Spencer III**[11], his father is a native of CA. His great grandfather was **Milton**[8] Severance who was pastor of the First Church of Bennington, VT."
     He was the son of **Milton Leonard**[8] Severance who married Emily Augusta Spencer. [Application for membership, S.A.R. 5-16-1916]

Children:
i   **Carlton Jr.**[10] b 1919 in AZ

(820) Edwin S.[9], (Martin Egbert[8], Samuel S.[7], Samuel[6], Ebenezer[5], Ebenezer[4], Ebenezer[3], John[2], John[1]), born 1880 in MA. He shows in MN and then in Dakota. [1880 DFC] He married Dora ___, who was born in IA, and a daughter. [1920 Stanfield, ORFC]

Children:
i   **Umatilla**[10].

(821) Leroy[9], (Martin Egbert[8], Samuel S.[7], Samuel[6], Ebenezer[5], Ebenezer[4], Ebenezer[3], John[2], John[1]), born 2- -1882. [1900 NDFC] **Roy C.**[9], age 36 was born in IA and his wife Anna N., age 31, was born in ND [1920 Owatonna, Steele Co. MNFC]

Children:
i   **Morris R.**[10], born 1916 in MN.

(822) Charles A.[9], (Benton[8], Ebenezer[7], Elijah[6], Abner[5], Ebenezer[4], Ebenezer[3], John[2], John[1]), born in December of 1861. He married to Mary A. Rist who was born in October of 1873 in WI. [1900 MNFC] They were living in Belgrade, MN. Julia, the mother, was living with them. [1900 MNFC] She was born in September of 1835. [Bryant p 675]

Children:
- i   **William J.**[10] b 6- -1895 in MN
- ii   **Charlie W.**[10] b 1910 in MN

(823) David J.[9], (Benton[8], Ebenezer[7], Elijah[6], Abner[5], Ebenezer[4], Ebenezer[3], John[2], John[1]), born in October of 1866 in NY state and later settled and lived in MN. [Bryant p675] He married to Camelia A. ___, who was born in 1866 in IN. [1920 MNFC]

Children:
- i   **Annie A.**[1c] b 2- -1892 in MN

(824) Ellsworth W.[9], (Willie L.[8], James Edwin[7], Elijah[6], Abner[5], Ebenezer[4], Ebenezer[3], John[2], John[1]), born in July of 1894 in CT. He married to Louise E. Zeiss who was born in 1894 in CT. [1920 CTFC]

Children:
- i   **Lucille E.**[10] b 1915 in CT
- ii   **William L.**[10] b 1917 in CT

(825) Milton Balcom[9], (Scott E.[8], James Edwin[7], Elijah[6], Abner[5], Ebenezer[4], Ebenezer[3], John[2], John[1]), born on 7-1-1887 in Shoreham, VT. [VTVR] He married Anne Mallory. **Milton**[9] lived in North Creek, Buffalo and Syracuse, NY. They lived their later adult lives in Buffalo and Syracuse, NY.

"**Milton**[9] went to high school at North Creek and was known as an excellent baseball pitcher, which was passing strange, as he had poor eyesight and wore glasses with lenses thicker than the bottom of a fruit jar. He could barely see home plate. He went to Syracuse University and was a star on the college team. After graduation he became a Civil Engineer for the city of Syracuse and remained there until retirement." [MESS]

Both **Milton**[9] and Anne were well known in Minerva and North Creek, NY.

Children:
- i   **Radford**[10]
- ii   **Jean**[10] was a twin to Don and never married. She lived in the Smokey Mountains of NC, and d at the age of 72 years. Her ashes

where spread on Oliver Pond in the
Adirondack Mountains of NY.
iii   **Don**[10] married to Niva ___ and they lived in
Syracuse, NY.

(826) Raymond Clarence[9], (Scott E.[8], James Edwin[7],
Elijah[6], Abner[5], Ebenezer[6], Ebenezer[3], John[2], John[1]),
born 5-10-1890 in Ticonderoga, NY. He married to
Kathryn A. Spain on 10-22-1913. They lived at
Mechanicville, NY. Kathryn was born in Athol, MA on
2-18-1885, daughter of William J. Spain and Abbie
M. Sumner. She died on 1-1-1969. **Raymond**[9] died on
5-1-1952.
    Raymond[9] was employed as an engineer for the
Boston and Maine Railroad. During the great
depression of the 1930's, the family temporarily
relocated to Granville, NY, where he and his
brother **Haswell**[9] were employed as bakers by their
father, **Scott**[8]. After the depression the family
returned ot Mechanicville, NY, where he again
worked for the railroad. **Raymond**[9] and Kathryn are
buried in the Catholic Cemetery at Mechanicville,
NY. [MESS]

Children:
    i   **Raymond Joseph**[10] b 8-28-1915 in
Mechanicville, NY and d in Granville, NY
on 3-12-1967. He m to Emily Caruso.
    ii   **Alton**[10] b 7-24-1918 in Mechanicville and
d on 1-6-1985 and is buried at the Catholic
Cemetery in Mechanicville. He m Margaret
Foley of Fair Haven, VT who was b on 9-14-
1919 and d on 11-28-1970. They had a
daughter b 9-25-1938 at Granville, NY.
Alton[10] and Margaret were divorced in 1940.
Alton[10] remarried to Margorie Nelson at West
Pawlet, VT. She d in October of 1984.
    iii **Dorothy**[10] b 8-27-1920
    iv   **Arthur Thomas**[10] b 2-12-1928

(827) Haswell Gordon[9], (Scott E.[8], James Edwin[7],
Elijah[6], Abner[5], Ebenezer[4], Ebenezer[3], John[2], John[1]),
born in 1895 in the state of NY. He married Sarah
"Sadie" Church, daughter of Scott Church and
Catherine B. Lane, on 7-4-1911. They were married
by Rev. Frank LaBar at the Church family homestead
in Irish Town at Minerva, NY. She was born in 1845
and died 7-4-1975. **Haswell**[9] owned various bakery
shops and was also an Adirondack Guide. **Haswell**[9] d

in May of 1947. **Haswell**[9] and Sadie are buried in North Creek. [MESS]

Children:
  i   **Denzel**[10] b 11-19-1918 d 1922 [MESS]
  ii   **Elizabeth**[1c]
  iii **Charles (Chuck) R.**[10] b circa 1920 [1920 NYFC] m Patrica (Tudy) Yandon, who was b in Schenectady, NY, and lived at North Creek, NY. **Chuck**[10] wrote Recollections of a Country Boy published by Minerva Historical Society, 1991.

(828) William Joseph[9], (Elias J.W.[8], Robert Murrell or Samuel[7], Robert[5], Thomas[5], John[4], John[3], John[2], John[1]), born circa 9- -1861 in Darlington Co. SC. [1900 SCFC] He married Mary Elizabeth Julia Gatlin. She was born in March of 1853 in SC. In 1900 **William**[9] and Bettie had been married 17 years with five children and 4 of them living. [SCFC]

Children: [MWS]
  i   **Mattie Viola**[10] b 4- -1889 m Peter Cassidy
  ii   **William James**[10] b 5-1-1891 m Malissie Cornelia McAlister
  iii **Lydia**[10] b 12- -1894 m Ben R. Odom
  iv   **Paul B.**[10] b 9-25-1896 d 1-3-1960

(829) Robert James[9], (Paul Elisha[8], Robert Murrell or Samuel[7], Robert[5], Thomas[5], John[4], John[3], John[2], John[1]), born 12-6-1873 and married to Lucy Watson. She died in 1949 and he died in 1931.

Children:
  i   **Robert Watson**[10] b 12-13-1907 m Katherine Maddry
  ii   **John**[10] b 1912 in SC. [1910-1920 Florence, SCFC]

(831) Martin Luther[9], (Paul Elisha[8], Robert Murrell or Samuel[7], Robert[6], Thomas[5], John[4], John[3], John[2], John[1]), was born 11-10-1885. He married Maggie Atwood Whitaker. They lived at Ridgetown, SC and by 1920 they were living in Nash Co. NC.

Children: [NCFC]
  i   **Martin W.**[10] b 1909 NC
  ii   **Cecil G.**[10] (male) b 1911 in NC

(836) William Elias⁹, (Robert Elifers⁸, Paul S.⁷, Robert M.⁶, Thomas⁵, John⁴, John³, John², John¹), born 9-7-1870 in SC. He lived in Ridgetown. He married to Leila Mae North. She was born on 6-17-1876 and died 1-9-1945. By 1920 they were living at Lake City in SC.

Children: [MWS]
i   **Kirby¹⁰** b 5-10-1903 d 5- -1904
ii   **Dorothy North¹⁰** b 8-3-1905 d 3-15-1910
iii   **William Ellis¹⁰** b 9-11-1908 d 10-28-1969
      m Elizabeth Cheatham
iv   **Elizabeth Gill¹⁰** b 3-29-1911 d 1- -1966 m
      Francis M. Brown
v   **Harry Wells¹⁰** b 11-29-1914 m Harriet Pripps
vi   **Frances S.¹⁰** b 9-15-1916 m Charles Winters
      Bailey

(837) Robert Calhoun⁹, (Thomas Glenn⁸, Robert Murrell⁷, Robert⁶, Thomas⁵, John⁴, John³, John², John¹), born 11-4-1861 in SC. He lived with his grandparents, **Robert M.⁷** and Elizabeth after his fathers death and lived in Timmonsville, Florence Co. He married first to Jessie M. Parrot who was born 10-2-1870 and died on 10-20-1902 and then **Robert⁹** married second to Janie Hines.
   Robert Calhoun⁹ shared in the estate of **Joseph H.⁹,** his uncle, and he received final settlement from the estate in December of 1882 from guardian **Robert M.⁷** Saverance Sr. **Paul A.⁸** was guardian from 1866 to 1871 and **Robert Murrell Sr.⁷,** from 1871 to 1887. [MWS]

Children of **Robert Calhoun⁹** and Jessie M. Parrot
i   **John¹⁰** b 11- -1889
ii   **Pheny¹⁰** b 4- -1891
iii   **Agnes¹⁰** b 8- -1894
iv   **Maggie¹⁰** b 5- -1897
v   **Jessie¹⁰** b 11- -1899 m Alzo Pierce

Children of **Robert Calhoun⁹** and Jannie Hines [1920 SCFC]
vi   **Julie¹⁰** b 1906
vii   **Mable¹⁰** b 1908
viii **Caroly¹⁰**
ix   **Murrell¹⁰** b 1912
x   **William¹⁰** b 1915
xi   **Robert Calhoun Jr.¹⁰**
xii   **Caroline¹⁰** b 1919

(838) Thomas Beauregard⁹ *Saverance*, (Thomas Glenn⁸, Robert Murrell⁷, Rcbert⁶, Thomas⁵, John⁴, John³, John², John¹), borr. on 10-8-1864 in Florence, SC. He married to Ella Parnell. Ella was born on 6-14-1865. She died 12-9-1935. **Thomas⁹** died 12-9-1923.

Thomas Beauregard⁹ also shared in the estate of his fathers brother, **Joseph⁹** Saverance. He was still living with his grandparents in 1885. The amount of his final settlement was not listed. Thomas told of walking on the streets of Florence and one day a man walked up to him and said "you look exactly like **Thomas⁸** Savernace, but you could not be, because I was with him when he died in MS. My grandfather, **Thomas⁸** Beauregard, said "I am **Thomas⁹** Saverance, the son of **Thomas⁸** you are speaking of". [MWS]

Children:

i   **James Bureon¹⁰** b 1-15-1887
ii   **Ellington Glenn¹⁰** b 9-2-1889
iii **Robert Paul¹⁰** b 8-9-1891
iv   **Thomas Ellis¹⁰** b 5-12-1896 d 2-1-1961 m Daisy Anderson who was b on 1-17-1899 and d 10-3-1983
v   **Warren Lerand¹⁰** b 3-29-1898
vi   **Rosa Lee¹⁰** b 2-5-1903 m Julius Kinly Brown who was b 12-16-1901 and d 12-1-1965. They had no children.
vii **Ocie Barton¹⁰** b 5-12-1905 d 6-2-1926
viii **John Edward¹⁰** b 9-27-1900
ix   **Effie Blance¹⁰** b 3-17-1908
x   **Theron L.¹⁰** b 11-2-1917

(842) Horace Wells⁹, (Samuel Orton⁸, Cyrus⁷, Matthew⁶, Matthew⁵, Joseph⁴, Joseph³, John², John¹), born 5-13-1844 at Scottsville, Monroe Co. NY. He married to Eleancr Ballantine, daughter of William Ballantine and Susan Ann Rippey, on 12-22-1869. They settled at Kansas City, Monroe Co. MO. Eleanor was born 7-28-1843. She died on 5-25-1932 in Kansas City. **Horace Wells⁹** died on 6-2-1897. [KSVR]

Horace⁹ was Secretary of Dain Manufacturing Co., Carrolton, MO for many years and was a controlling partner. Dain Mfg. was the largest Manufacturing plant in MO (located in Carrolton) outside of large cities. Mr. Dain invented and patented the Dain Center Draft Mower, The Dain Sweep Hay Rake, the Dain Power Life Push Rakes, and the Eureka Corn Harvester. [MDLB] In 1880 the family was living in NY state. [NYFC]

Children: [MDLB]
  i   **Frank Lewis**[10] b 1-6-1873 at Scottsville,
       NY. He was a bookkeeper for the Dain
       Manufacturing Company. In 1896 he moved to
       Kansas City and served as Vice-President of
       Irving Pitt Manufacturing Company at Kansas
       City, MO. In 1920 he moved to Chicago and
       was Vice-President of Wilson Jones
       Manufacturing. Then in 1932 he returned to
       Kansas City and was employed by the City
       Park Department until 1956, when he
       retired. He m to Carrie Elizabeth Patton,
       daughter of William G. Patton and Mary Ann
       Snider, on 4-29-1891. Carrie was b in
       Carrollton, MO on 6-8-1871 and d on 12-12-
       1962 at Kansas City, MO. **Frank**[10] d 4-5-1957
       at Kansas City, MO. They had children,
       Helen Frances[11] b 9-28-1895, m Frederick
       Wymer Erbes, 10-2-1920 and Robert
       Snelling; **Horace William**[11] b 1-12-1898, m
       Dorothy Elizabeth Smith, 6-24-1922; **Mary
       Eleanor**[11] b 12-25-1902, m Wiley Ecton
       Pendleton 9-5-1922; and **Margaret Elizabeth**[11]
       b 4-3-1905, m Watson Green 6-16-1928.
  ii   **William Orton**[10] b 1-13-1875 and d 7-11-1899
       in Kansas City, MO.
  iii **Orla Addison**[10] b 1-11-1877 d 6-11-1954 m
       Ruby Lewis 2-2-1914. In 1900 he was living
       with his mother in Kansas City, MO. [MOFC]

(843) Homer R.[9], (Samuel Orton[8], Cyrus[7], Matthew[6],
Matthew[5], Joseph[4], Joseph[3], John[2], John[1]), born on 6-
15-1846 at Scottsville, NY. He married Jeanette D.
Warren on 2-6-1873. She was born in May of 1848. He
married again in 1891. She was born 5-5-1876 and
died on 7-9-1952. [BR **Cyrus Wells**[8] Severance] [1900
NYFC] They apparently located at Chili, NY. [1880-
1900 NYFC]

Children:
  i   **Ellsworth**[10] b 9- -1874 in NY
  ii   **Horton**[10] b 4- -1882 in NY

(844) George Wells[9], (Cyrus Wells[8], Cyrus[7], Matthew[6],
Matthew[5], Joseph[4], Joseph[3], John[2], John[1]), born 1-15-
1870 in North Chili, NY and he died in Hobart, IN
on 7-19-1940. [BR **Cyrus Wells**[8] Severance] He
married to Agnes Jane Burns on 6-29-1891. **George
Wells**[9] was born at Rochester/North Chili, NY and
died at Crown Point, IN. [DARLR] Agnes Jane Burns

was born at Chicago, IL and died at Crown Point, IN. [DAR Nat's No. 48-312] [CRCH p 7]

He was working as a teamster in Chicago when he married Agnes Jane Burns in 1892. **George**[9] and Agnes moved to the family farm known as the Doctor Farm northeast of Merrillville, IN about 1898. [Fieler]

Children: [Fieler]

i   **Martha**[10] b 1893 in Chicago m Ray Burge in 1913. He d in May of 1957 and Martha d in February of 1977.

ii   **George Jr.**[10] b 6-6-1895 in Hobart, IN. He m Alberta in 1917. They were divorced in 1935. His second wife was Emily Thoreson in 1935. They both d in 1972.

iii   **Pearl**[10] b 1897 m George Yager in 1915, divorced and later m Glen Price in 1930.

iv   **Irving**[10] b 1899

v   **Nellie**[10] b 1900

vi   **Ralph J.**[10] b 1903 in IN m Florence Sears (Frantz) a widow

vii   **Charles H.**[10] b 1905 in IN, he moved to MI where he married

viii **Agnes Bertha**[10] b 2-9-1908 at Hobart, IN, m to Henry Phillip Fieler of Crown Point, IN. She was co-author of Severance-Fieler Families in America [Fieler]

ix   **Frank H.**[10] b 1910 in IN m Margarite Slade in 1936. They were divorced. He d in 1974

x   **Viola**[10] b 1913

xi   **Lester A.**[10] b 1915 in IN

xii   **Dorothy**[10] b 1920 m Andres Tyler in 1938

(845) Fayette George[9], (Anthony Peck[8], Cyrus[7], Matthew[6], Matthew[5], Joseph[4], Joseph[3], John[2], John[1]), born on 1-4-1857. He married Anna Bonnett on 1-24-1876. She was born in August of 1856 in England. They lived at Brownville, Jefferson Co. NY. **Fayette**[9] was also known as Rev. **Fayette George**[9] Severance since he was a clergyman of the Methodist Church and resided at Hillsboro, NY.

Children:

i   **Anna Maud**[10]

ii   **Cyrus William**[10]. He does not show on the 1900 census and perhaps he d young. [NYFC]

iii   **Fayette Bonnett**[10] b circa 1885 in NY. In 1920 he was living in Lost Springs, Marion County with his wife, Daisy Elliott, and their children, **Bernice**[11], **Leroy**[11], **Ester Ellen**[11], and **Isla Jean**[11]. Also living with him was his mother, Anna, and his mother in law, Helen M. Elliott. [1920 KSFC]

    iv   **Edna Frances**[10]

(846) Charles Nicholas[9], (Anthony Peck[8], Cyrus[7], Matthew[6], Matthew[5], Joseph[4], Joseph[3], John[2], John[1]), born 10-25-1858 in NY state. He married to Gertrude A. Calkins, daughter of Jesse W. and Lydia A. Calkins. They later settled in KS. [1900 KSFC] It shows the birth of their children as being in CT. (**Gertrude J.**[10] was born in NY and **Ruth**[10] was born in CT) There also appears to be other flaws in the census records as **Charles**[9] was listed with the middle initial of F. and the birth dates of **Gertrude**[10] were listed as 1885 and **Ruth**[10] as 1887.

    Charles N.[9] was a Congregational Minister and located at Garden City, Kansas. [Oakes Vol I]

Children:
    i   **Gertrude Jean**[10] b 8-23-1886
    ii   **Ruth**[10] b 1-1-1889[10]

(847) Frank B.[9], (Anthony Peck[8], Cyrus[7], Matthew[6], Matthew[5], Joseph[4], Joseph[3], John[2], John[1]), born 7-23-1860. He married to Charlotte Loretta Scott on 8-4-1890. She died on 5-1-1892. **Frank**[9] is shown living in Bridgewater and Mexico, NY.

    Frank B.[9] was a Methodist Clergyman, located at Frankfort, NY. [Oakes Vol I p633-634]

    Charlotte Loretta Scott died in April of 1891. **Frank**[9] remarried to Sarah Banfield on 7-17-1864. [VTVR]

    Frank B.[9] married to Mary P. ____, who was born in September of 1862 in NY. They were living in Boonville, Oneida Co. NY with a son **Frank B.**[10] born in September of 1898 in NY. [1900 NYFC]

(848) Cyrus Job[9], (Anthony Peck[8], Cyrus[7], Matthew[6], Matthew[5], Joseph[4], Joseph[3], John[2], John[1]), born 7-16-1862, He married Hattie E. Davis, daughter of Charles E. Davis, on 2-11-1883. Hattie was born in May of 1863. [1900 NYFC] They lived in Ellisburg, Jefferson Co. NY. They had one son who died in infancy.

    Cyrus J.[9] Severance M.D. grew up in Oswego Co. NY. but he was a practicing physician of Mannsville and a native of the town of Oswego County, NY. He

received his M.D. degree at the medical department of the University of the City of New York in 1888.
He was a member of the Jefferson County Medical Society and the New York State Medical Association, a Mason, and a member of Lodge No. 234 of Adams. [Oakes Vol I p634]

(850) Charles Dori[9], (William Sidney[8], Chester[7], Matthew[6], Matthew[5], Joseph[4], Joseph[3], John[2], John[1]), born 12-18-1868 in VT. He married to Henrietta E. ___. They lived in Greefield, MA.

Children:
i   **Charles Sydney[10]** b 1915

(853) Herman Waldo Deane[9], (Samuel Clesson[8], Cephas Clesson[7], Matthew[6], Matthew[5], Joseph[4], Joseph[3], John[2], John[1]), born 11-22-1881. [MAVR] **Samuel's[8]** family was living with **Herman's[9]** grandfather and **Samuels[8]** stepmother and their first three children in 1800. The remaining children which includes **Herman Waldo[9]** are indicated in 1900. [1880-1900 MAFC] His wife was Lillian L. ___, born in 1883.

Children:
i   **Waldo D[10]** b 1919 in MA. In 1920 **Herman Waldo[9]** was with his wife, Lillian L., born 1883 and their son **Waldo D.[10]** born 1919 in MA. [MAFC]

(857) Derrick Dutton[9], (Warren F.[8], Leonard[7], Zenas[6], Matthew[5], Joseph[4], Joseph[3], John[2], John[1]), born 4-13-1871 in VT. He married Olive M. Cutler on 10-29-1895. She was born in February of 1867. Olive was the daughter of Silas Cutler and Maria Woodward of Springfield, VT.

Children:
i   **Miriam Elsie[10]** b 5-29-1901
ii   **Cutler Frost[10]** b 7-10-1904 in Springfield, VT.

(859) Harold Craig[9], (George Craige[8], George[7], Consider[6], Matthew[6], Joseph[4], Joseph[3], John[2], John[1]), was born 7-1-1879 Chazy, NY.
He studied architecture and became one of leading influences on the 20th Century style of modern buildings in major cities throughout the world, namely New York City. He entered the office of his cousin, Charles A. Rich, and later with the

firm of Carrere & Hastings. In 1907, he opened his own practice in partnership with William Van Allen.

Perhaps his best known building was the Bank of Manhatten Building on Wall Street, NY. but the number of others throughout the city are very numerous.

He married twice and his second wife, Louise, served as head of the firm, *Severance Engineer Company and H. Craig Severance Associates,* Architects.

After the First World War, he made a survey of the devastation in France and Belgium for the American State Department.

He traveled extensively and enjoyed tennis, riding, golf, and fishing. [Encyclopedia of American Biography, Vol XVII, 1944]

Children:
  i   **Faith Douglas**[10] m George Hackl Jr.

(860) George Alvin[9], (Joseph Cordenio[8], Ruel[7], Ruel[6], Matthew[5], Joseph[4], Joseph[3], John[2], John[1]), born 7-22-1871 in MA. **George A.**[9] living in Franklin Co. with his wife Mary W. and their children. [1920 MAFC]

Children: born in MA
  i   **Thelma F.**[9] b 1907
  ii   **Alvin W.**[9] b 1911
  iii   **Donald F.**[9] b 1911

(861) Robert Graves[9], (Elmer D.[8], Luther[7], Ezra[6], Matthew[5], Joseph[4], Joseph[3], John[2], John[1]), born 10- - 1881 in MA or VT. He married to Janet Danforth. [DARLR Buffalo NY]

Children:
  i   **Roger Danforth**[10] b 8-30-1935 at Clarendon Place, Buffalo, NY

(865) Ralph[9], (William Dwight[8], William Sydney[7], Jesse[6], Jesse[5], Joseph[4], Joseph[3], John[2], John[1]), born 2-27-1870 in Phelps, Ontario Co. NY. He married Augusta Hyna and they had one child named **Marion**[10]. **Ralph**[9] died 2-9-1899. [HOCoNY Vol II]

Child:
  i   **Marion D.**[10] b 12- -1897. In 1900 she was living with her grandfather, **William Dwight**[8]. [NYFC Phelps].

(866) Frederick C.[9], (Samuel J.[8], Charles C.P.[7], David[6], Jesse[5], Joseph[4], Joseph[3], John[2], John[1]), born 11- -1882, In 1920 **Frederick**[9] was living in Alameda, Alameda Co. with his wife Kate E., age 35, born in CA. [CAFC]

Children: born in CA [1920 CAFC]
i   **Gladys**[10] b 1905
ii   **Jerome**[10] b 1911
iii **Vernon**[10] b 1915

(867) Alfred D.[9], (Samuel J.[8], Charles C.P.[7], David[6], Jesse[5], Joseph[4], Joseph[3], John[2], John[1]), born 5- - 1893 in CA. In 1920 he was living with his wife, Elizabeth, born 1893 in CA, and their daughter. [CAFC]

Children:
i   **Dorothy**[10] b 1916 in CA

(869) George W.[9], (Seth[8], Joseph A.[7], Seth[6], David[5], John[4], Joseph[3], John[2], John[1]), born 2-6-1876. He lived in IA and then later in SD. [1920 SDFC]. His wife was Nellie M., born circa 1874, in SD.

Children:
i   **Wales A.**[10] b 1916 in SD

(870) Martin Elbert[9], (John[8], James Taggart[7], Jonathan[6], Jonathan[5], Jonathan[4], Joseph[3], John[2], John[1]), born 6-2-1893 in Belfast, NY but grew up in Hutchinson, KS. He married to Fern Forman, daughter of Walter Forman and Lillie Shane of Alton, KS, on 8-31-1917 in Hutchinson. Fern was born on 3-12-1886 and died 3-9-1980. **Martin**[9] died on 8-23-1976. Both of them are buried in Pleasant Hill Cemetery, Concordia, KS.

Elbert[9] traveled with his parents to Hutchinson, KS in 1895. **Elbert's**[9] formal schooling included the Beloit City School system graduating from high school in 1911 and then the College of Emporia (KS) graduating in 1915. He then worked for the late William Allen White of the Emporia Gazette.

Fern was also an employee of William Allen White. In 1918 they moved to NY, NY, where **Elbert**[9] became a member of the Foreign Press Cable Service and worked under Murdock Pemberton. After WWI he was working with Pemberton as Assistant Publicity Manager of the New York Hippodrome. He was in charge of all Charles Dillingham Theaters and attractions and wrote the press and publicity books for many season's tours of John Phillip Sousa's Band. He later went to work for the Chanin Organization and worked for this organization for 48 years as Press Representative. He retired 7-1-1975 as Advertising and Promotional Manager of the organization. During WWII he obtained the rank of Lieutenant Colonel with the U.S. Air Force. **Elbert**[9] and Fern did not leave any children. [MHGS]

(871) Robert James[9], (John[8], James Taggart[7], Jonathan[6], Jonathan[5], Jonathan[4], Joseph[3], John[2], John[1]), born 11-17-1895 in Hutchinson, KS and died in Beloit. He married to Olive Mae Lukens, daughter of William Mathias Lukens and Sarah Beatrice Blackford of Beloit, KS, on 4-12-1922. She was born 9-7-1892.

   Robert[9] moved with his parents to Beloit, KS in 1906. His formal schooling was in Beloit, graduating from Beloit High School in 1914. He worked for the Beloit State Bank until 1933 except for the time of WWI service. He was a member of Co A., 353 Inft. Reg. 89th Division. He served as a scout on the front lines in France. As such he participated in the heavy fighting of the St. Mihiel and Meuse-Argonne offensives. He was awarded the Purple Heart for wounds recieved in action. He later served with the occupation forces in Germany following the Armistice.

   After his marriage and while still working at the bank, **Robert**[9] started a small dairy and milk delivery service at their farm on the east edge of Beloit where he later added crop farming. He was a long time member of the First Presbyterian Church, of Beloit where he was for several years one of its ruling elders and deacon. **Robert**[9] died on 3-14-1963 and Olive died 1-23-1990.

Children: [MHGS]
   i   **John William**[10] b 6-17-1925 m Virginia Lee Moss, daughter of David Leroy Moss and Eva Vanschoiack on 6-7-1947. In June 1944, prior to his graduation and because of World War II he was drafted into the Navy. He served in the south Pacific as a cook and with a gun crew while on board Various LST's. After the service he returned and graduated from high school in 1947. He farmed South West of Beloit until 1893. He

specialized in raising sheep and cash grain. He served one term as the Mitchell County Commissioner. Three daughters, **Anita Jean**[11] m Oliver Krannewitter, **Melanie Lynn**[11] m Larry Miltner, and **Susan Marie**[11] m Dale Engelbert, were b to **"Bill"**[10] and Virgina Lee. [MHGS]

ii   **Robert James Jr.**[10], b 12-10-1926 at Beloit, KS. He m Dorcas Rae Spear, daughter of Levi Wendell Speer and Effie Rae Jacques of Clearwater, on 6-8-1952. He graduated from Beloit High School in 1944. During World War II he served with the Navy as a musician with a Navy Band while stationed at Adak, AK and at Jacksonville, FL. He earned his Ph.D. (1974) from KS State University, Manhattan, KS. **"Bob"**[10] taught vocational agriculture at Simpson High School and Central Area Vocation Technical School where he later served as the director.

Children of **"Bob"**[10] and Dorcas are **Jean Elaine**[11], b 4-25-1953, m Timothy D. Ney; **Sara Joanne**[11], b 11-16-1954, m Lyle Weinert; **Rachal Lynn**[11], b 9-19-1958, m Rick Smith; **James Wendell**[11], b 4-18-1961 m Claudia K. Vines; and **Frederick John**[11] b 5-20-1963. [MHGS]

iii   **Wilford Lee**[10] b 10-7-1931 at Beloit, KS m 9-13-1955 to Sandra Jane Mc Millan, daughter of Gordon Benjamin and Mary Opal McMillan. They had two children, **Jeffrey Alan**[11] b 10-5-1957 and **Jennifer Ann**[11] b 10-30-1958. **Wilford**[10] remarried to Mary Elizabeth Harrison, daughter of Merle Otis and Margaret Genevieve Harrison of Pueblo, CO. They adopted two sons, David Michael and Gregory Martin. **Wilford Lee**[10] graduated from Beloit High School and attended KS State University, Manhattan, KS. He served with a division of the U.S. Marine Band while stationed at Camp Pendelton, CA and in Korea duting 1951 and 1954. He worked for the U.S. Bureau of Reclaimation. [MHGS]

iv   **Harold Gail**[10] b 5-1-1933 in Beloit, Kansas. He m Myrtle Anne Hilding, daughter of Carl Ephraim Hilding and

Myrtle Grace Powell, on 12-26-1959 at
Osage City, KS. Their two children are
Martin Kent[11] b 11-21-1962, m Sharon Kay
Brady of Warren, OH, and **Diane Mae**[11] b 9-
2-1965. **Harold**[10] earned his Ph.D degree
at IA State University, Ames, IA in
1972. He served in the U.S. Army from
May 1954 to May of 1956 with a majority
of time spent as a clerk with a Signal
Construction Battalion in Germany. His
profession as a vocational agriculture
teacher as been utilized at KS secondary
schools at Long Island, Lebanon, and
Jewell, KS. He spent two years in
Nigeria for the KS State University
Agency for the International Development
Team. [MHGS]

(872) John Long[9], (Louis Henry[8], Solomon Lewis[7],
Robert Bruce[6], Solomon[5], Jonathan[4], Joseph[3], John[2],
John[1]), born 5-8-1863 at Cleveland, Cuyahoga Co.
OH. [OHVR] He married Elizabeth Huntington DeWitt
on 11-3-1891. **John Long**[9] died on 1-16-1936 and
Elizabeth died 1-25-1929.

John[9] went to Oberlin College and graduated in
1885 with a Bachelor of Arts. He started work in
the Standard Oil Corporation of Cleveland and
quickly advanced to Treasurer and Secretary of the
Cleveland Linseed Oil Company. He later organized
the American Linseed Oil Co. and the Colonial Salt
Company. For several years he was Secretary and
Treasurer of the Linde Air Products Co., and Vice
President and Director of the Cleveland Steel Co.,
He was Chairman of the Board of Directors of the
Youngstown Steel Door Co., and Colonial Salt Co.,
President of the Cleveland Arcade Co., the
Cleveland Museum of Art, and the Cleveland
Orchestra Co., Director of the Youngstonw Sheet and
Tube Co., the Cleveland Trust Co., and the National
Carbon Co., a trustee of Oberlin College, Western
Reserve University, Nanking (China) University, and
Pekin University, and a sponsor of the Severance
Union Medical School and Hospital. He also held
various memberships at Pasadena, CA where he
settled in later life.

He gave the Severance Hall at Wellesley College,
Wellesley, MA. The Severance Music Hall of
Cleveland, OH is among the finest in the world,
Perhaps it is the very best of its kind. It is the
home of the Cleveland Symphony Orchestra. When it

was constructed in 1931, it cost nearly 3 million dollars. The hall was opened on 2-5-1931. **John L.**[9] made the presentation, and the Orchestra and Chorus gave the world premiere of Charles Martin Loeffler's "Evocation"

He contributed to the Lake Side Memorial Hospital and he built the base hospital of Seoul, Korea. He was a heavy financial contributor to Oberlin and Wooster Colleges and to Western Reserve University. [NEHGR Vol 15 p276]

(873) Elizabeth "Bessie Lill"[9], (Lewis/Louis Henry[8], Solomon Lewis[7], Robert Bruce[6], Solomon[5], Jonathan[4], Joseph[3], John[2], John[1]), born 11-16-1865 in Titusville, PA and died in Cleveland, OH on 1-4-1944. She studied for three years at Wellesley College and then spent a year studying in Berlin and Paris.

She married first to Dr. Dudley Peter Allen, past president of the Ohio State Medical Association and the American Surgical Association, who died 1-5-1915. She married secondly to Francis Fleury Prentiss, industrialist and philanthropist, in September of 1917. He died in Pasadena, CA on 4-1-1937.

Elizabeth[9] was "awarded the Cleveland Medal for Public Service as a patroness of Cleveland's humanitarian ideals." She gave millions of dollars to further many worthwile organizations. [NEHGR Vol XCVIII]

(874) William Rotch Morgan[9], (Pierre Clarke[8], Theodoric Cordenic[7], Robert Bruce[6], Solomon[5], Jonathan[4], Joseph[3], John[2], John[1]), born in MA in 1887. He married to Susan Williams Grinnell, daughter of Edmund Grinnell and Jennie G. Swift, on 2-18-1911. She was born 1-15-1888 in New Bedford. They lived at New Bedford and Boston, MA and later at Redlands, San Bernardino, CA. In 1920 he was living in CA, age 33, with his family and all the children. [1920 CAFC]

During his course at Harvard, he was captain of the varsity crew. **William Rotch[9]** was a mariner, sea captain, ship builder and owner.

Children: [Enery p281] born in MA except **Peter[10]**
i   **Rachel Lee[10]** b 11-3-1911
ii   **William Rotch[10]** b 2-21-1913
iii **Isabel Pierre[10]** b 7-28-1916
iv   **Peter G.[10]** b 1919 in CA

(875) Lyman Cathestes[9], (Oliver Cathestes[8], Otis Cathestus[7], Otis[6], Solomon[5], Jonathan[4], Joseph[3], John[2], John[1]), born 11-9-1866. He married to Nettie Bell who was born in November of 1864 in PA. The family was living in Carbondale, Lackawana Co. PA. in 1920. Anna Bell, age 75, his mother and her sister Ida Bell were living with them in 1900. [1900-1920 PAFC]

Children:
i   **Mildred[10]** b 6- -1898 in PA

(876) Burton Cordenio[9], (Otis Cordenio[8], Otis Cathestus[7], Otis[6], Solomon[5], Jonathan[4], Joseph[3], John[2], John[1]), born 2-8-1870 in Bloomsburg, Columbia Co. PA. He was living in Waverly, Tioga Co. NY with his wife, Emma A. ___ and their children in 1920. [NYFC]

Children: born in PA except **Helen[10]** [1900-1910 PAFC] and [1920 NYFC]
i   **Lena M.[10]** b 2- -1893
ii   **Cora[10]** b 1896
iii   **Stanley B.[10]** b 5- -1896
iv   **Alvin[10]** b 1903
v   **Cordean[10]** b 1906
vi   **George A.[10]** b 1912
vii   **Helen A.[10]** b 1915 in NY State
viii **Mary L.[10]** b 1917

(877) Ward O./Worden Oscar[9], (Oscar Alphonso[8], Otis Cathestus[7], Otis[6], Solomon[5], Jonathan[4], Joseph[3], John[2], John[1]), born 12-1-1875 in MN or PA. He married to Edna E. ___ who was born in May of 1876. [1900-1920 PAFC]

Children: born in PA
i   **Clayton M.[10]** b 10- -1896
ii   **Glenn R.[10]** b 2- -1898
iii   **Lilian R.[10]** b 5- -1899

(878) Charles[9], (Charles H.[8], Zacheus[7], Phillip[6], James[5], James[4], unconnected) was born 6- -1859 in Pierrepont or Canton, NY. He married to Matilda Ladison, daughter of Frank Ladison and Betsey LaGrow. She was born 5-3-1859 at Canton, NY and died on 5-10-1935. **Charles[9]** was killed in 1901.

Children: [1900 NYFC]
i   **Vernon[10]** b 12- -1880

```
ii    Hazel B.¹⁰ b 6- -1888
iii   Melvin¹⁰ b 6- -1890
iv    Byron G.¹⁰ b 5- -1896
v     female b 5-29-1893 at Canton [NYVR]
vi    son b 5-22-1896 at Canton [NYVR]
```

(904) William Henry⁹, (Waldron⁸, David⁷, Eben⁶, unconnected, Ebenezer³, Ephraim², John¹), was born in Mill Creek, OH on 10-16-1841. [MLM] He married 6-9-1867 to Rosanah Rhoades. She was born in 1849 [OHFC] **William⁹** died on 7-24-1907. [MLM] A pension was filed by the widow 10-2-1907 for service in C 111 OH Inf. [CWPR]

Children: [1880-1900 OHFC]
```
i     George¹⁰ b 6- -1869
ii    Daniel¹⁰ b 5-30-1872 [OHVR]
iii   James A.¹⁰ b 11- -1881
iv    Sylvia¹⁰ b 10- -1884
v     Joseph¹⁰ b 11- -1887
vi    Eliza¹⁰ b 11- -1891
```

(905) James⁹, (Waldron⁸, David⁷, Eben⁶, unconnected, Ebenezer¹, Ephraim², John¹), was born 10-1-1850 [MLM] at Hillsdale, OH. He married to Lydia Jessie Esterline, daughter of Henry Esterline and Christina Lyons in 1872 or 1873. [IGI] Lydia was born 4-11-1851 and died 11-8-1886. **James⁹** died 7-2-1880 at Millcreek. They are buried at Olive Branch Cemetery, Millcreek, Williams Co OH.

Children: [MLM]
```
i     Walden H.¹⁰ b 1873 in OH, m Rosa Del
      Camp on 3- 26-1893. He was killed in a
      train accident as a young man.
ii    Ella¹⁰ b 1875 in MI
iii   David E.¹⁰ b 10-8-1876 at Hillsdale,
      MI. He m to Florence Connor, daughter
      of Charles Gideon Connor and Mary Jane
      Cotton. They were divorced 1-5-1899 at
      Jackson, MI. He d 4-8-1943 and is buried in
      the Jackson, Jackson Co. MI. Children of
      David¹⁰ and Florence were: [MLM] George
      Eslie¹¹ b 10-19-1899 at Jonesville, MI. He m
      to Ida Nora Darrow on 3-14-1921 at
      Centerville, Turner Co. SD. He d 1-26-1978
      at Aberdeen, Spink County, SD. Evelyn May¹¹
      b 6-2-1909 at Allen, MI. She d on 11-18-
      1985 at Sun City, AZ. Emma Jane¹¹ b 1-3-
      1913 at Jackson, MI. She d 2-16-1976 at
```

Cedar Rapids, IA and was buried at San Deigo, CA.

(906) David W.[9], (Waldron[8], David[7], Eben[6], unconnected, Ebenezer[3], Ephraim[2], John[1]), was born 2-4-1855 in Jefferson Co NY. [MLM] He married to Sarah I. Bachman at Fulton Co., NY. She was born 12- -1860. [OHFC] **David**[9] died 4-27-1940. They are buried in the Olive Branch Cemetery. [MLM]

Children: [1900-1920 OHFC] [MLM]
i   **James**[10] b 6- -1881
ii   **Aldis**[10] b 7- -1883
iii **Myrtle**[10] b 11- -1885
iv   **Sylvester**[10] b 5- -1888
v   **Ruth**[10] b 7- -1891
vi   **Ida**[10] b 6- -1894
vii **Dewey**[10] b 1- -1899
viii **Russell**[10] b 1901
ix   **Amber**[10] b 1903

(907) Martin Ellsworth[9] *Severens*, (Charles Weaver Pulsipher[8], Franklin[7], Isaac[6], Joseph[5], Benjamin[4], Ephraim[3], Ephraim[2], John[1]), born on 8-12-1861 at South Rockingham, VT and died 6-19-1923. He married first to Dora A. Woolley of Grafton, VT. Dora died on 4-18-1889. **Martin Ellsworth**[9] married secondly to Abbie Susan Davis of Athens, VT on 12-24-1889. [Lovell]

Children of **Martin Ellsworth**[9] Severens and Dora A. Woolley
i   **Raymond Martin**[10], b on 6-25-1884 m Alice E. Sprowson of Concord Jt., MA on 6-16-1909. Children: **Edward Martin**[11] b 3-20-1910, resided in Fitchburg, MA, m Bertha Houghton on 11-26-1936. **Joseph Raymond**[11] b 1-19-1912, m 1st Helena Hazelburg on 9-21-1935 and 2nd to Gertrude Nivell Joynes on 10-6-1951. **Eleanor Alice**[11] b 1-1-1924, He m Robert F. Peck of Leominster, MA on 7-17-1944. **Norman Dana**[11] b on 5-16-1926 and lived in Townshend, MA, m to Lorraine Chalifoux on 1-10-1948.

Children of **Martin Ellsworth**[9] *Severens* and Abbie Susan Davis

ii   **Mildred Davis**[10], b on 5-16-1892, m Floyd B. Bowen of Dickerson Center, NY on 12-23-1918.

iii   **Marion Elizabeth**[10], b 4-26-1894

iv   **Ruth Winona**[10], b 5-14-1899 and d 9-9-1951 at South Rockingham, VT. She m to Walter George Hitchcock of Westminster West, VT on 12-27-1920.

v   **Ralph Weaver**[10], b 5-14-1899 at South Rockingham, VT and resided there. He m to Stella Lucia Hoxie of Proctorsville, VT on 8-9-1932. Their children were **Richard Hoxie**[11] b on 3-10-1934 who m to Barbara Ann Child of Syracuse, NY on 8-31-1957, and **Kenneth Warren**[11] who was b on 5-8-1936.

vi   **Martha Ester**[10], b 11-2-1906 and resided at E. Swanzey, m to Charles Frichofer on 6-7-1931 and they lived at Keene, NH.

(908) Jefferson Franklin[9] *Severens*, (Charles Weaver Pulsipher[8], Franklin[7], Isaac[6], Joseph[5], Benjamin[4], Ephraim[3], Ephraim[2], John[1]), born 10-26-1864. He married to Elizabeth Walsh on 12-24-1887. **Jefferson**[9] died on 3-27-1899. [Weaver]

Children:

i   **Hazel Katherine**[10] b 2-21-1890 at Saxtons River, VT

ii   **Albert Jefferson**[10], b 11- -1898 at Cavendish, VT, resided in Claremont, NH

(909) Charles H.[9] *Severens*, (James M.[8], Franklin[7], Isaac[6], Joseph[5], Benjamin[4], Ephraim[3], Ephraim[2], John[1]), born 1873 in MN. In 1920 **Charles**[9] was with his wife Marie F. who was born 1884 in MI. [MIFC]

Children: born in MI

i   **James M.**[10] b 1914

ii   **Beatrice I.**[10] b 1915

iii   **Richard L.**[10] b 1918

(910) George M.[9] *Severens*, (James M.[8], Franklin[7], Isaac[6], Joseph[5], Benjamin[4], Ephraim[3], Ephraim[2], John[1]), born 1875 in MN. In 1900 he was living alone at Grant Valley, Beltrami Co. In 1920 he was living in the same area with Anna _____ and his large family. [MNFC] There may have been more children.

Children: born in MN

i   **Vera** [10] b 1898
ii   **Clifford**[10] b 1904
iii **Lucile**[10] b 1908
iv   **James**[10] b 1911
v   **Lois**[10] b 1913
vi   **Doris**[10] b 1915
vii **Catherine**[10] b 1916
viii **Gladys**[10] b 1918

(911) Clinton Earl[9] *Sevrens*, (William P.[8], Urial[7], David[6], Joseph[5], Benjamin[4], Ephraim[3], Ephraim[2], John[1]), born 8-2-1889/91 and died in March of 1987.
C. Earl "Buster"[9] Sevrens was a Personnel Manager and Safety Engineer for Monsanto Chemical Co., of Everett, MA. He was married to Helen Flint Poole, whom he met while skating on the North Woburn Mill pond around 1910. Helen died in November of 1986. The couple had been married for 74 years.
    "Buster"[9] and several friends procured some land on Main Street in North Woburn and built a baseball field and skating rink for the public to use. This later became the North Woburn Playground. Mr. Sevrens showed a great interest in sports his entire life." [NSW *Daily Times Chronicle*-Woburn, MA Monday, October 5, 1987]
    William G.[11] Sevrens said of his grandparents "He met my grandmother, Helen Flint Poole, while skating on the North Woburn (MA) mill pond around 1910. this place I also haunted as a youth. It has now been damned to provide a resivoir twice as large. it feeds a water hungry Woburn whose population has increased ten times since those days."
    "I remember the smell in my grandmothers kitchen when she used to bake 'tomatoe soup cake' for my fathers' birthday."
    "I remember my grandfathers' cigars leasted for hours. I could always tell when Garmpa had been around. He was a veteran cigar smoker, often travelling in his car, windows rolled up, creating his own wheeled humider. The smoke didn't harm him, perhaps because he gave it up 10 years before his death at 98."
    "One of my favorite 'Garmpa' stories was based upon information I calculated in the 1970's while conversing with a friend. We were talking about our families. His grandfather had been a Boston Police Officer during the Boston Police Strike of 1918. My grandfather was serving in the National Guard at that time. His Unit had been activated for duty.

426

They patrolled Boston's mean streeets in lieu of
the police. This was an elucidation to us both.
Strange how things come around." [MWGS]

Children:
   i   **Palmer E.**[10]
   ii   **Jean**[10] m Harold MacLeod of Red Bank, NJ
   iii   **Freda**[10] m Colby Little of Woburn, MA
   iv   **Shirley**[10] m Gilmore Smith of Billerica,
       MA

(912) Chester S.[9] *Sevrens*, (William P.[8], Uriel[7],
David[6], Joseph[5], Benjamin[4], Ephraim[3], Ephraim[2],
John[1]), was born 11- -1891 in MA. In 1920 **Chester
S.**[9] *Sevrens* was living in Woburn, Middlesex Co.
with his wife, Marion C., born 1890 in MA, and
their family. MAFC]

Children: born in MA
   i   **William A.**[10] b 1916
   ii   **Elizabeth M.**[10] b 1917

(913) George W.[9], (William[8], Jonathan Thompson[7],
David[6], Joseph[5], Benjamin[4], Ephraim[3], Ephraim[2],
John[1]), was born 1- -1874 in Grafton, NH. **George
W.**[9] married Annie E. Graham, daughter of Emiline
Graham, on 4-4-1897. She was born 1879. [1910 NHFC]
Annie died 5-12-1927 in Tilton, NH. She had
previously lived in St. Petersburg, FL. He died
before 1927. They lived in Grafton, NH.

Children: born in NH
   i   **Hazel G.**[10] b 1897
   ii   **Verna E.**[10] b 1900 m 9-20-1919 at Laconia,
       Everett M. Brown, son of Melvin E. Brown
       and Etta A. Carr, [NHVR] b 1896 [1920
       NHFC]
   iii   **Georgianna M.**[10] b 10-28-1902 d 10-28-1912
       Grafton, NH [NHVR]
   iv   **Glen Graham**[10] b 1908 [1920 NHFC]

(914) Leon O.[9], (George[8], Jonathan Thompson[7], David[6],
Joseph[5], Benjamin[4], Ephraim[3], Ephraim[2], John[1]), was
born in February of 1885 at Wilmot, NH. [NHVR] His
father was born at Grafton. His mother was Anna
Bean. [NHVR] He married to Florence M. (Keniston)
Sanborn, daughter of James Keniston and Minnie
Swallow of Franklin, NH, on 8-19-1905 at Andover.
[NHVR] Florence was born in 1884. [1910 NHFC] They
show living in Wilmot, Franklin, and Andover, NH.

Children:
    i   **James George**[10] b 1906 d 1906 at Andover
          [NHVR]
    ii   **Irene**[10] b 1908 from Tilton, NH m William
          D. Buckley 8-9-1927. He was the son of
          Fred Buckley and Isabel Blan.
    iii   **Beryl S.**[10] b 1912 d 10-5-1983 m
          ___Garrett
    iv   **Olive**[10] b 1914
    v   **Leon Jr.**[10] b 1915 at Kennebunk, ME
    vi   **Henry**[10] b 1916
    vii   **Ave**[10] b 1917

(915) Willard William[9], (Joseph[8], Willard Colby[7],
Joseph[6], Joseph[5], Benjamin[4], Ephraim[3], Ephraim[2],
John[1]), born 1879 in Grantham, NH and lived in
Springfield, NH. [NHVR] He married first to
Blanche Emma Tenney, daughter of Kirk M. Tenney and
Emma Heath, on 10-19-1901. [NHVR] Blanche was born
on 8-20-1883 and died 2-26-1924. [NHVR] He married
secondly to Angie B. Beyer, of Union, ME, on 8-20-
1927. He was a mail carrier and stage driver.

Children:
    i   **Kirk T.**[10] b 1908 m Muriel B. Sleeper on
          8-30-1930 [NHVR] He was a truck driver.
    ii   **child** b 6-7-1923 (Hanover, NH)
    iii   **Beatrice**[10] b 1924 m Clarence L. Hastings,
          son of Burleigh Hastings and Melissa
          Barton, of Grantham, NH.

(916) Henry Seely[9], (Joseph C.[8], Willard Colby[7],
Joseph[6], Joseph[5], Benjamin[4], Ephraim[3], Ephraim[2],
John[1]), born 7- -1886 of Springfield, NH. He
settled in Grafton, Grafton Co. with his wife,
Amelia M., who was born in Canada in 1892. [1920
NHFC]

Children:
    i   **Bessie O.**[10] b 1911 in NH
    ii   **Evan M.**[10] b 1917

(918) Percy E[9]. *Sevrens*, (Alonzo Miner[8], Newell[7],
John[6], Joseph[5], Benjamin[4], Ephraim[3], Ephraim[2],
John[1]), born circa 1875 in Green Lake, WI. The
[1880 MNFC] shows him in MN with his wife Cora M.,
she was born in MN circa 1878. In 1920 **Percy E.**[9]
Sevrens was with his wife Cora M. and his children.
[SDFC]

Children:
i   **Fred E.**[10] *Sevrens* b 1899 in SD
ii   **Earl L.**[10] *Sevrens* b 1907 in SD

(919) Ernest A[9]. *Sevrens*, (Alonzo Miner[8], Newell[7], John[6], Joseph[5], Benjamin[4], Ephraim[3], Ephraim[2], John[1]), born in 1878/1879. He married to Jesse M. who was born in 1879 in NY. **Ernest**[9] was born in Green Lake, WI but settled in Carson Co. SD. He was living in Hilde, Walworth Co., with his wife and his brother, **Eugene H.**[9] *Sevrens* in 1900. [SDFC]

Chilren: born in SD [1920 SDFC]
i   **Faith**[10] b 1902
ii   **Donald**[10] b 1904
iii **Frank**[10] b 1909
iv **Dorothy**[10] b 1919

(920) John W.[9], (Fred G.[8], Leonard H.[7], John[6], Peter[5], Benjamin[4], Ephraim[3], Ephraim[2], John[1]), born in 1907 and died on 11-1-1989 at Manchester, NH. He was born and raised in Hooksett and resided most of his life in Allenstown and Pembroke, NH. At the time of his death he left Bernice (Stewart), his wife of 59 years, and children, (listed below) three brothers, **Charles**[9] of Londonderry, **Dean**[9] of Plant City, FL, and **William**[9] of Lakeland, FL, and two sisters, Mrs. **Ellen**[9] Willis and Mrs. **Nancy**[9] Kenney of Plant City, FL. Obituary [NSUL-Manchester, NH]

Children:
i   **Stewart**[10] Severance of San Jose, CA,
ii   **Jeannette**[10] (Mrs. Rudolph Plourde)
iii **Barbara**[10] (Mrs. Robert Marier)
iv **Debra**[10] (Mrs. Alan Turcotte) of Allenstown.
v   **Donna**[10] (Mrs. Robert Barker) of Hooksett.

(921) Washington Bainbridge[9], (Ambrose Warren[8], Warren[7], Rueben[6], Caleb[5], Joseph[4], Ephraim[3], Ephraim[2], John[1]), born on 6-19-1843 and died 9-24-1917. [MEVR] He was married to Ida M. ____, who was born in November of 1856. In 1900 **Washington**[9] shows living in Orrington and Bangor, ME. [MEFC]

Children:
i   **Virginia**[10] b 12- -1888

(922) Frederick E. Sr.[9], (William Henry[8], Russell Howard[7], Caleb[6], Caleb[5], Joseph[4], Ephraim[3], Ephraim[2], John[1]), born 11- -1891. He married to Catherine Carney, They lived in Lynn, Essex County, MA.

Children: [MFES]
i   **Frederick E.**[10] b 1916 d 12-29-1990. He m to Mary Fiveash. They lived Manchester, NH, Marblehead, MA, and St. Simons Island, GA. They left two children, **Frederick E. Severance III**[11] of Manchester, and Mrs. Gary (**Kay S.**[11]) Eisenhower of Marblehead.
        Frederick E.[10] Severance Jr. age 73, of St. Simons Island, GA, Founder, President, and Treasurer of Seal Tanning Co., in Manchester, NA, d at Worcester City Hospital in Worcester, MA. He was a graduate of Peabody High School in 1934 and a World War II Coast Guard Veteran. He was a Director and Trustee of the Manchester YMCA, Commissioner of the Boy Scouts of America, a member of the Kawanis Club, and a member of the Washington Lodge A.F. & A.M. The funeral was held at Marblehead, MA. [NSUL Manchester, NH]
ii   **Marie**[10] m ____Spencer

(924) William H.[9], (Preston P.[8], William B.[7], Benjamin[6], Joshua[5], Joseph[4], Ephraim[3], Ephraim[2], John[1]), born 6- -1877 in OR. In 1900 he was with his wife Daisy E., born 5- -1881 in OR and his grandfather **William B.**[7], born 3- -1823 in ME. [Portland, Multnomah Co. ORFC] In 1920 he was with his wife, Daisy, and their two daughters. [ORFC Portland]

Children:
i   **Dorothy E.**[10] b 1908 OR
ii   **Marvel E.**[10] b 1912 OR

(926) Harold E.[9], (Harry J.[8], Carlos Erastus[7], Benjamin[6], Joshua[5], Joseph[4], Ephraim[3], Ephraim[2], John[1]), was born 12-1-1897. He married to Jarvis O. Goodridge, born 1900, on 9-20-1922. [MEVR]
    An obituary notice from Kihei, Hawaii for **Harold's**[9] wife, Lucile Day, January 26, 1994 stated that Lucile Day, 75, of Kehei, died Saturday at Queen's Medical Center. She was born at Center

Lovell, ME. She and her husband, **Harold E.**[9] Severance, owned and operated the Severance Lodge, a well-known resort in ME, for 35 years.

Children:
i   **Craig**[10], of Hilo, HI
ii **Douglas**[10], of New Smyrna Beach, FL
iii **Carol**[10], m ____Taylor, Canton, CT

(928) Raymond Gerald[9], (Charles A.[8], Harvey A.[7], Benjamin[6], Joshua[5], Joseph[4], Ephraim[3], Ephraim[2], John[1]), was born 8-23-1909 in OR, married to Dorothy Alyce Bouvier on 12-19-1926, and died 6-15-1962 in CA. Dorothy died 5-15-1991. [MJDJ]

Children :
i   **Dorothy Jean**[10], b 1-3-___ m John Montgomery 2-7-1975

(933) Octavius W.[9], (George A.[8], John[7], John[6], John[5], Ephraim[4], Ephraim[3], Ephraim[2], John[1]), born 6-30-1865 in Hancock, ME. He married to Leah Osgood Miller, daughter of Eliza M. and George H. Miller, on 1-5-1887. [MEVR]

Children:
i   **Amanda**[10] b 1)- -1887
ii **Harriet E.**[1c] b 8-20-1895 [MEVR]
iii **George Austin**[10] b 9-30-1896

(933a) John W.[9], (Asa[8], Asa[7], John[6], John[5], Ephraim[4], Ephraim[3], Ephraim[2], John[1]), born in 1852/53 at Sandwich, NH. [1870 NHFC] He married to Helen M. Mills on 12-23-1876. [NHVR] **John**[9] was a school teacher. Helen was born in Boscawen, NH. After **John**[9] died on 10-20-1891 at the age of 39-4-0 at Gilford, NH. [NHVR] Helen remarried to George York. Helen was born 12-31-1850 and died 5-22-1922. [Lighton]

Children:
i   **Eva G.**[10] b 8-1-1883 d 8-26-1917 [NHVR] Single
ii   **Hermie**[10] d 1-15-1891 infant son
iii **Laura M.**[10] b 7-25-1881 d 9-30-1923 [NHVR] Single
iv   **Mary Elizabeth "Lizzie"**[10] b 1879 m Walter Bryant. Shortly after they were married they lived in **Lizzie's**[10] grandfather, **Asa**[8] Severance's house on the upper road

to North Sandwich, now owned by John and
Janet Laverack. When **Asa**[8] d in 1901,
title passed to Walter and **Lizzie**[10]. She
had been brought up in the house as her
parents. [SNHE 66th Excursion]

v   **Alice Frances**[10] b 1879. [1900 NHFC] She m
first to Ernest W. Glines, son of Erwin A.
and Etta Berry. They divorced. **Alice**[10] m
second to George Harry Elliott 4-9-1917.
[NHVR]

(933b) Clarke[9], (William H.[8], Levi[7], John[6], John[5],
Ephraim[4], Ephraim[3], Ephraim[2], John[1]), born in 10- -
1876 in MN. He was living with his parents. [1880
MNFC Spencer, Isanti Co.] **Clarke**[9] was living with
his wife, Lotte, who was born 7- -1878 in Iowa.
[1900 MNFC Spencer Brooks]

Children: [1920 MNFC]
   i   **Henry**[10] b 1901
   ii   **Blanche**[10] b 1906
   iii **Iris**[10] b 1912

(934) Fred Merserve[9], (William J.[8], Jacob Jewell[7],
John Jr.[6], John[5], Ephraim[4], Ephraim[3], Ephraim[2],
John[1]), born 4-2-1860. He married to Dora B. Noble,
daughter of Scamon G. and Lucrecia Jane Noble, on
3-31-1888. Dora was born on 11-26-1864 and died 10-
5-1936. **Fred**[9] died on 12-24-1920 at Laconia or Lake
Village, Belknap Co. NH. [NHVR]

Children:
   i   **Irwin J.**[10] b 11- -1893 m Olla Belle
Hunkins, daughter of Charles H. Hunkins
and ____ Lamprey, on 4-9-1922 [NHVR]
Irwin J.[10] was an electrician and Olla
was a telephone operator.

(935) Leroy J.[9], (William J.[8], Jacob Jewell[7], John
Jr.[6], John[5], Ephraim[4], Ephraim[3], Ephraim[2], John[1]),
born 12-17-1870. He married first to Ilsa M.
Sanborn on 6-27-1891. They were divorced on 4-26-
1921. He married secondly to Mary E. Robinson,
daughter of Charles Swain and Dell M. Goodwin, on
1-10-1928 and divorced on 5-15-1929. [NHVR] **Fred
J.**[9] was listed as living in Lakeport and Salem, NH.
   William J.[9] Severance and Etta were at Lakeport,
New Hampshire in 1900. [NHFC]

Children:

i   **Fred M.**[10]
ii   Ethel M. b 10- -1894 (the 1910 NH census
     says that she was an adopted daughter b in
     NH)

(936) William Hector[9], (William Norman[8], Sargeant
Jewell[7], John Jr.[6], John[5], Ephraim[4], Ephraim[3],
Ephraim[2], John[1]), was born 8- -1868. **William Hector**[9]
married to Lillian Perkins. They settled in
Wasioja, Dodge Co. MN. [Dodge Co. MNVR]

Children: [MHCS]
i   **Hazel**[10] b 1899
ii   **Pearl**[10]
iii **Jessie**[10] d young
iv   **Grace**[10]

(937) Lester Floyd[9], (William Norman[8], Sargeant
Jewell[7], John Jr.[6], John[5], Ephraim[4], Ephraim[3],
Ephraim[2], John[1]), born 2-20-1881 in SD. He married
to Marietta Dibble in 1901. Marietta was born on 2-
4-1884 and died on 2-4-1901. **Lester**[9] was a farmer
all his life, farming first in MN and Flandreau,
SD, then for many years in Ryder, Ward Co. ND. The
1920 ND census shows them living in McLean Co. Many
of his descendants still live within 100 miles of
Ryder. **Lester**[9] and Marietta are both buried at
Ryder, ND.

Children: [MHCS]
i   **Gladys V.**[10] b 6-20-1902
ii   **Sadie May**[10] b 11-25-1907
iii **Harley**[10] b 1912
iv   **Charlotte Elizabeth**[10] b 2-28-1918
v   **Walter H.**[10] b 1921
vi   **Raymond**[10] b 1924
vii **Curtis Leroy**[10] b 2-1-1927
The first 4 children. [1920 NDFC]

(938) Arthur Burton[9], (John Martin[8], Sargeant
Jewell[7], John Jr.[6], John[5], Ephraim[4], Ephraim[3],
Ephraim[2], John[1]), was born 4-16-1870. [MNVR] He
married to Emma Grow on 4-5-1892. [MHCS] Emma was
born 4-22-1870 and she died on 6-18-1902. **Arthur
B.**[9] died on 12-24-1939. After farming first in MN,
they moved to ND in April of 1916, first to
Parshall, then other farms in the general vicinity.
They are both buried there. The family shows on the
1920 NDFC with their children.

Harland[9] gives an excellent account of all the grand children of **Arthur Burton**[9]. [MHCS]

Children: The first 5 children were born in SD and the last were born in MN
- i   **Archie Floyd**[10] b 2-2-1893 and he shows in 1920 with his wife, Lela b in IN and children, **Floyd P.**[11] and **Ruth P.**[11] [NDFC]
- ii   **Clifford Franklin**[10] b 2-22-1895
- iii **Charles Burton**[10] b 6-23-1897
- iv   **Frances Willard**[10] b 3-15-1901
- v   **Giles Ernest**[10] b 7-29-1902
- vi   **Winnifred Edna**[10] b 12-3-1903
- vii **Ruth Phoebe**[10] **b** 4-27-1906
- viii **Hazel May**[10] b 5-9-1908
- ix   **Flossie**[10] b 1909 d 1910
- x   **Chester Alfred**[10] b 8-1-1911

(939) Edward Clifford[9], (John Martin[8], Sargeant Jewell[7], John Jr.[6], John[5], Ephraim[4], Ephraim[3], Ephraim[2], John[1]), born 10-5-1876. He married to Graca L. Babcock on 5-14-1903. **Eddie**[9] was a painter by trade. They lived first at Dodge Center, MN, then Gentry, AR and then to Milton, WI. [MHCS]

In 1920 **Edward**[9] and his wife were living in Farwin, IA with their children and his mother and father, **John**[8] and Phoebe. [IAFC]

Graca was born on 9-10-1875 at Garwin, IA. She died 1-1-1926. He died on 10-14-1956. They are both buried at Milton, WI.

Children: born in Gentry, AR
- i   **Mildred Fern**[10] b 5-20-1905
- ii   **Leonard Ozora**[10] b 3-3-1907
- iii **Elda Fae**[10] b 10-22-1911
- iv   **Illo**[10] b 1915 in AR [1920 IAFC]

(940) Louette Carl[9], (Hector Calbreth[8], Sargeant Jewell[7], John Jr.[6], John[5], Ephraim[4], Ephraim[3], Ephraim[2], John[1]), born 11-23-1879 in MN. He married to Corabelle Whitney on 9-30-1903. She was born on 8-29-1885 at Melotte, SD. She died 4-5-1923 at Grand Island, NE. **Louette**[9] died at North Loup, NE.

Soon after his marriage he moved first to AR. The around 1911 he moved his family back to NE, first to North Loup and later to Grand island, where he worked for many years in a sugar beet factory. After Corabelle's death, when their youngest daughter was just a baby, he moved to Battle Creek, MI, where his children grew up, and married. He never remarried but brought up the younger children with the help of the older ones. In his old age, he moved back to North Loup where he died. [MHCS] In 1920 the family was living at Grand Island, Hall Co. [NEFC]

Children: [MHCS]
i **Clifton Leroy**[10] b 8-8-1904 in AR
ii **Fern B.**[10] b 3-6-1905 in AR
iii **Lillian Vernette**[10] b 1-6-1908 in NE
iv **Leslie Nile**[10] b 5-2-1909 in NE
v **Cecil Floyd**[10] b 12-25-1910 in NE
vi **Chester Robert**[10] b 1-13-1913 in NE
vii **Cora Lucille**[10] b 9-19-1915 in NE
viii **Marie Evelyn**[10] b 1-8-1922 in NE

(941) Harland Claude[9], (Hector Calbreth[8], Sargeant Jewell[7], John Jr.[6], John[5], Ephraim[4], Ephraim[3], Ephraim[2], John[1]), was born 8-3-1904. He married to Vesta May Davison on 8-8-1922. She was born on 6-24-1904. **Harland**[9] and Vesta lived in several states including AR, CA, OR, WA, and AZ.

Harland[9] tells in his own autobiography, "My father had gone to Gentry, AR about 1900 or 1901 from WI to avoid the cold winters there, and in order to start farming for himself again. it was there that Hector died in 1907. Vesta and Harland were married in Montague, CA. They lived first in South Passadena, CA, then several places in OR. For a number of years he worked in sawmills as a lumber grader, then they operated a bakery in College Place, WA. After selling the bakery, they moved to Phoenix, AZ and for eight years travelled with a motor home as Field Representatives for the Seventh Day Adventist Missionary Foundation, over much of the U.S. and western Canada. He retired in 1986. [MHCS]

Harland[9] researched and wrote a vast amount of information on his family's genealogy. The author is indebted for his insight and dedication to his line of the Severance Family.

Children: [MHCS]
i **Harland Kenneth**[10] b 8-7-1923
ii **Norman Everett**[10] b 10-5-1926 m Margaret and they lived in WA State.
iii **Verna May**[10] b 10-1-1928 m and the had a daughter. Later widowed, he lived in OR.
iv **Sylvia Fern**[10] b 4-27-1934 m and had a son and they lived in NV.

v   **Virgil Lauren**[10] b 5-21-1939 m Lorena and had four daughters and they lived in OR.

vi   **James Lyle**[10] b 8-8-1944 m to Kathleen and they lived in OR.

vii   **Carol Corrinne**[10] b 4-21-1948 m Stanley and had 3 children and lived in OR.

(943) Rollo J.[9], (Thomas Burton[8], Sargeant Jewell[7], John Jr.[6], John[5], Ephraim[4], Ephraim[3], Ephraim[2], John[1]), was born 4-5-1870 in Wasioja, MN. [MHCS] He married to Mamie (Maxine) E. Saxton, born 3- -1879 in WI. [1900 MNFC Ashland, Dodge Co.] **Rollo**[9] was a Seventh Day Baptist Pastor in a number of churches for several years.

Children: born in MN
i   **Alberta M.**[10] b 2- -1897 m Godfrey ___
ii   **David R.**[10] b 5- -1900

(944) Frank E.[9], (Thomas Burton[8], Sargeant Jewell[7], John Jr.[6], John[5], Ephraim[4], Ephraim[3], Ephraim[2], John[1]), born 9- -1871 in Wasioja, MN. [MHCS] **Frank E.**[9] married to Ellen Sanford in October of 1896. She died 3-3-1916. [MNVR] Ellen was the daughter of Mr. Sanford and Jane Proper. [Dodge Co. MNVR E-127-7] **Frank**[9], his wife, and children lived at Wasioja, MN. [1900-1910 Wasioja, MNFC] In 1920 **Frank E.**[9] was living with his brother, **Barton Thomas**[9] at Dodge Center. [MNFC]

Children:
i   **Hazel E.**[10] b 2- -1898
ii   **Bernice**[10] b 3- -1901

(945) Burton T., "Bert"[9], (Thomas Burton[8], Sargeant Jewell[7], John Jr.[6], John[6], Ephraim[4], Ephraim[3], Ephraim[2], John[1]), born 1-21-1873 in Dodge Co. MN. He married to Anna Osborn on 2-12-1896, who was born in 1879. [MHCS] They settled in Ashland, Dodge Co. MN. The family lived at Dodge Center, MN. [1900-1920 MNFC]

Children: born in MN
i   **Lyle B.**[10] b 3- -1897
ii   **Lorna Augusta**[10] b 4-13-1899 [MNVR]
iii   **Irving (Erwin) O.**[10] b 1903
iv   **Belva (Belna)**[10] b 1905
v   **Luvern (Laverne) W.**[10] b 1910
vi   **Howard D.**[10] b 1913
vii   **Graydon Lewayne**[10] b 5-20-1918 [MNVR]

(946) Walter Edmund[9], (Alonzo[8], James M.[7], John Jr.[6], John[5], Ephraim[4], Ephraim[3], Ephraim[2], John[1]), born 4-12-1883 in North Sandwich, NH. As a child, **Walter**[9], lived in Laconia with his sister **Ruth Ann**[9]. At about 24 years of age he went to work as a fireman on the New Hampshire branch of the Boston and Maine Railroad, working out of Concord, West Lebanon and in the White Mountain area.

Walter[9] married to Florence Bessie (Porter) Hennessey, born 5-15-1875 as a daughter of Dennis Porter and Mary Ann Longever, at White River Junction on 5-18-1912. They settled at West Lebanon, NH. Florence had previously been married to Arthur F. Slayton. She died 3-23-1923 in West Lebanon, NH.

Walter[9] married secondly to Muriel Shea, daughter of William Shea and Celia Freeman, on 12-1-1923. They lived in West Lebanon until 1928 when **Walter**[9] was transferred to Boston and therefore moved to Oak Grove (Malden) MA. Then they moved to Greenfield, MA where they lived until his death on 7-14-1936 at the age of 53. Muriel died in Laconia, NH in 1962. [MDPS]

Walter[9] was a road foreman of engines, a position which was to avoid locomotive problems. He would intermittently watch for trouble by leaning out of the gangway between engine and its coal tender. He was killed at Charlemont, MA, when he was thrown to the ground between the east and west bound rails, dying instantly from a skull fracture. [NHVR]

Children:
  i   **Donald Porter**[10] b 4-13-1916

(947) Isaac L.[9], (Asa W.[8], James M.[7], John Jr.[6], John[5], Ephraim[4], Ephraim[3], Ephraim[2], John[1]), born on 8-22-1868 at Bradford, ME. [MECR Bradford] He died 6-20-1956 at Milo, Piscataquis Co. ME. He married to Flora E. Barter, daughter of Samuel Barter and Emma Tudor Rose, on 9-20-1896 in S. Lagrange, ME. [MEVR] Flora was born on 4-6-1875 and died on 10-17-1941. [MEVR]

Isaac[9] was a Grist-Sawmill operator, store clerk. He worked in the mills and store owned by his grandfather, Isaac Libbey. In 1918, he moved to Milo, ME and worked as a woodsman, at the American Thread Company. [MINB]

They are buried in the Mills Cemetery, Bradford, ME with his mother's (Elizabeth Libby) first husband, **Octavus W.**[8] Severance who d on 10-1-1864 at the age of 32-9-8. In 1920 they were living with their first two children. [MEFC]

Children: [MINB & MAM]
  i   **Lyman L.**[10] b 7-18-1897 in Bradford, ME. [MEVR] He d 12-23-1963 in Milo. [MEVR] He was a machinist in the B&ARR Shops at Derby. He m at Milo, ME, Miss Dorothy Minard Foss, daughter of Moses C. Foss and Harriett Towle of Milo, ME, on 10-16-1923. She d 12-28-1968. They are buried in Evergreen Cemetery, Milo, ME. They had five children all b in Miio, ME. **Viola May**[11] b 1-19-1924, **Carl Libby**[11] b 5-23-1926, **Priscilla**[11] b 4-27-1927, **Minard Foss**[11] b 1-1-1930, and **Wilbur Leigh**[11] b 10-27-1932.
  ii   **Gladys**[10] b 7-6-1901 [MEVR] m Perley John Buzzel, son of Herbert Eri Buzzell and Nellie May Hodgkis, 1-8-1921 in Bangor, ME. She d 1-23-1962 at Milo, ME.
  iii **Austin Earle**[10] b 2-6-1909 at Bradford, ME. ([MEVR] their 3rd child) He d on 2-12-1909 at Bradford.

(950) Charles F.G.[9] (Charles R.[8], Peter[7], Ephraim[6], John[5], Ephraim[4], Ephraim[3], Ephraim[2], John[1]), born 9-30-1858 at Needham, MA [MAVR] He married Fanny who was born in Joliet, IL. [MAVR]

Children:
  i   **Dora Isabella**[10] b 7-12-1891 at Boston, MA [MAVR]

(951) Ivy Coleman *Clark*[9], (Charles Coleman[8], Elbridge G.[7], Moses[6], John[5], Ephraim[4], Ephraim[3], Ephraim[2], John[1]), was born on 10-21-1888 at Ft. Winnebago, Columbia Co. WI. His surname was retained as *Clark*, although he was a Severance. He married to Emma Turner on 9-9-1889. He served in the First World War in France. When he returned from the war he became a cashier for the Bank of Kimberly, WI where he remained for twenty years. They later moved to Yakima, WA where he was in the Insurance Business until his death. **Ivy Coleman**[9] died on 1-12-1976 in Yakima, WA. Emma, his wife, died 1-28-1992 at Yakima.

Children: [MDCD]

i   **Betty Agnes**[10] b m Jack Lewellyn and
      __Montgomery
ii   **John Alexander**[10] Clark of Bonners Ferry,
      WA
iii   **Stewart**[10] *Clark* of Yakima, WA

(952) Harold Roberts *Clark*[9], (Charles Coleman[8],
Elbridge G.[7], Moses[6], John[5], Ephraim[4], Ephraim[3],
Ephraim[2], John[1]), born 8-9-1892 at Ft. Winnebago,
Columbia Co. WI. Although he retained the surname
of *Clark,* he was a Severance. He married to Lela
Eldora Peckham, daughter of William Harrison
Peckham and Abigail Mary Waite, on 6-23-1915.
Harold[9] remained in partnership with his father.
They prided themselves with a well organized farm
and prize livestock. **Harold**[9] and Lela farmed until
1947 when they moved to Pardeeville, WI. They were
active members of the North Marcellon Church and
the community. **Harold**[9] served on the school board
of the Berry School for many years. **Harold**[9] died on
5-16-1961 at Portage, WI and Lela Eldora died 1-31-
1965 at Portage.

Children: [MDCD]
i   **Carol Marie**[10] b 5-20-1917 m Sheldon F.
      Dewsnap 4-7-1939
ii   **Norma Elaine**[10] b 4-24-1921 m Eldon Audiss
      1-1-1944
iii   **Beverly May**[10] b 5-21-1929 m Orville L.
      Karow 10-21-1950

(953) Arthur Leason[9], (Charles Lamb[8], Charles[7],
Benjamin[6], Daniel[5], Ephraim[4], Ebenezer[3], Eprhaim[2],
John[1]), was born 9-19-1860 at Walled Lake, MI. He
died 11-15-1930 at Flint, MI. **Arthur**[9] married to
Almira who was born 5- -1858. [1900 MIFC] In 1910
Arthur[9] was living in Flint, Genesee Co. MI with
his wife, Celindas Susan Mascho, [MIFC] who was
born 12-23-1880 and died 5-16-1859, in MI. [Florida
Society of the National Society, Sons of the
American Revolution. Application for Membership of
Stephen Lewis[10] Severance 4-15-1967]

Children: born in MI
i   **Clarence Arthur**[10] b 8-25-1882 d 9-11-1883
ii   **Stephen Lewis**[10] b 6-11-1884 at Walled
      Lake, MI. He m Iva Lillian Shanck 11-25-
      1909. **Stephen**[10] was an Engineer student
      at MI State College. (1927) Children
      included **Stanley Edmond**[11] b 8-7-1910,

Wesley Arthur[11] b 4-22-1912, and **Russell Verne**[11] b 12-2-1913
iii **Jennie**[10] b 4-26-1886 m Lewis Martin Richmond
iv **Ora**[10] b 10-15-1889 m Mary Ellen Gekeler 2-24-1915. Children included **Clifford Arthur**[11] b 2-23-1917
v **Adah**[10] b 11-3-1891 m Porter J. Bentley 4-30-1913
vi **Maggie**[10] b 1-27-1893 m Clarence 2-24-1917
vii **Charlie Jacob**[10] b 2-9-1901 m Pearl Dickinson 12-23-1924. Children, **Bentley Jane**[11] b 11-17-1926

(954) Eugene[9], (Charles Lamb[8], Charles[7], Benjamin[6], Daniel[5], Ephraim[4], Ebenezer[3], Ephraim[2], John[1]), born 7-16-1862 Walled Lake, MI. He married first to Frances A. Patterson on 6-27-1894. They were divorced on 8-21-1916. He married secondly to Jewell Pearce who was born 12-2-1893. **Eugene**[9] can be found living in MI, IL, and later in Santa Anna and Riverside, CA. In 1920 he was living with his wife, Jewel, who was born in TN. [CAFC] He was a teacher, minister, rancher, and real estate dealer

Children of **Eugene**[9] Severance and Frances A. Patterson [HOS]
i **Evelyn Mary**[10] b 4-4-1899 m Thomas Henry Spohr
ii **Paul Donald**[10] b 1-17-1901 d 7-27-1921

Children of **Eugene**[9] Severance and Jewell Pearce [HOS]
iii **Eugenia Marie**[10] b 6-13-1924

(955) Palmer[9], (Charles Lamb[8], Charles[7], Benjamin[6], Daniel[5], Ephraim[4], Ebenezer[3], Ephraim[2], John[1]), born on 7-30-1864 Walled Lake, MI. He married to Mary A. Lowe on 9-8-1886. She was born 4-26-1868. They later settled in IL. **Palmer**[9] was a farmer, mason, and builder. [1900 MIFC]

Children: [HOS]
i **William**[10] b 10-6-1887 d 3-21-1908
ii **Elmer**[10] b 4-20-1890 was an insurance agent in Flint, MI m 9-18-1912 to Hattie Hutchinson b 9-22-1889. **Elmer**[10] had children **Dorothy Grace**[11] b 6-14-1913, **Ida Mary**[11] b 8-30-1914, **Palmer Elmer**[11] b 11-19-1915, **Donald Edwin**[11] b 12-25-1916,

Ruth Lucile[11] b 4-14-1922, **Walter Merlyn**[11] b 5-8-1924, and **Pearl Harriet**[11] b 6- - 1927.
- iii **Madcie**[10] b 6-9-1892 d 4-26-1905
- iv **Grace**[10] b 8-23-1894 d 4-13-1913
- v **Henry L.**[10] b 6-17-1899 merchant, Flint, MI m Myrtle Smith 4-18-1916
- vi **Rollin**[10] b 6-20-1901, Minister, Flint, MI m Henrietta De Young on 3-3-1924. Children included **Ellen Catherine**[11] b 8-19-1925 and **Robert Henry**[11] b 11-26-1926.
- vii **Alta May**[10] b 10-5-1903, m Judson Bigelow, Flint, MI 4-7-1921
- viii **Nora**[10] b 6-28-1908

(956) Henry Ormal[9], (Charles Lamb[8], Charles[7], Benjamin[6], Daniel[5], Ephraim[4], Ebenezer[3], Ephraim[2], John[1]), born 2-19-1867 at St. Johns, MI. He married to Anna M. Lane on 1-18-1898, who was born 7-7-1867. He earned his A.M., Ph.D, was Librarian at Columbia, MO. He was the Author of several books and papers, namely, The Severance Genealogy, which followed the lines of **Benjamin, Charles,** and **Lewis** lines of the seventh generation descending from **John**[1] Severance of Salisbury, MA. In 1920 he was living with his wife Anna and their children. [MOFC Columbia, Boone Co]

Children:
- i **Esther A.**[10] b 9-21-1904 in MI. Recieved a B.S. from University of MO and MI
- ii **Philip L.**[10] b 5-17-1907 in MI, He was a student at the University of MO and MI.
- iii Millie Bowling b 1903 in TN. (adopted)

(957) Charles[9], (Charles Lamb[8], Charles[7], Benjamin[6], Daniel[5], Ephraim[4], Ebenezer[3], Ephraim[2], John[1]), born on 11-4-1873 Andalusia, IL. He married to Carrie E. English on 4-28-1896, she died 5- -1896, he married secondly to Gertrude Emily Patch on 3-21-1900, she was born 4-19-1873. They lived at Bloomfield, MI and Rock Island, IL. **Charles**[9] was a farmer at Cass City, MI. [1900-1920 MIFC]

Children: [HOS]
- i **Stephen Henry**[10] b 5-21-1901 d 5-27-1901
- ii **Roy William**[10] b 12-24-1902 Graduate of MI State College, teacher
- iii **Vernon Elmer**[10] b 8-21-1904 m Erma Irene Smith 9-13-1926. **Vernon**[10] was a student

(1927) at University of MO and a postal clerk, Cass City, MI.
iv   **Charles Louis**[10] b 6-9-1907
v   **Harry Arthur**[10] b 2-6-1909
vi   **Helen Gertrude**[10] b 4-6-1912
vii **Lloyd Dean**[10] b 4-24-1916
viii **Bessie A.**[10] b 11-18-1919 d 11-18-1919
ix   **Clara Edith**[10] b 2-8-1921

(958) Thomas Chalkley Jr.[9], (Thomas Chalkley[8], Charles[7], Benjamin[6], Daniel[5], Ephraim[4], Ebenezer[3], Ephraim[2], John[1]), born 7-26-1863. He married to Julia Frances Mason on 12-27-1898. Julia F. was born on 12-27-1865. **Thomas**[9] received his A.B. in 1889 and his A.M. in 1893 from the University of MI. He was a teacher, merchant, and undertaker. She died 5-27-1944. **Thomas Chalkley Jr.**[9] died 9-11-1903 at Walled Lake, MI.

Children: [HOS]
i   **Wilbur**[10] b 11-8-1899 m Eleanor Frederick 1922 in Detroit, MI. They had children, **Frederick**[11] b circa 1927 and **Frances**[11] b 11-8-1930
ii   **Wilson Boyce**[10] b 11-8-1899 m Ethel Josephine Case 6-25-1925 of Oakland, MI. She was b 11-8-1899 and d 5-8-1978. Their children were **Thomas Homer**[11], **Kathryn Ann**[11] b 8-7-1933 m Gunther Kilsch, and **Wilson Karl**[11] b 4-11-1938.
iii **May**[10] b 1901 d 1902

(959) Lewis[9], (Thomas Chalkley[8], Charles[7], Benjamin[6], Daniel[5], Ephraim[4], Ebenezer[3], Ephraim[2], John[1]), was born in 1867. Settled in MN. He married to Lillie Clarrisa Holton in November of 1891. She was born on 11-2-1874. He received a A.B. from the University of MI in 1892 and was an Attorney at Law in Minneapolis, MN.

Children:
i   **Mark L.H.**[10] b 10-28-1899

(960) Ira[9], (Thomas Chalkley[8], Charles[7], Benjamin[6], Daniel[5], Ephraim[4], Ebenezer[3], Ephraim[2], John[1]), born 1-18-1869. He married to Blanche M. Lewis on 4-27-1899. She was born 7- -1876 in WI. They lived at Walled Lake, MI and later settled in Minneapolis, MN. [HOS]

Children:
   i   **Lewis**[10] b 4-13-1900
   ii   **Irene**[10] b 11-21-1907

(961) George[9], (Thomas Chalkley[8], Charles[7], Benjamin[6], Daniel[5], Ephraim[4], Ebenezer[3], Ephraim[2], John[1]), was born on 2-4-1874 in MI or OR and died in Portland, OR, (Pullman) on 3-9-1931. He was Vice Dean of the WA State College of Agriculture where he had served for thirty years. He left a wife, three daughters and one son. [NSOR-3-10-1931]
    He married Ethel E. Espy on 8-28-1908. She was born 4-9-1883. They were living in WA in 1920. [WAFC] **George**[9] received a B.S. from MI State College, Professor, State Agr. College, Pullman, WA.

Children: born in Pullman, WA
   i   **Percy Howard**[10] b 11-10-1908
   ii   **Mabel Grace**[10] b 2-26-1910
   iii   **Helen Katherine**[10] b 12-4-1913
   iv   **Ethel Jean**[10] b 7-6-1924

(962) Frank J.[9], (Nathan Ezra[8], Charles[7], Benjamin[6], Daniel[5], Ephraim[4], Ebenezer[3], Ephraim[2], John[1]), born 9-4-1873. He married to Amy V. Bullen on 5-1-1907.

Children: [HOS]
   i   **Lenore Janette**[10] b 2-18-1908

(963) Melvin[9], (John[8], Charles[7], Benjamin[6], Daniel[5], Ephraim[4], Ebenezer[3], Ephraim[2], John[1]), was born on 9-18-1865 at St. John, MI. He married to Minnie M. Murdock on 4-9-1887. [IGI] She was born in April of 1868 in MI.

Children: [HOS]
   i   **Frances May**[10] b 8-26-1891 m Jesse A.
           Winslow 5-4-1912
   ii   **Carrie Margaret**[10] b 7-7-1895
   iii   **Leslie Clark**[10] b 7-28-1902

(964) Lemuel[9], (John[8], Charles[7], Benjamin[6], Daniel[5], Ephraim[4], Ebenezer[3], Ephraim[2], John[1]), born 1-24-1868. He married to Laura May Chappell on 6-15-1898. She was born in May of 1868 in MI. He was a Minister and an Insurance Agent at Hastings, MI.

Children:

    i   **Alice Marian**[10] b 8-24-1899 m Wayne Frey
            on 6-30-1925. Alice was a student at
            Western Normal College
   ii   **Lois May**[10] b 10-8-1901
  iii   **Ernest Lemuel**[10] b 8-6-1903
   iv   **Hazel Margaret**[10] b 9-13-1905
    v   **Beulah Lucile**[10] b 7-28-1910

(965) Chester Cole[9], (John[8], Charles[7], Benjamin[6], Daniel[5], Ephraim[4], Ebenezer[3], Ephraim[2], John[1]), was born on 2-12-1879 at Walled Lake, MI. He married to Bessie Mabel Bone on 8-20-1898. She was born in February of 1879 in MI. **Chester Cole**[9] died 4-12-1926. They lived at Walled Lake, and Montrose, MI.

Children: [HOS]
    i   **Esther Lois**[10] b 12-4-1899
   ii   **Helen Janet**[10] b 2-16-1902
  iii   **Ines Leola**[10] b 5-15-1904
   iv   **Glen Russell**[10] b 10-18-1908
    v   **Donald Bertram**[10] b 11-17-1908

(966) Miraon (Myron)[9], (John[8], Charles[7], Benjamin[6], Daniel[5], Ephraim[4], Ebenezer[3], Ephraim[2], John[1]), born 10-7-1881. He married May Allen 11-19-1902.

Children:
    i   **Vernon**[9] b 1904 [1910 MIFC]

(967) Earl Lewis[9], (John[8], Charles[7], Benjamin[6], Daniel[5], Ephraim[4], Ebenezer[3], Ephraim[2], John[1]), born 8-3-1883 and settled at Ann Arbor, MI. He married to Grace DeGroot on 11-19-1903. She was born 3-3-1883. Grace died in 1956. He was elected to the Ann Arbor City Council from his ward without a descenting vote. He helped to bring about the rural electrification to parts of southern MI.

Children: [HOS]
    i   **Aaron**[10] b 8-19-1904 d before 1986, he m
            to M. Lucille Wagoner in 1932. **Aaron**[10]
            researched and maintained his family
            lines in MI
   ii   **Lena Rachel**[10] b 8-29-1907

(968) Charles Jotham[9], (King Jotham[8], Charles[7], Benjamin[6], Daniel[5], Ephraim[4], Ebenezer[3], Ephraim[2], John[1]), born 10-9-1872 at Walled Lake, MI. He married to Cora E. Slaybough on 9-1-1906. She was born 12-10-1878. The family lived in MI. [1910 MIFC]

Children:
   i   **Charles Stanley**[10] b 6-2-1907

(969) Edgar M.[9], (King Jotham[8], Charles[7], Benjamin[6], Daniel[5], Ephraim[4], Ebenezer[3], Ephraim[2], John[1]), born 4-22-1879 at Walled lake, MI. He married to Bessie M. _____. She was born in 1892. [1920 MIFC] They were living at St. John, MI in 1920. **Edgar**[9] was a brother in law of Ephraim Ford.

Children:
   i   **Leona I.**[9] b 1911
   ii   **Cecil M.**[9] b 1912
   iii **Joseph**[9]

(969a) Benjamin L.[5], (Frank[8], Ezra[7], Benjamin[6], Daniel[5], Ephraim[4], Ebenezer[3], Ephraim[2], John[1]), born 8- -1878 in Jordan, MI. In 1920 he was with his wife Mary Janet and their children. [MIFC Jordan] She was born in 1880 in MI.

Children: born in WA [1920 MIFC]
   i   **Franklin P.**[10] b 1910
   ii   **Helen L.**[10] b 1913
   iii **Elizabeth**[10] b 1916

(969b) William[9], (Frank[8], Ezra[7], Benjamin[6], Daniel[5], Ephraim[4], Ebenezer[3], Ephraim[2], John[1]), was born 5- - 1891 in Jordan, MI. He married to Marion, who was born in 1893 in MI. They lived in Antrim Co. [1920 MIFC]

Children: [MIFC]
   i   **Frank**[10] b 1916
   ii   **Lucile**[10] b 1917

(969c) Albert Henry/Bert Henry[9], (Orren J.[8], Daniel[7], Benjamin[6], Daniel[5], Ephraim[4], Ebenezer[3], Ephraim[2], John[1]), born 8-31-1876 in NH. He married first to Florence Adelaide Green, daughter of Bion Green and Lena Florence Norris, on 5-18-1905 but divorced 2-24-1909. [NHVR] Florence was born 2-7-1884 at Biddeford, ME and died 7-1-1955. He married secondly to Elizabeth Perkins on 9-11-1910. [MEVR] **Bert**[9] died 7-31-1924 in Maine. [BR of Mrs Judith Brindle] [MBGD]

Children:
    i   **Sarah Judith**[10] b 9-22-1905 at Merrimack, MA. [MAVR] m1 John Henry Norris 5-18-1921. She m2 to Everett Knight Greenleaf on 12-31-1928 at Kennebunk, ME. Her third marriage was to Joseph E. Brindle 6-20-1933 at Portsmouth, NH.

(970) Birney Charles[9], (Charles[8], Nathan[7], Benjamin[6], Daniel[5], Ephraim[4], Ebenezer[3], Ephraim[2], John[1]), born on 5-1-1862 at Claremont, NH and died on 11-12-1918 at Chester, VT. He married at Charlestown, NH to Florence Nightingale Grow, daughter of Watts Grow and Laura Clark Smith of Plainfield, NH, on 3-17-1880. She was born 10-29-1856 and died 11-10-1921 in Londonderry, VT. They are buried at Pleasantview Cemetery, Windsor, VT. [MBFS]

In 1900 Florence was with two of her sons but **Birney**[9] was not listed. [VTFC] **Birney**[9] moved around alot and Florence lived with a family where she kept house. [MBFS]

Children: [MBFS]
    i   **Edna Martha**[10] b 12-26-1880 in Chester, VT, m Frank Stevens Spencer, son of Joshua Spencer and Mary Jane Gould, 5-16-1900 at Springfield, VT. [VTVR] She d 6-27-1961 at Rutland, VT. [VTVR] They are buried at Evergreen Cemetery, Rutland, VT

    ii   **Albert Bernie**[10] b 5-11-1882, Claremont, NH m Lula Amy (Abbott) Carlisle, daughter of John E. Abbott and Addie L. Cook, at Chester, VT on 5-17-1904. He died 3-10-1953 and they are buried in the Pleasantview Cemetery, Chester, VT. [VTVR]

    iii **Wesley Charles**[10] b 5-21-1888 at Chester, VT. [VTVR] He m Florence Eva Lockwood, daughter of Edward John Lockwood and Nettie B. Davis, 4-12-1916 at Brattleboro, VT. They lived at Londonerry, VT where they died. **Charles**[10] died 11-10-1958 and Florence died 11-30-1964 and are buried in the Londonderry Cemetery. Children: **Mable Gladys**[11] b 8-26-1919 m William Otis Hart, 4-5-1938, **Gordon Wesley**[11] b 10-2-1920 m June Georgetta Buell, 1-26-1946, and **Edna May**[11] b 5-24-1918

iv **Dean Charles**[10] b 2-16-1896 at Weathersfield, [VTVR] lived at Chester, VT and died 10-5-1940 at Hanover, NH. He died 10-8-1940 and is buried in the Pleasantview Cemetery at Chester, VT. He m Arminalla Ruth Parmenter, daughter of Foster Cutler Parmenter and Lula May Morris, 12-7-1903. He entered WWI 5-16-1918 at Burlington age 22 years, discharged 2-11-1919 at NY, NY. [WWI] Manager of the Cloverdale Store, Chester, VT. They had a son, **Deane Charles Jr.**[11] b 1923

(971) Henry Lucien Don[9], (Charles Lucien[8], Benjamin[7], Benjamin[6], Daniel[5], Ephraim[4], Ebenezer[3], Ephraim[2], John[1]), born 6-17-1880 at Claremont and married to Marion Allene Doe, daughter of Warren W. Doe and Isabel C. Stevens, [DARLR, Vol 71] 6-28-1906. [NHVR] She was born on 10-26-1881 at Boston, MA. [Doe p114] **Harry**[9] was graduated from Dunbar Business College. He served as Post Office Clerk, Claremont, NH 1901-1909, Ass't Postmaster 1909-1923, and then Postmaster from 1923, commissioned by President Calvin Coolidge, 32nd degree Mason.

Children:
i **Ruth Ellen**[10] b 11-18-1915 d Easter Sunday 1989, m _____ Thompson

(972) George Henry Jr.[9], (George Henry[8], Benjamin[7], Benjamin[6], Daniel[5], Ephraim[4], Ebenezer[3], Ephraim[2], John[1]), born 4-8-1884. He married to Leila Parsons, on 7-22-1908. He received his A.B. at Middlebury College 1908, B.D. Gen Theolog. Sem., NY City, A.M. Columbia Univeristy 1913. Ordained to Episcopal Ministry 12-21-1911, Missionary in charge of Okanogan Co. WA, 1914. He was later a Minister in Detroit, MI. [HOS]

Children:
i **Hope Vietta**[10] b 10-27-1923 in Brattleboro, VT and d in 1976 at Brattleboro. She m Ralph Chapman.

(973) Laverne Stanard[9], (Morris Ripley[8], Lewis[7], Benjamin[6], Daniel[5], Ephraim[4], Ebenezer[3], Ephraim[2], John[1]), born on 10-28-1901. **Laverne**[9] was a banker, employed by the U.S. National Bank.

He was born in Detroit, MI and lived in the
Portland area 59 years. He had been employed by
U.S. National since 1927. He was a member of Mt.
Hood Lodge 157, AF&AM, OR White Shrine of Jerusalem
and a member of the Woodburn United Methodist
Church. He was survived by his wife Thelma, a son
L. Standard[10], a daughter , Mrs. Stanley A.
Admiston, and a sister, **Ruby L.**[9] Gripman of MI.
[NSOR Wednesday 4-8-1970]
    Thelma was b 8-17-1902 in Portland. She married
Laverne[9] in 1927 in the house where she was born
and grew up. She was a teacher in the David Douglas
School District, retiring in 1968. After Laverne
died in 197- she moved to Salem. She is survived by
her daughter, Sally Edmiston of Salem, and a son,
Laverne[9], of Oakton, VA. [NSOR 4-14-1990]

Children:
    i   **Laverne Stanard**[10] Severance Jr. was Rear
         Admiral and Commander of the U.S. Naval
         Base in Seattle. Severance joined the
         U.S. Navy Reserve as a sailor when he
         was a student at Jefferson High School.
         He won a competitive appointment to the
         U.S. Naval Academy at Annapolis, MD
         after 30 months in enlisted ranks and
         worked his way up to flag rank.
         He graduated from high school in
         Portland in 1951, and his unit was
         called to active duty in the Korean
         conflict [NSOR Thursday 6-6-1985 by
         Rolla J. Crick]

(975) Fred Allen[9], (George Walter[8], Walter Searles[7],
Abijah[6], Daniel[5], Ephraim[4], Ebenezer[3], Ephraim[2],
John[1]), born 1-31-1878 at South Abington, MA.
[MAVR] He married Elsie M. Leslie, daughter of
Arthur R. Leslie and Nellie B. Dunn, on 11-28-1900
in Hanson, MA [NHVR] She was born 7-15-1884 in
Brockton, MA and died 4-21-1943 in Quincy, MA. They
settled in E. Bridgewater, MA. **Fred**[9] was a farmer
and cobbler. [1920 MAFC] He was killed when his
tractor overturned on him. [MAM]

Children:
    i   **Raymond Leslie**[10] b 1902 m Bernice Cone
         Morrill 9-6-1926. [NHVR]
    ii   **Arthur Washburn**[10] b 11- -1903 in E.
         Bridgewater d 7-27-1922 in Duxbury, MA.
         He drowned saving 2 swimmers

iii **Grace F.**[10] b 1907
iv **Dorothy L.**[10] b 1909
v **LeRoy A.**[10] b 1910
vi **Miriam R.**[10] b 1918

(976) Lester Washburn[9], (George Walter[8], Walter Searles[7], Abijah[6], Daniel[5], Ephraim[4], Ebenezer[3], Ephraim[2], John[1]), born 10-26-1888. He married first to Hazel Anna Lincoln, daughter of Levi Prescott Lincoln, on 10-5-1913. She was born 7-1-1890 and died 10-20-1949. He married secondly to Ethel Florence Beals, daughter of Edward N. Beals and Alma Jenkins, on 2-3-1951. She was born 9-24-1888 and died 7-11-1967. He was a professional carpenter. **Lester**[9] died on 12-31-1978. [MAM]

Children:
i **Roger Lincoln**[10] b 4-25-1917 m Helen Mae Campbell, daughter of Frederick Weston Campbell and Ida Myrtle Cedarholm on 9-18-1944. He d 6-19-1983, all in Whitman, MA.

(977) Edwin John[9], (John M.[8], John[7], Ebenezer[6], Daniel[5], Ephraim[4], Ebenezer[3], Ephraim[2], John[1]), born 6-29-1870 in VT. [VTVR] He married to Zoe Barrow who was born in 1886 in VT. [1920 VTFC]

Children:
i **Caroline M.**[10] b 3- -1894
ii **Herbert J.**[10] b 6- -1895
iii **Harry Edwin**[10] b 5-4-1905 [VTVR]
iv **Madora Ellen**[10] b 8-27-1907 [VTVR]
v **Blanche**[10] b 1913 [1920 VTFC]

(978) Percey W.L.[9], (John M.[8], John[7], Ebenezer[6], Ebenezer[5], Ephraim[4], Ebenezer[3], Ephraim[2], John[1]), born 1-26-1882. He married to Josephine Etta Boyden on 2-21-1903 [VTVR]

Children:
i **Maurice Marvin**[10] b 4-22-1903 [VTVR]

(985) Spencer W.[9], (Benjamin Warren[8], William[7], Samuel[6], Ebenezer[5], Ephraim[4], Ebenezer[3], Ephraim[2], John[1]), born 12-16-1887. He married Ivy Ashley who was born in 1874. They lived in Pittsfield, MA. [1920 MAFC]

Children:

i   **Velma**[10] b 1913
ii   **Glen**[10] b 1914

(986) Karl W.[9], (Benjamin Warren[8], William[7], Samuel[6], Ebenezer[5], Ephraim[4], Ebenezer[3], Ephraim[2], John[1]), was born in 8-15-1894. He married to Pearl _____, who was born in 1898 in NY [1920 Phoenix, Oswego Co. NYFC].

Children:
i   **Marion**[10] b 1917
ii   **Bernice**[10] b 1919

(987) Frank Rollin[9], (Bert D.[8], William[7], Samuel[6], Ebenezer[5], Ephraim[4], Ebenezer[3], Ephraim[2], John[1]), was born in 12-7-1892 in Willsboro, NY. He died on 11-2-1949, unmarried.

"**Rolland**[9], who used the nick name "Doc" attended college at Princton. He was a member of the Musical and Dramatic Organization. He earned a degree in Literature. Doc. graduated with honors in Modern Languages and was awarded a scholarship to the Graduate School to continue his study of Romance Languages. After a year in graduate school, he entered General Theological Seminary in New York, to prepare for the priesthood of the Episcopal Church. After a short curacy in New York City, he left for the Philippines as a Missionary for six years. **Rolland**[9] took the first steps to the monastic life in 1936 leading a group of young Episcopal clergy to Nashdom Abbey in Buckinghamshire, England. He became a novice and took the name Paul and after final vows, returned again to America to found Three Rivers, Michigan, where he was known as Dom Paul, order of St. Benedict.

Rolland[9] was the author of various short plays and serious musical works. His "Symphonic Fantasy on the Exulet" premiered with the Philippine Symphony in 1925. A quote from the Princeton account of his death: "No classmate worked harder to gain heaven than Doc Severance. Saints like him will make it anything but a dull place." **Rolland**[9], who suffered a cerebral hemorrhage in 1946, was not well his last three years. He traveled to England to rest and speed his recovery. **Rolland**[9] died at Nashdom Abbey, Burnham, Bucks, England where his body was laid to rest." [MWLS]

(988) Raymond William⁹, (Bert D.⁸, William⁷, Samuel⁶, Ebenezer⁵, Ephraim⁴, Ebenezer³, Ephraim², John¹), born 12-1-1897 in Willsboro, NY. He married to Joyce M. McMurtrey on 9-20-1941. She was born at Wala Walla, WA on 11-14-1906. They married at Walla Walla. **Ray⁹** attended the University of MI. In 1922 he and his brother, **Vernon⁹**, moved to Seattle, WA and found work with the telephone company. **Ray⁹** also lived in Tacoma. After he married to Joyce, they lived in Seattle until circa 1969 when they moved to Hood Canal. The last year of his life was spent at Panorama City in Lacey, WA. **Raymon⁹** died on 11-11-1976. [MWLS]

Children:
i   **Warren Lee¹⁰** b 2-15-1944 in Seattle, WA

(989) Leroy E.⁹, (Bert D.⁸, William⁷, Samuel⁶, Ebenezer⁵, Ephraim⁴, Ebenezer³, Ephraim², John¹), was born on 8-21-1904 in Willsboro, NY. He married to Mildred Cowles on 3-12-1933. Mildred was born on 12-24-1907. **Leroy E.⁹** and Mildred settled in Springfield, MA. **Leroy⁹** attended Wesleyan University and he was a fine swimmer. He worked in the insurance business. He died in October of 1971. [MWLS]

Children:
i   **Virginia¹⁰** b 12-13-1933
ii   **Robert¹⁰** b 1-20-1937 m Patsy King who was b on 7-24-1945

(991) Fred Barton⁹, (Arthur F.⁸, Joel⁷, Joseph⁶, Rufus⁵, Ephraim⁴, Ebenezer³, Ephraim², John¹), born on 3-17-1880. He married first to Margaret E. Clark on 9-30-1903. [NHVR] They were divorced in November of 1905. [NHVR] He married secondly to Christina May Smith, daughter of Richard Smith and Ellen Hart of Nova Scotia, on 7-2-1906. [NHVR] She was born 1884. [NHVR]

Children:
i   baby b 1-27-1907 d same day [NHVR]
ii   **Richard F.¹⁰** b 1914 [NHVR] m Constance L. Ross 8-18-1934
iii **Madeline C.¹⁰** b 1907 [NHVR] m Anthony J. Rossetti 10-27-1925. [NHVR]

(993) Archie William⁹, (William J.⁸, Joseph⁷, Joseph⁶, Rufus⁵, Ephraim⁴, Ebenezer³, Ephraim²,

John[1]), was born in 1903, he married first to Ardis
M. Cilley, daughter of Leonard W. Cilley and Lina
M. Flanders, on 10-7-1923. They were divorced 1-25-
1928. He married secondly to Odena I. Gagnon,
daughter of Honore Gagnon and Rose Prire of Canada,
on 4-30-1932. [NHVR] They settled in Suncook, NH.

Children:
  i   **Richard N.**[10] b 1-16-1933, m first to
      Judith Jane (Wentworth) Drake, daughter
      of Harold and Evelyn Wentworth. Children
      by first marriage were, **Scott**[11] b 4-11-
      1958, **Randy**[11] b 4-30-1960, **Glenn**[11] b 1-20-
      1962, and **Mark**[11] b 7-4-1963. **Richard N.**[10]
      m second to Judith Ann Ellison, daughter
      of Clarence Ellison and Eleanor Farrell.
      No children.
  ii   **Pearl**[10] b 1-10-1935 m Kenneth Barnett
  iii **Norma**[10] b 1-28-1934 m Virgle Cripple
  iv **William**[10] b 2-27-1936 d same day

(994) George Oscar[9], (Frank E.[8], James[7], Jacob[6],
Ephraim/Nathaniel[5], Ephraim[4], Ebenezer[3], Ephraim[2],
John[1]), born on 8-7-1875 in Lewiston, ME. When he
was only 5 years he was taken to Butte, MT. **George
O.**[8] married to Bertha L. Palmer, daughter of Horace
Palmer and Nellie Hiscox, 9-12-1898 in Boston, MA.
In 1914 he moved to Somerville, as treasurer of the
Security Fence Company, which was located at No. 22
Kent Street, in Somerville. [Conklin]

Children: [Conklin]
  i   **George Palmer**[10] b 7-29-1900 Jersey City,
      NJ

(997) Orman John[9], (Orrin T.[8], Thatcher[7], Ephraim[6],
Ephraim[5], Ephraim[4], Ebenezer[3], Ephraim[2], John[1]), born
8- -1885. In 1920 **Orman J.**[9] was living with Herbert
G. Crockett as his son-in-law. [MEFC] He married
first to Azzie Adkins McSarley, born 1893 and
secondly to Hackett Ara Crockett. [MEVR]

Children:
  i   **Edward Byron**[10] b 6-8-1920 at Foxcroft as
      their 4th child

(998) Delbert A.[9], (Delbert A. Jr.[8], Daniel[7],
Ephraim[6], Ephraim[5], Ephraim[4], Ebenezer[3], Ephraim[2],
John[1]), born in 4- -1891 in ME. In 1920 he was

living with his wife, Jemima age 28 and their children in PA. [PAFC]

Children: born in PA
  i   **Dorothy**[10] b 1911
  ii   **Lucille**[10] b 1913
  iii **Raymond**[10] b 1915
  iv   **Glenn**[10] b 1917
  v   **Arlene**[10] b 1910

(1004) William R.[9], (Charles Almon[8], Samuel[7], Benjamin[6], Jonathan[5], Benjamin[4], Jonathan[3], Ephraim[2], John[1]), born in 1878. He married first to Edna W. Tyler, daughter of Fred M. Tyler and Laura E. Keyser, on 1-11-1900 at Stoneham, MA. [MAVR] She was born 9-13-1876. She died 9-29-1910 and he remarried to Grace Cropley, daughter of Solomon F. Cropley and Elizabeth H. Demeritt, on 11-5-1916. They lived in Stoneham, MA and Moultonboro, NH. **William**[9] was a butcher. [NHVR]

Children of **William R.**[9] Severance and Edna W. Tyler born in MA [MDW]
  i   **Gladys Matilda**[10] b 1901 m Berthold Cropley 8-27-1924
  ii   **Charles Almon.**[10] b 1903 m Meredith Griffin 9-27-1928
  iii **Roland T.**[10] b 1905, he m Katherine M. ___. **"Bill"**[10] d 7-26-1988 age 83 in Wolfeboro. His family included his wife, a son **Roland T. Jr.**[11] of Melvin Village, **Brian**[11] of Northwood, a daughter, Mrs. **Marianne "Molly"**[11] Huusko of Tucson, AZ, a brother, **Malcolm**[10] of Wolfeboro and a sister, Mrs. **Gladys**[10] Cropley of Chatham, MA. [NSUL-Manchester, NH]

Children of **William R.**[9] Severance and Grace Cropley
  iv   **William Malcolm**[10] b 2-10-1923 at Wolfboro, NH m Beverly Carlisle who d 9-16-1989 in York, ME.

(1005) Fred Burbank[9], (Fred Wiggin[8], Jonathan Burbank[7], Benjamin[6], Jonathan[5], Benjamin[4], Jonathan[3], Ephraim[2], John[1]), born 9-28-1889. He married to Eva May Swett, daughter of Frank Osgood Swett and Grace Mac Kenzie, on 11-27-1919. She born 2-8-1898 and died on 12-21-1974. **Fred Burbank**[9] died 8-3-1967. They lived at Amesbury, MA and Portsmouth and Stratham, NH.

Children: [MDW]
    i   **Ivene**[10] b 9-16-1920 m Garland William
         Patch Jr. 4-24-1945. They were the
         parents of Deborah (Patch) who m to
         Frank C. Wilson Jr.

(1011) Earl Longley (Volney)[9], (Lafayette[8], Rufus[7],
Rodney[6], Benjamin[5], Jonathan[4], Jonathan[3], Ephraim[2],
John[1]), born on 4-6-1883 in Juneau Co. WI. He
married to Louise Weiler. It is noted that he died
on 12-13-1944 in Fountain, MN.

Children:
    i   **Leila Jean**[10] b 3-23-1939 in Juneau Co. WI

(1015) Robert Cowill[9], (Fayette[8], Rufus[7], Rodney[6],
Benjamin[5], Jonathan[4], Jonathan[3], Ephraim[2], John[1]),
was born 10-1-1887 in WI. He was living in
Aberdeen, Brown Co in 1920 with his wife, Hazel M.
____, age 28, born in ND and their son. [SDFC]

Children:
    i   **Coburn R.**[10] b circa 1915 in SD

(1016) Arthur[9], (Rufus[8], Robert C.[7], Rodney[6],
Benjamin[5], Jonathan[4], Jonathan[3], Ephraim[2], John[1]),
was born 9- -1879. He was with his wife, Edith M.,
b 1881 in WI, and their children in 1920. [WIFC]

Children:
    i   **Charles H.**[10] b 1910 in WI
    ii   **Carleen M.**[10] b 1917 in WI

(1018) Sydney Semour[9], (Silas[8], Robert[7], Rodney[6],
Benjamin[5], Jonathan[4], Jonathan[3], Ephraim[2], John[1]),
born on 9-23-1877. He married to Ethel Johnson,
daughter of William R. and Emily Johnson, on 4-14-
1906. [WIVR] They lived in Mauston, WI and
Rochester, MN.

Children:
    i   **Milton W.**[10] b 1918 in MN

(1020) Robert L.[9], (Silas[8], Robert[7], Rodney[6],
Benjamin[5], Jonathan[4], Jonathan[3], Ephraim[2], John[1]),
born on 2-25-1889. He married to Ethel Vance
Snively, daughter of Scott Montogomery Snively and
Lennie Estelia Thompson, on 8-27-1916. Ethel Vance
Snively was born 8-5-1896, Sheridan, WY, and
married **Robert L.**[9] Severance on 8-27-1916 at Big

Moose Rance, Sheridan Co., WY, with Rev. Long, Presbyterian, officiating. **Robert**[9] Severance was the son of **Silas**[8] and Phoebe (Huntley) Severance. He died on 9-23-1941. Ethel married to William J. Dauderman 4-9-1950, he died on 11-7-1951. A secretary in Sheridan in 1960, Ethel died there 8-4-1982. [Washburn p416]

Children:
 i **Roberta Vance**[10] b 7-26-1918 m Ralph N. Cloyd on 6-9-1938
 ii **Chester Snively**[10] b 10-17-1923 m June (Meeker) Puzahanich on 8-17-1952 m2 Edith Geer on 2-27-1971. **Chester**[10] d 3-19-1975

(1021) Ernest Stillman[9], (Robert C.[8], Robert C.[7], Rodney[6], Benjamin[5], Jonathan[4], Jonathan[3], Ephraim[2], John[1]), was born 2-7-1893 in Mauston, Juneau Co. WI. He married to Catherine E. _____. She was born in 1898 in SD. They later settled in Faulkton, Faulk Co. SD.

Children: [1920 SDFC], there were likely more children)
 i **Catherine E.**[10] b 1918 in SD
 ii **Robert P.**[10] b 1919 in SD

(1023) Fred C.[9], (Arthur E.[8], Arthur Rodney[7], Rodney[6], Benjamin[5], Jonathan[4], Jonathan[3], Ephraim[2], John[1]), born in October of 1888. He was living in Parson, Labette Co. KS with his wife Mabel K. age 27, born in MO and their son. [1920 KSFC]

Children:
 i **Earl V.**[10] b 1917 in KS

(1026) Phillip[9], Silas[8], Benjamin[7], Rodney[6], Benjamin[5], Jonathan[4], Jonathan[3], Ephraim[2], John[1]), was born 10- -1880 in West Virginia. He married to Elizabeth M. _____. She was born in 1882 in OH. [1920 OHFC] They settled in Cleveland, Cuyahoga Co. OH.

Children: [1920 OHFC]
 i **Phillip Jr.**[10] b 1912
 ii **George O.**[10] b 1914 in OH

(1027) Bert[9] *Severans*, (Charles[8], Hazen[7], Hazen[6], Benjamin[5], Jonathan[4], Jonathan[3], Ephraim[2], John[1]), born 1- -1890 in OH. In 1920 he was living with his wife, Matilda, who was born 1891 in OH, and their children. [Perry Co. OHFC]

Children:
  i   **Lillian**[10] b 1914 in OH
  ii   **Charles E.**[10] b 1915 in OH

(1029) Arthur Winfred[9], (Herbert Winfred[8], George W.[7], (Silas or Hazen[6]), Samuel[5], Samuel[4], Jonathan[3], Ephraim[2], John[1]), born in 1905 at Kingston, NH. [MAVR] He died 7-6-1986. **Arthur**[9] married to Caroline Hopkins 8-5-1928, They lived in Haverhill, MA.

Children: Listed in **Arthur Winfred's**[9] obituary
  i   **Edna**[10] m Mr. Berry of Raymond, NH
  ii   **Janet**[10] m Mr. Simard of Manchester, NH
  iii   **Glenna**[10] m Mr. Dunphy of Danvers, MA
  iv   **Susan**[10] m Mr. Davis of Falmouth, ME
  v   **Richard**[10] of Hooksett, NH
  vi   **Dale**[10] of Boulder, CO

(1030) Roland L.[9], (Herbert Winfred[8], George W.[7], (Silas or Hazen[6]), Samuel[5], Samuel[4], Jonathan[3], Ephraim[2], John[1]), born in Haverhill, MA. He married to Dorothy Burnham of that same town. They had a baby born 9-24-1935 in Portsmouth, NH. [NHVR]

(1031) Leroy Warren[9], (Earle Leroy[8], John[7], Nathan[6], John[5], John[4], Jonathan[3], Ephraim[2], John[1]), was born on 1-23-1910 at Pembroke, NH. He married to Thelma Heath. They were divorced on 7-6-1934 and he remarried to Margaret Wilson Kent on 8-19-1934.

Children: The order of the children is not known
  i   **Thomas**[10] lived in Pembroke, NH
  ii   **Roy**[10] lived in Monroe, WA
  iii   **Edward P.**[10] b 1941 d 8-19-1993 in a Concord, NH., hospital after a brief illness. (NSUL-Mancherster, NH, Friday August 20, 1993) He lived the past 25 years in Epsom, NH. In 1958, he was graduated form Pembroke Academy. During the war in Vietnam, he served as a sergeant in the U.S. Marine Corps. Mr. Severance worked for the Pembroke Water Works. He left two sons, **Michael**[11] of NY, NY., and **Avery**[11] of Epsom, NH.

REFERENCES

Abbe........Abbe, Cleveland and Nichols, Josephine
           Genung, Genealogy in Memory of John Abbe and his
           Descendants, New Haven, CT, The Tuttle, Moore
           House & Taylor Co. 1916
ACA.........The American Congregation Association Bulletin
           Vol 28 written 1977, No. 2 p 6
Adams A.....Adams, Andrew Napoleon, A Genealogical History of
           Robert Adams of Braintree, MA, Also John Adams of
           Cambridge, MA, The Tuttle Co. Printers 1898-1900
Adams B.....Adams, Bertram, An Incomplete History of the
           Descendants of John Perry of London 1604-1954,
           compiled by Bertram Adams, printed by Utah Print,
           Co. 1955
Adams E.....Adams, Enid Eleznor, Ancestors and Descendants of
           Jeremiah Adams 1794-1883, published by Ancestor
           Hunters, 1974
AKFC........Arkansas Federal Census, National Archive
           Microfilm
Allen I.....Allen, Orrin Peer, Descendants of William Scott
           of Hatfield, Massachusetts 1668-1906 and John
           Scott of Springfield, Massachusetts 1659-1906
           Palmer, MA, published by author, 1906
Allen II....Allen, Orrin Peer, The Allen Memorial,
           Descendants of Samuel Allen of Windsor,
           Connecticut 1604-1907, Palmer, MA, published by
           author, Press of C.B. Fiske & Co., 1907
Alvord......Alvord, Samuel M, A Genealogy of the Descendants
           of Alexander Alvord, compiled by the author,
           originally published Webster, NY, A.D. Andrews,
           1908
Arms........Arms, William Tyler and Marsha E., History of
           Leyden, Massachusetts 1676-1959, Orange, MA,
           Enterprise & Journal, 1959
AZFC........Arizona Federal Census, National Archive
           Microfilm
Bardwell... Bardwell, Leila S., Vanished Pioneer Homes and
           Families of Shelburne, Massachusetts, Shelburne
           Historical Society, 1974
Bates.......Bates, George E., The Bates-Breed Ancestry,
           privately printed, Boston, Massachusetts, 1975
BioR........Biographical Review, Merrimack and Sullivan
           Counties, New Hampshire, Vol XXII, Boston, MA,
           Biographical Review Publishing Company, 1897
Birgham.....Birgham, Emma E. (Neal), The Neal Family,
           compiled by the author, 1938
Blackmar....Blackmar, Frank W., Kansas Cyclopedia of State
           History, Embracing Events, Institutions,
           Industries, Counties, Cities, Towns, Prominent
           Persons, Etc., edited by Frank W. Blackmar, A.M.
           Ph.D. Standard Publishing Co., Chicago
Blood.......Blood, Henry Ames, History of Temple, New
           Hampshire, Boston, Printed by G.C. Rand & Avery,
           1860
BMN.........Compendium of History and Biography of Central

```
                  and Northern Minnesota containing a History of
                  the State of Minnesota, George A. Ogle and Co.,
                  Chicago, 1904
Bond........Bond, Henry, M.D., Early Settlers of Watertown,
                  Massachusetts, Genealogies of the families and
                  descendants of the early settlers of Watertown,
                  MA, including Waltham & Weston to which is
                  appended the early history of the town. The New
                  England Historic Genealogical Society, Boston,
                  1860
Bowman......Bowman, Fred Q., 10,000 Vital Records of Central
                  New York, 1813-1850, Baltimore, Genealogical
                  Publishing Company, 1986
BR..........Bible Records researched from family
                  contributions
Brant.......Brant & Fuller, The History of Huntington County,
                  Indiana, Chicago, Brant & Fuller, 1887
Briggs......Briggs, Lloyd Vernon, History and Genealogy of
                  the Briggs Family, Vol III, Charles E. Goodspeed
                  and Company, 1938
BRJMS.......Bible Records of James M. Severance, 1840 copied
                  by Lenora White McQuesten-owned by Mrs. Elvira
                  (Severance) Smith, Auburn, NH
Brown.......Brown, Cyrus Henry, The Brown Genealogy 1628-
                  1907, The Everett Press Company, 1907
Browne......Browne, George Waldo, History of Hillsboro, New
                  Hampshire 1735-1921, Manchester, NH, John B.
                  Clarke Company Printers, 1921-22
BRPS........Bible Records of Phillip Severance, contributed
                  by Mrs. Roy S. McCord, Mary Ball DAR Chapter,
                  Tacoma, WA
BRRF........Bible Records of the Robinson Family
Bryant......Bryant, Charles S., History of the Minnesota
                  Valley, and History of the Sioux Massacre, Rev.
                  Edward D. Neill, North Star Publishing Company,
                  Minneapolis, 1882
Burleigh I..Burleigh, Charles, The Genealogy of the Burley or
                  Burleigh Family of America, Portland, ME, B.
                  Thurston & Co., 1880
Burleigh II.Burleigh, Charles, History of Guild, Guile, Gile,
                  Portland, ME, B. Thurston & Co., 1887
Burnham.....Burnham, Mrs. Walter E., Mrs. Elliot H. Taylor,
                  Mrs. Herbert P. Ware, and Mr. Thomas W. Watkins,
                  History and Traditions of Shelburne,
                  Massaschusetts, compiled by the authors, History
                  and Tradition Committee, Shelburne, 1958
BWNH........One Hundred and Fiftieth Anniversary of the
                  Settlement of Boscawen and Webster, Merrimack
                  Co., NH, Printed by the Republican Press
                  Association, printed 1884
Cabot.......Cabot, Mary R., Annals of Brattleboro, Vermont,
                  compiled and edited by author, Press of E.
                  Hildreth and Co., 1921-22
CAFC........California Federal Census, National Archive
                  Microfilm
Candage.....Candage, Charles Samuel, and Ralph Ernest Peak,
                  Heard-Hurd Genealogy, 1610-1987, Some Descendants
                  of John and Elizabeth (Hull) Heard of Dover, New
                  Hampshire, Picton Press, Camden, ME, 1988
```

Carleton....Carelton, Hiram, State of Vermont, Lewis
            Publishing Co., 1903
Catalfo.....Catalfo, Alfred Jr., The History of the Town of
            Rollinsford, New Hampshire 1623-1973,
            Somersworth, New Hampshire Printers, 1973
CEMNY.......Cemetery Records for New York
CH&B........Compendium of History and Biography of Central &
            Northern, Minnesota, Chicago, George A. Ogle &
            Co., 1904
Chase.......Chase, Benjamin, History of Old Chester from
            1719-1869, New Auburn, NH, published by the
            author, 1369
Clapp.......Genealogy of the Early Generations of the Coffin
            Family in New England, from the New-England
            Historical and Genealogical Register for 1870
            David Clapp and Son, Printers, 1870
Coates......Coates, William R., A History of Cuyahoga County
            and the City of Cleveland, assisted by a board of
            advisory editors, Chicago and New York, The
            American Historical Society, 1924
COFC........Colorado Federal Census, National Archive
            Microfilm
Coleman E...Coleman, Emma Lewis, New England Captives carried
            to Canada between 1677 and 1760 during the French
            and Indian Wars, Portland, ME, The Southworth
            Press, 1925
Coleman L...Coleman, Lyman D.D., Lyman Family in Great
            Britain and America, Albany, NY, J. Munsell, 1872
Conklin.....Conklin, Edwin P., Middlesex Conty and Its
            People, A History, Lewis Historical Publishing
            Company, Inc., NY 1927
Cooley......Cooley, John Clark, Rathbone Genealogy, Syracuse,
            New York, Press of the Courier Job Print, 1898
Coolidge....Coolidge, Emma Downing, The Descendants of John
            and Mary Coolidge of Watertown, Massachusetts,
            1630, Boston, Wright & Potter Printing Company,
            1930
Conrad......Conrad, Howard Louis, History of Milwaukee
            County, from First Settlements to 1895, American
            Biographical Publishing Co., Chicago and New
            York, 1895
CRBCoNH.....Court Records, Belknap County, Clerk of Court
            Records, Laconia, NH
CRBMA.......Cemetery Records of Bellevue, Lawrence, MA
CRBWI.......Cemetery Records of Beldenville, Pierce Co.,
            WI
CRCH........Records of Crown Hill Cemetery, Crown Hill, NY
CRHMA.......Church Records for Harwich, MA
CRMA........Court Records of MA
CRME........Various Cemetery Records of ME
CRNNY.......Church Records of Newtown Presbyterian NY
            (Book of the Newtown Presbyterian Church of
            Elmhurst, L.I.)
CRNY........Surrogate Court Records, Rochester, NY
CROGMA......Cemetery Records of Oak Grove, New Bedford, MA
CRPA........Census Pensioners for the Western District of PA
CRPCNH......Cemetery Records of Plains Cemetery, Kingston, NH
CRRME.......Cemetery Records of Revolutionary Grave in ME,
            Maine Old Cemetery Association, 2 Vols, DAR
            Library 1981

```
CRSC........Church Records, Christ Church Parish SC
CRSNH.......Cemetery Records of Smith's Corner, NH
CRTWI.......Cemetery Records of Thurston Hill Cemetery,
            Trimbelle Township, Pierce Co., WI
CRWMA.......Church Records of Watertown, MA, First Church
            Parish Records (Pope)
CRWNH.......Nute's Ridge Graveyard, John Fipphen's Cemetery
            Inscriptions of Wolfeboro, New Hampshire.
CRWNH.......Cemetery Records of Wolfboro, NH
CTFC........Connecticut Federal Census, National Archive
            Microfilm
CTVR........Connecticut Vital Records
Cumming.....Cumming, Robert Hugh, The Antecedents and
            Descendants of George Hosmer Cumming, updated by
            author, John Cumming, Mount Pleasant, MI, 1988
Currier.....Currier, Harvy L., Currier, John McNah, Genealogy
            of Richard Currier of Salisbury and Amesbury, MA
            (1616-1686/7) by Harvey L. Currier, Genealogy of
            Ezra Currier of Bath, New Hampshire (1749-1825)
            and his descendants by John McNah Currier. Issued
            under the auspices of the Orleans County
            Historical Society, Newport, Vermont, 1910
Cutter......Cutter, William Richard, A.M. and William
            Frederick Adams, Genealogical and Personal
            Memoirs relating to the families of the State of
            Massachusetts, Vol I, New York, Lewis Historical
            Publishing Company, 1910
CWPR........Civil War Pension Records
DARGRC......Daughters of the American Revolution,
            Genealogical Records Committe
DARLR.......Daughters of the American Revolution Lineage
            Records
DARGCLR.....Daughters of the American Revolution Grand
            Children Lineage Records
DARRW.......Daughters of the American Revolution, War Records
DARPI.......Daughters of the American Revolution Patriot
            Index
Davis.......Davis, Norman, Westchester Patriarchs, A
            Genealogical Dictionary of Westchester Co., New
            York, Families prior to 1755, Bowie, Maryland,
            Heritage Books, 1988
Deal........Deal, Babbie and McDonald, Loretta, edited by,
            The Heritage Book of Original Fergus County Area,
            Montana, Fergus County Bi-Centenial Heritage
            Committee, Lewiston Genealogical Society,
            Montana, 1976
DFC.........Dakota Federal Census, National Archive Microfilm
Doane.......Doane, Alfred Alder, I Deacon John Doane of
            Plymouth; II Doctor John Doane of Maryland and
            their descendants with notes upon English
            families of the name, Vol II, compiled by Doane
            Family Association of America, 1975-1976
Dodge.......Dodge, Christine Huston, Vital Records of Old
            Bristol and Nobleboro in the County of Lincoln,
            ME, Published under the authority of the Maine
            Historical Society, 1947-51
Doe.........Doe, Elmer E., The Descendants of Nicholas Doe,
            Orleans, VT., published by the author, 1918
Dow.........Dow, Robert Piercy, Genealogical Memoirs of the
            Descendants of Henry Dow 1637, Thomas Dow 1639
```

and others of the name, Immigrants to America
during Colonial times, also Allied family of
Nudd-Writter, compiled and edited by author,
Claremont, New Hampshire, R.P. Dow, J.W. Dow, and
S.F. Dow, 1929

Draper......Draper, Mrs. Amos, New Hampshire Pensions Records

Dunham......Dunham, Robert W., Fuller-Dunham Genealogy from
Edward Fuller of the Mayflower, Baltimore MD,
Gateway Press, 1990

Durant......Durant, Samuel W., & Pierce, Henry B., History of
St. Lawrence County, New York, Illustrations and
Biographical Sketches, Printed by St. Lawrence
County, Canton, New York, 1878

Eastman.....Eastman, J., History of Andover, New Hampshire
1751-1906, Rumford Printing Co., Concord, NH 1910

Easton......Easton, Augustus B., History of the St. Croix
Valley, Vol II H.C. Cooper Jr. & Co., Chicago,
1909

ECRR........Essex County, Massachusetts Probate Records, The
Probate Records of Essex County, MA, Salem, MA,
published by the Essex Institute, 1917

ECVR........Essex County, Massachusetts Vital Records, Salem,
MA, Published by the Essex Institute, 1917

Edson.......Edson, Hon Obed, Cyclopedia of Chautauqua Co.,
NY, 1891

Eldridge....Eldridge, William Henry, Henry Genealogy, The
Descendants of Samuel Henry & Lurana (Cady) Henry
(his wife), Press of T.R. Marvin & Son, Boston,
MA., 1915

Elliot......Elliot, Mrs Mary A., The Thompson Genealogy 1720-
1915, compiled by author, New Haven, CT, The
Thompson Family Association, 1915

Ellison.....Ellison, Dorothy M., Parades & Promenades,
Antrim, New Hampshire, The Second Hundred Years,
Canaan, NH, published for the Antrim History
Committee by Phoenix Publishing, 1977

Emery.......Emery, William M., The Howland Heirs, New Bedford
Massachusetts, E. Anthony & Sons Inc, New
Bedford, 1919

Farmer......Farmer, John, A Genealogical Register of the
Fisrt Settlers of New England, Reprinted with
additions and corrections by Samuel G. Drake,
Genealogist Publishing Co., Baltimore, 1976

Fellows.....Fellows, Dana Willis, History of the town of
Lincoln, Penobscot County, Maine 1822-1928,
Lewiston, ME., printed by the Dingley Press Inc.
1929

Fermald.....Fermald, Mrs. Natalie R., The Skinner Kinsmen,
The Pioneer Press, Washington, D.C.

Fieler......Fieler, Henry P., and Agnes Severance Fieler,
Severance-Fieler Families in America 1630-1982,
Life on an Indiana Farm 1900-1982, Merrillville,
IN, by authors, 1982

Flandrau....Flandrau, Judge Charles E., Encyclopedia of
Biography of Minnesota, History of Minnesota,
Chicago, The Century Publishing and Engraving
Company, 1900

FLFC........Florida Federal Census, National Archive
Microfilm

Folsom......Folsom, Elizabeth Knowles, Genealogy of the

Folsom Family, a revised and extended edition, including English records 1638-1938, Rutland, VT., Tuttle Publishing Co., 1938

Fuller......Fuller, William Hyslop, Genealogy of John Fuller of Lynn, Palmer, Massachusetts, compiled and printed for the compiler, 1914

Furman......Furman, Consuelo and the late Robert Furman M.D. (1863-1944) Descendants of Joseph Phillips of Newton, L.I. Zeroxed Manuscript 6-19-1951

Garland.....Garland, James Gray, Garland Genalogy, The Descendants of Peter Garland, Mariner, Watson's Illuminator Print, Biddeford, ME. 1897

Glavinick...Glavinick, Jacquelyn Gee, The 1885 State Census of Weld County, Colorado, copied and compiled by author for the Genealogical Society of Weld County, July 1984

Goss I......Goss, Mrs. Charles Carpenter, (Winifred Lane) Colonial Gravestone Inscriptions in the State of New Hampshire, published by the Historic Activities Committe of the State of New Hampshire from collections made by committee from 1913-1942, Dover, NH. 1942, Genealogical Publishing Co. Inc., Baltimore, 1974

Gove........Gove, William Henry, The Gove Book, History and Genealogy of the American Family of Gove and Notes of European Goves, Salem, MA., edited by Sidney Perley, 1922

Gray........Gray, Ruth, Maine Families in 1790, edited by the author, Picton Press, Camden, ME, 1988

Greeley.....Greeley, George Hiram, Genealogy of the Greely-Greeley Family, Boston, MA., F. Wood, Printer, 1905

Green II....Green, Mary Shaw, The History of Levi Greene and His Descendants, Andrian College Press, 1944

Greenlee....Greenlee, Ralph Stebbins and Robert Lemuel Greenlee, The Stebbins Genealogy, 2 Vols, Chicago, privately printed, 1904

Grow........Grow Family Genealogy

GRWNH.......Gravestone Records of Washington, NH. Searched by the author

GSNH........Gravestone Records of the Sandwich Baptist Church of Sandwich, NH. searched by the author.

H&LCoOH.....The Commemorative Biographical Record of the Counties of Huron and Lorain, Ohio, J.H. Beers and Co., Chicago, 1894

HACoCA......History of Amador Co., CA., Oakland, California, Thompson and West, 1881

HACoNY......History of Allegheny Co., NY, F.W. Beers & Co., 1879

HACoPA......History of Allegheny Co., Pennsylvania, A. Warner and Co. Publishers, 1889

Hammatt.....Hammatt, Abraham, The Hammatt Papers, Early Inhabitants of Ipswich, Massachusetts, 1633-1700, indexed by Robert Barnes, Genealogical Publishing Co. Baltimore, 1980

Hammond.....Hammond, Issac, W.A.M., The State of New Hampshire Rolls of the Soldiers in the Revolutionary War, Concord, NH, Parsons B. Cogswell, State Printer, 1885

Hanaford....Hanaford, Mary E. Neal, Meredith, New Hampshire

462

Annals and Genealogies, arranged by Mary E. Hanaford, Concord, NH., The Rumford Press, 1932

Hannum......Hannum, Curtis H., and Horace F. Temple, Genealogy of the Hannum Family, Horace F. Temple Publisher, 1911

Hardy.......Hardy, Hardy and Hardie, Past and Present, Samuel Hardy Family of Bererly, MA., printed 1935

Hayley......Hayley, Rev. John W., Publishments and Marriages in the Town of Tuftonboro, years 1796-1830, An Historical Sketch by Reverend John W. Hales, D.D., Tuftonboro, 1923

Hayward.....Hayward, Sylvanus, History of Gilsum, New Hampshire 1752-1879, Manchester, NH., printed for Sylvanus Hayward by J.B. Clarke, 1881

Hazen.......Hazen, Tracy Elliot Ph.D., The Hazen Family in America, edited for publication by Donald Lines Jacobus, Thomaston, CT, R. Hazen, 1947

Hazlett.....Hazlett, Charles A., A History of Rockingham Co., New Hampshire, Chicago, IL, Richmond Arnold Publishing Co, 1915

HBHCoIA.....History of Black Hawk County, Iowa, Chicago, Western Historical Company, 1878

HCCoVT......History of Chittenden Co., VT

Hemenway....Hemenway, Abby Maria, Vermont Historical Gazeteer, Montpellier, VT, edited by Abby Hemenway, Burlington, VT, 1868-91

Heverly.....Heverly, Clement F., Pioneer and Patriot Families of Bradford County, Pennsylvania, 1770-1800, Towanda, PA, Bradford Star Print 1913-15

HGVT........Official History of Guilford, VT 1678-1961, edited by Broad Brook Grange #151, printed by the Vermont Printing Co., Brattleboro, VT., 1961

HHCCoMO.....History of Howard and Chariton Co., MO., St. Louis, National Historical Company, 1883

Hills.......Hills, William Sanford, The Hills Family in America 1794-1806, A Genealogy of Joseph Hills, The Grafton Press, New York, 1906

HJCoMI......History of Jackson Co., MI Vol II, Interstate Publishing Co, 1881

HMCoCA......History of Marin Co., Saucelito Township, CA., San Francisco, CA., Alley & Bowen & Co., 1880

HOCoNY......History of Ontario County, New York and Its People, Vol II, Lewis Historical Publishing Company, 1911

HOPCoME.....Ames, Mrs. Edward W. & Mildred N. Thayer History of Brewer, Orrington, Eddington, ME, Brewer 150th Anniversary Committee, 1962

HOS.........Severance, Henry Ormal, The Severance Genealogy, The Benjamin, Charles, and Lewis Lines of the Severnth Generation, Columbia, Missouri, Luca Brothers, 1927

Hosier......Hosier, Kathleen E., Kingston New Hampshire, Early Families Patriots and Soldiers, Heritage Books, Inc. 1993

Hotten......Hotten, John Camden, edited by, The Original List of Persons of Quality 1600-1700, Genealogical Publishing Co., Inc, Baltimore, 1974

House.......House, Charles J., Names of Soldiers of the American Revolution who applied for State Bounty under resolve of 1835, edited by Charles J.

House, Published by order of the govener and executive Council, Augusta, ME., Burleigh & Flynt, 1893, Baltimore, Genealogical Publishing Co., 1967

Howard......Howard, Walter E., Charles E. Prentis, Catalogue of Officers and Students of Middlebury College in Vermont and others who have recieved degrees 1800-1900, Middlebury, VT., The College, 1901

Howe........Howe, Gilman Bigelow, Genealogy of the Bigelow Family, 1890, Worcester, MA, Printed by Charles Hamilton, Reprint-New England Historic Genealogical Society, 1929

Hoyt........Hoyt, David Webster, The Old Families of Salisbury and Amesbury, Massachusetts, 1897, Providence, R.I., reprinted, New England History Press, Somersworth, 1981 Genealogical Publishing Co., 1982,

HSRCA.......Historical Society Records of Endocina Co., CA

HWCoWI......History of Walworth Co., WI., Western Historical Company, Chicago, Illinois, 1892

HWNH........History of Washington, New Hampshire from 1768-1886, Washington History Committee, 1976

IAFC........Iowa Federal Census, National Archive Microfilm

IAPA........Iowa Pioneers-Ancestors and Descendants

IDFC........Idaho Federal Census, National Archive Microfilm

IGI.........International Genealogical Index, Micro Fiche

INFC........Indiana Federal Census, National Archive Microfilm

Jackson.....Jackson, James R., History of Littleton, New Hampshire, University Press, Cambridge, MA. Published for the Town, Genealogy by George C. Furber 1905

Jacobus.....Jacobus, Donald Lines and Edgar F. Waterman, Hale, House and Related Families Mainly of the Connecticut River Valley, Connecticut Historical Society, 1932, Genealogical Publishing Co. Inc 1978

JFS.........Severance, John F., The Severans Genealogical History, compiled by Rev. John F. Severance of Chicago, Il., R.R. Donnelley and Sons Company, 1893

Johnsen.....Johnsen, Betty, The Ephraim Severance Line of Kingston and Chester, New Hampshire, Ventura County Genealogical Society Quarterly, Ventura, California, March 1987

Johnson I...Johnson, Charles Owen, The Genealogy of Several Allied Families, (Briggs) New Orleans, Pelican Publishing Company, 1961

Johnson II..Johnson, Rev. William Wallace, Records of the Descendants of John Johnson of Ipswich and Andover, Massachusetts 1635-1794 with an appendix containing records of descendants of Timothy Johnson of Andover and poems of Johnson descendants, Salem, MA., Higginson Book Co., 1892

Jones.......Jones, Charles Henry, Genealogy of the Rodman Family 1620-1886, Philadelphia, printed by Allen, Lane, & Scott, 1886

Judd........Judd, Sylvester & Lucius M. Boltwood, History of Hadley, Early History of Hatfield, South Hadley, Amherst, & Granby, MA., also Family Genealogies

by Lucius M. Boltwood, H.R. Huntting & Company,
Springfield, MA., 1905

Judkins.....Judkins, Eliza Littlefield, Job Judkins of Boston
and his Descendants, Larchmont, New York, 1962

Kelsey......Kelsey, Harry Norman and Elias Isbell Kelsey, A
Genealogy of the Descendants of William Kelsey,
Vol IV

Kelley......Kelley, Louise H. & Dorothy Straw, compiled by,
The Vital Records, Town of Harwich, MA., 1694-
1850, published by the Harwich Historical
Society, Inc., 1982

Kennedy.....Kennedy, Ruth S., Marriage Returns for Oakland
Co. MI, 1836-1884, Oakland County Genealogical
Society, Birmingham, MI, 1989

Kidder......Kidder, Frederic, 1804-1885, History of New
Ipswich, Massachusetts, Boston, Gould & Lincoln,
1852

KSFC........Kansas Federal Census, National Archive Microfilm

KSVR........Kansas Vital Records

KYFC........Kentucky Federal Census, National Archive
Microfilm

LAFC........Lousianna Federal Census, National Archive
Microfilm

LCCEC.......Biographical Review-Leading Citizens of Clinton
and Esex Counties, New York, Biographical Review
Publishing Company, Boston, 1896

LCoOH.......Daniels, Jack E., Janice Mahlstrom, Frances H.
Slack, Darrell C. Webster, The Historical Society
Quarterly of Painesville, Lake County, OH.,
published by the Lake County Historical Society
and the Board of Lake County Commissioners,
Painsville Publishing Company, 1976

Leighton....Leighton, Perley M., A Leighton Genealogy, New
England Historic Genealogy Society, Boston, 1989

Lighton.....Mrs. Harriet (Vittum), Gravestone Inscriptions of
Sandwich, New Hampshire, collected and arranged
by Harriet Lighton, 1930

Lord........Lord, Myra Belle Horne, History of the Town of
New London, Merrimack Co., New Hampshire 1779-
1899, Concord, NH., Rumford Press, 1899

Lovell......Lovell, Mrs Frances Stockwell, Mr. Leverett C.
Lovell, History of the Town of Rockingham,
Vermont, 1907-1957 with family Genealogies,
published by the Town of Belows Falls, VT, 1958

LRME........Land Records of Maine

LRWI........Land Records of Wisconsin

LRNH........Land Records of New Hampshire

MA..........Maine Abstracts

Machias.....Machis, M.E., Downeast Ancestry, A Maine Verrill
Family, Vol 14, New Journal 1977-1993

MacIntire...MacIntire, Susan Holt and Witherell, Sanford
Stone, A Genealogical Register of the Early
Families of Shoreham, Vermont, 1761-1899,
Rutland, VT., 1984

MAFC........Massachusetts Federal Census, National Archive
Microfilm

Malone......Malone, Dumas, Dictionary of American Biography,
Edited by Dumas Malone, Charles Scribner's &
Sons, 1935

MAM.........Manuscript of Avis Munro, Round Pond, Maine

Mardecai....Mardecai, Major A., Sandwich, New Hampshire
             History, Originally Military Commissions to
             Europe 1855-56, 1935
Marvin......Marvin Family Descendants, Descendants of Reinold
             and Matthew Marvin 1635-1904
MASS........Massachusetts Soldiers and Sailors of the
             Revolutionary War, Secretary of the Commonwealth,
             17 Vols, Boston, 1905
MAVR........Massachusetts Vital Records
MAVRS.......Vital Records of Salisbury, MA., published by the
             Topsfield Historical Society, Topsfield, MA.,
             1915
MBB.........Manuscript of Mrs. Barion Bernash
MBD.........The United States Biographical Dictionary and
             Portrait Gallery of Eminent and Self-Made Men,
             Minnesota Volume, American Biographical
             Publishing Company, 1879
MBFS........Manuscript of Barbara Fallon Senecal, Portsmouth,
             VA
MBG.........Manuscript of Barton W. Griffin, Malden, MA
MBGD........Manuscript of Berenice G. Davis, Ogden, UT
MBJ.........Manuscript of Betty Johnsen, Ventura, CA
MBS.........Manuscript of Bert Severance, Willsboro, NY
MCoL........Multnomah County Library Index Files, Portland,
             Oregon. Vital Records from family sources
MDBS........Manuscript of David B. Senter, Freemont, NH
MDCD........Manuscript of David C. Dewsnap, De Pere, WI
MDFC........Maryland Federal Census, National Archive
             Microfilm
MDH.........Manuscript of Mrs. Harry and Gladys Deyo
MDJS........Manuscript of Dorothy-Jean Severance, Milwaukee,
             OR
MDLB........Manuscript of Dottie Lu Baber, Vancouver, WA
MDS.........Manuscript of Donald P. Severance, Wellesley, MA
MDW.........Manuscript of Debbie Wilson, Greenland, NH
MEFC........Maine Federal Census, National Archive Microfilm
Merrill I...Merrill, Joseph, History of Amesbury and
             Merrimac, Haverhill Press of Franklin P. Stiles,
             1880
Merrill II..Merrill, Rev. J.L., History of Acworth with the
             Proceedings of the Centennial Anniversary,
             Genealogical Records, and Register of Farms,
             Edited by Rev. J.L. Merrill, Acworth, 1869
Merrill III.Merrill, Samuel, A Merrill Memorial 1917-1928 on
             account of the descendants of Nathaniel Merrill,
             an early settler of Newbury, Massachusetts,
             Cambridge, MA., 1917-18/1928
MESS........Manuscript of R. Scott Severance, North Andover,
             MA
MEVR........Maine Vital Records
MFES........Manuscript of Frederick E. Severance III, Lynn,
             MA
MgBH........Bangor Historical Magazine, Address on the
             incorporation of the Town of Orrington, ME, 1787,
             of Worcester, MA., 1781 and later called Brewer,
             MA, 6 Vols, Bangor, Maine, Picton Press, 1992
MGC.........Manuscript of Gus Collins, Seattle, WA
MgOA........Magazine, Oberlin Alumni 2-1-1936
MgSC........South Carolina Historical and Genalogical
             Magazine, South Carolina Historical Society,

```
                    Charleston, SC
MHCS........Manuscript of Harland C. Severance, Medical Lake,
            WA
MHGS........Manuscript of Harold G.[10] Severance, Concordia, KS
MHS.........Manuscript of Helen Scholl, Indianapolis, IN
MIFC........Michigan Federal Census, National Archive
            Microfilm
MIHJCO......History of Jackson County, Michigan, Vol II Inter
            -State Publishing Company, 1881
MINB........Manuscript of Iris N. Buzzell, Bangor, ME
MIPH........Michigan Pioneer and Historical Collections
            1903, Annual Meeting, 1902 Vol 32
MISS........United States Civil War Soldiers living in
            Michigan in 1894, Clinton County Historical
            Society, New York
MIVR........Michigan Vital Records
MJJO........Manuscript of Joanne Joy Osborn, Le Seuer, MN
MJR.........Manuscript of John R. Reynolds, Westerly, RI
MLCK........Manuscript of Lucile C. Knight, Magalia, CA
MLM.........Manuscript of Lynn Merton, Jefferson, OR
MLSW........Manuscript of Lucile Swift White, Topeka, Kansas
MLWM........Manuscript of Lenora White McQuesten
MME.........Marriages of Maine
MMS.........Manuscript of Mary Severance, Mattawamkeag, ME
MNFC........Minnesota Federal Census, National Archive
            Microfilm
MNVR........Minnesota Vital Records
MO..........Manuscript of Osborn
MOFC........Missouri Federal Census, National Archive
            Microfilm
Moore I.....Moore, Howard P., (1696-1786) The Descendants of
            Ensign John Moore of Canterbury, New Hampshire,
            Rutland, VT., The Tuttle Company, 1918
Moore II....Moore, James W., Rev. John Moore of Newtown, Long
            Island and some of his descendants, Easton, PA.,
            Printed for the publisher by the Chemical
            Publishing Co., 1903
Moran.......Moran, Edward C., 1894, Descendants of James
            Bunker of Dover, New Hampshire (Rockland, ME),
            Bunker Family Association of America 1961-1965
Mosher......Mosher, Elizabeth M. & Isabel Morse Marsh,
            Marriage Records of Waldo County, Maine, Prior to
            1892, Picton Press, Camden, ME, 1990
Mower.......Mower, Ephraim, Cutler Family Genealogy, 1606-
            1897
MPN.........Manuscript of Peggy Nesbitt, Pheonix, AZ
MPV.........Manuscript of Pat Vandeveer, Fountain Valley, CA
MRS.........Manuscript of Robert[10] Severance, Natick, MA
MSJSM.......Manuscript of Sarah Jane Severance McDonald
MTFC........Montana Federal Census, National Archive
            Microfilm
Mudgett.....Mudgett, Mildred & Bruce D. Mudgett, Thomas
            Mudgett of Salisbury, MA and His Descendants
MVM.........Manuscript of Virginia Mills, Orrick, MO
MWBM........Manuscript of William B. Morse, Portland, OR
MWGS........Manuscript of William G. Sevrens, Woburn, MA
MWLS........Manuscript of Warren L. Severance, Seattle, WA
MWR.........Manuscript of William Reynolds, Waverly, RI
MWS.........Manuscript of William Saverance of Florence,
            South Carolina, privately printed, 1987
```

```
NCFC........North Carolina Federal Census, National Archive
            Microfilm
NDFC........North Dakota Federal Census, National Archive
            Microfilm
NEFC........Nebraska Federal Census, National Archive
            Microfilm
NEHGR.......New England Historical and Genealogical Register,
            multiple vols, The New England Historic and
            Genealogical Society
Newcomb.....Newcomb, Bethuel Merritt, Andrew Newcomb 1618-
            1686 and his Descendants, a revised edition of
            Genealogial Memoirs of the Newcomb family,
            published 1874 by John Bearre Newcomb, New Haven
            CT., privately printed for the author by Tuttle,
            Moorehouse & Taylor Co., 1923
NHPSP.......Provincial and State Papers, various volumes 1-
            40, published by authority of the legislature of
            New Hampshire, Concord 1867-1943
NHVR........New Hampshire Vital Records
NJFC........New Jersey Federal Census, National Archive
            Microfilm
NSAA........Newspaper, The American Advocate 3-8-1817
NSAL........Newspaper, Amador Ledger, CA
NSCA........Newspapers of CA
NSCC........Newspaper, Columbian Chronicle, MA
NSCOH.......Newspaper, The Cleveland Press, OH
NSDJ........Newspaper, Dunkirk Journal, Dunkirk, NY
NSEWI.......Newspaper, The Ellsworth Herald, WI
NSFG........Newspaper, Franklin Gazette, Philadelphia, PA
NSFR........Newspaper, The River Falls Advance, River Falls,
            Pierce Co., WI
NSG&B.......Newspaper, Gazette and Bangor Weekly, ME
NSHI........Newspaper, Huntington, Indiana Herald-Press
NSHMW.......Newspaper, Huntington Mid-Weekly Herald, IN
NSLD........Newspaper, Laconia Democrat, NH
NSMA........Newspapers of MA
NSME........Newspapers of ME
            Bangor Daily News, Bangor, Maine, began 6-18-1889
NSMWI.......Newspaper, Milwaukee Sentinel, WI
NSNBMA......Newspaper, The New Bedford Mercury, New Bedford,
            MA
NSOR........Newspaper, The Oregonian, Portland, Oregon
NSPCA.......Newspaper, Pacific Christian Advocate, OR
NSPT........Newspaper, Painesville Telegraph, OH
NSRFJ.......Newspaper, River Falls Journal, WI
NSSAR.......Newspaper, San Andreas Register, CA
NSUL........Newspaper, Union Leader, Manchester, NH
NSW.........Newspaper, Woburn News (Daily Times Chronicle),
            Worburn, Massachusetts, Monday, 10-5-1987)
NSWA........Newspapers of WA
NSYDR.......Newspaper, The Yakima (Washington) Daily Republic
NWI.........Necrology of Wisconsin, Wisconsin State
            Historical Society, Madison, WI
Nye.........Nye, Glen R., Jonathan Farnsworth Genealogy,
            Farnsworth Memorial II, Revised, 1974
NYFC........New York Federal Census, National Archive
            Microfilm
NYGBR.......New York Genealogical and Biographical Register,
            Vol XXIX, Published by the New York Genealogical
            & Biographical Society, 1948
```

```
NYVR........New York Vital Records
O'Gorman....O'Gorman, William, Scrapbook of Zerox copies of
            clippings of extracts from the Newtown Records,
            edited by William O'Gorman, Publisher in the
            Newtown Register, 1885
Oakes.......Oakes, R.A., Genealogical and Family History of
            the County of Jefferson, New York, Vol I, Lewis
            Publishing Co., 1905
OHFC........Ohio Federal Census, National Archive Microfilm
OHVR........Ohio Vital Records
OKCR........Chronicles of Oklahoma, Necrology, Vol 18 March
            1940, Oklahoma Historical Society, 1-1-1921 to
            present
ORFC........Oregon Federal Census, National Archive Microfilm
ORVR........Oregon Vital Records
Paine.......Paine, Josiah, A History of Harwich, Barnstable
            Co. MA 1620-1800, The Tuttle Publishing Co. Inc,
            Rutland, Vermont, 1937
P&BIA.......Portrait and Biographical Record of Jasper,
            Marshall and Grundy Counties Iowa, Biographical
            Publishing Co., Chicago, 1894
P&BOMI......Portrait and Biographical Album of Oakland MI.,
            Champman Bros., 1891
P&BRWI......Portrait and Biographical Album of Rock Co., WI.,
            Acme Publishing Co., 1889
PAFC........Pennsylvania Federal Census, National Archive
            Microfilm
PAVR........Pennsylvania Vital Records
Perley......Perley, Martin Van Buren, History and Genealogy
            of the Perley Family, Salem, MA., printed by the
            compiler, 1906
Pierce......Pierce, Frederick Clifton, Fiske and Fisk Family,
            being the Record of the descendants of Symond
            Fiske, Lord of the Manor of Stadhaugh, Suffolk
            Co., England, from the time of Henry IV to date
            including all the American members of the
            family, Chicago, IL., published by Frederick C.
            Pierce, Press of W.B. Conkey Co., 1896
Pope I......Pope, Charles Henry, Records of the First Church,
            Dorchester, Massachusetts, Boston, 1891
Pope II.....Pope, Charles Henry, Merriam Genealogy, of
            Charles Pierce Merriam in England and America,
            the collection of James Sheldon Merriam, Boston,
            C.H. Pope, 1906
Pope III....Pope, Charle Henry, 1841-1918, Pioneers of Maine
            and New Hampshire 1623-1660, a descriptive list
            drawn from records of the colonies, towns,
            churches, courts, and other contempory sources
            with forward by James Phinney Baxter, Baltimore
            Genealogical Publishing Company, 1965
PRCSC.......Probate Records of Charleston Co., SC., Original
            Will Book 1722-24
PRJWI.......Probate Records of Juneau Co., WI, researched by
            author
PRMA........Probate Records of MA, researched by author
PRMASC......Files for MA. Superior Court of Judicature Number
            27,319
PRME........Probate Records of ME, researched by Berenice G.
            Davis
PRNH........Probate Records of NH, researched by author
```

PRPCoME.....Abstracts of Penobscot Co. ME, Probate Records, 1816-1866, Edited by Ruth Gray, Picton Press, Camden, ME, 1990

PRMOAH......Probate Records of Morgan Co., OH, researched by author

PRNNY.......Probate Records of Newton, L.I. NY, research by author

PROVT.......Probate Records of Orange Co., VT, research by author

PRRNY.......Probate Records of Rochester, NY, research by author

PRSC........Probate Records of Charleston, SC, Court Of Probate, Index to Will of Charleston Co. SC, 1671-1868, Caroline Moore, compiled under the direction of the Charleston Free Library, Genealogical Publishing Co, Inc, 1974

PRVT........Probate Records of VT, research by author

PRWI........Probate Records of WI, Waukesha Co. research by author

Quinby......Quinby, Henry Cole, The Quinby-Quimby Family of Sandwich, NH, NY City, Rutland VT., The Tuttle Company 1915-23

Radasch.....Radasch, Arthur Hitchcock, The William Barstow Family, Genealogy of the Descendants of William Barstow, 1635-1965, Published by author, 1966

Reighard....Reighard, Frank H., A Standard History of Fulton County, OH., Vol I, 1920

Reynolds....Reynolds, Cuyler, Hudson-Mohawk Genealogical & Family Memoirs, New York, Lewis Publishing Co, 1911

Ridlon I....Ridlon, Gideon Tibbetts, Contribution to the Genealogy of the Burbank and Burbanck families in the U.S., Saco, ME, C.P. Pike, 1880

Ridlon II...Ridlon, Gideon Tibbetts, Saco Valley Settlements, Poingdestre-Pendexter, Portland, ME., 1895

Ridlon III..Ridlon, Gideon Tibbetts, History of the families Millegas & Millanges, published by the author, Journal Press, Lewiston, ME, 1907

Riker.......Riker, James Jr., 1822-1889, The Annals of Newtown in Queens County, NY., New York, D. Fanshaw, 1852/1982

RMOFMA......Representative Men and Old Families of Southeastern Massachusett Vol III, J.H. Beers and Co., Chicago, 1912

Robinson....Robinson, Timothy W., A Genealogical History of Morrill, Maine, copied and edited by Theoda Mears Morse, Belfast, Maine, City Job Print, 1944

Root........Root, James P., Root Genealogical Records, Seventh Generation-Harford Line, The Root Family of Hartford, Connecticut, New York, R.C. Root, Anthony & Co., 1870

Runnels.....Runnels, Rev. M.T., History of Sanbornton, New Hampshire, Vol II Genealogies, Boston, 1881-82

RWR.........Revolutionary War Records, National Archives, Washington, DC, microfilm

Salley......Salley, Alexander S. Jr., The Narrative of Early Carolina 1650-1708, New York, C. Scribner's & Sons, 1911

Sanders.....Sanders, Helen Fitzgerald, A History of Montana, Vol I, Lewis Publishing Co., 1913

SC.........Severance, Charles, Recollections of a Country
          Boy, Minerva Historical Society, 1991
SCCR.......South Carolina, Darlington Co., The Darlington
          County Historical Commission
SCFC.......South Carolina Federal Census, National Archive
          Microfilm
SCG........South Carolina Grants
SDFC.......South Dakota Federal Census, National Archive
          Microfilms
SFSC.......Bay of San Francisco, California-Its Cities and
          Suburbs, Lewis Publishing Co., 1892
Sheldon....Sheldon, George, A History of Deerfield,
          Massachusetts, New Hampshire Publishing company,
          1896 reprinted, New Hampshire Publishing Co.,
          Somersworth, in collaboration with the Pocumtuck
          Valley Memorial Association, Deerfield, 1972
ShipsR.....New Bedford, MA., Ship Registers of New Bedford,
          Massachusetts, Vol I 1796-1850, The National
          Archives Project
Shurtleff...Shurtleff, Roy C., Descendants of William
          Shurtleff, Benjamin Shurfleff 1866-1952, revised
          editions 1976, San Francisco, 1976
Sinnott....Sinnott, Mary Elizabeth, The Winslow Family,
          Sinnot, Rogers, Coffin, Corliss, Reeves, Bodine
          and allied Families
Slevin.....Slevin, Ruth M., Marriage Records of Huntington
          County, Indiana, Book E. Vol I 1976
Smith I....Smith, H.P. History of Warren Co., PA., 1981
Smith II....Smith, William C., History of Chatham, MA., 1913
Smith III...Smith, H.P., History of Essex Co., NY, Syracuse
          NY, D. Mason Company, publisher, 1885
SNHE.......Sandwich, New Hampshire Annual Excursions,
          Sandwich, New Hampshire Historical Society
Snow.......Snow, Nora Emma, The Snow-Estes Ancestry Vol I
          Hillburn, New York, 1939
Spalding....Spalding, Charles Warren, Spaulding Memorial,
          1897
Spofford....Spofford, Charles Byron, Gravestone Records from
          Ancient Cemeteries in the town of Claremont, New
          Hampshire with Historical and Biograpical notes,
          compiled by the author, Claremont, NH,
          G.I.Putnam, 1896
Spooner.....Spooner, Thomas, William Spooner of Plymouth,
          Massachusetts Vol I, Cincinati, Press of F.W.
          Freeman, 1883
Sterns.....Stearns, Ezra S., Genealogical and Family History
          of the State of New Hampshire, 2 Vols, Lewis
          Publishing Co, Chicago-New York, 1908
Stone......Simon Stone Genealogy, Descendants in America
Stout......Stout, Tom, Montana Its Story and Biography, 2
          Vols, Chicago and New York, The American
          Historical Society, 1921
Stowell....Stowell, William Henry Harrison, Stowell
          Genealogy, a Record of the Descendants of Samuel
          Stowell of Hingham, Vermont, The Tuttle Company,
          1922
Stratten....Stratten, Allen L., History Town of Isle La Motte
          Vermont, Northlight Studio Press, Barre, Vermont,
          1984
Strawn......Strawn, Anne White, The Ancestors and Descendants

of John White and Sarah Elizabeth Green, with
allied lines,, Salisbury Printing Co, Salisbury,
North Carolina, 1984

Street......Street, Mrs Mary A., The Street Genealogy,
printed by John Templeton, The News Letter Press,
Exeter, New Hampshire, 1895

Suddaby.....Suddaby, Elizabeth C., Nims-Munn Genealogy, The
Thankful Nims Munn Line, Seven Generations of
Descendants from Godfrey Nims / Elizabeth C.
Suddaby compiled for Greenville, SC., Southern
Historical Press, 1990

Swift.......Swift, Samuel, History of the Town of Middlebury
in the County of Addison, Vermont, Rutland,
Vermont, Charles E. Tuttle Company, 1971

Tasker......Tasker, Reverand, Sandwich, New Hampshire
Historical Records

Thurston....Thurston, Brown, Thurston Genealogies 1635-1892,
Portland, ME., B. Thurston and Hoyt, Fogg &
Donham, 1892

Tibbetts....Tibbetts, Charles W., The New Hampshire
Genealogcial Record, Vol I, July 1903-April 1904,
Vol 3, 1905-06, Vol 4, 1907, Vol 5, 1908, Vol 7,
1910' Harmon, George H., Harmon's Notes of
Kingston, New Hampshire, Kingston First Church
Records, A Collection of Notes compiled by George
H. Harmon Concerning Early Kingston, New
Hampshire Residents of Kingston First Church
Editor publisher (Tibbetts), 1904

Titus.......Titus, P.H. Titus Family in America, 1943

Torrey......Torrey, Clarence Almon, New England Marriages
Prior to 1700, Genealogical Publishing Co., Inc.,
Baltimore, MD 1991

TPNH........Town Papers of Laconia, NY

Trask.......Trask, Grace Martin & Adams, Rachel French,
Genealogy of the French Family, compiled 1971

TRBNY.......The Town of Bedford, Westchester Co., NY,
Historical Records, Vol I, Minutes of Town
Meetings 1680-1737

TRDNH.......Town Records of Danbury, NH

TRNINH......Town Records of New Ipswich, NH

Tuttle......Tuttle, William H., Names and Sketches of the
Pioneer Settlers of Madison Co, NY, Edited by
Isabel Bracy, Heart of the Lakes Publishing,
Interlaken, NY

Virkus......Virkus, Frederick Adams, The Abridged Compendium
of American Genealogy; First Family of America,
Vol 2, by author under direction of Albert Nelson
Marquis, Chicago, F.A. Virkus & Co., 1925/1926

Vittum......Vittum, Edmund March and Page, Linnie Bean, The
Vittum Folks, Muscatine, Iowa, Grinnell Herald
Press, printed for E. M. Vittum, 1922

Volkel......Volkel, Lowell M., The War of 1812 Bounty Lands
in Illinois, The National Archives, indexed by
Lowell,M. Volkel

VTFC........Vermont Federal Census, National Archive
Microfilm

VTVR........Vermont Vital Records, 1760-1890

WAFC........Washington Federcal Census, National Archive
Microfilm

Wallbridge..Wallbridge, William Gedney, Descendants of Henry

Wallbridge, who married Anna Amos, 12-25-1688 at
Preston, Connecticut and allied families,
Philadelphia, Press of Franklin Printing Company,
1898
Washburn....Washburn, Elizabeth F., The Swiss Ancestors and
American Descendants of Johann Jacob Schnebele
1659-1743 and other Snivelys and Snavelys of
Southeastern, Pennsylvania, Baltimore, Gateway
Press, Vestal, NY
WDCFC.......Washington D.C. Federal Census, National Archive
Microfilm
Weaver......Weaver, Lucius Egbert, History and Genealogy of a
branch of the Weaver Family, Rochester, NY, 1928
Wellman.....Wellman, Rev. Joshua Wyman D.D., Descendants of
Thomas Wellman of Lynn, Massachusetts, Boston, MA
Published by Arthur Holbrook Wellman, 1918
Wentworth...Wentworth, John, The Wentworth Genealogy, English
& American, 3 Vol's, Vol 2, Little Brown & Co.,
Boston, 1878
WIFC.......Wisconsin Federal Census, National Archive
Microfilm
WVFC.......West Virginia Federal Census, National Archive
Microfilm
Wheeler.....Wheeler, Albert Gallatin Jr., History of the
Wheeler Family in America, compiled by the
American College of Genealogy under the direction
of Albert Gallatin Wheeler, Boston, 1914
White I.....White, Emma Siggins, assisted by Martha Humphreys
Maltbey, Genesis of the White Family and The
Scotts of Scott's Hall, Tierman-Dart Printing
Co., Kansas City, MO, 1920
White II....White, Virgil D., Genealogical abstracts of
Revolutionary War Pension Files, Waynesboro, TN,
National Historical Publishing Co., 1990
Whitney.....Whitney, William Lebbeus, Some of the Descendants
of John and Elinor Whitney who settled in
Watertown, Massachusetts, 1635, Edition Private,
Pottsville, PA., M.E. Miller, 1890
Whittelsey..Whittelsey, Charles Barney, Genealogy of the
Whittlesey-Whittelsey Family, New York-London,
Whittlesey House, McGraw-Hill Book Company, Inc.,
1941
Whitten.....Whitten, Phyllis O., Samuel Fogg 1628-1672 His
Ancestors and Descendants, compiled by P.O.
Whitten, Annandale, Virginia, Whitten, 1976
Willard.....Willard, Joseph, & Charles Wilkes Walker, Willard
Genealogy, Boston, MA, Printed for the Willard
Association, 1915
Williams....Williams, George E., A Genealogy of the
Descendants of Robert Goodate/Goodell of Salem,
Massachusetts, West Hartford, CT, G.E. Williams,
1984
Williamson..Williamson, Lois Fooshee, Morrill Lineage, Vol 1
p 21, Augusta, Georgia, Williamson, 1977
Winslow.....Winslow, Kenelm, Winslows and their Descendants
in America, Vol II, Mrs Frances-K (Forward)
Holton, publisher, 1888
WWI.........WWI Roster of Vermont Men and Women in the
Military and Naval Service of Vermont

INDEX

___, Lotte 432
___, Louisa 395
___, Louise 305 395 416
___, Louise E. 295
___, Lucile Day 430
___, Lucinda 322
___, Lucy C. 120
___, Luela T. 315
___, Lyon 65
___, Mabel K. 395 455
___, Margaret 435
___, Margarett 369 387
___, Mariah 384
___, Marie F. 425
___, Marietta 331
___, Marion 445
___, Marion C. 427
___, Maritta/Addie 398
___, Martha 345
___, Martha J. 257 378
___, Martha M. 110
___, Martha R. 274
___, Mary 13 26 78 158 201
229 262 282 294 309 321
354 396 402 403
___, Mary A. 89 178 196 286
400
___, Mary E./A. 341
___, Mary Evaline 181
___, Mary I. 177
___, Mary Janet 445
___, Mary Margaret 170
___, Mary P. 414
___. Mary S. 168
___, Mary W. 416
___, Matilda 199 293 321 455
___, Maud B. 401
___, Maude 300
___, Melissa 166
___, Merle A. 393
___, Mollie 327
___, Myrtle 348
___, Nancy 61 122 300
___, Nancy A. 230 352
___, Nellie M. 197 417
___, Nellie R. 383
___, Niva 408
___, Oliver 47
___, Ollie R. 388
___, Ottie 297
___, Parks 297
___, Pearl 371 450
___, Polly 69 111
___, Rachell 103
___, Rena L. 402
___, Rosa M. 362
___, Ruth 155 337 391
___, Sadie F. 378
___, Sarah 5
___, Sarah A. 202 230 352

___, Sarah B. 216
___, Shipton 380
___, Signe 363
___, Snyder 380
___, Sophia B. 47
___, Stanely 436
___, Susan 201
___, Thelma 448
___, Thompson 447
___, Verleda 321
___, Vesta 350
___, Viola E. 286 399
___, Violet A. 182
___, W.L. 129
___, Winifred M. 333
Abbott, Alice 215 Jane 132
John E. 446
Kendall B. 52 Sophia
Anna 41 89
Abby, Joseph 12
Abel, Tracy 92
Abrams, William 31
Ackerman, Lucina 295
Adams, Aseneth G. 143 E.
George 35 36 Ezzie
(Lizzie) 378 Henry 36 37
John Quincy 106 Justus
379 Lucretia R. 260 May
Gertrude 334 Williams 15
Admiston, Mrs. Stanley A.
448
Alden, Fred C. 259
Aldrich, Everett F. 386 Mina
267 386
Alexander, Elvira 48 James
85 Polycarpus Cushman 47
Robert 85 William D. 163
Allbright, Allia Grover C.A.
188 314
Allen, Benjamin F. 338
Charles S. 175 David 22
Dr. Dudley Peter 316 421
Edith 95 Emily C. 193 315
Jacob and Lucy G. 247
John 13 Lucy A. 137 247
May 361 444 Mercy 27 49
Moses 42 175 Peter 315
Sylvanus Moses 42
Thomas 23 William Van 416
Allis, ___ 42
Allis, Joel 50 Rebecca 201
Alvord, John Pomeroy 91 Noah
20 Rhoda Crampton 190
Amazeen, Dorothy 117
Ambrose, Abigail 5 Dennis 62
Henry 4 Susanna 4
Ames, James M. and Eunice
103 Thurston 208 William
Ambrose 102 103
Amidon, Grace D. 405

475

Anderson, Daisy 411 Mrs.
Elvira 48 Samuel 42
Timothy 48

Andrews, James 83 Kezia 38 83
Stephen 232 William 2

Angier, Amey E. (Reynolds)
248

Appleton, Scott J. 210

Archdale, (Governor) 14, 87

Arey, Margaret Theresa
(Maloney) 323

Arkett, Isabelle 346 John 346

Arms, Daniel 25 Esther 16 25

Arnold, ___ 75 Amanda Julia
101 195

Arsdalen, Amber Mary Van 325

Arthur, Charlotte A. 93 184

Arvilus, Lucy 278

Ashley, Ivy 371 449 Katherine
371 Parson 41

Atcherson, Mary Angeline 173
304 Thomas and Charlotte
304

Atherton, Adonijah 26 Oliver
22

Atkins, Isaac 12

Atwood, Alba 283 Florence
Jane 160 283 Helen E. 163
292 Sadie 125

Audiss, Eldon 439

Austin, Abigail 28 52

Austine, Philura 353

Avery, John M.D. 163 Myrtle
393

Ayers, Mrs. Mabel Miles 404

Babcock, Graca L. 434 Ray H.
352

Bacchus, Eliza Elizabeth 100
192

Bachelder, Sarah 209

Bachman, Sarah I. 423 424

Bacon, Benjamin and Sylvania
L. 164 Martha S. 164

Badgley, Elisa F. 88 174

Bagnell, Ruth 243

Bagness, Edmund Joshua 243

Bailey, Albina Louise
(Powell) 384 Amanda A. 342
Charles B. 288 Charles
Winters 410 Harry H 377
Jesse B. 70 Joanna 51 101
Mary A. 384

Baine, Homer 292

Baker, ___ 125 Addino R. 164

Benomi 60 62 120 Gertrude A.
367 Loren and Cynthia 164
Mary 62 125 Mary A. 224
William 123

Balch, James Bird 326

Balcom, Carrie 166 295 Myron
295

Balderson, Eliabeth 157

Baldwin, Araminta Ann 89 177
Col. Nahum 68 Ella 286
399 Elvira 165

Ball, Frederic Augustus 45
Grace 104

Ballantine, Eleanor 299 411
William 411

Ballard, John 189

Ballou, Sarah 334

Bandt, John 361

Banfield, Sarah 303 414

Bangs, Judith Fox 243 Martha
43 92

Banks, James 37

Barber, Mary E. 105 197

Bardwell, Samuel 16
Tama/Zama 16 William
Ewing 44

Barker, Elisha 144 Mary 20
Mrs. Robert (Severance)
429 Sarah Dix 144 Vernal
144

Barkley, ___ 15

Barlow, Frank 259

Barnard, Allen 42 Capt Salah
25

Barnes, Augustus 140 Ellen
102 Sarah 11

Barnett, Kenneth 452

Barrett, Abram and mary E.
217 Dr. Amasa 101 Sewall
217

Barrow, Zoe 449

Barry, Mr. 456

Barstow, George 285 286 Lot
341 Mary Elizabeth 224
341 Rev T.E. 222

Barter, Flora E. 352 437
Samuel 437

Bartlett, Bert James 353
Joanna 19 37 Josiah 34
Merton E. 343

Barton, ___ 15 Ann 15 20
Anne 20 Emma 281 Joseph
20 Leslie C. 376 Melissa
428 Robert 376 Thomas 20

Bascom, Ezekiel 13 Moses 22

Batchelder, Hilas 66 Samuel
66 Sarah Jane (Severance)
66

Bates, Jane 204

Battles, Thirza 362

Beal, Matthew W. 336

Beale, Joseph S. 260 Sarah
Ann 260

Beals, Dolly (Mary) 41 90
Edward N. 449, Ethel

Beals (Cont.) Florence 449
Sophie Moore 367
Bean, Abby F. (Emily F.) 153
275 Alvin C. 244 Anna M.
330 Dolly 131 Emily 113
402 John 113 Nehemiah and
Rosanna 275 Rebecca W. 322
Sarah C. 71 143
Bearce, Anna 220
Beardsley, Sidney A. 246
Beazley, Florence M. 270
Richard T. and Jennis J.
270
Bedsome, Mary 332
Beeman, David 242 Frederick
C. 242
Been, Emma Jane 78 155 157
Belknap, Harriet 172
Belknapp, Mrs. Clarissa 52
Bell, Alfred 220 Anna 422 Ida
422 Louisa M. 124 220
Nettie 422 Sarah C. 195
318
Bellow, Jonathan 69
Bement, John 160 285 Mary W.
160 285
Benedict, Fannie Buckingham
193 316
Benjamin, H.D. 105
Bennett, Amie 29 Lizzie
(Marston) 131 Lydia 96
Matilda 195 318
Benson, James B. 334
Bent, John Henry 339
Bentley, Martha 96 Porter J.
440
Bently, Martha 47
Benton, Elbridge G. 142
Bentz, Clara Ester 221
Berce, Clara E. (McNaughton)
382
Berry, ___ 263 Almon L. 44
Etta 432 Eimoce 124 220
Mary 84 263 381 Mary E.
148
Beyer, Angie B. (Grace) 332
428
Bickford, Ellen L. 244 367
Eva M 216 336 Mary E. 152
274 Mini Grace 339 Mr. 153
Sumner H. 339
Bigelow, Judson 441
Biggart, Dora D. 290
Biglow, Elisha 139 Lucy/
Lucia 69 70 139
Bilicke, Albert S. 317
Billings, Celestia Matilda
289 405 Dexter 43 Mary
Ann 327 Mrs. Lucy 46
Nathaniel 15

Billington, Walter 357
Bingham, Joseph and Hannah
51 Sarah C. 116
Bird, Hannah 70 137 373
Birge, Nancy 82 164
Bisbee, Nancy 210
Biscoe, Bathsheba (Howe) 190
Thomas 190
Bishop, Stephen W. 367
Black, Nancy 328
Blackford, Sarah Beatrice
418
Blackman, Bradley 119
Charles N. 331
Blades, Rev. John T. 244
Blaisdell, Ella J. 235 236
356
Blake, Laura H. 241 Rev.
S.L. 162, William F. 363
Blan, Isabel 428
Blanchette, Joseph and
Jennie 376 Mary 376
Blethen, Greenleaf 148
Bliss, Jonathan 87
Blizzard, Edith May 382
Lemuel 382
Blodd, Ann C. 210
Blodgett, Araminta 240 Lucy
281
Bombard, Lillie E. 246 369
Bond, Dr. G.W. 249
Bone, Bessie Mabel 360 444
Bonnett, Anna 300 413
Bordwell, David 93
Bosh, Jennie M. 400
Botsford, Marian P 97 188
Marion 313
Bougler, John 21
Bouvier, Dorothy Alyce 339
431
Bowden, Eleanor Miranda 124
219 Jeremiah 125 220
Lydia 124 219
Bowen, Floyd B. 425
Bowker, Hattie E. 386 Mrs.
Edith M. 384
Bowlin, Sophie 96
Bowman, Susan G. 115
Boyden, Calista 90 91
Josephine Etta 369 449
Joshua and Laura 90
Boyton, Sarah/Sally 284
George 161 George P. 117
John 117 Richard and
Polly 161
Bradbury, Mary D. 343
William F. 343
Braddock, Gen 51
Bradley, Jonathan Jr. 240

477

Bradly/Bradley, Martha 134
240
Brady/Broody, Calista B.
324 Edmund T. 324
Brady, Sharon Kay 420
Braley, Martha A. 330
Brastow/Barstow, Elizabeth
E. 223
Bray, Lizzie 338
Briggs, Carrie 177 307 308
Colburn and Orianna 307
Ervin 279 Mary 165 Mary C.
279 Orrison C. 284
Briggsbur, George 267
Brigham, Dr. Amariah 101
Luther 136
Brindle, Joseph E. 446
Britton, Alexander 178
Elizabeth Clark 90 178
Broadbrooks, Abigail
(Severance) 10 Beriah 10
12
Brock, Sarah 284
Brooks, Abigail 87 Joshua 15
Brothers, George James 297
Brouse, Bernice 199
Brown, Isabella M. 330 Alvin
B. 259 Capt. Cyrus 63
Capt. Josiah 57 68 Charles
34 Charles and Margaret
269 Clara (Clarrisa) H.
212 David 118 212 Edmund
D. 118 Elias and Rebecca
75 Elizabeth B. 375
Everett M. 427 Francis M.
410 John R. 115 Jonathan
75 Julia 379 Julius Kinly
411 Laura Ann Frances 254
Mary 55 92 Mary (Marion)
Elizabeth 288 404 Mary E.
152 269 272 Mary Eliza 149
Mehitable 35 76 153 Melvin
E. 427 Sally / Sarah 75
Sarah 34 128 230 Sarah
Jane 363 Timothy 98
Bruce, Martha 33 69
Bryant, Elizabeth 267 386
Elizabeth Ann 386 Isaac
386 James W. 154 Walter
431
Bubier, John and Eliza 226
Buchan, George R. 250 Mrs.
Elizabeth Bird (Severance)
69
Buchanon, Mary 157 279
Buckley, Fred 428
Buell, June Georgetta 446
Bullak/Bullock, Sarah 95
185
Bullen, Amy V. 360 443

Bump, Hannah / Emma 403
Bumps, Susan T. 140
Bundy, Elizabeth 312
Bunker, Alexander Francis
251 Helen 151
Burbank, ___ 233 Elizabeth
77 151 Jonathan 151 Lydia
203 Mary 269 Capt. 39
Burchard, ___ 181
Burge, Ray 413
Burgess, John 17 Joseph 10
Mary (Warden) 10
Burgoyne, General 64
Burke, Capt. 27
Burleigh, Betsey 224 229
Harriet 224 341 Nathaniel
224 341
Burlingame, Asa 78 Asa
(Franklin) 78 Franklin
and Lucy Ann 124 Sarah
(Severance) 78 William N.
124
Burnap, Nancy 124 241
Burnes, Helen 364
Burnham, Dorothy 397 456
Florence M. 391 John 203
Mary 12 17 Melissa Sarah
111 203 R.DeWitt 391
Thomas Jr. Lt. 17
Burnip, Elizabeth J. 253
Burns, Agnes Jane 299 412
413
Burr, Betsy W. 119
Burrage, Edward C. 194
Johnson C. and Emeline
194
Burroughs, James 7
Burton, Elizabeth 128 228
Hazel S. 385
Buss, Cyrus 327 Zephenia 38
Buswell/Buzzell, Eliza J.
141 253 Joseph 56
Butler, B.C. 361 Grace 334
John C. 57 Rebecca 78 155
156
Butterfield, Hannah 135
Buttick, Charlotte M. 376
Buzzard, Mary 157
Buzzel, Perley John 438
Buzzell, Edward 253 Herbert
Eri 438
Cady, Delia Helen 162 289
Elva M. 284 Martha W. 162
Cahoon, Experience 53
Caldwell, Jane 78 156 157
279 Margaret 51 102
Calf, Mr. John 30
Calkins, Amos 204 Gertrude
A. 300 414 Jesse W. and
Lydia A. 300 414

Call, Capt. Silas 156
Callow, Maud 244 367
Cameron, Zaide L. 10
Commander, Sarah S. 298
Camp, Rosa Del 423
Campbell, ___ 303 Christiana
242 Frederick Weston 449
Helen Mae 449 Martha
Langston 169 Rev. 169
Cann, Enos Henry 243 James
366
Cantwell, Sarah 361
Carey, Caleb 328 Daniel F.
141 Ellen Cora 328
Carleton, Rose E. 340
Carlisle, Beverly 453 Lula
Amy (Abbott) 446
Carney, Catherine 338 430
Sophia (Arnie) 203
Carr, Ella A. 427 George Jr.
3 Mable 264
Carroll, James 364 James H.
364 Sophronia 354
Caruso, Emily 408
Case, Charles E. 143 Ethel
Josephine 442 John and Ann
143
Cassidy, Peter 409
Castrine, Baron Sair: 8
Caswell, Della 113 208 Julie
330
Catlin, Sarah 43
Cattle, Mary E. 279 394
Cedarholm, Ida Myrtle 449
Chadwick, John and Mary 66
Mary Jane 66 Rowena 378
Chalifoux, Lorraine 424
Challender, Alton Russell 314
Mary Maxine 314 Willard
Alton 314
Challis, Mary 35
Chamberlain, Sarah M. 240
Simeon 240 Clara Ann
(Holmes) 244 Flora 323
Chambers, Mable 192
Champney, Ebenezer 33 72
Chandler, George A. 209
Hannah 42 Loretta C.
(Lyon) 245 368
Chapin, Giles S. 96 Harriet
A. 85 168 Justin 168
Chapman, Ann Augusta 345 346
Cynthia 225 343 Florence
A. 220 Lorenzo A. 220
Rachel 158 280 Ralph 447
Roswell S. and Augusta 345
Sophronia M. 304
Chappel, Etiole 148 266
William H. 266 Laura May
360 443

Charles, Effie 397
Chase, Aquila and Mary 80
Bessie (Eaton) 337
Charles and Mary Ann 362
Eunice 38 80 George M.
236 John G. 385 Lucia 362
Lucy 240 Moses H. 141
Olive A. 202 322 Phoebe
E. 385 Samuel Brown Jr.
260 Savallah E. 253
Timothy W. 142
Cheatham, Elizabeth 410
Cheney, John Tirrell 165
Maria 70 140 Samuel 140
Chesbro, Charles A. and
Martha J. 306 George A.
306
Child, Barbara Ann 425
Hannah Swan 107 198 James
L. 107 James Loring 198
Childs, Experience 50
Choate, Margaret 18
Chubbuck, Flora Lois 267 385
Church, John 5 Jonathan 5
Mary 5 Sarah "Sadie" 296
408 Scott 408
Churchill, Emily A. 329 S.G.
235
Cilley, Aaron 114 115 116
Andrew Jackson 115 Ardis
M. 376 452 Benjamin Dodge
115 Leonard W. 376 452
Miriam 114
Clapp, Ann R. 147 261 262
Billins 261 Susanna 51
Clark / Morrill / Norris,
Susanna 126
Clark, Betty Agnes
(Severance) 439 Beverly
May (Severance) 439 Carol
Marie (Severance) 439
Charles 356 Eben and
Jennie 144 Edwin 236
Ephraim 100 Frank 377
George A. 144 George L
375 Grace Olive 357
Harold Roberts 357 Harold
Roberts (Severance) 439
Henry F. 102 Ivy Coleman
357 Ivy Coleman
(Severance) 438 John
Alexander (Severance) 439
John and Phebe 85 John H.
85 Luther 47 Margaret E.
375 451 Michael D. 100
Moses D. 377 Norma Elaine
(Severance) 439 Pearl
Naomi 357 Philander T. 96
Roxanna 342 Stewart

Currier (Cont.) 233 Gideon 55
Hannah 129 233 Harvey L.
55 John and Hannah 232
Lorinda 116 210 Lydia 114
115 Mary 258 mary A. 129
233 Sylvina 403
Curtis, Alberta L. 221 Cora
A. 398 Elizabeth 149 Ella
F. 398 Emma G. 382
Curtis, General 180
Horace T. and Caroline M.
398
Cushing, Ida M. 245
Cutler, Olive M. 305 415
Silas 306 415
Cutter, John 33 72
Cutting, Thankful 242
Dailey, Mary Ann 280
Daily, Mary Ann 158
Daken, Simon 15
Dakins, Leonard 81
Dane, James 112
Danforth, ___ 79 256 Janet
416 May A. 124 Nathaniel
C. and Rosetta M. 124
Polly Warner 158
Darby, Margaretta 216
Darrow, Ida Nora 423 Jedediah
83
Dauderman, William J. 455
Davis, Abbie Susan 327 424
Abel 141 Albert H. 345
Alva 256 Arvilda 111 202
Carrie (Severance), Mrs.
G.C. 165 Charles F. 335
Donald W. 387 Ephraim 141
Gaylon 138 Hattie E. 300
414 Issa (Elizabeth) T/L.
142 256 377 John 13 John
P. 238 John P. and Mary A.
238 Lucy 255 Mabel 377
Mary 71 127 141 227 234
Mr. 456 Nancy B. 132
Nettie B. 446 O.J. 280
Plummer M. 235 Sarah 201
Senator 319 Theodore M.
202 Virginia M. 335
Davison, Josiah 14 Vesta May
435
Day, Cornelius 267
Daye, Hardy Alfred 367
De Young, Henrietta 441
Dean, Abigail 56 112
Angenette 173 302
Deane, Stillman H. 125
Dearborn, Captain 64
Dearfield, Capt. Henry 64
Decora, Emma A. 166
DeGroot, Grace 361 444

Delvey, John C. and Mary S.
167
Demeritt, Elizabeth H. 389
453
Dennett, Nathaniel 61
Dennis, Ellen / Nettie A.
216 336 Hiram 402
Derby, Martha A> 120 217
Devore, Rosella 401 Ruth E.
401
Deweir, Martha 113
Dewey, Arlene Wendell 328
DeWitt, Elizabeth Huntington
316 420 Merab Abigail 298
Dewsnap, Charles 236 Sheldon
F. 439
Dibble, Abigail 9 10 John 8
9 10 John Jr. 9 Marietta
347 433, Mary 9 10 Sarah
9
Dickey, John and Sarah 126
Samuel 126
Dickinson, David 47 49 Pearl
440
Dill, Ansel S. 117
Dillingham, Charles 417
Dinsmore, Cassandana 285
Eliza J. 175 306 Mary 74
Dixon, Margaret 85
Doane, Julia E. 215 Noah 215
Dodge, Addison and Mary B.
270 Betsey 67 133 Joseph
134 William H. 270
Dods / Dodds, Catherine Ann
137 247
Doe, Marion Allene 364 447
Warren W. 364 447
Dole, David 255 Eliza J. 255
Enoch 44 Mehitable 141
Sarah 37
Dollard, Florence E. 126 222
Dolliver, Susan 62
Donavan, Sarah H. 345
Douglas, Hannah M. 66 174
Douglass, Cynthis Davy 44 93
David 448 Mary Elizabeth
174
Dow, Alice O. 238 Joel 204
John 12 William 323
Downing, Martha J. 241 363
Downs, Huldah 355 356
Drake, Francis 226 Judith
Jane (Wentworth) 452
Ransom 89
Draper, Henry O. 94 Lyman
and Mary Ann 94
Dresser, Carrie L. 155 391
Drew, Ray Sibley 360
Driscoll, Ella C. 392 Ellen
C. 278 John 278 392

484

Holcomb, Mr. 77 Rebecca
(Sweet) (Swett) 35 77 156
Holden, Elizabeth C. 322
Rachel Aldana 385
Holmes, Benjamin 244 Ruth 134
Holt, Sarah H. 245 William
and Susan A. 245
Holton, Lillie Clarrisa 359
442
Hood, General 180
Hooper, Frank 295 John 99
John and Jane 99
Hopkins, Albert B. 398
Caroline 397 456 Constance
62 Heber Augustus 398
Oscar 397 Stephens 62
Horton, Abraham 116 Nellie T.
332 Samuel Benjamin 116
Hosley, Adolphus 85 David 25
Luke M. 85 Theron and
Orilla 85
Houghton, James R. and
Frances 312 Mary F. 187
Mary E. 312
Houston, George 211
How, Ichabod 33
Howard, Belinda / Melinda 47
96 Elizabeth 98
Howland, Mary 28
Howlett, Mary 140
Hoxie, Mary 219 Stella Lucia
425
Hoyt, Charles S. 376 Edward
F. 376 Frederick A. 273
George A. and Sophia J.
273 Hannah 27 50 Jonathan
50 Sarah (West) 238
Hubbard, Daniel A. 264
Elizabeth 98 Wendell P.
264
Hubbell, Julius C. 174
Huff, Anna May 377 Persis E.
209
Huggins, ___ 15 Capt. John and
Clarissa 86 Elizabeth 87
Elizabeth Simmons 169
Hannah 39 85 169 Hester
(Severance) 169 John 85
86
Humphreys, Ann 21
Hunkins, ___ 65 Charles H. 432
Olla Belle 432
Hunt, Ellen C. 168 Emily B.
79 159 Linus and Emily 168
Hunter, Harvey M. 375 Mary L.
375
Huntley, Phebe 279 393 Phoebe
455
Huntoon, Frances A. 205

Hupp, Mary 78 157 Phillip
157 158
Hurd, Ruth Bertha 386
Hurlbut, Sarah 226
Hussey, Helen 259 380 Sarah
391 Sarah E. 153 275
Hutchin Capt. 30
Hutchins, H. 57 Lois A. 382
Lt. Col. Gordon 68
Hutchinson, ___ 83 George 211
Hattie 440
Huusko, Mrs. Marianne
"Molly" 453
Hyde, Luman C. 83
Hyna, Augusta 309 416
Ingales, Sellena 88
Ingalls, Mary C. 212 Sellena
B. 174
Irvins, Lucy 323
Jackman, Cora B. 391 Eli and
Hannah 391
Jackson, Charles 108
Jacobs, John 305 May
Gertrude 186
Jacoby, John 204
Jacques, Effie Rae 419
Frederic P. 212 Nathan E.
and Pamelia 212
Jamerson, Eunice S. 85 168
Wintrhop 168
Jameson, John 124
Jaques, Elbena 282
Jeffers, Family of 80
Jeffords, Samuel King 87
Jeffrey, Harriet Newell 98
189
Jenkins, Alma 449 Elizabeth
R. 165
Jenne, Henry 29
Jennes, Marion R. 392
William H. and Mrs.
Elizabeth 392
Jewell, Jacob 127 341 James
Pierce 139 Lydia 63 127
223 227 Martha (Quimby
127 Ruhama B. 234
Johnson, (Governor) 86 ___
248 Benjamin and
Elizabeth 122 charles E.
216 David 108 Elisha 138
250 Elisha and Elizabeth
216 Ethel 454 J. Brainerd
108 Julius Christopher 83
Mary 403 Mary Jane 138
250 Nelson W. 122 Rhoda
Eveline 108 Roxalene 88
173 Roy R. 293 William B.
210 William R. and Emily
454 Jama 300

Jones Asahel and Catherine
162 Corcina 81 Ebenezer
20 Harriet 281 395 Hattie
322 Myra 342 Rebecca 13
Jones 19 20 Sant 178 Sarah
126 221 William 335 348
Jordan, Amos 124
Joslyn, Arzelia 89 177
Charles 177
Joynes, Gertrude Nivell 424
Judkins, Hannah Jane 132 Joel
132 Mrs. Belle (Severance)
264 Obidia 112 Samuel 147
148
Kaime, Benjamin 225 343
Hannah J. 225 343
Kamehameha, King V. 106 198
Karow, Orville L. 439
Kaven, Herman 325 Nora 325
Keep, Rev. John 38
Keimbach, Fannie B. 373
Keith, Isaac 345 Lavina Delia
226 345
Kellam, Charles 327
Kelley, Naomi 119
Kellogg, ___ 319 Ann 167 Anna
10 16 Captain 16 19 Martin
16 Rollo 221
Kelly, Andrew and Mary 174
William 174
Kelsea, Robert 205
Kelsey, Ansel Wallace 289 405
Lena Adelia 289 405
Kendall, Hattie B. 210
Kendrick, Abigail 65 131
Keniston, James 427 Mary
Elizabeth 272
Kenney, Mrs. Nancy
(Severance) 429
Kenny, Laurana 168
Kent, Arthur Stevens 397
Margaret Wilson 397 456
Thomas 60
Keyser, Laura 389 Laura E.
453
Kidder, Aaron 33
Kilborn, Nathaniel 35
Kilburn, Hannah 220
Kilby / Kilbourne, Jerusha 69
136 246
Kiler, Isaac 178 John 178
Kilgore, Charlotte 152
Kimball, Abigail 3 4 7 9 14
55 John 94 Richard 3 58
Samuel and Electa 94
Thomas 2 Ursula (Scott) 3
57 William H. 202
King, Eli P. 33 Eliza 77 152
Flora H. 191 George 208
Patsy 451

Kinyon, T.L. 91
Kirby, Abraham 80 Clark 81
John S. 81 Mary 38 80 Mr.
38
Kingaman, Eliza 191
Knapp, Col. Lyman Enos 162
Esther 111 203 Samuel Jr.
and Deborah 203
Knapton, Roy C. 377
Knight, Andrew L. 226
Nathaniel and Sarah 226
Knowles, ___ 15
Koomry, Amelia 185
Korman, Emma B. 306
Krannewitter, Oliver 419
Kryzaniak, Josephine 376
Labar, Rev. Frank 408
Ladd, Hannah 56 115 Matilda
269 389 Samuel 389
Ladison, Frank 422 Matilda
321 422
Laferty, Fannie 397
Lagrow, Betsey 422
Lamb, Charles 358 Elvira L.
216 Martha 134 239 Rev.
Nehemiah 239 359 Susan
134 239
Lambert, Dell 202 323 Lewis
and Delvine 323
Lamprey, ___ 432
Lamson, Freedom and Isabel
J. 222
Lancaster, Frank 338 Lulu
Ethel 338 339 Sophia B.
123 218
Lance, Susan 58 118
Landon, E.P. 83 Henry and
Harriet 103 Mary A. 289
405 Nellie M. 103 Zelia
L. 177
Landry, Mary Jane 282
Lane, Anna M. 358 441
Catherine B. 408 Elijah
125 Frank 362 Joshua 146
Mary A.
Langdon, Woodbury 151
Larrabee, Angeline C. / J.
225 343 David 225 343
Latimer, Amos 240 Ida L. 290
405 John Mulford 182 Lucy
240 Mary T. 92 182
Laverack, John and Janet 432
Law, Emily Elizabeth
McKenzie 297
Lawry, Eliza Jane 259
Leach, Sarah 368
Lear, Frances Ann 214 John
and Clara 214
Learned, A.F./R.F. 217 218

Leavitt, Eben 231 Sally 64
129 231 233 Sarah E. 123
Lee, John S. 232 Samuel W.
99 Tobias 87
Leer, Francis Ann 118
Legate, Nancy 87
Leggett, John 172 Nancy P.
172
Legree, ___ 15
Leighton, Martha Augusta 275
Sarah 150
Leonard, David Cooley 41
Laura 161 286 Sylvester
and Lydia 91
Leslie, Arthur R. 448 Elsie
M. 367 448
Lester, Alice 307 Edward and
Olive 307
Lewellyn, Jack 439
Lewis, Effie E. 340 Elizabeth
40 George 340 Gladys 340
Jessie L. 320 Melissa 96
Muraluisa (Melissa) 187
Ruby 412 Susan 299
Libby / Libbey, Hanson 131
234
Libby, Elizabeth 224 342 437
Isaac 224 342 351 437
Joseph 342 Lizzie 351
Light, Capt. John 25
Lincoln, Hazel Anna 449 Levi
Prescott 449
Lindsay, Dulcena 252 James
252 Lucy C. 218
Linscott, Annie M. 267 386
Linsey, Mary E. 150 268
Linsley / Lindsley, Hannah
Maria 44 94
Little, Colby 427 elizabeth
394 Lt. 156
Littlefield, Fred 378 Mary E.
(Maud) 378
Locke, Lucinda L. 365
Lockwood, Edward John 446
Florence Eva 446 Karen C.
375
Loeffler, Charles Martin 421
Long, Dr. David 193 Diana 50
100 Ebenezer 29 mary H.
101 193 Rev. 455 Ruth 17
29 William 29
Longever, Mary Ann 351 437
Loomer, John and Annie 381
Mary 381
Lord, Joseph 15
Loveland, Rev. Samuel C. 243
Lovell, Lydia 61 122 Polly
121
Lovering, Sidney H. 382
Lowe, Mary A. 440

Lucas, E.M. 109
Lukens, Olive Mae 418
William Mathias 418
Lumbert, Mr. 10
Lunt, Almira/Elmira C. 62
125 Margaret 336
Lyman, Martha Elizabeth 172
300 301 Thomas 172 300
Lynch, Elizabeth 6 Gabriel 6
John 181
Lyon, C.H. 361 Charles 41
111 Isaac Keith 368 Sarah
368
Lyons, Christina 423 Rev.
Angus 384
Lyshow, Hattie 338
Mac Donald, John 390
Mac Kenzie, Grace 390 453
MaCall, Martha 359
MacDermaid, John 401 Maud E.
401
MacLeod, Harold 427
Maddox, Sarah A. (Clay) 322
Maddry, Katherine 409
Mahan, Caroline A. 226 John
A. and Harriet 226
Maier, Mrs. Abbie
(Severance) 264 265
Malcouson, Mary (J.H.) 139
251
Mallard, William 150
Mallory, Anne 296 407 Mrs.
Nola 384
Maloney, Margaret theresa
Arey 323
Maloon, Mehitabel 56 207
Mankey, Frank 361
Mann, Lucy 41
Mansfield, Allen 41 Robert
and Prudence 355 Sarah
232 355
Manuel, Margaret A. 150 267
Mapes, Ecrasny 101
March, John 29 30
Marier, Mrs. Robert
(Severance) 429
Markham, Lovilla Jane
(Jennie) 188 312 Ransom
312
Marsh, Chester 99 John 13
Samuel Esq. 58
Marshall, Ada E. 280 394
Col. 58 Mrs. Susan
(Bartlett) 115 Sarah J.
141 254 T.J. 394
Marston, Albion 131 Horace
T. 125 Jason P. 131 230
Shubael 131 William and
Elizabeth 125
Martell, John Raymond 367

Severance (Cont.) 369 Albert
89 123 140 165 166 167 176
211 239 269 282 Albert
Bernie 446 Albert Deloyd
249 Albert F. 341 Albert
G. 178 Albert Gallatin 176
Albert Henry/Bert Henry
363 445 Albert Jefferson
425 Albert M. 196 333
Albert T. 122 Albert Tefft
122 Albert W. 176 Alberta
M. 436 Alberto D. 253
Albertto D. 256 Albion 140
277 281 385 Albion J. 379
Aldis 424 Alexandria 103
319 Alfred 117 143 144 145
167 204 257 325 377 Alfred
D. 310 417 Alfred E. 289
Alfred H. 378 Alfred P.
117 212 377 Alice 155 156
157 216 228 232 293 344
404 432 Alice Amidon 338
Alice B. 172 Alice E. 345
Alice Edna 116 Alice Eliza
243 Alice Eva 261 Alice
Frances 432 Alice L. 344
Alice M. 168 344 Alice
Margaret 288 Alice Maria
306 Alice Marian 444 Alice
May 198 238 Alice N. 219
Alice W. 379 Allen 316
Allen Dudley 316 Allison
Augustus 385 Alma 311
Almeda 40 Almira 52 Almira
M. 93 Alonzo 229 232 273
350 354 Alonzo Clark 152
273 Alonzo F. 273 Alonzo
Miner 212 334 Alphonso/
Alphonzo 119 120 Alta May
441 Alton 408 Aluira G.
255 Alvah 82 Alvan A 91
Alvin 85 168 422 Alvin A.
181 Alvin W. 416 Alvira
111 223 224 Alzira 118
Amanda 50 75 208 431
Amanthus 171 Amber 424
Ambrose 288 336 402
Ambrose Warren 216 336
Amelia 91 208 Amelia J. 93
Amelia S. 91 Amittai 89
Ammarilla J. 280 Andrew
225 343 352 Andrew G. 200
321 Andrew J. 223 224 225
340 342 343 Andrew
Pettengill 65 Angeline 136
297 Angeline Melissa 103
Angeline Theresa 99 Angie
343 Angie L. 246 348 Angie
Leona 351 Anita Jean 419
Ann 114 178 211 Ann Barnum

Severance (Cont.) 81 Ann
Elisabeth 192 Ann
Elizabeth 21 Ann M. 125
240 Ann Maria 208 Anna
16 30 31 56 63 68 70 107
139 281 322 364 404 Anna
Douglas 305 Anna E. 294
Anna F. 213 Anna Frances
213 Anna Jane 135 Anna
Lois 364 Anna M. 197
Anna Maria 205 Anna Maud
300 413 Anna P. 219 396
Anne 127 Annetie Bell
(Nettie) 347 Annice A.
324 Annie 112 175 Annie
A. 295 407 Annie Belle
317 Annie Douglas 305
Annie Etta 365 Annie J.
277 Annie K. 273 Annie
M. 203 Annie Maria 366
Anson 251 Anson Biglow
139 251 Antionette 95
Anthony 238 Anthony Peck
171 299 Apollos 52 108
Archie Floyd 434 Archie
M. 379 Archie William 376
451 Ardela 117 Ardela K.
212 Ardella 140 Ardelle
253 Ardith M. 258 Arlene
382 453 Arlo J. 399
Arnold 242 Arnold Holmes
243 366 Arethusa 38
Ariel Kendrick 76 149
Arnold 135 Artemus 75 267
Artemus Cushman 267 385
Arthur 178 789 190 238
255 279 282 314 318 358
367 375 393 439 454 456
Arthur B. 348 433 Arthur
Burton 433 434 Arthur C.
190 Arthur E. 280 395 399
Arthur Edson 294 Arthur
Edwards 177 Arthur F. 255
375 391 Arthur G. 241
Arthur J. 164 Arthur L.
353 Arthur Leason 184 311
439 Arthur M. 158 280
Arthur Rodney 156 157 279
Arthur Thomas 408 Arthur
W. 397 Arthur Washburn
448 Arthur Winfred 456
Artimus 149 267 386
Artimus (Artie) 385
Artimus F. 267 Artimus
Jr.149 Artiss Eveline 402
Asa 34 43 68 70 71 74 75
89 90 91 127 129 143 145
225 232 233 341 344 351
352 431 432 434 Asa
Albion 155 277 Asa C. 233

Severance (Cont.) Asa F. 223
341 Asa French 224 341 Asa
W. 342 351 Asa Waldo 229
230 342 351 Asa Walter 228
229 Asabel Jones 162 Asaph
40 44 45 Asaph C./Asa C.
177 307 Asel C./Azel E.
218 219 Asel F./Azel 338
Aseph 88 Atwood 131 230
352 Augusta 390 Augusta J.
280 Augusta L. 166
Augustus 165 Augustus N.
83 161 164 Aurelia 89
Aurelia T. 114 115 Authur
J. 167 Austin Earle 438
Ava 217 Ave 428 Avery 84
166 186 456 Avery W. 95
Avesta 267 Azubah 38
Azubiah 81 Barbary Ann 122
B. Russell 399 Barbara 378
429 Barbara Lois 340
Barton Thomas 436 Baxter
398 Baxter Horace 398
Beatrice 181 428 Beatrice
C. 396 Beatrice I. 425
Beatrice May 340 Belle 91
148 264 Belle G. 324 Belva
(Belna) 436 Ben Jr. 156
Benjamin 5 6 7 9 18 19 29
30 35 56 62 63 66 67 73 75
77 78 79 80 110 112 115
117 123 124 125 132 133
134 142 146 147 151 153
154 155 156 157 158 156
157 158 200 217 219 238
241 262 271 279 362 365
374 441 Benjamin F. 200
241 280 365 395 Benjamin
Franklin (Frank) 90 94 178
200 Benjamin Jr. 147 155
156 241 Benjamin L. 445
Benjamin C. 123 Benjamin
Otis 217 Benjamin Samuel
204 Benjamin True 210
Benjamin W. Benjamin
Warren 247 249 371 137
Bentley Jane 440 Benton
165 166 294 Bernice 320
414 436 450 Bernice A. 379
Berniece 400 Bert 350 370
371 372 445 455 Bert D.
(Deloyd) 249 371 Bert V.
396 Bert Vernon 372 Bertha
197 396 Bertha (Beatrice
E.) 181 Bertha R. 193
Berton 350 Bertrand Ernest
246 369 Beryl S. 428
Bessie A. 442 Bessie C.
332 Bessie Eva 242 Bessie
Lill 316 Bessie Louisa 366

Severance (Cont.) Bessie O.
428 Betsa 76 Betsey
/Betsy 46 57 60 67 111
112 134 233 360
Betty/Betsey 65 Betty
Agnes 439 Beulah 311
Beulah Lucile 444 Beverly
Isaac 386 Beverly May 439
"Bill" 419 422 Billings
E. 323 Birney 446 Birney
Charles 363 446 Bishop
276 277 392 Bishop C. 276
Bishop Clayton/Clayton
Bishop 277 392 Blance M.
402 Blanche 432 449
Blanche M. 400 "Bob" 422
Bradley 133 Bradley W.
272 Brewer Samuel 119 215
Brian 453 Burnice 333
Burnice M. 318 Burt
Rowley 267 Burton
Cordenio 318 422 Burton
D. (B. Dean) 210 Burton
T. "Bert" 436 "Buster"
426 429 Byron 92 184 281
Byron G. 423   C. Earl
"Buster" 426 C. Oscar 176
C.E. 379 C.G. 251 Caleb
31 56 60 61 119 120 121
122 Calvin 44 98 190
Calvin Cuyler 94 Calvin
L. 110 198 321 Camilla 96
Camilla S. 95 Carl Libby
438 Carleen M. 454 Carlos
(Harlow Erastus) 124
Carlton 406 Carlton Jr.
406 Carlton Metcalf 191
Carlton Spencer 292 406
Carlton Spencer III 406
Carol 431 Carol Corrinne
436 Carol Marie 439
Carolina 45 Caroline 103
118 171 204 245 410
Caroline A. 125 Caroline
M. 369 449 Caroline Maria
122 Caroline Sarah 122
Caroline T. 122 Caroly
410 Carrie 206 262 326
385 405 406 Carrie Ann
196 Carrie C. 274 Carrie
E. 308 Carrie F. 352
Carrie H. 223 260 Carrie
Josephine 192 Carrie
Margaret 443 Carrie
Ophelia 101 Carrie R. 304
Carrie W. 103
Carroll/Harold 340
Carroll Clark 346 Carroll
Ernest 369 Carroll G. 340
Carroll Harold 340

Severance (Cont.) Cassell 196
319 320 Cassell Jr. 320
Catharine 25 Catharine
Mercy 99 Catherine 426
Catherine E. 455 Catten 35
Cecil 320 396 Cecil
Elizabeth 297 Cecil Floyd
435 Cecil G. 409 Cecil M.
445 Cephas Clesson 87 172
Chandler 84 167 173 303
304 Channing 244 Charles
52 85 89 90 100 103 105
106 108 109 118 119 120
134 145 155 156 157 161
168 178 179 192 199 201
212 213 217 220 235 236
239 267 271 275 278 284
286 289 300 302 305 309
321 326 339 341 345 355
356 359 363 384 385 389
391 396 399 401 414 422
425 429 441 446 Charles A.
124 219 294 406 Charles
Alfred 339 Charles Allen
89 Charles Almon 269 389
454 Charles Barber 198
Charles Burton 434 Charles
C. 166 174 291 305 322 391
Charles C. Sr 305 308
Charles C.P. 90 179
Charles Carlton 290 405
Charles Coleman 132 236
356 Charles Consider 88
174 Charles Curtis 84
Charles Dori 301 415
Charles Douglass 175
Charles E. 201 456 Charles
Earl 172 302 Charles Edgar
74 259 380 Charles Edwin
122 Charles Elijah 253
Charles Ezra 241 363
Charles F. 92 281 339 395
400 Charles F.G. 355 438
Charles Francis 173 303
339 Charles Frederic
Malcom 192 314 Charles
Frederick 245 Charles H.
160 199 202 213 284 318
321 322 327 389 413 425
454 Charles Harvey 339 342
Charles Herbert 169
Charles I 248 Charles
Jotham 361 444 Charles Jr.
109 Charles K. 217 Charles
L. 185 222 335 Charles
Lamb 239 358 Charles
Leland 369 Charles Louis
442 Charles Lucien 241 363
Charles Lucius 248 Charles
M 155 220 275 401 Charles

Severance (Cont.)Marcellan
284 Charles N. 171 221
414 Charles Nelson 401
Charles Nicholas 300 414
Charles O. 274 Charles R.
232 355 436 Charles
R.(Chuck) 409 Charles
Robinson 355 Charles
Ryland 403 Charles S. 213
Charles Sands 250 Charles
Sidney 301 Charles Sr.
174 Charles Stanley 445
Charles Sydney 415
Charles V. 329 Charles W.
92 105 144 179 197 200
206 226 246 257 310 345
393 395 Charles Walter
272 Charles Weaver
Pulsipher 326 Charles
Wesley 345 Charlie 220
Charlie Alfred 221
Charlie D. 304 Charlie
Jacob 440 Charlie R. 393
Charlie W. 407 Charlotte
21 82 213 Charlotte
Converse 103 Charlotte
Elizabeth 433 Charlotte
Emily 242 Charlotte Jane
377 Charlotte Louisa 122
Charlotte S. 122 Charry
M. 83 Chester 87 171 172
301 382 Chester Alfred
434 Chester C. (G.) 301
Chester Cole 360 444
Chester Gilbert 301
Chester L. 264 382
Chester M. 400 Chester
Robert 435 Chester S. 329
427 Chester S. (W.) 301
Chester Snively 455
Chester Wells 172 301
Christina 49 Christopher
144 145 248 257 258 378
Christopher/John Ellis
258 378 Christopher Jr.
258 Church 158 Church B.
280 Cinderilla 280 Clara
92 148 178 189 214 249
287 333 386 Clara Anna
260 Clara B. 263 Clara
Belle 185 314 Clara
Catherine 358 Clara Edith
442 Clara F. 381 Clara M.
197 Clara Mable 338 Clara
Maude 349 Clara May 182
Clara S. 332 Clarance 178
Clare Sullivan 365
Clarence 78 92 203 286
309 385 399 Clarence A.
369 Clarence Arthur 439

Severance (Cont.) Clarence B.
401 Clarence E. 256
Clarence L. 176 277 246
Clarence R. 395 Clarence
T. (O.) 381 Clarenda L.
277 Clarinda Arabella 175
Clariot P. 304 Clarissa 44
91 92 93 98 161 279
Clarissa Adeline 87
Clarissa Ann 158 281
Clarissa Champion 90
Clarissa Chapman 346
Clarissa F. 179 Clarissa
T. 310 Clark 226 Clarke
346 432 Clarrisa A. 173
Claud F. 325 Claude Milton
291 Claudia 378 Clayton
168 Clayton B. 277 Clayton
F. 185 Clayton M. 422
Clementine 145 Cliff B.
338 Clifford 287 400 426
Clifford Arthur 440
Clifford B. 379 Clifford
Franklin 434 Clifford H.
400 Clifford L. 330
Cliffton Eugene 432
Clifton Eugene 401 Clifton
Leroy 435 Clinton 286 399
Clinton D. 401 Clinton
Earle 329 426 Cloe 22
Clorinda 134 Clyde T. 362
Coburn R. 454 Coello B.
252 373 Colinda Elizabeth
122 Collamer 139 251
Collamer G. 251 Columbus
Robert 299 Consider 40 88
Cora 272 274 422 Cora Ann
361 393 Cora E. 204 Cora
L. 321 Cora Leslie 205
Cora Lucille 435 Cora M.
274 Cordean 422 Cordenio
319 Cordenio A. 319
Cordenio Arnold 196 319
Coresfelia 217 Corneily
284 Craig 431 Crotia L.
392 Curtis 89 176 297
Curtis D. 32 164 Curtis
Leroy 433 Cutler Frost 305
415 Cynthia 27 48 119
Cynthia Electa 300 Cyprian
62 125 Cyrus 68 87 124 137
171 247 243 Cyrus B. 124
Cyrus J. 414 Cyrus Job 300
414 Cyrus Wells 171 299
412 Cyrus William 300 413
Dale 456 Daniel 8 9 13 19
20 24 26 32 33 38 47 66 71.
72 81 96 133 134 146 148
150 151 187 240 244 263
264 287 363 423 Daniel

Severance (Cont.) Arms 47 96
Daniel D. 174 Daniel H.
233 Daniel Healey 96 187
Daniel Jr. 133 Daniel L.
159 Daniel N. 240 Darius
81 163 Darrow 201 David
26 41 43 45 46 56 90 96
111 112 113 114 151 189
201 203 204 207 209 212
271 324 331 390 423 424
David Allen 96 190 David
C. 331 David E. 271 390
423 David Edwin 272 390
David J. 294 407 David
Jr. 90 David R. 436 David
Smith 98 189 David W. 111
202 324 424 Dean 429 Dean
Charles 447 Dean Charles
Jr 447 Dean R. 335
Deborah 146 147 Debra 429
DeForest 265 383 Delbert
264 382 384 Delbert
A./Adelbert 266 382 383
452 Delia H. 374 Della
323 382 397 Della M. 256
402 Delphina Arabelle 148
Delvia Clara Bell 148
Delvina 385 386 Denzel
409 Denzil 296 Derrick
Dutton 305 415 Detta 251
Dewey 424 Dewitt 369
Diana H. 142 374 Diana
Long 175 Diane Mae 420
Diantha Smith 132 Dinah
12 Don 408 Donald 350 429
Donald Bertram 444 Donald
C. 378 Donald Edwin 440
Donald F. 416 Donald
James 206 Donald M. 400
Donald Michael (Adopted)
419 Donald Porter 437
Donna 429 Donna North 378
Donna P. 315 Dora 384 390
Dora Isabella 438 Dorance
H. 401 Doris 429 Doris
Amidon 405 Dorotha 27
Dorothy 34 232 281 382
398 408 413 417 429 453
Dorothy E. 430 Dorothy
Grace 440 Dorothy H. 377
Dorothy Jean 431 Dorothy
L. 449 Dorothy North 410
Douglas 362 Douglass 431
Durward Lawrence 387
Drucilla 26 E. 231 234
331 E. Scott 295 E.W. 264
Earl Clarendon 302 Earl
D. 182 Earl Ernest 325
Earl Franklin 387 Earl J.
201 Earl L. 283 334 429

Severance (Cont.) Earl Lee
385 Earl Lewis 361 444
Earl Longley (Volney) 392
454 Earl Ross 405 Earl V.
455 Earle Leroy 397 Eben
205 Eben F. 111 203 Eben
Jr. 111 Ebenezer 3 4 5 6 7
8 10 11 12 13 17 18 20 24
28 29 33 34 111 136 137
139 162 165 173 246 373
Ebenezer Jr. 111 136 Eddie
249 434 Edgar 365 448
Edgar Carlos 242 365 Edgar
F. 219 338 Edgar M. 361
445 Edith 146 160 197 263
Edith F. 395 Edith I 396
Edith L. 330 Edith Leila
303 Edith Lilian 371 Edith
M. 196 384 Edmund 289 405
Edmund Kirby 162 289 404
405 Edna 456 Edna Frances
300 414 Edna Martha 446
Edna May 446 Edson J. 165
293 294 Edson S. 168 296
Edward 3 165 268 333 348
383 434 Edward Byron 452
Edward (Alfred) 143 Edward
Clark 163 Edward Clifford
348 434 Edward D. 374
Edward E. 91 201 Edward
Hitchcock 102 Edward J.
211 Edward Martin 424
Edward P. 456 Edward W.
265 383 Edward Woodman 254
255 Edwin 100 178 202 309
369 Edwin C. 288 Edwin
Cuthbert 89 Edwin J. 295
369 Edwin James 166 Edwin
John 449 Edwin K. 191
Edwin Percy 273 Edwin S.
293 406 Edwin W. 191 Effa
K. 333 Effie A. 144 Effie
Blance 411 Effie E. 376
Egbert 265 Egbert D. 265
Ela Eliza 274 Elbert 313
417 418 Elbridge 234 235
236 Elbridge G. 131 223
227 230 234 235 236 Elda
348 Elda Fae 434 Eleaner
26 140 Eleanor Alice 424
Eleanor May 318 Eleanor S.
373 Electa E. 89 Eliab 110
201 Elias J./Elias James
112 205 206 Elias J.W. 169
Elias James W. 297 Elihu
27 28 41 50 52 90 Elijah
/Elisha 24 28 38 43 70 83
92 93 139 328 344 Elijah
Charles 226 344 Elisha F.
205 325 Eliphalet G. 231

Severance (Cont.) Eliza 60
83 87 120 128 229 287 423
Eliza Ann 169 Eliza E.
263 Eliza J. 303 Eliza
Jane 210 Eliza K. 149
Eliza Pendleton 121
Elizabeth 3 5 6 13 14 17
19 30 37 48 56 57 63 78
87 89 97 99 146 148 150
190 204 240 250 268 275
277 279 338 341 379 409
421 445 Elizabeth A. 118
Elizabeth Adelaide 270
Elizabeth "Bessie Lill"
421 Elizabeth (Lizzie)
Belle 314 Elizabeth Bird
69 250 Elizabeth Bulah
170 298 Elizabeth C. 147
Elizabeth Gill 410
Elizabeth Grace 108
Elizabeth H. 163
Elizabeth Hall 116
Elizabeth Isabel 213
Elizabeth J. 170 280
Elizabeth L. 241
Elizabeth M. 102 427
Elizabeth N. 305
Elizabeth Nancy 175
Elizabeth S. 126
Elizabeth T. 181 185
Elizabeth Turner 182 Ella
214 215 253 284 313 325
333 423 Ella F. 144 336
Ella Jane 397 Ella M. 313
Ella Marguerite 313 Ella
Maud 299 Ella May 318
Ella R. 286 Ellan Jane
400 Ellen 104 177 198 288
429 Ellen B. 282 Ellen
Catherine 441 Ellen D. 93
Ellen Josephine 191 Ellen
Maria 100 246 288 Ellen
R. 91 Ellen S. 335 Ellen
Sophronia 242 Ellenor 374
Ellie 321 322 Ellington
Glenn 411 Ellis V. 126
Ellis W. 379 Ellsworth
412 Ellsworth W. 295 406
Elly H. 144 Elma 203 214
Elma May 206 Elmer 197
307 310 320 440 Elmer D.
177 307 Elmer W. 182
Elmer Warren 310 Elmira
239 264 Elmira (Clarissa
L.) 125 Elmira M. 97
Elnora 278 394 Eloi 251
Elsie Aline 323 Elsie C.
304 Elsie Helen 238 Elsie
L. 323 Elva 105 328
Elvira 85 214 Elvira

Severance (Cont.) Electa 176
Elvira Janette 167 Elvira
M. 248 Elvira Minerva 248
Elwood L. 393 Elzina 71
142 Emelia J. 94 Amelia T.
56 Emeline 146 Emeline L.
147 Emeline M. 126
Emerancy 87 Emerson 306
Emerson M. 176 Emery 160
163 195 283 284 Emilla 71
Emily 45 50 114 116 133
153 171 265 284 Emily
Aileen 372 Emily J. 132
Emily L. 241 Emily M. 355
Emily Morgan Rotch 317
Emily William 93 Emma 141
157 162 166 178 217 220
221 243 248 251 262 270
292 325 362 400 401 Emma
A. 120 121 Emma Adelia 162
Emma H. 109 Emma J. 115
214 Emma Jane 195 361 423
Emma L. 163 Emma/Lovisa
403 Emma M. 278 Emma R.
231 284 Emma S. 248 Emma
Sophia 242 Emma Viola Jane
294 Emmie (Elizabeth) 347
Enoch 233 Enoch A. 139 252
375 Enoch Q. 233 Enoch
Quimby 129 233 Enos 38 82
83 Ephraim 4 6 7 11 12 17
18 29 30 31 32 33 62 64 70
71 72 73 74 75 126 129 132
139 140 141 143 144 145
146 147 148 149 150 225
231 232 233 263 266 356
Ephraim/Nathaniel 73 147
Ephraim Carlton 131
Ephraim F. 232 Ephraim
Hubbard 99 190 Ephraim Jr.
73 Ephraim Sr. 70 73
Erahaman 132 Erasmus 195
Erasmus Cordenio 101 195
Erasmus Darwin 101 Erastus
40 Erastus Kendrick 131
Ernest 251 257 292 334 377
378 429 Ernest A. 429
Ernest B. 377 Ernest
Bertrand 256 377 Ernest E.
184 Ernest Elton 311
Ernest Lemuel 444 Ernest
Sprague 380 Ernest
Stillman 394 455 Ernest
Walter 337 Erwin L. 395
Estella Bertha 325 Estelle
369 Ester Ellen 414 Esther
26 135 Esther A. 441
Esther G. 356 Esther Lois
444 Esther May 335 Esther
R. 401 Ethel 333 384 Ethel

Severance (Cont.) C. 395
Ethel Estelle 323 Ethel
Jean 443 446 Ethel M. 257
365 Ethel May 346 Ethel
N. 364 Ethel Pearl 381
Ethell 267 Ethelyn Daisy
185 Etta 265 Etta Alma
377 Etta C. 368 Etta M.
255 Etta May 301 Ettie C.
246 Eugene 176 249 287
358 405 440 Eugene E. 247
Eugene H. 249 334 429
Eugene Kincaid 195 318
Eugene L. 401 Eugenia G.
222 Eugenia Marie 440
Eunice 22 41 46 80 81 195
199 325 Eunice A. 120
Eunice M. 112 Eusebia 38
81 Eva 239 262 286 287
312 348 Eva E. 187 Eva
Florence 388 Eva G. 431
Eva M. 381 Eva Mable 380
Eva P. 259 Evaline 85
Evan M. 428 Evander O.
217 337 Eveline 247
Evelyn C. 168 Evelyn
Kendall 302 Evelyn Mary
440 Evelyn May 423 Evelyn
Searles 368 Everett 283
Everett L. 385 Everett N.
272 390 Everett W. 382
Evon M. 387 Experience 16
25 27 40 88 Ezra 40 48
134 239 240 F.A. 264 F.E.
258 F.H. 193 Fairfield 44
93 Faith 429 Faith
Douglas 416 Fannie 220
Fanny 118 218 Fayette 278
393 413 Fayette Bonnett
300 413 Fayette George
300 413 Fern B. 435 Fern
E. 392 Fidelia 117 Flora
267 280 287 346 384 Flora
A. 121 123 132 Flora
Annette 109 Flora J. 210
Flora Irene 102 Florance
A. 285 Florance Maude 370
Florence 310 Florence E.
330 Florence H. 245
Florence J. 311 Florence
Lillian 390 Florence M.
293 Florence Maude 367
Florence May 124 Florence
W. 203 Flossie 434 Floyd
D. 402 Floyd P. 434
Forest/Joseph 386
Francelia G. 93 Frances
87 108 214 308 312 338
353 445 Frances A. 108
Frances Ann 162 Frances

Severance (Cont.) Agnes 303
Frances Carroll 387
Frances E. 221 Frances F.
353 Frances Ellen 252
Frances J. 171 Frances L.
125 Frances M. (Fannie)
218 287 Frances Matilda
367 Frances May 443
Frances S. 410 Frances
Willard 434 Francesa
(Angela F.) 225 Francis
327 400 Francisa 225
Francis Edwin 124 Francis
H./Herbert Frances 93
Frank 146 167 193 202 209
211 229 232 238 259 262
263 264 278 282 283 300
325 346 350 361 370 373
379 380 386 397 404 412
414 429 436 445
Frank/Francis 240 Frank A.
229 344 Frank B. 270 300
315 414 Frank Bidwell 196
Frank Burbank 270 Frank E.
177 259 308 379 436 Frank
Edmund 289 404 Frank
Edward 148 267 386 387
Frank G. 181 206 208 325
Frank H. 370 413 Frank
Hayward 249 370 Frank J.
360 443 Frank Jr. 289
Frank L. 258 286 379 400
446 Frank L. (Francis
Lewis) 403 Frank Leslie
385 Frank Lewis 412 Frank
N. 221 274 Frank Norman
222 Frank M. 105 Frank
Oliver 290 405 Frank P.
381 Frank P./Clyde Henry
209 330 331 Frank Rix 167
Frank Rolland 372 Frank
Rollin 450 Frank Roy 378
Frank S. 164 263 Frank T.
405 Frank Tyrel 406 Frank
W. 121 233 373 Frank W./H.
288 Frank Ward 250 373 250
373 Frank Ward Jr. 250
Franklin 112 206 287 303
Franklin C. 51 102 104 196
Franklin E. 187 Franklin
Grant 326 Franklin Orrin
148 265 Franklin P. 330
331 445 Franklin Sanborn
147 263 Franklin Sawyer
302 Franklin W. 262 Fred
164 179 193 259 261 266
267 281 309 310 314 335
346 380 384 389 390 396
432 449 Fred A. 148 150
259 265 379 380 Fred Allen

Severance (Cont.) 368 448
Fred Barton 375 451 Fred
Burbank 390 453 Fred C.
164 177 310 395 455 Fred
Clark 346 Fred D. 335
Fred E. 261 293 334 429
Fred Ellsworth 261 Fred
G. 335 Fred Henry 404
Fred J. 432 Fred Jr. 384
Fred Leon 267 384 Fred M.
433 Fred Merserve 347 432
Fred N. 342 Fred R. 256
Fred W. 202 Fred Wiggin
271 389 Fred Wilmot 290
Freda 427 Freddie 272
Freddie G. 215 335
Frederic A. 306 Frederic
Almon 168 Frederic C. 309
Frederic Henry 175
Frederic Hollister 100
Frederick 119 146 160 179
193 262 285 305 310 420
442 Frederick C. 179 310
417 Frederick E. 430
Frederick E. III 430
Frederick Earle Sr. 338
430 Frederick Henry 123
Frederick Hollister 193
Frederick Jefferson 58
Frederick John 419
Frederick Lewis 343
Frederick Mortimer 260
Frederick Sawyer 345
Frederick V. 179 310
Fredrick 118 Fredrick W.
400 Freeman 155 251 G.B.
193 Galen 80 110 Garnett
O. 395 Geneva B. 397
Geneva May 283 George 62
73 74 88 100 104 110 111
117 120 135 136 138 141
142 149 150 151 161 164
172 174 175 176 186 190
192 195 196 208 209 221
243 244 246 252 253 266
267 268 278 282 286 287
306 315 325 330 339 342
343 344 352 359 367 368
385 387 391 398 402 413
423 443 452 George A. 122
143 212 224 253 257 340
342 343 416 422 George
Albert 253 George Alvin
306 416 George Arnold 253
George Arthur 123 George
Austin 431 George B. 401
George Bertrand 369
George Craige 175 305
George E. 238 285 286 324
345 348 398 400 402

Severance (Cont.) George
Edgar 250 George Edward
385 George Elias 211
George Elmer 199 321
George Emerson 306 George
Eslie 423 George F. 167
George Franklin 325 George
Freeman 276 392 George G.
166 George H. 259 364
George Harold 385 George
Henry 241 302 364 George
Henry Jr. 364 447 George
I. 304 George Jr. 413
George L. 190 219 284
George M. 221 289 327 339
405 425 George Malcom 305
George N 124 135 219
George O. 452 455 George
Oscar 145 379 455 George
P. 132 George Palmer 452
George Quimby 129 George
R. 279 394 397 George Rose
167 George S. 142 George
Specer 174 George Stanley
405 George V. 275 391 394
George W. 51 57 89 104 126
170 173 176 186 197 205
221 252 254 283 299 312
330 342 399 417 427 George
Walter 245 367 George
Washington 58 116 117 121
140 159 252 253 283 374
George Wells 412 Georgia
217 Georgia A. 171 Georgia
Ann 387 Georgiana 244 253
Georgianna M. 427 Georgie
254 Gerald A. 386 Gersham
136 Gershom 200 Gershon E.
322 Gertie G. 169 Gertrude
414 Gertrude Ann 347
Gertrude Child 198
Gertrude Elizabeth 206
Gertrude Iowa 187 Gertrude
J. 414 Gertrude Jean 300
414 Gertrude M. 381
Gertrude R. 193 Giles 122
Giles Ernest 434 Gladis
336 Gladys 340 347 417 426
438 453 Gladys E. 311 340
343 Gladys Matilda 453
Gladys V. 433 Glen 371 450
Glen Graham 427 Glan
Russell 444 Glen W. 371
Glenn 382 452 456 Glenn L.
191 Glenn R. 422 Glenn
456 Gordon Wesley 446
Grace 201 257 309 386 433
441 Grace B. 193 Grace
Ella 398 Grace F. 449
Grace M. 201 402 Grace

Severance (Cont.) Olive 357
Gratia Ethel 303 Graydon
Lewayne 436 Greenleaf 323
Greenleaf Frank 323 327
Gregory Martin (adopted)
419 Guilford 323 Guy 46
50 103 405 Guy Carlton 52
103 290 405 Guy Eugene
328 Guy Raymond 303
Hannah 10 12 13 17 18 19
20 26 36 38 46 48 81 112
118 144 151 204 208 272
343 Hannah Alberta 323
Hannah Angeline B. 169
Hannah E. 205 Hannah Edna
116 Hannah F. 133 Hannah
Godfrey 119 Hannah J. 126
140 Hannah Jane 93 127
Hannah L. 129 Harland 229
350 437 434 435 Harland
Claude 349 350 435
Harland Kenneth 435
Harley 433 Harlons
Erastus 220 Harlow 171
Harlow Wells 171 Harold
155 175 396 420 430 439
Harold Clyde 395 Harold
Craige 305 415 Harold E.
308 339 430 431 Harold G.
188 Harold Gail 419
Harold Henry 391 Harold
J. 340 Harold Judson 315
Harold Roberts 357 439
Harriet 13 50 52 109 124
165 226 189 199 205 208
229 254 308 353 374
Harriet A. 38 53 54 67 68
75 81 83 84 88 112 137
139 140 Harriet Ann 173
Harriet Augusta 93
Harriet Augustus 122
Harriet Charlotte 84
Harriet E. 431 Harriet
Gertrude 303 Harriet
Lovilla 256 Harriet
Newell 114 Harriet S. 171
Harriet Susannah 169 297
Harris 85 167 Harrison 79
158 161 235 236 281 356
Harrison Cushing 121
Harrison R. 236 356
Harrison Roberts 236
Harry 84 197 201 205 278
367 401 447 Harry/Henry
Lucien Don 364 447 Harvey
A. 124 378 376 381 Harry
Arthur 442 Harry C. 273
Harry Edwin 449 Harry F.
342 Harry H. 346 Harry J.
220 338 339 374 Harry

Severance (Cont.) Mildred 397
Ida P. 169 Ida S. 364 Ida
Sophronia 364 Ida V. 388
Ila M. 222 Illa M. 225
Illo 348 434 Imogene 402
Ines Leola 444 Inez Ethel
384 Ira 232 273 274 356
359 402 442 445 Ira E. 232
Ira G. 232 355 Ira Leavitt
233 Ira O. 152 274 Irene
359 403 428 443 Irene
Laura 337 Irene M. 401
Irene Velma 384 Iris 432
Irving 413 Irving (Erwin)
O. 436 Irvin J. 139 422
Irving Lindsley 94 Isaac
56 69 112 139 141 230 252
352 437 Isaac L. 342 351
437 Isaac Libby 352 Isabel
D. 376 Isabel Maria 192
Isabel Pierre 421 Isabell
Annett 167 Isabella 158
284 Isla Jean 414 Iva 401
Iva L. 392 Ivene 454 Ivory
144 145 147 Ivory 258
Ivory E. 144 257 Ivy
Coleman 357 438 J. Arthur
400 404 J. Frank 327 J.
Fred 327 J.D. 217 J.E. 164
J.G. 217 354 J.T. 212
Jacob 18 32 66 67 68 70 74
110 132 145 147 149 201
227 259 260 322 380 396
Jacob A. 396 Jacob H. 202
281 322 Jacob Jewell 127
226 227 Jacob Jr. 146 259
James 7 12 17 28 52 56 57
74 83 110 112 113 114 117
123 145 147 165 188 197
202 204 205 208 214 227
229 230 242 245 252 258
259 269 290 323 324 327
351 423 424 426 James A.
83 112 146 165 287 401 423
James Anslie 275 James B.
219 James Bureon 411 James
D. 147 James David 387
James E. 214 James Echard
334 James Edwin 84 165 169
James F. 135 245 James
George 428 James H. 105
197 201 226 312 James
Henry 118 214 385 James
Hervey 94 James Horn 152
James Hubbard 190 James
Jr. 323 James L. 323 James
Leonard 348 Jaems Lyle 436
James M. 58 117 128 206
223 227 229 320 327 350
402 425 James Madison 228

Severance (Cont.) 229 James
Martin 229 James P. 201
James Ralph 102 196 James
Seymour 194 James Sr. 323
James Royal 114 James
Taggart 97 188 191 313
James Wendell 419 Jane 97
118 136 150 153 374 Jane
A. 112 Jane Ann 55 Jane
Eliza 246 Jane Isabella
189 Jane Tuttle 176 Janet
378 456 Jason F. 298
Jason S. 282 Jasper
Nelson 152 Jeamette 315
Jean 407 427 Jean Elaine
419 Jean G. 221 Jeanette
312 360 Jeannette 429
Jefferson 206 216 425
Jefferson F. 327
Jefferson Franklin 425
Jeffrey Alan 419 Jennie
189 190 267 268 293 387
440 Jennie A. 200 289
Jennie Ann Maria 163
Jennie B. 215 Jennie H.
368 Jennie Harriet 189
Jennie L. 185 Jennie M.
323 Jennie N. 239 246
Jennifer Ann 419 Jennis
L. 166 Jennis M. 326
Jenny 169 Jemima 49 79
Jennette E. 41 Jeremiah
242
Jeremiah/Michael/Micah 68
134 135 Jerome 417 Jerome
P. 126 221 Jerry 322
Jerusha/Jeremiah 62 Jesse
22 41 89 90 128 146 230
386 Jesse Forest 386
Jesse P. 178 309 Jesse W.
365 Jessie 324 336 352
353 355 410 433 Jessie F.
206 Jessie M. 327 Jessie
R. 312 Jewell 225 Jimmi
Edwin 403 Joe E. 399 Joe,
(Uncle) 40 Joel 42 67 71
141 142 255 374 Joanna 22
28 John 3 4 5 6 7 8 9 10
13 14 15 16 18 19 20 21
22 24 25 26 32 37 39 40
45 48 49 54 55 56 57 63
64 67 70 71 75 76 78 79
80 81 94 97 98 99 113 116
118 127 133 136 138 139
140 150 153 155 159 160
163 138 186 188 189 197
203 204 210 211 214 215
223 224 225 227 232 234
239 241 243 245 246 257
267 268 282 283 312 313

Severance (Cont.) 239 361
Kirby 410 Kirk Eugene 319
Kirk T. 428 L. Standard
448 L.F. 273 Lafayette 171
277 392 Lagrange 73 74 75
131 230 352 353 354
Lanawee 204 Laura 42 113
208 268 403 Laura A. 174
Laura Ann 88 210 Laura
Belle 250 Laura E. 144
Laura M. 431 Laura Mae 361
Laura May 385 Laura
Mitilda 101 Laura S. 125
Laurae 281 Laurence Pooler
337 Laverne 447 448
Laverne Stanard 366 447
448 Lavica 347 Lavina 278
Lavinda 281 Lavinia 117
Lawrence C. 401 Layette
281 Lefy 144 Leigh Pearson
285 Leila Jean 454 Lemira
D. 305 Lemuel 360 443 Lena
297 Lena A. 312 Lena J.
186 Lena M. 422 Lena
Rachel 444 Lenrie J. 258
Lenora 117 Lencre Janette
443 Leo 322 402 Leola 120
Leon 384 387 398 Leon E.
382 Leon Henry 303 Leon
Jr. 428 Leon Morse 398
Leon O. 330 427 Leona 199
321 394 Leona C. 394 Leona
I. 445 Leonard 85 88 162
168 173 215 304 348
Leonard H. 118 215 Lecnard
Ozora 434 Leonard S. 174
304 305 Leonora 155 156
157 279 Lephe Wells 171
Leroy 293 346 406 414 451
LeRoy A. 449 Leroy E. 372
451 Leroy J. 347 432 Leroy
Warren 397 456 Leslie 306
403 Leslie Clark 443
Leslie Nile 435 Leslie P.
288 403 404 Leslie T. 306
398 Lester 433 449 Lester
A. 413 Lester Floyd 347
433 Lester H. 213 Lester
Washburn 368 449 Leta May
296 Lettie 402 Levi 69 127
137 138 153 155 225 225
276 277 345 373 391 Levi
A. Warren 137 247 Lewis 84
134 199 241 242 278 279
321 359 396 441 442 443
Lewis A. 394 Lewis B. 394
Lewis Cap 394 Lewis D. 239
Lewis Eggleston 187 312
Lewis Harry/Louis H. 392
Lewis Howard 191 Lewis J.

Severance (Cont.) 342 Lida
35 Lidea 19 Life A. 143
Lila 346 Lilain R. 422
Lillian 246 275 456
Lillian E. 301 140
Lillian Louise 301 302
Lillian M. 343 Lillian
Vernette 435 Lillie 262
Lillie M. 138 Linette 268
Linton Garfield 328
Lisa/Louisa 200 Lizzie
224 230 265 272 322 341
431 432 434 Lizzie B. 169
Lizzie Barbes 196 Lizzie
Ethel Daisy 290 Lizzie
Helen 190 Lizzie J. 256
Lizzie Munroe 341
Llewellen 212 Lloyd 327
398 Lloyd Dean 442 Lloyd
Dewey 380 Lloyd Earl 393
Lloyd Elbert 384 Lloyd
Francis 323 Lloyd M. 340
Loammi 134 Loammie 241
Loana 352 Logan 383 Lois
41 426 Lois F. 285 Lois
May 444 Lona 352 Loren P.
256 Lorenzo 44 94 Lorenzo
F. 273 Lorenzo Fisk 152
272 273 Lorenzo
B.(G.)(Lonny) 126 223
Loretta 144 145 257
Lorrimer R. 329 Lorna 350
Lorna Augusta 436 Lottie
Louise 368 Lou Virginia
191 Louette 434 Louette
Carl 349 434 Louis 316
Louis (Lewis C.) 281
Louis (Lewis) Henry 316
Louis H. 285 Louis Henry
193 316 Louis R. 203
Louisa 190 200 320 321
Louisa A. 210 Louisa M.
190 Louisa Maria 243 366
Louise 351 352 Lovell
Bullock 186 Lovica A. 254
Lovina/Louisa B. 288
Lovina 47 49 82 96 Lowell
323 Lowes 35 Lucia 288
Lucia Ann 175 Lucia Jane
306 Lucia M. 363 Lucia
Marion 139 Lucian 92 93
Lucie J. 275 Lucien 240
Lucile 426 445 Lucile
Norma 372 Lucille 282 286
385 410 453 Lucille E.
407 Lucina M. 83 Lucinda
134 204 232 Lucinda E.
209 241 244 Lucinda J.
142 Lucius E. 362 Lucius
Warren 137 248 Lucretia

Severance (Cont.) 82 392
Lucretia M. 83 Lucretia
Scott 45 Lucy 41 42 60 80
89 131 141 275 361 387
Lucy A. 219 Lucy Ann 363
Lucy Anne 142 Lucy B. 131
230 Lucy J. 110 253 275
Lucy L. 111 Lucy M. 137
178 Lucy Malanda 76 Lucy
Maria 103 Lucy N. 55 Lucy
Ward 100 Luella 321 Lulie
222 Lulu 117 212 Lulyn 239
Lura 212 Luther 44 52 93
105 106 107 109 110 177
198 Luther Jr. 201 Luther
N. 89 177 Luther R. 110
200 Luther S. 168 Luther
U. 324 Luvern (Laverne) W.
436 Lyde Miller 250 Lydia
13 19 47 53 56 76 83 112
127 409 Lydia A. 224 241
Lydia C. 253 Lydia
Dulcinia 253 Lydia E. 203
Lydia Ella 253 Lydia
Estelle (Estelle L.) 283
Lydia J. 226 Lydia Lovisa
205 Lydia M. 147 Lyle B.
436 Lyle E. 362 Lyman 164
165 Lyman Cathestes 318
422 Lyman L. 438 Lyman M.
83 164 165 168 Lynn 393
Lynn Earl 393 Mabel 265
326 350 Mabel Clair 349
Mabel Connelly 359 Mabel
E. 168 375 Mabel Grace 405
443 Mabel Kelsey 405 Mabel
L. 155 391 Mable 260 410
Mable Gladys 446 Mable R.
203 Madaline 253 Madeline
A. 295 Madeline C. 451
Madgie 441 Madora Ellen
449 Maebelle 335 Margaret
18 Margarit 51 Maggie 299
410 440 Mahala 287 Malcolm
453 Malcolm B. 334 338
Malcom 214 Mamie 297 Mande
253 Manly C. 161 286
Marcella 263 Marcus 286
Marcus M. 400 Margaret 201
387 396 Margaret Elizabeth
412 Margie T. 326 Margorie
334 Marguerite 401
Marguerite Fredal 248
Maria 161 164 241 433
Maria H. 105 Maria P. 141
Mariah 98 Marian 361 372
Marian Jane 366 Marianne
"Molly" 453 Marie 430
Marie Evelyn 435 Mariette
259 Marinda 278 Marilla 82

Severance (Cont.) Marion 152
199 307 311 321 401 416
450 Marion A. 277 Marion
Alton 349 Marion C. 125
Marion D. 416 Marion
Elizabeth 425 Marion
Irene 328 Marion Isabel
401 Marion L. 333 Marion
L.C. 177 Marjorie S. 317
Mark 317 452 Mark L.H.
442 Mark Sibley 195 317
320 Marquerite 303
Marrian 199 321 Marrianne
208 Marrietta 208 Marsey
10 Martha 9 13 14 27 38
40 72 82 83 113 139 172
201 208 257 293 294 359
413 Martha A. 289 Martha
Agnes 162 Martha Ann 94
122 Martha Ellen 172
Martha Ester 425 Martha
F. 128 Martha H. 388
Martha Helen 302 Martha
I. 171 Martha J. 174
Martha Jane 87 Martha M.
201 Martha Mary 201
Martha W. 217 Martin 16
22 23 24 25 41 42 43 44
66 133 313 417 Martin
Egbert 163 292 Martin
Elbert 188 313 417 Martin
Ellsworth 327 424 Martin
Harrison 188 312 314
Martin Joan 91 179 Martin
Jr. 42 Martin Kent 420
Martin L.W. 360 Martin
Lafayette 393 Martin
Luther 297 409 Martin
Oliver 318 Martin W. 409
Marvel E. 430 Marvel
Louisa 399 Marvin 161 286
Mary 5 7 8 9 11 12 13 18
20 22 25 32 35 43 52 53
72 83 84 85 87 88 90 92
99 103 104 105 106 108
133 136 140 158 159 165
171 209 216 221 226 230
232 244 246 247 268 284
311 316 359 383
Mary/Polly 80 111 119 150
Mary A. 117 125 135 140
170 201 274 390 Mary
Addine 75 Mary Alice 168
Mary Ann 97 118 126 128
130 204 230 231 243 281
Mary Augusta 228 Mary C.
173 Mary Catharine 162
Mary Catherine 314 Mary
E. 117 124 148 166 222
231 263 333 234 Mary

Severance (Cont.) Eleanor 412
Mary Electa 306 Mary
Elizabeth 94 203 393 Mary
Elizabeth "Lizzie" 431
Mary Ellen 262 276 Mary
Emelia 246 Mary Emilla 84
Mary Emma 299 Mary Eveline
369 Mary F. 280 Mary
Frankie 167 Mary Helen 316
Mary I 118 Mary J. 208 209
238 Mary Jane 122 134 135
208 Mary Joanna 102 Mary
Josephine 233 Mary L. 131
422 Mary Latimer 182 Mary
Louisa 103 Mary Lucretia
175 Mary M. 140 Mary
Margaret 87 Mary Mehitable
172 Mary Meroa 173 Mary P.
403 404 Mary Parthena 82
Mary R. 254 Mary S. 145
232 402 Mary Sophia 133
Mary T. 132 Mary Weare 121
210 Mason 282 Mason
Samuel/Samuel Mason 159
282 Massa/Mercy 53 Matilda
157 279 322 Matthew 18 22
39 87 172 Matthew Stebbins
172 Mattie 92 Mattie Lois
396 Mattie viola 409 Maud
286 333 340 430 Maud
(Manda) E. 330 Maud Annie
388 Maud B. 381 Maud E.
295 Maud Emily 295 Maude
Emily 292 Maude M. 340
Maudly 161 164 Maurice 385
Maurice Marvin 369 449 Max
Elwin 334 May 442 445 May
Florence 191 May L. 239
May S. 94 Mazzini 244 367
Mehitable 87 89 113 150
208 Melanie Lynn 419
Melinda 117 Melissa 137
Melissa Maude 222 Melville
B. 126 Melvin 92 181 222
333 340 360 377 423 443
Melvin A. 91 Melvin A./Asa
Melvin 181 Melvin B. 222
340 Melvin J. 256 377 378
Melvin J. II 378 Melvin J.
III 378 Mercy 399
Mercy/Marcy (Mary) 28 49
63 Merite 374 Merl L. 320
Merle 386 Merton L. 258
Michael 456 Michael
Benjamin 135 243 Mildred
182 277 315 348 371 392
422 Mildred (Frances) 277
Mildred Davis 425 Mildred
E. 303 307 Mildred F. 383
Mildred Fern 434 Mildred

Severance (Cont.) M. 181
Mildred May 404 Millie
287 404 Millie Wing 380
Milton 291 292 406 407
Milton Balcom 296 407
Milton G. 253 Milton
George 405 Milton L. 405
Milton Leonard 162 290
292 406 Milton W. 454
Minard Foss 438 Minerva
251 Minerva B. 137 Mini
Katherine 339 Minnie 177
178 282 309 Minnie B. 142
360 Minnie L. 214 Minot
F. 367 Minot Forrest 245
368 371 Miranda 40 50 87
254 Miranda E. 174 Miraon
(Myron) 361 444 Miriam
Elsie 305 415 Miriam R.
449 Mitilda 282 Mollie M.
381 Molly 33 34 35 77
Morris 366 Morris A. 340
Morris R. 406 Morris
Ripley 242 365 Moses 16
17 27 28 32 38 51 52 53
64 65 66 80 83 108 110
127 129 131 133 161 165
234 Moses H. 108 Muriel
398 Murray 191 Murrell
410 Myra Evangeline 350
Myron Albert 346 Myron D.
363 Myrtic 239 Myrtie 369
Myrtle 236 252 356 424
Myrtle E. 379 Myrtle H.
362 Myrtle L. 281 Nabby
Bailey 140 Nancy 99 113
202 204 229 429 Nancy
Augusta 208 Nancy B. 335
Nancy Colby 115 Nancy J.
142 159 Nancy Judson 115
Nancy Wilbur 175 Naomi 34
361 396 Nathan 37 67 79
80 113 134 159 159 208
209 240 330 359 Nathan C.
226 Nathan E. 360 Nathan
Ezra 239 359 Nathan N. C.
226 345 Nathaniel 25 63
74 113 128 208 230 231
354 Nathaniel C. 226 346
Nathaniel S. 128
Nathaniel Smith 63 129
Nellie 145 281 284 287
353 360 413 Nellie A. 144
257 Nellie Allice 281
Nellie C. 304 Nellie F.
217 Nellie J. 258 Nellie
Lorette 203 Nellie M. 289
Nellie Maud 185 Nelson 82
163 200 287 Nelson Chase
161 287 Nettie J. 181

Severance (Cont.) Nettie Jane
144 Nettie L. 280 Nettie
Maria 387 Newell 116 211
272 Newell Atchison 152
272 Nicholas 282 Nicholas
Jr. 54 Nichols 35 158
Nicholson 11 29 54
Nickelson 159 Nickerson 29
136 Nicols/Nicholas 78 79
158 Nixon/Nickerson 136
Noble D. 95 186 Nola 384
Nora 402 441 Norma 452
Norma Elaine 439 Norman
278 394 396 400 Norman
Dana 424 Norman E. 286
Norman Everett 435
Obed/Obid 20 39 84 85 Ocie
Barton 411 Octava/Octavia
98 Octavius 224 342 351
352 Octavius W. 224 431
Octavius Webster 224 342
Octavus 224 230 342
Octavus W. 342 438 Ola A.
382 Olive 61 63 428 Olive
Elvira 161 Olive June 339
Olive L. 125 Oliver 81 162
208 289 290 331 394 Oliver
Cathestus/Oliver Cathestes
195 318 Oliver F. 328
Oliver P. 328 Oliver S.
280 394 Ollie E. 395 Ora
41 111 159 440 Ora P. 79
159 Oralin S. 254
Oren/Orrin 39 46 84
Oresamus 195 Orla Addison
412 Orla Avery 186 Orland
Lane (Allen) 386 Orlie E.
195 Orman 263 Orman J. 381
452 Orman John 452 Orren
362 363 Orren J. 240 362
363 Orrin 381 Orrin Frank
148 Orrin P. 263 Orrin T.
381 Orson Seymour 194
Orwell/Roswell 240 Oscar
124 163 177 308 318 Oscar
Alphonso 195 318 Oscar F.
286 Osman 303 Otis 50 101
198 Otis C. 326 Otis
Cathestus 101 195 Otis
Cordenio 195 318 Otis F.
218 Otis R. 296 Otto 251
Otto R. 373 Owen 314
Palmer 329 358 440 Palmer
E. 427 Palmer Earl 329 443
Palmer Elmer 440 Palmer W.
329 Pansy Maud 335 Parker
150 Pascal 114 Patience 25
43 44 Patty /Martha 58 70
81 Paul 39 85 86 169 170
297 Paul A. 170 173 410

Severance (Cont.) Paul B.
409 Paul Donald 440 Paul
Elisha 169 297 Paul Frame
316 Paul Frederick 380
Paul S. 85 169 Paul W.
333 Pauline 280 382
Pauline M. 382 Pauline
Smart 390 Pearl 287 413
433 452 Pearl Harriet 441
Pearl Naomi 357 Pearl W.
373 Peaslie (Pearl) 249
Percey E. 222 Percey W.L.
449 Percy E. 334 428
Percy H. 340 Percy Howard
443 Percy W.L. 369 Perley
C. 392 Perley V./Perly B.
309 Perry 358 Persis A.
149 Peter 11 30 32 56 57
58 64 65 117 129 131 231
368 Peter G. 421 Phebe 37
Phebe Ann Wood 76 Phebe
E. 324 Pheny 410 Phidelia
141 Phil H. 315 Philena
39 83 Philip L. 441
Phillip 10 17 28 53 110
158 280 395 455 Phillip
Jr. 53 54 455 Phillip
Smith 173 Phillip Sr. 53
Phillis J. 374 Philo 292
Philo S. 292 Philo
Spencer 163 292 Pilsbury
122 Phimela 178 Phyllis
374 Pierre 317 Pierre C.
317 Pierre Clarke 195 317
Pliny 49 100 193 Polly 25
58 60 76 79 Polly M. 128
Porter 90 Porter A. 272
Preston 218 Preston P.
338 Preston Phillip 218
338 Priscilla 438
Priscilla Ann 232
Priscilla M. 124 Proctor
206 Ptolemy Philadelphus
51 102 103 Quantus 173
303 Quentin Roosevelt 339
R. Scott 166 R.L. 400
Rachael 386 Rachal Lynn
419 Rachel 26 42 47 61
111 160 Rachel Lee 421
Redford 407 Ralph 101 133
309 416 Ralph Abercrombie
51 101 Ralph H. 315 339
Ralph J. 383 413 Ralph
Nelson 273 Ralph S. 193
318 Ralph Weaver 425
Randy 452 Ransom 116 210
Ray 306 451 Ray (Sydney)
333 Ray C. 197 Raymon 372
451 Raymond 382 385 408
433 453 Raymond C. 400

508

Severance (Cont.) Adams 210
Sarah B. 117 135 Sarah C.
105 176 Sarah E. 324 Sarah
Elizabeth 323 Sarah D. 141
Sarah Ellen 187 Sarah F.
121 Sarah Isabel 121 Sarah
J. 117 255 287 Sarah Jane
66 118 243 367 Sarah
Judith 446 Sarah L. 89
Sarah M. 108 213 258 400
Sarah Melvina 143 Sarah
Permela Carpenter 76 Sarah
R. 133 Sarah S. 263 Sarah
Susana 87 Sarah T. 115 276
Sarah V. 158 280 Sarah
Zama 96 Sargeant 341 347
348 Sargeant French 224
341 Sargeant Jewell 128
228 229 349 Sargent 228
Scott 295 408 452 Scott E.
296 Scott Ellsworth 166
295 Selah 25 44 Selena
Emeline 170 Sephas 41 Seth
46 95 96 148 186 194 266
267 312 384 Seth Lawrence
266 267 Seth Lawrence Jr.
266 Seth W. 95 Seth
Washburn 99 Sewell 155 276
Seymour 46 328 Seymour B.
206 321 327 Shirley 427
Sibil 155 Sible J. 310
Sidney 278 Signe I. 363
Silas 78 79 157 158 278
279 393 455 Silas O. 280
395 Silvia E. 381 Smith 63
223 Solinda 149 Solomon 27
49 51 103 193 385 Solomon
Lewis 101 193 316 Solon
Long 193 315 Sophia 25 42
52 83 89 Sophia M. 147
Sophrona 139 Sophronia 47
118 360 Spencer W. 371 449
Stanley 398 402 Stanley B.
422 Stanley Edmond 439
Stephen 69 70 78 138 140
152 153 250 274 439
Stephen Henry 441 Stephen
Lewis 439 Stephen Nute 152
274 Stephen Samuel 169
Stewart 429 438 Submit 25
Sukey (Sarah) 127 Susan
145 456 Susan A. 125 Susan
E. 155 Susan Frances 211
Susan Marie 419 Susan W.
137 Susanna 49 58 Susannah
63 205 Susi Augusta 245
Sybil 391 Sydney Semour
393 454 Sylvania 165
Sylvester 288 402 424
Sylvester Chase 287 401

Severance (Cont.) Sylvester
Edwin 153 275 Sylvia 287
333 423 Sylvia Fern 435
Sylvia K. 165 Tabitha 20
38 79 Teresa 179 Thankful
27 Thankful N. 126
Thatcher 148 150 263 381
Thelma F. 416 Theo Clyden
386 Theodore 178 Theodore
R. 396 Theodoric 194
Theodoric Cordenio 101
194 Theresa 171 Theron L.
411 Thersha 216 Thomas 10
11 17 21 29 39 54 55 61
79 87 122 123 159 169 216
243 260 298 350 359 411
442 456 Thomas B. 230 261
Thomas Beauregard 170 298
411 Thomas Benton 146 260
Thomas Burton 350 Thomas
Chalkley 239 359 Thomas
Chalkley Jr. 359 442
Thomas Edwin 122 Thomas
Ellis 411 Thomas Freeman
155 276 391 Thomas Glenn
170 173 298 Thomas Homer
442 Thomas J. 120 216
Thomas Sr. 159 Thomas,
Capt. 55 Thompson Burton
229 Thirza 27 42 Tirzah
C. 91 Tracy P. 375 Truth
E. 386 Tryphena 35
Ulysses Grant 301
Umatilla 406 Unrico 288
403 Uriel 113 207 210
Ursula 226 Ursula M.W.
231 Vance L. 320 Varna
222 Velma 371 450 Velma
L. 393 Vera 426 Verna E.
427 Verna May 435 Verne
C. 339 Vernon 272 372 417
422 441 444 451 Vernon
Elmer 441 Vernon P. 391
Verra 352 Vesty 352
Victor 293 Victor Lyman
294 Victoria 386 389
Victoria Jennie C. 294
Victorine W. 338 Viena
131 Vienah A. 218 Viola
83 165 402 413 Viola
Emeline 318 Viola May 438
Virgil Lauren 436
Virginia 314 336 429 451
Virginia Emma 192
Virginia Lu Etta 314 W.F.
186 Waldon H. 423 Waldo
229 230 351 Waldo D. 415
Waldron 204 324 Waldron
M. 204 Wales A. 197 312
417 Wales Frank 186

Severance (Cont.) Wallace L.
104 Walter 222 244 262 298
324 350 351 387 437 Walter
A. 344 Walter Allen 368
Walter B. 262 Walter E.
275 360 363 398 Walter
Edmund 351 437 Walter F.
216 336 340 Walter H. 203
324 433 Walter Harris 368
Walter Henry 313 Walter I.
197 320 Walter L. 177 307
400 Walter M. 308 Walter
Merlyn 441 Walter Searles
135 244 Warden 149 Warner
E. 307 Warren 92 120 182
304 335 383 Warren Decatur
95 185 Warren F. 174 304
Warren Lee 451 454 Warren
Lerand 411 Washington 216
429 Washington Bainbridge
336 429 Wesley 360 368
Wesley Arthur 440 Wesley
Charles 446 Wesley Forrest
368 Wilbert 314 Wilbur 442
Wilbur Leigh 438 Wilburt
Nathaniel 291 Wilford 419
Wilford Lee 419 Wilhelmina
301 Willard 313 332
Willard Colby 115 210
Willard Lorenzo 188 312
313 Willard Murry 297
Willard Wilkens 301
Willard William 332 423
William 3 11 17 21 29 30
51 54 55 56 57 60 67 70 83
96 111 112 118 120 121 133
137 146 150 158 161 164
166 177 186 189 199 207
208 213 214 218 243 246
248 249 254 255 261 268
269 286 287 293 295 298
300 321 322 323 325 332
333 329 331 333 334 336
345 346 347 362 387 403
410 423 429 440 445 452
453 William (Wesley) Hardy
367 William A. 288 300 427
William Albion 252 William
B. 120 123 218 219 338 430
William Bernard 334
William C. 170 William
Chester 301 William D. 141
202 222 254 374 William
Daniel 135 242 243 366
William Darling 111 202
William Dwight 177 308 416
William Edgar 355 William
Elias 298 410 William
Ellis 410 William F. 146
William G. 113 338 426

Severance (Cont.) William H.
126 171 211 216 218 226
245 300 331 336 337 338
345 346 430 William
Hayward 211 William
Hector 347 433 William
Henry 126 174 217 243 300
324 327 337 423 William
J. 228 294 346 407 432
William James 409 William
Jewell 228 William Joel
256 376 William Joseph
297 409 William Jr. 268
William L. 266 382 383
407 William Lyman 301
William M. 92 218 272 275
289 338 William Malcolm
453 William Mead 338
William Morgan 182
William Mulholland 191
William N. 157 164 293
347 William Norman 229
347 William O. 189
William Orton 412 William
P. 208 328 329 Willaim R.
389 453 William Rotch 317
421 William Rotch Morgan
421 William S. 305
William Sidney 89 172 177
300 301 William Sr. 54
William T. 161 285
William W. 275 331 335
William Wallace 260 261
William Warren 216 332
335 388 Williams 204
Willie 166 376 Willie B.
283 Willis E. 122 Willie
Frank 290 Willie H. 274
Willie L. 166 295 Willis
E. 375 Willis Edgar 122
123 Wilmer 404 Wilmer L.
404 Wilson Boyce 442
Wilson Karl 442 Wilson V.
399 Winfield S. 126 222
Winnie Floss 349
Winnifred Edna 434
Winthrop G. 181 Worden
Oscar/Ward O. 318 422
Young 334 Zacheus 110 199
200 321 Zama 47 Zama
Sophia 96 Zebina
Henderson 93 Zella 309
Zella G. 179 310 313
Zenas 40 87 Ziba 113 114
209 Zua A. 401
Severans, Samuel 2
Severns, Sarah 2
Sewell, John W. 123
Seymour, Caroline M. 101 194
Orson 194

513

514

Walker, Annie J. 380 Col.
William 61 John 250 Joshua
380 Sarah Jane 273 392
Wall, Elizabeth 333
Wallace, Daniel H. 373
Florence (Walker) 250 373
Olive 157
Walsh, Elizabeth 327 425
Walsworth, James 49
Walton, William 370
Ward, Benjamin 61 Charles and
Sarah 328 Elva / Alva 208
328 Jennie Phoebe 155 277
Warden, Samuel 10 martha 5 10
Mary 10 Peter Jr. 10
Wardner Phebe 247
Ware, Angeline Laura 93 185
Warmer, Garce E. 307
Warner, ___ 79 Caroline A. 308
Chester 308 Oliver 49
William Phelps 49
Warren, Charles B. 290
Jeanette D. 299 412 Julia
A. 310 Martha F. 150 269
Susannah 69 Sussan 137
Sylva Estella (Worth) 397
Zenas 137
Washburn, Allen 367 Celia
Phillips 245 367
Waste, Warren E. 359
Waters, Elizabeth 73 287
Sylvanus 287
Watkins, Nettie 181
Watson, ___ 15 Abraham 12
Achsah 275 Ann 15 21 Emily
397 Etta M. 217 337 Henry
Butler 276 391 Lucy 114
409 Nicodemus 114 Sally
225 343
Weare, Sarah Ann 114 209
Timothy 209
Weatherford, C.A. 182
Weatherhead, Albert George
358
Weaver, Daniel 112
Webster, ___ 229 Capt.
Ebenezer 54 Charles F.
241 Daniel 6 Ebenezer 6
Hannah M. 225 344 Horace
H. and Nancy E. 241 John
Jr. 127 Josiah T. 129
Rhoda 127 225 232 344
Rhoda (Severance) 129
Weed, William M. 223
Weegar, Mary Jane 199 321
William 199 321
Weiler, Louise 392 454
Weinert, Lyle 419

Welch, Benjamin F. and Mary
F. 187 Mary Ann 96 Mary
G. 187 Ruth 271
Weld, Mary 17
Weller, Fearietta 191
Zechariah 191
Wellman, Melissa Ann 254 255
Nelson 254
Wells, Abigail 46 95 Agrippa
Capt. 26 46 David 42 47
Elisha 27 87 Fannie 95
John 42 46 180 Lephe
Louisa 87 171 Mary 46 87
Reuben 27 Sarah 403
Wendell, Frank H. 208 Henry
and Julia A. 208
Wentworth, Joseph 210
Margaret 202 Sarah 110
201
Wentzell, Lucinda 277
Wesson, Charles H. 203
Elizabeth J. 111
West, Charles H. 116 Josiah
238 Mary E. 182 311
Westcot, Abigail 53
Elizabeth 97 188
Weston (Westers) Lydia
Frances 148 264
Weston, Susanna 137
Wetherbee, Alfred Grout 252
Henry and Prudence 252
Carrie Celestia 195 318
Wheelden, Addie R. 125
Benjamin Frank and Marion
125
Wheeler, Cornelia Augusta
175 Jonathan 240 Marion
(Mary S.) 209 330 Persis
71 Tripena 402
Whilden, ___ 15 John 86 87
Whipple, James 213 Sarah M.
213
Whitaker, Maggie Atwood 297
409
White, Aaron 49 Abriah 160
284 Charles W. 128 Elihu
187 Jacob F. 117 John 6
15 86 Loomis and Harriet
187 Lucile Swift 156
Polly 177 Samuel 284
William 15 William Allen
417
Whitmarsh, Mrs. Esther
(Gazley) 98
Whitney, Corabelle 434 Emily
262 George W. 354 Joseph
42 Lucy 25 42
Whittier, Benjamin 57
Whittlesey, Austin 326